Policing in the U.S.

Past, Present, and Future

Lorenzo M. Boyd

Melissa S. Morabito

Larry J. Siegel

 Cengage

Australia • Brazil • Canada • Mexico • Singapore • United Kingdom • United States

Policing in the U.S.: Past, Present, and Future,
First Edition
**Lorenzo M. Boyd, Melissa S. Morabito,
Larry J. Siegel**

SVP, Product: Cheryl Costantini

VP, Product: Thais Alencar

Portfolio Product Director: Jason Fremder

Portfolio Product Manager: Conor Allen

Product Assistant: Isaiah Johnson

Learning Designer: Mara Vuillaume

Content Manager: Chip Cheek

Digital Project Manager: John Smigielski

Director, Product Marketing: Neena Bali

Product Marketing Manager: Morgan Gauthier

Content Acquisition Analyst: Andrea White

Production Service: Lori Hazzard, MPS Limited

Designer: Erin Griffin

Cover Image Source: April30/E+/Getty Images

For product information and technology assistance, contact us at
**Cengage Customer & Sales Support, 1-800-354-9706
or support.cengage.com.**

For permission to use material from this text or product, submit all requests online at **www.copyright.com.**

Library of Congress Control Number: 2023913590

ISBN: 978-0-357-12548-9

Cengage
5191 Natorp Boulevard
Mason, OH 45040
USA

Cengage is a leading provider of customized learning solutions. Our employees reside in nearly 40 different countries and serve digital learners in 165 countries around the world. Find your local representative at **www.cengage.com.**

To learn more about Cengage platforms and services, register or access your online learning solution, or purchase materials for your course, visit **www.cengage.com.**

Printed at CLDPC, USA, 12-23

Dedication

To my parents, Grover and Lucille, for unyielding support and love, and to my daughters LaKeyva and LaTasha, my bonus-son Joe III, and my grandkids Joe IV and Karley.
All I do is for you!

—LMB

To my husband, Andrew, and our children, Leah and Ben.

—MSM

To my wife, Therese J. Libby; my children, Julie, Andrew, Eric, and Rachel; my grandchildren, Jack, Kayla, Brooke, and Elliot; and my sons-in-law, Jason Macy and Patrick Stephens.

—LJS

About the Authors

LORENZO M. BOYD, PH.D., is the Stewart Professor of Community Policing at the University of New Haven (CT). He formerly served as the university's vice president for Diversity and Inclusion and former director of the Center for Advanced Policing. He effectively translates research and theory into practice, making him a sought-after consultant, trainer, and speaker for police agencies, seminars, and communities across the country. Boyd served over a decade as a deputy sheriff in Suffolk County, Massachusetts, and currently serves as a police consultant. He spent eight years as the primary adviser and consultant for the Fayetteville, North Carolina, Police Department. He develops police promotional assessments and training in such areas as trauma-informed policing, community policing, and cultural competence. He served as the president of the Academy of Criminal Justice Sciences (ACJS) from 2016 to 2017 and is a life member of the National Organization of Black Law Enforcement Executives (NOBLE). He has been published in numerous scholarly journals, including the *Journal of Ethnicity in Criminal Justice; Policing, An International Journal; Race, and Justice*; and *Criminal Justice Policy Review.* Boyd received his Ph.D. in sociology from Northeastern University, M.S. in applied sociology, and B.A. in sociology and political science from the University of Massachusetts.

MELISSA S. MORABITO, PH.D., is a professor in the School of Criminology and Justice Studies at the University of Massachusetts–Lowell. She earned a B.A. in political science from the University of Pennsylvania and an MSW from Columbia University before attending American University and graduating with a Ph.D. in justice, law, and society. After graduation, she was awarded a postdoctoral fellowship with the Center for Criminal Justice and Mental Health Services Research. Her research focuses on the intersection between policing and public health issues and most notably she regularly conducts research regarding enhancing the police response to people with mental illnesses as an academic partner to police agencies. To date, she has published more than 50 peer-reviewed articles.

LARRY J. SIEGEL, PH.D., was born in the Bronx, New York. He attended Christopher Columbus High School, and then NYU and City College (CCNY). After graduating in 1968 with a degree in sociology, he was admitted to the Ph.D. program in criminal justice at the State University of New York at Albany. He began his teaching career at the College of Criminal Justice at Northeastern University in Boston, Massachusetts, where he served for nine years. He has also held teaching positions at the University of Nebraska–Omaha, Saint Anselm College in New Hampshire, and then the School of Criminology and Justice Studies at the University of Massachusetts at Lowell (UML); he is now a professor emeritus. During his career, Larry published 16 books on topics such as juvenile law, delinquency, criminology, courts, corrections, criminal justice, and criminal procedure. He is a court-certified expert on police procedure and has testified and consulted on numerous legal cases involving police misconduct and/or failure to act.

Brief Contents

Contents

Part 1
The History and Development of Police

Chapter 1 Police and Society 2

Chapter 2 The Development of Policing: From Past to Present 26

Chapter 3 Becoming a Police Officer 56

Part 2
Police Practice and Organization

Chapter 4 Patrol and Investigation 86

Chapter 5 The Evolving Responsibilities of Responding to Tragedy and the Accompanying Promise of Police Reform...................118

Chapter 6 Contemporary Policing: Community, Problem-Oriented, Broken Windows, and Other Police Innovations 156

Part 3

Challenges of Policing

Chapter 10 Police Misconduct: Corruption and Abuse of Power 278

Chapter 11 Legal Controls...304

Part 4

Contemporary Issues in Policing

Chapter 12 Modern Challenges of the Job 340

Chapter 13 Technology and the Future of Policing 368

American policing has become a lightning rod for controversy. While some citizens worry about public safety, others demand greater police presence and more forceful law enforcement. While many citizens want the police to take action, others fear that the call for aggressive policing will lead to incidents of excessive force and police brutality. The demand to "defund the police" has been heard in a number of communities. Because of this increased interest in law enforcement and the focus the media has put on police officers and police agencies, it has become evident that a book that reviews the current state of policing in America is needed. Rather than rely on traditional, outdated, and sometimes invalid perspectives on police, our text reviews the challenges now being faced by law enforcement agencies across the United States and how they are being met by modern police administrators. In the book *Policing in the United States: Past, Present, and Future,* we take a fresh look at contemporary issues in policing. We examine police topics while adding perspective and context and expanding the typical sound-bite explanations of interactions between the police and the community.

Why We Wrote This Text

We wrote this text for people who want to challenge students to think critically about police action, illuminate problems in policing, and consider workable solutions. This text, written from a social justice perspective, addresses controversial issues in policing in a fair and balanced way with the intention of presenting detailed information. We pull no punches and focus on levels of accountability and professional responsibility. Our aim is to allow students to rethink traditional policing and consider more efficient, user-friendly methods of providing unbiased police services in all communities.

This text allows readers to reimagine the profession of policing in a comprehensive way by considering practical examples to illustrate the complexities of the issues. This text is not just about what the police do on a daily basis, but also how police actions and strategies affect citizens and neighborhoods as well.

We address the most important concerns that have divided the public and captivated the media, ranging from accountability, defund-the-police protests, the Black Lives Matter movement, the George Floyd Justice in Policing Act of 2020, diversity issues in policing, to the use of technology to identify criminals and track their movements. We draw a visible line from the origins of policing to some of the concerns faced today. We dissect patrol functions and discuss differences between the concept of *policing* and *law enforcement.* This text examines more modern problems facing local police like mass shootings, school shootings, and domestic terrorism. We explore important legal cases that shape the way police officers carry out their duties. In a similar fashion, we look at how technology has changed police practices. Also discussed is community policing as a philosophy that guides policing in the twenty-first century.

Goals of This Text

While people are fascinated by stories and issues relating to crime and justice, we have been able to channel this interest into a career as professors in a variety of university settings. Many of our students are pre-service and in-service so that we engage with law enforcement professionals on a daily basis. Between the three of us, we have had years of active law enforcement experience, consulted with police departments, conducted research on policing, and testified as experts in numerous legal cases involving police. Our goal in writing this text is to help students generate the same enthusiasm for policing and law enforcement that we have developed over the years. What could be more important or fascinating than a field of study that deals with such wide-ranging issues as the proper use of deadly force to the development of computer models to direct patrol? Its dynamism and variety make policing an important and engrossing area of study.

Because interest in policing is so timely, this text reviews the most critical ongoing issues and cover the field of policing and law enforcement in an organized and comprehensive manner. It is meant as a broad overview of the field, designed to whet the reader's appetite and encourage further and more in-depth exploration. The key elements of the text include:

- **Diversity and social justice** Diversity and social justice are critical issues in law enforcement today, and the text attempts to integrate racial, ethnic, gender, and cultural diversity throughout.

- **Current research** Every attempt has been made to use the most current research and present it in a balanced fashion, looking at each side of important social debates is presented in full.

- **Social policy** There is a focus on social policy throughout the book so that students can see how research on policing has been translated into effective crime prevention programs.

- **The reality of police work** One of the main goals of the text is to present the reality of police work. Because the media often gives people a distorted picture of how police function, focusing on the most sensational cases, it has become essential to help students separate the rhetoric from the reality. Are most police officers violent? Is racial bias rampant in some police departments? Do police catch most criminals? We try to address and amplify current notions, perceptions, and biases. Each chapter opens with a provocative real-life case or incident that is used to help students envision what police face in their typical shift and how they address these problems.

- **Competing viewpoints** There are still ongoing debates about how police should act and how they should interact with the community. We try to present the various viewpoints on each topic and then draw a conclusion based on the weight of the existing evidence. It is important for us to present an unbiased and objective analysis of leading issues, actions, and policies.

- **Critical thinking** It is important for students to think critically about police and their role in the justice system. Throughout the book, students are asked to think critically about important issues.

The primary goals, then, in writing this text are as follows:

- To separate fact from fiction about police and law enforcement

- To provide students with a thorough knowledge of policing past present and future

- To be as thorough and up to date as possible

- To be objective and unbiased

- To offer a more complete view of policing as a profession

In sum, the text has been carefully structured to cover relevant material in a comprehensive, balanced, and objective fashion. Every attempt has been made to make the presentation of material interesting and contemporary.

Features

The book has a number of features that will allow students to move beyond basic memorization and consider deeper issues in the profession of policing. Each feature is designed to complement different teaching and learning practices. We are mindful that there is rarely enough time in a semester to utilize all of these features, but their availability gives the instructor the option to assign some and draw attention to others.

- **Policing & the Law** This feature looks at classic and recent cases that have created legal precedence that guide police behavior. For example, Chapter 13 reviews a case, *Kyllo v. United States*, that asked the Supreme Court to decide whether technology such as thermal imaging intrudes on people's right to privacy. In Chapter 11, a Policing & the Law feature on the cases *Riley v. California, US. v. Wurie,* and *Torrey Dale Grady v. North Carolina*, looks at how the Supreme Court set out the meaning of a search in the age of digital technology. Another Police and the Law in Chapter 11 on *Kansas v. Glover* sets out important elements of the propriety of a search and seizure of an automobile.

- **Focus on Policing** These features provide an in-depth analysis of important research, police initiatives, and events that have had an impact on policing. In Focus on Policing: Kansas City Preventative Patrol Experiment, the purpose of the experiment was to determine the effectiveness of random preventative patrol practices—a staple of traditional policing—on crime, citizen fear, and satisfaction with the police. Another objective was to determine if the police could establish and maintain experimental conditions for social science research. In Chapter 10, a Focus on Policing feature called Overtime Scam looks at an infamous case in which Boston police officers were arrested and charged with committing overtime fraud and went to prison for claiming hundreds of thousands in pay they did not actually earn.

■ **Careers in Policing** These features provide a look at the various careers students can have in law enforcement ranging from becoming a detective (Chapter 4) to a police dispatcher, someone who answers calls for service, gathers information from the caller, and then directs the response of police officers and emergency service providers (Chapter 12). Another covers the public information officer (PIO) who is responsible for maintaining official communications between the police department and the media (Chapter 12).

■ **Other Features** Each chapter contains several other feature types that support student learning. Each chapter begins with a **Chapter Outline** and a list of chapter **Learning Objectives**. The learning objectives are called out in the margin of the text to help readers navigate where each objective's corresponding content begins within the chapter. In addition, each **Chapter Summary** is organized by the chapter learning objectives.

Throughout the book, **Critical Thinking** questions, designed to spur classroom discussion and debate, are placed near relevant text. Each chapter also contains a number of **On the Web** features that direct students to sites that provide more in-depth material than is contained in the text. Lastly, wherever a **Key Term** first appears in the text, it is highlighted and a definition for it is provided in the margin.

Organization of the Text

Policing in the United States is divided into four main sections containing 13 chapters.

■ **Part 1: The History and Development of Police** This section contains three chapters that set out the role of police in society, tracing the development of law enforcement from ancient times to today's modern police force. The role of police within the criminal justice process is covered in detail.

■ **Part 2: Police Practice and Organization** What are the day-to-day activities of police officers? How is patrol and investigation carried out? What is being done now to modernize policing, ranging from community policing to intelligence-led policing?

■ **Part 3: Challenges of Policing** The challenges of policing in modern society are covered in detail. We look at the significant effort being made to increase the role of women and people of color in policing and how this diversity affects policing. Another challenge is how police use their discretion and how it can lead to misconduct and abuse of power.

■ **Part 4: Contemporary Issues in Policing** How does the stress of police work affect the health and well-being? And is stress increasing as budgets are cut, workloads increase, and the media places its focus on police behavior? Can digital technology improve the situation and how has it impacted policing today?

Chapter Contents

■ **Chapter 1: Police in Society** This introductory chapter provides a foundation for understanding the role of the police within the community as well as in the criminal justice system. The chapter begins with a description of modern policing and the police role with an emphasis on the differences between policing and law enforcement. This includes a discussion of how the police act as agents of social control and how this role fits with the competing models of due process and crime control. The responsibility of enforcing social control has direct impacts on the relationship between police officers and the community. Further, the chapter places policing within the context of the larger criminal justice system—exploring how police decision-making both affects latter stages of the criminal justice system and how police discretion affects overall outcomes. These decisions all factor into police legitimacy—the next part of the chapter. Police legitimacy is not determined by the lawfulness of police conduct; instead, it is determined mostly by procedural justice or the perceived fairness of the specific police action. Finally, this chapter concludes with a discussion of myths associated with policing in the United States as well as the CSI effect. There are two Career features in this chapter. The first feature explores the role of patrol officers in U.S. police agencies. The second feature details the role and responsibilities of detectives or investigators in police departments.

■ **Chapter 2: The Development of Policing: From Past to the Present** Chapter 2 details the antecedents to modern policing in the United States. While the roots of policing can be traced back before the first organized police existed in Egypt in about 300 BC, much of policing in the United States has its roots in early English society. One of the most well-known contributors to modern policing is Sir Robert Peel who created the Metropolitan Police Act, which established the first organized police force in London. Its members would be known from then on as bobbies, after their creator. This was the first time that policing is seen as a career option and not simply a task that must be performed by men in the city. Early policing in the colonies was neither proactive nor organized. One of the chapter Feature highlights the uniquely American slave patrols—a cruel and dehumanizing part of early policing that can't be traced back to early English society. The chapter then discusses the challenges associated with the first organized police departments in the United States and what is now known as the political era of policing before delving into the reform efforts of the 1960s and the civil rights era. Next, the adoption of community and problem-oriented policing is discussed, ending with the state of policing In the present day. This final section includes a survey of the different federal, state, and local police agencies that comprise modern policing.

■ **Chapter 3: Becoming a Police Officer** Chapter 3 begins with a discussion of the current landscape of policing in the United States. Most municipal police departments in the United States are independent agencies within the executive branch of government, operating without specific administrative control from any higher governmental authority. In particular, this chapter details the bureaucratic nature of policing, including some of both the positive and negative aspects of bureaucracy that affect all government organizations generally and the police specifically. Next, the chapter explores the recruitment and selection processes to explain the characteristics of officers who comprise police agencies in the United States, with a special emphasis on the crucial role of diversity in policing. The specific example of

the recruitment and selection criteria of the Dallas Police Department is offered to provide specific information for students interested in pursuing a career in policing. This section includes a general description of the types of examinations that are included in the selection process. Next, the chapter includes a discussion of the importance of education and educational requirements within policing. While most police agencies still do not require recruits to have an advanced degree, the number requiring some higher education in the hiring and promotion process is growing. Finally, this chapter ends with information about accreditation and training, including the role of national accreditation through CALEA or accreditation at the state level. The specific example of the Texas Commission on Law Enforcement (TCOLE) is used.

■ **Chapter 4: Patrol and Investigation** Chapter 4 begins Part 2 of the text and moves beyond introductory information about policing to more in-depth discussion about patrol and investigation. There are numerous boxed features in this chapter, including two research sections on the Kansas City Preventative Patrol Experiment and the RAND Detective Study—both seminal research studies in the history of policing. The chapter begins with a discussion of the roles and responsibilities of patrol officers—namely order maintenance and peacekeeping. The police engage in practices that involve handling minor offenses and conflicts and disorders before they escalate into serious crimes to keep communities safe. The chapter involves the different logistical aspects of patrol as well as the various types of patrol: foot, automobile, motorcycle among others. Next, the myth of the value of quick response time is explored. Finally, hotspot policing and other patrol innovations are included. The chapter concludes with details about the role of detectives and research on investigations and investigator workloads with emphasis on the challenges of measuring the effectiveness of investigations. The role of forensic evidence is put into context as well. This section also presents the big picture, including the experience of victims of crime in dealing with both patrol and detectives.

■ **Chapter 5: The Evolving Responsibilities of Responding to Tragedy and the Accompanying Promise of Police Reform** Chapter 5 starts with detailing the changing role of the police, particularly regarding mass shootings, domestic terrorism, and mass casualty incidents. The frequency and complexity of the various types of mass shootings have forced the police to rethink their strategies of response and training. Added to that complexity is when these mass shootings happen at schools. The question asked is, is it possible to prevent these incidents? Terrorism has increasingly been added to the list of responsibilities for local police since the attacks of 9/11. The Focus on Policing box highlights the problems and successes that the police had in dealing with the Boston Marathon bombing. Terrorism is no longer events that come from other countries, increasingly domestic terrorism is a main issue for police. We explore the roles of local, county, state, and federal law enforcement efforts to combat terrorism. Then the chapter moves into a discussion of police reform, helping the police become more efficient, effective, and more user friendly. The chapter then gives a detailed overview of the George Floyd Justice in Policing Act of 2020, which addresses a wide range of policies and practices in policing and law enforcement accountability.

- **Chapter 6: Contemporary Policing: Community, Problem-Oriented, Broken Windows, and Other Police Innovations** Chapter 6 explores the transition from traditional policing to strategies that include community involvement from the start. After the tumultuous 1960s and 1970s police departments began experimenting with initiatives to improve the relationship between police and the community. The chapter outlines the development of community involvement in policing and introduces the concept of problem-solving and problem-oriented policing. Police Community Relations Units were developed in the 1960s and 1970s and had programs with the general title of police–community relations designed to make citizens more aware of police activities, alert them to methods of self-protection, and improve general attitudes toward policing. The chapter also illuminates problems or challenges faced in deploying community policing projects and explores the effectiveness of each new strategy. In contrast, the chapter outlines the broken-windows and zero-tolerance policing initiatives. As policing moves toward data-driven initiatives, the era of CompStat (Computer Statistics) is ushered in to mixed reviews.

- **Chapter 7: Ethical Issues in Policing** Chapter 7 takes a big picture view of ethical policing. The chapter starts with defining ethics as well as an overview of ethical policing practices. We ask that the reader think about a definition of justice, as we offer a working definition of justice to frame the concepts in this book. Included in this chapter is the idea of accountability as described in the context of whistleblowing and the duty of police officers to intervene when a colleague is doing something wrong or using excessive force (among other things). The chapter examines accountability through qualified immunity, special commissions that examine the police and legal remedies. In our focus on policing, we introduce the term *blue fragility* and explore officer demeanor and attitude after an outcry to hold rogue officers accountable. The chapter wraps up with a discussion of citizen review boards and police officer and agency accreditation. Many of these concepts are explored through the lens of procedural justice.

- **Chapter 8: The Changing Rank and File** Chapter 8 explains the idea of policing as a subculture. A subculture is a subdivision within the dominant culture that has its own norms, beliefs, values unwritten rules, values, and worldview. Subcultures can be both positive and negative. The discussion of subculture leads to the discussion of the blue curtain in policing. The chapter then explains various police styles or personalities that determine a working attitude through which the officer approaches policing. The chapter also shows the history and challenges of women in policing as well as the legal challenges that they have had to face. Then there is a discussion of the tumultuous history of people of color in policing from the mid-1800s, through the civil rights era until modern policing today. The recruitment and retention of officers of color is considered, and ways to increase diversity within the ranks of policing. Because many Black officers found themselves marginalized within their departments, many banded together and or joined police affiliate organizations based on their shared heritage. The focus is on Black and Latinx officers as well as from other underrepresented populations. Tension within policing is discussed and the chapter ends with a discussion of intersectionality within policing by exploring the experiences of people of color who are also women. The chapter then asks, "Does diversity matter?" Representative bureaucracy theory states that a heterogenous police department is valuable.

- **Chapter 9: Police Discretion** Chapter 9 starts with a discussion and definition of police discretion. Discretion has always been an element of police work but was only formally identified in the 1950s when municipal police officers were observed in the field and found that they do not always follow the letter of the law. Police officers exercise a great deal of discretion in their dealings with the public and were found to ignore violations of the law sometimes. The chapter also debates full enforcement versus selective enforcement to determine which is more realistic and practical. Then the chapter explores factors influencing discretion such as legal, extra-legal, and situational factors. We also explain the CSI factor that drives the interest in forensics and investigations. Also discussed are legal controls such as oversight and accreditation that should improve the use of discretion. There is also discretion in the use of force. The use of force is one of the most controversial aspects of policing. Because police officers are the only government officials who routinely use force, it is important to know how it is being used and to take steps to make sure it is applied fairly and efficiently.

- **Chapter 10: Police Misconduct: Corruption and Abuse of Power** Chapter 10 looks at police misconduct, forms of misbehavior that traditionally has taken two separate paths: corruption and abuse of power. The chapter begins with an analysis of police corruption that occurs when officers engage in behavior that violates the same criminal law that they have sworn to uphold. Some may demand bribes and gratuities from law violators and business owners while others may engage in crimes such as burglary and larceny. Some forms of corruption take place within police agencies themselves, including wage theft, embezzlement, and other crimes. The chapter then reviews a second form of misconduct—abuse of power—that occurs when police officers make false arrests, use excessive force; falsify evidence, and employ racial profiling in violation of a citizen's civil rights. Racial profiling is of particular concern because the practice violates civil rights and differentiates based on race or ethnicity. The chapter then reviews the causes of misconduct, including departmental culture, gender, personality, prior history, and work-related issues. Several departments have taken steps to reduce misconduct. The chapter reviews a number of these initiatives, including creating organized outside review boards and

special prosecutors to investigate reported incidents of corruption. This chapter also shows why change is difficult because of the police code of silence, which demands that officers do not cooperate with outside authorities.

- **Chapter 11: Legal Controls** Chapter 11 reviews the law that controls the balance between the law enforcement agent's need for a free hand to investigate crimes and the citizen's constitutional right to be free from illegal police behavior. The chapter's main focus is on the law controlling searches for evidence, arrest, and the subsequent interrogation of suspects. Special emphasis is placed on the changes in the law that reflects the Supreme Court justices' evolving legal philosophy that impacts their view of how the need to maintain public safety can impact the civil liberties of criminal defendants. There is a thorough investigation of the Fourth Amendment and how it controls searches and seizures of evidence and people. There are sections on what happens when an arrest is made, what the law requires for a legal arrest, when an arrest warrant can be issued, and what the legal rules are for serving a warrant. There is also discussion about when a warrantless search and arrest can be made. This chapter also covers the interrogation of suspects after they have been arrested, what the police can do to get someone to talk, and how has their behavior been controlled by the courts in order to preserve the suspect's right to remain silent. The chapter also devotes considerable time to explaining the exclusionary rule that states that all evidence obtained by illegal searches and seizures is inadmissible in criminal trials.

- **Chapter 12: Modern Challenges of the Job** Chapter 12 reviews the stresses in policing that were unknown to earlier generations. These challenges range from the health and well-being of police officer and their self-care to dealing with budgetary crises, relationships with the media, and policing protests all while under the scrutiny of the media in the new 24-hour news cycle. The chapter begins with an analysis of the health concerns created by police stress. It is more likely for police officers to suffer injury and death due to poor nutrition, lack of exercise, sleep deprivation, and substance abuse than to be injured on the job. the chapter covers such issues as police suicide, chronic disease, and physical and mental health problems. Another source of stress is a reduction in police budgets, resulting in departments across the country being forced to do more with fewer resources. Still another source of stress is the way police are portrayed in the media whose coverage portrays police as violent and racist. The widespread availability of cell phone cameras provides a steady supply of highly damaging video footage. Another modern challenge is the proper response to mass protests. This sometimes results in charges of excessive force and negative attention from the media. There are two Career features in the chapter.

■ **Chapter 13: Technology and the Future of Policing** Chapter 13 looks at how police departments are now employing advanced technology in all facets of their operations. It shows that technology has revolutionized almost all elements of policing, from assigning patrol routes to streamlining investigations to gathering evidence. The chapter begins with a discussion of the origin of police technology, going back to the contributions of August Vollmer, considered to be the father of modern policing. There is a discussion of how more than 100 years ago the first police cars became widespread, followed by the two-way radio, a device that eliminated communication problems. We cover the work of the Law Enforcement Assistance Administration (LEAA) that funded innovative research on police work and advanced training of police officers. Technological innovations involving computers transformed the way police kept records, investigated crimes, and communicated with one another. The chapter covers what is referred to as hard technology, which typically involves tangible equipment that is designed to help police prevent crime, identify suspects, and bring them to justice. This includes such equipment as body-worn cameras (BWCs), thermal imaging, and gunshot detection technology. The chapter reviews the recent employment of small, unmanned surveillance drones used to track crime and monitor neighborhoods. Their use has also brought warnings that a big brother mentality may be developing. The Focus on Policing feature looks in depth at a device that uses a network of weatherproof acoustic sensors that locate and record gunshots. The new technology also involves software and information systems that improve the effectiveness of police operations. This soft technology helps identify geographic "hotspots" where a majority of crimes are concentrated. Computer

mapping now allows departments to identify problem areas for particular crimes, such as drug dealing or burglary.

Online Learning Platform: MindTap

MindTap, today's most innovative online learning platform, powers your students from memorization to mastery. The MindTap for *Policing in the U.S.* gives you complete control of your course to provide engaging content, challenge every individual, and build student confidence. This MindTap introduces students to core concepts from the beginning of your course using a simplified learning path that progresses from understanding to application.

We built MindTap for this title with you in mind. We talked to current Criminal Justice and Policing instructors, as well as MindTap users, to find out what they liked and what they wanted more of. With that feedback, we built a learning path that consists of applicable and useful activities for student learning and instructor teaching and assessment. We hope you're happy with it. Universal learning path features include:

■ **Why Does [Topic] Matter to Me?** Immediately engage students with new "Why Does [Topic] Matter to Me?" activities. These activities connect the upcoming chapter to an authentic, real-world scenario designed to pique engagement and emphasize relevance. Use these activities to ensure students read material before class and to trigger lively in-class discussion.

■ **Chapter-Level eTextbook** Foster student engagement with a dynamic eTextbook that brings the value, concepts, and applications of the printed text to life. Students open an active-learning experience as each chapter provides opportunities to interact with content using the approach that's best for the individual learner.

■ **"Learn It" Video Cases** "Learn It" activities offer small sections of instruction that highlight the most important concepts in each chapter via a Video Case. Each activity reinforces the text's instruction and approaches concepts in a different way to promote student choice and autonomy with personalized learning. You can assign "Learn It" Video

Cases to ensure students have read and understand key concepts before class.

- **"You Decide"** Our "You Decide" branching activities encourage students to apply their knowledge as they role-play scenarios specific to Criminal Justice and the Policing profession. Assign these carefully designed, practically focused activities as chapter homework to ensure your students know how to apply what they have learned in the real world.

- **"Listen and React"** Comprised of an authentic audio clip followed by a critical thinking prompt, "Listen and React" activities require the learner to apply key chapter concepts to real-world scenarios while also practicing crucial writing and listening skills.

- **Chapter Quizzes** Use carefully curated chapter quizzes to assess student performance and immediately identify class-wide learning needs.

Learn more about MindTap at: http://www.cengage.com/mindtap

Ancillary Package

Additional instructor resources for this product are available online. Instructor assets include an Instructor's Manual, Educator's Guide, PowerPoint® slides, and a test bank powered by Cognero®. Sign up or sign in at http://faculty.cengage.com to search for and access this product and its online resources.

The Cengage Instructor Center is an all-in-one resource for class preparation, presentation, and testing. The instructor resources available for download include:

- **Instructor's Manual** Includes key terms with definitions, a chapter outline, and additional activities and discussion questions that may be conducted in an on-ground, hybrid, or online modality.

- **Solution and Answer Guide** Provides answers to all Critical Thinking questions presented in the text.

- **PowerPoint Slides** Helping to make lectures more engaging, these handy Microsoft PowerPoint slides

outline the chapters of the main text in a classroom-ready presentation. The PowerPoint slides reflect the content and organization of the text and provide ample opportunities for generating classroom discussion and interaction.

- **Test Bank** A comprehensive test bank, offered in Blackboard, Moodle, Desire2Learn, and Canvas formats, contains learning objective-specific multiple-choice and essay questions for each chapter. Import the test bank into your LMS to edit and manage questions and to create tests.

- **Cengage Learning Testing, Powered by Cognero** This assessment software is a flexible, online system that allows you to import, edit, and manipulate test bank content from the *Policing in the United States* test bank, or elsewhere, including your own favorite test questions; create multiple test versions in an instant; and deliver tests from your LMS, your classroom, or wherever you want.

Acknowledgments

Many people helped make this book possible. We would like to give special thanks to both our Product Manager Conor Allen and our wonderful Content Manager Chip Cheek. We would also like to thank our Learning Designer Mara Vuillaume for her guidance and perspective on this first edition. We are thankful to the whole team at Cengage, who managed this process from start to finish, and to Senior Project Manager Lori Hazzard at MPS Limited, who guided us through the production process. We are appreciative of the collaboration and support.

Professor Boyd would like to give additional thanks to Kimberly Conway Dumpson, JD, CFRE, for technical support and guidance while writing this book, and to Ann and Shelley Stewart for establishing the professorship that allowed him to give back to the community and work on this book. Thank you all.

Lorenzo M. Boyd
Melissa S. Morabito
Larry J. Siegel

Part 1

The History and Development of Police

This section contains three chapters discussing the role of police in society, the development of policing from its origins in ancient times, and law enforcement today, including its culture and style. The section also covers the duties of police and law enforcement agents in contemporary society, their role in the criminal justice system, and the interactions they have with members of the community.

Chapter 1
Police and Society

Chapter 2
The Development of Policing: From Past to Present

Chapter 3
Becoming a Police Officer

Police and Society

Learning Objectives

LO1 Analyze what the police do.

LO2 Describe the patrol, investigation, and administration functions.

LO3 Compare policing vs. law enforcement.

LO4 Recognize what is meant when we say that police are social control agents.

LO5 Compare and contrast the crime control and due process models.

LO6 Explore the role of the police in the community.

LO7 Describe the role of the police in the criminal justice process.

LO8 Explain the concept of police legitimacy.

LO9 Describe common myths about policing.

Chapter Outline

What Is Policing?

What the Police Do

Force and Discretion

Patrol, Investigation, and Administration

Policing vs. Law Enforcement

Police and Social Control
   Police as Social Control Agents

Two Traditional Models of Criminal Justice Policy: Crime Control vs. Due Process
   Due Process vs. Crime Control in Action: Using Technology

Policing the Public

Police and the Criminal Justice Process

Police and the Pretrial Stage of Justice

Police and the Trial Process

Police and Corrections

Police Legitimacy

Myths in Policing
   Super Cop Image
   CSI Effect

Jamey Lee Matthews went on a crime spree in Alabama. Among the local stores that he robbed included Mike's Quick Stop convenience store, a Dollar General store, Winn Dixie supermarket, a Gas Station, and a pharmacy. He first robbed the convenience store, where he entered with a shotgun, threatening a female clerk ordering her to open the cash register, she complied. In a series of armed robberies that followed, he wore a Halloween mask as he entered the stores carrying a firearm. He threatened employees and customers and demanded money. During one robbery at a pharmacy, he changed his routine. Instead of looking for quick cash, Matthews demanded prescription medication. As a result of this robbery, he ended up with more than 3,000 pills which contained controlled substances.

Matthews wore distinctive Halloween style masks during most of the robberies. One of which was a caricature of a devil. The weapons that he used were equally distinctive. Many had different colored tape on them. One gun had a clear ammunition magazine, another was a silver sawed-off rifle, and yet a final weapon was an Uzi-style assault weapon.

The case took a potentially deadly turn when Matthews robbed a gas station, brandished a gun, and threatened employees. When he left the station, employees chased him down the street and Matthews fired at them, hitting and severely wounding one of his pursuers.

Because of the seriousness of these crimes, a team of law enforcement officers assigned to the case included agents from the the Bureau of Alcohol, Tobacco, Firearms, and Explosives (ATF); the Federal Bureau of Investigation (FBI); the Birmingham Alabama Police Department; and the Blount County and Jefferson County (Alabama) Sheriff's Office.

The case was cracked open when a seriously injured man was found under a remote bluff outside of Birmingham, Alabama, and taken to a hospital. Law enforcement officers responding to the scene found a pickup truck a short distance away with various firearms leaning up against the vehicle and others on the ground nearby, as well as evidence inside the truck seemingly tied to the series of Birmingham robberies. The truck was registered to a Birmingham woman who was the mother of the man found under the bluff: Jamey Lee Matthews.

Among the items recovered from the pickup truck that Matthews drove, as well as his mother's house were some of the firearms and masks matching eyewitness descriptions, clothing similar to what the robber had worn, a customer's check written out to the victim gas station, and prescription bottles from the victim pharmacy.

One reason that local authorities asked for federal help in the case was their desire to prosecute Matthews under the Hobbs Act, which is an anti-racketeering law passed by Congress in 1946. The Hobbs Act makes it illegal for anyone to obstruct or affect interstate trade in any way or by any degree by committing robbery or extortion. It prohibits the committing of, attempting, or conspiring to commit robbery or extortion that would have even a slight harmful effect on interstate or foreign commerce. Showing that a business's assets or an individual's assets were being drained is sufficient in proving that commerce had been affected. The person or business need not be involved in interstate or foreign commerce. Although state criminal statutes exist prohibiting robbery, if committing such a robbery impedes, delays, or affects trade or business in any way, prosecutors may also apply the Hobbs Act in addition to the statutes, which substantially increases the penalties involved. In the face of overwhelming evidence, and the fear of a very long prison sentence, Matthews agreed to plead guilty and was sentenced to 25 years in prison.[1]

Do you think offenders like Matthews should be allowed to take a plea to get a reduced sentence or should they face the maximum for violent crimes? While inter-agency cooperation has its benefits, what can be some drawbacks?

Internet crime

Any illegal activity involving one or more components of the Internet, such as websites, chat rooms, and/or email. Internet crime involves the use of the Internet to communicate false or fraudulent representations to consumers. These crimes may include, but are not limited to, advance-fee schemes, nondelivery of goods or services, computer hacking, or employment/business opportunity schemes.

What Is Policing?

The Matthews case illustrates a number of facets of contemporary law enforcement. First, it demonstrates the changing police role and the emerging crime patterns police must confront on a daily basis. One of Matthews's crimes took place at a local drug store. Pharmacy crime is a growing problem in the United States.[2] Pharmacy crime has captured national attention because of the opioid epidemic sweeping the United States and creating another problem for contemporary law enforcement.[3] As criminal acts become more complex involving criminal, health, and social issues, ranging from robbing pharmacies to international conspiracies and transnational cybercrimes, law enforcement agencies by choice or necessity are finding it critical to pool resources and cooperate in order to be effective. The Focus on Policing feature on the next page discusses another type of inter-agency cooperation to fight **Internet crimes**.

These cases also illustrate that in order to work effectively in the modern world, contemporary law enforcement agents must be aware of a wide range of issues, ranging from the legal to the scientific, from computer monitoring to the effectiveness of nonlethal weapons. This includes collaboration between federal, state, and local agencies. In the Matthews case, local law enforcement agents, aware of an obscure federal law, asked the cooperation of federal agencies in order to apply an element of the U.S. criminal code to a local case in order to (a) bring pressure on the suspect and (b) get them to plea bargain and (c) enhance their sentence. In response to cybercrime, federal law enforcement must rely on local police to encourage victims to report to the federal government.

LightField Studios/Shutterstock.com

Police officers today must be aware of a wide range of issues, ranging from the legal to the scientific. They must also be willing to collaborate with other federal, state, and local agencies.

Internet Complaint Center

According to the Internet Crime Complaint Center (www.IC3.gov), people who are the victim of Internet scams often do not know where to go for assistance. In response to this need, the Internet Crime Complaint Center (IC3) is a collaboration between the FBI and the National White Collar Crime Center. It was started in 2000 to receive complaints of web-based crimes. IC3 receives complaints about a wide range of crimes, including fraud, economic espionage, hacking, online extortion, and identity theft. Staff also gather national statistics on Internet crime, inform police agencies and the public of national cybercrime trends, and issue public service announcements and "scam alerts" regarding current types of fraud that are occurring.

The IC3 issues warnings and notices designed to help people avoid being scammed. For example, one popular Internet fraud scheme, the confidence fraud/romance scam, encompasses those designed to pull on a victim's "heartstrings." In 2022, the IC3 received almost 20,000 reports from victims who lost $700 million in romance scams; this type of fraud accounts for the third-highest losses reported by victims. Romance scams arise when a criminal assumes a fake identity online to gain a potential victim's affection and confidence. The scammer then uses the deception of a romantic or close relationship to manipulate or steal from the victim. The criminals who carry out romance scams are experts at what they do and will seem genuine, caring, and believable. The scammer's intention is to quickly establish an online relationship, endear themselves to the victim, gain trust, and eventually ask for money. Scammers may propose and make false plans to meet in person to get married. They tell the victim that they are out of the country or in the military, or a trades-based industry engaged in projects outside the United States. That makes it easier to avoid meeting in person—and more plausible when they request money be sent overseas for a medical emergency or unexpected legal fee. Other scammers are present on most dating and social media sites.

In 2022, the IC3 received thousands of complaints from victims of online relationships resulting in sextortion or investment scams. Sextortion occurs when someone threatens to distribute private and sensitive material, for example, compromising photos, if their demands are not met. In 2022, the IC3 reports an uptick in sextortion involving the threat of releasing fake images or videos created from content posted on social media sites or web postings. Many victims of romance scams report being pressured into investment opportunities, especially using cryptocurrency. In 2022, there have been around 5,000 complaints made by victims who reported the use of investments and cryptocurrencies, or "pig butchering"—so named because victims' investment accounts are fattened up before draining, much a like a pig before slaughter. Another variation on this kind of Internet fraud are grandparent scams, where criminals impersonate a panicked loved one, usually a grandchild, nephew, or niece of an older person. The loved one claims to be in trouble and needs money immediately.

The FBI's IC3 provides the American public with a direct outlet to report cybercrimes to the FBI. They analyze and investigate the reporting to track the trends and threats from cyber criminals and then share this data with intelligence and law enforcement partners. The FBI, alongside their partners, recognizes how crucial information sharing of cyber activities is to prepare our partners to combat the cyber threat, through a whole-of-government approach. Critical to that approach is public reporting to IC3, enabling them to fill in the missing pieces with this valuable information during the investigatory process. Not only does this reporting help prevent additional crimes, but it also allows them to develop key insights on the ever-evolving trends and threats faced from malign cyber actors. IC3 analysts are able to connect what may seem like small incidents to make cases against bigger perpetrators. Internet crime is rarely targeted against one city or town. Rather, many police departments may receive complaints about scams ranging from $500 to $1,000. Pulled together, this can be evidence of a substantial scam. www.ic3.gov

(Continued)

Critical Thinking

1. Why would some people refuse to report being scammed to the IC3? Might victims of sextortion be reluctant to report the incident?

2. Why would someone trust a person who proposes marriage before they have ever met?

Sources: Internet Complaint Center, Internet Crime Report 2022, https://www.ic3.gov/Media/PDF/AnnualReport/2022_IC3Report.pdf; Police Executive Research Forum, *Critical Issues in Policing Series, The Role of Local Law Enforcement Agencies In Preventing and Investigating Cybercrime* (Washington, DC, April 2014), https://www.policeforum.org/assets/docs/Critical_Issues_Series_2/the%20role%20of%20local%20law%20enforcement%20agencies%20in%20preventing%20and%20investigating%20cybercrime%202014.pdf.

This first chapter introduces the concept of policing and distinguishes between policing and law enforcement. Among the issues discussed are the police role in contemporary society and the role of the police in the criminal justice system.

L01

Analyze what the police do.

▶ What the Police Do

The term "police" refers to an institution of state authority that represents the will of the government through the enforcement of criminal laws and the maintenance of civil order. In the narrowest sense, police departments are assigned the duty of maintaining law and order—fighting crime—in the jurisdiction they serve. This extremely narrow viewpoint is what the media presents to society. In countless books, movies, and TV shows, the public has been presented with a view of policing that romanticizes cops as fearless crime fighters who think little of their own safety as they engage in daily high-speed chases and shootouts.

How close is this portrayal of a crime fighter to real life? Not very close, according to most research. It is true that police officers routinely investigate crimes. When someone calls the police department after a crime is committed, officers in the area respond to the call. They take statements from parties involved in the incident as well as any witnesses to get additional information and statements. Officers also gather up any evidence immediately accessible and help section off areas where the crime occurs so forensic scientists can come and do more thorough evidence searches.

Nonetheless, a police officer's crime-fighting efforts are only a small part of their overall activities. Police officers are called on to deal with increasingly difficult and unpredictable situations—many of which are noncriminal acts—including minor disturbances, service calls, and administrative duties. It is more likely for an officer to administer first aid and/or emergency medical care, direct traffic, enforce parking regulations, or take charge of dangerous animals than it is for them to be involved in a shoot-out.

The evidence, then, shows that unlike their TV and film counterparts, the police engage in many activities that are not related to crime. Although officers in large urban departments may be called on to handle more felony cases than those in small towns, they too will probably find that most of their daily activities are not crime related. Many of the calls for service that the police handle can be better characterized as problems that need to be addressed, or order maintenance issues than criminal offenses.

Police officers today can be viewed as problem-solvers, who, while serving the public, are more concerned with addressing quality-of-life issues in a community than they are arresting felons. **Policing** deals with the day-to-day issues in a community and tries to address problems before they become crimes. Whether officers engage in preventive patrol, respond to calls for service, forge relationships with citizens, or aggressively target a small list of known criminal suspects, they have to be constantly vigilant and prepared. Being a police officer is a daunting task.

policing

The maintenance of public order, law enforcement, and crime prevention by police officers, the duly sworn agents of the civil authority of government.

It is often a thankless task in which officers face potentially dangerous situations on a daily basis and have to draw on their training and basic knowledge to keep themselves safe as well as the general community, and often the suspects too. Focus on Policing: Improving Police Community Relations discusses one such instance.

Force and Discretion

Police are an agency of the civil government and not a quasi-military organization. However, like the military, they have the authority to use force, coerce behavior, and detain citizens. The police are the only agency of a civil government

Focus on Policing

Improving Police Community Relations

In 2008, the city of Fayetteville, North Carolina, was dealing with issues of high crime rates and very low citizen satisfaction with the police. With over 30 years of policing experience, **Fayetteville Police Chief Thomas Bergamine** was committed to addressing the problems in the city. So, he elicited the help of criminal justice professors from the local Fayetteville State University, Drs. Boyd and Brown.

They realized that the city had high rates of unemployment, drug use, and transiency. Most of the people who lived in the city rented their housing units, and many did not take as good of care of the unit as an owner probably would. After much consideration and planning, the team decided that the city of Fayetteville was a socially unhealthy city; instead of building just a community policing plan, they built a community wellness plan.

The police department moved from a strict reliance on law enforcement and moved toward addressing community *problems* before they became crimes. They enlisted the help of other city departments. The parks were cleaned up, many pieces of broken playground equipment were fixed, and abandoned houses boarded up or torn down. Landlords were held accountable for their properties and were heavily fined when the properties were not up to code. Abandoned cars in the streets were towed away.

City leaders then encouraged the community members to help spruce up the neighborhoods by cutting grass and planting flowers. Within a year or two, many neighborhoods within the city of Fayetteville started to transform into places where people were proud to live. Crime rates in some areas were reduced and many reported a higher level of satisfaction with the police. This alone is not the magic cure to stop all crimes, but when the police moved from strict law enforcement mode into a community-oriented strategy

© Thomas Bergamine

Fayetteville Police Chief Thomas Bergamine

of policing, they became part of the community, and police–citizen relations improved.

Critical Thinking

1. Can the Fayetteville model be easily adopted in larger cities? What might be the impediments to implementation?

2. Considering recent incidents, does the public trust the police to deal with problems in their community before they become crimes?

authorized to use force and it is this element of the police role that has created a great amount of controversy. When the right to use force should be exercised, and against whom, has become a critical public issue.

One reason the use of force has become so controversial is because the police exercise levels of discretion in doing their job that are afforded to few other professionals. Police discretion and how it's employed can have profound effects on the lives of community members. It is expected that police agents handle calls differently, using their discretion to deal with the situation in either an official or unofficial manner. It is routine to expect that if two people are caught speeding, one is let go with a warning, and another issued a citation. Despite the fact that their use of discretion may involve a split-second decision, police officers are expected to make the right decisions and do the right things every time. Without appropriate guidance, at best these decisions may be at inconsistent and at worst discriminatory.[4]

One reason that the use of discretion matters so much is that we hold the police to a much higher standard than other occupations (and rightly so) is because the police have the authority to use deadly force. Take for instance the 2016 shooting death of Philando Castile. While driving in a suburb of St. Paul, Minnesota, with his girlfriend, Diamond Reynolds, and her 4-year-old daughter, Mr. Castile was stopped by Officer Jeronimo Yanez. Castile told the officers he had a firearm that he was licensed to carry. When Officer Yanez asked to see identification and registration, Mr. Castile went to find it. Yanez then fired seven shots at point-blank range, killing him instantly. Yanez was later acquitted on all charges. These highly publicized incidents, often accompanied by cell phone video, exacerbate public debate over the relationship between the police and the public they serve.

Serve and Protect

While their duties are vast and complex, police officers are charged with protecting and serving the public while protecting the constitutional rights of all citizens. This includes upholding democratic principles such as:

- Individualism
- Civil Rights
- Human Dignity
- Social Justice
- Constitutionalism
- Majority Rule
- Rule of Law

In fact, the phrase "serve and protect" is common in the credo of many police agencies. Police officers are responsible for protecting all members of the community—including the most vulnerable citizens. Providing services to people who are experiencing homelessness, who have mental or physical illnesses, and youth can be challenging for police. Police officers are also required to serve their communities by helping citizens in times of crisis and emergency, such as when a natural disaster hits. To protect citizens on the road, they issue

Shironosov/iStock/Getty Images

While the media focuses on crime fighting, police are involved in many public service roles ranging from speaking at schools and businesses, organizing athletic activities, and instructing in rape aggression defense (RAD) programs.

tickets to dangerous and careless drivers. To protect them in their communities, they make arrests that deter illegal and dangerous behaviors.

While the media focuses on crime fighting, the efforts by many departments to nurture community involvement often get overlooked. These public service roles include speaking at schools and businesses, where officers educate people on how to avoid dangerous situations and handle emergency situations. Other forms of community involvement that create a better rapport between law enforcement and citizens include athletic activities, rape aggression defense (RAD), and driver safety programs.

Patrol, Investigation, and Administration

LO2

Describe the patrol, investigation, and administration functions.

To carry out their duties, the typical police department is divided into at least two, and sometimes three or more, segments.

- **Patrol.** Assigned an area in which to enforce the law and render service, patrol officers may ride in a car or a bicycle, walk, use a boat, or even ride on a horse.

- **Investigation.** Large jurisdictions maintain an investigative or detective branch whose main duty is to identify a culprit after a crime has been completed. Not all local police departments have investigative units; it is routine for small-town police departments to rely on state or county agencies to provide investigators.

- **Administration.** Police departments are independent agencies that maintain a management staff, including the day-to-day management of the department including such tasks as hiring, training, and record keeping.

Whether in administration, patrol, or investigation, police officers take part in a wide range of duties: from purchasing equipment to responding to emergency calls, from rendering first aid to controlling dangerous animals. Each element of policing—patrol, investigation, and even administration—requires split-second decision making based on experience and training. Some of the typical duties performed by each element of a municipal police department are set out in Exhibit 1.1.

Police work, then, involves much more than catching offenders but a variety of administrative, patrol, and investigation tasks that will be discussed in greater detail throughout this book.

Policing vs. Law Enforcement

LO3

Compare policing vs. law enforcement.

Typically, the terms *policing* and *law enforcement* are used by people interchangeably. Although this may be acceptable in many situations, there are discernable differences between the two concepts. Policing is a much broader concept than law enforcement and police agencies carry out many different tasks than simply enforcing laws. Police officers perform a wide range of activities—from delivering babies to returning stray pets—that do not involve criminal law violations or enforcement. Policing often involves officers trying to solve problems before they become crimes. The majority of citizens' calls to local police departments are calls for service that do not involve enforcing laws; because of this, the service-provider side of policing must be maintained and prioritized.

Exhibit 1.1

Duties of Police Officers

Patrol Officers' Duties

- Patrol a designated area of the city on foot, on a motorcycle, or in a radio cruiser to preserve law and order.
- Prevent the commission of crime.
- Answer calls and complaints involving misdemeanors and felonies.
- If a crime is committed, identify and apprehend criminal offenders.
- Secure a crime scene.
- Conduct preliminary investigations, gather evidence, obtain witnesses, and make arrests; testify as a witness in court.
- When necessary, administer first aid or emergency medical care.
- Interview people with complaints and inquiries and attempt to make the proper disposition or direct them to proper authorities.
- Enforce traffic and parking regulations.
- Check parking meters for overtime parking violations and issue traffic tickets.
- Direct traffic at intersections; participate in escorting funerals and house-movers.
- Conduct accident investigations providing first aid for those injured, taking safeguards to prevent further accidents.
- After an accident, interview principles and witnesses, take written statements from drivers and witnesses; examine vehicles and roadways, observe traffic control devices and obstructions to view; take necessary street measurements; clear the scene of obstructions and wreckage.
- Escort prisoners to and from court; ensure that prisoners are properly guarded.[5]
- Act as custodian of personal property and evidence being held for court presentation.
- Maintain records of property, evidence, and automobiles held or impounded.

Investigative Officers' Duties

- Responsible for responding to the scene of a crime and conducting preliminary and follow-up investigations.
- Prepare investigative reports that are used by prosecutors when bringing the case to trial.
- May be asked to travel to other jurisdictions to extradite suspects wanted in connection with crimes committed in their own district.
- May be asked to coordinate and liaison with other law enforcement agencies in task forces aimed at particular criminal enterprises such as drug trafficking.

law enforcement

The activities of an agency of the Federal, State or local government, authorized by law to engage the prevention, detection, investigation, or prosecution of violations of the criminal law.

In contrast, the term **law enforcement** is pretty direct and narrow in its scope and definition; it is the action of enforcing laws, investigating criminal activities, and arresting offenders. There are many municipal, state, and federal laws that must be enforced on a daily basis. These laws may be as simple as traffic infractions, loitering, or shoplifting from a local convenience store. But they may also be as serious as rape, homicide, terrorism, or treason. This is the

- May be assigned to special units formed to specifically address particular crime problems, such as sex crimes, gangs, or homicide.

- As part of their investigation, they may maintain surveillance over people and places suspected of vice operations.

- Perform court liaison functions working with prosecutors while a trial is underway.

- Often called as witnesses to testify about what they saw and heard during their investigation.

- Some are specially trained to use electronic equipment ranging from surveillance equipment to polygraphs.

- Conduct missing persons investigations.

- Collect and examine evidence at crime scenes and tasked with maintaining custody of physical and drug evidence.

- Provide protective services for witnesses and victims who are expected to testify at trial.

- Conduct background checks on applicants and businesses who have applied for permits to engage in controlled or licensed commerce such as bars and taverns.

- When assigned, participate in training activities at the police training academy; may instruct or establish curriculum for instructional purposes.

Administrative Officers' Duties

- Senior staff conduct performance evaluations, and document the need for improvement, training requests, and acknowledgment of accomplishment.

- Administrative staff officers monitor training opportunities, recommend which officers need to attend training classes, enroll officers in training classes, and schedule employees to attend training classes.

- Most departments assign an administrative officer to coordinate hiring, which involves assessment, testing, and recommending candidates to hire for vacant positions within the department.

- An administrator, typically the chief, prepares a departmental budget and presents that document to the legislative or executive body.

- An administrative public information officer disseminates information to the public regarding crimes, crime prevention, emergencies, and all other information related to police actions.

- An important element of administration involves the purchase of supplies and equipment, ranging from bullets to patrol cars. This includes a request for bids, if required, and preparation of all associated documents needed to affect a purchase. After purchase, the department staff has to keep track and account for all inventory and equipment issued to employees.

- Police administrators routinely oversee purchase, equipment, and daily maintenance on all departmental vehicles.

- Liaison with law enforcement agencies such as the FBI and other federal agencies as well as the state police.

classic role of the police, and the role that most people think of when they envision as police work, or what they think an officer actually does. Crime control is the occupational mandate of law enforcement agencies. We pay law enforcement officers to do what they can to control crime.

Typically, municipal police agencies deal with a full range of activities, acting as traffic control monitors, first responders, law enforcers, and so on. There are

VDB Photos/Shutterstock.com

While the terms policing and law enforcement are often used interchangeably, there are discernible differences between the two concepts. Police agencies carry out many noncriminal law-related tasks—ranging from delivering babies to returning stray pets. In contrast, crime control is the occupational mandate of law enforcement agencies such as the FBI. However, they do not generally respond to calls for service as do policing agencies.

Critical Thinking

Which police role or function do you think is most important: the service provider function or the law-enforcing function? Why?

arrest

To deprive a person of their freedom of movement. A police officer can legally arrest someone if a warrant has been issued or without a warrant if probable cause exists that the person has committed a crime at the time of the arrest.

Critical Thinking

Would you consider being a police officer? If you answered "yes," what would be your motivation? If "no," why not?

LO4

Recognize what is meant when we say that police are social control agents.

also law enforcement agencies whose mandate is narrow in focus. While FBI agents enforce federal criminal laws, they do not generally respond to calls for service (unless it's from a local law enforcement agency).

Many police officers may say that law enforcement is an easier mandate than policing. Law enforcement is pretty straightforward; when people violate the law, they are arrested. Policing is more fluid in its actions. It involves solving problems and quality-of-life issues. These things may not be as cut-and-dry as simply enforcing laws. Policing may involve a lot more gray areas and uncertainty.

Unlike many criminal justice agencies, the average citizen encounters police on a routine basis. Most of us (we hope) have little contact with prosecutors, probation and parole officers, correctional officers, or even local politicians, but few of us have not encountered the police at some time in our lives. Many of us will even get to know a local police officer by name. For many, police are the face of not only the criminal justice system but also local government overall.

The breadth of police–citizen interaction is underscored by a national survey of police contacts with civilians that found that about 54 million people have at least one contact with police each year, and very few of them were offenders in the conventional sense of the term.[6] More than half of the contacts are for traffic-related matters, and about 30 percent are to report problems or ask for assistance—for example, responding to a neighbor's complaint about music being too loud during a party or warning kids not to shoot off fireworks.

Each year, about 80,000 local, county, and state police officers make about 14 million **arrests**, or about 20 each. Of these, about 2 million (approximately three per officer) are not only for serious crimes such as murder, rape, or robbery but also larceny, prostitution, or vandalism.

Given an even distribution of arrests (which we know is untrue), it is evident that the average police officer makes fewer than two arrests per month and fewer than a single felony arrest every 4 months. These figures should be interpreted with caution because not all police officers are engaged in activities that allow them to make arrests; about one-third of all sworn officers are in such units as communications, antiterrorism, administration, and personnel. Even if the number of arrests per officer were adjusted by one-third, it would still amount to 9 or 10 serious crime arrests per officer per year, or less than one a month, and these include arrests for larcenies such as shoplifting and petty theft.

So even though the nation's police departments handle millions of calls each year, relatively few result in an arrest for a serious crime such as a robbery, burglary, or a homicide. In suburban and rural areas, years may go by before a police officer makes a felony arrest.

Police and Social Control

Modern policing in a free, democratic society involves the delicate and proper balance between invoking police powers, the use of coercion, and the constitutional rights of American citizens. Social control of its citizens is actually a core element of the policing role. Moreover, if society is to continue to function in a seemingly orderly fashion, the police must be able to establish and maintain public order. For order maintenance to be established in a community, the public behavior of its citizens must be predictable and able to be controlled to some extent. The seventeenth-century English philosopher Thomas Hobbes, in his seminal work *Leviathan*, referred to this agreement between society and the government as society's **Social Contract**.

According to Hobbes, the Social Contract is a condition in which citizens give up some individual liberties or rights in exchange for some common security provided by the government.[7] For instance, individuals give up the right, and in return citizens are protected from the crimes of murder and assault. In order for citizens to enjoy the constitutional or inalienable rights that we so richly deserve, we must all agree to not violate or infringe on the rights of our fellow citizens. Maintaining this agreement and protecting the citizenry is a job that belongs to the police. In fact, order maintenance is a major role of policing.

Joseph Prezioso/AFP/Getty Images

Social control of its citizens is actually a core element of policing. It is essential that police be able to establish and maintain public order. This element of policing can be controversial since it requires them to get involved in political and social disputes between opposing groups, attempting to maintain order without taking sides. Here, police separate people from fighting as rally attendees and counter protesters get into an argument during a pro-police and Trump rally organized by "Super Happy Fun America," outside the State House in Boston, Massachusetts, on June 27, 2020.

Police as Social Control Agents

The police represent several different systems of social control and carry out a number of tasks to maintain social order.

Gatekeepers

Police are the gatekeepers of the criminal justice system. Most people who come in contact with the criminal justice system do so through contact with the police. Keep in mind that this contact, however, is mostly citizen initiated, meaning that members of the community call on the police for help. People can also enter the criminal justice system directly through the courts, but, by and large, most people enter the criminal justice system after contact with the police. The police have a great deal of discretion when handling calls for service. They can choose to ignore the call, choose to be peacemakers, or they can choose to be problem-solvers and handle things informally. The police can also decide to use force when they effect an arrest. If the police choose to invoke their police powers, then the person or case will move to the next stage in the criminal justice process. If the police choose to use discretion and ignore a violation or if an officer chooses to handle a situation informally, then a person's contact with the criminal justice system will likely end at that point.

social contract
A condition in which citizens give up some individual liberties or rights in exchange for some common security provided by the government.

Social Service Agents

Police officers also act as agents of the social service system. The police are called after regular business hours, on weekends, and holidays when social service workers or other government officials tend not to be available. The police represent the government 24 hours per day, 7 days per week, and 365 days per year. If there is a social services issue with a family member, you have a lost loved one, or a noncriminal situation that is out of hand, many people will ask the local police to handle the situation. Police are on the frontlines of the opioid crisis and are frequently on scene for calls involving people with mental illnesses. In fact, anytime there is a need for some sort of government intervention after regular business hours, many people will rely on the police to act as the surrogate part of the government that can address that situation. The police are called for broken water main pipes, power outages, downed power lines, malfunctioning traffic lights, neighborhood disputes, and often general questions about city/town ordinances. Anytime there needs to be government intervention after regular business hours, many citizens call on the police for help.

Political Representatives

The police are also governmental agencies subject to federal, state, city, and county laws, rules, and ordinances. Within municipal policing, the police chief or commissioner is an appointed position who answers directly to the mayor, city or town manager, or the city council. Sheriffs tend to be directly elected by the people. The head of the state police is appointed by the governor. County police department chiefs or commissioners answer to the county commissioners or the board of selectmen. The head of the FBI, which is a federal law enforcement agency, is appointed by the president of the United States and then confirmed by the Senate. County sheriffs have to run for election and serve a fixed term. So there is a direct connection between politicians and the heads of police agencies. Crime and safety will often be a main part of political platforms. It is an issue that appeals to citizens regardless of whether they are actually at risk of victimization. If crime rates rise in a given year, political figures may promise to increase funding for public safety, particularly in election years. If crime rates decrease, many politicians will use that as a marker of success in their time in office. So the issue of crime, and thus the police, are main issues of debate in politics.

LO5

Compare and contrast the crime control and due process models.

► Two Traditional Models of Criminal Justice Policy: Crime Control vs. Due Process

The structure and form of all criminal justice policy typically falls into one of two categories: the crime control model or the due process model that can be applied to policing. First developed by distinguished Stanford University law professor Herbert Packer in his book *Two Models of the Criminal Process and The Limits of the Criminal Sanction*, the models serve as a way of understanding how agents of the criminal justice system approach their role and mission.

crime control model

A view of justice that places primary emphasis on the protection of citizens and the control of criminal behavior.

Those who embrace the **crime control model** see their most significant role as getting offenders off the street and protecting citizens. They believe that the absence of harsh punishment enables criminal offending while producing a fear of crime in the general population. Fear encroaches on individual liberty and social freedom. When crime is rampant, people don't go out at night and lock their doors, fearing intrusions. If, on the other hand, offenders are swiftly apprehended and punished, it sends a message to others that crime will not be tolerated and that the streets are safe. While quick solutions can produce errors, those who espouse the crime control model are reassured that existing legal protections mean that those likely innocent are screened out from the system while those likely guilty will receive their just desserts. The presumption of guilt is an important element of the crime control model, that is, cops do not arrest innocent people, and allow the criminal justice system to deal efficiently with large numbers of offenders using swift and routine procedures.

The **due process model** is in direct opposition to the crime control model. The due process model focus is primarily on using the proper *process* and findings of guilt are secondary to individual constitutional rights. According to Packer, the due process model is designed to protect the rights of the accused person by presenting challenging obstructions to moving the accused through each step in the legal process. The Fourteenth Amendment to the U.S. Constitution guarantees due process and equal protection under the law. The due process clause acts as a protection from the arbitrary denial of life, liberty, or property by the government outside the sanctioning provisions of the law. Due process further ensures the rights and equality of all citizens.

The due process model is closely aligned with the words of English jurist Sir William Blackstone when he wrote in 1765 that it is better that 10 guilty men go free than that one innocent person suffer. Both the Fifth and Fourteenth Amendments to the U.S. Constitution contain a "due process clause" that is guaranteed to all. The Fourteenth Amendment guarantees equal protection under the law. The term *due process* deals directly with the administration of justice, particularly in criminal cases, and thus the term acts as a safeguard from random denial of life, liberty, or property by the government outside the sanction of law. The U.S. Supreme Court interprets this clause more generally and broadly because the due process clause provides several primary protections.

> **due process model**
>
> A view of justice that emphasizes the protection of the rights of the accused person as they move through the system.

Due Process vs. Crime Control in Action: Using Technology

The use of technology amply illustrates the eternal conflict between due process and crime control policing. Technology represents an avenue to increase police effectiveness. But does this newfound efficiency come at too high a price? Does it interfere with hard-earned due process rights?

Some U.S. police departments have turned to complex computer algorithms to try to forecast crime. There are four categories of predictive methods: (1) those that identify places and times with an increased risk of crime, (2) those that identify people most likely to be offenders, (3) those that predict profiles of likely offenders, and (4) those that predict likely victims. Determining who will commit a crime and where that crime will occur in the future, in an effort to prevent it from occurring, is often referred to as *predictive policing*. This approach combines the fundamental principles of traditional policing with strategies such as increased attention to high-crime areas and closely monitoring those most likely to offend.

The recent development of federally funded, computerized predictive analytics and data mining by law enforcement agencies for crime projections is part of a larger trend by government agencies and corporations to examine criminal behavior. Researchers working with the police to develop the predictive algorithms claim they can come closer to figuring out who is likely to commit future crimes, where crimes will occur, and who is likely to be victimized than can be done with traditional detective work. This type of technology, and others like it, have been employed by several major city police departments, such as Miami, Los Angeles, and Nashville. It has also been employed by the Manhattan and Philadelphia district attorneys' offices.[8]

Other police departments have begun borrowing technology from the military and using facial recognition software to identify and track down known gang members, drug dealers, and other potentially dangerous suspects. This state-of-the-art technology was originally used by the U.S. military and federal intelligence agencies for years in foreign countries to identify potential terrorists. But because local police agencies are using it with few guidelines and very little oversight or public disclosure, it is raising questions of privacy and concerns about potential misuse. Police officers claim the facial recognition technology is faster than using traditional fingerprint methods to identify suspects, but it is still uncertain how much this technology is helping the police make arrests.[9]

What Are the Concerns?

The downside to relying on these new methods is the concern that technology is not unbiased. Human beings must decide what data are included in the algorithms or where to scan faces. Even something as simple as arrest data can be indicative of where police officers are deployed rather than where more crime occurs. The use of this type of technology can allow for interference with due process rights vis-a-vis racial profiling and for guilt by association. These are enormous civil liberties issues that must be addressed when these approaches are used. This strategy is likely to disproportionately target people who live in poverty or in high-crime communities that may have done nothing wrong, other than be related to, or have close ties to, known offenders or where police officers are disproportionately assigned. In essence, you could be targeted because the computerized predictive modeling software asserts that you might commit a crime at some point in the future mainly because of your past criminality or because you live in an area that has high crime rates. These are clear violations of due process for the sake of effective crime control. Is this fair?

LO6

Explore the role of the police in the community.

▶ Policing the Public

In carrying out these critical tasks, local police and law enforcement agents are given a great deal of discretion in their decision making. Some critics believe that the police use this freedom in a biased fashion. Because of the repeated allegation that police officers engaged in law enforcement activities based solely on race, the term *racial profiling* has become part of the vernacular. This concept is so ingrained in our culture and with citizens from racial minority groups that there are terms to describe the concept when Black drivers are stopped and/or harassed by the police: driving while Black (DWB). This concept has moved into other facets of life and has spawned the terms *shopping while Black*, *walking while Black*, and so on.

In response, many police departments have undertaken efforts to train police officers in implicit bias to enhance sensitivity toward the community that they are sworn to protect and serve. Programs have been created to improve relations between police and community as well as to help police officers on the beat be more sensitive to the needs of the public and cope more effectively with the stress of their jobs. Police officers have also become better educated and now some attend college. After graduation, they seem willing to stay on the job and contribute their academic experiences to improve police performance and enhance police–community relationships.[10]

But many challenges still exist. Take what happened a decade ago when Boston, Massachusetts, community leaders called for an independent review of the Boston Police Department in the wake of reports claiming the department lacked diversity. In the midst of the public outcry Darnell Williams, president of the Urban League of Eastern Massachusetts, said, "The numbers are not pretty, that's one thing we know," after news reports showed that the number of minority cops in Boston has decreased slightly in the past year and a half and now represented 33.5 percent of all 2,123 officers in the departments; only 17 percent of the ranking officers, lieutenants are Black; Boston has a 53 percent minority population. In one noted case, a Black sergeant with 25 years of experience and a law degree was passed over for promotion in favor of a White sergeant with identical test scores. Representation can send an important signal to the community—when it is absent, community relations become strained and frayed.[11] While progress has been made since Williams made his statement, the racial makeup of the department has not appreciably changed.

Police and the Criminal Justice Process

◀ **L07**

Describe the role of the police in the criminal justice process.

The police serve as the gatekeepers of the criminal justice process that takes an offender through a series of decision points, beginning with investigation and arrest and concluding with reentry into society. During this process, key decision makers decide whether to maintain the offender in the system or discharge the suspect without further action. This decision making is often a matter of individual discretion, based on a variety of factors and perceptions. Legal factors, including the seriousness of the charges, available evidence, and the suspect's prior record, are usually considered legitimate influences on decision making. A troubling fact is that extralegal factors such as the suspect's race, sex, gender, class, and age may also influence decision outcomes. Some critics believe that a suspect's race, class, sex, and gender largely determine the direction a case will take, whereas supporters argue that the system is relatively fair and unbiased. The police are the critical players early in the process but remain active throughout. What are their main activities and duties?

Initial Contact

In most instances, an offender's initial contact with the criminal justice system takes place as a result of a police action:

- Patrol officers observe a person acting suspiciously, conclude the suspect is under the influence of drugs, and take them into custody.

- Police officers are contacted by a victim who reports a robbery; they respond by going to the scene of the crime and apprehending a suspect.

- An informer tells police about some ongoing criminal activity in order to receive favorable treatment.

- Responding to a request by the mayor or other political figure, the local department may initiate an investigation into an ongoing criminal enterprise such as gambling, prostitution, or drug trafficking.

- A person walks into the police station and confesses to committing a crime— for example, killing their spouse after an altercation.

Investigation

The purpose of the criminal investigation is to gather sufficient evidence to identify a suspect and support a legal arrest. An investigation can take only a few minutes, as in the case where a police officer sees a crime in progress and can apprehend the suspect quickly. Or it can take many years and involve hundreds of law enforcement agents. During the investigatory stage, police are guided by the rule of law. They may wish to search and seize evidence, freely interrogate suspects, and bring witnesses in to identify their alleged attackers, but the courts have laid down strict rules of procedure that police officers must follow.

Because the person in custody is only suspected of a crime and has not yet been tried or convicted, suspects' rights must be protected. This often creates tension between police who want a free hand to carry out their duties and the courts who want to protect citizens' civil rights.

Arrest

If during their investigation police are able to gather sufficient evidence (probable cause) to identify an alleged lawbreaker, they are permitted to make an arrest by taking the suspect into custody and depriving them of their freedom of movement. An arrest is considered legal when all of the following conditions exist: (1) the police officer believes there is sufficient evidence, referred to as *probable cause,* that a crime is being or has been committed and the suspect is the person who committed it; (2) the officer deprives the individual of freedom; and (3) the suspect believes that they are now in the custody of the police and has lost their liberty. The police officer is not required to use the word "arrest" or any similar term to initiate an arrest, nor does the officer have to bring the suspect to the police station. To make an arrest in a misdemeanor, the officer must have witnessed the crime personally, a provision known as the in-presence requirement. Some jurisdictions have passed laws allowing misdemeanor arrests based on victim complaints in cases involving child or domestic abuse. Arrests can also be made when a magistrate, presented with sufficient evidence by police and prosecutors, issues a warrant authorizing the arrest of the suspect.

Custody

After an arrest and while the suspect is being detained, the police may wish to search them for evidence, conduct an interrogation (which is a process of in-depth questioning from police officers), or even encourage a confession. Witnesses may be brought to view the suspect in a lineup or in a one-on-one confrontation. Again, because these procedures are so crucial and can have a great impact at trial, the U.S. Supreme Court has granted suspects in police custody protection from the unconstitutional abuse of police power, such as illegal searches and intimidating interrogations.

Custodial Interrogations

The police must also inform the suspect of their guaranteed rights during an interrogation while in custody. The landmark 1966 case of *Miranda v. Arizona* ruled that all criminal suspects must be informed of their right against self-incrimination and their right to consult with an attorney before being questioned by police while in custody. The suspect also has to be informed that if they cannot afford an attorney, one will be provided to them.

Police and the Pretrial Stage of Justice

The role of the police does not end at the arrest stage of the criminal justice process. Many times the work of police detectives continues through the pretrial stage. Detectives continue to gather information, interview witnesses, interview the suspect, gather evidence, conduct forensic searches, and have evidence examined for DNA, fingerprints, and the like. When prosecutors investigate crimes, it is mostly local police that are doing the day-to-day investigations. Often, the police are required to keep all evidence collected and preserve the chain of custody until the final disposition of the criminal case.

Recent research suggests that police may consult with prosecutors before the arrest decision is made. Police work with prosecutors to determine if a case requires more investigation to improve the evidence. While police are concerned with whether they have probable cause to make an arrest, prosecutors must decide if they can prove that a defendant is guilty beyond a reasonable doubt in court. This consultation is largely informal and occurs before the trial process.

Once a suspect has been arraigned and issued bail, or released on bond, that suspect is expected to return to court on the appointed date and time. If the suspect does not return to court for the trial, then a warrant is likely issued and the local police search for the suspect, arrest them, and return them to court. Most prosecutors do not have an investigative division. When prosecutors conduct criminal investigations, typically the actual investigation work is done by the police with oversight of the prosecutor's office. The local district attorney uses local police officers. The state attorney general's office tends to use the state police, and the U.S. attorney general uses the FBI or other federal law enforcement/investigative agency to conduct the bulk of the actual criminal investigations.

Police and the Trial Process

The police have a very critical role in a criminal trial. While most complaints do not end up going through the trial process, the actions or inactions of the police can make or break a trial. Police officers properly trained in collecting and preserving evidence, as well as maintaining the chain of custody is crucial in any criminal trial. Police officers initiate crime reports, investigate crimes, gather and protect evidence, give testimony during the court process, and conduct follow-up investigations, if needed. It is the quality of the police report and consistency of evidence that will make or break a criminal trial.

Every part of the police process is held under great scrutiny during the trial. The police actions will be held against and compared to the constitutional rights granted to citizens and previous case laws. The police may be challenged on the Fourth Amendment, which protects against illegal searches and seizures during the arrest. They may also get challenged on the Fifth Amendment

Abaca Press/Alamy Stock Photo

The police have a very critical role in a criminal trial; their actions can have significant impact on the outcome. Therefore, officers must be properly trained in collecting and preserving evidence. Here U.S. Capitol Police Officer Caroline Edwards and documentary filmmaker Nick Quested are sworn in to testify before the U.S. House Select Committee to investigate the January 6 attack on the United States Capitol, on Capitol Hill in Washington, D.C., June 9, 2022.

rights against self-incrimination if the suspect's *Miranda* warning was not read to them. Was there a proper field interrogation prior to the arrest as outlined in the court case *Terry v. Ohio* (1968)? The officer may also be challenged at trial on their adherence to the Fourteenth Amendment, which guarantees equal protection under the law for all citizens. Virtually everything that the police officer has said, written, and done in affecting the arrest may be under scrutiny by the defense. This can be challenging for police officers. For example, a police officer may purposely not ask questions or take notes about a victim seeking mental health services because the officer can't keep this information confidential. The officer could be asked by a defense attorney at trial about the mental health of the victim or any services received and would have to answer truthfully. So the role of the police officer is to justify their actions during all phases of this criminal justice process, and these actions will be reviewed at trial.

Police and Corrections

While not directly involved in post trial process, police officers play a role when offenders are sentenced to community corrections or when they return from a correctional facility. Police officers may work with correctional officers in programs designed to reduce crime and lower recidivism rates. Take, for instance, Operation Night Light, a joint program designed to stem youth violence, described in Focus on Policing: Operation Night Light.

LO8

Explain the concept of police legitimacy.

▶ # Police Legitimacy

Typically, when there is contact between the police and citizens, the officers' actions are examined and judged as to whether or not the actions of the officer are fair and just. Citizens in a democratic society absolutely have the inalienable right to question the government, including police legitimacy or authority. Although Americans often see the police as heroes who are doing a very important and dangerous job, often the police are viewed as having crossed the line of what is a legitimate police action. Many times there is a distinct disconnect between what the police do, and what citizens think the police should do.

That is where the concept of police legitimacy comes in. Tracey Meares and Peter Neyroud have defined "police legitimacy" or "rightful policing" as an effort to consider how citizens judge police actions (on the continuum of fairness).[12] Police legitimacy, like any other form of governmental legitimacy, needs to be established in order for cooperative governance to occur. Jacinta Gau simplifies this concept by writing that any police department or other government agency that possesses coercive authority over its citizens must be able to explain to its citizens the reasons that it is necessary or proper for citizens to submit to this authority. A police department that can successfully articulate and explain these reasons is said to have legitimacy.

Police legitimacy is not necessarily the same as lawful policing. Just because the police are authorized to conduct a certain action, it does not always mean that the action is the right thing to do (e.g., violently arresting a 15-year-old for allegedly trespassing at a pool party, or giving a speeding ticket to a person rushing to the hospital with a medical emergency). Often citizens' perception of the fairness of police actions dictates the behavior of the citizens toward the police. In other words, a citizen's perception often colors their reality. If citizens believe

Focus on Policing

Operation Night Light

The overarching purpose for Operation Night Light was to successfully enforce the terms and conditions of juvenile offenders on probation while ensuring the protection of the public and also trying to rehabilitate the juvenile offender.

In the early 1990s, the city of Boston experienced a severe youth violence and youth homicide problem. At that time, the Boston Police Department examined the juvenile gun violence problem in the city and discovered that nearly three-quarters of both the victims and offenders were under 17 years of age and also had been on probation in the juvenile court. The youth violence spilled over into the schools and even in the court house. Operation Night Light began in the fall of 1992 as a partnership between Anti-Gang Violence Unit police officers and probation officers in Boston. Gang-involved young people in the city who were also on juvenile court probation were targeted for enforced conditions of probation including nighttime curfews, being prohibited from associating with known gang members, and orders to stay away from specific locations including some parks, neighborhoods, or street corners.

Prior to the implementation of Operation Night Light, probation officers worked primarily alone, independent of local or state police officers. Nighttime curfews for probationers were typically not imposed by the courts because they were difficult for probation officers to enforce. In response to these issues, probation officers and police officers met informally to develop a strategy that would address these problems and help probation officers do their jobs. Operation Night Light was the strategy that was employed as a more effective way to prevent juvenile violence and youth homicides in the city.

Operation Night Light matches up probation officers with the police to make unannounced visits to the homes, schools, and workplaces of high-risk youth probationers. Many of these visits happened during nontraditional times, often between 7:00 P.M. to midnight rather than the more traditional probation hours of 8:00 A.M. to 5:00 P.M.

The probation officer decides which of the probationers to visit each evening based on which youths were not compliant with the conditions of their probation. The probation and police officers wear plain clothes and use an unmarked car in these community visits These restrictions are designed to keep juvenile probationers from reoffending and strictly enforced. Probation officers also have been instrumental in convincing judges to impose expanded conditions.

This proactive strategy has enhanced the safety of the probation officers and given officers in the Boston Police Department an opportunity to meet people in the community in a nonconfrontational manner in order to increase their community policing role. These probation and police officers discussed prominent issues like substance abuse prevention and treatment options with the juvenile offenders who were on probation and their families. Some parents of juvenile probationers welcomed these interactions because they wanted to protect their children from becoming victims or perpetrators of violence. These unannounced home visits by probation and police officers also gave potential juvenile offenders an excuse for staying in at night and putting off their gang leaders or friends engaged in criminality with the argument that they would face serious sanctions if they violated their curfew. The results from the Operation Night Light initiative in Boston showed that Boston did not have a juvenile homicide in the city for well over a year.

Critical Thinking

Does your community have an "operation night light" in place? What should be the main focus of this event?

Source: Operation Night Light, to learn more about Operation Night Light visit http://www.ojjdp.gov/pubs/gun_violence/contents.html.

that the police are acting in a way that is harmful or contrary to what the citizen feels is fair or just, the citizen may try to resist, act out, or blatantly disregard the commands of the officer. Police legitimacy differs from lawful policing and effective policing in several ways.

First, police legitimacy is not determined by the *lawfulness* of police conduct; instead, it is determined mostly by procedural justice or the *perceived fairness* of the specific police action. Second, police legitimacy is not determined by whether or not the police can prevent crimes or maintain a greater degree of order. Police depend heavily upon citizens' view of their legitimacy as a means of securing the public's cooperation, compliance, and support. Research has shown that citizens who have positive views of the police, and see the actions of the police as being legitimate, are more likely to cooperate with officers. This level of citizen compliance may assist the police in moving toward strategies that are substantially more democratic. Finally, establishing police legitimacy yields positive results for police officers on the streets as well. Increasing legitimacy in policing will not only encourage citizens to comply with the law and police directives, but it also encourages behaviors during the encounters that tend to keep officers and community members safe.

Jacinta Gau goes further into detail with the issues of global and specific attitudes toward police. Global attitudes toward the police are those attitudes that are informed by various sources that often include such things as a citizen's personal experiences with the police, as well as hearing about their friends' experiences with the police and also how the popular media (including social media) portray the police and their behavior. Global attitudes tend to come from second-hand experiences with the police. Specific attitudes toward the police tend to be more personal and immediate. Specific attitudes are the impressions citizens are left with after they have face-to-face or one-on-one contact with the police. Procedural justice or *perceived fairness* has been measured by both citizens' global attitudes toward the police and citizens' specific attitudes toward the police. Police legitimacy is sometimes used to measure citizens' attitudes about their interactions with officers and sometimes to capture more detailed beliefs about the general quality of treatment police give citizens.[13]

LO9

Describe common myths about policing.

▶ Myths in Policing

Policing is an extremely stereotypical profession. These stereotypes are perpetuated by the media as well as police officers themselves.

Super Cop Image

The lines are becoming blurred between fiction and reality within policing. There are many myths of police officers and sometimes they are portrayed as almost mythical beings. Often there is a significant difference between what sworn police officers are trained, allowed, and able to do and what the general public expects them to do. Many times, police officers are portrayed in the media as heroes who are larger than life and will always win in the end. Officers are often shown to be the most courageous of humans and will stop at nothing to right the wrongs of citizens and victims. Sometimes the public may look the other way or ignore when an officer bends the rules, just a little bit, in order to catch the bad guys.

Many images of officers in popular television police shows portray an image of officers who will continue to chase the bad guys, regardless of their injury, and we will see that they almost always are perfect marksman with their weapons. They usually make the right decision and they come out victorious in the end. This vision of the "super cop" is not only fictitious, but it is not healthy (or fair to the officers) to hold police officers to such lofty superhuman tasks. This overly lofty view of the police is often referred to as the "super cop image."

CSI Effect

The general public tends not to be very savvy regarding the limits and boundaries of criminal and constitutional laws. They tend to know or understand even less about the technical aspects of what detectives, police investigators, crime scene technicians, and forensic technicians are capable of doing. Because of this divide, there is a lot of disappointment with the results of police actions, investigations, courtroom procedures, and trial outcomes. We have come to accept a romanticized version of technical crime fighting and crime solving.

Because of the vast numbers of crime-related television shows that depict the good guys defeating the bad guys every week within a 60-minute span of a prime-time television show, the public tends to have an unrealistic view of what is truly achievable within the realm of good and honest police work. This perception is growing because of such widely popular reality-television networks like Court-TV and Real-TV, as well as prime-time American television shows like *CSI: Crime Scene Investigation*. This popular crime drama first aired on October 6, 2000, on the CBS network and quickly became the gold standard for popular crime dramas. These shows glamorize the job of the police officer and presumably drive thousands of people toward the interest of policing as a career option. This phenomenon is known as the "CSI effect."

It seems that the popular term **CSI effect** first entered the common-usage vocabulary through a *Time* magazine article in 2002 written by Jeffrey Kluger about the use of science to solve crimes.[14] Since that time, the media has caught on and popularized the term to now account for any and all linkages of crime-fighting techniques and technology. This effect is so popular that it spawned several spin-off television shows. According to a 2009 *Stanford Law Review* article by Simon Cole and Rachel Dioso-Villa, the term became so popular that it rose to its height in 2006 with 76 different newspaper and magazine articles mentioning the CSI effect. This particular show, based in Las Vegas, Nevada, became so popular that it spawned several spin-off shows like *CSI Miami* and *CSI NY*. Another version, based on the FBI labs in Quantico, Virginia, called *CSI-Cyber*, added to the franchise. Although the public will all agree that the plotlines are fictitious, many may still believe that the outcomes shown on television may, in fact, be real.[15]

The popular television show *CSI: Crime Scene Investigation*, and others like it are driving popular myths in policing that the police always get their culprit, and modern technology is available and can be used at all crime scenes to positively point out the perpetrator. Often students will report that they want to pursue a career in policing, but they do not want to spend the years on the street in uniform as a patrol or traffic officer in order to make their way through the promotional process to eventually reach detective. Many students want to graduate from the police academy, put on a suit, and start their careers as detectives. This overglamorizing of police work does the profession a disservice and gives the public an unrealistic view of policing that has repercussions for police and the communities that they serve.

CSI effect

Refers to the influence television shows like *CSI: Crime Scene Investigation*, have on jurors and, as a result, juries now place heavy emphasis on forensic science in making their decisions and reaching a verdict.

Summary

LO1   Analyze what the police do.

The role of the police is multifaceted and complex—ranging from maintaining order to making arrests. As part of the community, police must work to solve ongoing problems. Police must also work with other actors in the criminal justice system to address the crime problem.

The term *police* refers to an institution of state authority that represents the will of the government through the enforcement of criminal laws and the maintenance of civil order. A police officer's crime-fighting efforts are only a small part of their overall activities. Police officers are called on to deal with increasingly difficult and unpredictable situations—many of which are noncriminal acts, including minor disturbances, service calls, and administrative duties. Police officers today can be viewed as troubleshooters or problem-solvers, who, while serving the public, are more concerned with addressing quality-of-life issues in a community than they are arresting felons.

LO2   Describe the patrol, investigation, and administration functions.

To carry out their duties, the typical police department is divided into patrols, investigation, and administration. Large jurisdictions maintain an investigative or detective branch whose main duty is to identify a culprit after a crime has been completed. Not all local police departments have investigative units; it is routine for small-town police departments to rely on state or county agencies to provide investigators. Police departments are independent agencies that maintain a management staff who conducts the day-to-day management of the department, including such tasks as hiring, training, and record keeping.

LO3   Compare policing vs. law enforcement.

Policing is a much broader concept than law enforcement and police agencies carry out many different tasks, from delivering babies to returning stray pets that do not involve criminal law violations or enforcements. The majority of citizens' calls to local police departments are calls for service that do not involve enforcing laws. Because of this, the service–provider side of policing must be maintained and prioritized. In contrast, the term *law enforcement* is pretty direct and narrow in its scope and definition; it is the action of enforcing laws, investigating criminal activities, and arresting offenders. Law enforcement is pretty straightforward; when people violate the law, they are arrested. Policing is more fluid in its actions. It involves solving problems and quality-of-life issues. These things may not be as cut and dry as simply enforcing laws. Policing may involve a lot more gray areas and uncertainty.

LO4   Recognize what is meant when we say that police are social control agents.

The police represent several different systems of social control. Police are the gatekeepers of the criminal justice system. Most people who come in contact with the criminal justice system do so through contact with the police. Police officers also act as agents of the social service system. The police are called for broken water main pipes, power outages, downed power lines, malfunctioning traffic lights, neighborhood disputes, and often general questions about city/town ordinances. The police are also governmental agencies subject to federal, state, city, and county laws, rules, and ordinances.

LO5   Compare and contrast the crime control and due process models.

Those who embrace the crime control model see their most significant role as getting offenders off the street and protecting citizens. They believe that the absence of harsh punishments enables criminal offending while producing a fear of crime in the general population. The due process model is in direct opposition to the crime control model. The due process model focus is primarily on using the proper *process* and findings of guilt are secondary to individual constitutional rights.

LO6   Explore the role of the police in the community.

Many police departments have undertaken efforts to train police officers in implicit bias to enhance sensitivity toward the community that they are sworn to protect and serve. Programs have been created to improve relations between police and community as well as to help police officers on the beat be more sensitive to the needs of the public and cope more effectively with the stress of their jobs.

LO7   Describe the role of the police in the criminal justice process.

The police serve as the gatekeepers of the criminal justice process that takes an offender through a series of decision points, beginning with investigation and arrest and concluding with reentry into society. Recent research suggests that police may consult with prosecutors before the arrest decision is made. Police work with prosecutors to determine if a case requires more investigation to improve the evidence. The role of the police does not end at the arrest stage of the criminal justice process.

LO8   Explain the concept of police legitimacy.

How police do their jobs is as important, if not more than, the outcomes and outputs of their work. Police legitimacy is a measurement of perceptions of how police officers do their jobs. Police legitimacy is not determined by the *lawfulness* of police conduct; instead, it is determined mostly by procedural justice or the *perceived fairness* of the specific police action.

LO9   Describe common myths about policing.

Much of what we know about the police comes from fictionalized accounts. This gives way to a mythologized perspective of the police role. It is important to recognize fact from fiction when evaluating how the police do their jobs and the outcomes of their work.

Key Terms

Internet crime, 4
policing, 6
law enforcement, 10

arrest, 12
Social Contract, 13
crime control model, 14

due process model, 15
CSI effect, 23

Notes

1. Federal Bureau of Investigation, Serial Armed Robber Gets Substantial Prison Term Joint Law Enforcement Effort Pays Off, June 5, 2015.
2. Tara O'Connor Shelley. *Pharmacy Robbery and Burglary: The Offender Perspective*. (Fort Collins, CO: Center for the Study of Crime and Justice, Department of Sociology, Colorado State University, 2014).
3. "America's Opioid Epidemic Is Worsening, States Are Losing the Battle Against Deadly Drugs Like Heroin and Fentanyl," *The Economist*, March 6, 2017, http://www.economist.com/blogs/graphicdetail/2017/03/daily-chart-3.
4. National Initiative for Building Community Trust & Justice, "Implicit Bias," 2015, http://trustandjustice.org/resources/intervention/implicit-bias, accessed May 25, 2023.
5. Baton Rouge, LA, Police Department, "Duties & Responsibilities of Police Officers," http://brgov.com/dept/brpd/pdf/police_duties.pdf.
6. Susannah Tapp and Elizabeth Davis, Contacts Between Police and the Public, 2020, Bureau of Justice Statistics, 2022, https://bjs.ojp.gov/library/publications/contacts-between-police-and-public-2020.
7. Social Contract Theory, https://www.iep.utm.edu/soc-cont/.
8. John Eligon and Timothy Williams, "Police Program Aims to Pinpoint Those Most Likely to Commit Crimes," *The New York Times,* September 24, 2015.
9. Timothy Williams, "Facial Recognition Software Moves from Overseas Wars to Local Police," *The New York Times,* August 12, 2015.
10. David Jones, Liz Jones, and Tim Prenzler, "Tertiary Education, Commitment, and Turnover in Police Work," *Police Practice and Research* 6 (2005): 49–63.
11. "Calls to Review Boston Police Department's Diversity; Boston's Black Leaders Want Independent Probe," May 14, 2015, http://masspolicereform.org/2015/05/calls-to-review-bpds-diversity-bostons-black-leaders-want-independent-probe/
12. Tracey L. Meares with Peter Neyroud. Rightful Policing. New Perspectives in Policing Bulletin. (Washington, DC: U.S. Department of Justice, National Institute of Justice, 2015). NCJ 2484, https://www.ncjrs.gov/pdffiles1/nij/248411.pdf.
13. Jacinta M. Gau, "Procedural Justice and Police Legitimacy: A test of Measurement and Structure," *American Journal of Criminal Justice* 39 no. 2 (2013): 187–205.
14. Jeffrey Kluger, "How Science Solves Crimes. From Ballistics to DNA, Forensic Scientists Are Revolutionizing Police Work—on TV and in Reality. And Just in Time," *Time*, October 21, 2002.
15. Simon A. Cole and Rachel Dioso-Villa, "Investigating The '*CSI* Effect' Effect: Media and Litigation Crisis in Criminal Law," *Stanford Law Review* 61 (2009): 1335.

The Development of Policing: From Past to Present

Learning Objectives

LO1 Discuss the historical antecedents to policing in the United States.

LO2 Discuss the development and evolution of law enforcement in the United States.

LO3 Describe the path to police reform and how it has changed over time.

LO4 Examine contemporary law enforcement.

Chapter Outline

The first organized police existed in Egypt in about 300 BC. The nation was then divided into 42 separate jurisdictions which were administered by a local official appointed by the pharaoh and a chief of police, who bore the title *sab heri seker*, or "chief of the hitters" (men responsible for tax collecting). Egyptian police officials provided assistance to people of even the lowest levels of society when crimes were committed. Victims from all over the countryside of Egypt called on local law enforcement officials to investigate crimes; hold trials; and arrest, question, and sometimes even imprison wrong-doers. This early police system was efficient, effective, and largely independent of central government controls. No other law enforcement organization exhibiting such a degree of autonomy and flexibility appears in extant evidence from the rest of the Greco-Roman world.[1] Though policing may seem like a relatively new concept, efforts to protect the community from external and internal threats actually date back thousands of years.[2]

The word *police* is actually taken from the Greek word *polis*, meaning "city," indicating that even in ancient times citizens worked together to bring order to the community. In ancient Greece policing duties were assigned to local magistrates. Ten *astynomoi* were responsible for municipal upkeep and cleanliness in the city of Athens and the port of Piraeus; 10 *agoranomoi* kept order in the marketplace, and ten other *metronomoi* monitored measurement standards. The magistrates depended in part on the military, whose duties were focused on external state security, to help keep order. Slave battalions were also assigned to the magistrates and acted as their enforcement arm.[3]

The Roman government was rarely involved in criminality, considering it a private matter to be resolved between citizens in a civil proceeding. However, one of the earliest forms of organized policing occurred when in 7 BCE Emperor Augustus Caesar divided the city into 14 *regiones* (wards), each consisting of *vici* (precincts) overseen by *vicomagistri*, who were responsible for fire protection and other administrative and religious duties. This was eventually expanded into a corps of *vigiles* (firefighters and watchmen), that was responsible for fire and at night, police protection. Augustus created three cohorts of police, which were part of the army who could call upon the Praetorian Guard, the emperor's bodyguards, for assistance.[4]

Efforts at policing the community stretches back thousands of years. Early forms of policing can also be found in ancient England and, from these roots, eventually into the American colonies. How English policing developed and helped our contemporary police organizations is set out below.

LO1
Discuss the historical antecedents to policing in the United States.

▶ Policing in Early English Society

The origin of U.S. police agencies, like that of criminal law, can be traced to early English society.[5] England had no regular police force before the eleventh-century Norman Conquest, which was the invasion by the armies led by Duke William II of Normandy. Every person living in the villages scattered throughout the countryside was responsible for aiding their neighbors and protecting the settlements from outside thieves and marauders. This was known as the pledge system.

Most scholars credit the development of this early form of community self-protection to King Alfred the great in 871–899, in which every male 12 years of age and older would take a pledge to protect the kingdom against invasions and catching criminals. Every family was responsible for the safety and welfare of the other members of their families. Beyond the individuals in each family, the families were further grouped together. People were convened in groups of 10 families, called tythings (or tithings), and were entrusted with policing their own minor problems such as dealing with disturbances, fire, wild animals, or other threats. The leader was called the tythingman. When trouble occurred, he was expected to make a hue and cry to assemble his helpers and warn the village. The hue and cry is like the early precursor to the modern call to 9-1-1. Ten tythings were gathered into groups called a hundred. The affairs of the hundred were supervised by a hundredman appointed by the local nobleman. The hundredman, which would later to be called the parish constable, may be considered the first real police officer, and he dealt with more serious breaches of the law.[6]

Shires, which resembled the counties of today, were controlled by the shire reeve, who was appointed by the Crown or local landowner to supervise the territory and ensure that order would be kept. The shire reeve, a forerunner of today's sheriff, soon began to pursue and apprehend law violators as part of his duties. Just as the parish constable was the lead law enforcement person in urban areas, the **shire reeve** was the lead law enforcement person in county and rural areas.

shire reeve (later became sheriff)
The lead law enforcement person in county and rural areas.

The Winchester Statute

During the reign of King Edward I of England, he was determined to enforce law and order within his kingdom. He complained that local people were reluctant to do justice to (or enforce laws upon) strangers. So, in 1285, he enacted the Winchester Statute which reformed the watch system in England and revived the jurisdiction of the local courts. The Winchester Statute, a primitive form of criminal justice system, was the primary legislation that regulated the policing of the country between the times of the Norman Conquest and the Metropolitan Police Act of 1829. The Winchester Statute declared that each area or hundred would be held responsible for resolving the unsolved crimes in their district.

The Winchester Statute had four major parts. The statute formally established (1) the **watch and ward**, which was the establishment of groups of men to deter crime, stand watch at the city gates, and provide law enforcement; (2) the establishment of the **hue and cry**, which is a process by which bystanders are summoned to assist in capturing criminals or assist the watch as needed. The statute further stated that every man in the hundred shall be answerable for any crimes committed in their area and in effect a form of collective responsibility, or collective guilt to protect the hundred; (3) the requirement that all men between the ages of 15 years and 60 must **bear arms**, or keep weapons in their home

watch and ward
The establishment of groups of men to deter crime, stand watch at the city gates, and provide law enforcement.

hue and cry
Bystanders summoned to assist law enforcers.

bear arms
The ability or requirement to keep weapons in defense of the city or town.

for keeping the peace; and (4) establishing the position of the parish constable to oversee the parish and uphold the compliance to the statute.

The watch system was created to help protect people and property in England's larger cities and towns. Watchmen patrolled at night and helped protect against robberies, fires, and disturbances. Many cities and towns had nighttime curfews in place to maintain law and order. A bell would ring (typically from a church steeple) at dusk, warning residents to end their workday and go inside for the night. Anyone found milling around outside after curfew had to justify their actions to the night watchmen. The watchmen reported directly to the area **constable**, who became the primary municipal law enforcement agent. In larger cities, such as London, the watchmen were organized within church parishes and were typically members of the parish they protected.

In 1326, the office of **justice of the peace** was created to assist the shire reeve in maintaining order in the county. Eventually, these justices took on judicial functions in addition to their primary role as peacekeeper. The local constable became the operational assistant to the justice of the peace, supervising the night watchmen, investigating offenses, serving summonses, executing warrants, and securing prisoners. This system helped delineate the relationship between police and the judiciary, which has continued for more than 600 years.

Private Police and Thief Takers

As the eighteenth century began, rising crime rates in the cities stimulated a new form of private, paid police force, who were able to profit both legally and criminally from the lack of formal police departments. These private police people, referred to as **thief takers**, were generally corrupt, taking profits not only from catching and reporting on criminals but also from receiving stolen property, blackmail, theft, intimidation, and perjury. Thief takers typically took money and stolen goods from their prisoners and made more income by accepting hush money, giving perjured evidence, swearing false oaths, and operating extortion rackets. Petty debtors were especially easy targets for those who combined thief taking with the keeping of alehouses and taverns. While prisoners were incarcerated, their health and safety were entirely at the whim of the keepers, or thief takers, who were virtually free to charge what they wanted for board and other necessities. Court bailiffs who also acted as thief takers were the most passionately detested legal profiteers. They seized debtors and held them in small lockups, where they forced their victims to pay exorbitant prices for food and lodging.

The thief takers' use of violence was notorious. They went armed and were prepared to maim or kill in order to gain their objectives. Before he was hanged in 1725, Jonathan Wild, the most notorious thief taker, "had two fractures in his skull and his bald head was covered with silver plates. He had seventeen wounds in various parts of his body from swords, daggers, and gunshots, [and] . . . his throat had been cut in the course of his duties."[7]

Henry Fielding, who is the famed author of the book *Tom Jones,* along with Saunders Welch and Sir John Fielding (Henry's brother), sought to clean up the thief-taking system. Appointed as a city magistrate in 1748, Fielding operated his own group of private police out of Bow Street in London, directing and deploying them throughout the city and vicinities, deciding which cases to investigate and which streets to protect. His agents were carefully instructed on their legitimate powers and duties. Fielding's Bow Street Runners were a marked improvement

constable
The primary municipal law enforcement agent in urban areas.

justice of the peace
Assists the shire reeve or constable in maintaining order.

thief takers
Private citizens who were paid to catch criminals.

Bow Street Runners
A group of private police out of Bow Street in London.

over the earlier monied police because they actually had an administrative structure that improved record-keeping and investigative procedures. The **Bow Street Runners** did not patrol the streets of London, but they served legal warrants and subpoenas and arrested offenders. Their jurisdiction eventually grew and over time they began to travel across England to capture criminals. Many times former constables, after having some formal legal training, were selected for the positions of Bow Street Runners when their service as constables was over.

Although an improvement, Fielding's forces were not adequate, and by the nineteenth century, state police officers were needed. Ironically, almost 200 years later, private policing is now considered indispensable. Private police forces are a rapidly growing entity, and in many instances local police forces work closely with private security firms and similar entities. In some gated communities and special tax assessment districts, property owners pay a special levy, in addition to their tax dollars, to hire additional private police, who may work in partnership with local law enforcement to investigate criminal activities.[8]

The London Metropolitan Police

Building on some of the successes of the watchmen and the Bow Street Runners, in 1829 Sir Robert Peel, England's home secretary, guided through Parliament an "Act for Improving the Police in and near the Metropolis." Peel argued his point in Parliament on the grounds that this new type of policing would be more efficient than the existing systems. Peel said that the current level of protection was as inefficient. He argued that some boroughs had seemingly effective Watch patrols but they tended to displace crime into areas of the city that were not patrolled as well. Peel's version of policing would standardize the protection of the city and surrounding areas.

The Metropolitan Police Act established the first organized police force in London. Composed of more than 1,000 men, the London police force was structured along military lines. Its members would be known from then on as *bobbies,* after their creator. They wore a distinctive uniform and were led by two magistrates, who were later given the title of commissioner. This was the first time that policing is seen as a career option and not simply a task that must be performed by men in the city. However, the ultimate responsibility for the police fell to the home secretary and consequently Parliament.

The early bobbies suffered many problems. Many of them were corrupt, they were ineffective at stopping crime, and they were often influenced by the wealthy. Owners of brothels who in the past had guaranteed their undisturbed operations by bribing watchmen now turned their attention to the bobbies. Metropolitan police administrators fought continuously to terminate officers who were cowardly, corrupt, or who had alcohol use disorders. In the beginning, they dismissed about one-third of the bobbies each year.

Despite its recognized shortcomings, the London police experiment proved to be a vast improvement over previous police endeavors. It was considered so successful that the metropolitan police soon began providing policing assistance to outlying areas that requested it. An act of Parliament allowed justices of the peace to establish local police forces, and by 1856 every region and county in England was required to form its own police force. Although every officer conducted some level of investigations, the earliest record of the position of detectives was in 1842, and there were only a few people assigned the task of full-time investigations. The modern, fully functioning Criminal Investigation Unit did not appear until 1877.

Sir Robert Peel and the Development of Modern Policing

Because of the overwhelming success of the London Metropolitan Police, Sir Robert Peel became known as the father of modern policing. His mantra was that the police force should be "policing by consent" of the people. One of his more famous sayings was "The Police are the People and the People are the Police."

The London Metropolitan Police were organized around the *beat system,* in which officers were assigned to relatively small permanent posts and were expected to familiarize themselves with the community within their beat, making the officer a part of the neighborhood life. According to the British government's publication, *Policing By Consent*, the institution of policing should be guided by the following nine principles, often referred to as Peel's Nine Principles (1829).[9] There is growing evidence that these principles were not devised by Peel. Susan Lentz and Robert Chaires uncovered the origins of the principles that are believed to be derived from the General Instructions. However, these principles are not included in the language of the Metropolitan Police Act and there is no evidence that the General Instructions was more than a document meant for public relations purposes.[10] The principles included in Exhibit 2.1 are perhaps more of an idealistic view of Peel's intentions created by textbook authors.

As cities developed and populations grew, the focus of many police departments started to change. No longer were police departments focused primarily on providing serves and seeking to preserve the public favor as outlines in Peel's principles, police departments took up the mantle of enforcing laws and bringing suspected offenders to justice as their main priority. The influx of citizens from rural areas in America to more urban cities brought about a slow but steady change in focus from policing to law enforcement.

GL Archive/Alamy Stock Photo

Sir Robert Peel, 2nd Baronet FRS, was a British Conservative statesman who is credited with establishing the first modern police force. He also served twice as Prime Minister of the United Kingdom, as Chancellor of the Exchequer, and twice as Home Secretary. He died in 1850.

Law Enforcement in Colonial America

◀ LO2

Discuss the development and evolution of law enforcement in the United States.

Policing in colonial America paralleled the British model. In the colonies, the county **sheriff** became the most important law enforcement agent. In addition to enforcing laws, catching criminals, and keeping the peace, sheriffs had municipal duties such as collecting taxes, supervising elections, and handling a large amount of other legal business.

The colonial sheriff did not patrol or seek out crime. Instead, he reacted to citizens' complaints and investigated crimes that had occurred. His salary, related to his effectiveness, was paid on a fee system. Sheriffs received a fixed fee for every arrest made. Unfortunately, their tax-collecting duties were more lucrative than fighting crime, so law enforcement was not one of their prime concerns.

sheriff (formerly shire reeve)

The lead law enforcement person in county and rural areas.

Exhibit 2.1

Peel's Principles of Policing

- To prevent crime and disorder, as an alternative to their repression by military force and severity of legal punishment.

- To recognize always that the power of the police to fulfil their functions and duties is dependent on public approval of their existence, actions, and behavior and on their ability to secure and maintain public respect.

- To recognize always that to secure and maintain the respect and approval of the public means also the securing of the willing cooperation of the public in the task of securing observance of laws.

- To recognize always that the extent to which the cooperation of the public can be secured diminishes proportionately the necessity of the use of physical force and compulsion for achieving police objectives.

- To seek and preserve public favor, not by pandering to public opinion; but by constantly demonstrating absolutely impartial service to law, in complete independence of policy, and without regard to the justice or injustice of the substance of individual laws, by ready offering of individual service and friendship to all members of the public without regard to their wealth or social standing, by ready exercise of courtesy and friendly good humor, and by ready offering of individual sacrifice in protecting and preserving life.

- To use physical force only when the exercise of persuasion, advice, and warning is found to be insufficient to obtain public cooperation to an extent necessary to secure observance of law or to restore order, and to use only the minimum degree of physical force that is necessary on any particular occasion for achieving a police objective.

- To maintain at all times a relationship with the public that gives reality to the historic tradition that the police are the public and that the public are the police, the police being only members of the public who are paid to give full time attention to duties that are incumbent on every citizen in the interests of community welfare and existence.

- To recognize always the need for strict adherence to police-executive functions, and to refrain from even seeming to usurp the powers of the judiciary of avenging individuals or the state, and of authoritatively judging guilt and punishing the guilty.

- To recognize always that the test of police efficiency is the absence of crime and disorder, and not the visible evidence of police action in dealing with them.

Source: Definition of policing by consent and historic principles of British policing, https://lawenforcementactionpartnership.org/peel-policing -principles/.[11]

In cities, policing was the sphere of the town marshal, who was aided, often unwillingly, by a variety of constables, night watchmen, police justices, and city council members. However, local governments had little oversight or enforcement of the criminal law was largely an individual or community responsibility. After the American Revolution, larger cities relied on elected or appointed officials to serve warrants and recover stolen property, sometimes in cooperation with the thieves themselves. Night watchmen, who were often referred to as *leatherheads* because of the leather helmets they wore, patrolled the streets calling the hour while equipped with a rattle to summon help and a nightstick to ward off lawbreakers. Initially watchmen were not widely respected. Rowdy young men enjoyed tipping over watch houses with a watchman inside, and a favorite saying in New York was "While the city sleeps the watchmen do too."[12]

Slave Patrols

An early form of law enforcement included patrols charged with recapturing escaped enslaved people (and sometimes free Black citizens if they did not have proper papers). These patrols first appeared in the Caribbean before moving on to rural areas in the South.[13] Although the requirements varied over time and from place to place, units typically consisted of 10 people who in some jurisdictions would then be exempt from serving in the militia. Some patrols pulled members from the low-income White communities while others were staffed from the upper classes looking to avoid military service. Fines were levied against individuals who shirked their patrol duties.[14]

As the enslaved population increased, so did the presence of these horrific patrols; they began to operate in urban areas. Officials in Charleston, South Carolina, created mounted daytime slave patrols in 1704.[15] By 1837, Charleston had a patrol of approximately 100 people, which at the time made it one of the largest police forces in the nation. This growth was not surprising: As the enslaved population steadily increased, so did the desire among slaveholders for the formalized mechanism for controlling insurrections by those enslaved.

Southern slave patrols were a form of social control used to maintain the economic order and the institution of slavery by enforcing restrictive laws and putting fear into the hearts of those enslaved. These patrols were instrumental in capturing enslaved runaways, restricting their movement after hours on the plantation, and protecting White slaveholders from insurrections. Patrols were also authorized to enforce laws against Black literacy, trade, and gambling. In spite of being on a patrol, they also enjoyed some benefits as well. For instance,

slave patrols

A government-sponsored force paid to patrol specific areas to prevent insurrection by those enslaved against the White community.

Focus on Policing

The Long-Term Effect of Slave Patrols

The role of the slave patrols can't be ignored because they were a government-sponsored force that was well organized and paid to patrol specific areas to prevent crimes and insurrection by those enslaved against the White community. The history of the **slave patrols** is also crucial to understanding modern-day relationships between racial and ethnic minority communities and the police.

The Washington, DC Metropolitan Police Department has developed 10 hours of training that includes a trip to the African American History Museum so that officers can learn about and gain an appreciation of the interactions between the police and people of color. The National Museum of African American History and Culture (NMAAHC) is the only national museum devoted exclusively to the documentation of Black life, history, and culture in the United States. It was established

by Congress in 2003. The museum visit is specifically intended to allow officers to confront the uglier and more uncomfortable moments of police interactions with marginalized groups throughout history. This training is required of all 3,800 sworn officers and 660 civilian personnel.

Critical Thinking

1. Based on the difficult relationship between the police and many communities of color, do you think it is an affective training strategy to have officers make trips to the NMAAHC?

2. If more officers visit the NMAAHC, what outcome do you think would be beneficial? How would you know if the visit was effective?

Source: https://www.cnn.com/2018/04/17/us/dc-police-to-learn -black-history-trnd/index.html

men who served on the patrols were often exempt from public, county, and parish taxes and fees during their term of service. In addition to the bounties paid by the slaveholders, some on patrol were paid additional sums with surplus money.

Vigilantes

vigilante
A self-appointed private citizen who undertakes law enforcement in their community without legal authority.

In the western territories of the United States, an individual initiative was encouraged by the practice of offering rewards for capturing felons. If trouble arose, the local vigilance committee might form a posse to chase offenders. These **vigilantes** were often called to eradicate social problems, such as the theft of livestock, through force or intimidation. For example, the San Francisco Committee of Vigilance actively pursued criminals in the mid-nineteenth century.

As cities grew, it became exceedingly difficult for local leaders to organize ad hoc citizen vigilante groups. Moreover, the early nineteenth century was an era of widespread urban unrest and mob violence. Local leaders began to realize that a more structured police function was needed to control demonstrators and keep the peace. Both Northern and Southern civil authorities used the military to enforce various laws and as peace keeping forces. Local elections after the civil war were no exception. The violence and fraud related to elections had been increasing since the emancipation of those enslaved in Southern states, with disruption of meetings, killing and intimidation of many Black people, and a suppression of the Black vote by military and paramilitary groups.

Early Police Agencies

The modern American police department was born out of the urban mob violence that wrecked U.S. cities in the nineteenth century. In 1838, the city of Boston created the first formal U.S. police department. New York city formed its police department in1844 and Philadelphia followed suit in 1854. The new citywide police departments replaced the previous night watch system and relegated constables and sheriffs to serving court orders and maintaining jails. The early Boston police department consisted of 250 officers. Each officer received payment of $2 per shift, walked his own beat, carried a 14-inch night stick, and was forbidden to hold outside employment.

Initially city police departments inherited the functions of the organizations they replaced. For example, Boston police officers were charged with maintaining public health until 1853, and the New York city police department was responsible for sweeping and cleaning streets until 1881. Politics dominated the departments and determined the recruitment of new officers and the promotion of supervisors. An individual with the right connections could be hired despite a lack of qualifications. Early police agencies were corrupt, brutal, and inefficient.[16]

In the late nineteenth century, police work was highly desirable because it paid more than most other blue-collar jobs. By 1880, the average factory worker earned $450 per year, while a metropolitan police officer made double that amount. For immigrant groups, having enough political clout to be appointed to the police department was an important step up the social ladder.[17] However, job security was uncertain because it depended on the local political machine staying in power.

Police work itself was primitive. Few of even the simplest technological innovations common today, such as call boxes or centralized recordkeeping, were in place. Most officers patrolled on foot, without backup or the ability to call for help. Officers were frequently taunted by local thugs and responded with force

Focus on Policing

The Posse Comitatus

Another form of vigilantism was the "posse," a group familiar to all who enjoy the Western genre. The term *posse* comes from the Latin phrase, *posse comitatus,* which means "power of the community." Historically, *posse comitatus* was the old English common-law or statute law authority of a county sheriff, or other law enforcement officer, to enlist or deputize any able-bodied local man to assist him in maintaining order, keeping the peace, or to track and capture a known felon. *Posse comitatus* is similar to the concept of the *hue and cry* that was used in old England.

The **Posse Comitatus Act of 1878** was passed as an amendment to an army appropriation bill following the end of Reconstruction and used to limit the powers of the federal government in using its military personnel to act as domestic law enforcement personnel. Originally, it was passed with support from the Southern states so that the military could not be used to enforce equal rights after Reconstruction ended. Practically speaking, it also protects us from military coups.

The Posse Comitatus Act was back in the news in 2018 as President Donald Trump requested that states activate National Guard troops to head to the southern border to assist U.S. Customs and Border Patrol. Secretary of Defense James Mattis authorized the movement of up to 4,000 troops to the southern border to support the Department of Homeland Security.

While governors in Texas and Arizona were quick to comply with this request, there are limitations to what National Guard troops can do at the border. Federal law prohibits the military from being used to enforce laws, meaning troops cannot actually participate in immigration enforcement. In the past, they've served in support roles like training, construction, and intelligence gathering.[18] Governors generally call upon the Guard to respond to natural disasters in their states. Guard units can also be mobilized by the president in the case of federal emergency or to deploy overseas. Most famously, President Dwight D. Eisenhower called up and federalized the National Guard in 1957 to escort the "Little Rock Nine" to public school following desegregation for student safety.

These limitations are a direct result of the Posse Comitatus Act of 1878.

Critical Thinking

1. Based on the information in the Posse Comitatus Act of 1878, there is a clear differentiation between the military and the police? Do you think there are situations where it would be appropriate for the military to "police" or patrol streets within the United States?

2. Should there be restrictions on how the U.S. military should be used (if at all) in American cities?

3. Should the military be allowed to train civilian police departments?

---

and brutality. The long-standing conflict between the police and the community started in the difficulty that untrained, unprofessional officers had in patrolling the streets of nineteenth-century U.S. cities and in breaking up and controlling labor disputes. Police were not the crime fighters they are known as today. Their major role was maintaining order, and their power was almost unchecked. The average officer had little training, no education in the law, and a minimum of supervision, yet the police became virtual judges of law and fact, with the ability to exercise unlimited discretion.[19]

At mid-nineteenth century, a detective bureau was set up as part of the Boston police. Until then, thief taking had been the province of amateur bounty hunters who hired themselves out to victims for a price. When professional police departments replaced bounty hunters, the close working relationships that developed between police detectives and their underworld informants produced many scandals and, consequently, high personnel turnover.

Posse Comitatus Act of 1878

Bars federal troops from participating in civilian law enforcement except when expressly authorized by law.

Police officers in the nineteenth century were typically regarded as incompetent and corrupt, and they were often disliked by the people they served. The police role was only minimally directed at law enforcement. Its primary function was serving as the enforcement arm of the reigning political power, protecting private property, and keeping control of the increasing numbers of immigrants.

Police agencies evolved slowly in the second half of the nineteenth century. Uniforms were introduced in 1853 in New York. The first technological breakthroughs in police operations came in the area of communications. The linking of precincts to central headquarters by telegraph began in the 1850s. In 1867, the first telegraph police boxes were installed. An officer could turn a key in a box, and his location and number would automatically register at headquarters. Additional technological advances were made in transportation. The Detroit Police Department outfitted some of its patrol officers with bicycles in 1897. By 1913, the motorcycle was being used by departments in the eastern part of the nation. The first police car was used in Akron, Ohio, in 1910, and the police transport wagon became popular in Cincinnati in 1912.[20] Nonpolice functions, such as care of the streets, began to be abandoned after the Civil War, with a focus more on enforcing criminal laws and stopping corruption.

Big-city police were still disrespected by the public, unsuccessful in their role as crime stoppers, and uninvolved in progressive activities. The control of police departments by local politicians impeded effective law enforcement and fostered an atmosphere of graft and corruption. There was rampant avarice, vice, and nepotism within early police departments, and many officers tried to line their own pockets instead of helping the community.

Twentieth-Century Reform

In an effort to reduce police corruption, civic leaders in a number of jurisdictions created police administrative boards to lessen local officials' control over the police. These tribunals were responsible for appointing police administrators and controlling police affairs. In many instances, these measures failed because the private citizens appointed to the review boards lacked expertise in the intricacies of police work.

Underwood Archives/Archive Photos/Getty Images

A New York policeman from the 77th Precinct patrolling the lake in Central Park, New York, in the early 1920s. At that time, big city police were disrespected and accused of corruption and vice.

Another reform movement was the takeover of some big-city police agencies by state legislators. Although police budgets were financed through local taxes, control of police was usurped by rural politicians in the state capitals. New York City temporarily lost authority over its police force in 1857. It was not until the first decades of the twentieth century that cities regained control of their police forces.

One of the key events that brought about reform was the Boston police strike, discussed in the following Focus on Policing.

August Vollmer and the Emergence of Professionalism

Following the turn of the century, a number of nationally recognized leaders called for measures to help improve the professionalism of the police. In 1893, the International Association of Chiefs of Police (IACP), was formed. Under the direction of its first president (Washington D.C. Chief of Police Richard Sylvester), the IACP became the leading voice for police reform during the first two decades of the twentieth century. The IACP advocated creating a civil service police force and for removing political influence and control. It also encouraged centralized organizational structure and recordkeeping reducing the power of politically aligned precinct captains. Another professional reform the IACP fostered was the creation of specialized units, such as delinquency control squads.

The most famous police reformer of the time was August Vollmer. While serving as the first police chief of Berkeley, California (1909–1932), and before that Berkeley city marshal (1905–1909), Vollmer instituted university training for young officers and advocated hiring college-educated officers.[22] Vollmer petitioned the University of California at Berkeley with a revolutionary idea to approach the profession of law enforcement through academic research and introduced police science as an academic discipline. He also helped develop the School of Criminology at the University of California at Berkeley, which became the first formal criminal justice academic degree program and the model for justice-related programs around the United States.

The primary focus of the new academic program at Berkeley was to professionalize American policing in order to end corruption and institute structured protocols for basic police functions, patrol procedures, and investigations. The initial courses in the newly established program addressed police functions and were more like professional training courses rather than traditional academic courses. The Berkeley program quickly evolved into a respected, rigorous academic program as new concepts and procedures were analyzed, tested, and evaluated. Vollmer initiated such technological advances in policing as putting officers on bicycles, then on motorcycles, and then in patrol cars. Vollmer put radio communication in the cars in the late 1920s. He created a centralized police records system, and insisted that his department use blood, fiber, and soil analysis to solve crimes. Vollmer's emphasis on scientific investigation spurred the creation of several crime laboratories around the state. He also banned the use of brutal interrogation tactics (the third degree) by the police when questioning suspects. His motto was that the role of police is to prevent crime rather than just to solve it.

August Vollmer was well ahead of his time in such areas as crime records, retroactive investigations, patrol force distribution, and police communications. Vollmer developed a comprehensive theory of police professionalism that was adopted by J. Edgar Hoover when he became the director of the Federal Bureau of Investigation (FBI) in 1924. When Vollmer took over the Berkeley Police Department, police officers were known more for their brutality and corruption than their crime-solving skills. Much of the police reforms that swept the country in the early part on the century started with Vollmer in Berkeley. Vollmer wrote in *The National Police Journal* (April 1920), "an effort ought to be made to obtain men who are capable, honest, active in mind and body, industrious, cool headed, actuated by sentiment of humanity and kindness, well educated, experienced in dealing with men, women, and children, able to solve difficult problems quickly, and prompt to act on decisions formed on the basis of practical common sense and sound judgment. A police force composed of such material would be a good investment for any city." Because of these advances in criminal justice police studies and practices, **August Vollmer** is affectionately known as the father of modern American policing for his dedication to groundbreaking practices and professionalism in policing.

August Vollmer

First police chief of Berkeley, California, and a leading figure in the development of the field of criminal justice in the United States.

The Boston Police Strike

The evening of Tuesday September 9, 1919, was when policing as we knew it would change forever. That was the night that uniformed patrolmen in the city of Boston would go on strike, leaving the city in chaos. As America was still recovering from World War I, the police action in Boston heightened the interest in police reform across the nation. Though this strike is sometimes regarded as an obscure event in American history, the Boston police strike of 1919 would prove to be one of the most significant events in policing history. It was widely known that police officers in Boston were dissatisfied with their status in society. At the time, other professions were being unionized and with that, they were getting increases in pay and benefits. That was not the case for the police. It was notable that the police at the time were not reaping the same benefits and officers were becoming increasingly unhappy with their weakened status in society.

In Boston, officers noticed that not only was their pay lagging during the war, but so was their respect from the average citizen. Their pay had not increased in decades, their shifts were often 12 hours lone, and officers were required to be on call at the police station several nights per week. It was widely accepted that the Boston policemen of 1919 had a valid complains in their work-related demands. The biggest complaints fell into three primary categories: their less than adequate working conditions, the length of working shifts, and, most importantly for them, their low wages. Despite their low pay, officers also had to purchase their own uniforms and boots. Finally, the officers objected to the conditions under which they were forced to work, and often sleep, in the crowded decay and disrepair of the police station.

The Boston police commissioner, Edwin Upton Curtis, was publicly anti-union and believed that if the police were allowed to unionize, the whole department would take orders from the union and not the command staff. That would hamper the officers' discipline and ultimately, his authority to command the department. Curtis feared that the union concerns would not protect the interests of the city or its business leaders. The commissioner banned the officers from associating with any outside organizations and flatly refused to sanction a police union.

Representatives from the Boston Social Club, Boston police officers' fraternal organization, underwent a month-long labor dispute, but ultimately voted to defy the commissioner's orders and unionize to become affiliated with the American Federation of Labor (AFL). Commissioner Curtis then began the process of suspending 19 Boston police officers, including the president and other union leadership, for violation of his orders not to unionize. That evening, the Policemen's Union voted to protest the suspensions by striking at evening roll call the next day.

On Tuesday, September 9, 1919, around 5:45 P.M. at the beginning of the evening shift, approximately 1,117 Boston policemen conducted a work stoppage

Vollmer's disciples included O. W. Wilson, who pioneered the use of advanced training for officers when he took over and led reforms to reduce corruption in the Wichita (Kansas) Police Department in 1928. Wilson instituted professionalism in the Wichita Police Department, requiring all new police hires to be college educated. He also introduced such police innovations as the use of mobile radios, police patrol cars, and a mobile crime laboratory. Wilson believed that officers using two-way radio allowed for better communications, more efficient supervision of patrol officers, and therefore more efficient policing. Wilson was also instrumental in applying modern management and administrative techniques to policing. His text, *Police Administration,* became the single most influential work on the subject.

During this period, police professionalism was equated with an incorruptible, tough, highly trained, rule-oriented police departments which should be organized along militaristic lines. The most respected department was the Los Angeles Police Department (LAPD), which emphasized police as incorruptible crime fighters who would not question the authority of the central command.

and walked off the job. This action removed 70 percent of the police force from protecting the city. This was the first strike by public safety workers in U.S. history. With the city of Boston virtually unprotected, petty crimes escalated into looting, and rioting took place throughout the city. Disorder in the central downtown business district of Boston was almost instantaneous as people took advantage of the strike, looting stores and breaking windows. With the police on strike, reported assaults, rapes, vandalism, and looting went unpunished as the city struggled to get replacement police in place. Boston's Mayor Andrew Peters asked Governor Calvin Coolidge to mobilize the state militia to take over protecting the city.

As crime rose and people were victimized, public support quickly turned against the police. The violence began to subside when the militia fired into a crowd, killing five men. Most people in Boston blamed the turmoil on the police for abandoning their posts and leaving the city defenseless, and the strike was broken. Eventually, all the striking officers were fired and replaced by new recruits. The Boston police strike ended police unionism for decades and solidified power in the hands of reactionary, autocratic police administrators and local officials.

The striking policemen in Boston were not rehired, and their jobs went overwhelmingly to servicemen returning from the war. Despite repeated appeals from the American Federation of Labor requesting reinstatement of the striking officers, they were not allowed to return to work. The new officers, however, were granted higher pay as well as paid holidays and they gained the additional benefit of free uniforms. The irony is that the Boston police strike was effective in obtaining its objectives, just not for the police officers who went on strike. It would be nearly 50 years before Boston's police were allowed to finally unionize. In the aftermath of the strike, various local, state, and federal crime commissions began to investigate the extent of crime and the ability of the justice system to deal with it and made recommendations to improve police effectiveness.[21] However, with the onset of the Great Depression, justice reform became a less important issue than economic revival, and for many years, little changed in the nature of policing.

Critical Thinking

1. It seems that the Boston police strike of 1919 was effective in getting future officers better pay and working conditions, even though many people were hurt in the ensuing crimes. Do you think that first responders should be allowed to go on strike or conduct a work stoppage?

2. What can be done to keep citizens safe when first responders go on strike?

3. What can be done to protect the rights of first responders if they do not have the right to conduct an organized work stoppage?

Sources: Roll Coll—Researching the Men Behind the 1919 Boston Police Strike. 2019 Joseph P. Healey Library at University of Massachusetts Boston. Lorenzo M. Boyd, "The Boston Police Strike of 1919," *Encyclopedia of Police Science*, 3rd ed., 2 vols., ed. Jack R. Greene (New York: Routledge, 2006).

The Modern Era of Policing: 1960 to the Present

 LO3
Describe the path to police reform and how it has changed over time.

The modern era of policing can be traced from 1960 to the present day. The modern era of policing started with the police actions during the civil rights struggles and continues to the modern-day strategies of CompStat. Also included is an overview of the causes and consequences of the urban riots and how they change community views of the police. Also included is the move toward the "professionalism era" as well as community policing and the age of technology.

What are the major events that occurred during this period?

Policing in the 1960s

Turmoil and crisis were the hallmarks of policing during the tumultuous 1960s. Throughout this decade, the U.S. Supreme Court handed down several major decisions intended to regulate police operations and procedures. Police officers were now required to obey strict legal guidelines when questioning suspects, conducting searches and wiretapping, and so on. As the civil rights of suspects were significantly expanded, police complained that they were being "handcuffed by the courts."

Also during this time, civil unrest produced a growing tension between police and the public. Black citizens, who were battling for increased rights and freedoms in the civil rights movement, regularly found themselves confronting police lines. When riots broke out in Detroit, Harlem, Chicago, Watts, and other U.S. cities in the 1960s, the spark that ignited conflict often involved the police. The following Focus on Policing addresses one of the most notorious events that helped shape the future of policing.

Focus on Policing

The Watts Riot

Many of the racial problems that came from a post-antebellum America spread from the South to other parts of the country, including Los Angeles. The summer of 1965 in Los Angeles experienced excruciating heatwaves. Many residents did not have air conditioning in their homes, and this was particularly true in low-income areas. So, to beat the heat in their homes, many residents spent their evenings outside trying to catch a breeze. So whenever something happened in the neighborhoods, there were lots of community members on the streets watching.

Tensions were already high in many parts of the city because Black and Latino residents were constantly being excluded from the high-paying jobs, affordable housing, and political advancements made available to the White residents of Los Angeles. There was also frustration in the Watts section of Los Angeles regarding their long-standing grievances and growing dissatisfaction with high unemployment rates, substandard housing, and inadequate schools. Racial and ethnic minority residents also had serious unanswered complaints about the Los Angeles Police Department (LAPD). This military-like urban police force had a long history of complaints of discrimination, severe brutality, and racial bias. The stifling heat in the summer of 1965 did not help matters at all.

The inciting event to the Watts riots began on August 11, 1965, when a White California highway patrol officer stopped a Black motorist from Watts,

21-year-old Marquette Frye and his brother, Ronald, for suspicion of drunk driving in their neighborhood. The LAPD was called for backup as a crowd, including Frye's mother, gathered to watch the ensuing arrest. The incident quickly escalated when an officer pushed Frye's mother. Frye's brother and mother then struggled with the arresting officers and were subsequently arrested by LAPD officers. Rumors spread that the police used brutality to arrest Frye's family, which angered the crowd and tensions between the police and the crowd erupted in a violent exchange.

The riot was concentrated in the commercial section of Watts, an extremely impoverished Black neighborhood in South Central Los Angeles, and lasted for six days, with close to 30,000 people involved. Rioters overturned and burned vehicles, set fire to buildings, looted and damaged several stores, resulting in more than $40 million in property damage. The Watts riots proved to be the biggest and most expensive urban uprising of the entire civil rights era. Fourteen thousand California National Guard troops were mobilized in South Central Los Angeles and a curfew zone encompassing over 45 miles was established in an attempt to restore law and order in the area. By the time the rebellion was over, the rioting claimed 34 lives and over 1,000 residents reported various levels of injuries.

Civil Rights Era

In 2013, Montgomery, Alabama, Police Chief Kevin Murphy and Congressman John Lewis met to discuss attacks on the Freedom Riders during a trip to Montgomery in May 1961. Representative Lewis and other civil rights activists were beaten by a mob after arriving at Montgomery's Greyhound station. In 2013, Chief Murphy apologized and offered his badge in a gesture of reconciliation. Specifically, Chief Murphy apologized for the Montgomery Police Department's failure to protect the Freedom Riders and the enforcement of unjust laws. Representative Lewis was moved by the gesture.[23]

This meeting between two former adversaries illustrated a sharp difference from their first encounter during the civil rights era when Lewis suffered an arrest

When the riots were over, a full investigation was ordered by Governor Pat Brown. In spite of the findings of the commission appointed by the governor, city leaders and state and federal officials failed to implement sustainable measures to improve the social and economic conditions of Black people living in the Watts neighborhood and the surrounding impoverished Los Angeles communities. In the ensuing decades, many of the issues of police brutality, poverty, and systemic discrimination still plagued the Watts section of Los Angeles. This area, however, has shifted demographically from predominantly Black to mostly first- and second-generation Latino.

The 1965 Watts riot kicked off a series of civil rights–involved, Black-led urban riots in what was termed the "long, hot summers." Prior to Watts, race riots had almost always involved White people going into racial and ethnic minority neighborhoods, similar to the Tulsa race riots of 1921. After the Watts riots, the norm became a series of often-oppressed people of color setting fires and rioting in their own communities in response to White offenses and oppression. While many people did not understand the social uprising and rebellion of members of communities of color, many saw these actions as vital insurrections that brought much-needed attention to the issues of civil rights, police brutality, and biased policing in many impoverished neighborhoods and communities of color. Many scholars and historians see these types of riots and rebellions as the language of a voiceless class. Many would argue that without these types of civil unrest, there may not have been the types of improvements in the lives of people of color in America that followed.

The Watts riots, as an event, are still considered by many to have been one of the key turning points in the civil rights movement of the 1960s, and helped to shape public understanding of race riots, uprisings, and the development of race relations in the United States. But the Watts riots also helped usher in the era of militaristic policing. It was during the Watts riots that many middle-class Americans began to fear crime in general, and urban crime in particular, in a way that they never did prior to the summer of 1965. Based on the history of brutality against nonviolent protesters in the 1950s and early 1960s, the police were ill equipped to deal with citizens who actually fought back and used violence as a means to an end. The LAPD went to the U.S. military for guidance and training in urban warfare. This military style of policing in Los Angeles, led by a young lieutenant named Daryl Gates, was the precursor to the modern-day police SWAT teams.

Critical Thinking

1. The Watts riots illuminated several problems in society. Other than a negative relationship with the police, what other issues contributed to the riots?

2. What are some of the things that the police can do to avoid situations like the Watts riots from happening again?

Sources: H. Edward Ransford, "Isolation, powerlessness, and violence: A study of attitudes and participation in the Watts riot," *American Journal of Sociology* 73 (1968): 581–591; D. Sears and J. McConahay, *Politics of Violence—The New Urban Blacks and the Watts Riot* (Boston: Houghton Mifflin, 1973).

for leading a protest. The conflict between the police and civil rights groups was a product of the 1954 decision *Brown v. Board of Education* in which the Supreme Court ruled unanimously that racial segregation in public schools was unconstitutional. Yet, by the 1960s, few Southern schools were integrated. The civil rights movement picked up steam in response to this Supreme Court decision. In 1957, National Guard troops under orders from President Eisenhower enforced the desegregation of Little Rock Central High School in Arkansas. Even after the Little Rock incident, integration was slow.

In February 1960, four Black college students sat down at a Woolworth's lunch counter in Greensboro, North Carolina, and requested service. They were declined service, and they refused to leave their seats. Sit-ins and other protests swept across the South in early 1960, touching more than 65 cities in 12 states. Roughly 50,000 young people joined the protests that year. Seating on public buses in the South was also segregated, along with bus station waiting rooms, restrooms, and restaurants. In May 1961, the Congress of Racial Equality (CORE), led by James Farmer, organized integrated Freedom Rides to defy segregation in interstate transportation. Freedom Riders were arrested in North Carolina and beaten in South Carolina by the police. The police and protesters were clashing on a regular basis.

When students across the nation began marching in anti–Vietnam War demonstrations, local police departments were called on to keep order. Police forces were ill equipped and poorly trained to deal with these social problems. Confounding these problems was a rapidly growing crime rate. The number of violent and property crimes increased dramatically. Drug addiction and abuse grew to become national concerns, common in all social classes. Urban police departments could not control the crime rate, and police officers resented the demands placed on them by dissatisfied citizens. With no other strategy to employ, many local police departments started to engage in a militaristic form of policing, which further enraged urban communities and citizens of color. Not surprisingly, the 1960s were marked by a number of bloody confrontations between the police and the public.

The Emergence of Legal Rights

Terry v. Ohio

A Supreme Court case that established that the police could stop, detain, question, and search a person based only on an officer's reasonable suspicion.

Another policing milestone was the 1968 ruling of the U.S. Supreme Court, which grew out of a field interrogation in Cleveland, Ohio, and expanded police authority. The Supreme Court ruled in *Terry v. Ohio* (1968) that the police could stop, detain, question, and search a person based only on an officer's reasonable suspicion that a person has committed or is about to commit a crime, and nothing more. This court decision would arguably become the most impactful decision on the criminal justice system to date. Other critical cases included *Mapp v. Ohio* (1961), which limited the scope of police search, and *Miranda v. Arizona* (1966), which required police to warn suspects about their right to remain silent and have an attorney present if they are to be questioned about a case.

These cases still influence police behavior today. Take, for instance, *Terry v. Ohio* (1968), in which the Supreme Court developed the idea of reasonable suspicion, ruling that an officer must act on more than a hunch and on what "a reasonably prudent man would have been warranted in believing . . ." before they can stop and frisk (pat down search) a suspect in the field.[24] For example, it would be reasonable for police officers to question and frisk a suspect if they see them lurking in a mall parking lot at midnight after all the stores have been closed.

This power is not without its limits; for example, deciding to search based on racial profile is illegal. Most recently, in *Commonwealth v. Warren* (2015), the Supreme Judicial Court of Massachusetts ruled that Black people may have a legitimate reason to run from the police. Subsequently, running from the police is not enough to establish reasonable suspicion in Massachusetts.[25]

Policing in the 1970s

The 1970s witnessed many structural changes in police agencies themselves. The end of the Vietnam War significantly reduced tensions between students and police. However, the relationship between police and marginalized groups was still rocky. Local fears and distrust, combined with conservative federal policies, encouraged police departments to control what was perceived as an emerging "minority-group threat."[26]

Increased federal government support for criminal justice agencies and policy greatly influenced police operations. During the decade, the Law Enforcement Assistance Administration (LEAA) dedicated a significant portion of its funds to police agencies. Although a number of police departments used this money to purchase little-used hardware, such as anti-riot gear, most of it went to supporting innovative research on police work and advanced training of police officers. Perhaps most significant, LEAA's Law Enforcement Education Program helped thousands of officers further their college education. Hundreds of criminal justice programs were developed on college campuses around the country, providing a pool of highly educated police recruits. LEAA funds were also used to import or transfer technology originally developed in other fields into law enforcement. Technological innovations involving computers transformed the way police kept records, investigated crimes, and communicated with one another. State training academies improved the way police learned to deal with such issues as job stress, community conflict, and interpersonal relations. More women and people of color were recruited to police work. Affirmative action programs helped, albeit slowly, alter the ethnic, racial, and gender composition of U.S. policing.

The 1970s were full of police corruption in many U.S. cities. Stamford, Connecticut, was arguably one of the most corrupt cities in the country. The FBI investigated the Stamford police department and found that a police commander was taking $1,800 a week from the Gambino crime family and a detective sergeant was running a drug ring out of police headquarters.

The New York City Police Department (NYPD) was also plagued with corruption when undercover police officer **Frank Serpico** blew the whistle on police within his department in the early 1970s. Serpico provided credible evidence of widespread systematic police corruption that originally was ignored. During a drug raid in which he was under cover, other officers failed to back him up and he was subsequently shot in the face. Other officers refused to put out a call that an officer was shot. The circumstances surrounding Serpico's shooting quickly came into question. At the scene, he realized that the two other officers who had accompanied him to the scene did not follow him into the apartment, raising the question whether Serpico had actually been brought to the apartment by his colleagues to be murdered. NYPD launched no formal investigation of the shooting. Based on Serpico's allegations of corruption, the mayor appointed the landmark Knapp Commission to investigate the corruption in the NYPD.

Frank Serpico
A former NYPD detective, best known for whistleblowing on police corruption.

Policing in the 1980s

As the 1980s began, the police role seemed to be changing significantly. A number of experts acknowledged that the police were not simply crime fighters and called for police to develop a greater awareness of community issues, which resulted in the emergence of the community policing concept.[27] This decade is sometimes thought of as the "bending granite years" of policing as departments struggled to change their orientation and focus; the term **bending granite** refers to the fact that police departments are reluctant to innovate and are set in their ways.

There were a number of factors that contributed to changing the police culture. First, in a 1982 article written in *Atlantic Monthly* magazine, criminologists James Q. Wilson and George Kelling argued that the focus of policing should be aimed at community-level problems such as improving neighborhood living conditions and away from simply just enforcing laws.[28] This article used the metaphor of *broken windows* to explain quality-of-life issues in potentially decaying neighborhoods. A neighborhood with lots of un-mended broken windows sends a message: crime and disorder will be tolerated here. Wilson and Kelling devised a *Broken Windows Model* of policing that suggests police forces garner community support to improve neighborhoods. The emphasis was on reducing fear while getting community members involved with police efforts to reduce crime. Similarly, some departments began to experiment with *Problem Oriented Policing*. In 1986, problem-oriented policing programs were implemented in Baltimore County, Maryland, and Newport News, Virginia.[29] For example, in Newport News, the police worked with the community members to help solve burglaries in the area.

From 1988 to 1990, the National Institute of Justice sponsored the *Perspectives on Policing Seminars* at Harvard University's Kennedy School of Government. These seminars helped popularize scholars and practitioners refine and synthesize the mixture of ideas and approaches labeled community- and problem-oriented policing, setting the stage for widespread implementation in the 1990s. Research was also conducted to support these changes. For example, in 1988, the Police Foundation funded a multiyear study in Madison, Wisconsin, to uncover how community policing could improve officer attitudes as well as citizen perceptions about crime and the police.[30]

Police unions, which began to grow in the late 1960s, continued to have a great impact on departmental administration in the 1980s. Unions fought for and won increased salaries and benefits for their members. In many instances, unions eroded the power of the police chief to make unquestioned policy and personnel decisions. During the decade, chiefs of police commonly consulted with union leaders before making major decisions concerning departmental operations.

Although police operations improved markedly during this time, police departments were also beset by problems that impeded their effectiveness. State and local budgets were cut back during the Reagan administration, and federal support for innovative police programs was severely curtailed with the demise of the LEAA.

Police–community relations continued to be a major problem. Riots and incidents of urban conflict occurred in some of the nation's largest cities.[31] They triggered continual concern about what the police role should be, especially in inner-city neighborhoods. The Miami Police Department was plagued by scandal during the 1980s: more than a dozen officers were charged with

---

bending granite
Refers to the fact that police departments are reluctant to innovate and are set in their ways.

crimes ranging from drug dealing to murder. The department was the focus of an inquiry by the FBI into drug-related corruption. Twenty-five other police officers, some of them of high rank, were subpoenaed as witnesses or as targets of the investigation.[32]

Policing in the 1990s

The 1990s began on a troubled note and ended with an air of optimism. The incident that helped change the face of U.S. policing occurred on March 3, 1991, when two Black men, Rodney King and Bryant Allen, were driving on the interstate highway in Los Angeles. They refused to stop when signaled by the California Highway Patrol, instead increasing their speed, exiting the highway, and driving through the city. According to the LAPD officers, King, who was driving, appeared to be under the influence of drugs or alcohol. When LAPD, along with the highway patrol, finally stopped the car, they delivered 56 baton blows and six kicks to King in a period of two minutes, producing 11 skull fractures, brain damage, and kidney damage. They did not realize that their actions were being videotaped by an observer, who later gave the tape to the media.

The officers involved were tried and acquitted in a suburban court by an all-White jury. The acquittal set off six days of rioting in South Central Los Angeles, which was brought under control by the California National Guard. In total, 56 people were killed, 2,383 were known to have been injured, and 13,212 people were arrested.[33] The police officers involved in the beatings were later tried and convicted in federal court.

The Rodney King case prompted an era of police reform. Several police experts decreed that the nation's police forces should be evaluated on their courteousness, deportment, and helpfulness instead of their crime-fighting ability. Interest renewed in reviving an earlier style of police work featuring foot patrols and increased citizen contact. Police departments began to embrace new forms of policing that stressed cooperation with the community and problem solving; this is referred to as the community policing model. Ironically, urban police departments began to shift their focus to becoming community organizers at a time when technological improvements increased the ability to identify suspects.

An ongoing effort was made to bring diversity to police departments, and Black people began to be hired in greater numbers, particularly in Los Angeles. As a result of the reform efforts, the intellectual caliber and emotional intelligence of the police rose dramatically, and they became smarter, better informed, and more sophisticated than ever before. Management skills became more sophisticated, and senior police managers began to implement sophisticated information technology systems. As a result, policing became more intellectually demanding, requiring specialized knowledge about technology, forensic analysis, and crime. Although a few notorious cases of police corruption and violence made headlines, by and large, the police began to treat the public more fairly and more equitably than before.[34]

The LAPD also went through another major scandal involving its officers. The LAPD's specialized anti-gang unit, called the Community Resources Against Street Hoodlums (CRASH) unit was plagued with complaints of harassment, brutality, and corruption in the Rampart section of the city. With roughly 165,000 residents occupying a roughly 5.5-square-mile area, the Rampart section of the city is one of Los Angeles's most densely populated communities. This challenging community led to police officers being more aggressive in doing their

The Community Resources Against Street Hoodlums (CRASH) was a group of elite anti-gang units within the LAPD set up to tackle gang-related crime. There were complaints and allegations that CRASH handed out rough street justice including harassing and abusing suspects and falsifying reports. Before it was disbanded, some argued that they had become a street gang themselves.

jobs, and some would say many officers were overzealous. LAPD-CRASH officers have been accused of such offenses as unprovoked beatings and shootings of suspects, officers planting and falsifying evidence, stealing from drug dealers and selling narcotics, bank robbery, perjury, and covering up evidence to protect other officers.

More than 70 Los Angeles police officers assigned to or associated with the Rampart CRASH unit were implicated in some form of misconduct, making it one of the most widespread cases of documented police misconduct in U.S. history. Of those 70 officers implicated in wrongdoing, enough evidence was found to bring 58 officers before an internal affairs disciplinary board. The result was that 24 LAPD officers were found to have committed wrongdoing, with 12 being suspended, 7 were forced to resign or retire, and 5 were terminated.

As a result of the investigation into falsified evidence and police perjury, over 100 prior criminal convictions were overturned. The LAPD Rampart-CRASH scandal resulted in more than 140 civil lawsuits against the city of Los Angeles, costing over $125 million in settlements. The full extent of Rampart police corruption is not known, and several rape, murder, and robbery investigations involving Rampart officers remain unsolved.[35]

LO4

Examine contemporary law enforcement.

Policing and Law Enforcement Today

Contemporary law enforcement agencies are still undergoing transformation. There has been an ongoing effort to make police "user friendly" by decentralizing police departments and making them responsive to community needs. Police and law enforcement agencies are also adapting to the changing nature of crime: they must be prepared to handle terrorism, Internet fraud schemes, and identity theft, as well as rape, robbery, and burglary.[36]

Law enforcement duties are distributed across local, county, state, and federal jurisdictions. There are approximately 750,340 sworn law enforcement officers in the United States, employed in almost 18,000 different agencies.[37] Police and law enforcement agencies can be found in a variety of levels of government. In the following sections the most important agencies of Federal, State, County, and Municipal policing and law enforcement will be discussed in some detail.

Federal Law Enforcement

Federal law enforcement authorities have authorization to enforce the laws contained within the United States Code (U.S.C.). In recent years, the scope of federal law enforcement has been greatly expanded; more than 40 percent of all federal criminal provisions have been enacted since 1970. This means that dozens of offenses what were once considered state crimes now fall under federal jurisdiction. With the passage of the USA PATRIOT Act in October 2001, the reach of federal law enforcement agencies has become even broader.

It is now commonplace for federal law enforcement agencies to work closely with state and local law enforcement agencies to bring federal criminals to justice.[38]

The most important of these agencies are described below.

Federal Bureau of Investigation

Today's FBI is not a police agency but an investigative agency, with jurisdiction over all law enforcement matters in which the United States is or may be an interested party. However, its jurisdiction is limited to federal laws, including all federal statutes not specifically assigned to other agencies. Areas covered by these laws include espionage, sabotage, treason, civil rights violations, murder and assault of federal officers, mail fraud, robbery and burglary of federally insured banks, kidnapping, and interstate transportation of stolen vehicles and property.

The FBI headquarters in Washington, DC, oversee more than 56 field offices, approximately 350 satellite offices known as resident agencies, four specialized field installations, and more than 60 foreign liaison posts. The foreign liaison offices, each of which is headed by a legal attaché or legal liaison officer, work abroad with U.S. and local authorities on criminal matters within FBI jurisdiction. In all, the FBI has approximately 35,000 employees, including approximately 13,000 special agents and 20,000 support personnel, who perform professional, administrative, technical, clerical, craft, trade, or maintenance operations.[39]

The FBI also offers important services to local law enforcement agencies, including use of its vast fingerprint file and a sophisticated crime laboratory that aids local police in testing and identifying evidence, such as hair, fiber, blood, tire tracks, and drugs. The FBI's National Crime Information Center is a computerized network linked to local police departments by terminals. Through it, information on stolen vehicles, wanted persons, stolen guns, and so on is made readily available to local law enforcement agencies. In the post-9/11 world, the FBI has shifted its priorities to counterintelligence, counterterrorism, and cyberterrorism.

Pressmaster/Shutterstock.com

Interagency collaboration among law enforcement agencies is now being developed and encouraged. For it to succeed it must be perceived as being appropriate and acceptable to all participating organizations. There is evidence that interagency collaboration promotes greater efficiency while improving the quality and quantity of service.

The Department of Homeland Security (DHS)

Following the September 11, 2001, attacks, a new cabinet-level agency called the Department of Homeland Security (DHS) received congressional approval. DHS was assigned the mission of preventing terrorist attacks within the United States, reducing America's vulnerability to terrorism, and minimizing the damage and aiding the recovery from attacks that do occur. Since September 11, 2001, roughly $1 trillion was spent on the infrastructure that is homeland security.[40] There are five basic homeland security missions:

■ Prevent terrorism and enhancing security

■ Secure and manage our borders

■ Enforce and administer our immigration laws

■ Safeguard and secure cyberspace

■ Ensure resilience to disasters

DHS is the third-largest cabinet department in the federal government, after the Department of Defense and the Department of Veterans Affairs. It has more than 260,000 employees. The Department of Homeland Security has a number of independent branches and bureaus.[41] Of them, three are well-known law enforcement agencies: Customs and Border Protection, Immigration and Customs Enforcement, and the U.S. Secret Service.

Customs and Border Protection (CBP)

This agency is responsible for protecting our nation's borders in order to prevent terrorism, human and drug smuggling, illegal immigration, and agricultural pests from entering the United States, while improving the flow of legitimate trade and travel.

Customs and Border Protection (CBP) employs nearly 60,000 personnel, among them approximately 22,000 Border Patrol agents and CBP Air and Marine agents who patrol the country's borders and points of entry. CBP also partners with other countries through its Container Security Initiative and the Customs-Trade Partnership Against Terrorism program. The goal of each is to help ensure that goods destined for the United States are screened before they are shipped.[42]

CBP made headlines in 2018 for enacting a policy change made by the president. The CBP was running family detention centers at the southern border of the United States. Thousands of children had been separated from their parents, who were seeking asylum, and were housed in these CBP facilities. These events underscored the differences between federal and local police both in mission and responsibilities.[43]

Immigration and Customs Enforcement (ICE)

As the largest investigative arm of the Department of Homeland Security, Immigration and Customs Enforcement (ICE) is responsible for identifying and shutting down vulnerabilities in the nation's border, and for economic, transportation, and infrastructure security. ICE executes its mission through the enforcement of more than 400 federal statutes, and focuses on smart immigration enforcement, preventing terrorism, and combating the illegal movement of people and trade. Immigration enforcement is the largest single area of responsibility for ICE. There are four main components of ICE:

1. The Office of Investigations investigates a wide range of domestic and international activities arising from the movement of people and goods that violate immigration and customs laws and threaten national security.

2. The Office of Detention and Removal Operations is responsible for public safety and national security by ensuring the departure from the United States of all removable aliens through the fair enforcement of the nation's immigration laws.

3. The Office of Intelligence is responsible for the collection, analysis, and dissemination of strategic and tactical intelligence data for use by ICE and DHS.

4. The Office of International Affairs (OIA) conducts and coordinates international investigations involving transnational criminal organizations responsible for the illegal movement of people, goods, and technology into and out of the United States.[44]

The Secret Service

The U.S. Secret Service has two significant missions. The first is to protect the president and vice president, their families, heads of state, and other high-level officials. Part of this function involves investigating threats against protected officials and protecting the White House, the vice president's residence, and other buildings within Washington, DC.

The second mission is to investigate counterfeiting and other financial crimes, including financial institution fraud, identity theft, computer fraud, and computer-based attacks on our nation's financial, banking, and telecommunications infrastructure. Criminal investigations cover a range of conduct:

> . . . counterfeiting of U.S. currency (to include coins); counterfeiting of foreign currency (occurring domestically); identity crimes such as access device fraud, identity theft, false identification fraud, bank fraud, and check fraud; telemarketing fraud; telecommunications fraud (cellular and hard wire); computer fraud; fraud targeting automated payment systems and teller machines; direct deposit fraud; investigations of forgery, uttering, alterations, false impersonations, or false claims involving U.S. Treasury Checks, U.S. Saving Bonds, U.S. Treasury Notes, Bonds, and Bills; electronic funds transfer (EFT) including Treasury disbursements and fraud within the Treasury payment systems; Federal Deposit Insurance Corporation investigations; Farm Credit Administration violations; and fictitious or fraudulent commercial instruments and foreign securities.[45]

Drug Enforcement Administration (DEA)

Drug Enforcement Administration (DEA) agents assist local and state authorities in investigating illegal drug use and carrying out independent surveillance and enforcement activities to control the importation of narcotics. For example, DEA agents work with foreign governments in cooperative efforts aimed at destroying opium and marijuana crops at their source—hard-to-find fields tucked away in the interiors of Latin America, Asia, Europe, and Africa. Undercover DEA agents infiltrate drug rings and simulate buying narcotics to arrest drug dealers.

According to the DEA website, their mission is "to enforce the controlled substances laws and regulations of the United States and bring to the criminal and civil justice system of the United States, or any other competent jurisdiction, those organizations and principal members of organizations, involved in the growing, manufacture, or distribution of controlled substances appearing in or destined for illicit traffic in the United States; and to recommend and support nonenforcement programs aimed at reducing the availability of illicit controlled substances on the domestic and international markets."[46]

Drug Enforcement Administration (DEA)

The federal agency that enforces federal drug control laws.

Bureau of Alcohol, Tobacco, Firearms, and Explosives (ATF)

The **Bureau of Alcohol, Tobacco, Firearms, and Explosives (ATF)** helps control sales of untaxed liquor and cigarettes and, through the Gun Control Act of 1968 and the Organized Crime Control Act of 1970, has jurisdiction over the illegal sale, importation, and criminal misuse of firearms and explosives. At its core, the ATF is a law enforcement agency that is part of the Department of Justice, designed to protect people from gun violence, violent criminals, illegal guns, and the trafficking of firearms of any type. The ATF also guards against the illegal use or storage of explosives, acts of terrorism, and the illegal use and distribution of alcohol and tobacco products.

Bureau of Alcohol, Tobacco, Firearms, and Explosives (ATF)

Federal agency with jurisdiction over the illegal sale, importation, and criminal misuse of firearms and explosives and the distribution of untaxed liquor and cigarettes.

U.S. Marshals Service

The **U.S. Marshals Service** is America's oldest federal law enforcement agency and one of the most versatile. The Office of the U.S. Marshall was created in

U.S. Marshals Service

Federal agency whose jurisdiction includes protecting federal officials, transporting criminal defendants, asset forfeiture, and tracking down fugitives.

September 1789, with the passage of the Judiciary Act by Congress. The U.S. Marshals Service (USMS), however was created nearly a century later in 1969 to assist the U.S. Marshals throughout the nation. Its over 3,500 deputy marshals and criminal investigators perform a number of functions, including judicial security, fugitive investigations, witness protection, prisoner transportation, prisoner services (the agency houses nearly 60,000 federal detainees each day), and administration of the U.S. Justice Department's Asset Forfeiture Program. The basic mission of the U.S. Marshals is to enforce federal laws and provide support to the federal justice system.

State Law Enforcement Agencies

Unlike municipal police departments, state police were legislatively created to deal with the growing incidence of crime in nonurban areas, a consequence of the increase in population mobility and the advent of personalized mass transportation in the form of the automobile. County sheriffs—elected officials with occasionally corrupt or questionable motives—had proved ineffective in dealing with the wide-ranging criminal activities that developed during the latter half of the nineteenth century. In addition, most local police agencies were unable to protect effectively against highly mobile lawbreakers who randomly struck at cities and towns throughout a state. In response to citizens' demands for effective and efficient law enforcement, state governors began to develop plans for police agencies that would be responsible to the state, instead of being tied to local politics and possible corruption.

The Texas Rangers, created in 1835, was one of the first state police agencies formed. Essentially a military outfit that patrolled the U.S.–Mexico border, it was followed by the Massachusetts State Constables in 1865 and the Arizona Rangers in 1901. The states of Connecticut (1903) and Pennsylvania (1905) formed the first truly modern state police agencies.[47]

Today, about 23 state police agencies have the same general police powers as municipal police and are territorially limited in their exercise of law enforcement regulations only by the state's boundaries. They provide investigative services to smaller communities when the need arises. The remaining state police agencies are primarily responsible for highway patrol and traffic law enforcement.

Some state police direct most of their attention to the enforcement of traffic laws. Others are restricted by legislation from becoming involved in the enforcement of certain areas of the law. For example, in some jurisdictions, state police are prohibited from becoming involved in strikes or other labor disputes unless violence erupts.

The nation's 93,000 state police employees (about 61,000 officers and 32,000 civilians) carry out a variety of functions besides law enforcement and highway safety, including maintaining a training academy and providing emergency medical services.[48] State police crime laboratories aid local departments in investigating crime scenes and analyzing evidence. State police also provide special services and technical expertise in such areas as bomb-site analysis and homicide investigation. Some state police departments, such as California's, are involved in highly sophisticated traffic and highway safety programs, including the use of helicopters for patrol and rescue, the testing of safety devices for cars, and the conducting of postmortem examinations to determine the causes of fatal accidents.

County Law Enforcement Agencies

The county sheriff's role has evolved from that of the early English shire reeve, whose primary duty was to assist the royal judges in trying prisoners and enforcing sentences. From the time of the westward expansion in the United States until municipal departments were developed, the sheriff was often the sole legal authority over vast territories.

Today, sheriffs' offices contain about 350,000 full-time employees, including about 183,000 sworn personnel. Employment has risen an average of about 4 percent per year since 1990.[49] The duties of a sheriff's department vary according to the size and degree of development of the county. In some jurisdictions, sheriffs' offices provide basic law enforcement services such as performing routine patrols, responding to citizen calls for service, and investigating crimes.

Other standard tasks of a typical sheriff's department are serving civil process (summons and court orders), providing court security, and operating the county jail. Less commonly, sheriffs' departments may serve as coroners, tax collectors, overseers of highways and bridges, custodians of the county treasury, and providers of fire, animal control, and emergency medical services. In years past, sheriffs' offices also conducted executions. Typically, the law enforcement functions of a sheriff's department are restricted to unincorporated areas of a county, unless a city or town police department requests its help.

Some sheriffs' departments are exclusively law enforcement oriented; some carry out court-related duties only; some handle civil process; some are involved solely in correctional and judicial matters with limited law enforcement duties. However, a majority are full-service agencies that carry out judicial, correctional, and law enforcement activities. Typically, agencies serving heavily populated areas (over 1 million) are devoted to maintaining county correctional facilities, whereas those in areas of smaller population are focused on law enforcement.

There are also county police departments that are separate from the sheriff's department. County police are municipal police that operate on a countywide basis, but typically do not have any non-law enforcement duties. While the sheriff's department typically handles court security, civil process, and some correctional duties as well as law enforcement, county police primarily have only law enforcement duties. Some of the larger county police departments include Suffolk County (NY), Nassau County (NY), Broward County (FL), Charlotte-Mecklenburg County (NC), Fairfax County (VA), Miami-Dade County (FL), and Las Vegas (NV) Metropolitan Police.

Municipal Law Enforcement Agencies

Local police form the majority of the nation's authorized law enforcement personnel. Municipal police departments range in size from the New York City Police Department, with almost 40,000 full-time officers and 10,000 civilian employees, to rural police departments, which may consist of a single officer. At last count, nearly 13,000 local police departments nationwide had an estimated 600,000 full-time employees, including about 460,000 sworn personnel.[50]

Municipal police departments are attracting applicants who value an exciting, well-paid job that also offers them an opportunity to provide valuable community service. Salaries in municipal police agencies are becoming more competitive.

Most TV police shows feature the crime-fighting efforts of big-city police officers, but the overwhelming majority of departments have fewer than 50 officers and serve a population of less than 25,000. Recent data reveal that nearly three-quarters of all local police departments serve populations of less than 10,000 people. Roughly 650 municipal agencies employ just one sworn officer.

Municipal police officers' responsibilities are immense, and they are often forced to make split-second decisions on life-and-death matters. At the same time, they must be sensitive to the needs of citizens who are often of diverse racial and ethnic backgrounds. What's more, local police perform multiple roles, including (but not limited to) investigating crimes, identifying suspects, and making arrests.

Smaller agencies can have trouble carrying out many of the same functions as their big-city counterparts; the hundreds of small police agencies in each state often provide duplicate services. Whether consolidating smaller police agencies into "superagencies" would improve services is often debated among police experts. Smaller municipal agencies can provide important specialized services that might have to be relinquished if they were combined and incorporated into larger departments. Another approach has been to maintain smaller departments but to link them via computerized information sharing and resource management networks.[51]

Summary

LO1   Discuss the historical antecedents to policing in the United States.

U.S. police agencies trace their beginnings to early English society. Under the pledge system, people were grouped into tithings and were entrusted with policing their own minor problems. Ten tithings were grouped into a hundred, supervised by a constable. Ten hundreds were organized into shires overseen by the shire reeve, the precursor to the modern sheriff. Early thief takers were private police who apprehended criminals for reward payments. Henry Fielding's Bow Street Runners improved on the thief-taking system. The first organized police force was founded by Sir Robert Peel in London.

LO2   Discuss the development and evolution of law enforcement in the United States.

In the colonies, the county sheriff became the most important law enforcement agent. The first true U.S. police departments were formed in Boston, New York, and Philadelphia in the early nineteenth century. During the period ranging from 1960 to 1980 police departments underwent significant change. Questions about the effectiveness of law enforcement led to changes such as the hiring of women and people of color. The fact that police officers were viewed as "outsiders" in the neighborhoods they served led to the development of community policing. Police departments began to embrace new forms of policing that stressed cooperation with the community and problem solving.

LO3   Describe the path to police reform and how it has changed over time.

A number of sources brought about police reform. The International Association of Chiefs of Police (IACP) called for creating a civil service police force and for removing political influence and control. The organization fostered the creation of specialized units, such as delinquency control squads. August Vollmer, the first police chief of Berkeley, California (1909–1932), was another influential reformer. He instituted university training for young officers and advocated hiring college educated officers. These reform movements that began in the 1920s culminated in the concept of professionalism. Police professionalism was interpreted to mean tough, rule-oriented police work featuring advanced technology and hardware. The view that these measures would quickly reduce crime proved incorrect.

LO4   Examine contemporary law enforcement.

There are several major law enforcement agencies. At the federal level, the FBI is the largest federal agency. Other agencies include the Drug Enforcement Administration and the U.S. Marshals Service. Most states maintain state police agencies who investigate crimes and patrol the roadways. County-level law enforcement is provided by sheriffs' departments, who run jails and patrol rural areas. Local police agencies engage in patrol, investigative, and traffic functions, as well as many support activities.

Key Terms

shire reeve, 28

watch and ward, 28

hue and cry, 28

bear arms, 28

constable, 29

justice of the peace, 29

thief takers, 29

Bow Street Runners, 30

sheriff, 31

slave patrols, 33

vigilantes, 34

Posse Comitatus Act of 1878, 35

August Vollmer, 39

Terry v. Ohio (1968), 42

Frank Serpico, 43

bending granite, 44

Drug Enforcement Administration (DEA), 49

Bureau of Alcohol, Tobacco, Firearms, and Explosives (ATF), 49

U.S. Marshals Service, 49

Notes

1. John Bauschatz, *Law and Enforcement in Ptolemaic Egypt* (Cambridge, England: Cambridge University Press, 2013)
2. Clive Emsley, *The English Police* (London: Routledge, 2014); Robert Wadman and William Thomas Allison, *To Protect and to Serve: A History of Police in America,* 1st ed. (Upper Saddle River, NJ: Prentice Hall, 2003); Wilfried Nippel, *Public Order in Ancient Rome* (Cambridge, England: Cambridge University Press, 1995).
3. Virginia J. Hunter, *Policing Athens* (Princeton, NJ: Princeton University Press, 1993).
4. Lesley Adkins and Roy Adkins, *Handbook to Life in Ancient Rome* (London: Oxford University Press, 1998).
5. Malcolm Sparrow, Mark Moore, and David Kennedy, *Beyond 911: A New Era for Policing* (New York, NY: Basic Books, 1990); Daniel Devlin, *Police Procedure, Administration, and Organization* (London: Butterworth, 1966); Robert Fogelson, *Big-City Police* (Cambridge, MA: Harvard University Press, 1977); Roger Lane, *Policing the City, Boston 1822–1885* (Cambridge, MA: Harvard University Press, 1967); J. J. Tobias, *Crime and Industrial Society in the Nineteenth Century* (New York, NY: Schocken, 1967); Samuel Walker, *A Critical History of Police Reform: The Emergence of Professionalism* (Blue Ridge Summit: Lexington Books, 1977); Samuel Walker, *Popular Justice* (New York, NY: Oxford University Press, 1980); John McMullan, "The New Improved Monied Police: Reform Crime Control and Commodification of Policing in London," *British Journal of Criminology* 36 (1996), 85–108.
6. Malcolm Sparrow, Mark Moore, and David Kennedy, *Beyond 911: A New Era for Policing* (New York: Basic Books, 1990); Daniel Devlin, *Police Procedure, Administration, and Organization* (London: Butterworth, 1966); Robert Fogelson, *Big-City Police* (Cambridge, MA: Harvard University Press, 1977); Roger Lane, *Policing the City, Boston 1822–1885* (Cambridge, Mass.: Harvard University Press, 1967); J. J. Tobias, *Crime and Industrial Society in the Nineteenth Century* (New York, NY: Schocken, 1967); Samuel Walker, *A Critical History of Police Reform: The Emergence of Professionalism* (Lexington, MA: Lexington, 1977); Samuel Walker, *Popular Justice* (New York, NY: Oxford University Press, 1980); John McMullan, "The New Improved Monied Police: Reform Crime Control and Commodification of Policing in London," *British Journal of Criminology* 36 (1996), 85–108.
7. Devlin, *Police Procedure,* p. 3.
8. John L. McMullan, "The New Improved Monied Police: Reform, Crime Control, and the Commodification of Policing in London," *British Journal of Criminology* 36 (1996), 92.
9. Elizabeth Joh, "The Paradox of Private Policing," *Journal of Criminal Law & Criminology* 95 (2004), 49–132.
10. Susan A. Lentz and Robert H. Chaires, "The Invention of Peel's Principles: A Study of Policing 'Textbook' History." *Journal of Criminal Justice* 35, no. 1 (2007), 69–79.
11. Wilbur Miller, "The Good, the Bad, and the Ugly: Policing America," *History Today* 50 (2000), 29–32.
12. Wilbur Miller, "The Good, the Bad, and the Ugly: Policing America," *History Today* 50 (2000), 29–32.
13. Phillip Reichel, "Southern Slave Patrols as a Transitional Type," *American Journal of Police* 7 (1988), 51–78.
14. K. B. Turner, David Giacopassi, and Margaret Vandiver, "Ignoring the Past: Coverage of Slavery and Slave Patrols in Criminal Justice Texts," *Journal of Criminal Justice Education* 17, no. 1 (2006), 181–195.
15. Andrea Diaz, "DC Police Officer Training Now Includes Trips to the African American History Museum," *CNN*, April 17, 2018, https://www.cnn.com/2018/04/17/us/dc-police-to-learn-black-history-trnd/index.html.
16. Walker, *Popular Justice,* p. 61.
17. Ibid., p. 8.
18. https://www.cnn.com/2018/04/06/politics/national-guard-troops-border/index.html.
19. Dennis Rousey, "Cops and Guns: Police Use of Deadly Force in Nineteenth-Century New Orleans," *American Journal of Legal History* 28 (1984), 41–66.
20. Law Enforcement Assistance Administration, *Two Hundred Years of American Criminal Justice* (Washington, DC: Government Printing Office, 1976).
21. National Commission on Law Observance and Enforcement, *Report on the Police* (Washington, DC: Government Printing Office, 1931), pp. 5–7.
22. Willard M. Oliver, *August Vollmer: The Father of American Policing* (Durham: Carolina Academic Press, 2017).
23. Craig Giammona, NBC News. March 3, 2013, https://www.nbcnews.com/news/us-news/alabama-police-chief-apologizes-freedom-rider-congressman-flna1c8655005;
24. https://www.oyez.org/cases/1967/67.
25. https://www.bostonglobe.com/metro/2016/09/20/sjc-judges-must-consider-high-rate-fios-between-boston-police-and-men-color/0baqga4wecvXxsWZwSnNll/story.html.
26. Pamela Irving Jackson, *Minority Group Threat, Crime, and Policing* (New York, NY: Praeger, 1989).
27. James Q. Wilson and George Kelling, "Broken Windows," *Atlantic Monthly,* March 1982, pp. 29–38.

28. James Q. Wilson and George Kelling, "Broken Windows," *Atlantic Monthly,* March 1982, pp. 29–38.

29. John E. Eck and William Spelman, "Who Ya Gonna Call? The Police as Problem-busters," *Crime & Delinquency* 33, no. 1 (1987), 31–52.

30. Mary Ann Wycoff and Wesley K. Skogan, Community Policing in Madison: Quality from the Inside Out. An Evaluation of Implementation and Impact, 1993, https://www.ojp.gov /pdffiles1/Digitization/144390NCJRS.pdf

31. Frank Tippett, "It Looks Just Like a War Zone," *Time,* May 27, 1985, pp. 16–22; "San Francisco, New York Police Troubled by Series of Scandals," *Criminal Justice Newsletter* 16 (1985), 2–4; Karen Polk, "New York Police: Caught in the Middle and Losing Faith," *Boston Globe,* December 28, 1988, p. 3.

32. https://www.nytimes.com/1986/08/03/us/police-corruption -plaguing-florida.html.

33. The Staff of the Los Angeles Times, *Understanding the Riots: Los Angeles Before and After the Rodney King Case* (Los Angeles: Los Angeles Times, 1992).

34. David H. Bayley, "Policing in America," *Society* 36 (December 1998), 16–20.

35. Peter Boyer, "Bad Cops," *The New Yorker Magazine*, May 21, 2001, https://www.newyorker.com/magazine/2001/05/21 /bad-cops.

36. Ronald Burns, Keith Whitworth, and Carol Thompson, "Assessing Law Enforcement Preparedness to Address Internet Fraud," *Journal of Criminal Justice* 32 (2004), 477–493.

37. Brian A. Reaves, *Census of State and Local Law Enforcement Agencies, 2008* (Washington, DC: Bureau of Justice Statistics, 2011).

38. Federallawenforcement.org, The Scope and Mission of Federal Law Enforcement, http://www.federallawenforcement.org /what-is-federal-law-enforcement/.

39. Federal Bureau of Investigation, https://www.fbi.gov/about/faqs /how-many-people-work-for-the-fbi (accessed May 25, 2023).

40. Steven Brill, "Is America Any Safer?," *The Atlantic*, September 2016 issue, https://www.theatlantic.com/magazine/archive /2016/09/are-we-any-safer/492761/.

41. Department of Homeland Security, http://www.dhs.gov/history (accessed May 25, 2023).

42. Customs and Border Protection, https://www.cbp.gov/trade /basic-import-export (accessed May 25, 2023).

43. Nomaan Merchant, "Immigrant kids seen held in fenced cages at border facility," *AP News*, June 18, 2018, https://apnews.com /6e04c6ee01dd46669eddba9d3333f6d5 (accessed June 13, 2013).

44. Immigration and Customs Enforcement, https://www.justice .gov/criminal-oia / (accessed May 25, 2023).

45. U.S. Secret Service, US Secret Service Handbook Volume 1 Strategic Information, Developments, Contacts. International Business Publications, Washington, DC (accessed May 25, 2023).

46. United States Drug Enforcement Administration, https://www .dea.gov/who-we-are/about (accessed June 12, 2023).

47. Bruce Smith, *Police Systems in the United States* (New York, NY: Harper & Row, 1960).

48. Brian J. Reaves, *Census of State and Local Law Enforcement Agencies, 2008* (Washington, DC: Bureau of Justice Statistics, 2011).

49. Reaves, *Census of State and Local Law Enforcement Agencies, 2008.*

50. Reaves, *Census of State and Local Law Enforcement Agencies, 2008.*

51. See, for example, Robert Keppel and Joseph Weis, *Improving the Investigation of Violent Crime: The Homicide Investigation and Tracking System* (Washington, DC: National Institute of Justice, 1993).

Becoming a Police Officer

Learning Objectives

LO1 Discuss the current landscape of policing in the United States.

LO2 List the steps taken to attract and recruit police officers.

LO3 Describe the state of police education.

LO4 Examine the role of accreditation.

LO5 Compare and contrast police academies and POST certification.

Chapter Outline

The Craigslist Robbers were a gang of thieves, based in the San Francisco Bay Area, who stole more than $500,000 in jewelry from victims. How did the case unfold? The gang got on police radar when they robbed a Bay Area man who was selling his watch on Craigslist. The seller was contacted by a local who arranged to meet in a public place—a coffee shop in Fremont, California. After they met up, the so-called buyer grabbed the Rolex and took off running.

Video surveillance and the so-called buyer's cell phone number turned up an identity that police were able to link to two more robberies in Bay Area cities. In each case, the victims were selling Rolex watches on Craigslist and the potential buyer grabbed the goods and ran. Two months later, the lead detective, Michael Gebhardt, received word that police in Oakland were investigating five similar robberies. After three men were arrested in Oakland, they revealed the identity of the Fremont "watch thief," who as it turns out, was part of a gang being run by his father, an inmate at the California Men's Colony state prison.

The gang by then had come up with a new ploy: to ease the mind of sellers, they sent airplane tickets to jewelry sellers and had a limo meet them at the airport. Who would suspect that robbers would send someone an airline ticket! But it was a relatively small investment for the robbers: a $500 airline ticket in order to steal a $30,000 diamond. One Wisconsin woman, who took the airplane ticket to sell the $19,000 diamond ring she had listed on Craigslist, was robbed instead. The gang spread its wings and began attacking victims around the nation—from Florida, Oregon, and Colorado—all with the same prime suspects and associates.

In the end, detectives conducted a sting operation. They posted an ad on Craigslist, hoping to attract the attention of the robbery crew's leader in prison and it worked. Gebhardt was contacted and a pickup was arranged. The gang was busted; the robbery crew's mastermind was in prison and his son was arrested. After their trial, five gang members received sentences ranging from 41 months to 30 years. The father was given an additional seven years in prison for his role.[1]

The detective work by Michael Gebhardt in busting the Craigslist Crew was dramatic enough to be made into a feature film. But while glamorous, it represents only a tiny fraction of local police work. This chapter looks at the nature and extent of local policing in the United States, why people become police, and the roles they carry out on the job.

L01

Discuss the current
landscape of policing in
the United States.

Critical Thinking

1. Many students are
   drawn to the profession
   of policing because of
   the allure and notoriety
   of the detective unit.
   Identify some attributes
   or characteristics of being
   a good detective that are
   attractive or appealing to
   prospective police officers.

2. Which skills do you think
   are necessary for an
   effective detective to solve
   crimes and close cases?

▶ An Introduction to Police Organizations

Most municipal police departments in the United States are independent agencies within the executive branch of government, operating without specific administrative control from any higher governmental authority. Although they often cooperate and participate in mutually beneficial enterprises, such as a joint task force with state and federal law enforcement agencies, local police agencies are functionally independent organizations with unique sets of rules, policies, procedures, norms, budgets, and so on.

Most local police departments are organized in a hierarchical manner. Within this organizational model, each element of the department normally has its own paramilitary style chain of command. In a large municipal department, there may be a number of independent investigation units headed by a captain who serves as the senior administrator, a lieutenant who oversees cases and investigations and acts as liaison with other police agencies, and sergeants and inspectors who carry out fieldwork. Smaller departments may have a captain or lieutenant as head of a particular branch or unit.

The Bureaucratic Nature of the Police

To understand the organization of police departments, it is also important to understand the bureaucratic nature of the police. Most departments are modeled after the military model that is bureaucratic by nature. This includes a hierarchical command structure with a military rank structure. It can be argued that the police are not really using a true military model. A true military model emphasizes supervision, teamwork, and team-involved operations. In contrast, most police work is conducted more independently and without much supervision. The rank structure is further supported with an authoritarian management style. Efficiency is an important element of bureaucracy.

Patrol officers in Miami set out to counter and control a spate of recent shootings using high-powered assault weapons. Though most police departments employ a military like structure, officers are more likely to act independently without much supervision.

Joe Raedle/Getty Images News/Getty Images

Bureaucratic Characteristics

Police departments are not the only public bureaucracy. All government agencies are similarly segmented with structures that are hierarchical with a clear division of labor among workers, supervisors, and executives. Bureaucratic organizations are complex, performing multiple tasks in pursuit of a common goal. For police, that goal is maintaining public safety. In bureaucracies, tasks are grouped into divisions or bureaus with a clear chain of command. There is also a clear unity of command where employees answer to one supervisor. In bureaucracies, the responsibility for specific tasks is delegated to lower-ranking officials. Written rules exist for conformity and consistency. In a bureaucracy, information flows up and down the organization. In addition, formal career paths exist in an orderly fashion.

There are a number of problems associated with bureaucracies, but it is important to remember that these issues are not limited to policing. Bureaucracies have been described as rigid, inflexible, and poorly adapted to change. For example, police were criticized in the 1960s (and today) for not responding to changing social conditions. This is a common critique of all bureaucratic organizations—and particularly the police. Another criticism of bureaucracies is that communication often breaks down because of all these formal layers. It is difficult for patrol officers to share information with command staff. Conversely, the message of the command staff often gets diluted when it travels through the layers of the hierarchy.

Bureaucracies can also become inward looking, insular, and self-serving. This can cause police to become isolated from people that they serve. There becomes a huge disconnect between the police and various communities. It is somewhat related that bureaucracies can come to exist to sustain themselves. This means that bureaucratic imperatives prevail and the organization focuses less on its mission and more on promoting itself. Bureaucracies have also been described as not using the talents of people within the organization. Similarly, bureaucracies can also stifle creativity by pushing workers to just follow orders and not develop their own ideas. In bureaucratic organizations, it is difficult to move up the chain of command—limited opportunities for promotions create morale issues.

Despite these problems, police departments continue to model at least a quasi-military-based bureaucratic organizational model. While these characteristics are important, they are not the only predictors of organizational behavior. In his book, *Becoming Bureaucrats*, Zachary Oberfield follows two sets of public employees—police officers and welfare caseworkers—from their first day on the job through the end of their second year. He finds that while the bureaucracy did affect the development of workers' personalities, how they did their jobs was really tied to the views, identities, and motives that they held before entering public service. Accordingly, how bureaucracies function depends somewhat on supervision and culture but also on the beliefs and ideas held by who gets hired. Thus, more attention should be paid to patterns of self-selection and recruitment.[2]

Pros and Cons of Police Administrative Organization

Police administrative organization has both its pros and cons. Because most departments are civil service organizations, administrators must rise through the ranks to get to command positions. To be promoted, they must pass a battery of tests, profiles, interviews, and so on. Most police departments employ a time-in-rank system for determining promotion eligibility. This means that before moving up the administrative ladder, an officer must spend a certain amount of time in the next lowest rank; a sergeant cannot become a captain without serving an appropriate amount of time as a lieutenant.

This system has both benefits and shortcomings. On the plus side, it is designed to promote stability and fairness and to limit favoritism and political patronage. The chief's favorite officer cannot be promoted over a more experienced officer who is better qualified. Once earned, a rank can rarely be taken away or changed if new management takes over. The rank system is supposed to protect police agencies from losing talented officers who are trained at public expense to other departments who offer more money or other incentives. The time-in-rank system is also supposed to reward officers who are loyal to the department and have paid their dues in service to the department and the community. Many times, better-performing officers may be stuck on off-shifts because more senior officers pick the favorable shifts, regardless of their performance.

On the downside, the rank system restricts administrative flexibility. Unlike in the private sector, where the promotion of talented people can be accelerated in the best interests of the company, the time-in-rank system prohibits rapid advancement. A police agency would probably not be able to hire a computer systems expert with a PhD and give them a command position in charge of its data-analysis section in some systems. The department may be forced to hire the expert as a civilian employee under the command of a ranking senior officer who might not be as technically proficient. Because senior administrators are typically promoted from within only after years of loyal service, time-in-rank may render some police agencies administratively conservative. Although once a command rank is not in the union bargaining unit, more flexibility may happen.

Even when police executives adopt new programs, such as CompStat (see later in this chapter for more on CompStat), they are most likely to choose those elements that confer legitimacy on existing organizations, and on implementing them in ways that minimize disruption to existing organizational routines, rather than embracing truly innovative changes.

Most police work entails relatively mundane tasks, such as responding to service calls, random routine motorized and foot patrols, and completing administrative tasks, as illustrated in Exhibit 3.1. Television programs and movies almost completely ignore this side of police work. Instead, they focus on the crime-fighting role.

Chain of Command

In a large municipal department, there may be a number of independent units headed by a bureau chief who serves as the senior administrator, a captain who oversees regional or precinct units and acts as liaison with other police agencies, a lieutenant who manages daily activities of the shift as a shift commander, and sergeants and patrol officers who carry out fieldwork. At the head of the organization is the police chief (sometimes called the commissioner or similar), who sets policy and has general administrative control over all the department's various operating branches. The chief is responsible for budgeting, resource allocation, overseeing policy changes, and liaising with local politicians, like the mayor, city manager, or city council.

Critical Thinking

1. With the level of bureaucracy listed here, do you think it is harder for the police to do their jobs?
2. How would you streamline the police bureaucracy?

Within this organizational model, each element of the department normally has its own unique chain of command and rank system. A department the size of New York City's police department, which employs roughly 55,000 employees with 35,000 sworn police officers, contains many specialized investigative units, such as special victims or sex crimes, whereas many smaller departments do not employ detectives at all and rely on county or state police investigators to probe unsolved crimes, as illustrated in Exhibit 3.2.

┌───┐

Exhibit 3.1

Core Functions of Municipal Police

Law Enforcement Functions

■ Identifying criminal suspects

■ Investigating crimes

■ Apprehending offenders and participating in their trials

■ Deterring crime through patrol

■ Enhancing public safety by maintaining a visible police presence

Order Maintenance Functions

■ Resolving conflict and keeping the peace

■ Maintaining a sense of community security and public order (i.e., peacekeeping) within the patrol area

■ Keeping vehicular and pedestrian movement efficient

■ Promoting civil order

Service Functions

■ Aiding individuals in danger or in need of assistance

■ Providing emergency medical services

■ Providing public education and outreach

■ Maintaining and administering police services

■ Recruiting and training new police officers

└───┘

Elements of Police Organization

It is important to note that there is more than one type of police structure. Because police departments are local, the structures are not uniform. Included below is a list of divisions that might be typically found in police departments. This is not an exhaustive list, nor is it a representation of all police departments in the United States.

Field services is also known as patrol services or field operations. As you may recall (Chapter 1), patrol divisions comprise the largest portion of field services; approximately, 68 percent of local police officers were assigned to patrol operations.[3] Larger departments employ various forms of detective and investigative divisions. Traffic enforcement is typically conducted by patrol, but in larger departments traffic enforcement is a separate division. Traffic accident reports can take up a lot of time, which is why a separate division is needed in larger agencies. Some police departments also maintain community service (or community engagement) divisions. If an agency has adopted community-oriented policing, then patrol officers will need to attend neighborhood meetings and assist with neighborhood projects.

Exhibit 3.2

New York City Ranks include the following, from Lowest to Highest:

- Cadet
- Police officer
- Detective specialist
- Detective investigator
- Sergeant (symbol of rank: 3 chevrons)
- Lieutenant (symbol of rank: 1 gold bar)
- Captain (symbol of rank: 2 gold bars)
- Deputy inspector (symbol of rank: gold oak leaf)
- Inspector (symbol of rank: gold eagle)
- Deputy chief (symbol of rank: 1 gold star)
- Assistant chief (symbol of rank: 2 gold stars)
- Bureau chief (symbol of rank: 3 gold stars)
- Chief of department (symbol of rank: 4 gold stars)
- Deputy commissioner (symbol of rank: 3 gold stars)
- First deputy commissioner (symbol of rank: 4 gold stars)
- Police commissioner (symbol of rank: 5 gold stars)

Source: New York City Police Department.

Administrative services in police departments consist of staff or support services. Administrative services are responsible for:

1. Recruitment
2. Training
3. Planning and research
4. Communication
5. Crime lab
6. Records

As the model of a typical police department indicates, not all members of a department engage in what the general public regards as real police work—patrol, detection, and traffic control. Even in departments that are embracing community- and problem-oriented policing, a great deal of police resources are devoted to support and administrative functions.

Many police departments maintain their own human resources, or personnel service, that carries out such functions such as recruiting new police officers, creating exams to determine the most qualified applicants, and handling promotions and transfers. Innovative selection techniques are constantly being developed and tested. To give you an idea, the Behavioral-Personnel Assessment Device (B-PAD) requires police applicants to view videotaped scenarios and respond as though they were officers handling the situation. Reviews indicate that this procedure may be a reliable and unbiased method of choosing new recruits.[4]

Larger police departments often maintain an **internal affairs** (or Office of Professional Standards) division, which is charged with policing the police and investigating many police actions, misconduct, and complaints. The internal affairs division processes citizen complaints of police corruption, investigates allegations of unnecessary use of force by police officers, and even probes allegations of police participation in criminal activity, such as burglaries or narcotics violations. In addition, the internal affairs division may assist police managers when disciplinary action is brought against individual officers.

Internal affairs is often seen as having a controversial function because investigators are feared and distrusted by fellow police officers. Nonetheless, rigorous self-scrutiny is the only way that police departments can earn citizens' respect. Internal affairs units represent one avenue to increase citizen perceptions of police integrity and legitimacy, but internal complaint review systems will continually be challenged because opportunities for police misconduct are prevalent due to the use of police discretion.[5] Some type of citizen oversight of police practices and civilian review boards with the power to listen to complaints and conduct investigations has become commonplace in police departments. Most police departments are responsible for the administration and control of their own budgets. This task includes administering payroll, purchasing equipment and services, planning budgets for future expenditures, and auditing departmental financial records.

internal affairs

An element of a law enforcement agency investigating incidents and plausible suspicions of lawbreaking and professional misconduct attributed to officers on the force.

Who Are Today's Police?

Who fills these tasks? How many police officers are there and who makes up their ranks? There are now more than 700,000 sworn officers—meaning that they have general arrest powers—working the nation's local police, state, and sheriff's departments.[6] Municipal and township police departments employ about 2 officers per 1,000 residents. This average has steadily decreased over time—in 2003, there were 2.5 officers per 1,000 residents.[7] More than half of local police officers are employed in larger cities and towns with 100,000 or more residents. This means that while there are more small police departments, larger agencies actually employ more officers.

In fact, about half (48 percent) of local police departments employ fewer than 10 officers. On the other end of the spectrum, the New York City Police Department (NYPD) remains the largest local police department, employing roughly 35,000 full-time officers. The NYPD is 1 of 43 police departments that employ more than 1,000 officers. This suggests that there is wide diversity in local police departments in the United States. Accordingly, the conditions and experiences of police officers in these agencies will also vary.

Police departments are becoming more diverse:

■ About 1 in 7 local police officers and about 1 in 10 first-line supervisors are women.

■ About 1 in 4 local police officers and about 1 in 5 first-line supervisors are Black or Hispanic.

Openly lesbian, gay, bisexual, transgender, and queer (LGBTQ) officers are also increasingly commonplace in policing. This was unheard of as late as the 1980s. The San Francisco Police Department did not have openly gay or lesbian officers as late as 1980 and the Chicago Police Department did have anyone as recently as 1991.[8] It is difficult, however, to measure the numbers of LGBTQ officers in police departments because there are no official statistics collected on sexual orientation. As part of his effort to increase relational policing in Houston, TX, enhanced outreach to the LGBTQ community, in 2017, Chief Acevedo created a new "Pride Car" with rainbow decals on every side, saluting Houston's LGBTQ+ community. Chief Acevedo is quoted as saying, "By actually participating … we send a very powerful message that we're an inclusive department, … where every segment of society is welcome, is respected, and will be protected by the Houston Police Department." This sentiment was shared by the police union: "We're supportive of the pride parade and all our members who are LGBTQ," said Houston Police Officers Union Vice President Joseph Gamaldi.[9]

Race and Gender

In 1987, women comprised 7.5 percent of the sworn police employees and by 2000 this had increased to 10.6 percent. The gains in the percentage of female police officers have not kept up at the previous pace and, in fact, have slowed between 2000 and 2007, moving from 10.6 to 11.9 percent. In 2020, 86 percent of police officers were men.[10] The percentage of Black officers increased from 9.3 percent in 1987 to 11.7 percent in 2000 and then stalled roughly at that level (i.e., at 12 percent) until 2007.[11] In 2020, about 70 percent of full-time sworn officers in local police departments were White, while around 30 percent were Black, Hispanic, or another race (Asian, Native Hawaiian, or Other, Pacific Islander, American Indian, or Alaska Native, or two or more races).[12]

Aggregate statistics, however, do not tell the whole story. Indeed, representation for women and people of color is hardly stable across agencies, with some agencies employing no (or few) women or people of color while others are more representative of the communities they serve.[13] In Ferguson, Missouri, at the time of the controversial shooting of Michael Brown, only 5.6 percent of the police force was Black, compared to 67 percent of the population. It is not unusual for smaller cities like Ferguson to lack diversity, as much of the recent progress in representation of people of color has been observed in larger agencies. Research suggests that most police agencies do not represent the communities that they serve.[14]

Departments in larger jurisdictions are typically more diverse than those in smaller ones—probably a function of the populations that they serve.[15] Amie Schuck examined 4,000 agencies to evaluate the effects of community, organization, and economic factors on the representation of women in police departments.[16] Higher levels of female officer representation are associated with organizations that emphasize community policing; have higher education requirements, more incentives and benefits, minimal physical fitness screening criteria, and few collective bargaining rights; belong to the Commission on Accreditation for Law Enforcement Agencies; and serve larger and more racially and ethnical diverse communities. Many people of color and women may not apply to more traditional and less innovative police agencies based on negative images of police in their communities or bad personal experiences. Others note that a competitive market and higher education requirements cause qualified women and applicants of color to choose private-sector jobs over law enforcement.[17]

Does Diversity Matter?

Sam Walker, a police historian and civil rights scholar, has repeatedly called for increased diversification in law enforcement and has made it one of the hallmarks of a successful police department.[18] According to the 2020 U.S. Census, there are over 350 languages spoken in U.S. homes; increasing the cultural diversity of officers will help officers better serve the community.[19] A heterogeneous police force can thus be instrumental in gaining the confidence of racial and ethnic minority communities by helping dispel the view that police departments are generally bigoted or biased organizations. In a study of two separate police departments, Lorenzo Boyd found that there may be situations where there exist measurable differences in the attitudes of Black and White officers regarding quality-of-life policing in communities of color .

There are also consequences related to gender diversity. For example, in a study of gender diversity in police departments and domestic violence, researchers found that the more gender-representative an agency is, the fairer it is viewed, regardless of whether the agency has a low or high arrest rate for that crime.[20] This is important because the increased legitimacy of police units that results from increased representation could also increase the willingness of citizens to report crimes to the police. Increased reporting will increase police awareness and may also increase arrests and possibly safety in the community. Thus, representativeness can allow police the opportunity to better do their jobs.

Critical Thinking

What are several ways that you think your local police department could use to recruit a diverse applicant pool to become police officers?

Who Becomes a Police Officer, and Why?

There are a variety of reasons someone might decide to become a police officer. Are the motivations the same for women and people of color? To answer these questions, Anthony Raganella and Michael White surveyed 278 New York City Police Department recruits. They found that regardless of race or gender, the motivations for becoming a police officer are very similar.[21] There are some common reasons why policing is an attractive profession:

- Opportunity to help people in the community
- Job security and benefits
- Excitement of the job
- Fighting crime

In particular, a desire to help one's community is an important motivation for becoming a police officer. Take for instance what happened after a tragic ambush of police officers in Dallas, Texas. This ambush resulted in the death of five police officers and injuries of nine more. Following these deadly attacks, now retired Chief David O. Brown delivered a call to action. He called for citizens of Dallas to "Become a part of the solution, serve your communities. Don't be part of the problem." In the weeks after the attack, 467 people applied to join the Dallas Police Department, nearly a 250 percent increase in applications compared to the same time frame a month before.[22]

Critical Thinking

Are you considering a career in policing? What is your motivation to do so?

Becoming a Police Officer

Integrity, honesty, trustworthiness, helpfulness, and *dependability* are all words that should be associated with the ideal of policing. The objective of any police department is to hire applicants with these personal traits or at the very least try to instill them in all who complete the police training. Recruiting and selecting its potential officers is an extremely important task. Going through the selection and hiring process to become a police officer today is very different from most other jobs for which you could apply. For the right person, becoming a police officer could be the perfect career option with good pay, decent benefits, and the satisfaction of helping others. But the screening process is often quite extensive and rigorous. Police officers today are often better trained, better educated, better compensated, and more representative of the entire community than almost any other time in history. But a career in policing is not for everyone. Personnel costs comprise 75 to 85 percent of police department budgets, meaning that recruiting, selecting, and retaining the best candidates are of the utmost importance for police departments.[23] Once the decision has been made to apply, how does the recruitment and selection process work?

LO2

List the steps taken to attract and recruit police officers.

▶ # Recruitment

The purpose of recruitment and selection is to get the best eligible pool of applicants for open positions. The quality of the department's officers depends on successful recruitment and selection procedures. The recruitment and selection process can take several months and is often delayed by administrative and economic factors. At last count, the process of screening and testing applicants, basic academy training, and field training averaged 31 weeks in small agencies and 43 weeks in large agencies.[24]

Police departments rely heavily on newspaper ads, career fairs, and the Internet to recruit applicants. Other programs commonly utilized for this purpose are college internships, explorer programs, and school resource officers.

One reason that some police departments struggle to recruit women and other marginalized people to become officers is that many police agencies do very little in the way of designing recruitment campaigns that target marginalized groups, a method that has been shown to produce more hires of marginalized people.[25] Who are targeted: more than a third (36 percent) of agencies targeted applicants who possessed prior law enforcement experience for sworn positions, including about half of agencies employing 100 or more officers? Smaller percentages of agencies targeted applicants who were military veterans (17 percent), multilingual (16 percent), or four-year college graduates (14 percent).[26]

What can be done to help recruiting efforts? Strategies such as maintaining a recruiting department or committee that remains in effect year round and directs activities around a specific recruiting plan can be beneficial for maintaining a strong pool of applicants.[27] Greg Ridgeway and colleagues suggest that agencies might also consider a department's civilian staff for sworn positions, a strategy that would create "feeder" networks of existing employees.[28] Another strategy is to partner with the community.

Selection

Once a pool of candidates is recruited, it is important to ensure that the right person is selected, hired, and trained. At this point, the selection process begins and applicants are subject to a range of criteria and a battery of tests before being sworn in as a police officer. Although many jurisdictions have similar types of selection standards, most departments have agency-specific goals and some are stricter than others.

bona fide occupational qualifications

Employment standards linked to specific job tasks.

Selection standards must have **bona fide occupational qualifications**. This means that employment standards must be linked to specific job tasks in

Exhibit 3.3

Requirements for the Massachusetts State Police[29]

- Must be at least 21 years old and less than 35 years old before the start of training;

- Pass a physical fitness test, medical examination and a psychological text

- Must not smoke any tobacco product

- Must not have been convicted of a felony or drug law violations

- Must not have been convicted of a misdemeanor and confined to any jail or house of correction as punishment for a crime

- Demonstrate themselves to be of good moral character, sound work ethic, decision making consistent with the Oath of Office, and otherwise suitable for appointment to the Massachusetts State Police Academy

- Be qualified and deemed suitable to possess a valid Massachusetts Firearms License

- Possess a high school diploma or a General Educational Development (GED) certificate

- Satisfy the department's physical fitness standards for initial appointments

- Satisfy the department's medical and psychological standards for initial appointment

- Be a U.S. citizen upon appointment

- Possess a valid Massachusetts driver's license upon appointment

- Be a Massachusetts resident upon appointment

All candidates shall have tattoos, body art, brands, or scarifications that are visible when the candidate is dressed in the department's summer Class B duty removed prior to appointment.

order or else they could be considered discriminatory. It is essential for a new recruit to have a driver's license in order to become a police officer. This is linked to specific job tasks like driving a patrol car—an important aspect of patrol for most police departments in the United States.

In Exhibits 3.3 and 3.4, the qualifications for two large police departments in different parts of the United States are provided. In order to be considered for the Massachusetts State Police, candidates considered for appointment must meet the requirements set out in Exhibit 3.3; the requirements for applicants to the Dallas Police Department are set out in Exhibit 3.4.

These selection standards represent minimally acceptable standards for becoming a police officer. Given the strength of the applicant pool, however, agencies can make the decision to hire candidates with more qualifications. The agency can never hire someone with fewer qualifications. These basic minimum qualifications are designed to maintain the professionalism of the agency.

Some police agencies have very strict height and weight requirements for police officer applicants; although these standards have relaxed over time. In fact, few police agencies maintain a height requirement. Instead, most police agencies have preferences of the height and weight ratio of applicants. As Exhibit 3.5 shows, the Dayton, Ohio, Police Department has a fairly rigid scale of height and weight standards for applicants and those that are outside of these standards may not be considered for employment.[30]

Exhibit 3.4

Requirements for the Dallas Police Department

- Must be a citizen of the United States
- Must be a high school graduate or possess a GED
- Must be between 19 years of age and 44 years of age.
- Applicants that are 19 years of age must have a minimum of 60 semester college hours with a 2.0 GPA from an accredited college or university
- Applicants between 21 and 44 years of age must have a minimum of 45 semester college hours with a 2.0 GPA from an accredited college or university
- Have a valid driver's license
- Military Exemption: College credit hours requirement is waived for military personnel who served at least three years on active duty and were conferred an honorable discharge as stipulated on their DD Form 214
- Previous Law Enforcement Experience. College credit hours requirement is waived for current and former law enforcement officers if they:

  1. Have worked for any Law Enforcement Agency as a sworn Police Officer with powers of arrest in the United States or U.S. Territories.
  2. Have 36 months certified law enforcement experience with any city, county or state law enforcement agency.
  3. Have not been separated as a police officer for more than four months.

- No worse than 20/100 vision rating in each eye, correctable to 20/20
- Must be certified by a city physician to be medically fit in accordance with state law
- Must be certified by a staff psychologist to be mentally fit in accordance with state law
- Must pass the physical fitness test
- Must be of good moral character

Source: Dallas Police Department, https://dallaspolice.net/joindpd/Pages/Qualifications.aspx

Applicant Processing

Police departments will all use different versions of the application process depending on their needs and policies. Below is a fairly standardized set of criteria that applicants can expect to go through when seeking employment as a police officer.

Civil Service Written: Test

Many police departments in the United States hire police officers based on scores from civil service exams. But there are some municipalities, however, that do not hire based on the civil service test. You should consult your local agency to see if they require civil service testing. The types of questions and exams given by civil service agencies may vary by state. Take, for instance, the test given

Exhibit 3.5

Height and Weight Standards Dayton, Ohio, Police Department

	Height	Minimum weight	Maximum weight
Allowable Minimum	5'7"	140 lbs	180 lbs
Recommended Minimum	5'8"	140 lbs	180 lbs
	5'9"	145 lbs	185 lbs
	5'10"	150 lbs	190 lbs
	5'11"	155 lbs	195 lbs
	6'0"	160 lbs	205 lbs
	6'1"	165 lbs	210 lbs
	6'2"	170 lbs	220 lbs
	6'3"	175 lbs	225 lbs
	6'4"	180 lbs	230 lbs
	6'5"	185 lbs	235 lbs

Source: Dayton (OH) Police, http://www.wright.edu/~jim.adamitis/physical_req/requirements.html.

in the State of Louisiana where this test is administered by the Office of State Examiner for Municipal Fire and Police Civil Service. They provide a study booklet for applicants to prepare for the exam. Applicants do not need to have a prior knowledge of law enforcement in order to pass the civil service exam. The test has been designed to evaluate knowledge, skills, and abilities that are needed in order to successfully complete police officer training. For example, in order to successfully complete the police academy, you must be able to read and comprehend material on law enforcement procedures. Therefore, part of the written examination contains a section of questions on reading comprehension of material similar to that which must be read on the job.

The Louisiana civil service exam, police officer test consists of two parts: a test in following oral directions and a multiple-choice written examination. Because of the potentially hazardous nature of the job, police officers must be able to comprehend and precisely follow oral directions given by supervising officers in physically or psychologically demanding or intense situations. The Oral Directions Test has been designed to determine how well you are able to follow oral directions in accomplishing simple tasks.

The second part of the exam for a police officer is a written test consisting of 73 multiple-choice questions. Some of the areas covered in this exam are English usage, reading comprehension, prioritizing and following written instructions, logic, classifying information, attention to details, reading codes and abbreviations, estimating and measuring time and distance, interpreting maps, recognizing similar and different patterns, form completion, and evaluating two-dimensional maps. Recruits have 1 hour and 30 minutes in which to complete this part of the examination.[31]

Other departments have similar standards. The first step in becoming a Dallas Police Officer in many cities and towns starts with registering for and taking the civil service examination. The passing score for the civil service examination

Critical Thinking

Should there be minimum and maximum ages to become police officers? If so, what are those ages and why?

typically is 80 percent and 2 hours are allotted to complete the 100-question test. Depending on how many people qualify, many departments may only take the top scores on a test but departments have considerable leeway in how to consider the scoring of these exams. The decision on how to evaluate the written tests can be controversial and the courts have weighed in. One of the most well-known challenges to the value of these exams was the case *Jordan v. City of New London* set out in the feature below.

Preliminary Interview and Oral Boards

Applicants answer a series of questions to confirm they meet the minimum requirements and have no disqualifying factors. Many times this interview is done by a board of seasoned officers who typically are recruiters or trainers for the police department as well as other members of local government and a representative from the community. Personal interviews are used in more than 95 percent of police agencies' selection efforts.[32] Such interviews often take the form of an "oral board" protocol and are designed to determine how well the applicant fits with the organizational culture. The oral board asks a set of predetermined questions and evaluates the responses. Some of these are trick questions designed to confuse the applicant and see if they will contradict themselves. Sometimes

Police & the Law

Jordan v. City of New London (2000)

On March 16, 1996, plaintiff Robert Jordan and 500 other applicants took a written screening process conducted by the Law Enforcement Council of Southeastern Connecticut, Inc. a coalition of 14 cities and towns, for a position as a police officer. The testing material included the Wonderlic Personnel Test and Scholastic Level Exam ("WPT"), which purports to measure cognitive ability. The test manual listed recommended scores for various professions and cautioned that overqualified candidates may become bored with unchallenging work and quit. Jordan scored a 33 on the WPT, above the median for any listed occupation, and well over the normative median of 21 suggested for a police patrol officer.

In the fall of 1996, Jordan learned that the city of New London was interviewing candidates and Jordan was not among the candidates. Because Jordan was 46 years old, he suspected age discrimination and filed an administrative complaint with the Connecticut Commission on Human Rights and Opportunities. The city responded that it removed Jordan from consideration because he scored a 33 on the exam, and that to prevent frequent job turnover caused by hiring

overqualified applicants the city only interviewed candidates who scored between 20 and 27. Jordan brought a civil rights action in the District Court for the District of Connecticut alleging that the city denied him equal protection in violation of the Fourteenth Amendment and Article 4, Section 20, of the Connecticut Constitution.

On August 29, 1999, the district court granted defendants' motion for summary judgment, finding no suspect classification and that defendants had shown a rational basis for the policy. The U.S. Court of Appeals agreed that New London's use of an "upper cut" did not violate the equal protection clause and affirmed the judgment of the district court. The Appeals Court noted that there exists no fundamental right to employment as a police officer. Furthermore, they stated that even if the scoring guidelines are unwise, the upper cut was a rational policy instituted to reduce job turnover and thereby lessen the economic cost involved in hiring and training police officers who do not remain long enough to justify the expense.

Source: *Jordan v. City of New London,* https://www.anylaw.com/case/jordan-v-city-of-new-london/second-circuit/08-22-2000/qoC6PWYBTITomsSBYalb.

questions will involve hypothetical situations created to engage the applicant in discussion about misconduct or corruption. Most interviews will try to tease out whether applicants have common sense, verbal communication skills, motivation, and quick thinking. Interviews are also designed to uncover racism, sexism, or other forms of bigotry but it can be difficult for interviewers to do so. While oral boards are a popular method of assessing recruits for policing, there have long been questions about their effectiveness.[33]

ZUMA Press, Inc./Alamy Stock Photo

A trainer helps a recruit while he does sit-ups during a fitness test held for potential police cadets in Napa Valley. The police academy program involves taking a written test, as well as a physical test, which includes sit-ups, push-ups, and a 1.5-mile run.

Physical Fitness Test

Applicants must pass a series of physical agility tests which will test a general fitness for duty as a police officer. The courts have generally been accepting of physical requirements as long as they are related to the job. Sample physical requirements are below:

- Shuttle run (25 seconds)
- Sit-ups (14 in 1 minute)
- 300-meter run (110 seconds)
- Push-ups (4 in 1 minute)
- 1.5-mile run (19.5 minutes)
- Vertical jump (6.5 inches)
- Bench press, free weights (50–55 percent of your body weight)
- Vertical jump (6.5 inches)

Physical standards are constantly evolving and have been monitored by the Department of Justice and the courts. Recently, the Department of Justice reached a settlement with the city of Corpus Christi, Texas, to resolve the department's claim that the city violated Title VII of the Civil Rights Act of 1964 by engaging in a pattern or practice of discrimination against female applicants for entry-level police officer positions. The Justice Department's complaint, filed in the U.S. District Court for the Southern District of Texas, alleges that Corpus Christi's use of a physical abilities test between 2005 and 2011 violated Title VII because it unlawfully screened out female applicants for entry-level positions with the police department without the required evidence showing that the test did not properly evaluate whether a candidate was in fact qualified for a police officer position.[34] Between 2005 and 2009, only 19 percent of the female applicants who took the test passed it, compared with 63 percent of the male applicants.

Polygraph Examination

Preemployment screening polygraph examinations of police applicants are widespread in the United States and elsewhere, and are intended as an aid in the selection of suitable applicants. Unlike diagnostic tests, which are used for criminal investigation polygraphs, screening examinations are conducted in the absence of any known incident or allegation. Screening polygraphs and screening tests, in general, are often constructed to investigate, in a cost effective and expedient manner, the applicant's history of involvement in a range of possible activities of concern to hiring officials.[35] One additional benefit of a police preemployment polygraph screening polygraph program is that it may deter less suitable candidates from applying for positions in police work or public service. There are two general testing approaches with selection tools: screening-in and screening-out. Screening-in refers to those methods by which employers test applicants for the competencies needed to perform well in an organization. Screening-in assessments include tests of knowledge, skill, and ability.

Screening-out, in contrast, is the process of identifying vulnerabilities that would make a candidate a risk to the potential employer. One current challenge in the field is a lack of standardization in test administration across the profession. Practitioners and researchers have urged the polygraph profession toward more data-driven field practices[36] and the American Society of Testing and Materials[37] has developed standards for a variety of polygraph tests and settings. While polygraph test results should not be the sole basis for the selection or rejection of a police candidate without other information, they can be a useful tool for evaluating the fitness of police applicants.

Background Investigation

Applicants who pass all the previous steps proceed to the background investigation. A detective conducts an extensive background investigation to include, but not limited to, contacting all prior/present employers, references, coworkers, exspouses, family members, neighbors, and schools. Also, the applicant's residential history, previous drug use, financial responsibility including a credit report, military records, and driving history are investigated. The background investigation can take from two to four months to complete. Most of the delay is caused by the lack of reference response.

As the California Peace Officer Standards and Training (POST) notes:

> ...There are very few *automatic* bases for rejection. Even issues of prior misconduct, such as prior illegal drug use, driving under the influence, theft, or even arrest or conviction are usually not, in and of themselves, automatically disqualifying. However, deliberate misstatements or omissions can and often will result in your application being rejected, regardless of the nature or reason for the misstatements/omissions. In fact, the number one reason individuals "fail" background investigations is because they deliberately withhold or misrepresent job-relevant information from their prospective employer.[38]

Psychological Examination

Applicants complete psychological written tests and are interviewed by a staff psychologist. Psychological screening is a well-established process used in the selection of police officers. These tests are typically used to screen out applicants with the most severe psychological problems. There are questions about the usefulness of these instruments. Jonathan Lough and Kathryn Von Treuer examined the psychological instruments most commonly used by police departments.[39] Specifically, they assess the Minnesota Multiphasic Personality Inventory (MMPI), the California Personality Inventory (CPI), the Inwald Personality Inventory (IPI), the Australian Institute of Forensic Psychology's (AIFP) test battery, and a few others. No test is foolproof and many current screening practices are likely to be adding minimal value to the selection process by way of using instruments that are not "cut out" for the job.

Medical Examination

The applicant's physical and medical conditions are evaluated to ensure that they can function safely as a police officer. Under the American with Disabilities Act (ADA), subjecting applicants for employment to medical questions and examinations is generally not permitted before a conditional offer of employment is made. It is, however, permissible to obtain a medical clearance from the applicant's personal physician to participate in a physical agility test. After a conditional offer of employment has been made, a physician chosen by the law enforcement agency conducts the preplacement (also called "post-offer") examination. There are some medical conditions that would exclude an applicant from working as a full-duty law enforcement officer. One example that comes to mind is significant visual impairment—an officer with severe visual impairment would not be able to drive or recognize suspects and weapons. Medical conditions that could create a risk of sudden incapacitation higher than that which is acceptable include epilepsy, heart disorders, uncontrolled diabetes, and the use of certain blood thinning medications. Individualized assessment by a qualified police physician is necessary to make sure that the medical condition is actually causing that risk in the applicant. The mere diagnosis of epilepsy, heart disease, or diabetes should not lead to an automatic disqualification.[40]

Drug Screening

Applicants provide samples and these are analyzed to detect the use of illegal drugs. Once these steps are successfully completed, the applicant's file is routed through the chain of command for review and approval. If the applicant is approved for hire, they are tendered a conditional offer of employment.

Victor Kappeler notes that police departments set *drug usage standards*. Most departments today have specified what drug-related behaviors are acceptable and which ones are not. When developing policy, departments often consider the following areas:

1. Recency of usage
2. Patterns or frequency of usage
3. Types of drugs used
4. Involvement in sale and distribution of drugs

There is substantial variability in police drug standards for police applicants. Many departments consider applicants who have experimented with soft drugs such as marijuana but have strict prohibitions against long-term usage or the use of hard drugs such as cocaine, LSD, or opiates. Moreover, a department's drug standards likely change over time. Many departments have loosened their requirements as a result of shortages in officers and applicants. Kappeler writes that having a history of drug use does not preclude someone from becoming a police officer. It is really dependent upon what that history entails. A person who has an extensive history of using hard drugs over an extended period of time, or recently or has been involved in the sale or distribution of illegal drugs, will likely not be hired by a major municipal police department. On the other hand, experimental drug use in one's youth will not likely bar police employment in many agencies.[41]

Given the changes in drug laws across the country, whether a person who formerly used drugs can become a successful police officer will continue to be a topic for discussion.[42] Police departments will likely have to adapt to evolving community standards.

Education

LO3

Describe the state of police education.

August Vollmer, when he was chief of police in Berkeley, California, helped start police and criminal justice courses at the University of California, Berkeley and other West Coast universities. He also required new police recruits to be college educated. Today, most police departments simply require a high school diploma or a high school equivalent—GED certificate—to be hired. Some police agencies require some college credits, while others may require an associate's degree. Although most law enforcement agencies still do not require recruits to have an advanced degree, the number requiring some higher education in the hiring and promotion process is growing. Today, nearly all local police departments (98 percent) have an education requirement for new officer recruits:

- About 16 percent of departments have some type of college requirement.

- About 9 percent require a two-year degree.

- Only 1 percent of local police departments require a four-year degree.

- When asked, most departments express a preference for criminal justice majors, usually because of their enhanced knowledge of the entire criminal justice system and issues in policing.[43]

- Yet, in a recent census of local police departments, it was uncovered that nearly 1 in 4 local police officers worked for a department that required entry-level officers to have at least a two-year college degree.[44]

Some examples of police educational requirements include:

- The Milwaukee, Wisconsin, Police Department requires either a two-year associate's degree from a Wisconsin technical college system district or its accredited equivalent from another state, or a minimum of 60 college-level credits from an accredited college or university, within five years of hire. If this requirement is not met by the end of the fifth year of employment, the police officer will be decertified by the Wisconsin Law Enforcement Standards Board (LESB), and will be separated from employment. If someone has been decertified by the LESB, the 60-credit requirement must be fulfilled before they are eligible to reapply for a police officer job.[45]

- In the Nassau County Police Department (NY), no college education is required to take the written examination; however, 32 credits of college

As police responsibilities increase in both complexity and sophistication, having an educated force takes on even greater importance. Nor does classroom training end after appointment. These officers in Austin, Texas, are participating in a post appointment training session.

Bob Daemmrich/Alamy Stock Photo

education are required for appointment. Those candidates who have not attained that level of education but are otherwise eligible for appointment will remain on the eligible list and will become eligible for appointment after they have obtained the necessary college credits.[46]

- The Chicago Police Department requires 60 semester hours (90 quarter hours) from an accredited college or university, or three years of active duty, or one year active duty and 30 semester hours (45 quarter hours) for employment. The city of Lakewood, Colorado, requires a four-year degree with "no exceptions." Jacksonville, Florida, Sheriff's Department requires 60 college credits. Elgin, Illinois, requires a bachelor's degree from an accredited college or 60 college credit hours *and* three years of *active* military service.

As part of the Assessing Police Use of Force Policy and Outcomes project, a National Institute of Justice (NIJ) funded a multi-method study of eight police departments, Eugene Paoline and colleagues examined the role of higher education in shaping officer attitudes.[47] They used a 116-item survey designed to capture a variety of use of force, organizational climate, and occupational culture dimensions. The survey also gleaned information on officers' background characteristics. The authors said that educational background had little effect on occupational attitudes. They speculated that individual differences that are part of such background characteristics tend to get eliminated (or lessened) once the socialization of officers takes shape.

They specifically asked respondents when they received their degrees (i.e., prior or after police hiring) and the results revealed little variation across the seven departments, as 92.5 percent completed their education prior to being hired as a police officer. As such, officers were predominantly coming into the occupation with their college education, just as they were coming in with their gender and race. In the end, it could be that the various experiences that occur during interactions with other police officers and citizens are what produce variation in officers' conceptions of their role.

In contrast, Rob Worden, utilizing survey data of officers collected as part of the Police Services Study (PSS) of 24 police departments in the late 1970s, examined whether having an associate's or bachelor's degree was attributed to differences in attitudes toward the police role, the organization, legal restrictions, discretion, morale, and supervision.[48] Worden conducted seven multivariate analyses of over 1,400 officers, controlling for gender, race, length of service, and rank. He also accounted for whether the associate's or bachelor's degree was obtained prior to police employment. Although the magnitude was small, Worden reported that those with associate's and bachelor's degrees held less favorable views toward legal restrictions and were more discretion-control oriented than their less educated peers. In addition, those officers with preservice bachelor's degrees held more expansive role orientations, while those with associate's degrees perceived their supervisors to be less restrictive.

Accreditation and Certification

 LO4

Examine the role of accreditation.

Public safety accreditation is a progressive and contemporary way of assisting police agencies evaluate, analyze, and improve their overall performance. Accreditation provides formal recognition that an organization meets or exceeds general expectations of quality in the field. Accreditation acknowledges the implementation of policies that are conceptually sound and operationally effective. The goals of police accreditation include increasing the effectiveness and efficiency of public safety agencies utilizing existing personnel, equipment, and facilities to the extent possible. Accreditation is also intended to promote increased cooperation and coordination among public safety agencies and other organizations of the criminal justice services. The intent is to ensure the appropriate training of public safety personnel; and to promote public confidence in the police.

Accreditation programs are comprised of a set of standards developed to further enhance the capabilities of an agency, and tend to be divided into three categories (administrative, training, and operations). Standards in the administrative section have provisions for such topics as agency organization, fiscal management, personnel practices, and records management. Training standards encompass basic and in-service instruction, as well as training for supervisors and specialized or technical assignments. Operations standards deal with such critical and litigious topics as high-speed pursuits, roadblocks, patrol, and unusual occurrences.[49] Independent jurisdictions may have their own individual standards of evaluation, but there tend to be some overarching ideals that are generally agreed upon when evaluating police organizations and agencies.

The Commission on Accreditation for Law Enforcement Agencies (CALEA)

Although there are various commissions, organizations, and agencies that provide guidance, training, and service to public safety agencies, the Commission on Accreditation for Law Enforcement Agencies, Inc. (CALEA), is often regarded as the gold standard in accreditation. CALEA was created in 1979 as a credentialing authority through the joint efforts of the following law enforcement major executive associations:

- International Association of Chiefs of Police (IACP);
- National Organization of Black Law Enforcement Executives (NOBLE);
- National Sheriffs' Association (NSA); and
- Police Executive Research Forum (PERF).

The purpose of CALEA's Accreditation Programs is to improve the delivery of public safety services, primarily by maintaining a body of standards, developed by public safety practitioners, covering a wide range of up-to-date public safety initiatives; establishing and administering an accreditation process; and recognizing professional excellence. Specifically, CALEA's goals are to strengthen crime prevention and control capabilities, formalize essential management procedures, establish fair and nondiscriminatory personnel practices, improve service delivery, solidify interagency cooperation and coordination, and increase community and staff confidence in the agency. The CALEA Accreditation Process is a proven modern management model that promotes the efficient use of resources and improves service delivery—regardless of the size, geographic location, or functional responsibilities of the agency.[50] Each state also has an accrediting body that oversees the standards of training for public service agencies within their jurisdiction.

There are inconsistent results regarding the potential effectiveness of accreditation. Doerner and Doerner examined 260 law enforcement agencies in Florida and found that CALEA accreditation had no influence on agency clearance rates for violent or property crime offenses.[51] At the micro-level, Richard Johnson found that CALEA accreditation does not change the organizational practices of rank-and-file officers.[52] Other studies show that there is no association between CALEA accreditation and officer work attitudes.[53] Stephen Mastrofski and colleagues on the other hand, surveyed police executives and found that, in the opinions of these executives, CALEA accreditation increased agency success in implementing community-oriented policing (COP).[54]

Due to the cost of CALEA, some states have developed their own accreditation agencies. These agencies have standards similar to CALEA but more aligned with state law and policies. For example, Exhibit 3.6 explores the Texas Commission on Law Enforcement.

Training

Many police academy training programs vary by jurisdiction, but it is not uncommon for police academy training to last for six months. As of year-end 2018, a total of 681 state and local law enforcement academies provided basic training to entry-level recruits in the United States. Academies prepared trainees for a law enforcement career in a variety of settings. Ninety-two percent of academies trained and certified recruits who were employed as local police officers. On average, academy training programs included 833 hours of classroom training (about 19 weeks). A third of academies had an additional mandatory field training component with an average length of 508 hours. Nearly all recruits received reality-based scenario training and specialty firearms training.[55]

In many situations, the recruits often spend 8–10 hours in training per day for as many as 40–55 hours per week. Some of the topics covered include, but are not limited to, principles of law enforcement, criminal law, constitutional law, rules and evidence, search and seizure, laws of arrest and control methods, traffic laws, juvenile laws, first aid, care and use of firearms, patrol theory/methods, the criminal justice system, physical conditioning, and self-defense.

For example, in Fayetteville, North Carolina, new police recruits report to the facility Monday–Friday from 6:00 A.M. to 5:00 P.M. During their time in the academy, trainees are compensated with salary, benefits, and are provided uniforms. Trainees undergo 25 weeks of intensive Basic Law Enforcement Academy

---

Exhibit 3.6

The Texas Commission on Law Enforcement (TCOLE)

The mission of the Texas Commission on Law Enforcement (TCOLE), as a regulatory state agency, is to establish and enforce standards to ensure that the people of Texas are served by highly trained and ethical law enforcement, corrections, and telecommunications personnel. TCOLE shall set reporting standards and procedures for the appointment and termination of officers and county jailers. It also provides that the chief administrative officer of a law enforcement agency is responsible for compliance with the reporting standards and procedures prescribed by the commission. A person may not be appointed to serve as an officer, county jailer, or public security officer unless the person holds an appropriate license issued by the commission.

Source: The Texas Commission on Law Enforcement (TCOLE), https://www.tcole.texas.gov.

training and an Intensive Physical Fitness Program. This training is followed by a 15-week period of field training. The new officer is assigned to work with a field training officer for on-the-job training and evaluation.[56]

The Dallas police basic training is 36 weeks long and consists of 1,431 hours of instruction. The Basic Training Academy is mentally challenging and physically demanding. Police recruits should arrive for training at their peak physical fitness. After the training academy, new officers are assigned to one of the seven patrol divisions for 24 weeks of field training under the tutelage of experienced field training officers (FTO).[57] To become a Massachusetts state police officer (state trooper), recruits must successfully complete the training and live at the academy Monday through Friday during this period.

It can be difficult for some recruits to succeed during the training phase. To provide support for new recruits, some police agencies have offered programs and policies. For example, the Los Angeles Police Department has a Candidate Assistance Program (CAP) that helps potential police candidates become successful in the hiring process. The CAP will assist the candidate in attaining a satisfactory level of physical fitness and assist in achieving a passing score on the physical abilities test. The CAP also will help prepare the candidate for the physical portion of the police academy training as well as familiarize the candidate with the quasi-military protocol and self-discipline expected of a recruit officer in the Los Angeles Police Academy.

Similarly, in recognition that despite scoring well on tests and passing background checks, women were being dismissed from the Newark, New Jersey, police academy, the Women's Leadership works in partnership with the Newark Police Superior Officers' Association to:

1. increase the retention rate of female recruits attending the Newark Police Academy.

2. create a sororal community among the female members of the Newark Police Department, where women support women in meeting their career objectives.

3. increase the number of women in supervisory and management positions.

4. advocate for women's access to career development training and assignments.

LO5

Compare and contrast police academies and POST certification.

Police Academies and POST (Peace Officer Standards and Training) Certification

Many jurisdictions determine their own academy standards, based on the minimum standards of qualification assigned by their state government. Other jurisdictions seek higher individual and department wide certification of their academies and training staff. The State of California has the commission on Peace Officer Standards and Training (POST) to regulate police training within the state. POST was established by the California legislature in 1959 to set minimum selection and training standards for law enforcement. POST funding comes from money from penalty assessments on criminal and traffic fines. Therefore, the POST program is funded primarily by people who violate the laws that peace officers are trained to enforce. No tax dollars are used to fund the POST program. The POST program is voluntary and incentive-based. More than 600 participating agencies agree to abide by the standards established by the POST.[58]

Does Everyone Who Enters the Academy Become a Successful Police Officer?

Policing is not a profession for everyone but how do we identify those officers who will be least successful? Adrienne Meier and her colleagues found that peer evaluations in the police academy can be a good way to determine which new recruits will leave the profession.[59] Three peers, who were top in their class and three who needed the most improvement during the 7th and 16th week of a 24-week basic police training academy, were nominated by 1,248 police recruits. Using this approach, recruits who dropped out or were terminated during probation could be determined with 91.7 percent specificity. This means that peer evaluations could be another way to predict which officers will have trouble in the field once they have left the academy.

ZUMA Press Inc/Alamy Stock Photo

The police academy experience can help identify recruits that have the potential to become successful officers. Here the Albuquerque Police Department's 111th cadet class walks to the track outside of Albuquerque Police Roger Hoisington Training Academy for physical fitness running tests. The basic training will last for about 27 weeks and includes crisis intervention, New Mexico law, city ordinances, constitutional and criminal law, traffic regulations and investigation technique, physical fitness and defensive tactics.

In-Service (On-the-Job) Training and Ongoing Professional Development

The institution of policing is arguably one of the most complex and constantly changing professions there is. This is due partially to new laws, policies, procedures, court decisions, or new technologies. That is a lot for officers to keep track of.

Legal Issues in Training

In the 1989 court case *Canton v. Harris*, a person in custody needed medical care and it was not provided. It was suggested that police commanders were not provided with any special training to make a determination as to when to summon such care for an injured person in their custody. The court ruled that a municipality may, in certain circumstances, be held liable for constitutional violations resulting from its failure to train its employees.[60] In order to maintain municipal levels of certification, accreditation, and/or licensure as well as avoid harm to the public and resulting potential lawsuits, police agencies must ensure that their personnel go through regular refresher courses and requalification every year. This annual training is referred to as in-service training. The length, type, and style of that training may differ, but all police officers must go through it.

In the requirements of the Texas Commission on Law Enforcement (TCOLE), once an individual is licensed, there are required training courses that must be completed in order to keep the license active. The commission has a minimum 40-hour continuing education requirement for each 24-month training unit for peace officers. Along with refresher courses of the subjects covered in police academy training, some of the topics for those holding a Basic Peace Officer Certificate include in-service training classes on civil rights, racial sensitivity, cultural diversity; crisis intervention techniques; as well as recognition and documentation of cases that involve child abuse, child neglect, family violence, sexual assault, and

Careers in Policing

Police Officer

Duties and Characteristics of the Job

- Police officers are responsible for enforcing the written laws and ordinances of their jurisdiction.

- Police officers patrol within their jurisdiction and respond to calls wherever police attention is needed.

- Duties can be routine, such as writing a speeding ticket, or more involved, such as responding to a domestic disturbance or investigating a robbery.

- Non-patrol duties include testifying in court and writing reports of their law enforcement actions.

- Some officers will choose or be chosen to work in specialized units such as the well-known special weapons and tactics (SWAT) or canine corps (K9).

- Police officers patrol jurisdictions of various sizes and have varying duties based on the nature of their jurisdiction. For example, sheriffs and their deputies enforce the laws within a county. State police primarily patrol state highways and respond to calls for backup from police units across their respective state. Institutions such as colleges and universities often have their own police forces as well, which enforce laws and rules in this specific area.

- Police work can be an intense and stressful job; it sometimes entails encounters with people who are hostile and potentially violent. Police are asked to put their lives on the line to preserve order and safety. Their actions are watched closely and reflect upon their entire department.

- Because the places that police protect must be watched at all times, police work shifts that may fall on weekends and holidays. Quite often it is the younger police officers who take these less desirable shifts. Additionally, police officers will often have to work overtime; 45-hour work weeks are common.

Job Outlook

- Government spending ultimately determines how many officers a department has.

- Overall opportunities in local police departments will be good for individuals who meet the psychological, personal, and physical qualifications. In addition to openings from employment growth, many openings will be created by the need to replace workers who retire and those who leave local agencies for federal jobs and private-sector security jobs.

- Police work is appealing to many because of the good benefits and retirement policies.

issues concerning sex offender characteristics.[61] Many agencies require more in-service training hours based on the needs of the agency and/or community.

Retention

In 2010, RAND published a report, "Recruitment and Retention for the New Millennium," describing the issues and challenges associated with police: personnel practices of police agencies in the United States that employ 300 or more officers.[62] RAND reports that police departments are having difficulties maintaining their authorized strength. Much of the difficulty police agencies face in maintaining their workforce levels is a product of attrition. Attrition is not always bad. An officer who retires after a full career or one who leaves after deciding they are not committed to being effective, high-performing officers is good for police agencies. People who are not well suited to policing should not stay in the organization.

- For the better-paying positions, there may be more applicants than available positions. This competition means those with qualifications such as a college education will have better chances of being hired.

- After several years, those with a reputation for good work as well as the proper education can rise in the ranks of their department or be assigned to other desirable positions such as detective or investigator.

Salary

- Police patrol officers have median annual wages of more than $55,000. The middle 50 percent earn between $39,000 and $65,000. The lowest 10 percent earned less than $30,000, and the highest 10 percent earned $80,000 and beyond.

- Median annual wages are $46,620 in federal government, $57,270 in state government, $51,020 in local government, and $43,350 in educational services.

- In Chicago, officers earn $72,510 after 18 months of service.

- In the Nassau County (NY) Police Department, the starting annual salary is $34,000, and officers earn $107,319 after nine years.

Qualifications

- To be a police officer, you must be in good shape mentally and physically, as well as meet certain education requirements and pass written tests.

- New police officers go through rigorous training and testing—normally in the form of a local police academy for 16 to 36 weeks—before they go out on the streets.

- During training, new officers learn diverse skills that will be necessary for their job, such as knowledge of laws and individual rights, self-defense, and first aid. Applicants can also expect to be asked to pass lie detector and drug tests.

- Because of the enormous responsibility associated with being a police officer, certain personal qualities are considered key for future officers, such as responsibility, good communications skills, good judgment, and the ability to make quick decisions.

Education and Training

- In most cases, a high school diploma is required to be a police officer, but more and more jurisdictions are requiring at least some college education.

- Although some college credits are enough to obtain a position in the police force, to be promoted and move up in rank, more education, generally in the form of a bachelor's degree in a relevant field, especially criminal justice, is necessary.

The Bureau of Justice Assistance found that about half (52 percent) of officers who leave state agencies did so because of nonmedical retirements, compared to less than a quarter from local police departments (23 percent) and sheriffs' offices (19 percent). Resignations, on the other hand, accounted for more than half of the separations from sheriffs' offices (56 percent) and local police departments (55 percent), compared to less than a third from state agencies (30 percent).[63]

Nevertheless, attrition can be a problem when it occurs in waves, resulting in large proportions of staff retiring within a short time of one another. There are a number of other reasons why police officers, however, might decide to leave a police agency. First, younger workers have different expectations than those from previous generations. The Rand report notes that younger workers do not have the same organizational commitment and may expect to change agencies throughout the course of their career. Budget crises can also affect retention. Uncompetitive wages and salary freezes can lead police officers to seek better opportunities elsewhere.

Military call-ups can also affect retention. These call-ups pose not just manpower but fiscal challenges to police departments. Federal law requires that health benefits of these officers be maintained and their positions held until they return.[64]

While turnover can pose many problems for police agencies, its extent, particularly in comparison to that in other professions, is unclear. How policing compares to attrition in other sectors is somewhat unclear. Police turnover rates are lower than the rates for teachers, at 17 percent.[65] It is important to remember, however, that although turnover rates appear lower in police agencies than in many other sectors, police officer turnover can carry greater costs than turnover elsewhere because of the expense of selecting and training officers. In response to this issue, some agencies are requiring that new recruits sign a minimum time of service agreement, requiring them to stay in the agency for two to three years.[66] Other agencies use financial incentives to increase officer retention. About two-thirds (65 percent) of agencies offer free uniforms or a financial allowance for uniform-related expenses to officers. Another tool for retaining officers is the use of incentive pay. About half of agencies offer increased pay at specific service milestones, for educational attainment or take-home vehicles.[67] It is clear that more time, effort, and research must be dedicated to enhancing retention in police organizations.

Summary

LO1 Discuss the current landscape of policing in the United States.

Most municipal police departments in the United States are independent agencies within the executive branch of government, operating without specific administrative control from any higher governmental authority Most departments are modeled after the military model that is bureaucratic by nature. Department size is the biggest predictor of the number of subunits within the agency.

LO2 List the steps taken to attract and recruit police officers.

The first step in becoming a police officer is recruitment, to get the best eligible pool of applicants for open positions. The recruitment and selection process can take several months and police departments rely heavily on newspaper ads, career fairs, and the Internet to recruit applicants. Once a pool of candidates is recruited, it is important to ensure that the right person is selected, hired, and trained. Some police agencies have very strict height and weight requirements for police officer applicants, although these standards have relaxed over time.

Applicants must pass a series of physical agility tests, which will test a general fitness for duty as a police officer. The courts have generally been accepting of physical requirements as long as they are related to the job. The applicant's physical and medical conditions are evaluated to ensure that they can function safely as a police officer. Applicants provide samples and these are analyzed to

detect the use of illegal drugs. Once these steps are successfully completed, the applicant's file is routed through the chain of command for review and approval. If the applicant is approved for hire, they are tendered a conditional offer of employment.

LO3 Describe the state of police education.

August Vollmer helped start police and criminal justice courses at the University of California–Berkeley and other West Coast universities. Today, most police departments simply require a high school diploma or a high school equivalent to be hired. Some police agencies require some college credits, while others may require an associate's degree. Departments requiring some higher education in the hiring and promotion process are growing. Today, nearly all local police departments (98 percent) have an education requirement for new officer recruits.

LO4 Examine the role of accreditation.

Accreditation provides formal recognition that an organization meets or exceeds general expectations of quality in the field. The goals of police accreditation include increasing the effectiveness and efficiency of public safety agencies utilizing existing personnel, equipment, and facilities to the extent possible. Accreditation is also intended to promote increased cooperation and coordination among public safety agencies and other organizations of the criminal justice services; to ensure the appropriate training of public safety personnel; and to promote public confidence in the police.

Programs are comprised of a set of standards developed to further enhance the capabilities of an agency, and tend to be divided into three categories (administrative, training, and operations). Standards in the administrative section have provisions for such topics as agency organization, fiscal management, personnel practices, and records management. Training standards encompass basic and in-service instruction, as well as training for supervisors and specialized or technical assignments. Operations standards deal with such critical and litigious topics as high-speed pursuits, roadblocks, patrol, and unusual occurrences. Independent jurisdictions may have their own individual standards of evaluation, but there tend to be some overarching ideals that are generally agreed upon when evaluating police organizations and agencies.

LO5   Compare and contrast police academies and POST certification.

Many jurisdictions determine their own academy standards, based on the minimum standards of qualification assigned by their state government. Other jurisdictions seek higher individual and department wide certification of their academies and training staff. The State of California has the commission on Peace Officer Standards and Training (POST) to regulate police training within the state. POST was established by the California Legislature in 1959 to set minimum selection and training standards for law enforcement. POST funding comes from money from penalty assessments on criminal and traffic fines. Therefore, the POST program is funded primarily by people who violate the laws that peace officers are trained to enforce. No tax dollars are used to fund the POST program. The POST program is voluntary and incentive-based.

Key Terms

internal affairs, 63

bona fide occupational qualifications, 66

Notes

1. Department of Justice, U.S. Attorney's Office, Northern District of California.
2. Zachary W. Oberfield, *Becoming Bureaucrats: Socialization at the Front Lines of Government Service* (Philadelphia, PA: University of Pennsylvania Press, 2014).
3. Shelley S. Hyland and Elizabeth Davis, "Local Police Departments, 2016," P. Bureau of Justice Statistics, 2019, https://bjs.ojp.gov/content/pub/pdf/lpd16p.pdf.
4. William Boerner and Terry Nowell, "The Reliability of the Behavioral Personnel Assessment Device (B-PAD) in Selecting Police Recruits," *Policing* 22 (1999), 343–352.
5. John Liederbach, Lorenzo M. Boyd, Robert W. Taylor, and Soraya K Kawucha, "Is It an Inside Job?: An Examination of Internal Affairs Complaint Investigation Files and the Production of Non-sustained Findings," *Criminal Justice Policy Review* 18, no. 4 (2007), 353–377.
6. Sean E. Goodison, Local Police Departments Personnel, 2020 Bureau of Justice Statistics, 2022, https://bjs.ojp.gov/sites/g/files/xyckuh236/files/media/document/lpdp20.pdf.
7. Ibid.
8. David Alan Sklansky. "Not Your Father's Police Department: Making Sense of the New Demographics of Law Enforcement," *Journal of Criminal Law and Criminology* 96 (2005), 1209.
9. http://www.houstonchronicle.com/news/houston-texas/houston/article/Houston-Police-Department-s-rainbow-cruiser-11243917.php.
10. https://datausa.io/profile/soc/police-officers#demographics.
11. William T. Jordan, Lorie Fridell, Donald Faggiani, and Bruce Kubu, "Attracting Females and Racial/Ethnic Minorities to Law Enforcement," *Journal of Criminal Justice* 37, no. 4 (2009), 333–341.
12. https://datausa.io/profile/soc/police-officers#demographics.
13. Shelley S. Hyland and Elizabeth Davis, "Local Police Departments, 2016," Bureau of Justice Statistics, 2019, https://bjs.ojp.gov/content/pub/pdf/lpd16p.pdf.
14. Melissa Morabito and Tara O'Connor Shelley, "Representative Bureaucracy Understanding the Correlates of the Lagging Progress of Diversity in Policing," *Race and Justice* 5, no. 4 (2015), 330–355.
15. U.S. Equal Employment Opportunity Commission. Advancing Diversity in Law Enforcement. U.S. Department of Justice Equal Employment Opportunity Commission. October 2016. https://www.eeoc.gov/advancing-diversity-law-enforcement#_Toc463016101.
16. Amie M. Schuck, "Female Representation in Law Enforcement: The Influence of Screening, Unions, Incentives, Community Policing, CALEA, and Size," *Police Quarterly* 17, no. 1 (2014), 54–78.
17. Lisa Kay Decker and Robert G. Huckabee, "Raising the Age and Education Requirements for Police Officers: Will Too Many Women and Minority Candidates Be Excluded?," *Policing: An International Journal of Police Strategies & Management* 25, no. 4 (2002), 789–802.
18. S. Walker, What a Good Police Department Looks Like: Professional, Accountable, Transparent, Self-Monitoring (Technical Report) (Omaha, NE: University of Nebraska Omaha, 2014).
19. https://www.census.gov/newsroom/archives/2015-pr/cb15-185.html.
20. Norma M. Riccucci, Gregg G. Van Ryzin, and Cecilia F. Lavena, "Representative Bureaucracy in Policing: Does It Increase Perceived Legitimacy?," *Journal of Public Administration Research and Theory* 24, no. 3 (2014), 537–551.

21. Anthony J. Raganella and Michael D. White, "Race, Gender, and Motivation for Becoming a Police Officer: Implications for Building a Representative Police Department," *Journal of Criminal Justice* 32, no. 6 (2004), 501–513.

22. http://www.cbsnews.com/news/dallas-police-ambush-chief-david-brown-call-inspires-hundreds-to-apply-to-join-force/.

23. W. Dwayne Orrick, *Recruitment, Retention, and Turnover of Police Personnel: Reliable, Practical, and Effective Solutions* (Springfield, IL.: Charles C. Thomas, 2008).

24. Christopher S. Koper, Edward R. Maguire, and Gretchen E. Moore, Hiring and Retention Issues in Police Agencies: Readings on the Determinants of Police Strength, Hiring and Retention of Officers, and the Federal COPS Program, Research Report (Washington, DC: The Urban Institute, October 2001, NCJ 193428).

25. Bruce Kubu, Lorie Fridell, Carter Rees, Tom Jordan, and Jason Cheney, "The Cop Crunch: Identifying Strategies for Dealing with the Recruiting and Hiring Crisis in Law Enforcement" (Washington, DC: Police Executive Research Forum, 2005).

26. http://www.bjs.gov/index.cfm?ty=pbdetail&iid=4514.

27. National Center for Women and Policing, Recruiting and Retaining Women: A Self-Assessment Guide for Law Enforcement. (Washington, DC: 2003).

28. Greg Ridgeway, Nelson Lim, Brian Gifford, Christopher Koper, Carl Matthies, Sara Hajiamiri, and Alexis Huynh, *Strategies for Improving Officer Recruitment in the San Diego Police Department* (Santa Monica, CA: RAND Corporation, MG-724-SDPD, 2008). As of June 24, 2010: http://www.rand.org/pubs/monographs/MG724/.

29. https://www.mass.gov/guides/becoming-a-state-trooper.

30. Dayton (OH) Police. http://www.wright.edu/~jim.adamitis/physical_req/requirements.html.

31. Pre-Examination Booklet for Police Officer Entrance Level Examination. State of Louisiana, https://ose.louisiana.gov/wp-content/uploads/2020/11/PO-STUDY-GUIDE-2021.pdf.

32. Matthew J. Hickman and Brian A. Reaves, Local Police Departments, 2003 (Washington, DC: Department of Justice, Office of Justice Programs, Bureau of Justice Statistics, NCJ 210118, April 1, 2006a). As of June 24, 2010: http://bjs.ojp.usdoj.gov/index.cfm?ty=pbdetail&iid=1045.

33. William G. Doerner, "The Utility of the Oral Interview Board in Selecting Police Academy Admissions," *Policing: An International Journal of Police Strategies & Management* 20, no. 4 (1997), 777–785.

34. http://www.justice.gov/opa/pr/justice-department-settles-sex-discrimination-lawsuit-against-corpus-christi-texas-police.

35. Mark Handler, Charles R. Honts, Donald J. Krapohl, Raymond Nelson, and Stephen Griffin, "Integration of Pre-employment Polygraph Screening into the Police Selection Process," *Journal of Police and Criminal Psychology* 24, no. 2 (2009), 69–86.

36. Donald J. Krapohl, "Validated Polygraph Techniques," *Polygraph* 35, no. 3 (2006), 149–155.

37. American Society of Testing and Materials International (2008). Committee E52 on Forensic Psychophysiology, http://www.astm.org.

38. https://post.ca.gov/peace-officer-candidate-selection-process.

39. Jonathan Lough and Kathryn Von Treuer, "A Critical Review of Psychological Instruments Used in Police Officer Selection," *Policing: An International Journal of Police Strategies & Management* 36, no. 4 (2013), 737–751.

40. Fabrice Czarnecki, "Medical Screening of Police Applicants," *The Police Chief* 81 (March 2014), 46–48.

41. http://plsonline.eku.edu/insidelook/can-you-become-police-officer-history-drug-use.

42. http://www.governing.com/gov-data/state-marijuana-laws-map-medical-recreational.html.

43. Brian Reaves, *Local Police Departments, 2007* (Washington, DC: Bureau of Justice Statistics, 2010).

44. Brian Reaves. *Local Police Departments, 2013: Personnel, Policies, and Practices.* (2015). http://www.bjs.gov/content/pub/pdf/lpd13ppp.pdf.

45. Milwaukee, WI Police: http://city.milwaukee.gov/jobs/PO#.VruvEVKGNj8.

46. https://www.pdcn.org/148/Recruitment.

47. Eugene A. Paoline III, William Terrill, and Michael T. Rossler, "Higher Education, College Degree Major, and Police Occupational Attitudes," *Journal of Criminal Justice Education* 26, no. 1 (2015), 49–73.

48. R. E. Worden, "A Badge and a Baccalaureate: Policies, Hypotheses, and Further Evidence," *Justice Quarterly* 7 (1990), 565–592, doi: 10.1080/07418829000090731.

49. New York State Division of Criminal Justice Services. https://www.criminaljustice.ny.gov/ops/accred/accred04.htm.

50. The Commission on Accreditation for Law Enforcement Agencies (CALEA), https://www.calea.org/.

51. W. M. Doerner and W. G. Doerner, "Police Accreditation and Clearance Rates," *Policing: An International Journal* 35, no. 1 (2012), 6–24. https://doi.org/10.1108/13639511211215423.

52. Richard R. Johnson, "Examining the Effects of Agency Accreditation on Police Officer Behavior," *Public Organization Review* 15, no. 1 (2015), 139–155.

53. Manuel P. Teodoro and Adam G. Hughes, "Socializer or Signal? How Agency Accreditation Affects Organizational Culture," *Public Administration Review* 72, no. 4 (2012), 583–591. doi: 10.111/j.1540-6210.2012.02531.x.

54. Stephen D. Mastrofski, James J. Willis, and Tammy Rinehart Kochel, "The Challenges of Implementing Community Policing in the United States," *Policing* 1, no. 2 (2012).

55. Census of State and Local Law Enforcement Agencies, 2008, https://bjs.ojp.gov/sites/g/files/xyckuh236/files/media/document/slleta18st.pdf.

56. Fayetteville (NC) Police Department, https://www.fayettevillenc.gov/city-services/police/recruiting.

57. Dallas Police Department, https://dallaspolice.net/joindpd/Pages/Qualifications.aspx

58. Commission on Peace Officer Standards and Training, https://post.ca.gov/home.aspx.

59. Adrienne M. Meier, Timothy J. Arentsen, Luann Pannell, and Katharine M. Putman, "Attrition of Police Officers as Predicted by Peer Evaluations during Academy Training," *Policing and Society* (2016), 1–10.

60. *Canton v. Harris*, 1989, http://caselaw.findlaw.com/us-supreme-court/489/378.html#sthash.f4pEzuYw.dpuf.

61. Texas Commission on Law Enforcement. https://www.tcole.texas.gov/content/training-requirements

62. Jeremy M. Wilson, Erin Dalton, Charles Scheer, and Clifford A. Grammich, "Police Recruitment and Retention for the New Millennium," (Santa Monica, CA: RAND Corporation, 2010).

63. Brian Reaves, *Hiring and Retention of State and Local Law Enforcement Officers, 2008—Statistical Tables.* 2012, https://www.bjs.gov/content/pub/pdf/hrslleo08st.pdf.

64. Matthew J. Hickman, "Impact of the Military Reserve Activation on Police Staffing," *Police Chief* 73, no. 10 (October 2006), 12–14.

65. Michael Planty, Stephen Provasnik, William J. Hussar, Thomas D. Snyder, and Grace Kena, *The Condition of Education 2008* (Washington, DC: Claitors Publishing Division, June 2008). As of June 24, 2010: http://nces.ed.gov/pubsearch/pubsinfo.asp?pubid=2008031.

66. Brian Reaves, *Hiring and Retention of State and Local Law Enforcement Officers, 2008—Statistical Tables.* 2012, https://www.bjs.gov/content/pub/pdf/hrslleo08st.pdf.

67. Brian Reaves, *Hiring and Retention of State and Local Law Enforcement Officers, 2008—Statistical Tables.* 2012, https://www.bjs.gov/content/pub/pdf/hrslleo08st.pdf.

Part 2
Police Practice and Organization

This section focuses on the day-to-day activities of police officers. How are patrol and investigations carried out? How do police deal with tragedies such as terrorist and mass casualty attacks? We also cover what is being done now to reform police responses to these events in order to ensure that the public is both protected and served. One area that gets special attention is how police departments are evolving and formulating new approaches to traditional policing, ranging from community policing to intelligence-led policing that places heavy emphasis on data-generated tactical responses.

Chapter 4
Patrol and Investigation

Chapter 5
The Evolving Responsibilities of Responding to Tragedy and the Accompanying Promise of Police Reform

Chapter 6
Contemporary Policing: Community, Problem-Oriented, Broken Windows, and Other Police Innovations

Patrol and Investigation

Learning Objectives

LO1 Describe the reality of the police role.

LO2 Analyze 9-1-1 and patrol operations.

LO3 Explain how police patrol can be a deterrent to crime.

LO4 Evaluate alternative methods of patrol.

LO5 Summarize the organization of a detective bureau.

LO6 Appraise the effectiveness of investigation operations.

Chapter Outline

Robyn Beck/AFP/Getty Images

In Socorro, a city in El Paso County, Texas, a community member saw flames erupt from a mobile home in Texas, and recorded a video as a local police officer out on patrol ran into the burning building to save a family trapped inside. Socorro police officer Joshua Gonzalez was filmed wearing a bulletproof vest and face mask as he was running out of the flames carrying a child. Later, Gonzalez told the media: "As I parked my patrol unit I could feel the heat coming from the residence . . . Once I made myself present to the people standing by, I asked them what was going on and they said somebody was inside the residence, that there were people in there . . . it was well within my heart and soul to run in and try and get these people out." The officer said that when he entered he found two adults, one who was an older adult, and an eight-year-old boy.

"The house was already full of smoke, I could barely breathe and I even advised them, 'cover your mouths,' to try to get out as soon as possible safely . . . From that point, I grabbed the child and I held him tight in my arms and I ran out with him and got him to the street where there was a couple of neighbors . . . to take care of him." The other two adults inside the home were brought to safety by an off-duty firefighter that was on the scene. The boy didn't sustain any injuries, but the older adult was treated at the scene for smoke inhalation. The Socorro Police Department issued a statement praising Officer Gonzalez and going on to say, ". . . thank you to the residents and emphasize that what we saw happen yesterday was an example of friends and neighbors helping one another under extreme circumstances." When the rescued boy told Gonzalez that he was really sad his football cleats were lost in the fire, the officer offered to buy him new ones.[1]

■ Would you agree that while the rescue of a family from a burning home by an individual police officer does not seem particularly dramatic when compared to the mammoth shootouts and fights depicted in the media, it is a much more accurate portrayal of the day-to-day activities of police officers?

■ Do you think that the media often presents an overly romanticized version of policing that is far from the truth? As Officer Gonzalez's heroics show, policing is a multifaceted and complex occupation.

- Right now, police engage in such activities as responding to accidents, helping people in distress, dispensing emergency medical care, and controlling family disputes. Do you think it would be best for them to stick to law enforcement and have other social agencies respond to social and individual problems?

- Many officers say that they love that every day is different: Not knowing who you will meet, not knowing what to expect, and not knowing who you may help on any given day has its appeal. While this uncertainty has appeal, do you think that it may also lead to unpleasant encounters with the public?

In this chapter, we will first look at the reality of how a police officer spends their time on the job. We divide the police role into two broad segments, patrol and investigation, and discuss how officers assigned to each segment operate on a daily basis.

LO1

Describe the reality of the police role.

The Police Role

In countless books, movies, and TV shows, the public has been presented with a view of policing that romanticizes police officers as fearless crime fighters who think little of their own safety as they engage in daily shootouts and car chases while frequently encountering psychopathic serial killers and organized crime professional killers. Occasionally, but not often, fictional patrol officers seem aware of departmental rules, legal decisions, citizens' groups, civil suits, or physical danger. They are rarely faced with the economic necessity of moonlighting as security guards, taking on extra details, caring about an annual pay raise, or focused on collective bargaining and retirement benefits.

How close to real life is this portrayal of a selfless crime fighter? Not very, according to most research efforts. Police officers are asked to deal with hundreds of incidents each year, and crime fighting is only a small part of the daily routine.

Studies of police work indicate that a significant portion of an officer's time is spent handling minor disturbances, service calls, and administrative duties. Police work, then, involves much more than catching criminals.[2] The single largest number of these involve some form of motor vehicle or traffic-related issues. Millions of contacts are initiated by citizens asking for assistance—requesting police help for things like asking neighbors to turn down loud music during a party, warning kids not to shoot fireworks, and so on.

While the number of residents who experience interactions with police has been in decline, more than 60 million people now have interactions with the police each year. Violent encounters are actually quite rare: about 2 percent of police contacts involve the threat or use of force.

Contacts with the Public

The most recent report on police citizen contacts shows that the number of residents (16 or over) who experience interaction with police has been in decline. In 2020, about 58 million people now have dealings with the police each year.[3] White citizens (22 percent) were more likely than Black (18 percent), Hispanic (17 percent), or Asian citizens (16 percent) to have had contact with police; these differences are not statistically significant.

The media has focused attention on the police use of force, which is portrayed as a routine occurrence. In reality, most police citizen contacts were force free:

Among those who had contact with police, 2 percent experienced a nonfatal threat or use of force by police. However, Black people were more than twice as likely (3.8 percent) than White people (1.5 percent) to experience force.

This survey indicates that the police role is both varied and complex. The majority of a police officer's activities do not involve handling calls for serious violent felonies nor do they involve violent interactions.

These results are not surprising when we consider the Uniform Crime Report (UCR) arrest data collected by the Federal Bureau of Investigation (FBI):

- The most recent data indicates that law enforcement officers make more than 10 million arrests each year. Of these arrests, about 500,000 are for serious violent crimes, and about 1 million were for serious property crimes.

- The highest number of arrests for less serious crimes were for drug violations (more than 1.5 million arrests) and driving under the influence (slightly more than 1 million),

- Each year, about 3,000 people per 100,000 inhabitants are arrested. The arrest rate for serious violent crime (including murder and nonnegligent manslaughter, rape, robbery, and aggravated assault) is about 160 per 100,000 inhabitants, and the arrest rate for serious property crime (burglary, larceny-theft, motor vehicle theft, and arson) is almost 350 per 100,000 inhabitants.[4]

With approximately 800,000 active police officers in the United States, this means that the average police officer makes fewer than two serious crime arrests per year. Of course, since crime is not evenly distributed, we know that many police officers who work in rural and suburban departments in areas with very low crime rates make even fewer annual arrests for serious crimes; others working in large metropolitan areas such as Chicago and Miami probably make many more annual arrests.

These figures should also be interpreted with caution because not all police officers are engaged in activities that allow them to make arrests, such as patrol or detective work. About one-third of all sworn officers in the nation's largest police departments are in such units as communications, training, anti-terrorism, administration, and personnel.

Even if the number of arrests per officer were adjusted by one-third, it would still amount to about four serious crime arrests per officer per year, and these figures include such crimes as shoplifting and other larcenies. So, although police handle thousands of calls each year, relatively few result in arrests for serious crimes, such as a robbery or burglary; in suburban and rural areas, years may go by before a police officer makes a felony arrest.

Order Maintenance and Peacekeeping

If making arrests for felonies is only a small part of the job, what is the most important function of police? Most experts agree that the bulk of patrol effort is devoted to what has been described as **order maintenance**, or **peacekeeping**: maintaining order and civility within the officer's assigned jurisdiction.[5] Order-maintenance policing generally targets behavior that falls somewhere between criminal and noncriminal, such as asking noisy kids to leave the area or dealing with neighborhood disputes.

The patrol officer's discretion often determines whether a noisy neighborhood dispute involves the crime of disturbing the peace or whether it can be controlled with street-corner diplomacy and the combatants sent on their

Critical Thinking

Based on the statistics above, what do you think should be the main objective of local police?

order maintenance

Police practice that involves handling minor offenses and conflicts and disorderly conduct before they escalate into serious crimes.

peacekeeping

The goal of policing to create a secure and stable neighborhood environment.

way. Similarly, teenagers milling around in the shopping center parking lot can be brought in and turned over to the juvenile authorities or handled in a less formal and often more efficient manner. While peacekeeping may be the backbone of policing, the visible presence of police officers on the street also creates crime prevention outcomes: more cops, less crime. The police may be the most important and effective crime reducing element of the criminal justice system.[6]

LO2

Analyze 9-1-1 and patrol operations.

▶ The Patrol Function

A great deal of the police role is carried out by uniformed patrol officers, considered to be the backbone of policing. Patrol officers typically account for about two-thirds of a department's personnel.[7] The patrol division delivers the bulk of police services and makes the bulk of the daily decisions. The police organization is unique in that those at the bottom of the agency hierarchy make the most important decisions. At the same time, patrol often consists of the least experienced officers in the department. This dissonance may account for some of the problems encountered by police agencies. When George Floyd was killed at the hands of four Minneapolis police officers, two of them were rookies, who had only been on the job for a few days and were actually in field training at the time of his death.[8] This case will be discussed in detail in later chapters.

Some officers elect to stay in patrol for their entire careers because they enjoy the variability of the work while others try to move into other divisions as soon as they can. For the officers who stay in patrol, seniority provides benefits including selecting shifts and days off. If the most senior officers choose to work on the day shift, this means that the least experienced patrol officers are working the higher crime shifts in late afternoon and evening hours.

Patrol officers are the most highly visible members of the entire criminal justice system and their interactions with the public color opinions of courts and corrections as well. They are charged with supervising specific zones within their jurisdiction, designated areas traditionally called **beats**, whether in a patrol car, or by motorcycle, horse, bicycle, helicopter, or boat, or even on foot in some departments. Generally, most agencies rely on three shifts to provide patrol services but some larger departments may have a fourth shift that could run from 6 P.M. until 2 A.M. Typically, shifts are either 8, 10, or 12 hours. Officers may prefer longer shifts because the more hours worked during one shift results in more days off. Recent research by the Police Foundation suggests that 10-hour shifts might be best for preventing fatigue and promoting the best overall performance of patrol officers.[9]

While patrol is the most common police activity, it is also a highly complex procedure. Patrol officers must engage in a deterrence function: the presence of a patrol officer, in uniform and often behind the wheel of a distinctively marked police car, is aimed at proactively preventing potential offenders from committing crimes. At the same time, patrol officers must swiftly respond to emergencies ranging from a citizen in medical distress to an armed robbery in progress. This dual purpose required efficient management aimed at a diverse array of goals: minimize emergency response times.

beats

Specific zones designated as areas of police patrol.

Motorized Patrols

Modern-day patrol is dominated by the automobile. Nearly every police department in the United States relies on the automobile to conduct routine patrol. Motor vehicles make up the bulk of patrol and this is unlikely to be changed in the near future.

In addition to patrol cars, about 80 percent of large agencies use motorcycles as some part of their routine patrol activities. This means that the majority of agencies had a motorcycle unit that did some of the regular patrol. More than three-quarters of agencies rely on bicycles to provide patrol services and two-thirds of police agencies use foot patrol. There are also some less commonly used methods for providing patrol. About 20 percent of police agencies that have a body of water within their jurisdiction employ some form of marine patrol. Other agencies use aviation patrol, mounted or horse patrol (about 15 percent), or make use of two-wheel, motorized segways.[10]

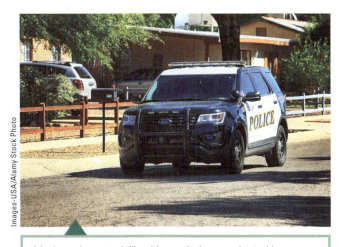

Images-USA/Alamy Stock Photo

Modern-day patrol, like this one being conducted in Tucson, Arizona, is dominated by the automobile. Motor vehicles make up the bulk of patrol and this is unlikely to change in the near future. Can you think of a more effective way for the police to patrol? Would a drone system work better?

9-1-1 and Patrol Operations

In 1957, the National Association of Fire Chiefs recommended use of a single number for reporting fires.[11] This was followed by the President's Commission on Law Enforcement and Administration of Justice recommending in 1967 that a "single number should be established" nationwide for reporting emergency situations. In 1968, AT&T announced that it would establish the digits 9-1-1 (nine-one-one) as the emergency code throughout the United States. 9-1-1 was chosen because it best fit the needs of all parties involved.

First, and most important, it met public requirements because it is brief, easily remembered, and can be dialed quickly. Second, because it is a unique number, never having been authorized as an office code, area code, or service code, it best met the long-range numbering plans and switching configurations of the telephone industry. On February 16, 1968, Senator Rankin Fite completed the first 9-1-1 call made in the United States in Haleyville, Alabama. The serving telephone company was then Alabama Telephone Company. This Haleyville 9-1-1 system is still in operation today. At the end of the twentieth century, nearly 93 percent of the population of the United States was covered by some type of 9-1-1 service. Ninety-five percent of that coverage was *Enhanced 9-1-1.* Approximately 96 percent of the geographic United States is today covered by some type of 9-1-1.

As a result of the development of 9-1-1, patrol is largely deployed by citizen calls. While police are considered to be the gatekeepers of the criminal justice system, when citizens call 9-1-1 or their local police directly, they are deploying department resources (see the following feature for the history). Most modern police work is reactive, driven by communication and technology. Citizen use of 9-1-1 drives police work and causes it to be incident driven and reactive in nature. Modern communications allow the public to call the police to fix everything and act as "social repair person" ready to take on all challenges.

There are a number of reasons why citizens call 9-1-1 for police assistance. Most notably, citizens call because it is convenient. People have been socialized into calling the police to solve their problems rather than having to do it for themselves; people want the police to restore order. This can involve asking the police to remove a trespasser or people loitering in front of a business. Sometimes people call the police to point police attention away from their own illegal actions and draw scrutiny to other offenders in the community. Other callers are malicious and provided "misleading" information about the events they report. Citizens may accidentally or purposely mislead police operators, describing, for example, events as more legally serious than they know them to be in order to prompt a faster police response.[12]

swatting

A practice of calling 9-1-1 and faking an emergency that draws a response from law enforcement. The purpose is to harass or injure a victim.

The misuse of 9-1-1 calls now includes a practice called **swatting**: calling 9-1-1 and faking an emergency that draws a response from law enforcement—usually a SWAT team; hence the term *swatting*. These calls usually can "spoof" or clone someone else's phone number when making this call. The callers often tell tales of hostages about to be executed or bombs about to go off. The community is placed in danger as responders rush to the scene, taking them away from real emergencies.[13] Swatting can have deadly consequences: When police surrounded the Wichita, Kansas, home of Andrew Finch, 28, they believed the man inside had killed his father and was holding family members hostage. Finch was shot and killed when he made a sudden move after coming outside to face police. It turned out that the call was a swatting attack and, tragically, Finch was not the actual target. The swatters had given the police the wrong address; one of the conspirators received a 20-year prison sentence.[14] In 2022, Representative Marjorie Taylor Greene was swatted after she had introduced a bill in Congress that would make it a felony to provide gender-affirming care to transgender minors.

9-1-1 Communications Centers

9-1-1 call centers are the nerve centers of modern policing and are typically staffed by civilians. At call centers, there is an incoming call that gets answered by an operator or call taker who retrieves information and determines if a police response is necessary. They are information brokers. The operator sends information to the dispatcher who then finds the next-available patrol officer or stacks the call using computer-aided dispatch (CAD). This is not an easy job because there is often tension between dispatchers and the officers. This is due in large part because they do not have enough information from the 9-1-1 operator. People calling 9-1-1 are often having their worst possible life experiences. As a result, they can provide vague, incomplete, and inaccurate information that eventually will frustrate the responding officer. In some departments, dispatchers and police spend time learning about each other's jobs to better understand these frustrations, enabling dispatchers to directly address problems they encounter.[15]

L03

Explain how police patrol can be a deterrent to crime.

► # The Nature of Patrol

Once a call is dispatched, officers respond, but when there are no calls, officers will patrol their assigned areas. Police work is divided between committed time (handling a call) and uncommitted (in-service, waiting for a call) time. Patrol officers often have a lot of uncommitted time left over and the amount of this time will vary by department, shift, and day of week. On average, over three-quarters of a patrol officers' shift is unassigned. During this time, officers primarily self-initiate routine patrol, or back up other officers on calls to which they were not dispatched. Research shows that just 6 percent of unassigned time activities are directed by supervising officers, dispatchers, other officers, or citizens.[16]

Calls also vary in the amount of time needed to clear them. If an officer makes an arrest, it takes much longer to process and book the suspect and complete paperwork (often several hours). This depends on how far the county jail is, the personal property owned by the individual and if they have health problems that need to be cleared by a hospital.

Uncommitted time is largely spent on patrol. Each beat, or patrol area, is covered 24 hours a day by different shifts. Generalist patrol officers not only respond to calls for service and make arrests but also may conduct traffic enforcement, warrant searches, follow-up investigations, community presentations, directed patrols in high-crime areas, and many other activities.[17] As this list should make clear, patrol officers' responsibilities are immense. While police are typically responding to mundane violations of the law like loitering or other misdemeanors, patrol officers never know when this routine work will be punctuated with the more dangerous and exciting activities. More commonly, patrol officers are responding to noncrime calls, such as community members needing information or are having a noncrime crisis. They call the police when they are unsure who else will call because they know that police will show up.

Patrol and Order Maintenance

Patrol officers mainly spend their time maintaining order—making sure that public spaces are open and available for use by community members. Police encounter many troubling incidents that need to be addressed, but rarely do they require formal intervention such as an arrest. Rather, the real police role is that of a community problem solver. Police officers practice a policy of selective enforcement, concentrating on some crimes but handling the majority in an informal manner.

Patrol and Deterrence

Random preventive police patrol was long considered one of the greatest deterrents to criminal behavior. The visible presence of patrol cars on the street and the rapid deployment of police officers to the scene of the crime were viewed as particularly effective law enforcement techniques. Since, the vast majority of policing is reactive, the police tend to only be called after the commission of a crime, or at best while the crime is still in progress.

It is widely assumed that people who offend can be caught if the police can simply get to the scene of a crime quickly. In a classic statement, Lawrence W. Sherman asserted

> . . . the shorter the police travel time from assignment to arrival at a crime scene, the more likely it is that police can arrest offenders before they flee. This claim is then extended to rapid response, producing three crime prevention effects. One is a reduction in harm from crimes interrupted in progress by police intervention. Another, more general benefit of rapid response time is a greater deterrent effect . . . The third hypothesized prevention effect comes from the incapacitation through imprisonment of offenders. . . .[18]

But does the research support this view?

Critical Thinking

If you were a police commander, how do you think officers should spend uncommitted time?

Critical Thinking

Thinking about your own neighborhood, what effect do you think random preventive police patrol has on crime rates?

Response Time

The prevailing wisdom is that the faster a patrol officer can respond to a crime in progress the greater the chance they will apprehend the perpetrator. There are four factors that influence how quickly the police can respond to a call for service.

- **Discovery time:** This is the interval between the commission of the crime and its discovery. Time intervals are largely unknown for property crimes. If a college student leaves campus for winter break to visit family and their apartment is burglarized, it is typically impossible to know if that burglary occurred the evening that they left or an hour before they returned home (unless there is some sort of home security camera system).

- **Reporting time:** This is the interval between discovery of the crime and when the citizen actually calls the police. After discovering a crime, it is not unusual to call a family member or try to assess the damage. Even if the crime was just committed, this delay prevents police from finding the offender.

- **Processing time:** This is the interval between the call and the dispatch of the patrol car. While this is not a very long period of time, it can add to the total time elapsed.

- **Travel time:** This is the length of time it takes officers to reach the scene.

Because response time is considered critical, the ability to arrive quickly is the central assumption of the random preventative patrol. This approach depends on police being spread out all over a town or a city so that officers can respond quickly to any given crime. But is it important for police to respond quickly? For most crimes that come to the attention of the police, it is not clear that a quick response time will impact apprehending offenders or clearance overall. The meaning of crime clearance is discussed in Exhibit 4.1.

Exhibit 4.1

Crime Clearance

According to the FBI, a law enforcement agency reports that an offense is cleared by arrest, or solved for crime reporting purposes, when three specific conditions have been met. The three conditions are that at least one person has been:

- Arrested.

- Charged with the commission of the offense.

- Turned over to the court for prosecution (whether following arrest, court summons, or police notice).

- Crimes can also be cleared by exceptional means. In certain situations, elements beyond law enforcement's control prevent the agency from arresting and formally charging the offender. When this occurs, the agency can clear the offense exceptionally. Law enforcement agencies must meet the following four conditions in order to clear an offense by exceptional means. The agency must have:

  - Identified the offender.

  - Gathered enough evidence to support an arrest, make a charge, and turn over the offender to the court for prosecution.

  - Identified the offender's exact location so that the suspect could be taken into custody immediately.

  - Encountered a circumstance outside the control of law enforcement that prohibits the agency from arresting, charging, and prosecuting the offender.[19]

More than 30 years ago, the most well-known study of police patrol effectiveness was conducted in Kansas City, Missouri. Known as the Kansas City Preventative Patrol Experiment, the findings challenged long-held beliefs, and to some, called into question the utility of random preventative police patrol. This classic study is described in detail in the following Focus on Policing: Kansas City Preventative Patrol Experiment feature.

Focus on Policing

Kansas City Preventative Patrol Experiment

Beginning in October 1972 and continuing through September 1973, the most famous police experiment was administered by the Kansas City Police Department and evaluated by the Police Foundation. The purpose of the experiment was to determine the effectiveness of random preventative patrol practices—a staple of traditional policing—on crime, citizen fear, and satisfaction with the police. Another objective was to determine if police could establish and maintain experimental conditions for social science research.

To conduct the experiment, 15 beats were selected with similar crime rates, calls for service, and neighborhood demographics to conduct the experiment. Each of the 15 beats included in the study was assigned varying levels of patrol for the 12-month study period. Five of the beats were designated as reactive beats and received no preventative patrol. This area was all but completely devoid of a police presence unless there was a call for service. Police vehicles assigned to patrol these beats entered them only to respond to a call. Once finished answering the call for service, they patrolled other beats. The next five beats were designated as proactive beats with patrol officers providing two to three times more preventative patrol. The final five beats were designated as control beats that received the same levels of patrol as before the experiment. Again, this experiment went on for one full year.

To measure the impact of different levels of patrol, the following data were collected:

1. Crime rates—Uniform Crime Reports (UCR)
2. Response times
3. Arrest data
4. Community surveys
5. Interviews with citizens who had encounters with the police during the experiment

6. Survey of business owners
7. Observation of police behavior and practices
8. Survey of officer attitudes
9. Observers rated citizen satisfaction during interaction

So what did the researchers find? Variations in patrol levels had no significant impact on crime. In fact, the number of arrests remained the same, regardless of the level of police presence. No significant impact existed on citizens' or business owners' perceptions of safety and fear of crime created by adding or subtracting patrol. Despite wide variations in the levels of patrol across the beats, response time remains unchanged.

Critical Thinking

1. The Kansas City study affected policing like no other. Other research efforts, conducted in the United States and abroad confirmed the Kansas City study's less-than-stellar findings. This research caused police administrators to think of better uses of officer time than just randomly patrolling neighborhoods. But what should they do to improve the situation?

2. Think of different techniques police departments could use to bring the crime rate down, or is it not possible?

Sources: George Kelling, Tony Pate, Duane Dieckman, and Charles Brown, Kansas City Preventive Patrol Experiment: A Technical Report, Police Foundation, 1974, https://www.policinginstitute .org/wp-content/uploads/2015/07/Kelling-et-al.-1974-THE-KANSAS -CITY-PREVENTIVE-PATROL-EXPERIMENT.pdf; and Jordi Blanes I Vidal and Giovanni Mastrobuoni, Police Patrols And Crime, Cato Institute. Research Briefs in Economic Policy No. 112, May 9, 2018, https://www.cato.org/publications/research-briefs-economic -policy/police-patrols-crime.

▶ Approaches to Patrol

Modern police departments generally rely on motorized patrol to cover wide areas, to maintain a visible police presence, and to ensure rapid response time. Although effective and economical, the patrol car removes officers from the mainstream of the community, alienating people who might otherwise be potential sources of information and help to the police. Below, a number of approaches that have been tried are set out in some detail.

Foot Patrol

To improve on community relations, a number of urban police departments began experimenting with foot patrols, returning the police to the street rather than having to patrol in cars. The goal was to increase visibility of officers, increase their contact with the community, and develop greater understanding of community needs and issues. By forming a bond with community residents and acquainting them with the individual officers who patrolled their neighborhood, letting them know that police were caring and available, the **foot patrol** was seen as a proactive method of crime control.[20] Three of the most famous foot patrol experiments are described below.

foot patrol

A policing initiative that took
officers out of cars and has
them walking in neighborhood
beats.

Newark Foot Patrol

In 1973, the New Jersey state legislature passed the Safe and Clean Neighborhoods Act, and researchers conducted a yearlong study to find the effectiveness of police foot patrol in Newark, New Jersey. The goal was to determine if the advantages of foot patrols in urban areas were worth the expense of implementation. Police foot patrol was specifically mandated as part of an effort to expand the presence and visibility of police protection. Newark was selected as the primary evaluation site. The evaluation began in February 1978 and ended in February 1979.

Researchers matched sets of patrol beats in Newark to compare the effects of continuing and discontinuing foot patrols. Outcome measures included reported crimes, arrests, victimization, citizens' fear, and satisfaction of residents and merchants. The Police Foundation posed the following questions:

- Does foot patrol improve police-citizen relationships?
- Do citizens feel safer when officers patrol on foot?
- Does foot patrol reduce crime?
- Will citizens report more crime when they have closer contact with the police?
- Will more arrests be made in foot-patrolled areas?
- Will foot patrol officers be more satisfied with their jobs and have more positive attitudes about citizens?
- Will citizens' fear of victimization be lessened?

The study found that when foot patrol was added in neighborhoods, citizens reported that levels of fear decreased significantly, and fear subsequently increased

San Francisco Chronicle/Hearst Newspapers/Getty Images

Police officers walk up Powell Street on foot patrol in San Francisco, California. Research indicates that foot patrols reduce citizen fear of crime and in some cities have actually reduced crime rates.

significantly when the foot patrol was withdrawn. It was also noted that citizens' satisfaction with police increased when foot patrol was added in their neighborhoods. Officers who patrolled on foot seemed to have a greater appreciation for the values of neighborhood residents, had greater job satisfaction, less fear of the community, and higher morale than police who patrolled in cars.

A more surprising finding was that *actual* crime levels were not affected by foot patrols. Perceptions of foot patrol effectiveness also varied between individuals and businesses: Although residents were aware of the foot patrols and felt that crime was diminished by their presence, commercial respondents did not note an increase in patrols and perceived an increase in the crime problem. These contradictory responses probably resulted from the fact that foot patrols were used mainly at night when commercial establishments were closed.

Moreover, multiple layoffs and unrest among police during the last stages of the experiment had a greater influence on merchants than on residents. Residents in areas with added foot patrols indicated greater reduction in use of protective measures than persons in other experimental areas. Overall, foot patrols improved citizens' feelings of safety under the most difficult urban circumstances. These improved feelings were not shared by merchants in the area.[21] So the results were mixed: while there was no significant effect on crime rates, Newark residents were less fearful of crime and more satisfied with the police when a foot patrol was added to their respective neighborhoods.

Flint, Michigan, Foot Patrol

Another well-known effort was the Neighborhood Foot Patrol Program (NFPP) in Flint, Michigan, which was conducted in 14 neighborhoods between January 1979 and January 1982. The program included three efforts. First, citywide planning meetings were held as far as a year in advance of the formal beginning of the program. Second, assigned officers were expected to be familiar with their neighborhoods, to recognize potential problems, and to make referrals to the appropriate social agencies when it was necessary to do so. Third, the Flint program operated on the assumption that citizens themselves had an important role to play in the prevention of crime and maintenance of public order as the "eyes and ears" of their neighborhoods.[22]

Three methods of data gathering and evaluation were used: (1) several hundred interviews were conducted with community residents, block club leaders, businesspeople, clergy, foot patrol officers, and others; (2) members of the research team talked with community residents and police officers informally; and (3) the daily, weekly, and monthly reports of the foot patrol officers were sampled to determine how they had used their time. For the formal evaluation, information was developed through five primary sources: personal interviews, crime statistics and calls for service, monitoring (daily, weekly, and monthly reports submitted by foot patrol officers), media content analysis, and intervening variables that could not be controlled during the three-year experiment. An evaluation of the Flint foot patrol program found that in the foot patrol jurisdictions, calls for police service were down 43.4 percent during the evaluation period. In the areas with foot patrol, reported crime was down 8.7 percent during the project's life while crime rates in other Flint neighborhoods were rising.[23]

Of the 280 residents interviewed during the third year, 42 percent said they knew exactly what the duties of the foot patrol officers were; additionally, more than 64 percent said they were satisfied with the program, and more than

61 percent said that protection for women, children, and older adults had been increased. Finally, more than 90 percent of the 280 residents interviewed were aware of the Foot Patrol Program; most agreed that foot patrol officers were more effective than motorized officers. Moreover, residents in Flint, Michigan, despite having the highest unemployment in the nation, voted in 1982 and 1985 to raise their taxes in order to support extended foot patrols throughout the entire city.[24]

Philadelphia, Pennsylvania, Foot Patrol

With over 6,600 officers, Philadelphia is the fourth-largest police department in the United States and police a city of nearly 1.5 million people. The city is ranked the 30th most dangerous in the country. Philadelphia assigned more than 200-foot patrol officers in the summer of 2009. To determine their effectiveness, researchers examined 60 violent crime hotspots within the city. The term "hotspots" refers to crime clusters (or addressed) within highly specific geographic locations. The results identified a substantial reduction in the level of violent crime in the areas studied. After 12 weeks of foot patrol, target areas had considerably less violent crime during the period studied. Target areas outperformed the control sites by 23 percent, resulting in a total net effect of 53 violent crimes prevented. The results suggest that targeted foot patrols in violent crime hotspots can significantly reduce violent crime levels provided that a threshold level of violence already existed. This study suggests that intensive foot patrol efforts in violent hotspots may achieve deterrence at a micro-spatial level, primarily by increasing the certainty of disruption, apprehension, and arrest.[25]

These and other foot patrol efforts have been considered successful. Not only have they been shown to reduce specific crimes such as disorderly conduct, their crime-reducing capabilities can reduce crime in neighboring areas, even those that have not already adapted foot patrol strategies.[26] When surveyed, police officers expressed the belief that foot patrols can improve police-community relations, facilitate intelligence gathering, reduce crime, and provide needed exercise. The officers critiqued foot patrol for being resource intensive, potentially decreasing officer safety, physically demanding, and limiting access to vital equipment.[27] Nonetheless, there are still questions to be answered, including whether it works to reduce only specific crimes such as assault but not others such as robbery, whether there is a displacement effect, and whether it can have utility in lower-populated rural and suburban areas.[28] There are also questions raised about whether foot patrols strain departmental budgets because they are personnel and resource intensive.[29]

Hotspot Policing

Another innovative policing effort, **hotspot policing**, is a methodology that involves focusing police patrol resources on small units of geography like neighborhoods, street blocks, or even single addresses that have extremely high levels of criminal activity. The idea behind this approach is that since the highest amounts of crime are concentrated in selected geographic regions, increasing police presence specifically in these areas would likely produce substantial reductions in crime. Research shows that less than 5 percent of places in a city—streets, addresses, and other geographic coordinates—are places for 50 percent or more of crime incidents and this concentration of crime is relatively stable; high-crime hotspots remain that way for decades.[30] The use of computer algorithms can be used to identify high-crime areas while helping position patrol cars so that they can effectively and efficiently cover target areas.[31]

Critical Thinking

1. How do you feel when you see police officers walking around your neighborhood?
2. Does seeing officers patrol on foot make you feel safe? Do you think it has an effect on crime?

hotspot policing

Focusing police patrol on small units of geography like street blocks or even single addresses that have extremely high levels of criminal activity.

What makes this so different is that hotspot policing is a place-based strategy in contrast to traditional policing and crime prevention, which typically focus on people.[32] Hotspot interventions typically target serious offenses, including aggravated assault, robbery, firearm-related crime, and street-level drug trafficking.[33] This approach is well researched and all results show that this is an effective law enforcement strategy for achieving short-run reductions in crime.

The results from the first hotspots study, the Minneapolis Hot Spots Patrol Experiment, indicated that increased police presence alone leads to reductions in crime.[34] In this study, officers were instructed to spend more patrol time in crime hotspots but were not given directions about what types of activities they should engage in at the hotspots. Officers from the Minneapolis Police Department provided intensive patrol services to the high-crime areas of Minneapolis. The program focused on increasing the police presence in hotspots of crime, rather than the specific activities conducted by officers during patrols. The crime hotspots that did not receive intensified patrol had twice as much observed disorder as those that benefited from the increased police presence.[35]

Police can use a number of strategies in hotspot policing including directed patrol, foot patrol, or enhanced drug enforcement. **Situational crime prevention (SCP)** strategies have proven to be effective.[36] They focus on efforts to disrupt the dynamics that allow crime to occur. Situational prevention increases risks or efforts for offenders or reduces the attractiveness of potential targets. Such approaches include things like razing abandoned buildings and cleaning up graffiti.

situational crime prevention (SCP)
Crime prevention strategies that are aimed at reducing criminal opportunities that arise from the routines of everyday life.

Directed patrol is the most common method used in hotspot policing. It involves assigning officers to a specific geographic area that is considered to be high crime and freeing them up from calls for service on the radio. This means that officers have time to engage with the community proactively—rather than reactively responding to calls for service.[37] Another approach for dealing with crime hotspots that has been met with some success is having officers incorporate principles from problem-oriented policing namely approaching individual problems proactively rather than responding reactively to individual incidents.

An innovative study randomly assigned foot patrol officers to crime hotspots in the London, England subway system. A careful analysis, using rigorous experimental design features, found that the patrol effort was able to reduce public calls for service by more than 20 percent on treated platforms relative to control areas that did not experience the foot patrols.[38] In addition to the direct effects of hotspot-oriented patrols, there also seems to be a residual effect: Hotspot areas that are targeted experience significant crime reductions for up to four days after the patrols are removed.[39] In sum, there is growing empirical evidence that hotspot policing efforts can reduce crime at a minimal cost.[40]

Hotspot Concerns

Despite its proven efficacy, there are still some concerns about hotspot policing. For example, the issue of "crime displacement"; if potential offenders perceive increased police patrol activity in their neighborhood, they can simply relocate (i.e., just move down the block) in order to commit crimes.[41] Existing research, however, tells us that this is not in fact the case: hotspot intervention has the ability to reduce criminal activity without merely shifting crime to another location.[42] Nonetheless, while crime may not simply move down the block, patrol cars might. There is evidence that when a hotspot initiative is prolonged, police will be spending less time in the target area and more in surrounding neighborhoods.[43] Patrol officers may expect crime to shift and are thereby acting on their predictions of changing crime locales.

In reality, crime does not move because some places have characteristics that make them attractive for criminal activity. Vacant or abandoned buildings on one block can provide an attractive landscape for drug dealing or drug use. The next block, however, may not have those same buildings, thus making it less attractive to offenders. By focusing police resources on the block with the vacant buildings, hotspot policing reduces overall crime rates.

Most research on the effect of hotspot policing has been conducted in urban areas like Minneapolis, Philadelphia, and New York City. Little is known about whether this approach can also be effective in rural and suburban areas that do not have the same population density. Given how people and crime are dispersed in rural and suburban areas, different police strategies might be necessary even in hot spots.

police legitimacy

Refers to the public belief that there is a responsibility and obligation to voluntarily accept and defer to the decisions made by authorities.

Another concern is that we do not know enough about the effects of hotspot policing on **police legitimacy**; there exists little evidence detailing how the public feels about the initiative.[44] There is evidence that the public supports some forms but not others. There are also racial differences (e.g., hotspots receiving greater approval from White citizens than from communities of color).[45] This may come as no surprise given that hotspot policing typically involves communities of color whose residents may be (or believe they are being) unfairly targeted.[46]

This level of uncertainty is further complicated by the fact that hotspot policing varies greatly depending on the type of strategies used by local police in conducting the approach. In some instances, police use a situational prevention approach, identifying targets and taking measures to protect them from harm. Another approach is to use aggressive methods: stopping, frisking, detaining, and so on. The public is more approving of the former than the latter.[47]

Police administrators who back the hotspot approach may believe that crime control gains outweigh the feelings of the public. However, if hotspot policing does negatively impact perceptions of legitimacy, then crime control gains in the short run may be offset by reduced cooperation and compliance by citizens in the long term. In short, this could be an overall loss to the police.[48]

Other Patrol Innovations

Another approach used by many police agencies is the use of civilian staff, who are not sworn officers, to respond to nonemergency calls for service. Most police agencies traditionally were organized in such a way that nearly all functions were performed by sworn officers. Currently, it is not unusual to see some departments employ non-sworn staff. Civilian staff can be helpful for police operations and typically cost less than sworn personnel. In relation to patrol operations, they can serve as community service officers and can also respond to community members' requests for service, identify and report criminal activities, assist citizens in identifying crime-prevention techniques, and assist in traffic control for special events.[49] Do we really need a sworn officer with a gun to respond to a fender-bender car accident in order to take a report?

Patrol effectiveness can also be enhanced by providing alternatives for citizens to report crimes and accidents. In most communities, police officers are dispatched to the scene of an incident to gather information for a report that citizens may need for their own purposes (such as insurance claims), even though for many incidents there is little likelihood the case will be solved. Providing alternative means, such as telephone reporting units or officer response by appointment, for reporting of many incidents can help free up time of sworn personnel for other duties.[50]

A good example is the method used by the Yakima Police Department in Washington. In 2004, they established the Telephone Reporting Unit (TRU) to relieve patrol officers from report writing to allow them more time to patrol in their assigned districts. The TRU utilizes noncommissioned personnel who answer phones and handle walk-in business at the station. Approximately 38 percent of the reports taken by the Yakima Police Department are TRU reports. Today, reports taken as TRU calls include mostly vandalisms, thefts, identity thefts, some misdemeanor assaults (non-domestic violence related), auto thefts at the counter, runaway juveniles, some civil disputes, some threats and harassment calls, and other information reports.

Determining factors would be whether the suspect is still present at the scene, how long before the call the incident took place, if there is possibly evidence at the scene to be collected, and whether there is a public safety issue to consider. Victims and reporting parties receive the same service as if an officer came to the scene. They then get a case number. Any cases with significant leads are assigned to a detective for follow-up. Insurance companies do not require that reports be taken by commissioned officers.[51]

Policing Reality: How Does the Public View Patrol?

Notwithstanding all of these innovations, most citizens never actually come into contact with their local police.[52] Regardless of well-publicized incidents of police misconduct, the vast majority of those who do request police assistance report that the officer acted properly during the encounter. Whether having an officer respond improved the situation, however, is something of a different story. But importantly, if police failed to improve the situation, it may be through no fault of their own. For example, if someone wakes up in the morning to find their car was broken into overnight, reporting the crime to the police may come a little too late; it is difficult to catch perpetrators when the trail has gone cold. These results also mask important details. Police receive much higher approval for their responses to noncrime emergencies (70 percent approval) than reports of problems such as neighborhood disturbances (58 percent approval).[53]

Critical Thinking

1. What are your views of your local police department? What factors influenced your opinion?
2. What can be done to improve police/citizen relations?

Detectives and Investigations

 L05

Summarize the organization of a detective bureau.

In the event that a suspect escapes from responding patrol officers, or the crime has occurred long before police are summoned, police detectives are called in to gather evidence, use it to identify the criminal suspect, and bring them to trial. To do so, investigators must be able to process crime scenes and gather physical evidence; interview witnesses and victims; conduct surveillance; and, in the event a suspect is identified, interview them and prepare formal reports. Another key task it to testify in court, where officers will be called upon to explain their actions and motivations, how they conducted the inquiry, and whether they followed the law during the investigation. Detectives then must be part forensic specialist, psychologist, and criminal lawyer in addition to being a law enforcer.

Gina Ferazzi/Los Angeles Times/Getty Images

Detectives investigate the specific elements of a crime and attempt to identify the individuals or groups responsible for committing particular offenses. Pictured are Irvine, California, police detectives who are investigating the mysterious disappearance of Amber Aiaz and her daughter Melissa Fu from their Irvine apartment in 2019. Despite the ongoing efforts of these detectives, the case remains unsolved.

The Investigative Function

Since the very first independent detective bureau was established by Sir Robert Peel's London Metropolitan Police in 1842, police investigators have been fairly romanticized figures vividly portrayed in popular novels, movies, and television series. The fictional police detective is usually depicted as a loner who is willing to break departmental rules, perhaps even violate the law, to capture the suspect. The average fictional detective views departmental policies and U.S. Supreme Court decisions as unfortunate roadblocks to police efficiency. Civil rights are either ignored or actively scorned.[54] Modern criminal investigators are experienced civil servants, trained in investigatory techniques, knowledgeable about legal rules of evidence and procedure, and at least somewhat cautious about the legal and administrative consequences of their actions.[55]

Detectives investigate the specific elements of a crime and attempt to identify the individuals or groups responsible for committing particular offenses. They typically engage with a case after patrol officers have made initial contact with the victim when the crime is reported.

Organization of Detective Bureaus

Investigative services can be organized in a variety of ways. Larger departments have specialized units that focus on individual crimes like homicide, sexual assault, and narcotics. Other larger agencies will have major crimes divisions that focus on solving all felony offenses. Smaller agencies will have detectives who focus on investigating all crimes. Many police departments have moved to a decentralized method of assigning detectives. In New York City, each borough or district has its own detective division that supervises investigators assigned to neighborhood police precincts. Local squad detectives work closely with patrol officers to provide an immediate investigative response to crimes and incidents.

New York City also maintains specialized borough squads—homicide, robbery, and special victims—to aid local squads and help identify suspects whose crimes may have occurred in multiple locations. There are also specialty squads that help in areas such as forensics. Other departments maintain special divisions with a prime responsibility for addressing specific types of crimes. According to the most recent Law Enforcement Management and Administrative Statistics Survey, approximately 16 percent of U.S. police personnel worked in the investigations area.[56]

Some jurisdictions maintain **vice squads**, which are usually staffed by sworn officers who work in plain clothes, and not in traditional uniforms, or detectives specializing in victimless crimes, such as prostitution or gambling. Vice squad officers may set themselves up as customers for illicit activities to make arrests. This covert type of police activity has often been criticized as violating the personal rights of citizens, and their appropriateness and fairness have been questioned.

vice squads

Police units assigned to enforce morality-based laws, such as those addressing prostitution, gambling, and pornography.

Critical Thinking

What can detectives do to get citizens to assist in solving crimes?

Careers in Policing

Detective

To become a detective in a large police department typically requires working as a uniformed officer for a stated number of years before applying to the detective branch. In larger departments, the rank of detective is considered a promotion based on a written examination, performance as a patrol officer, and personal characteristics.

Like many patrol officers, detectives engage in a wide ranging and diverse set of job-related activities, from going undercover to testifying in court, but their biggest tasks involve reactive investigations. According to the U.S. Bureau of Labor Statistics, below are some of the most important daily activities of a police detective:

- Testify at legal or legislative proceedings.
- Check the physical condition of people or animals.
- Prevent unauthorized individuals from entering restricted areas.
- Examine crime scenes to obtain evidence.
- Interview people to gather information about criminal activities.
- Record information about suspects.
- Prepare investigation or incident reports.
- Document legal or regulatory information.
- Analyze crime scene evidence.
- Process forensic or legal evidence in accordance with procedures.

- Record crime or accident scene evidence with video or still cameras.
- Examine records or other types of data to investigate criminal activities.
- Use databases to locate investigation details or other information.
- Detain suspects or witnesses.
- Communicate situation details to appropriate personnel.
- Serve court-ordered documents.
- Observe individuals' activities to gather information or compile evidence.
- Apprehend criminal suspects.
- Direct criminal investigations.
- Request emergency personnel.
- Block physical access to restricted areas.
- Record information about environmental conditions.
- Maintain surveillance of individuals or establishments.
- Collaborate with law enforcement or security agencies to share information.
- Collaborate with outside groups to develop programs or projects.

Source: U.S. Bureau of Labor Statistics, Occupational Outlook Handbook Police and Detectives, https://www.bls.gov/ooh /protective-service/police-and-detectives.htm.

The Purpose of Investigations

Investigations have many purposes. The first is to determine whether or not a crime has actually been committed. This means determining if there is enough evidence to go forward with an investigation or if there was a false report of crime. In these circumstances, the detective would unfound the case—and it would no longer be considered a crime. There has been a great deal of discussion about the use of the unfounded disposition and sexual assault. Researcher David Lisak and colleagues examined 10 years' worth of rape complaints and found that false reports account for between 2 percent and 10 percent. These dispositions are assigned based on determinations by police. Interestingly, they also found that police believe the rate is much higher than what the numbers suggest.[57]

Detectives are, for the most part, conducting follow-up or reactive investigations. It is also worth remembering that patrol officers are almost always the first to arrive on scene, which means that the patrol officer has conducted the preliminary investigation. The information that a patrol officer collects for the incident report is then sent to the detectives either in a bureau or in smaller departments. A case can be assigned to detectives after an arrest is made by patrol. In this case, the clock starts ticking for arraignment and detectives will work with the prosecutor to collect all of the necessary evidence to successfully try the case in court. If an arrest has not been made, detectives will start with the incident report.

Detectives may elect to wait before making an arrest—even if they know the identity of the suspect. If the suspect is not a public safety risk—meaning that there is not an immediate risk that they will reoffend—the detective, in consultation with the prosecutor, may decide to wait to make an arrest so that there is more time to build a strong case. This approach is referred to as a **downstream orientation**, where detectives consider the prosecutor's response as well as the next steps in the criminal justice system when making decisions rather than solely the merits of the complaint. Similarly, prosecutors consider how judges and juries will respond to the evidence collected.[58]

downstream orientation
When detectives consider the prosecutor's response when making decisions about a case.

Types of Investigations

Most detective work is reactive since it is dependent on citizen crime reporting or a police officer witnessing a crime. Some investigative work can be *proactive,* where investigators are building cases against people or groups. This proactive work tends to be in response to the so-called "victimless crimes" like drugs or prostitution, where the victim might not be willing to file a complaint with the police. This proactive work is not typical and most work is reactive since detectives are overwhelmed with caseloads. This means that detectives have little time to devote to the labor-intensive work of a proactive investigation.

Jack Kuykendall says there are three types of follow-up investigations that detectives can conduct. There are:

- **Walk-Throughs:** These types of investigations involve those cases where suspect has been identified and apprehended. Since the arrest has already been made, the detective's primary responsibility is to process the materials and evidence so the prosecutor can file charges. Some detectives may do additional follow-up work to better the case.

- **Where Are They's:** These are cases where the suspect has been identified but officers were unable to make an apprehension. Detectives must find them so that they can be arrested. An example of this is a perpetrator who is involved in a hit-and-run accident. The detectives will find the perpetrator and make an arrest.

- **Whodunits:** In these cases, the preliminary investigation did not result in identification of the offender. Detectives must start over. This usually begins with a review of the original report, document files, and with the detective attempting to find witnesses and victims.[59]

Workloads

A detective's workload is an important determinant of investigative success: Higher long- and short-term workloads are associated with a reduced chance of a case being cleared.[60] Therefore, the optimum number of cases in a detective's caseload will vary based on the type of crime being investigated. Adequate staffing is essential to successfully solving cases. In fact, the police agencies most successful at clearing homicides are those where, given the annual number of homicides in a jurisdiction, each investigator is the lead investigator for three homicides per year. While this may seem low, the researchers explain that lead investigators have a large number of responsibilities including maintaining case files, briefing supervisors, and meeting with forensic analysts. These same detectives can assist on other cases but should be limited in the number to achieve optimum success.[61]

Jurisdictional and Other Issues

An important element of case processing is a determination of whether the crime was actually committed within the investigator's jurisdiction. This can be difficult as victims do not always remember crossing over borders from one city or town to the next or even to another state. For example, a sexual assault victim may have met their assailant at a bar (or a ride-sharing program) in one municipality, but the crime may have actually occurred in a neighboring suburb. Police must first determine that they have jurisdiction to investigate the criminal offense: Is it where the victim and offender met, where they traveled, or the actual scene of the crime? Was the victim kidnapped at location 1, threatened in location 2, and assaulted in location 3? If not, the case must be handed to the correct investigating agency where the criminal activity occurred. To solve some of these issues, it has become routine to set up multi-jurisdictional task forces to investigate crimes and identify culprits. The following Focus on Policing: A Multi-Jurisdictional Investigation feature discusses one such effort.

Solving Cases

Once it has been determined that a crime has been committed and that it is in the appropriate jurisdiction, cases are assigned to a detective. Detectives and/or their supervisors must screen cases to decide how many resources to put into each one. These screenings are based on the seriousness of the crime and a number of solvability factors, including the cooperation of the victim.

Detectives must cover all facts pertaining to the complaint by gathering and preserving evidence and following up on clues. They are responsible for recovering stolen property. The detectives are responsible for identification of the perpetrator as well as for locating and apprehending the perpetrator. Finally, detectives have direct contact with prosecutors. They aid in the prosecution of the offender by providing evidence of guilt that is admissible in courts, and usually involves testifying as a witness in court.

Gathering Information

Detectives may successfully identify a criminal suspect if these methods pan out. But that is only the beginning of building an airtight case. Next, the detectives attempt to gain as much information as possible from their suspect, perhaps even getting them to confess.

In a study of investigation techniques, Martin Innes found that police detectives rely heavily on interviews, emerging technologies, and forensic evidence to reconstruct or manufacture a narrative of the crime, creating in a sense the "story" that sets out how, where, and why the incident took place.[62] To create their story, contemporary detectives typically use a three-pronged approach as follows:[63]

Focus on Policing

A Multi-Jurisdictional Investigation

Recently, the Olympia Police Department in Washington received a report of two armed robberies, one at a local Taco Bell and the second at a nearby Bank of America. In the days following, 14 similar robberies were carried out in the surrounding area, all committed by an unknown subject with similar physical descriptions and patterns of behavior. The suspect, a White man in his 30s, was seen armed with a handgun, wore a mask, and had a hooded sweatshirt pulled over his head. Then, during a robbery at a *Pizza Time* restaurant, the suspect fired his weapon during a struggle with an employee, ratcheting up the seriousness of his crimes. More *Pizza Time* stores were robbed, and another bank was robbed. Soon after, the same man robbed the Umpqua Bank located in Olympia; this was followed up with five more armed bank robberies.

Local detectives and analysts from the Olympia PD, and nearby agencies including Pierce County Sheriff's Department, Puyallup PD, Thurston County Sheriff's Office, and Kent PD, began working together to develop possible leads. The detectives conducted surveillance details at regional banks. During a stakeout at one of Olympia's westside banks, detectives from the Olympia Police Department noted a suspicious dark gray vehicle that was slowly rolling through the parking lot. While trying to follow the car, they were able to capture the license plate. About 30 minutes after losing sight of the vehicle, another bank, the Columbia Bank, was robbed at gunpoint.

Local detectives soon spotted the dark gray sedan and followed it to a residence in the Shelton,

Washington, area where it was pulled into a garage. When the driver reemerged and drove away, the detectives noted the vehicle had switched license plates from the time the driver pulled into the garage. They continued to follow the unknown suspect to Olympia, Washington, where he began driving around local banks, parking just prior to closing hours at the Olympia Federal Bank. Detectives, already in place, observed the subject exit his vehicle, wearing similar items that were worn in previous robberies, and begin walking toward the front door of the bank. The suspect, Eric M. Collier, was then taken into custody by police; though armed with a handgun, he submitted without an escalation of force. Collier eventually pleaded guilty and received a 29-year prison sentence.

Critical Thinking

1. What other agencies aside from law enforcement might help police solve crimes?

2. In *The Silence of the Lambs,* the FBI called on a psychiatrist to help identify a serial killer (of course, it turns out the psychiatrist was also a serial killer!!). But who else might help? Social workers? Accountants? Programmers?

Sources: FBI Seattle, Public Affairs Specialist Ayn Dietrich-Williams, "Prolific Bank Robber Captured with FBI Assistance," January 21, 2015, https://www.fbi.gov/contact-us/field-offices/seattle/news/press-releases/prolific-bank-robber-captured-with-fbi-assistance; Amelia Dickson, "Eric M. Collier, 36, Was Sentenced to 29 Years, Three Months in Prison after Pleading Guilty Thursday to a String of Bank and Pizza Restaurant Robberies," *The Olympian,* August 31, 2015.

- **Specific focus.** Detectives interview witnesses, gather evidence, record events, and collect facts that are available at the immediate crime scene.

- **General coverage.** This process involves detectives who (a) canvass the neighborhood and make observations; (b) conduct interviews with friends, families, and associates; (c) contact coworkers or employers for information regarding victims and suspects; and (d) construct victim/suspect timelines to outline their whereabouts before the incident.

- **Informative data gathering.** Detectives use modern technology to collect records of cell phones and pagers, computer hard drives (tablets, laptops, notebooks, desktops, and servers), diaries, notes, and documents. Information includes data used by persons of interest in the investigation that tell about their lives, interactions with others, and geographical location.

Solvability Factors

Certain solvability factors can increase the probability of clearing a case. There is a lack of consensus among researchers about what factors affect solvability. In aggregate the research has shown that extralegal or those characteristics of victims that are unrelated to the crime, as well as the location of their homicide, do not influence **clearance** rates.[64]

So what influences the solvability of cases for detectives? Incidents with more physical evidence, witnesses, and information are easier to investigate and solve. The most common predictor of whether a case is cleared is if the suspect is named. Most clearances are in fact due to the identification of a known perpetrator.

Violent crime receives more investigative attention than property since the nature of violent crime means that the victim had direct contact with the suspect and they can identify the offender.[65] It is important to remember that while witnesses can be crucial to solving a crime, there are some issues associated with their use. Human memory often is unreliable and distorted. Police are, and must be mindful of, challenges associated with eyewitness testimony. Regardless of evidence, detectives develop a working style and orientation. These styles are discussed in the following Focus on Policing: Detective Types feature.

clearance

The identification of the offender and the development of sufficient evidence to charge them and take them into custody.

Focus on Policing

Detective Types

Not all detectives approach an investigation in the same fashion. On TV, we see that some detectives rely on their instincts; in a big case, they rely on inferences and hunches. In reality, most detectives trust their knowledge gleaned from experience and training and assume human behavior follows familiar and routine patterns. In a case of murder, many assume that the victim knew their attacker because that is the typical pattern they have encountered during their careers. Others are more science-oriented and believe that modern forensics is the key to unraveling a case; an eyewitness may err, but DNA is infallible.

To better understand how detectives approach their job, Dean Dabney conducted interviews with homicide investigators in a metropolitan police force located in the Southeast. He found that detectives can be placed into one of four different and distinct groups based on their investigation style. The four include:

Victim-centered detectives: While these detectives would normally focus on the victim, because of the nature of homicide (there is no living victim), the detective becomes involved with friends and family members, who are pressing them to apprehend the assailant as a means of getting closure. The detective views themself as an advocate for the victim and the family, while others either avoid or dislike the emotionally charged issues surrounding homicide victims and their families.

Avenging the death and bringing closure to the victim's family become primary motivators underlying their work as homicide detectives. To a detective with this orientation, making the phone call and telling the family that the perpetrator has been found guilty is what counts the most. The victim-centered homicide detective is focused on the end game of the investigation (i.e., the arrest and conviction), not the process. These detectives rely on emotion more than calculated logic to guide the direction and substance of their investigation.

Offender-centered detectives: Offender-centered detectives are driven by a desire to match wits with suspects, track down the guilty party, and personally hold them accountable for their crimes. A sense of competitiveness and righteousness lead them to fixate on the person suspected of murder rather than the victim. Rather than comfort families and waste time on "bonding" they want to get criminals off the street so they cannot do it again. These investigators exhibit clear disdain for the "criminal element" and see it as their core mission to hunt them down and bring them to justice. The last thing they want is for the culprit to "get away with it" and plan their

(Continued)

next attack. It should come as no surprise that, without exception, these detectives display fierce interrogation skills and are dogged in their pursuit of confessions. Conversely, they are not smooth talkers and generally lack confidence and results when talking with witnesses or conducting impromptu canvass activities in the community seeking to generate leads.

Case-centered detectives: These detectives are puzzle-solvers. Rather than focus on the human element, they fixate on the available evidence and seek to arrange the clues into a sound casefile that will achieve an arrest and conviction. They gather information on the victim, suspect if any, and try to tie all the information together. They try to out-think their opponents, the criminal suspect, and use the information to shake them up. They try to think outside the box and stay one step ahead of the perpetrator. For them, solving the case is more of a process of piecing together the case more than it is about the thrill of the outcome or achievements along the way. For the case-centered detective, the moves one makes during the chess game are more important than beating the opponent. The case-centered detectives prefer to work alone as opposed to collaborating with others along the way.

These detectives adopt a very unemotional approach to the cases they work; instead, they are very methodical and practical, with high levels of focus and determination in connecting the dots to solve the case. They pose few challenges for supervisors who trust their approach and success. They avoid the human side of the job (e.g., the limelight and camaraderie of the unit) and choose to engulf themselves in the case and all of the possibilities that it presents.

Hybrid detective: These investigators exhibit characteristics from two or more work styles. They may care about the family and friends of the victim but are still focused on catching the perpetrator. Their interests and goals are split rather than focused. Some investigators who fall into the hybrid category do so because they are new to the unit and are still making sense of the work world. Consequently, they are finding their way around and not ready to commit to one style or another.

Critical Thinking

Which detective type do you think would be most effective? Or do you think they are probably equally likely to solve crimes?

Sources: D. Dabney, "Doing death work: A typology of how homicide detectives orient to their work," *Policing and Society* 30 (2020), 777–794; S. Tong and B. Bowling, "Art, craft and science of detective work," *The Police Journal* 79 (2006), 323–329.

LO6

Appraise the effectiveness of investigation operations.

▶ Evaluating Investigations

Serious criticism has been leveled at detectives for getting bogged down in paperwork and being relatively inefficient in clearing cases. One famous study of 153 detective bureaus conducted by Peter Greenwood and Joan Petersilia found that a great deal of a detective's time was spent in unproductive work and that investigative expertise did little to solve cases. Half of all detectives could be replaced without negatively affecting crime clearance rates, a topic covered in more detail in the following Focus on Policing: RAND Detective Study feature.[66]

DC Studio/Shutterstock.com

Evaluations of detective work such as the RAND study have found it to be ineffective. Some departments are working to improve investigation effectiveness by using technology. Here investigators are shown discussing crime scene evidence with a remote team during an online video call meeting. Technological advances in DNA and fingerprint identification have also boosted investigation effectiveness.

Are Investigations Effective?

Generally speaking, police departments spend a great deal of time, money, and other resources to operate the investigative function. Nonetheless, little is known about how effective investigations are and whether the detective function is a good use of agency resources. One of the most well-known studies that sought to help us better understand the effectiveness of criminal investigations was the RAND Detective Study.

Focus on Policing

RAND Detective Study

In 1973, the RAND Corporation researched criminal investigation practices that are used in major metropolitan police agencies across the United States. The purpose of the study was to assess the value and effectiveness of various investigatory tactics and activities. The study sought to:

1. Describe investigation and organizational practices related to felonies.
2. Assess the contribution of police investigations to the achievement of criminal justice goals.
3. Assess the use of new technology and systems that enhance investigative performance.
4. Examine how investigative effectiveness is related to organizational variables such as staffing procedures and scheduling.

Research Design

The researchers sent surveys to all municipal and county law enforcement agencies with 150 or more full-time employees or jurisdictions with a population over 100,000, resulting in a sample of 300 agencies. The researchers achieved just over a 50 percent response rate. This response rate, while not unusual, is somewhat of a limitation. The final sample was 153 agencies. The survey included questions about the following topics:

- Department characteristics
- The process of investigator deployment
- Training
- The use of evidence techniques
- Types of specialization
- Police and prosecutor interaction
- How cases are assigned
- The use of technology
- Clearance and arrest rates

The researchers also conducted case studies of 29 agencies in the sample. These agencies were selected based on survey responses, with an emphasis on Kansas City since the researchers had detailed information on their detectives. The researchers first conducted on-site interviews with detectives about their work, including in-depth observations of the detectives to better understand the processes and their interactions. As part of the case study, they also talked to prosecutors and victims.

Findings

The most important finding was that this study confirmed prior research that clearance and arrest rates are not good measures of the effectiveness of investigations. These outcomes are sometimes measuring different results. For example, one arrest can sometimes clear multiple crimes if the same offender is responsible for multiple crimes. If the police catch a burglar, the police may find evidence of several burglaries; thus, the one identified perpetrator is responsible for several unsolved crimes.

The researchers found that most detective work is superficial, routine, and nonproductive. In fact, most cases only receive cursory attention and some are not investigated at all. This means that the most attention given to some crimes is reading the incident report. Of the cases that do get attention, detectives often spend less than one day. Most of the time, a detective spends is devoted to reviewing reports, files, and attempting to locate and interview witnesses.

The RAND Study shows that the critical factor to solving a case is the information the victim and witness provide and not necessarily what the police do as part of evidence collection and sleuthing. This tells us that community trust matters and that detectives that have better relationships with the community may have better outcomes. More specifically, the researchers found:

- In 30 percent of cases, patrol makes the arrest at the crime scene or shortly thereafter;
- In 50 percent of the cases, the perpetrator is already known, so all that has to be done is locate them and make the arrest;
- Twenty percent of the cases are solved through detective work—most of which includes help from the community, which provides information; and

(Continued)

- The RAND researchers estimated that really as little as 2.7 percent of cases are solved by detective work. In many agencies, detectives have high caseloads but only work a few and the rest remain backlogged.

There were other findings as well. Researchers found that the investigative process is more complicated than previously thought. While the work of a detective results in issuance of an arrest warrant, sometimes patrol officers arrest the suspect rather than the detective. For example, if the suspect is also known to be in a gang, the warrant may be given to the gang unit to execute. Researchers found that police organizations can always make clearance rates go up by rating many crimes as unfounded (no evidence to support the claim). If there are fewer crimes to solve, there is a better chance you can increase clearances.

Critical Thinking

Despite the fact that detective work is glamorized in the media, the research shows that investigations are not as effective as hoped. Would police agencies be better off defunding detectives and putting the money elsewhere?

Source: P. Greenwood and J. Petersilia, *The Criminal Investigation Process: Summary and Policy Implications*, ed. Peter Greenwood et al. (Santa Monica, CA: RAND Corporation, 1975), http://www.rand.org /pubs/papers/P6352.html.

Post-RAND Evaluations

In addition to the RAND Study, researchers looked more closely at Kansas City to see how detectives spend their time. They found that detectives spend 45 percent of their time on non-case specific activities such as administration and general surveillance or intelligence. Fifty-five percent of a detective's time is spent on actual cases, many of which do not get solved. The RAND Study found that for the agency's studies, the lack of resources is not the reason for low clearances and that adding more detectives will not improve this rate. They recommended that "walk-through cases" be handled by patrol to free up detectives for more difficult cases and that detectives work with a patrol in a team policing environment.

In a more recent effort to evaluate the effectiveness of investigations, Anthony Braga and Desiree Dusseault studied the adoption of a problem-solving approach by homicide detectives in the Boston Police Department. Boston police engaged a problem-oriented policing approach to improve their post-homicide criminal investigation processes and practices in response to lower-than-average clearance rates. Their analyses suggest that the intervention significantly increased key investigative activities and improved Boston homicide clearance rates.[67]

Although some questions still remain about the effectiveness of investigations, police detectives do make valuable contributions to police work because their skilled interrogation and case-processing techniques are essential to eventual criminal conviction.[68] In a majority of cases that are solved, the perpetrator is identified at the scene of the crime by patrol officers, witnesses, or victims. Research by the Police Executive Research Forum (PERF) shows that if a crime is reported while in progress, the police only have about a 33 percent chance of making an arrest. The probability of arrest declines to roughly 10 percent if the crime is reported after one minute of being committed. The chance of arrest falls to 5 percent if the crime is reported 15 minutes after it occurs. As the time between the crime and the arrest grows, the chances of a conviction are also reduced, probably because the ability to recover evidence is lost. To put it another way, the longer the gap between commission of a crime and the placing of the investigation into the hands of detectives, the less likely the perpetrator will be identified and arrested.[69]

Forensic Issues

One issue with investigation effectiveness is the accuracy of forensic evidence. The *Chicago Tribune*'s "Forensics Under the Microscope" series suggests that all is not well in the world of forensic sciences. Such concerns were echoed in a more recent National Academy of Sciences (NAS) report entitled *Strengthening Forensic Science in the United States: A Path Forward.* The authors of the report highlighted a series of problems with the forensic sciences, many of which are not well known to people on the outside—and particularly not to those who owe their knowledge of forensics and investigations to fictional television programs.

A National Research Council (NRC) of the NAS report asserts that aside from DNA testing, no forensic method had been rigorously shown to consistently and reliably establish a connection between evidence and a specific person. The report calls for major reforms and new research. The report states that rigorous and mandatory certification programs for forensic scientists are currently lacking as are strong standards and protocols for analyzing and reporting on evidence.[70] Here are some of those problems.

- **Case backlog.** The NAS called attention to another report in which it was learned that federal, state, and local laboratories reported a backlog of nearly 500,000 requests for forensic analysis. This backlog has been made even more serious by requests for quick test results. Labs are having a difficult time keeping up.

- **DNA demands.** The ascendancy of DNA evidence and the opportunities to use it during investigations has further burdened crime labs. Although the NAS, along with other experts and commissions, has heralded the advent of DNA testing as valuable for criminal investigation, there is only so much it can do. According to the NAS report, "DNA evidence comprises only about 10 percent of case work and is not always relevant to a particular case. Even if DNA evidence is available, it will assist in solving a crime only if it supports an evidential hypothesis that makes guilt or innocence more likely. For example, the fact that DNA evidence of a victim's spouse is found in the house in which the couple lived and where the murder took place proves nothing. The fact that the spouse's DNA is found under the fingernails of the victim who put up a struggle may have very different significance."

- **Questionable evidence.** Now that DNA evidence is regarded as a gold standard in criminal investigations, this has started to cast doubt on convictions secured through other, more traditional types of evidence. According to the report, "The fact is that many forensic tests—such as those used to infer the source of tool marks or bite marks—have never been exposed to stringent scientific scrutiny . . . Even fingerprint analysis has been called into question."

- **Errors.** The NAS also called attention to several disturbing examples of errors and fraud in the forensic sciences. In one case, a state-mandated examination of the West Virginia State Police laboratory revealed that the convictions of more than 100 people were in doubt. Another scandal involving the Houston Crime Laboratory came to light in 2003. An investigation revealed "routine failure to run essential scientific controls, failure to take adequate measures to prevent contamination of samples, failure to adequately document work performed and results obtained, and routine failure to follow correct procedures for computing statistical frequencies."

- **Incompatible fingerprint identification systems.** Law enforcement agencies around the country have developed and put in place automated fingerprint identification systems in an effort to solve crimes. The problem, according to the NAS, is that there is inadequate integration of these systems.

- **Lack of preparation for mass disasters.** According to the NAS, "Threats to food and transportation, concerns about nuclear and cyber security, and the need to develop rapid responses to chemical, nuclear, radiological, and biological threats underlie the need to ensure that there is a sufficient supply of adequately trained forensic specialists . . . [but] public crime laboratories are insufficiently prepared to handle mass disasters."

- **The CSI effect.** The so-called "CSI effect," named for the popular television programs, is concerned with the real-world implications of Hollywood's fictional spin on the forensic sciences and criminal investigations. The NAS found that some prosecutors believe they must make their in-court presentations as visually appealing as possible in an effort to please jurors who think they understand forensic work from having watched their favorite television programs. Attempts to satisfy such unrealistic expectations may possibly compromise the pursuit of justice.

Improving Investigations

A number of efforts have been made to revamp and improve investigation procedures. One practice has been to give patrol officers greater responsibility for conducting preliminary investigations at the scene of the crime. In addition, specialized units, such as homicide or burglary squads, now operate over larger areas and can bring specific expertise to bear. Technological advances in DNA and fingerprint identification have also boosted investigation effectiveness. Investigations also improve with cooperative victims. If there are better relations between the police and the community, then more information will likely be shared with the police, helping them solve more crimes.

One reason for investigation ineffectiveness is that detectives often lack sufficient resources to carry out a lengthy ongoing probe of any but the most serious cases. Research shows the following:[71]

- **Unsolved cases.** Almost 50 percent of burglary cases are screened out by supervisors before assignment to a detective for a follow-up investigation. Of those assigned, 75 percent are dropped after the first day of the follow-up investigation. Although robbery cases are more likely to be assigned to detectives, 75 percent of them are also dropped after one day of investigation.

- **Length of investigation.** The vast majority of cases are investigated for no more than four hours stretching over three days. An average of 11 days elapse between the initial report of a crime and the suspension of the investigation.

- **Sources of information.** Early in an investigation, the focus is on the victim; as the investigation is pursued, the emphasis shifts to the suspect. The most critical information for determining the case outcome is the name and description of the suspect and related crime information. Victims are most often the source of information. Unfortunately, witnesses, informants, and members of the police department are consulted far less often. However, when these sources are tapped, they are likely to produce useful information.

■ **Effectiveness.** Preliminary investigations by patrol officers are critical. In situations in which the suspect's identity is not known immediately after the crime is committed, detectives make an arrest in less than 10 percent of all cases.

Given these findings, the effectiveness of detective work may be improved if greater emphasis is placed on collecting physical evidence at the scene of the crime, identifying witnesses, checking departmental records, and using informants. The probability of successfully settling or clearing a case is significantly improved if patrol officers gather evidence at the scene of a crime and effectively communicate it to detectives working the case. Cooperation of community members is crucial in this step of the investigation. Also recommended is the use of targeted investigations that direct attention at a few individuals, such as career criminals, who are known to have engaged in the behavior under investigation.

The Victim Experience

In examining the role of detectives, we must also consider how victims fit into the picture. Research suggests that some crime victims are traumatized during the criminal justice process, a phenomenon dubbed *secondary victimization.* Rape victims in particular often relive certain aspects of the initial incident, perhaps when testifying at trial or while interacting with investigators soon after calling police. Shana Maier conducted interviews with a number of rape victim advocates, one of whom reported:

> . . . a lot of police don't have training on sexual assault. And if you have just been raped by a man and you have a man coming in who is talking down to you in a way or making it feel like it is your fault, asking questions like, "Well, did you go with him to his room? Were you alone with him in his room?" Things like that, it tends to make you feel like it was your fault.[72]

This is not to suggest that the police are uniformly insensitive to the plight of sexual assault victims. Much has changed in the past few decades. More attention is now being paid to the victim experience, especially in sensitive cases involving sexual assault. Serious strides have been made in the criminal justice system and beyond to ensure victims are not forgotten, and the police are often trained in how to deal appropriately with crimes in which the secondary victimization potential looms large.

The Big Picture

Moving into other areas of criminal activity, some domestic violence victims have reported unpleasant experiences in the investigative process. Others believe that the system did not take their case seriously enough. Additional research published by the National Institute of Justice (NIJ) confirms as much. Domestic violence victims who felt the police did not handle the initial incident effectively were less likely to report subsequent incidents, which of course makes it more difficult to identify and apprehend the perpetrator. This line of research thus suggests that the police need to take great care in investigating such cases, not just to make victims "feel good," but to make sure offenders are held accountable.

Homicide is a special case. Obviously, the immediate victim cannot be "revictimized," but surviving family members, other close relatives, and friends sometimes are. These "co-victims" are often impacted by post-traumatic stress disorder (PTSD) symptoms, stress, physical illness, loss of trust, intense grief, and a host of other ailments. And they, too, occasionally report unpleasant interactions with criminal justice officials. A study by Paul Stretesky and his colleagues found that the vast majority of homicide co-victims were dissatisfied with their level of communication with investigators, especially in so-called "cold cases," those in which the offender has successfully eluded authorities for a long time. Co-victims reported frustration with a dwindling level of communication over time, staff turnover, and a general lack of updates concerning the status of the case. Their experiences are not particularly surprising, though; investigators have a lot on their plates and it is difficult to pour slim resources into the pursuit of perpetrators who may never be found. Even so, steps should be taken to encourage victim involvement, communication, and cooperation for as long as possible during the investigative process.

Summary

LO1   Describe the reality of the police role.

Police officers are asked to deal with hundreds of incidents each year, and crime fighting is only a small part of their daily routine. A great deal of an officer's time is spent handling minor disturbances, service calls, and administrative duties. It is more common for police officers to respond to a complaint about music being too loud during a party than being asked to deal with a serious violent felony. Although police handle thousands of calls each year, relatively few result in an arrest for a serious crime such as a robbery or burglary.

LO2   Analyze 9-1-1 and patrol operations.

As a result of the development of 9-1-1, patrol is largely deployed by citizen calls. Therefore, most modern police work is reactive driven by citizens' use of 9-1-1. This mode of communication allows the public to call the police to fix everything and places the police as "social repair people" who must be ready to take on all challenges.

Many citizens use 9-1-1 because it is convenient; some have been socialized into calling the police to solve their problems and restore order. This can include wide-ranging circumstances, including neighbors who are too noisy, a family conflict, or a fight on the street. Sometimes people call the police with malicious intent. They provide "misleading" information as a prank called swatting, that draws law enforcement into fake emergencies. Officers are placed in danger as unsuspecting residents may try to defend themselves.

LO3   Explain how police patrol can be a deterrent to crime.

According to deterrence theory, the visible presence of patrol cars on the street and the rapid deployment of police officers to the scene of the crime are viewed as particularly effective law enforcement techniques. Nonetheless, the prevailing research shows that patrol response time has little effect on the ability of police to deter crime. One reason is that the interval between the commission of the crime and its discovery is often significant, especially for property crimes. After discovering a crime, it is not unusual to delay calling the police. There is also a significant interval between a call and the dispatch of the patrol car; there is also travel time to reach the crime scene.

LO4   Evaluate alternative methods of patrol.

Alternative methods of patrol such as foot patrol and hotspots involve focusing police patrol resources on small units of geography like street blocks or even single addresses that have high levels of criminal activity. Since the highest amounts of crime are concentrated in selected geographic regions, increasing police presence specifically in these areas should produce substantial reductions in crime. These interventions typically target serious offenses, including aggravated assault and robbery, firearm-related crime, and street-level drug trafficking. Research shows the hotspot strategy is an effective law enforcement tool for achieving short-run reductions in crime. Hotspot strategies focus on efforts to disrupt the dynamics that allow crime to occur. There are a number of strategies that police can use in hotspots, including directed patrol, foot patrol, or enhanced drug enforcement.

While effective, there is concern about a displacement effect, merely moving crime to other locales. There is also some concern that aggressive police tactics will harm public perceptions of police: crime control gains in the short run may be offset by reduced cooperation and compliance by citizens in the long term.

LO5   Summarize the organization of a detective bureau.

Larger departments have specialized units that focus on individual crimes like homicide, sexual assault, and narcotics. Other larger agencies will have major crimes divisions that focus on solving all felony offenses. Smaller agencies will have detectives who focus on investigating all crimes. Many police departments have moved to a decentralized method of assigning detectives. There are also specialty squads that help in areas such as forensics. Some jurisdictions maintain vice squads, which are usually staffed by sworn officers who work in plain clothes, and not in traditional uniforms, or detectives specializing in victimless crimes, such as prostitution or gambling.

LO6   Appraise the effectiveness of investigation operations.

Like many patrol officers, detectives engage in a wide ranging and diverse set of job-related activities, from going undercover to testifying in court, but their biggest tasks involve reactive investigations. Detective work is unlike what we see on television. This section includes research like the Rand Detective Study that examines the effectiveness of different investigatory tactics. Further, case solvaibility factors as well as the different organization.

Key Terms

order maintenance, 89
peacekeeping, 89
beats, 90
swatting, 92

foot patrol, 96
hotspot policing, 98
situational crime prevention (SCP), 99

police legitimacy, 100
vice squads, 102
downstream orientation, 104
clearance, 107

Notes

1. Amanda Jackson, "A Texas Officer Runs into a Burning House and Saves an 8-year-old Boy," *CNN*, July 8, 2020.
2. Elizabeth Davis, Anthony Whyde, and Lynn Langton, "Contacts Between Police and the Public," 2015 (Washington, DC: Bureau of Justice Statistics, 2018).
3. Susannah N. Tapp and Elizabeth J. Davis, "Contacts Between Police and the Public," 2020 (Washington, DC: Bureau of Justice Statistics, 2020), https://bjs.ojp.gov/sites/g/files/xyckuh236/files /media/document/cbpp20.pdf.
4. Federal Bureau of Investigation, Crime in the United States 2019, Persons Arrested.
5. Yue Zhang and Donald E. Brown, "Police Patrol Districting Method and Simulation Evaluation Using Agent-based Model & GIS," Security Informatics (accessed May 25, 2023).
6. Jacob Kaplan and Aaron Chalfin, "More Cops, Fewer Prisoners?" *Criminology and Public Policy* 18 (2019), 71–200.
7. Brian A. Reaves, *Local Police Departments, 2013: Personnel, Policies, and Practices.* (Washington, DC: Bureau of Justice Statistics, May 2015), p. 2.
8. Bernard Condon and Todd Richmond, "Duty To Intervene: Floyd Cops Spoke Up but Didn't Step In," *Associated Press,* June 7, 2020, https://www.wkrg.com/news/duty-to-intervene-floyd-cops -spoke-up-but-didnt-step-in/, accessed May 25, 2023.
9. Karen L. Amendola, David Weisburd, E. Hamilton, Greg Jones, Meghan Slipka, and Anneke Heitmann, "The Shift Length Experiment: What We Know About 8-, 10-, and 12-hour Shifts in Policing," *Police Foundation. Advancing Policing Through Innovation and Science* (2011).
10. Shelley S. Hyland and Elizabeth Davis, Local Police Departments, 2016: Personnel.
11. https://www.nena.org/?page=911overviewfacts.
12. David A. Klinger and George S. Bridges, "Measurement Error in Calls-for-Service as an Indicator of Crime," *Criminology* 35, no. 4 (1997), 705–726.
13. FBI, "Don't Make the Call The New Phenomenon of 'Swatting,'" February 4, 2008.
14. Ryan W. Miller, "His 'Swatting' Prank Call Caused a Man's Death. Now He'll Serve 20 Years in Prison," *USA Today*, March 30, 2019, https://www.usatoday.com/story/news /nation/2019/03/30/swatting-tyler-barriss-get-20-years-hoax -911-call-andrew-finch-death/3320061002/, accessed May 25, 2023.
15. Carlena Orosco and Janne E. Gaub. 2022. "I am doing my part, you are doing your part": the sworn-civilian divide in police dispatching. *Policing: An International Journal*, Vol. 46 No. 1, pp. 164–178. https://doi.org/10.1108/PIJPSM-07-2022-0090.
16. Christine N. Famega, James Frank, and Lorraine Mazerolle, "Managing Police Patrol Time: The Role of Supervisor Directives," *Justice Quarterly* 22, no. 4 (2005), 540–559.
17. Officer Luke Bonkiewicz, Lincoln (NE) Police Department, "The IMPACTT of a Patrol Officer: Evaluating Productivity Metrics," July 13, 2020, nij.ojp.gov, https://nij.ojp.gov/topics/articles /impactt-patrol-officer-evaluating-productivity-metrics.
18. Lawrence W. Sherman, "Policing for Crime Prevention," in *Preventing Crime: What Works, What Doesn't, What's Promising*, eds. Lawrence W. Sherman, Denise C. Gottfredson, Doris L. MacKenzie, John Eck, Peter Reuter, and Shawn W. Bushway (Washington, DC: National Institute of Justice, 1998), Ch. 8.
19. FBI, Uniform Crime Reporting Program, 2022, https://www.fbi .gov/services/cjis/ucr.
20. Police Foundation, *The Newark Foot Patrol Experiment* (Washington, DC: Police Foundation, 1981).
21. Robert C. Trojanowicz, Richard Gleason, Bonnie Poland, and David Sinclair, "Community Policing: Community Input Into Police Policy-Making. The National Neighborhood Foot Patrol Center," U.S. Department of Justice. Office of Justice Programs. NCJ Number 105158.

22. Robert Trojanowicz, Evaluating a Neighborhood Foot Patrol Program: The Flint, Michigan Project. In Dennis Rosenbaum (ed.), *Community Crime Prevention: Does It Work?* (Beverly Hills, CA: SAGE Publications, 1987).

23. Charles Stewart Mott Foundation, Community Policing—Making the Case for Citizen Involvement, 1987, https://www.ncjrs.gov/App/Publications/abstract.aspx?ID=104831.

24. David Levinson, *Encyclopedia of Crime and Punishment,* Vol. 1. (Thousand Oaks, CA: SAGE Publications, 2001).

25. Jerry H. Ratcliffe, Travis Taniguchi, Elizabeth R. Groff, and Jennifer D. Wood, "The Philadelphia Foot Patrol Experiment: A Randomized Controlled Trial of Police Patrol Effectiveness in Violent Crime Hotspots," *Criminology* 49, no. 3 (2011).

26. Cory Haberman and Wendy Stiver, "The Dayton Foot Patrol Program: An Evaluation of Hot Spots Foot Patrols in a Central Business District" *Police Quarterly* 22 (2018), 247–277.

27. Cory Haberman and Wendy Stiver, "Using Officers' Perspectives to Guide the Implementation of Hot Spots Foot Patrols," *Policing & Society* 30 (2020), 920–932.

28. Eric L. Piza and Brian A. O'Hara, "Saturation Foot-Patrol in a High-Violence Area: A Quasi-Experimental Evaluation," *Justice Quarterly* 31 (2014), 693–718.

29. Cory Haberman and Wendy Stiver, "Using Officers' Perspectives to Guide the Implementation of Hot Spots Foot Patrols," *Policing and Society* 30 (2020), 920–932.

30. David Weisburd, "The Law of Crime Concentration and the Criminology of Place," *Criminology,* 53 (2015), 133–157.

31. Johanna Leigh, Sarah Dunnett, and Lisa Jackson, "Predictive Police Patrolling to Target Hotspots and Cover Response Demand," *Annals of Operations Research,* 283 (2019), p395–410.

32. David Weisburd, "Place-Based Policing." In *Ideas in American Policing*, Police Foundation, 2008.

33. Anthony Braga, Andrew Papachristos, and David Hureau, "Hot Spots Policing Effects on Crime," *Campbell Systematic Reviews* 8 (2012), 1–96.

34. Lawrence W. Sherman and David Weisburd, "General Deterrent Effects of Police Patrol in Crime 'Hot Spots': A Randomized, Controlled Trial," *Justice Quarterly* 12, no. 4 (1995), 625–648.

35. https://www.crimesolutions.gov/ProgramDetails.aspx?ID=58.

36. Anthony A. Braga and Brenda J. Bond, "Policing Crime and Disorder Hot Spots: A Randomized Controlled Trial," *Criminology* 46 (2008), 577–607.

37. Cordner, Gary W. 1981 The effects of directed patrol: A natural quasi-experiment in Pontiac. In J. Fyfe (ed.), *Contemporary Issues in Law Enforcement* (Beverly Hills, CA: SAGE).

38. Barak Ariel, Lawrence W. Sherman, and Mark Newton, "Testing Hot Spots Police Patrols against No Treatment Controls: Temporal and Spatial Deterrence Effects in the London Underground Experiment," *Criminology* 58, no. 8 (2019).

39. Geoffrey Barnes, Simon Williams, Lawrence W. Sherman, Jesse Parmar, Paul House, and Stephen A. Brown, "Sweet Spots of Residual Deterrence: A Randomized Crossover Experiment in Minimalist Police Patrol," file:///C:/Users/lboyd/Downloads/Sweet%20Spots%20Pre-Print%202020-07-13-1730-1.pdf, accessed May 25, 2023.

40. Roberto Santos and Rachel Santos, "Proactive Police Response in Property Crime Micro-time Hot Spots: Results from a Partially-Blocked Blind Random Controlled Trial," *Journal of Quantitative Criminology,* 2020, https://doi.org/10.1007/s10940-020-09456-8.

41. David Weisburd, Laura A. Wyckoff, Justin Ready, John E. Eck, Joshua C. Hinkle, and Frank Gajewski, "Does Crime Just Move around the Corner? A Controlled Study of Spatial Displacement and Diffusion of Crime Control Benefits," *Criminology* 44, no. 3 (2006), 549–592.

42. Richard Rosenfeld, Michael J. Deckard, and Emily Blackburn, "The Effects of Directed Patrol and Self-Initiated Enforcement on Firearm Violence: A Randomized Controlled Study of Hot Spot Policing," *Criminology* 52, no. 3 (2014), 428–449.

43. Evan T. Sorg, Jennifer D. Wood, Elizabeth R. Groff, and Jerry H. Ratcliffe, "Explaining Dosage Diffusion During Hot Spot Patrols: An Application of Optimal Foraging Theory to Police Officer Behavior," *Justice Quarterly* 34, no. 6 (2017), 1044–1068, doi: 10.1080/07418825.2016.1244286.

44. Ibid.

45. Christi Metcalfe and Justin Picketti, "The Extent and Correlates of Public Support for Deterrence Reforms and Hot Spots Policing," *Law & Society Review* 52 (2018), 471–502.

46. Andrew Wheeler, "Allocating Police Resources While Limiting Racial Inequality," *Justice Quarterly,* June 26, 2019, 842–868.

47. Ibid.

48. David Weisburd and Cody W. Telep, "Hot Spots Policing: What We Know and What We Need to Know," *Journal of Contemporary Criminal Justice* 30, no. 2 (2014), 200–220.

49. https://cops.usdoj.gov/html/dispatch/09-2021/civilian_personnel.html.

50. https://cops.usdoj.gov/html/dispatch/09-2021/civilian_personnel.html.

51. The Yakima Police Department, https://yakimapolice.org/online-police-reporting/

52. https://www.bjs.gov/index.cfm?ty=pbdetail&iid=2229.

53. Police Public Contacts Survey, https://www.bjs.gov/index.cfm?ty=pbdetail&iid=2229.

54. Alex Macleod, "The Contemporary Fictional Police Detective as Critical Security Analyst: Insecurity and Immigration in the Novels of Henning Mankell and Andrea Camilleri," *Security Dialogue* 45, no. 6 (2014), 515–529, http://www.jstor.org/stable/26292929, accessed May 26, 2023.

55. For a view of the modern detective, see William Sanders, *Detective Work: A Study of Criminal Investigations* (New York, NY: Free Press, 1977).

56. Brian Reaves, "Local Police Departments, 2013: Personnel, Policies, and Practices," Bureau of Justice Statistics, 2013, https://www.bjs.gov/content/pub/pdf/lpd13ppp.pdf.

57. David Lisak, Lori Gardinier, Sarah C. Nicksa, and Ashley. M. Cote, "False Allegations of Sexual Assault: An Analysis of Ten Years of Reported Cases," *Violence Against Women* 16 (2010), 1318–1334.

58. April Pattavina, Melissa Morabito, and Linda M. Williams, "Examining Connections between the Police and Prosecution in Sexual Assault Case Processing: Does the Use of Exceptional Clearance Facilitate a Downstream Orientation?," *Victims & Offenders* 11, no. 2 (2016), 315–334.

59. Jack Kuykendall, "The Municipal Police Detective: An Historical Analysis," *Criminology* 24 (1986), 175–202. doi:10.1111/j.1745-9125.1986.tb00382.x.

60. Aki Roberts and John M. Roberts, "Crime Clearance and Temporal Variation in Police Investigative Workload: Evidence from National Incident-Based Reporting System (NIBRS) Data," *Journal of Quantitative Criminology* 32, no. 4 (2016), 651–674.

61. Peter W. Greenwood, Jan M. Chaiken, Joan Petersilia, and Linda Prusoff, "The Criminal Investigation Process Volume III: Observations and Analysis," The National Institute of Law Enforcement and Criminal Justice, LEAA. Department of Justice, October 1975.

62. Martin Innes, *Investigating Murder: Detective Work and the Police Response to Criminal Homicide* (Clarendon Studies in Criminology) (London, England: Oxford University Press, 2003).

63. John B. Edwards, "Homicide Investigative Strategies," *FBI Law Enforcement Bulletin* 74 (2005), 11–21.

64. David L. Carter and Jeremy G. Carter, "Effective Police Homicide Investigations: Evidence from Seven Cities with High Clearance Rates," *Homicide Studies* 20, no. 2 (2016), 150–176.

65. Aki Roberts, "Adjusting Rates of Homicide Clearance by Arrest for Investigation Difficulty: Modeling Incident- and Jurisdiction-Level Obstacles," *Homicide Studies* 19, no. 3 (2015), 273–300.

66. Peter Greenwood and Joan Petersilia, *The Criminal Investigation Process: Summary and Policy Implications*, ed. Peter Greenwood et al. (Santa Monica, CA: RAND Corporation, 1975).

67. Anthony A. Braga and Desiree Dusseault, "Can Homicide Detectives Improve Homicide Clearance Rates?," *Crime & Delinquency,* 2016, https://doi.org/10.1177/0011128716679164.

68. Mark Willman and John Snortum, "Detective Work: The Criminal Investigation Process in a Medium-Size Police Department," *Criminal Justice Review* 9 (1984), 33–39.

69. Police Executive Research Forum, *Calling the Police: Citizen Reporting of Serious Crime* (Washington, DC: Police Executive Research Forum, 1981).

70. National Academy of Sciences, Strengthening Forensic Science in the United States: A Path Forward, 2009, https://www.nap.edu/read/12589/chapter/1.

71. John Eck, *Solving Crimes*: *The Investigation of Burglary and Robbery* (Washington, DC: Police Executive Research Forum, 1984).

72. Larry J. Siegel and John L. Worrall, *Introduction to Criminal Justice* (Cengage Learning, 2019), 219.

Chapter

5

The Evolving Responsibilities of Responding to Tragedy and the Accompanying Promise of Police Reform

Learning Objectives

LO1 Analyze the role of police in mass shootings and anti-terrorism activities.

LO2 Evaluate whether prevention is possible.

LO3 Describe the extent of terrorism against U.S. citizens.

LO4 Explain the effects that responding to mass casualties has on the police.

LO5 Recognize the concept of police reform.

LO6 Summarize the George Floyd Justice in Policing Act of 2020.

LO7 Analyze the concept of defunding the police.

LO8 State why reform efforts fail.

Chapter Outline

The role of policing is ever-changing based on the unpredictable events that happen in American society. While some police officers find this randomness an attractive part of the job, others may find it confusing and destabilizing. Take, for instance, the January 6, 2021, storming of the Capitol building by a group of insurgents looking to circumvent the outcome of the 2020 election. As the attack unfolded, a mob armed with chemical mace, hammers, poles, lances, and other weapons overcame the unarmed Capitol Police, stormed through barricades, entered the capitol building, and broke into the Senate chamber. Members of Congress were forced to flee just as they had begun counting Electoral College votes to confirm the presidential victory of Democrat Joe Biden. The mob seemed intent on finding and killing high-ranking government officials, including then–Vice President Mike Pence and House Speaker Nancy Pelosi. Frantic calls from senior officials were made as rioters pummeled Capitol police officers and vandalized the building. Vice President Pence tried to assert control, called the acting secretary of defense, and demanded that he "Clear the Capitol." Senate Majority Leader Chuck Schumer and Speaker Nancy Pelosi made similar appeals to military leaders, asking the U.S. Army to deploy the National Guard.

In addition to the vandalism and destruction of property, the attack left several police officers injured and resulted in the death of three Capital police officers, including U.S. Capitol Police Officer Brian Sicknick, who physically engaged with protesters. At the time, police made at least 68 arrests, 41 of them on Capitol grounds. Six months later, more than 580 people had been charged for their role in the insurrection.

The Capitol riot was merely one of a slew of unpredictable, high-tension events that have occurred during the past three decades, ranging from school shootings such as the one that occurred on April 20, 1999, at Columbine High School in Columbine, Colorado, to the terrorist attacks of September 11, 2001, that brought down the Twin Towers in New York. The police have been thrust into a response role in dealing with mass-casualty events. Events like these have made the term *active shooter* common in the American lexicon and have changed the way the police respond to active shooter events in public places.

How have these events and these new responsibilities affected the police and their role as public servants? In this chapter, we will first review the unpredictable and stress-producing acts that police must cope with and the mechanisms designed to effectively control these events. We then will turn to how coping with these incidents of random violence may have affected the average police officer and influenced police community relations.

LO1

Analyze the role of police in mass shootings and anti-terrorism activities.

active shooter

An individual actively engaged in killing or attempting to kill as many people as possible using a firearm.

Mass Shootings and Domestic Terrorism

Police have increasingly been called to respond to active shooter and mass shooting situations in a variety of settings ranging from schools like in Newtown Connecticut to music concerts as in Las Vegas, Nevada. An **active shooter** is an individual actively engaged in killing or attempting to kill as many people as possible using a firearm.[1] The shooter is an individual actively engaged in killing or attempting to kill people in a confined and populated area. In most cases, active shooters use firearms to attack as many victims as possible. For police, active shooter situations are unpredictable and evolve quickly. Because active shooter situations are often over within 10 to 15 minutes, a great deal of violence can occur before police are even able to arrive on the scene. Joel Capellan adds four additional elements:[2]

1. It may involve more than one individual at multiple locations.

2. It may include instances where the violence spills to other unintended victims.

3. Failed attempts or attempts where victims were only wounded will be included.

4. While the primary weapon must be a firearm, the offender is not limited to just firearms (e.g., knives, bats, explosives).

mass shootings

Shootings that involve four or more victims, taking place in a public location, with victims chosen randomly or for symbolic purposes.

hostage and barricaded suspect incidents

Incidents in which a suspect, usually armed with high-powered weapons or multiple weapons, has confined themselves in a building, structure, or area with limited access and egress and have taken a victim or victims hostage.

These situations overlap with rampage shootings. As Michael Rocque and Grant Duwe note that *rampage shooting* is a relatively new term used to describe **mass shootings** (generally defined as involving four or more victims), taking place in a public location, with victims chosen randomly or for symbolic purposes.[3] The Gun Violence Archive defines a mass shooting as an incident in which four or more people are shot or killed, excluding the shooter.[4] Regardless of how these shootings are categorized, they have dominated the media in recent decades and placed a strain on police resources and police officers themselves. The International Association of Chiefs of Police (IACP) also compares an active shooter incident to those of **hostage and barricaded suspect incidents**, where the suspect is typically armed with high-powered weapons or multiple weapons. These suspects often confined themselves in a building, structure, or area with limited access and egress and they have taken a victim or victims hostage. There are, however, some large differences between a barricaded suspect and an active shooter. Barricade suspect incidents may differ greatly from a characteristic active shooter incident because barricade situations typically give the initial arriving officers sufficient time to secure the immediate and adjacent areas and call for tactical back-up and a negotiator. The luxury of time allows officers time to keep bystanders at a safe distance. Active shooting situations are generally very different because they tend to develop and end very quickly and typically involve a fatal shooting involving three or more victims.[5] Take, for instance, the May 14, 2022, incident when an 18-year-old White man wearing military tactical gear with body armor and a rifle, drove over 200 miles and shot 13 people at a grocery store in a predominately Black neighborhood in Buffalo, New York, killing 10 and wounding three others in what authorities described as "racially motivated violent extremism." According to Buffalo police, the shooter shot 11 Black victims and two White victims in his rampage shooting, which he live-streamed on Twitch, a social media platform. After the shooting he surrendered to local police.[6] He reportedly posted a hate-filled racist manifesto to social media before the shooting. It is reported that he planned to shoot up a second location after leaving the store. Shortly after, on Sunday, May 16, 2022, a lone gunman walked into a church in Laguna Woods, California, and shot six people, killing one and critically wounding four. The gunman was rushed by churchgoers, subdued, and held until the police got there. He had two handguns in the incident.[7]

These situations can also be fluid where a mass shooting can transition into a hostage/barricade situation, such as what occurred on June 12, 2016, when Omar Mateen, a 29-year-old man, killed 49 people and wounded 53 more in a mass shooting at Pulse, a gay nightclub in Orlando, Florida. The siege ended when Orlando police officers shot and killed him after a three-hour standoff. As a result, police must be prepared to address these changing situations.

On a picturesque summer morning, Monday, July 4, 2022, a mass shooting took place during an Independence Day parade in Highland Park, Illinois. The shooting occurred at 10:14 A.M., roughly 15 minutes after the parade began. From a nearby rooftop, high above the parade route, a gunman fired down more than 70 rounds at the floats, parade watchers, and participants. Members of the high school marching band ran for their lives, still carrying their instruments. Bystanders scooped up young children and fled, while others tried to help people who were injured. When the shooting stopped, seven people were killed and at least 46 others were injured.

The accused shooter was 21-year-old Robert Eugene Crimo III, who had posted violent content on social media. The weapon used in this shooting was a high-powered rifle similar to the semiautomatic AR-15, was legally purchased with the help of his father. The gunman, using a high-capacity magazine, fired the weapon in rapid succession, emptied the magazine twice, and reloaded each time, using three magazines. After the shooting, the gunman left the rifle and evaded immediate capture in the minutes after the carnage by dressing as a woman and blending into the panicked crowd and walked to his mother's nearby house.

Authorities traced the gun left at the scene to the suspect and released his photo. He was apprehended later that afternoon, following a nine-hour-long search involving more than 100 law enforcement agencies. He was apprehended after a traffic stop and was taken into custody without incident. He was charged with seven counts of first-degree murder. At his first court hearing, he admitted to the shooting. The suspect previously purchased five firearms, including the rifle found at the scene, one found in his car, and other weapons seized from his father's home.[8]

Mass shooting events are more common than ever before. Let's take a snapshot in time and count mass shootings. July 4, 2022, was the 185th day of the year. There were 309 mass shootings reported in that time period.[9] That averaged out to more than 11 mass shootings per week in the United States in 2022. Mass shootings are a growing problem that the police must face every day. It clearly is a daunting task for officers.

School Shootings

school shooting

An armed attack involving the use of a firearm at any educational institution, such as an elementary, middle, or high school or university.

A **school shooting** is an armed attack involving the use of a firearm at any educational institution, such as an elementary, middle, or high school, or university. Fatal school shootings, such as the one that occurred at Sandy Hook Elementary School in Connecticut and the Robb Elementary School in Uvalde, Texas, are tragedies that have focused national attention on school violence. The most recent available data indicates that under 100 shootings occur each year and, of these, about 30 result in fatalities.[10] While this means there are about two or three school-associated shootings each week , this number must be balanced by the fact that there are about 50 million children in school and about 3 percent of students report carrying a weapon on school property. While this number has actually declined over the past decade, it still means about 1.5 million armed students come to school every day. Most violent deaths occur during transition times—immediately before and after the school day and during lunch. Violent deaths are more likely to occur at the start of each semester. Nearly 50 percent of homicide perpetrators gave some type of warning signal, such as making a threat or leaving a note, prior to the event. Firearms used in school-associated homicides and suicides come primarily from the perpetrator's home or from friends or relatives.

One of the more notorious shootings in recent years occurred in Parkland, Florida, at the Marjory Stoneman Douglas High School. Brief details of the shooting are included in the following Focus on Policing: Marjory Stoneman Douglas Shootings feature.

Joe Raedle/Getty Images News/Getty Images

A memorial at Marjory Stoneman Douglas High School for the 17 students and staff members killed on February 14, 2019, in Parkland, Florida. Responding to school shootings in an effective manner has become a significant aspect of contemporary policing.

Police Response

While these events are increasing, they are still relatively rare, making it difficult to plan for an effective response. Police agencies continue to adapt policies, procedures, and training to reflect the lessons that are learned from each new tragedy. The Police Executive Research Forum (PERF) notes, individuals involved in mass shootings rarely just snap—rather there is a buildup over time. They recommend that police work with other agencies to "connect the dots" and help troubled people before they have the opportunity to engage in violence.[11]

As for the shooting situations themselves, because these events evolve so rapidly, police must respond equally fast and with limited information. In these situations, response time does matter. Not waiting for SWAT teams and responding even a few minutes faster can save many lives. Time lost or time wasted by officers in delaying their response to these shootings most likely caused

Focus on Policing

Marjory Stoneman Douglas Shootings

On February 14, 2018, Nikolas Cruz brought a legally purchased .223-caliber AR-15 rifle concealed in a soft black case to the school and started shooting. He had previously been expelled from school for disciplinary reasons. Cruz had been troubled—adopted and then orphaned, he experienced behavioral health-related issues and had a fascination with weapons.

On this day, he went to the school with the intent of shooting and killing as many of his classmates as possible. Cruz entered the high school's Freshman Building on campus, which was mostly filled with freshmen students, and at 2:21 P.M. unpacked his rifle in a stairwell. In just under two minutes, he murdered 11 people and injured 13 others. In total, Cruz's attack lasted less than four minutes and left 17 dead at the school, making this the deadliest school shooting in the United States since Sandy Hook Elementary School in Newtown, Connecticut.

The shooter was able to blend in because he was recently a student at the school. He also knew and had participated in all of the training that students had received to respond to this type of tragedy.

Sheriff's deputies lost time retrieving bulletproof vests and did not go into the building immediately. There were problems with radio traffic and officers from various agencies were unable to communicate.

Cruz slipped away. He bought a drink at a Subway sandwich shop inside a nearby Walmart.

Later, he sat at a McDonald's for a few minutes before he was eventually caught and arrested by police. Broward sheriff's deputy school resource officer, Scot Peterson, who was assigned to the school that day, would later be accused of retreating during the shooting while victims were still under attack. Peterson was arrested in June 2019 and charged with seven counts of child neglect, three counts of culpable negligence, and one count of perjury. On November 2, 2022, after the jury deadlocked on whether he should be given the death penalty, Cruz was sentenced to life without parole.

Critical Thinking

1. Was there a delinquency problem in your high school? If so, how was it dealt with?

2. Should violent youths be suspended from school? Does this solution hurt or help?

3. Should teachers be trained in firearms and allowed to carry guns while in class?

Sources: Ray Sanchez, "'My school is being shot up,'" *CNN*, February 18, 2018, https://www.cnn.com/2018/02/18/us/parkland-florida-school-shooting-accounts/index.html; History.com Editors, "Teen gunman kills 17, injures 17 at Parkland, Florida high school," *History Channel*, February 14, 2018, https://www.history.com/this-day-in-history/parkland-marjory-stoneman-douglas-school-shooting.

more fatalities.[12] At the same time, there are limits to this quick response; solo entry by a police officer is more dangerous for the officer than a coordinated response.

Given the often lack of available planning time, training can be critical for these situations. The IACP recommends training and planning for all agencies and personnel likely to respond to active shootings. They advocate that this should include:[13]

■ "Practical, scenario-based exercises in operational environments such as schools, shopping malls, or office buildings;

■ Special emphasis on the primary mission objective of stopping the threat as opposed to rendering trauma care, extracting victims, and performing other actions; and

■ Joint training with local fire/EMS providers to ensure that all involved personnel understand their roles and responsibilities and those of other involved emergency responders;

■ Ensuring that resources between emergency responders are coordinated so appropriately trained personnel can gain access to victims as soon as possible;

- Establishing unified command practices in advance of an incident;
- Providing necessary equipment and related training for those tasked with immediate action, to include patrol rifles, helmets, enhanced ballistic and load-bearing vests, ballistic shields, window access and forced entry tools, and trauma kits."

Assessing Response

After tragedies like the shootings at Marjory Stoneman Douglas High School, there is frequently a call for prevention and questions about why no one noticed or intervened before the violence as well as for enhancing the police response. After the shooting, the Marjory Stoneman Douglas High School Public Safety Commission was created to understand what happened before, during, and after the attack. They wrote a 446-page report that included recommendations. In particular, the commission criticized the school district's security program that members believe allowed the shooter into the building with a weapon and the policies of the sheriff's department that prevented deputies from confronting him. Officers from nearby Coral Gables Police Department were praised for immediately entering the school. Several deputies from the sheriff's office resigned and the sheriff himself was suspended in 2019.

While police response is usually measured by the number of casualties, it is important to remember that these shootings can unfold in very different ways and the lessons learned from one active shooter situation may not always apply to the next one. For example, the Las Vegas Route 91 Harvest Festival shooting in October 2017 required a very different response. Stephen Paddock checked into a suite at the Mandalay Bay hotel in Las Vegas, Nevada, on September 25, 2017, with a total of 21 pieces of luggage. He was a regular visitor to the hotel and considered a high roller, which meant he received preferential treatment. The hotel security staff considered him to be low risk and he was not on anyone's radar as a threat. Less than a week later, Paddock opened fire on an outdoor concert during the closing act of the three-day Route 91 Harvest Festival. Police had little time to respond because in less than a minute, more than 100 rounds rained down on the crowd. A security guard had been alerted to a room alarm immediately before the shooting began and went to investigate. Paddock had barricaded himself in the suite and shot at hotel staff through the door. In fact, he had fired at the guard six minutes before he began firing on the crowd. Hotel security was initially confused and thought the gunfire was coming from outside. Concert attendees called 9-1-1. Police arrived quickly and were also under fire. They helped get many of the wounded to safety and secured the remaining people in the hotel. When they arrived at Paddock's suite, they found him dead of a self-inflicted gunshot wound, along with an arsenal of weapons and more than 1,000 spent shell casings. The violence was over and 58 people were dead. In the end, the police do not know exactly how many officers responded to the shooting; many of them were off duty and came to help in one of the deadliest mass shooting massacres in the history of the United States.[14]

Since the shooting, the hotel has instituted new security measures, including using K-9 units to conduct random checks of luggage. Federal, state, and local police looked for a motive to explain this tragedy but years later were unable to do so. Despite meticulously planning the shooting, Paddock left no note or manifesto explaining why he committed the massacre.

Critical Thinking

1. What type of training should civilians have in the case of a mass shooting happening where they are?
2. Should these trainings be offered in schools? For what ages?

Is Prevention Possible?

This begs the question: Are there limits to what the police can do? It is important to remember, however, even an enhanced police response as proposed by the commission would have been purely reactive to a shooting already in progress. In the Marjory Stoneman Douglas case, Cruz's mother had repeatedly called police for assistance with her son's violent outbursts. He had been expelled from the school prior to the shooting. School mental health counselors were well aware that the shooter was troubled but did not have the full picture, since he declined services. Even if there was a voluntary desire for treatment, it is not clear that Cruz would have received it. On the flip side, Stephen Paddock was described as a regular guest in Las Vegas. He gambled and ate at restaurants. His family reported no changes in behavior and no mental health concerns—yet, he killed 58 people and left 850 more injured. Surely, this is not the behavior of a healthy individual.

Given these behavioral health failures, could local police have stopped him before the shooting? Prevention is difficult, even with available information, for a variety of reasons. First, police must sort through an enormous amount of intelligence to determine which is valid and what tips are dead ends. This can be difficult given that police agencies do not have unlimited resources. Next, there are challenges associated with information sharing. If the Federal Bureau of Investigation (FBI) gets a warning about an individual threat, it is not necessarily true that the local agency at risk would get that same information. Finally, as in the case of the Stoneman Douglas shootings is that for prevention to work, there must be appropriate mental health services available to assist at-risk people before they engage in violence.

The United States has more mass shootings than any developed country in the world and the rate of incidence has been increasing over time. As Joel Capellan and Carla Lewandowski point out, there are steps that police can take to address and minimize mass violence.[15] First, threat assessment tools must be fine-tuned to be able to not only incorporate the large amounts of data that are available to not only the police but community partners but also determine the likelihood for violence. Next, they call for increased information sharing across police agencies to make sure that all pertinent information can be combined.

Finally, police must educate the public on warning signs for mass shootings. Joel Capellan and Carla Lewanowski also caution that this public education comes with increased responsibility for police. Friends and family members must trust that police will act on their information in a way that endangers their lives for reporting and that the person causing the threat will be treated fairly under the rule of law.

Beyond the Police: A Collaborative Approach

Following the shootings at Marjorie Stoneman Douglas High School, survivors have vigorously campaigned for increased gun control to prevent future tragedies. Within days of the shooting, students began speaking out against sending thoughts and prayers and asked for concrete

◀ **LO2**

Evaluate whether prevention is possible.

Critical Thinking

Instead of only training for these mass shooting events, what type of prevention do you think might work to stop them before they happen?

Bob Daemmrich/Alamy Stock Photo

Interagency cooperation is one key element for combating mass casualty events. Here, on March 21, 2018, members of various federal, state, and local law enforcement agencies can be seen working together to secure the Pflugerville, Texas, neighborhood around the home of Mark Conditt, who was the suspected serial bomber terrorizing Austin for three weeks. Conditt detonated a bomb, killing himself, during a car chase, as officers closed in.

action to prevent another school shooting. Not satisfied with the response, less than six weeks later, students organized "March for Our Lives" to be held in Washington, DC.

The march had three main demands: to pass a law banning assault weapons; to stop the sale of high-capacity magazines; and to make background checks on all gun purchases, including online and at gun shows, required.[16] There has been little legislative change in the aftermath of these activities. Despite their efforts, tightening of gun regulations has stalled. In the absence of removing the dangerous weapons from perpetrators, communities continue to search for other ways to prevent or minimize the harm associated with these tragedies. It is clear, however, that local police are just one piece of a comprehensive response to active shooter situations and gun violence more generally; some of these methods are described in the sections that follow.

The Media

The media can also play a role in prevention by decreasing the notoriety and attention that shooters receive. Media can assist in prevention by not using the names of perpetrators of mass violence. This is because with their names and pictures plastered all over the news, shooters achieve a level of fame that may be desirable to some. By not posting names and pictures, the victims, not the perpetrators, get the attention. Researchers have also suggested that these shootings are "contagious," meaning that they can encourage "copy-cat" responses. One way to prevent future violence is for media outlets to stop using the name and pictures of perpetrators in their coverage.[17] By only reporting on the victims, the media can reduce opportunities for fame and notoriety that perpetrators seek and that result from these tragedies.

Training Students

Another approach taken by some communities is to train students and community members to react to active shooter situations in a way to minimize harm. Some communities have opted for training students and employees to effectively respond to an active threat. One popular program is Active Aggressor Response (ALICE) training.[18] ALICE stands for Alert, Lockdown, Inform, Counter, and Evacuate. The ALICE system is preparing people to react in an active shooter situation. Some practitioners believe that it is not enough to teach people to hide or flee. Rather, more options are necessary since escape is not always an option. In particular, Counter refers to creating a distraction to reduce the shooter's ability to shoot accurately. The training is quick to note that this is not fighting but instead creating opportunities for escape. ALICE has been adopted in schools and other public areas across the country. This approach is not without its critics, however.

It has been argued that ALICE and similar trainings can cause unnecessary anxiety and trauma for students, particularly in light of the frequency of school shootings.[19] Jaclyn Schildkraut, Amanda Nickerson, and Thomas Ristoff found in an evaluation of Run, Hide, Fight, a similar approach to ALICE, that students expressed enhanced emergency preparedness but did not report feeling any safer. They speculate that some of these feelings may be the result of repeated drills that highlight the vulnerability of students.[20]

Schools, churches, and other public organizations have adopted a variety of other policies and procedures to minimize the harm associated with shootings.

One example of this is tourniquet training. After the Stoneman Douglas shootings, the Department of Homeland Security (DHS) offered a grant to an awardee to develop a program and training curriculum to teach high school students to use tourniquets. The School-Age Trauma Training grant aims to train teens on how to "assist victims with traumatic injuries" in emergency situations before responders arrive during mass-casualty events.[21]

Careers in Policing

School Resource Officer

In schools across the country, there are more than 10,000 full-time police working as school resource officers, or SROs. They are sworn law enforcement officers, most fully armed, who are assigned to work, either full or part time, in a school setting. In most jurisdictions safety officers are under the jurisdiction of the local police departments, while in others they are part of an independent organization administered by the Department of Education (DoE).

Main Duties

SROs have a number of different functions and activities. In addition to helping make the school environment safe for students and teachers, school resource officers work closely with staff and administrators in developing delinquency prevention programs. They also act as a liaison between the school administration and the police department.

As the main law enforcement officer in a school, they will respond quickly to problems in the schools, ranging from breaking up fights to preventing bullying. However, their job is more complex than simply policing school grounds. For example, schools routinely employ safety protocols to ensure students and staff can operate in a safe environment. SROs help to develop the best safety practices and then coordinate drills, such as active shooter scenarios, for students and teachers to help prepare for the potential of a hostile threat to the school.

They may also be asked to teach classes or hold seminars and training sessions on topics ranging from traffic and fire safety to character building. The SRO will also conduct informational presentations to parent groups concerning emerging drug trends. The SRO may be asked to speak to school clubs about relevant issues such as driver safety.

In some instances, SROs are responsible for traffic control, monitoring people entering and leaving school grounds. They are charged with maintaining school security, making sure exterior doors are checked and locked so that nonstudents and others cannot enter the school without first signing in at an entry office.

In addition to these duties, SROs interact with students in order to create bridges between young people and the local police departments. They may be asked to mentor a student who is having a tough time adjusting to the school environment.

Training

Because most SRO candidates are active police agents, they are expected to meet all the qualifications of a serving police officer. In addition, good communication skills and knowledge of such topics as security, crime prevention, drug/alcohol education, citizenship, and community responsibility, are a must. SROs may also be asked to take special training courses to help them deal effectively with the problems they encounter. For example, in 1985, the Florida attorney general's office developed the first 40-hour basic training course to train SROs with the basic knowledge and skills necessary to implement crime prevention programming in a school setting. In addition, the attorney general's office awards a designation to experienced SROs who attend a minimum of 130 hours of juvenile-related courses. To earn the School Resource Officer Practitioner Designation, a participant must successfully complete a 40-hour SRO basic training course and then 90 hours of SRO instruction offered in the form of workshops and seminars.

Source: Florida Crime Prevention Training Institute, School Resource Officer Practitioner Designation, http://www.fcpti.com/fcpti.nsf /pages/SROPD#:~:text=To%20earn%20the%20School%20 Resource,form%20of%20workshops%20and%20seminars.

Finally, some have advocated for bulletproof backpacks, which saw an increase in sales following these same shootings. The effectiveness of these backpacks is limited because they aren't rifle-proof. They can only protect against bullets from handguns and pistols, which typically aren't as strong as rifles. Mass shooters increasingly seem to prefer rifles like the AR-15, making bulletproof backpacks potentially less useful.[22]

In short, an effective approach to mass-casualty events involves collaboration and coordination. While there are steps that police can take to minimize harm to the public and themselves, it is not a problem that they can address themselves. Local police alone do not have the resources to prevent these events from occurring and can, at best, minimize casualties. Considering the need to address school shootings and violence, the role of the school resource officer has become crucial. The Careers in Policing: School Resource Officer feature looks at this element of the job.

LO3

Describe the extent of terrorism against U.S. citizens.

Terrorism against U.S. Citizens

Terrorism has increasingly been added to the list of responsibilities for local police and is another example of a mass-casualty event. After 9/11, responding to terrorist threats was also added to the responsibilities of local police. This fear was realized in 2013, with the Boston Marathon bombings. More information about this event is included in the following Focus on Policing: The Boston Marathon Bombers feature.

Yet, while it may seem intuitive to focus on foreign enemies, domestic terrorism continues to plague the United States. The growing concerns in the United States about the rise in hate crimes and activities led multiple components of the executive branch to shift focus to this threat. The DHS acknowledged in 2019 that hate crimes and far-right groups "represent a growing share of the threat to the Homeland."[23] On June 4, 2019, FBI officials testified before the U.S. House of Representatives Subcommittee on Civil Rights and Civil Liberties and emphasized the rise in reported hate crimes and related acts of violence linked to White supremacist groups, and the impact of these violent incidents on communities.[24] Such concerns led eventually to the decision of the Biden administration to formulate the National Strategy for Countering Domestic Terrorism (NSCDT), which focuses on several vectors of response.[25]

The NSCDT increased efforts to collect and analyze data on far-right extremism and its commitment to support community/local programs and partnerships with tech firms, to address both offline and online radicalization. In addition, the NSCDT aims to elevate the focus on domestic terrorism within law enforcement and intelligence agencies, as well as engage in educational, training, and screening efforts to prevent the infiltration of radical elements into the military and law enforcement. Lastly, the NSCDT emphasizes the need to enhance international collaboration, especially considering the growing ties between domestic and foreign far-right groups.

In 2017, University of Maryland scholars published an analysis of the Global Terrorism Database which showed a sharp increase in the domestic terrorism attacks by right-wing extremist. That increase grew from 6 percent in the 2000s to 35 percent a decade later. The number of attacks by religious extremists also grew, from 9 percent to 53 percent between the same two decades. By comparison, the number of attacks by left-wing terrorist groups and environmentalist extremists dropped from 64 percent in the 2000s to 12 percent 10 years later.[25] The hate crime data support that this continues (Figure 5.1). Since 2008, there

Figure 5.1   Number of Violent Hate Incidents per Year in the United States*

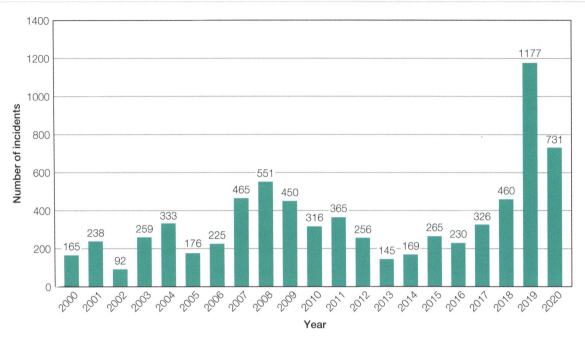

*UML Dataset of far-right violence incidents in the US. For more information on the dataset, see here—Arie Perliger, *American Zealots: Inside Right-Wing Domestic Terrorism* (New York: Columbia University Press, 2020).

is an overall increase in hate violence in the United States. While in the 1990s, the average number of attacks per year was consistently below a hundred, since 2008, the United States is experiencing several hundred violent incidents per year. Moreover, in 2019, there was another unprecedented rise, as the number of incidents crossed 1,000 for the first time since at least early 1990.

This type of terrorism played out in Charlottesville, Virginia. In August 2017, hundreds of White supremacists, neo-Nazis, and militia groups descended on Charlottesville for a "Unite the Right Rally." The purpose of the gathering was to protest the removal of a statue of Robert E. Lee. Counterprotesters were on scene in opposition to the rally. Among the chaotic events of the day, neo-Nazi sympathizer James Fields Jr. drove his car into a crowd of protesters, killing Heather Heyer. In December 2018, Fields was found guilty of murder and sentenced to life in prison.

right-wing

A description referring generally to an individual, a political party, or faction that advocates very conservative policies and typically favors socially traditional ideas. Hierarchy, separatism, and inequality may be seen as natural results of traditional right-wing ideology.

Right-Wing Political Groups

The term **right-wing** generally refers to an individual, a political party, or faction that advocates very conservative policies and typically favors socially traditional ideas. Hierarchy, separatism, and inequality may be seen as natural results of traditional right-wing ideology. As noted above, in recent decades, domestic terrorism has spiked in the United States. These groups tend to be heavily armed and organized around such themes as White supremacy, anti-abortion, militant tax resistance, and religious revisionism. Identified groups

AFP/Stringer/Getty Images

On April 15, 2013, victims of one of the blasts set off by the Tsarnaev brothers at the Boston Marathon lay near the finish line. Three people were killed and hundreds were wounded. Identified by federal agents, the brothers had a shootout with the police. Tamerlan was shot several times, run over by his escaping brother, and died at the scene. Dzhokhar was apprehended and, after numerous legal proceedings, sentenced to death.

The Boston Marathon Bombers

On April 15, 2013, two men, Dzhokhar and Tamerlan Tsarnaev, set off bombs at the finish line of the Boston Marathon, killing three people, and maiming and injuring many more. The two had conspired for many months to use improvised explosive devices (IEDs) to harm and kill people in the crowds of spectators who were cheering the runners on toward the marathon finish line. The IEDs were constructed from pressure cookers, explosive powder, shrapnel, adhesives, and other items and were designed to shred skin, shatter bone, and cause extreme pain and suffering, as well as death.

After carefully poring over footage from surveillance cameras and other sources, on April 18, 2013, the FBI released photographs to the media of the Tsarnaevs, identifying them as suspects in the marathon bombings. These photographs were widely disseminated on television and elsewhere online, and the brothers must have realized their identification and arrest were imminent. Soon after, the Tsarnaevs, armed with five IEDs, a Ruger P95 semiautomatic handgun, ammunition, a machete, and a hunting knife, drove to the MIT campus, where they shot Officer Sean Collier in an attempt to steal his service weapon. After killing Officer Collier, the brothers carjacked a Mercedes, kidnapped the driver, and forced him to drive to a gas station, robbing him of $800 along the way. After the driver managed to escape, the brothers drove the vehicle to Watertown, Massachusetts, where city police officers located the pair and a gunfight ensued. Attempting to escape, Dzhokhar Tsarnaev reentered the carjacked vehicle and drove it directly at the officers, running over and killing his brother Tamerlan, who had already been wounded in the shootout. Gravely wounded and injured, Dzhokhar Tsarnaev hid in a dry-docked boat in a Watertown backyard until he was spotted and taken into custody by police. He was later tried, found guilty, and sentenced to death.

Who were these killers? Tamerlan Tsarnaev was born in the Kalmyk Autonomous Soviet Socialist Republic, North Caucasus; Dzhokhar in Kyrgyzstan. Because their father was a Chechen, they identified themselves as being of Chechen descent. Though the family prospered in the United States and Dzhokhar attended a state university, the brothers clung to radical Islamic views and blamed the U.S. government for conducting a war against Islam in Iraq and Afghanistan. The brothers viewed the Boston bombing victims as "collateral damage" in their war against the West. Their actions were disavowed by Islamic, Chechen, and other groups, all of whom quickly distanced themselves from the atrocity.

The Tsarnaev brothers were motivated by their sensitivity to what they perceived as the oppression of Muslim people by the West. A note that Dzhokhar Tsarnaev wrote while hiding from authorities on a dry-docked boat said in part: "God has a plan for each person. Mine was to hide in this boat and shed some light on our actions. . . . Stop killing our innocent people and we will stop."

Critical Thinking

The Tsarnaev brothers were identified partially through the use of public surveillance cameras and private cell phone footage from the marathon event. Do you think that surveillance cameras and other sources like facial recognition in public places is an invasion of privacy or a needed tool for public safety?

Source: U.S. Department of Justice, "Federal Grand Jury Returns 30-Count Indictment Related to Boston Marathon Explosions and Murder of MIT Police Officer Sean Collier," June 27, 2013, http://www.fbi.gov/boston/press-releases/2013/federal-grand-jury-returns-30-count-indictment-related-to-boston-marathon-explosions-and-murder-of-mit-police-officer-sean-collier, accessed March 2022.

have included, at one time or another, the Aryan Republican Army, the Aryan Nation, the Posse Comitatus, and the Ku Klux Klan. These groups want to shape U.S. government policy over a range of matters, including ending abortion rights, extending the right to bear arms, and eliminating federal taxation. According to federal officials, they are often organized into paramilitary groups that follow a military-style rank hierarchy. They tend to stockpile illegal weapons and ammunition, trying illegally to get their hands on fully automatic firearms or attempting to convert weapons to fully automatic. They also try to buy or manufacture improvised explosive devices and typically engage in wilderness, survival, or other paramilitary training.

Many militia extremists view themselves as protecting the U.S. Constitution, other U.S. laws, or their own individual liberties. They believe that the Constitution grants citizens the power to take back the federal government by force or violence if they feel it's necessary. They oppose gun control efforts and fear the widespread disarming of Americans by the federal government. Militia extremists often subscribe to various conspiracy theories regarding the government. One of their primary theories is that the United Nations—which they refer to as the New World Order, or NWO—has the right to use its military forces anywhere in the world.

These extremists often train and prepare for what they foresee as an inevitable invasion of the United States by United Nations forces. Many militia extremists also wrongly believe that the federal government will relocate citizens to camps controlled by the Federal Emergency Management Agency (FEMA), or force them to undergo vaccinations. Although unlikely to topple the government, these individualistic acts of terror are difficult to predict or control. On April 19, 1995, in the most deadly right-wing attack, 168 people were killed during the Oklahoma City bombing, the most severe example of domestic political terrorism in the United States so far.

Some right-wing militants target specific groups. Pro-life, anti-abortion activists have demonstrated at abortion clinics, attacked clients and patients, bombed offices, and killed doctors who perform abortions. On October 23, 1998, Dr. Barnett Slepian was shot and killed by a sniper in his Buffalo, New York, home. He was one of a growing number of abortion providers believed to be the victims of terrorists who ironically claim to be "pro-life."

A favorite target is law enforcement officers. Between 1990 and 2013, far-right extremists killed 50 federal, state, and local law enforcement officers in the line of duty in 33 separate incidents. More than two-thirds were killed during ideologically motivated attacks; the remaining officers were killed in non-ideological confrontations (e.g., while arresting an individual during a bank robbery). In addition, corrections officers, private security guards, and a judge have been killed during ideologically motivated attacks.[26]

The budget for the DHS contains $131 million to help distinct, innovative, and community-driven strategies to prevent domestic terrorism. The DHS does this while showing respect for the civil liberties and civil rights of U.S. citizens.[27] Yet, this represents something of a mismatch. Most of the concern has been on preventing and thwarting foreign-born terrorists while research and funding has been reduced to address domestic and right-wing militants.

Terrorism and the Local Police

While local police in the United States had dealt with terrorists both domestic and foreign, these had been isolated incidents. The approach of local police dramatically changed after the September 11, 2001, terrorist attacks. On the morning of September 11, 2001, 19 terrorists from al-Qaeda hijacked four commercial airplanes, deliberately crashing two of the planes into the upper floors of the North and South towers of the World Trade Center complex and a third plane into the

Pentagon in Arlington, Virginia. The Twin Towers ultimately collapsed because of the damage sustained from the impacts and the resulting fires.

After learning about the other attacks, passengers on the fourth hijacked plane, Flight 93, fought back, and the plane was crashed into an empty field in western Pennsylvania about 20 minutes by air from Washington, DC. The terrorist attacks on September 11 resulted in the deaths of nearly 3,000 people from 93 different nations. The vast majority of the victims (2,753 people) were killed in New York City, 184 people were killed at the Pentagon, and 40 people were killed when Flight 93 crashed in Pennsylvania.[28]

The terrorists were from four different countries in the same region. Fifteen of the 19 terrorists that day came from Saudi Arabia. Two of the terrorists were from the United Arab Emirates (UAE), one was from Egypt and the other from Lebanon.

By attacking the symbols that represent power and prestige in America, it is believed Al-Qaeda hoped that the attacks would cause widespread fear throughout the nation and that it would severely weaken the national standing of the United States around the world. The weakening of the United States, it was thought, would eventually support the religious and political agenda in the Middle East and throughout the Muslim world.

The National Commission on Terrorist Attacks Upon the United States

The National Commission on Terrorist Attacks Upon the United States (also known as the 9-11 Commission), an independent, bipartisan commission created by congressional legislation and President George W. Bush in 2002, was chartered to prepare a full and complete account of the circumstances surrounding the September 11, 2001, terrorist attacks, including preparedness for and the immediate response to the attacks. The Commission was led by Thomas Kean, the former governor of New Jersey. The Commission was also mandated to provide recommendations designed to guard against future attacks. On July 22, 2004, the Commission released its final report. The report calls for changes to be made by the executive branch and Congress to more effectively protect the United States in an age of modern terrorism and provides 41 concrete recommendations.

The commission called for a number of changes. For example, the report noted:

- The U.S. border security system should be integrated into a larger network of screening points that includes our transportation system and access to vital facilities, such as nuclear reactors.

- The president should direct the DHS to lead the effort to design a comprehensive screening system, addressing common problems and setting common standards with system-wide goals in mind. Extending those standards among other governments could dramatically strengthen America and the world's collective ability to intercept individuals who pose catastrophic threats.

- The DHS, properly supported by the Congress, should complete, as quickly as possible, a biometric entry/exit screening system, including a single system for speeding qualified travelers.

Critical Thinking

1. Do you think local police are equipped to address and investigate terrorism at the local level?
2. What help or oversight might they need?

The National Commission on Terrorist Attacks Upon the United States

Also known as the 9-11 Commission, an independent, bipartisan commission created by congressional legislation and President George W. Bush in 2002 to prepare a full and complete account of the circumstances surrounding the September 11, 2001, terrorist attacks, including preparedness for and the immediate response to the attacks.

One of the biggest changes following 9/11 was the creation of the DHS. This cabinet level agency is discussed in the sections below.

Consequences of 9/11 for the Police

Clearly, 9/11 was a national tragedy that affected all Americans. Local emergency personnel particularly suffered, as they were largely unprepared to deal with this attack. 9/11 also laid bare some of the deficiencies in the public safety response to large scale attacks. For example, police radio tapes include clear warnings transmitted 21 minutes before the building fell. Officials say that these warnings were in fact relayed to police officers, most of whom managed to escape, however, never heard those warnings. Their radio system failed frequently that morning and was not linked to the police system. Furthermore, the police and fire commanders guiding the rescue efforts did not talk to one another during the crisis. Reviews of both the police and fire response revealed that big changes had to be made in order to respond to future disasters.[29] Changes in internal structures, such as the creation of a counterterrorism unit, tended to occur only in larger metropolitan and state police agencies—not in the typically smaller police organizations. Changes in organizational processes or operations tended to be far more universal and typically involve an increased collaboration among police departments, specifically greater openness toward information sharing.[30]

There were other consequences for emergency personnel. Suicide ideation in police officers who worked in the proximity of the September 11, 2001 (9/11), World Trade Center (WTC) terrorist attack has been recognized as a problem. Data were obtained for a period of four years (2001–2004) from Cop 2 Cop, a statewide New Jersey confidential phone hotline provided exclusively for police officers and their families. Results suggest that calls related to suicidal thoughts or ideation increased from pre-9/11 through three years post-9/11 and that the risk for urgent care suicide calls post-9/11 increased more quickly over time when compared to pre-9/11 urgent calls.[31]

Local Law Enforcement Efforts to Combat Terrorism

After 9/11, local police began to take terrorism much more seriously. Philosophically, there was a shift toward "intelligence-led policing," which seeks to collect information about possible perpetrators and intervene before a crime is committed. In the counterterrorism context, proponents of intelligence-led policing believe that analyzing even innocuous or disparate pieces of information can help "connect the dots" and reveal potential terrorist plots. Intelligence-led policing collects information about possible perpetrators and intervenes before a crime is committed. In the counterterrorism context, proponents of intelligence led policing believe that analyzing even innocuous or disparate pieces of information can help "connect the dots" and reveal potential terrorist plots. The use of intelligence led policing has been contested as it has been suggested that collecting information about specific communities or social movements can lead to perceptions of harassment.[32]

In New York City—one of the main targets of the 9/11 attacks, a Counterterrorism Bureau was established.[33] Teams within the bureau have been trained to examine potential targets in the city and are attempting to insulate those targets from possible attack. Viewed as prime targets are the city's bridges, the Empire State Building, Rockefeller Center, and the United Nations. Bureau detectives are assigned overseas to work with the police in several foreign cities, including cities in Canada and Israel. Detectives have been assigned as liaisons with the FBI and with INTERPOL in Lyon, France. The city is recruiting detectives with language skills ranging from Pashtun and Urdu to Arabic, Hokkien, and other tongues.

The existing New York City Police Intelligence Division has been revamped, and agents are examining foreign newspapers and monitoring Internet sites. The Counterterrorism Bureau has assigned more than 100 city police detectives to work with FBI agents as part of a Joint Terrorist Task Force. In addition, the Intelligence Division's 700 investigators now devote 35 to 40 percent of their resources to counterterrorism—up from about 2 percent before January 2002. The department is also drawing on the expertise of other institutions around the city. For example, medical specialists have been enlisted to monitor daily developments in the city's hospitals to detect any suspicious outbreaks of illness that might reflect a biological attack. And the police are conducting joint drills with the New York Fire Department to avoid the problems in communication and coordination that marked the emergency response on September 11.

New policies and bureaus, however, are not enough. The police must also continue to engage the community. Tom Tyler also argues the police benefit when they have the active willing cooperation of the people in the communities that might be inclined to provide support for terrorist activities.[34] For example, if immigrant communities fear the police because of aggressive policies, they may be less likely to share information about radicalization. Policing against terrorism requires a focus on how police practices are perceived by the people living in policed communities. The police must maintain good relationships with all communities in their jurisdictions. This may be considered to be a holdover from the community policing era—but it still applies to policing terrorism.

The IACP lists a number of activities that local police agencies can engage in to involve the community. These include sharing training materials, holding information sharing sessions, engaging programs such as Neighborhood Watch and Volunteers in Policing as well as attending community meetings. The IACP also notes the importance of social media to engage with the community as well as to share information.[35]

There is some evidence to suggest that Twitter can improve police legitimacy by increasing transparency into police work.[36] Twitter in particular can also be an outreach tool. For example, during the 2011 riots in London, UK police used Twitter as an outreach channel. British police saw huge growth in the number of Twitter followers. They also, for the first time, engaged with the public regularly using social media.[37] Similarly, following the 2013 Boston Marathon bombing, Police Commissioner Ed Davis instructed his media relations office to utilize all social media tools to help find the bombers. The goal was to share accurate information with the public about what the police were doing. Most notably, they were able to correct misinformation that was spreading throughout Boston.[38] Other research suggests that while large police departments have a strong social media presence[39] and interact with the community, they are not engaged in actual dialogue with the community. Beyond major events, scant research has examined how police departments actually make daily use of these tools and how this usage could improve community connections.

The 2013 Law Enforcement Management and Administrative Statistics (LEMAS) survey included one social media question. Of police agencies responding, 28 percent use Twitter, 58 percent use Facebook, and 15 percent use YouTube. According to the 2015 IACP Social Media survey,[40] 96.4 percent of agencies surveyed use some kind of social media, with 83.4 percent reporting that the intent was for citizen engagement and outreach; 48.6 percent of surveyed agencies had not identified measurable goals for social media use and 31.2 percent do not measure success. Yet 83.5 percent reported improving citizen engagement and outreach.[41] Based on available data, it is unclear if police departments are engaging the community through social media, or how police departments measure impact.[42] Finally, there are no comprehensive standards for social media use,[43] though the 2015 Final Report on 21st Century Policing dedicates one of their six pillars (Pillar 3) to Technology & Social Media. The report states that the police can utilize social media to communicate with and engage the community on important issues and to gauge community sentiment about agency policies and practices.[44]

County Law Enforcement Efforts to Combat Terrorism

Some counties are also now engaging in anti-terror and homeland security activities. For example, the Harris County, Texas, Office of Homeland Security & Emergency Management (OHSEM) is responsible for an emergency management plan that prepares for public recovery in the event of natural disasters or human-caused catastrophes or attacks. It works in conjunction with state, federal, and local authorities, including the city of Houston and other municipalities in the surrounding Harris County area when required. If needed, the OHSEM activates an emergency operations center to facilitate coordination of all support agencies to provide continuity of services to the public.

OHSEM is responsible for advisement, notification, and assembly of services that are in the best interest of the citizens of Harris County. It prepares and distributes information and procedures governing the same.[45] Similarly, in Montgomery County, Maryland, the Homeland Security Department plans, prevents, prepares, and protects against major threats that may harm, disrupt, or destroy the community, its commerce, and institutions. Its mission is to effectively manage and coordinate the county's unified response, mitigation, and recovery from the consequences of such disasters or events, should they occur. It also serves to educate the public on emergency preparedness for all hazards and conducts outreach to diverse and special populations to protect, secure, and sustain critical infrastructures and ensure the continuity of essential services.[46]

State Law Enforcement Efforts to Combat Terrorism

In the wake of the 9/11 attacks, a number of states have beefed up their intelligence-gathering capabilities and aimed them directly at homeland security. For example, Arizona maintains the **Arizona Counter Terrorism Information Center** (ACTIC), a statewide intelligence system designed to combat terrorism.[47]

Arizona Counter Terrorism Information Center

A statewide intelligence system designed to combat terrorism. It consists of two divisions; one is unclassified and draws together personnel from various public safety agencies and the other operates in a secretive manner and is made up of personnel from the FBI's Joint Terrorism Task Force.

It consists of two divisions. One is unclassified and draws together personnel from various public safety agencies. The other operates in a secretive manner and is made up of personnel from the FBI's Joint Terrorism Task Force. According to its website:

> The Arizona Counter Terrorism Information Center provides an increased level of readiness by distributing focused, concentrated, and applicable incident alerts. The Fusion Center is responsible for sharing early, reliable, and consistent incident information about conditions that may affect local authorities. Situational readiness is increased when agencies are empowered to become aware of potential occurrences in their jurisdictions. The ACTIC Fusion Center utilizes thousands of varied data sources to provide early warning of potential incidents or events at the local, county, state, and regional levels.[48]

ACTIC also has an outreach program known as the Community Liaison Program (CLP). Community partners, including religious groups, businesses, and community crime watches, provide intelligence information to ACTIC personnel as the need arises.

Federal Efforts to Address Terrorism

The Department of Homeland Security (DHS)

Department of Homeland Security

Agency assigned the mission of preventing terrorist attacks within the United States, reducing America's vulnerability to terrorism, and minimizing the damage and aiding the recovery from attacks that do occur.

Following the September 11, 2001, attacks, a new cabinet-level agency called the **Department of Homeland Security** (DHS) received congressional approval and was assigned the mission of preventing terrorist attacks within the United States, reducing America's vulnerability to terrorism, and minimizing the damage and aiding the recovery from attacks that do occur. DHS is the third-largest cabinet department in the federal government, after the Department of Defense and the Department of Veterans Affairs. DHS has approximately 240,000 employees in various employment categories which vary from aviation type jobs and border security and protection to emergency response units, as well as from cybersecurity analyst to chemical facility inspectors.[49] The 2022 budget for DHS is over $90 billion.[50] The DHS has a number of independent branches and bureaus.[51] Of them, three are well-known law enforcement agencies: Customs and Border Protection, Immigration and Customs Enforcement, and the U.S. Secret Service.

Customs and Border Protection (CBP)

This agency is responsible for protecting our nation's borders in order to prevent terrorism, human and drug smuggling, illegal immigration, and agricultural pests from entering the United States, while improving the flow of legitimate trade and travel. Customs and Border Protection (CBP) employs nearly 60,000 personnel, among them approximately 22,000 Border Patrol agents and CBP Air and Marine agents who patrol the country's borders and points of entry. CBP also partners with other countries through its Container Security Initiative and the Customs-Trade Partnership Against Terrorism program. The goal of each is to help ensure that goods destined for the United States are screened before they are shipped.[52]

Immigration and Customs Enforcement (ICE)

As the largest investigative arm of the DHS, ICE is responsible for identifying and shutting down vulnerabilities in the nation's border, and for economic, transportation, and infrastructure security. There are four main components of ICE:

■ *Enforcement and Removal Operations (ERO)* upholds U.S. immigration law within and beyond U.S. borders. ERO manages all aspects of the immigration enforcement process, including identification and arrest, domestic transportation, detention, bond management, and supervised release.

■ *Homeland Security Investigations (HSI)* is responsible for investigating, disrupting, and taking down transnational criminal organizations and terrorist networks. HSI conducts investigations of terrorism, narcotics smuggling, transnational gang activity, and human smuggling/trafficking among other transnational crimes.

■ The *Management and Administration (M&A)* identifies and tracks the agency's performance, recruits agents, and directs and maintains the budget while providing integrated information technology infrastructure.

■ With more than 1,300 attorneys, the *Office of the Principal Legal Advisor (OPLA)* is charged with litigating all removal cases, including those against criminal noncitizens, terrorists, and human rights abusers.

■ The *Office of Professional Responsibility (OPR)* is responsible for upholding the agency's professional standards through a multidisciplinary approach of security, inspections, and investigations.[53]

The Secret Service

The U.S. Secret Service has two significant missions. The first is to protect the president and vice president, their families, heads of state, and other high-level officials. Part of this function involves investigating threats against protected officials and protecting the White House, the vice president's residence, and other buildings within Washington, DC. The second mission is to investigate counterfeiting and other financial crimes, including financial institution fraud, identity theft, computer fraud, and computer-based attacks on our nation's financial, banking, and telecommunications infrastructure. Criminal investigations cover a range of conduct:

> . . . counterfeiting of U.S. currency (to include coins); counterfeiting of foreign currency (occurring domestically); identity crimes such as access device fraud, identity theft, false identification fraud, bank fraud and check fraud; telemarketing fraud; telecommunications fraud (cellular and hard wire); computer fraud; fraud targeting automated payment systems and teller machines; direct deposit fraud; investigations of forgery, uttering, alterations, false impersonations or false claims involving U.S. Treasury Checks, U.S. Saving Bonds, U.S. Treasury Notes, Bonds and Bills; electronic funds transfer (EFT) including Treasury disbursements and fraud within the Treasury payment systems; Federal Deposit Insurance Corporation investigations; Farm Credit Administration violations; and fictitious or fraudulent commercial instruments and foreign securities.[54]

The Federal Bureau of Investigations (FBI)

The FBI mission has been evolving to keep pace with world events. After 9/11, the FBI was charged with coordinating intelligence collection with the Border Patrol, the Secret Service, the CIA, and other law enforcement agencies. At the center of this initiative, the Counterterrorism Division of the FBI collects, analyzes, and shares critical information and intelligence on (a) international terrorism operations both within the United States and in support of extraterritorial investigations, (b) domestic terrorism operations, and (c) counterterrorism related to both international and domestic terrorism.

Based in Washington, DC, the Counterterrorism Division has the following responsibilities:

- Manage a team of analysts who work to put together information gathered by the field offices.

- Operate a national threat-warning system that enables the FBI to instantly distribute important terrorism alert bulletins to law enforcement agencies and public safety departments.

- Send out "flying squads" of specially trained officers to provide counterterrorism knowledge and experience, language capabilities, and analytical support, as needed, to FBI field offices.

- Maintain the Joint Terrorism Task Force (JTTF), which includes representatives from the Department of Defense (DoD), Department of Energy (DoE), Federal Emergency Management Agency (FEMA), Central Intelligence Agency (CIA), Customs Service, Secret Service, and Immigration and Naturalization Service. Additionally, there are 66 local joint terrorism task forces in which representatives from federal agencies, state and local law enforcement personnel, and first responders work together to track down terrorists and prevent acts of terrorism in the United States.[55]

Anti-Terrorism Coordination

National Criminal Intelligence Sharing Plan

A formal intelligence-sharing initiative that identifies the security and intelligence-sharing needs recognized in the wake of the 9/11 terrorist attacks.

fusion center

Often located in police departments, a mechanism for sharing information and intelligence within specific jurisdictions and across levels of government.

The leading terrorist information dissemination process is through the **National Criminal Intelligence Sharing Plan** (NCISP) is a formal intelligence-sharing initiative that identifies the security and intelligence-sharing needs recognized in the wake of the 9/11 terrorist attacks.

As part of this process, many states and large cities have formed **fusion centers**. According to the National Fusion Center Guidelines, a fusion center is "an effective and efficient mechanism to exchange information and intelligence, maximize resources, streamline operations, and improve the ability to fight crime and terrorism by analyzing data from a variety of sources."[56] Often located in police departments, these centers are set up for the purpose of sharing information and intelligence within specific jurisdictions and across levels of government. Fusion centers often emphasize terrorism prevention and crime fighting with extensive use of technology. They frequently resemble a department's technological "nerve center" and are usually housed in a central location where information is collected and then shared with decision makers. There are four main goals for fusion centers:

- Provide support for a range of law enforcement activities, including anticrime operations and terrorism prevention

- Provide help for major incident operations and support for units charged with interdiction and criminal investigations

- Provide the means for community input, often through tip lines

- Provide assistance to law enforcement executives so they can make informed decisions about departmental priorities[57]

Fusion Centers

A fusion center is a mechanism to exchange information and intelligence, maximize resources, streamline operations, and improve the ability to fight crime and terrorism by analyzing data from a variety of sources. Fusion centers are intended to provide a mechanism through which government agencies, law enforcement, and the private sector can work together for the common purpose of protecting the homeland and preserving public safety. They are based on a model of collaboration. Collaboration between agencies and across levels of government has been lacking throughout history, but the events of 9/11 affirmed a need for change. The concept of fusion centers will continue to catch on, and more will probably be developed as law enforcement becomes increasingly aware of the benefits they can yield.

International Efforts to Address Terrorism

There are also international efforts to address terrorism. The United States works in collaboration with international law enforcement given the globalization of crime and the necessity for this type of cooperation.

INTERPOL

INTERPOL (officially the International Criminal Police Organization) is the world's largest international police organization, with members from 195 countries. Its mission is to prevent criminal activities as well as fight crime through heightened innovation and collaboration on matters of police and security issues. INTERPOL is not a law enforcement organization with arrest powers and all the other hallmarks of modern policing. Rather, its job is to provide technical and operational support to police organizations the world over. It is mostly an intelligence-gathering entity that helps member countries fight complicated international crime problems.

INTERPOL
The world's largest international police organization, with members from 195 countries.

The idea of INTERPOL was born back in 1914 at the first International Criminal Police Congress. Representatives from 24 countries met in Monaco to find ways to solve crime, centralize record-keeping, and develop arrest and extradition policies. INTERPOL was officially created in 1923 and has since seen its membership grow markedly (only five formally recognized countries are not members). Today, the organization is headquartered in Lyon, France. Each member country maintains a National Central Bureau, or NCB. The United States' NCB is housed within the U.S. Department of Justice.

INTERPOL Activities

Amidst an increasingly complex international criminal landscape, INTERPOL helps law enforcement agencies combat problems such as corruption, organized crime, international drug trafficking, financial crime, high-tech crime, terrorism, and human trafficking. To assist in this regard, INTERPOL manages a variety of databases with information on wanted criminals, including fingerprints and DNA profiles.

INTERPOL also disseminates information through several types of international notices. A Red Notice seeks "the location and arrest of wanted persons with a view to extradition or similar lawful action." A Blue Notice seeks "to collect additional information about a person's identity, location or activities in relation to a crime." A Green Notice provides "warnings and intelligence about persons who have committed criminal offenses and are likely to repeat these crimes in other countries." Several other types of notices also exist, all with the intent of sharing information and/or gathering additional information on groups and persons suspected of involvement in criminal activity.

INTERPOL's Limitations

INTERPOL's focus is on common criminals. Article 3 of its constitution states, "It is strictly forbidden for the Organization to undertake any intervention or activities of a political, military, religious, or racial character."

LO4

Explain the effects that responding to mass casualties has on the police.

Responding to Mass Casualties: Effects on Officers

Not surprisingly, these events affect not only the victims and their families but also the police and other emergency responders. Regardless of assignment, police are exposed to a wide variety of stressors—frequently interacting with people at their worst moments. This is considered to be secondary trauma—while these emergency service providers are not "victims" of these events, they are also severely affected by the violence. The IACP notes that these events can have lasting effects on first responders long after the event has occurred.[58]

For example, Omar Delgado, an officer with the Eatonville Police Department in Florida, was the first officer to arrive on scene for the Pulse Nightclub shootings in 2016 where 49 people were killed and dozens of others were injured. He developed post-traumatic stress disorder (PTSD) following the events and was unable to return to work. He was not the only one. Three years later, the Orange County Board of Commissioners voted to fund a mental health program designed to help first responders who were still experiencing the effects of the shootings. The training program, created and run by the St. Petersburg College Center for Public Safety Innovation, is intended to teach first responders how to care for themselves after crisis events and recognize peers who may need help coping with PTSD.[59]

Another form of secondary trauma is known as compassion fatigue. Compassion fatigue is a way to describe the prolonged exposure to this trauma. Charles Figley (1995) first coined the term "compassion fatigue" to describe this "cost of caring for those who suffer"— a type of secondary or vicarious traumatic stress. In other words, being in proximity to people who have been traumatized can affect caregivers and first responders. Helping people in harm's way while also being in danger themselves can be traumatizing.[60] It is clear that in any coordinated response to mass violence or terrorism, we should consider the long-term needs of the first responders.

This new focus on mass casualty events, terrorist acts, active and mass murder shooter incidents, and similar emergency/violent situations have extended to every element of law enforcement and have affected the way police interact with the public. These new demands along with unresolved trauma issues tend to be a recipe for disaster for all but the best adjusted officers. Sometimes it seems that with the heightened level of hyper-arousal and sensitivity to danger, real or perceived, some officers have a hard time distinguishing

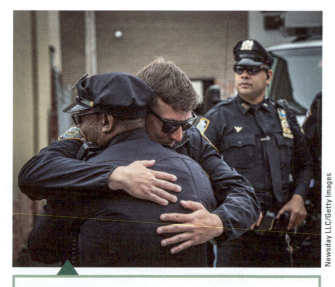

Newsday LLC/Getty Images

Police danger and death on a routine basis can take a toll on an officer's emotional well being. Here a New York Police Department highway patrol officer hugs Anastasios Tsakos' partner, Eric Cassidy (center), after Tsakos' body arrived at Farenga Funeral Home in Astoria, New York, April 29, 2021. Tsakos had been run down and killed by Jessica M. Beauvais, who is accused of driving drunk, running a roadblock in Queens, and striking Officer Tsakos, before fleeing the scene.

what is an imminent threat from citizens questioning police authority. Some would argue that while trying to protect the public, the police have moved too far toward the warrior mode and away from their guardian roles.[61] When police officers are in a constant state of hyper-arousal, they may miss important cues and can default to an aggressive stance when such a response is not warranted. Ultra-aggressive police responses and use of lethal force with unarmed citizens have been highlighted in recent years.

Recently there has been a call for police reform from many segments of the population as well as from elected officials. As a result of high-profile incidents, there have been calls for reform that range from calls to defund the police, to calls for an all-out dismantling of traditional policing services. A major sticking point is the lack of consensus not only on the term *reform* but also on what police actions need reforming. The police often want as little change as possible, with cries that reform will make society less safe. Many under-represented communities that often feel the brunt of police aggression are calling for more serious and instrumental reform measures. But what is reform, how will it work, and what is its purpose?

Police Reform

◄ **L05**

Recognize the concept of police reform.

In recent years, there has been a lot of talk, and legislative action surrounding the term "police reform." Although many have used the term, and even more have heard of it, many are confused as to what that term actually means, and if it is needed. Although at its core, policing is a noble and honorable profession, their exposure to violence, mass shootings, and other emotionally laden experiences may have influenced some officers to make violence a routine part of the job. There have been many high-profile cases of police misdeeds that have eroded confidence and trust in the police. Take for instance, the 2021 case involving police officer Everett Maynard, who was found guilty by a federal jury of violating an arrestee's civil rights by using excessive force. While serving as a police officer with the Logan, West Virginia, Police Department, Maynard assaulted a man in the precinct bathroom before dragging him into an adjoining room, hauling him across the room, and ramming his head against a doorframe. The assault initially rendered the victim unconscious and left him with a broken shoulder, a broken nose, and a cut to his head that required staples to close. Assistant Attorney General Kristen Clarke of the Justice Department's Civil Rights Division that prosecuted the case said:

> The Constitution and its Bill of Rights afford all people in our nation the right to be free from unlawful abuse by police officers. The Department of Justice will not tolerate criminal misconduct by law enforcement officials and will hold accountable those who commit civil rights violations.

U.S. Attorney Will Thompson for the Southern District of West Virginia added:

> Everett Maynard abused his authority as a police officer and betrayed the public's trust when he violated an arrestee's civil rights, while the overwhelming majority of law enforcement officers perform their duties with honor and professionalism, those who violate the rights of others will be held accountable. The prosecution of cases like this is important to my office, the citizens of West Virginia and the policing profession.[62]

Focus on Policing

Tyre Nichols and Memphis Police Scorpion Unit

On the evening of January 7, 2023, Tyre Nichols, a 29-year-old Black man, was driving home from his job at FedEx when he was stopped by the Memphis Police for alleged reckless driving. According to video from body-worn cameras, the officers yelled expletives at Nichols as they ordered him to get out of the car and lay on the ground. When he hesitated, the officers opened Nichols's car door, violently pulled him from the car, and forcibly placed him on the ground. When Nichols protested that he had done nothing wrong, the officers hit him and shocked him with a Taser. Nichols, still believing he had done nothing wrong, got off the ground and fled from the officers.

After being chased down and apprehended, video footage showed that at least five police officers kicked, punched, Tased, beat him with a baton, and sprayed Nichols with pepper spray for several minutes as he repeatedly asked, "What did I do?" A few minutes later, several other officers arrived on the scene. Minutes after that, emergency medical personnel arrived. Despite all the police and medical personnel at the scene, Nichols received no medical attention or care for at least 20 minutes after the beating. Tyre Nichols was transported to a local hospital in critical condition; he died three days later. Media coverage of the incident sparked outrage throughout the United States.

The officers involved in the beating were part of the Memphis Police Department's elite Scorpion Unit (*Street Crimes Operation to Restore Peace In Our Neighborhoods*), which was an aggressive, proactive crime suppression unit designed to increase the visibility of police presence in the community. The unit's area of responsibility was composed of three parts, crime suppression, auto theft, and gang activity; they were also allowed to tackle reckless driving. At its height, the unit had 40 officers that consisted of four, 10-men teams.

Investigations into the incident revealed extremely troubling behavior. According to a Memphis police report, after being beaten by the police, Tyre Nichols was propped against a police car, bloodied, dazed, and handcuffed, and one of the Scorpion Unit officers took a picture of him with a cell phone and sent it to several people.

The five officers who beat Nichols, all of whom were also Black men, with five years or less on the job, have been fired and were charged with various felonies, including second-degree murder. A sixth officer at the scene was later fired and another was suspended. Also, two sheriff's deputies have been relieved of duty, and three Memphis Fire Department employees have been fired for failure to render aid. There were ongoing investigations into other officers as well. As a result of these inquiries, the Scorpion Unit has since been disbanded.

While the Maynard case clearly shows a case of police rage, violence, and misconduct, there are numerous others where police use lethal force against unarmed suspects and in many instances the force is later ruled justified. The outcome of these cases may frighten the public and destroy faith in the justice system. Take for instance the following:

■ In 1994, Kim Groves, a resident of the Lower 9th Ward section of New Orleans, filed a civil rights complaint against Len Davis, a veteran officer in the New Orleans Police Department (NOPD), who was operating protection services for local known drug dealers. Groves told investigators that she saw Davis brutally beating and pistol-whipping her nephew. Groves filed a police complaint, which she was told was confidential, but within 24 hours Davis was informed of the complaint. The FBI, which was already targeting Davis as well as other NOPD officers with a wiretapping operation, recorded Davis tracking down Groves's address and ordering fellow NOPD officer Paul "Cool" Hardy to kill her. On October 13, 1994, Hardy shot Groves once in the head in front of her home. Two months later, officers arrested both Davis and Hardy. Davis was convicted and

These types of specialized police units are not unique to Memphis. Many major police departments have similar types of crime suppression units. Famously, the Los Angeles Police Department employed its CRASH anti-gang unit, Baltimore used a Gun Trace Task Force (GTTF) unit, and Washington, DC, formed crime-suppression teams and gun recovery unit. Other departments have similar units that are known as gang units, or violence suppression units; many times they are referred to as "jump-out" units because of the way they swarm assumed perpetrators. Known for their aggressive style of proactive policing, there have been numerous incidents where unit members used excessive force and violence.

Specialized units like the Scorpion or other "jump-out" units are not like SWAT units which are reactive and are dispatched after an incident is taking place. These crime suppression units tend to be more proactive, looking for potential crime and stopping potential and known criminals. They actively seek crimes in progress or crimes that are about to happen. The problem is that these units tend to be very aggressive and often violent, and often go beyond the scope of legal enforcement activities.

Often these units start off with well-meaning officers trying to make communities safer, but they often form into ultra-aggressive street units that run roughshod over the rights of citizens. The problem is that procedural policing is often omitted and many of these units operate with little supervision and oversight,

causing overzealous policing to turn tragic. They are focused on individual stats like how many arrests are made and the number of guns and drugs recovered. This incentivizes officers to take full advantage of the broad discretion under law and push the bounds of legal police tactics. This wayward discretion usually focuses on pretext stops and the ability to detain and search people based on little more than a hunch or a profile. This approach has been proven to be inefficient, alienating, and confrontation-provoking, even as its impact on crime is uncertain. If units like these were given more clear and direct guidance and intense supervision, perhaps they would be able to thrive without violating citizens' basic rights.

Critical Thinking

1. Elite units such as the Scorpion Unit are not unique. Many police departments have them. Do you think that crime-suppression units like the Scorpion Unit are effective at doing their jobs?

2. Would you like a unit like a Scorpion Unit in your community?

3. What can be done to make elite units like these better and more user-friendly?

Sources: https://abcnews.go.com/US/tyre-nichols-video-released-confrontation-memphis-police/story?id=96719253; https://www.nytimes.com/article/tyre-nichols-memphis-police-dead.html; https://abcnews.go.com/US/live-updates/tyre-nichols-police-video-release/?id=96703032#96705289; and https://www.nytimes.com/2023/02/07/us/tyre-nichols-photo-memphis-demetrius-haley.html.

sentenced to death for federal civil rights offenses and Hardy was sentenced to life imprisonment.[63]

- In 1997, Abner Louima, a Haitian-American, was living in New York City when he was arrested during an altercation between the police and other club patrons. Louima was physically attacked, brutalized, and raped by NYPD officers. He was dragged into a police station bathroom, where the officers kicked him in the testicles and jammed a broken wooden broom stick in his rectum. The injuries were so severe that it required three different operations to repair the damage. Two of the offending officers were sentenced to 30 and 15 years, respectively, for the aggravated assault.[64]

- In the late 1990s, the Rampart Division of the LAPD was the most populous area of Los Angeles for officers to patrol. This division had a primarily Latino

AP Images/City of Memphis

The Tyre Nichols case made national headlines and is viewed as a clear-cut example of unrestrained police brutality. Shown here leaning against a car after a brutal attack by five Memphis Police officers, Nichols later died of blunt force injuries to the head after he was beaten during an attempted arrest for reckless driving.

population. To combat the rising violent gang crime, the department created a group of elite anti-gang units called CRASH (**C**ommunity **R**esources **A**gainst **S**treet **H**oodlums). CRASH officers developed a culture in which they began to emulate the violence and tactics of gang members in dress and manner. They had a reputation for being tough and promoting violence. It was later discovered that many of them also engaged in corruption, such as stealing and selling drugs. More than 70 officers were implicated in misconduct, including unprovoked beatings and shootings, planting and covering up evidence, stealing and dealing drugs, as well as perjury.[65]

■ Joseph Miedzianowski was a 22-year city of Chicago police officer. He was often referred to as the most corrupt cop in the history of the Chicago Police Department. He served as both police officer and drug kingpin using his knowledge of the streets and local gangs to shake down drug dealers. During most of his police career he served as the head of the Chicago Police gang unit. He received multiple citations for valor and arrests and he was publicly praised for his high number of street-level drug and illegal weapon busts. He was also secretly working a criminal enterprise, revealing the identity of undercover police officers to known gang members, protecting drug organizations, distributing street-level drugs including crack cocaine, and supplying gang members with weapons and ammunition. In 2001, Joseph Miedzianowski was convicted of 10 counts, including drug conspiracy and racketeering, and was sentenced to life in prison.[66]

■ In 2005, two notorious Baltimore Police Department (BPD) officers, William King and Antonio Murray, were investigated by the FBI and convicted of robbery, extortion, and drug and handgun offenses. King and Murray were veteran officers assigned to BPD's public housing drug unit. The officers distributed the drugs they seized to rival drug dealers with whom they had a financial agreement. The officers pocketed cash and collected money from subsequent drug sales. King described learning to commit crimes as a form of on-the-job training, and blamed immense pressure to reduce crime as the reason he and some colleagues went bad. He said that his actions came as a result of departmental pressure to reduce crime and that there was a tacit acceptance of breaking the rules within the BPD.[67]

These are just a very few of the many cases that have helped to erode confidence in the police over the years. Are the courts too lenient with police when they use excessive force and violence? Are police more inclined to use violence now because of the dangerous mass killing and shooting situations they hear about on a daily basis? And if so, what can be done to ameliorate the current state of affairs?

Andrew Goldstein suggests that the absence of public trust in police is what characterizes the current negative state of police-community relations in the United States. Without having public trust in the police, the concept of "policing by consent" is difficult or impossible to achieve and the ideal of public safety suffers.[68] These well-documented cases of police abuse of power have further eroded the confidence that the police must have in the public. Former "FBI director James Comey has asserted that the federal government lacks comprehensive data on police-involved shootings. Thus, while the number of tragic deaths caused by police use of lethal force that are captured on film has increased, this may be the result of technology (particularly cell phone cameras) rather than indicative of a surge in police use of lethal force."[69] Admittedly, most police officers are well-intentioned officers and good at their job, but what is needed is for these good officers to step in more often to stop the action of the bad officers. In order to try to rebuild that trust, reform efforts must be taken by the entire profession of policing.

Some would argue that complete reform of policing would be expensive and time consuming. Although that is true, not reforming the system is even more costly to cities and towns, and can devastate a local budget. In the summer of 2020, Denver, Colorado, citizens were protesting against racism and police brutality when they claimed police officers acted dangerously and mishandled the response to the protests. In so doing, they endangered the citizens they had sworn to serve and protect. They also failed to follow their own policies and procedures, failing to document the incident and, in many instances, turning off their body-worn-cameras.[70]

An eight-member panel found that the policies and practices at the highest level of the Denver Police Department (DPD) led officers to deploy tear gas, pepper balls, and other weapons against peaceful demonstrators. It was argued that the police actions violated the plaintiffs' First and, in some cases, Fourth Amendment rights. It is clear that the jury has taken the First Amendment rights (to peacefully assemble) very seriously and are willing to hold government officials (the police) responsible for maintaining that right.

According to the judge's ruling, in addition to the monetary damages awarded to the plaintiffs in this case, District Court Judge R. Brooke Jackson could still order specific policy changes within the DPD through a process known as injunctive relief. Most plaintiffs in this case are expected to receive $1 million each from the city of Denver in damages. One plaintiff, who experienced a severe head injury, will receive $3 million in damages. The prosecutors in this case argue that many of the protesters in Denver were not peaceful protesters, but rather part of a riotous mob. The prosecutor argued that the Denver police officers should have been able to distinguish between violent demonstrators and peaceful protestors when deploying tear gas, pepper balls, and other crowd control weapons.[71]

The term "police reform" is not a new concept. In fact, the term was first used in the 1930s to address a general malaise and lack of professionalism in policing. This idea was so prominent in American policing that the period from 1930 to 1970 was referred to as the "Reform Era" of policing. Prior to this point, the structure of policing was the product of changing political systems, and often varied after each election, depending on which politician was in office. The reform era of American policing was a time in which officials attempted to address rampant police corruption, and an overall lack of professionalism. During this period, American policing struggled to develop a professional crime-fighting mantra with the bulk of the police resources dedicated to arresting offenders. This pursuit was relatively ineffective and overwhelmingly reactive in nature.

So, what is police reform? Reform is an assertion that the institution of policing should move beyond traditionally superficial and reactionary changes in policies, procedures, and practices. Policing as an institution should fundamentally rethink its strategies of public safety by proactively reducing the scope of traditional, reactive policing and investing in preventative and proactive

police reform
A way to reimagine policing in the twenty-first century, in order to produce a more effective, more efficient, more user-friendly version of public safety.

community-based services. Accountability is at the heart of this change. **Police reform** also insists that violent, abusive, and rogue officers are held accountable for their actions. Ultimately, the term reform simply means *to introduce positive change into the conduct and functioning of American Policing.* Police reform is a way to reimagine policing in the twenty-first century, in order to produce a more effective, more efficient, more user-friendly version of public safety. Police reform and professionalism are not new concepts. They have been tried various times over the years with varied results. As you will read below, August Vollmer tried with less than stellar results.

August Vollmer's Failed Attempts at Professionalization

August Vollmer, often touted as the father of modern American policing, was the first police chief in Berkeley, California. Vollmer was a true reformer in the twentieth century and was ahead of his time. Among other things, Vollmer is credited as being the first to establish a bicycle patrol unit and he created the first centralized police records system. Regarding police investigations, he also streamlined and organized criminal investigations. He also began to militarize his local police department, based partly on his military experience in the military during the Spanish-American war.

Vollmer was wildly successful in the implementation of reform and the adoption of innovation in Berkeley, California. His successes made him a candidate for the police chief's job in the Los Angeles Police Department (LAPD) and this was a challenge that he was eager to embrace. However, he did not achieve the same successes in LA and only stayed in the chief position for a year. The city of Los Angeles was riddled with corruption and had a high crime rate. City administrators hired Vollmer because they believed he was a small-town police chief who would be easily controlled by political interests and he would not interfere with lucrative levels of vice and corruption in the city.

However, accepting levels of corruption and graft went against Vollmer's nature and he immediately moved to clean up criminality in Los Angeles. Local politicians tried to undermine his efforts at every turn. In his book, *August Vollmer: The Father of American Policing*, William Oliver documents the animosity between Vollmer and the city's politicians. Although Vollmer left the position too soon to make all the changes he had planned for LAPD, he was able to implement some reforms. Interestingly, Oliver shares that before leaving Los Angeles, Vollmer completed a study that included several recommendations to improve the LAPD. That study remained on a shelf for 25 years, until William Parker became chief in 1950, and he found and implemented many of Vollmer's ideas.

LO6

Summarize the George Floyd Justice in Policing Act of 2020.

▶ ## George Floyd Justice in Policing Act of 2020

One such reform action is the *George Floyd Justice in Policing Act of 2020.* This act was passed by the U.S. House of Representatives on June 25, 2020, one month after the murder of George Floyd by former Minneapolis Police Officer Derek

Chauvin. This legislation was spurred on by nationwide protests, in all 50 states, various riots, and a national outcry for police reform.

On May 25, 2020 in Minneapolis, Minnesota, George Floyd, a 46-year-old Black man, purchased a pack of cigarettes with a $20 bill that a local convenience store clerk believed to be counterfeit. The clerk then called the police to report the incident. Four Minneapolis police officers (Derek Chauvin, J. Alexander Kueng, Thomas Lane, and Tou Thao) responded to the scene and engaged Floyd. During the arrest, Floyd was handcuffed and taken to the ground. Officer Chauvin kneeled on Floyd's neck for approximately nine minutes while officers Kueng and Lane assisted Chauvin in restraining Floyd by kneeling on his back and legs. The fourth officer, Tou Thao, prevented bystanders from interfering with the arrest and intervening to help Floyd as events unfolded.

While on the ground in handcuffs, George Floyd complained about being unable to breathe, became more distressed, and expressed the fear he was about to die and called for his mother, as Officer Chauvin continued to kneel on his neck. After several minutes, Floyd stopped speaking and laid motionless. Officer Kueng found no pulse when urged to check on Floyd. Despite this, Chauvin refused onlookers' pleas to lift his knee off Floyd's neck. Chauvin stayed in that position until directed by paramedics to get off his neck. Seventeen minutes after the first police car arrived at the scene, Floyd was unconscious and pinned beneath three police officers, showing no signs of life.

Those events were recorded and broadcast over social media and the world watched George Floyd's death. Various video footage shows Minneapolis officers engaging in a series of actions of brutality that violated the policies of the Minneapolis Police Department and turned fatal, leaving Floyd unable to breathe, even as he and onlookers begged for help. The next day, after onlooker and security camera videos became public, all four officers were fired. Two separate autopsies ruled that George Floyd's death was a homicide. Derek Chauvin was charged with second-degree unintentional murder and second-degree manslaughter. Kueng, Lane, and Thao were charged with aiding and abetting second-degree murder. All four former police officers will stand trial for their actions.

In a Minneapolis courtroom, Chauvin was charged with second-degree unintentional murder, third-degree murder, and second-degree manslaughter in state court. He was found guilty, and on June 25, 2021, he was sentenced to 22.5 years in state prison.[72] He was then charged by the federal government for violating George Floyd's civil rights. On July 9, 2022, after a guilty plea, Chauvin was sentenced to 21 years in federal prison for violating the civil rights of George Floyd. Those sentences will run concurrently.[73]

On May 18, 2022, former Minneapolis police officer, Thomas Lane, pleaded guilty to a state charge of aiding and abetting second-degree manslaughter in the killing of George Floyd. Lane admitted that he intentionally helped restrain Floyd in a way that created an unreasonable risk and caused his death. As part of his plea agreement, the more serious charge of aiding and abetting second-degree unintentional murder was be dismissed, meaning that he will avoid what could have been a lengthy state sentence if he was convicted of the murder charge. Lane along with former Minneapolis police officers Tou Thao and J. Alexander Kueng were previously convicted in federal court of several counts of willfully violating George Floyd's rights. The three disgraced officers are all free on bond while waiting to be sentenced on the federal charges.[74]

George Floyd Justice in Policing Act of 2020

Bill that increases accountability for law enforcement misconduct, restricts the use of certain policing practices deemed reckless, enhances police transparency and data collection, and establishes best practices and training requirements for cadets and in-service training for veteran officers.

This **George Floyd Justice in Policing Act of 2020** addresses a wide range of policies and practices in policing and law enforcement accountability. The bill increases accountability for law enforcement misconduct, restricts the use of certain policing practices deemed reckless, enhances police transparency and data collection, and establishes best practices and training requirements for cadets and in-service training for veteran officers. The bill enhances existing enforcement tools to address violations by police officers. The bill does the following (among other things):

- Lowers the criminal intent standard—from willful to knowing or reckless—to convict a law enforcement officer for misconduct in a federal prosecution,

- Limits qualified immunity as a defense to liability in a private civil action against a law enforcement officer, and

- Grants administrative subpoena power to the Department of Justice (DOJ) in pattern-or-practice investigations.[75]

The George Floyd Justice in Policing Act of 2020 establishes a framework to prevent and address racial profiling by law enforcement at the federal, state, and local levels. It also limits the unnecessary use of force and restricts the use of no-knock warrants, chokeholds, and carotid holds. The bill also creates a national registry (the National Police Misconduct Registry) to compile data on complaints and records of police misconduct. It also establishes new reporting requirements, including on the use of force, officer misconduct, and routine policing practices (e.g., stops and searches). Finally, the George Floyd Justice in Policing Act of 2020 directs the Department of Justice to create uniform accreditation standards for law enforcement agencies and requires law enforcement officers to complete training on racial profiling, implicit bias, and the duty to intervene when another officer uses excessive force.[76]

Police reform is a simple and promising concept. It seems like a concept that everyone could agree on and get behind. But yet there are people who shun the idea, and even when implemented, it often faces obstacles. Yet other, more progressive police entities will champion the idea of reform. The Washington (State) Fraternal Order of Police, which represents more than 2,500 police officers, decided early on to support police reform, and it continues to play a positive role in implementing the changes. The laws, passed by the legislature in the wake of the George Floyd murder and community outcry, dramatically changed many aspects of policing, including when officers can use physical force and respond to calls that don't involve criminal activity. Considered among the nation's most ambitious police reforms, these efforts, in theory, strengthen accountability, help undo racial injustice, and reduce unnecessary violence by law enforcement.

When addressing levels of accountability, perhaps reform should start in police training academies and their on-the-job-training with their field training officers (FTOs). In a 2014 study published by Ryan Getty, John Worrall, and Robert Morris, they assert that much of the problem related to bad police behavior can be tracked to how they were trained, and specifically who trained them. A bad FTO could predict negative behavior of newer officers when on patrol. This study, which utilizes both individual- as well as organizational-level data, examined the relationship between FTOs and the subsequent allegations of misconduct by the rookie officers that they trained. Getty, Worrall, and Morris found that approximately one-quarter of the trainees' allegations of misconduct after their supervision period was over could be linked specifically to their FTO training. They suggest that the apple (the police trainee) does not fall far from the tree (the FTO).[77]

Calls to Defund the Police

◀ **LO7**
Analyze the concept of defunding the police.

Since the 2020 killing of George Floyd in police custody, many communities have made the provocative call to defund the police. This event led to historic protests and reform movements across the United States and the world that has continued into 2021. "Not since the civil rights movement of the 1960s has America seen such a magnitude of people calling for both the recognition of institutionalized racism and radical policing reforms."[78] The argument is that the repeated use of lethal force causing fatalities against unarmed people of color has driven global protests against police violence and fueled criticism of policing as a mechanism for public safety.

Nationwide, demands to abolish the police as well as calls to reform or at least transform American policing have resurfaced with a central focus on eliminating the structural racism within the system.[79]

Calls for defunding have generally focused on resource reallocation. That is moving resources from traditional police action to other community services that may improve the quality of life within marginalized communities. **Defunding the police**, or better stated, budgeting less money for police and reinvesting those monies in other (preventative) public safety strategies, has become a prominent idea in the national conversation around police reform. Typically, the calls for defunding are made in the context of communities that have experienced or been on the losing end of an "us-versus-them" mentality between the police and the community. This relationship is most often expressed by community members as a punitive action against the police agency for perceived misconduct.[80]

defunding the police
A call for budgeting less money for police and reinvesting those monies in other (preventative) public safety strategies. It has become a prominent idea in the national conversation around police reform.

According to Vera Institute, nationally, the cost for policing is $115 billion annually.[81] Calls for defunding have generally focused on shifting resources away from reactive law enforcement agencies to other preventative public services that may improve the quality of life within marginalized communities.[82] The argument for defunding the police is that the police handle many public encounters and complex issues that they are not well equipped to handle, or should not handle at all.[83]

Some researchers have expressed general support for the request to reallocate some portions of police budgets toward various community-based or local government initiatives whose primary purpose is to improve the quality of life of community members instead of simply continuing to operate as instruments of pre-adjudication punishment and state-sanctioned, legitimized coercion.

One commonly raised suggestion is to reduce the police responses to 9-1-1 calls associated with mental health episodes and transferring these calls and the accompanying resources to mental health providers. Those calling for the defunding of police have also argued for reducing police response to calls for service for non-felonies, minor crimes, and community concerns such as quality-of-life issues or juvenile delinquency

Simone Hogan/Shutterstock.com

Calls to defund the police have grown after the highly publicized killing of Black people in police custody. Moving money from reactive aggressive policing into preventative community programs is what is being called for. Many protesters feel their voices and perspectives are not being heard, so taking to the streets to protest appears to be the best option available.

within schools. According to the Vera Institute, more than 80 percent of all arrests nationwide are for low-level, nonviolent offenses.[84] It is argued that these calls for service can be the beginning of a harmful cycle of arrest, systemic disparity, use of force, and unnecessary involvement in the criminal justice system. At the heart of the defunding debate is simply issues of the public safety needs of the community and who should be responsible for addressing them.[85]

Citizens are also complaining of disparate enforcement between protests in communities of color and other protests. It was widely documented the overly militaristic response to police in Washington, DC, during the largely peaceful Black Lives Matter (BLM) protests. There were scenes of the military and police in riot gear guarding national monuments and the like during the BLM protests, but very little police response to the January 6, 2021, insurrection at the U.S. Capitol on the day that the presidential election was being certified. According to Chris Burbank, vice president of law enforcement strategy for the Center for Policing Equity and the former chief of police of Salt Lake City, he "fears the seemingly muted response at the Capitol marks a step back in the reckoning over racism in policing, even as it proves the need for further reform. The divide is significant and very difficult to repair."[86] Even as there are calls to reduce or reallocate funding of police departments, law enforcement spending as a share of general expenditures rose slightly in 2021 from 13.6 percent to 13.7 percent, according to data compiled by Bloomberg CityLab.[87]

It could be argued that reform is needed because the police are inherently set up to fail. The problem may be that we ask the police to do too many things. Almost without exception, the police have been made to be the front line in addressing a significant amount of society's problems, even those that may not be crimes. The police often have to deal with mental health calls, lost relatives, juvenile complaints of a nonthreatening nature (such as skateboarding), graffiti, loud music or loud party complaints, noninjury traffic accidents, to name a few. Most police training may be designed for fundamentally different situations and outcomes that might be difficult to reconcile; Americans nevertheless expect the police to be able to seamlessly shift between these roles.

Perhaps we should have other services available to handle noncrime-related calls in order to remove the police (the gun and arrest powers) from calls that are not crimes. We should consider that some communities might want to contemplate whether removing incompatible responsibilities from police might be a more effective effort than trying to better train police officers to address a vast array of roles. Maybe with reform efforts comes a distinguishable set of calls that are appropriate for police intervention, and another type of response organization or team to handle the rest. The concept of "defunding the police" can look quite different, when the policy focus is not on punishing the police by cutting their budgets, but instead productively taking the police and the criminal justice system more broadly off the front line for responding to noncrime-related calls.[88]

LO8

State why reform efforts fail.

Why Reforms Often Fail

Even with the best of intentions, some reform efforts are destined to fail even before they get a chance to be fully implemented. Change is hard for many people, and even harder when people believe their current level of comfort or privilege will be affected. Some people avoid or even try to hamper some of the reform efforts because they are often seen as changed to the status quo. Any change in an officer's day-to-day routine is seen as disrupting habits and many will feel upset to see the end of the old ways of doing things. Many people like doing things because "we have always done things that way."

Many people resist change due to the fear of the unknown or not understanding what is happening or what comes next. Many changes happen without fully informing the rank-and-file officers, which makes them skeptical and non-trusting. Or officers may resist change because they feel that they are being targeted. Sometimes people want to avoid levels of responsibility when reforms affect their actions. It sometimes feels like *reform* is a code word for punishment, so people balk at the idea of reform.

Many people feel that reform is not needed and that the status quo is fine. Or people can experience embarrassment or have feelings of inadequacy or humiliation because it appears that the old ways weren't good ways. Sometimes middle managers or frontline supervisors may feel that levels of authority and oversight are being taken from them. They will fight to retain their perceived power. Many times officers do not believe that the problem lies solely with their actions, they want to push back on community members actions and deflect attention and responsibility. They may ask if the police are being reformed, what actions are taken to hold community members accountable.

Some reforms fail because they are not fully thought out or are just reactionary. Typically, knee-jerk policy changes are doomed to fail from the beginning. In order for a reform to work, the issue has to be well studied and the reform has to be appropriate and sustainable. The problem has to be examined from its origins and not just from the action itself. It's helpful if you can get buy-in from the community, the officers, or politicians. All three may not be needed, but the more people who get involved to help develop the reform, the more likely that it will be sustained and successful.

For any of the reform measures to work, there has to be a basic acknowledgment that there is a problem. There are still too many people who believe that the current form of traditional, reactive, aggressive police is working just fine. Many would say that the level of force used in these encounters was reasonable, or the resulting death would not have happened if the suspect/citizen would have just complied. The retort to that is in many instances the citizen did comply or was already in police custody when they died (or were killed). The main issue is that most people, particularly unarmed citizens, should not die due to a police encounter. Because the frequency of death seems to be increasing, perhaps reform is the logical next step. As we consider reforming local police, we must ensure that we do not strip them of their ability to conduct their core mission of protecting citizens.

Summary

LO1 Analyze the role of police in mass shootings and anti-terrorism activities.

Police have increasingly been called to respond to active shooter and mass shooting situations in a variety of settings ranging from schools to music concerts and more. The Police Executive Research Forum notes,

individuals involved in mass shootings rarely just snap—rather there is a build up over time. They recommend that police work with other agencies to "connect the dots" and help troubled people before they have the opportunity to engage in violence. Because these events evolve so rapidly, police must respond equally fast and with limited information. It is important to remember that even an enhanced police response would have been purely reactive to a shooting already in progress.

LO2   Evaluate whether prevention is possible.

It is important to remember that even an enhanced police response is purely reactive for a shooting already in progress particularly for a suspect that has mental health concerns. Prevention is difficult even with available information on possible suspects. The police must sort through an enormous amount of intelligence to determine which is valid and what tips are dead ends. This can be difficult given that police agencies do not have unlimited resources. There are also challenges associated with information sharing. If one agency gets a warning about an individual threat, it is not necessarily true that the local agency at risk would get that same information. There must be appropriate mental health services available to assist at risk people before they engage in violence. Finally, police must educate the public on warning signs for mass shootings.

LO3   Describe the extent of terrorism against U.S. citizens.

Terrorism has increasingly been added to the list of responsibilities for local police. After 9/11, responding to terrorist threats was also added to the responsibilities of local police. While it may seem intuitive to focus on foreign enemies, domestic terrorism continues to plague the United States. The growing concerns in the United States about the rise in hate crimes and activities led the executive branch to shift focus to this domestic terrorism. The DHS stated that hate crimes and far-right groups represent a growing share of the threat to the Homeland. The rise in reported hate crimes and related acts of violence linked to White supremacist groups, and the impact of these violent incidents on communities is a major focus of home-grown terrorists. These groups tend to be heavily armed and organized around such themes as White supremacy, anti-abortion, militant tax resistance, and religious revisionism. Identified groups have included, at one time or another, the Aryan Republican Army, the Aryan Nation, the Posse Comitatus, and the Ku Klux Klan. These groups want to shape U.S. government policy over a range of matters, including ending abortion rights, extending the right to bear arms, and eliminating federal taxation.

LO4   Explain the effects that responding to mass casualties has on the police.

Mass casualty events affect not only the victims and their families but also the police and other emergency responders. Regardless of assignment, police are exposed to a wide variety of stressors—frequently interacting with people at their worst moments. This is considered to be secondary trauma. While the police

are not "victims" of these events, they are also severely affected by the violence and can have lasting effects long after the event has occurred. It is clear that in any coordinated response to mass violence or terrorism, consideration should be given to the long-term needs of the first responders.

LO5   Recognize the concept of police reform.

Police reform is an assertion that the institution of policing should move beyond traditionally superficial and reactionary changes in policies, procedures, and practices. Policing as an institution should fundamentally rethink its strategies of public safety by proactively reducing the scope of traditional, reactive policing and investing in preventative and proactive community-based services. Accountability is at the heart of this change. Police reform also insists that violent, abusive, and rogue officers are held accountable for their actions.

LO6   Summarize the George Floyd Justice in Policing Act of 2020.

The George Floyd Justice in Policing Act of 2020 establishes a framework to prevent and address racial profiling by law enforcement at the federal, state, and local levels. It also limits the unnecessary use of force and restricts the use of no-knock warrants, chokeholds, and carotid holds. The bill also creates a national registry to compile data on complaints and records of police misconduct. It also establishes new reporting requirements, including on the use of force, officer misconduct, and routine policing practices.

LO7   Analyze the concept of defunding the police.

Defunding the police generally focuses on resource reallocation, which is moving resources from traditional reactive police action to other preventative community services that may improve the quality of life within marginalized communities. Defunding the police or, better stated, budgeting less money for police and reinvesting those monies in other (preventative) public safety strategies, has become a prominent idea in the national conversation around police reform.

LO8   State why reform efforts fail.

Even with the best of intentions, some reform efforts are destined to fail even before they get a chance to be fully implemented. Many people like doing things because they have always done things a certain way. Many people resist change due to the fear of the unknown or not understanding what is happening or what comes next. Sometimes officers do not believe that the problem lies solely with the police and want to push back on community members actions and deflect attention and responsibility. Some reforms fail because they are not fully thought out or are just reactionary knee-jerk policy changes. For any of the reform measures to work, there has to be a basic acknowledgment of the problem. There are still too many people who believe that the current form of traditional, reactive, aggressive police is working just fine, and no checks and balances are needed. As we consider reforming the police, we must ensure that we do not strip them of their ability to conduct their core mission of protecting citizens.

Key Terms

active shooter, 120
mass shootings, 120
hostage and barricaded suspect incidents, 120
school shootings, 122
right-wing, 129
The National Commission on Terrorist Attacks Upon the United States, 132

Arizona Counter Terrorism Information Center, 135
Department of Homeland Security, 136
National Criminal Intelligence Sharing Plan, 138
fusion centers, 138
INTERPOL, 139
police reform, 146

George Floyd Justice in Policing Act of 2020, 148
defunding the police, 149

Notes

1. U.S. Department of Homeland Security (DHS), "Active Shooter: How to Respond," *Office of Intelligence and Analysis Assessment,* 2008, http://www.dhs.gov/xlibrary/assets/active _shooter_booklet.pdf.
2. Joel A. Capellan, "Lone Wolf Terrorist or Deranged Shooter? A Study of Ideological Active Shooter Events in the United States, 1970–2014," *Studies in Conflict & Terrorism* 38, no. 6 (2015), 395–413.
3. Michael Rocque and Grant Duwe, "Rampage Shootings: An Historical, Empirical, and Theoretical Overview," *Current Opinion in Psychology* 19 (2018), 28–33.
4. https://www.gunviolencearchive.org/explainer.
5. https://www.theiacp.org/sites/default/files/2018-08/Active ShooterPaper2018.pdf.
6. Dave Collins, Carolyn Thompson, Michael Balsamo and John Wawrow. *Associated Press.* 10 Dead in Buffalo Supermarket attack, police call Hate Crime, https://apnews.com/article /buffalo-supermarket-shooting-442c6d97a073f39f99d006 dbba40f64b.
7. https://www.ocregister.com/2022/05/15/multiple-people -wounded-in-shooting-at-laguna-woods-church/?fbclid =IwAR1TeDos1JbeKs66tiVsc5biOmOm8mofAqOTVKm 0umgHsthPQFAZY3a5wvc.
8. Madeline Buckley, John Keilman, Jake Sheridan, Emily Hoerner, Gavin Good, Megan Crepeau, Tracy Swartz and Annie Sweeney. "Alleged shooter in Highland Park July 4th parade attack charged with 7 counts of murder in 'premeditated and calculated attack'" https://www.chicagotribune.com /news/breaking/ct-highland-park-shooting-day-after -20220705-2bfeprry5vckpjhugmn5oiuaj4-story.html.
9. Saeed Ahmed. America has seen at least 601 mass shootings so far in 2022. November 20, 2022 https://www.npr.org/2022/05/15 /1099008586/mass-shootings-us-2022-tally-number.
10. Véronique Irwin Ke Wang, Jiashan Cui, and Alexandra Thompson, Report on Indicators of School Crime and Safety: 2021. Institute of Educational Sciences. National Center for Educational Statistics.
11. https://www.policeforum.org/assets/docs/Critical_Issues _Series/the%20police%20response%20to%20active% 20shooter%20incidents%202014.pdf.
12. https://www.theiacp.org/sites/default/files/2018-08/Active ShooterPaper2018.pdf.
13. https://www.theiacp.org/sites/default/files/2018-08/Active ShooterPaper2018.pdf.
14. Bill Hutchinson, Juju Chang, Jasmine Brown, Josh Margolin, Katie Muldowney, and Eamon McNiff,. The Anatomy of the Las Vegas Mass Shooting, the Deadliest in Modern US History. *ABC News*' "Nightline" Takes a Comprehensive Look at Las Vegas Mass Shooting, December 23, 2018.
15. Joel A. Capellan and Carla Lewandowski, "Can Threat Assessment Help Police Prevent Mass Public Shootings? Testing an Intelligence-Led Policing Tool," *Policing: An International Journal of Police Strategies and Management* 42, no. 1 (2018).
16. https://www.cnn.com/2018/03/26/us/march-for-our-lives/index .html.
17. Adam. Lankford and Eric Madfis, "Don't Name Them, Don't Show Them, but Report Everything Else: A Pragmatic Proposal for Denying Mass Killers the Attention They Seek and Deterring Future Offenders," *American Behavioral Scientist* 62, no. 2 (2018), 260–279.
18. https://www.alicetraining.com/wp-content/uploads/2018/04 /ALICE-In-Action.pdf.
19. https://hechingerreport.org/is-the-trauma-of-training-for-a -school-shooter-worth-it/.
20. Jaclyn Schildkraut, Amanda B. Nickerson, and Thomas Ristoff, "Locks, Lights, Out of Sight: Assessing Students' Perceptions of Emergency Preparedness across Multiple Lockdown Drills," *Journal of School Violence*, 2019, doi: 10.1080/15388220.2019 .1703720.
21. https://www.dhs.gov/science-and-technology/news/2018/11/16 /news-release-funding-awarded-school-age-trauma-training.
22. https://time.com/5650839/bulletproof-backpacks-shootings/.

23. Department of Homeland Security Strategic Framework for Countering Terrorism and Targeted Violence, September 2019, https://www.dhs.gov/sites/default/files/publications/19_0920 _plcy_strategic-framework-countering-terrorism-targeted -violence.pdf.

24. Michael McGarrity and Calvin Shivers, "Testimony in Front of the Subcommittee on Civil Rights and Civil Liberties in a Hearing Titled 'Confronting White Supremacy.'" Their testimonies are available at https://docs.house.gov/meetings /GO/GO02/20190604/109579/HHRG-116-GO02-Wstate -McGarrityM-20190604.pdf.

25. Seth G. Jones, Catrina Doxsee, and Nicholas Harrington, *The Tactics and Targets of Domestic Terrorists* (Washington, DC: Center for Strategic and International Studies, 2021).

26. https://qz.com/1435885/data-shows-more-us-terror-attacks -by-right-wing-and-religious-extremists/.

27. https://www.researchgate.net/profile/Joshua_Freilich/publication /304194034_National_Security_and_Domestic_Terrorism_The _US_Case/links/5796ae8c08aeb0ffcd05959f.pdf.

28. FY 2022 Budget in Brief, Department of Homeland Security, https://www.dhs.gov/sites/default/files/publications/dhs_bib _-_web_version_-_final_508.pdf.

29. http://www.911memorial.org/faq-about-911.

30. http://www.nytimes.com/2002/07/07/nyregion/fatal-confusion -troubled-emergency-response-9-11-exposed-deadly-flaws -rescue.html?pagewanted=all.

31. Daniel E. Marks and Ivan Y. Sun, "The Impact of 9/11 on Organizational Development among State and Local Law Enforcement Agencies," *Journal of Contemporary Criminal Justice* 23, no. 2 (2007), 159–173.

32. John M. Violanti, Cherie Castellano, Julie O'Rourke, and Douglas Paton, "Proximity to the 9/11 Terrorist Attack and Suicide Ideation in Police Officers," *Traumatology* 12, no. 3 (2006), 248.

33. Michael Price, "National Security and Local Police," 2013, *Brennan Center for Justice at New York University School of Law, New York.*

34. William K. Rashbaum, "Terror Makes All the World a Beat for New York Police," *The New York Times*, July 15, 2002, p. B1; Al Baker, "Leader Sees New York Police in Vanguard of Terror Fight," *The New York Times*, August 6, 2002, p. A2; Stephen Flynn, "America the Vulnerable," *Foreign Affairs* 81 (January– February 2002), 60.

35. Tom R. Tyler, "Toughness vs. Fairness: Police Policies and Practices for Managing the Risk of Terrorism." In *Evidence- Based Counterterrorism Policy* (New York, NY: Springer, 2012), pp. 353–363.

36. https://www.theiacp.org/sites/default/files/2018-07/BCOT GuidanceForCommunityLeaders.pdf.

37. Stephan G. Grimmelikhuijsen and Albert J. Meijer, "Does Twitter Increase Perceived Police Legitimacy?," *Public Administration Review* 75, no. 4 (2015), 598–607.

38. Sebastian Denef, Petra S. Bayerl, and Nico A. Kaptein, "Social Media and the Police: Tweeting Practices of British Police Forces during the August 2011 Riots," *Proceedings of the SIGCHI Conference on Human Factors in Computing Systems*, ACM, 2013.

39. Edward F. Davis, Alejandro A. Alves, and David Alan Sklansky, "Social Media and Police Leadership: Lessons from Boston," (2014), 10, https://www.ojp.gov/pdffiles1/nij/244760.pdf.

40. Lori Brainard and Mariglynn Edlins, "Top 10 US Municipal Police Departments and Their Social Media Usage," *The American Review of Public Administration* 45, no. 6 (2015), 728–745.

41. The survey was sent electronically and 553 law enforcement agencies in 44 states participated.

42. International Association of Chiefs of Police, 2015, "2015 Social Media Survey Results," https://www.valorforblue.org /Clearinghouse/549/International-Association-of-Chiefs-of -Police-2015-Social-Media-Survey-Results, accessed May 30, 2023.

43. Lori Brainard and Mariglynn Edlins, "Top 10 US Municipal Police Departments and Their Social Media Usage," *The American Review of Public Administration* 45, no. 6 (2015), 728–745.

44. Lauri Stevens, "Social Media in Policing: Nine Steps for Success," *Police Chief Magazine* LXXVII, no. 2 (February 2010).

45. Final Report of President's Task Force on 21st Century Policing, 2015, https://cops.usdoj.gov/pdf/taskforce/taskforce _finalreport.pdf.

46. Harris County Homeland Security & Emergency Management, http://www.hcoem.org, accessed May 2014.

47. Montgomery County, Maryland, Homeland Security, http:// www.montgomerycountymd.gov/oemhs/, accessed May 2014.

48. Arizona Department of Public Safety, "*Arizona Fusion Center,*" https://www.azdps.gov/about/programs/actic. Also refer to http://www.azactic.gov, sites accessed May 30, 2023

49. Arizona Counter Terrorism Information Center, http://www .azactic.gov/About/Operation/, accessed May 2014.

50. Department of Homeland Security, https://www.dhs.gov /about-dhs.

51. FY 2022 Budget in Brief. Department of Homeland Security, https://www.dhs.gov/sites/default/files/publications/dhs _bib_-_web_version_-_final_508.pdf.

52. Department of Homeland Security, http://www.dhs.gov/history, accessed May 2014.

53. Customs and Border Protection, https://www.cbp.gov/border -security/ports-entry/cargo-security/examination, accessed June 2022.

54. Immigration and Customs Enforcement, https://www.ice.gov /about-ice, accessed June, 2022.

55. U.S. Secret Service, https://www.secretservice.gov/sites /default/files/reports/2021-03/USSS2010AYweb.pdf, accessed June 2022.

56. Federal Bureau of Investigation, *Protecting America Against Terrorist Attack: A Closer Look at the FBI's Joint Terrorism Task Forces*, https://www.fbi.gov/investigate/terrorism/joint -terrorism-task-forces, accessed June, 2022.

57. *Fusion Center Guidelines: Developing and Sharing Information and Intelligence in a New Era*, http://www.it.ojp.gov/documents /fusion_center_guidelines.pdf, accessed June 2022.

58. Charles R. Swanson, Leonard Territo, and Robert W. Taylor, *Police Administration: Structures, Processes, and Behavior*, 7th ed. (Upper Saddle River, NJ: Prentice Hall, 2008), pp. 77–78.

59. https://www.theiacp.org/topics/mass-casualty-events-and -terrorism.

60. https://www.orlandosentinel.com/2019/01/09/orange-county -starts-program-to-aid-first-responders-struggling-with -traumatic-pulse-memories/. C. R. Figley, "Compassion Fatigue: Toward a New Understanding of the Costs of Caring." In B. H. Stamm (Ed.), *Secondary traumatic stress: Self-care issues for clinicians, researchers, and educators*. (Baltimore, MD: The Sidran Press, 1995), pp. 3–28.

61. Seth Stoughton, Law Enforcement's Warrior Problem, 128 HARV. L. REV. F. 225.

62. Department of Justice, Office of Public Affairs, Former Police Officer Found Guilty of Violating an Arrestee's Civil Rights by Using Excessive Force, November 18, 2021,

63. https://www.nola.com/news/courts/article_c15cb712-c60a -5950-b299-d8b73638005a.html.

64. https://www.vanityfair.com/magazine/1997/12/louima199712.

65. https://www.pbs.org/wgbh/pages/frontline/shows/lapd /scandal/cron.html.

66. https://chicago.suntimes.com/crime/2021/7/7/22567247/judge -denies-sentencing-break-corrupt-ex-chicago-cop-joseph -miedzianowski.

67. https://www.baltimoresun.com/news/crime/bs-md-ci-cr-king-murray-sentence-reduced-20210525-7a2n7xjwd5hinnqutje3rjkvyq-story.html.

68. Andrew Goldsten, "Police Reform and the Problem of Trust," *Theoretical Criminology* 9, no. 4, (2005), 443–470.

69. American Bar Association Task Force on Building Public Trust in the American Justice System, January 25, 2017, https://www.americanbar.org/content/dam/aba/administrative/office_president/2_8_task_force_on_building_trust_in_american_justice_system.authcheckdam.pdf.

70. Denverite. March 25, 2022. https://denverite.com/2022/03/25/dpd-verdict-protesters-to-get-more-than-13-million-over-police-response-to-george-floyd-rallies/.

71. Ibid.

72. https://www.npr.org/sections/trial-over-killing-of-george-floyd/2021/06/25/1009524284/derek-chauvin-sentencing-george-floyd-murder.

73. https://www.vibe.com/news/national/derek-chauvin-sentenced-george-floyd-civil-rights-1234674825/.

74. https://apnews.com/article/death-of-george-floyd-minneapolis-thomas-lane-tou-thao-677bca9f4e263a28db3ab7a14a3db93c.

75. Congress.gov, https://www.congress.gov/bill/116th-congress/house-bill/7120.

76. Ibid.

77. R. M. Getty, J. L. Worrall, and R. G. Morris, "How Far From the Tree Does the Apple Fall? Field Training Officers, Their Trainees, and Allegations of Misconduct," *Crime & Delinquency* 62 (2016), 821–839.

78. C. Lum, C. S. Koper, and X. Wu, "Can We Really Defund the Police? A Nine-Agency Study of Police Response to Calls for Service," *Police Quarterly*, 2021, https://doi.org/10.1177/10986111211035002.

79. J. E. Cobbina and D. Jones-Brown, "Too Much Policing: Why Calls Are Made to Defund the Police," *Punishment & Society*, 2021, https://doi.org/10.1177/14624745211045652.

80. M. J. D. Vermeer, D. Woods, and B. A. Jackson, "Would Law Enforcement Leaders Support Defunding the Police? Probably—If Communities Ask Police to Solve Fewer Problems," RAND Corporation, 2020.

81. Vera Institute of Justice (N.D.), "What Policing Costs: A Look at Spending in America's Biggest Cities."

82. S. Andrew, "Crime Is Surging in U.S. Cities. Some Say Defunding the Police Will Actually Make It Fall," *CNN News,* July 14, 2020, https://www.cnn.com/2020/07/14/us/police-violence-defund-debate-trnd/index.html.

83. C. Lum, C. S. Koper, and X. Wu, "Can We Really Defund the Police? A Nine-Agency Study of Police Response to Calls for Service," *Police Quarterly*, 2021, https://doi.org/10.1177/10986111211035002.

84. Vera Institute of Justice (N.D.), "What Policing Costs: A Look at Spending in America's Biggest Cities."

85. C. Lum, C. S. Koper, and X. Wu, "Can We Really Defund the Police? A Nine-Agency Study of Police Response to Calls for Service," *Police Quarterly*, 2021, https://doi.org/10.1177/10986111211035002.

86. F. Akinnibi, S. Holder, and C. Cannon, "Cities Say They Want to Defund the Police. Their Budgets Say Otherwise," January 12, 2021, Bloomberg CityLab, https://www.bloomberg.com/graphics/2021-city-budget-police-funding/.

87. Ibid.

88. M. J. D. Vermeer, D. Woods, and B. A. Jackson, "Would Law Enforcement Leaders Support Defunding the Police? Probably—If Communities Ask Police to Solve Fewer Problems," RAND Corporation, 2020.

Contemporary Policing: Community, Problem-Oriented, Broken Windows, and Other Police Innovations

Learning Objectives

LO1 Discuss the development of community involvement in policing.

LO2 Explain the concept of community policing.

LO3 Explain the challenge of community policing.

LO4 Compare and contrast community-oriented policing (COP) and problem-oriented policing (POP).

LO5 Assess the relationship between the broken windows hypothesis and zero tolerance policing.

LO6 Evaluate the effectiveness of police response to crime achieved by broken windows and zero tolerance policies.

LO7 Describe intelligence-led policing and predictive policing approaches.

Chapter Outline

The Alameda County (California) Sheriff's Office Youth & Family Services Bureau sponsored a symposium on the roles and responsibilities needed to build healthy and safe communities. The symposium featured a play written and performed by Alameda County Sheriff's Deputy Jinho "Piper" Ferreira titled *Cops and Robbers*. Ferreira performs 19 characters with different perspectives, convictions, and prejudices about a local shooting. The play encourages everyone to consider taking action to improve their communities.

Prior to his career in law enforcement, Deputy Ferreira performed as a rapper but decided to become a sheriff's deputy to promote positive relationships between law enforcement and communities of color in Northern California and around the nation. The symposium brought together Alameda County law enforcement officers, school officials and high school students, public service agencies, nonprofit organizations, and other community partners for the day to discuss how each can work in a professional and personal capacity to address the concerns of youth and their communities. After his performance, Ferreira closed the symposium by discussing the critical issues addressed in the play as well as highlights of the Alameda County Sheriff's Office Youth & Family Service Bureau, including the Reach Ashland Youth Center, the Deputy Sheriff's Activity League and training opportunities such as Dig Deep Farms & Produce.[1]

Do you think that a lone police officer putting on a one-person play is an effective tool for community engagement? What are other ways the police can engage the community?

Efforts by police agencies to reach out and interact with the community have become routine. What are these efforts and why are they now considered so important?

"Trust between law enforcement agencies and the people they protect and serve is essential in a democracy. It is key to the stability of our communities, the integrity of our criminal justice system, and the safe and effective delivery of policing services."[2] With that ideal in mind, it is crucial for police agencies to foster a healthy relationship with the communities that they serve, and ultimately are part of. Before we can move forward and work toward a realistic version of effective community policing, it is imperative that we acknowledge the historic developments of police/community relations and learn from these developments.

LO1

Discuss the development of community involvement in policing.

The Development of Community Involvement in Policing

The 1960s was a time of turmoil for both the police and the public. Demonstrations on college campuses and in cities across the country were the result of poor relationships with communities of color and anger over the Vietnam War. Crime seemed out of control. The Federal Bureau of Investigation (FBI) had reported 288,460 violent crimes in 1960; by the end of the decade, this number had skyrocketed to 661,870 though the population rose only about 12 percent from 179 million to more than 200 million people.[3] Lack of trust in and disrespect for the police became the norm. Police administrators began to realize that something must be done to confront the twin problems of escalating crime rates and poor community relations. This realization became even clearer when the results of one of the most famous police experiments—The Kansas City Study (discussed in Chapter 4)—was released to the public.

As you may recall, this policing experiment was quite unique because never before had there been an attempt to determine through such extensive scientific evaluation the value of visible police patrols. The year-long experiment tested the effectiveness of the long-held traditional police strategy of routine preventive patrol to deter crime and found that random patrols had little effect on crime rates. Kansas City Police Chief Clarence M. Kelley said, "Many of us in the department had the feeling we were training, equipping, and deploying men to do a job neither we, nor anyone else, knew much about."[4] Given these less than encouraging results, police administrators began to ponder, "Could the resources that the Police Department ordinarily used for preventive patrol be safely dedicated to other, possibly more productive strategies?"

In the aftermath of the Kansas City Study, police administrators began to reevaluate how departments could gain community trust, considered a key element of improving police effectiveness. The urban riots in cities such as Newark and Detroit in the late 1960s convinced police administrators that aggressive action to reform traditional patrol techniques were desperately needed. Police departments began experimenting with initiatives to improve the relationship between police and the public. Three of the most prominent efforts—police community relations, foot patrol and team policing, are described in some detail below.

Critical Thinking

What does community policing look like in your neighborhood? How should it look?

Community Relations Initiatives

"[T]he history of American police strategies cannot be separated from the history of the Nation as a whole. Unfortunately, our police, and all of our other institutions, must contend with many bitter legacies from that larger history. No paradigm—and no society—can be judged satisfactorily until those legacies have been confronted directly."[5]

When discussing community relations initiative successes and failures, it is important to understand how policing developed in the early history because it can be noted that over time policing in the United States became a blend of traditions and practices. Changes in laws as well as the development and implementation of professional standards, and changes in societal norms have arguably improved many aspects of U.S. policing. However, with all of the changes and advances related to policing, communities of color still experienced differential enforcement as some officers still behave in ways that reinforce bias and injustice.[6] What was needed was comprehensive police reform that included community policing strategies.

The community policing movement can be traced back to programs with the general title of police–community relations (PCR). These initial PCR programs were designed to make citizens more aware of police activities, alert them to methods of self-protection, and improve general attitudes toward policing.

Police–community relations units were developed in the 1960s and 1970s. Consistent with this movement are:

- Store-front auxiliary police offices
- Neighborhood watch
- Drug awareness programs
- Project ID

These units were designed to improve relationships with marginalized and low-income communities. PCRs were created as a way to "make friends" with members of the community.

Rightfully so, community members saw through these units as window dressing designed to improve the police image without making actual change. They were often referred to as "Wave & Grin" squads, since non-sworn personnel were assigned to PCRs and not officers with arrest power. For example, in 1962, the San Francisco Police Department established a specialized unit based on the concept that police would help to reduce crime by reducing despair by acting as a social service agency to communities of color. Almost from the very beginning, the unit found itself hindered by the uncertainty of its mission. Officers were not sure which strategies they should apply to serving which population.[7]

Although PCR efforts showed a willingness of police agencies to cooperate with the public, some experts believed that law enforcement agencies needed to undergo a significant transformation to create meaningful partnerships with the public. In their view, community relations and crime control effectiveness cannot be the province of a few specialized units housed within a traditional police department. Instead, the core police role must be altered if community involvement is to be won and maintained. To accomplish this goal, police departments needed to return to an earlier style of policing, in which officers on the beat had intimate contact with the people they served. This would be more closely aligned with the principles of policing's founder, Sir Robert Peel, in his ideal of policing by content. Peel felt that the police need to be an integral part of the community in which they serve.

Team Policing

Team policing, first implemented in the 1970s, emphasized the delivery of continuous decentralized patrol services in a specific geographic area by a team of officers, usually under the direction of a sergeant or lieutenant. Rather than responding to specific crimes, team commanders were responsible for conditions in the patrol area.[8] Patrol is meant to be reorganized to include one or more teams, with a joint purpose of improving police services to the community and increasing job satisfaction of the patrol officers. Usually the team is based in a particular neighborhood. Each team has responsibility for police services in its neighborhood and is intended to work as a unit in close contact with the community to prevent crime and maintain order. At its peak in 1974, approximately

team policing

Continuous decentralized patrol services in a specific geographic area by a team of officers, usually under the direction of a sergeant or lieutenant.

60 departments claimed to practice the approach.[9] It is doubtful, however, that each of these agencies had actually adopted the core elements of team policing but merely applied the term to any new reorientation of patrol operations.

There are three core elements of team policing: geographic stability of patrol, maximum interaction among team members, and maximum communication among team members and the community. With team policing, conventional patrol strategies are reorganized and police teams are assigned to fixed districts usually operating out of a facility separate from police headquarters, that is, a storefront. Police were meant to become more familiar with the people of their districts and their problems and concerns. This would entail assembling highly trained and motivated members of the police department and assigning them full-time to a specific area of the city comprised of neighborhoods sharing similar concerns and challenges unique to their common environment. Team policing units were then expected to engage all matters concerning traffic, crime, and quality of life, while building collaborative and interactive relationships with area residents. They are assigned to provide customized services and protection that is both responsive to community needs and in partnership with the people living in the community.

While at first glance team policing appeared to be effective and have crime reducing utility, the program did not last. Its demise could be linked to a variety of reasons. First, mid-management of the departments saw team policing as a threat to their power. They were not happy with the ideas and strategic visions coming from line officers in the community replacing traditional top-down approach to policing strategies. As a result, they subverted and, in some cases, actively sabotaged the team policing plans.

Another problem was the lack of organizational support. The dispatching technology did not permit patrol officers to remain in their neighborhoods, despite the stated intentions of adjusting that technology to the pilot projects. Poor communication meant that the patrols never received a sufficiently clear definition of how their behavior and role should differ from that of a regular patrol.

Another impediment was that the benefits of team policing were unclear. Many police administrators have viewed team policing as a fad which had some merits in theory but was impossible to implement. This might be because the goals of team policing are unclear. Policing is also a number-driven occupation. It is easy to count the number of crimes reported and the number of arrests made but it is not easy to quantify the numbers of crimes prevented by this new community-based policing strategy. Team policing had the perception that the members were an elite group of officers, and their peers often resented not having been chosen for the project.

The Demise of Team Policing

As Samuel Walker notes, despite the promise of the approach, few people even remember team policing.[10] This is because we are often reticent to discuss failures. Yet, there was a great deal to learn from the effort as there is from all experiments in policing as this was the precursor to the COP approach implemented a decade later. Widely publicized cases of police-community conflict suggested that there was a need for structural changes in the way the police dealt with the public and even more assertive programs than foot patrols and team policing were needed. One case that focused national attention on police and the community was the arrest and beating of motorist Rodney King, discussed in the following Focus on Policing: LAPD and Rodney King. The King incident as well as other violent encounters helped spur the development of a variety of new and innovative programs designed to improve policing that are described in detail below.

Focus on Policing

LAPD and Rodney King

In March 1991, California Highway Patrol officers attempted to stop Black motorist Rodney King for speeding on a Los Angeles area highway. King also had two adult male passengers in his car. King failed to stop his vehicle and a high-speed chase ensued and traveled onto the city streets of Los Angeles where the Los Angeles Police Department (LAPD) ultimately joined in the chase and took over the incident. Eventually, the police cornered King and he was again not cooperative when ordered to exit his car. The two passengers in the car did exit the vehicle and by their accounts were manhandled and beaten by the police. Early in the encounter with LAPD, King allegedly lunges at officers (this is not on the tape that is later made public). King eventually got out of the car but was nonresponsive to verbal commands to get on the ground and was acting in a bizarre manner. LAPD officers tased him several times. LAPD officers claimed that the taser had no effect since King was not in compliance with verbal commands. The supervisor on scene, Sgt. Stacey Koon, ordered the use of batons and the LAPD officers ended up hitting King 56 times and kicking him while he was on the ground. After a long and brutal ordeal, officers finally handcuffed him and took him to the hospital for multiple injuries. The next day, King's brother tried to file a complaint with the LAPD. He claimed to be harassed and left the police department unable to file the report. Los Angeles resident George Holliday videotaped the beating from his apartment balcony. His amateur video (5+ minutes in length) of the incident was released to the press resulting in national outrage and condemnation of the LAPD. Rodney King was released without being charged and four LAPD officers, Sgt. Stacey Koon, Laurence Powell, Timothy Wind, and Theodore Briseño, were indicted by a grand jury in connection with the beating. After the officers were found not guilty at a controversial trial held in the predominantly White Los Angeles suburb of Simi Valley, rioting ensued in Los Angeles.

The Christopher Commission was created to investigate the incident and the subsequent response by the LAPD. The Christopher Commission found that there was a significant number of LAPD officers who repeatedly used excessive force against the public and constantly ignored the written guidelines of the department regarding force. The report also stated that the failure to control these officers was an administration issue that was at the core of the problem noting, that of the over 9,000 LAPD officers,

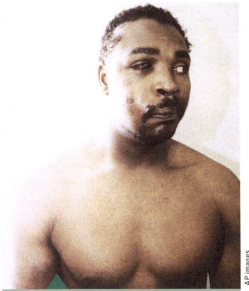

AP images

This photograph of Rodney King was taken on March 9, 1991, three days after his beating in Los Angeles. The acquittal of the four police officers who conducted the assault on King sparked rioting that spread across the city and suburbs. Cars were demolished and homes and businesses were burned. Before order was restored, 55 people were dead, 2,300 injured, and more than 1,500 buildings were damaged or destroyed.

there were approximately 1,800 officers against whom an allegation of excessive force or improper tactics was made from 1986 to 1990. The department not only failed to deal with the group of problem officers, but it often rewarded them with positive evaluations and promotions. In short, the LAPD response to Rodney King, and their general standard operating procedures, were evidence that there was still a great deal of work to be done.

Critical Thinking

1. The King case occurred more than 30 years ago. Do you believe that police community relations have improved since then or are they on a decline?

2. What can be done to improve the current climate?

Sources: *CNN*, Timeline: Rodney King from 1991–2012, http://news.blogs
.cnn.com/2012/06/17/rodney-king-what-happened-in-1991/; Christopher Commission report, p. iii and p. 31; Independent Commission on the Los Angeles Police Department, *Report of the Independent Commission on the Los Angeles Police Department* (Los Angeles, 1991), p. ii.

▶ The Community Policing Concept

By the 1980s, police officers were more educated and diverse. With the advent of government programs like the Law Enforcement Education Program (LEEP), more officers earned college degrees. Police departments slowly increased their employment of racial and ethnic minorities as well. By 1988, 65 percent of officers had some college education, up from 20 percent in 1960.[11] David Carter reports that in 1970, only 6 percent of officers held a bachelor's degree and today it is estimated about 30 percent of officers hold a college degree. There was not only change in the personnel of police organizations but also an overall dissatisfaction with traditional policing. During the late 1980s, the National Institute of Justice (NIJ) funded Executive Sessions at Harvard's Kennedy School. At these sessions, practitioners and researchers met to discuss the future of policing in the United States.

The 1980s had become known as the "bending granite" years when police agencies were set in their ways and not open to change.[12] Police agencies had just been "professionalized" and were unwilling to accept much change despite the recommendations. The experts who attended the Kennedy sessions at Harvard advocated an emphasis on peacekeeping, prevention, and order maintenance in the community. There was agreement that policing should move away from the crime-fighting orientation and the war on crime and put the focus on community control. Slowly the era of community policing took hold.

What Is Community Policing?

community policing
An attempt to involve the community as active partners with the police in solving community problems such as crime or quality-of-life issues.

The term "**community policing**" entered the popular lexicon with the passage of the Violent Crime Control and Law Enforcement Act of 1994 and the subsequent creation of the Office Community Oriented Policing Services (COPS) under the U.S. Department of Justice. The COPS office was responsible for providing funds to local police departments to hire new officers and to implement community policing. Specifically, the COPS office added 100,000 officers to the street, upgraded technology by making funds available for mobile computers in cars, and providing training and technical assistance around community policing implementation. To help fund these initiatives, the COPS office gave out over $1 billion to local police departments.

Some would like to attribute the reduction in crime during the 1990s to the creation of the COPS office, this link has been hard to prove.[13] As of 1999, more than 90 percent of American police agencies serving populations larger than 25,000 reported having adopted community policing activities and strategies with the majority of smaller departments following suit.[14] There was widespread adoption of community policing in police departments across the United States.

Kali9/E+/Getty Images

Community policing is based on the concept that police and private citizens working together and getting to know one another can help solve community-level problems of crime, disorder, and neighborhood decay. The underlying theme is that police should be open to interacting with different community groups, including teens, such as this interaction between a police officer and two neighborhood youths.

Community-Oriented Policing

Community-oriented policing (COP) is best known as a philosophy and not a program or special unit. COP is based on the concept that police and private citizens working together in creative ways can help solve contemporary community problems related to crime, fear of crime, disorder, and neighborhood decay. COP has been implemented in large cities, suburban areas, and rural communities.[15] The underlying theme is that police should partner with the community to develop programs for specific problems. COP promotes interaction between officers and citizens and gives officers the time to meet with local residents to talk about crime in the neighborhood and to use personal initiative to solve problems.

Crucial to community policing is giving line-level officers more discretion and time to work with community members. The main idea is the police cannot fight crime alone—they need the community to be successful! Police and the community act as coproducers of public safety. It is important to note that the implementation of community policing looks different in almost every community. Local police departments must adopt the tactics that are appropriate for the communities that they serve. Tactics like foot patrol and bicycle patrol work well in densely populated areas but are a waste of resources in rural areas where people do not live close to one another.

Three Key Components of COP

COP comprises three key components: community partnerships, organizational transformation, and problem-solving. Each of these components will be explained in detail below.

Community Partnerships

Community partnerships are collaborative between the police agency and the individuals and organizations they serve to develop solutions to problems and increase trust in police. These partnerships work well when there is local agenda setting—meaning that the community groups help the police prioritize problems in the community. This also means these community groups share in the responsibility of addressing problems of crime and disorder. Examples of groups that police may elect to partner with are:

- Other government agencies
- Community members/groups
- Nonprofits/service providers
- Private businesses
- Media

Organizational Transformation

Organizational transformation refers to the alignment of organizational management, structure, personnel, and information systems to support community partnerships and proactive problem solving. The community policing philosophy focuses on the way that departments are organized and managed and how the infrastructure can be changed to support the philosophical shift necessary to implement community policing. It encourages the application of modern management practices to increase efficiency and effectiveness. Community policing emphasizes changes in organizational structures to institutionalize its adoption

community-oriented policing (COP)

I concept that police and private citizens working together in creative ways can help solve contemporary community problems related to crime, fear of crime, disorder, and neighborhood decay.

and infuse it throughout the entire department, including the way it is managed and organized, its personnel, and its technology.

Agency management is the first component of organizational transformation. Some examples of how organizational transformation might affect agency management are changing climate and culture and leadership to support the changes necessary to adopt community policing. Leadership is particularly important for making police organizational changes. Leaders, therefore, must constantly emphasize and reinforce community policing's vision, values, and mission within their organization and support and articulate a commitment to community policing as the predominant way of doing business. Labor relations and police unions are also crucial to the adoption of community policing. Police unions and similar forms of organized labor must be a part of the process and function as partners in the adoption of the community policing philosophy. Including labor groups in agency changes can ensure support for the changes that are imperative to community policing implementation.

There are other organizational components that are crucial elements of community policing. It is important that the organizational structure of the agency ensure that local patrol officers have decision-making authority and are accountable for their actions. This can be achieved through long-term assignments, the development of officers who are generalists, and using special units appropriately. The geographic assignment of officers is an important part of the community policing philosophy in that it adds to the expertise of officers. With community policing, there is a shift to the long-term assignment of officers to specific neighborhoods or areas.

Geographic deployment plans can help enhance customer service and facilitate more contact between police and citizens, thus establishing a strong relationship and mutual accountability. Beat boundaries should correspond to neighborhood boundaries, and other government services should recognize these boundaries when coordinating government public-service activities. Despecialization is important because officers have to be able to handle multiple responsibilities and take a team approach to collaborative problem-solving and partnering with the community. Finally, police agencies must allocate the necessary resources and finances to change organizational structure in a way that allows for community policing implementation.

The principles of community policing need to be infused throughout the entire personnel system of an agency. This includes recruitment, hiring, selection, and retention of all law enforcement agency staff, from sworn officers to civilians, and volunteers. Personnel evaluations, supervision, and training must also be aligned with the agencies' community policing views as well. For community policing to be implemented, there must be a recalibration of incentives. This means that officers must be recognized and rewarded for reducing crime and enhancing citizen relationships—rather than a big bust. This change can be difficult for police agencies to make. To accomplish this task, police agencies must undergo planning and policy changes that involve input from police personnel at all ranks as well as community members and local leaders.

The final aspect of organizational transformation is the implementation of technology—specifically, information systems. Community policing is information-intensive, and technology plays a central role in helping to provide ready access to quality information. Accurate and timely information makes problem-solving efforts more effective and ensures that officers are informed about the crime and community conditions of their beat. In addition, technological enhancements can greatly assist with improving two-way communication with citizens and in developing agency accountability systems and performance outcome measures. Technology can be used to enhance transparency thereby adding to a culture of accountability. By making crime data, complaints and even body-worn camera footage available to the public, organizations become more accountable to the people that they serve.

Problem Solving

The third and final core component of COP is **problem solving**, defined as the process of engaging in the proactive and systematic examination of identified problems to develop and rigorously evaluate effective responses. To facilitate problem-solving, police expert John Eck developed the following four-step SARA model:

- **S**canning: Identifying and prioritizing problems.

- **A**nalysis: Researching what is known about the problem.

- **R**esponse: Developing solutions to bring about lasting reductions in the number and extent of problems.

- **A**ssessment: Evaluating the success of the responses.[16]

The steps in SARA are interconnected: Each step relies on information provided in the previous step and prepares information for the following step.

To effectively problem-solve, an officer must be given time during their shift to engage in the SARA process. This means an officer will not be responding to calls for service from the radio but instead will be working through the steps in the problem-solving process. For example, an officer might notice that thefts from motor vehicles increase over the weekend in an area surrounding a new nightclub. In the Scanning stage, the officer would confirm that this is in fact a problem and determine for how long the thefts have occurred. Once this has been established, an officer will begin the Analysis phase. To do this, the officer will collect and review relevant data that might include information about the nightclubs, reports of what has been stolen during these incidents, as well discussions with victims. The officer might also document current responses to the problem and identify resources to address the problem. Since the thefts from motor vehicles are occurring in the vicinity of a nightclub—the business owners should be considered a resource.

Finally, the officer should develop a hypothesis or reasonable explanation for why the problem is occurring. In the Response phase, the officer must brainstorm possible responses. This can include researching what other communities have done to address similar problems. Once a response has been selected, action must be taken to implement it. Finally, the Assessment stage allows the officer to evaluate whether or not the intervention has been successful in reducing the thefts from motor vehicles.

problem solving
The process of engaging in the proactive and systematic examination of identified problems to develop and rigorously evaluate effective responses.

U-T San Diego/ZUMA Press Inc./Alamy Stock Photo

The problem-solving process involves engaging with the community to learn about their concerns and issues. Here, during the STEP UP after-school student mentoring program at Libby Elementary School, Oceanside Police Department Neighborhood Police Team Officer Jose Munoz demonstrates his stun gun to the kids and their teen mentors.

▶ The Challenge of Community Policing

Since the advent of these programs, the federal government has encouraged the growth of community policing by providing millions of dollars to hire and train officers.[17] The U.S. Justice Department's Office of Community Oriented Policing Services is the go-to source for community policing funding.[18] Thousands of communities have adopted innovative forms of decentralized, neighborhood-based community policing models. Recent surveys indicate that a significant increase is evident in community policing activities in recent years and that certain core programs such as crime prevention activities have become embedded in the police role.[19]

While these programs are being implemented, they still face many challenges. First, community policing involves giving patrol officers a great deal of discretion. Specifically speaking, officers are expected to engage in problem solving which means that command stuff must trust that police are actually scanning and analyzing—activities that can be time-consuming and sometimes do not yield measurable results. Furthermore, unchecked discretion can result in the abuse of power. The community can also have an influence on policing and serve as an obstacle to the implementation of COP. For example, community members might have conflicting preferences about which local problems the police should focus on as part of the local agenda setting. Police must then decide which problems to address first and how to gain consensus. There are also many unpopular laws on the books as discussed in other chapters of this text. Community members may try to wield improper political influence and demand that the police do improper things, some of which may even be illegal. These all can make community partnerships difficult to maintain.

Another major obstacle in the adoption of community policing is that the approach is difficult to define. There are many different definitions of community policing and ways to implement it. That community policing looks different in almost every jurisdiction it is implemented in, means that evaluation is difficult.

Police chiefs can choose the definition that they are most comfortable with and varying community policing tactics can be implemented in different locations. This really makes it impossible to truly evaluate the effectiveness of the approach at a macro level. To compound the problem, the COP philosophy was the victim of rapid expansion issues. Many chiefs were eager to get started and implement community policing. As a result, they jumped in and did not plan fully for organizational transformation. In many agencies evaluation and promotion criteria were not changed to reflect changes in departmental philosophy.

Similarly, agencies did not adjust training enough to truly adopt community-oriented policing. This means that there are questions about whether the widespread adoption of community policing was rhetoric or reality. With all of these different definitions and various ways to adopt the approach, David Bayley referred to community policing as "old wine in new bottles."[20] He argued that community policing was really traditional policing wrapped up in a new package with little actual change taking place across American policing. Part of the reason it is so difficult to pinpoint the birth of community policing is that the approach means different things to many people.[21]

Although there are formidable obstacles to overcome, growing evidence suggests that community-oriented policing can work and fit well with traditional police practices.[22] For example, Kyle Peyton and colleagues conducted a randomized trial with the New Haven, Connecticut police department. They found that positive contact with police through brief door-to-door nonenforcement community policing visits improved residents' attitudes toward police, including legitimacy and willingness to cooperate. These effects remained more than 20 days after the initial contact were largest among people of color within the community.[23] Yet, these results should be taken with some caution. Joseph Ruckus and another group of researchers found no effect of community policing on rural and suburban areas suggesting that the same strategies that work in urban metro areas may not affect smaller communities.[24]

Many police experts and administrators have embraced these concepts as revolutionary revisions of the basic police role. Community policing efforts have been credited with helping reduce crime rates in large cities such as New York and Boston. The most professional and highly motivated officers are the ones most likely to support community policing efforts.[25] In addition, Amie Schuck's research finds that police organizations with more women may be better suited to adopting this and other police innovations.[26]

Community Policing in Action

There are community policing programs in operation around the nation. In New York City, the Neighborhood Policing program is a comprehensive crime-fighting strategy that relies on cooperation with community residents. The Neighborhood Policing program divides precincts into four or five fully staffed sectors that correspond, as much as possible, to the boundaries of actual established neighborhoods. Officers work in the same neighborhoods on the same shifts, increasing their familiarity with local residents and local problems. Sector officers and sector cars do not leave the boundaries of their assigned sectors, except in precinct-wide emergencies. When not responding to calls, officers engage with neighborhood residents, identify local problems, and work toward solutions. The sector officer plays the role of a generalist cop who knows and feels responsible for the sector, and who provides the full range of policing services there.

The NY model employs officers designated as the Neighborhood Coordination Officers (NCOs) who serve as liaisons between the police and the community. NCO's meet with residents and understand community problems by attending meetings with neighborhood leaders and clergy, visiting schools, following up on previous incidents, and using creative techniques and adaptive skills. This enables them to respond swiftly to incidents and develop a sense of belonging and responsibility that fosters a willingness to do whatever it takes to keep the neighborhood safe and secure.

Has the program worked? In 2017, the city of New York experienced some of its lowest violent crime numbers in decades. CBS News reported that NYC had a historic drop in crimes including reductions in robberies, burglaries, shootings, and murders, In fact, the number of shootings fell below 800 and the number of murders fell below 300. This is New York C'ty's lowest per-capita murder rate in almost 70 years.[27] The Patrol Services Bureau has systematically reorganized its patrol methods to achieve the goal of establishing neighborhood policing in every precinct, citywide.[28]

New York is not alone. Boston Police Commissioner William G. Gross made community policing a top priority. In September 2018, when he announced his first major initiative in the creation of the Community Engagement Bureau. Gross said that "ending 'senseless youth violence'" is the main reason he decided to put community policing at the forefront of his administration. He stated "before, we had great individual community service, but now we're going to bring more uniformity." The focus of this community policing initiative in Boston is to have Boston police officers mentor the city's youth and help create opportunities.[29]

These results are encouraging, but there is no clear-cut evidence that community policing is highly successful at reducing crime or changing the traditional values and attitudes of police officers involved in the programs.[30] A recent meta-analysis of existing studies by Charlotte Gill and associates found somewhat ambiguous results.[31] Their analysis suggests that COP strategies have positive effects on citizen satisfaction, perceptions of disorder, and police legitimacy, but limited effects on crime and fear of crime. Some research does show that the arrest rate actually increases after COP programs have been implemented.[32] However, crime rate reductions in cities that have used COP may be the result of an overall downturn in the nation's crime rate, rather than a result of community policing efforts.

Despite these professional obstacles, community policing has become a common part of municipal police departments. The concept is also being exported around the world, with varying degrees of success; some nations do not seem to have the stability necessary to support community policing.[33] Where it is used, citizens seem to like community policing initiatives, and those who volunteer and get involved in community crime prevention programs report higher confidence in the police force and its ability to create a secure environment.[34] They also tend to be more likely to report crime.[35]

Implementing Community Policing

While the community policing approach is now operating around the world there are still issues to be faced before community policing can be fully implemented. Some of the most significant include the following:

■ **Defining community.** Police administrators must be able to define the concept of community as an ecological area characterized by common norms, shared values, and interpersonal bonds.[36] After all, the main focus of community policing is to activate the community norms that make neighborhoods more crime resistant. If, in contrast, community policing projects cross the boundaries of many different neighborhoods, any hope of learning and accessing community norms, strengths, and standards will be lost.[37]

■ **Defining roles.** Police administrators must also establish the exact role of community police agents. How should they integrate their activities with those of regular patrol forces? For example, should foot patrols have primary responsibility for policing in an area, or should they coordinate their activities with officers assigned to patrol cars?

■ **Changing supervisor attitudes.** Some supervisors are wary of community policing because it supports a decentralized command structure. This would mean fewer supervisors and, consequently, less chance for promotion and a potential loss of authority.[38] Those supervisors who learn to actively embrace community policing concepts are the ones best able to encourage patrol officers to engage in self-initiated activities, including community policing and problem-solving.[39]

■ **Reorienting police values.** Research shows that police officers who have a traditional crime control orientation are less satisfied with community policing efforts than those who are public service oriented.[40] In some instances, officers holding traditional values may go as far as looking down on their own comrades assigned to community policing, who as a result feel "stigmatized" and penalized by lack of agency support.[41]

■ **Revising training.** Community policing requires that police departments alter their training requirements, especially during field training.[42] Future officers must develop community-organizing and problem-solving skills, along with traditional police skills. Their training must prepare them to succeed less on their ability to make arrests or issue citations and more on their ability to solve problems, prevent crime effectively, and deal with neighborhood diversity and cultural values.[43]

■ **Reorienting recruitment.** To make community policing successful, mid-level managers who are receptive to and can implement community-change strategies must be recruited and trained.[44] The selection of new recruits must be guided by a desire to find individuals with attitudes that support community policing. They must be open to the fact that community policing will help them gain knowledge of the community, give them opportunities to gain skill and experience, and help them engage in proactive problem-solving.[45]

■ **Reaching out to every community.** Because each neighborhood has its own particular needs, community policing must become flexible and adaptive. In neighborhoods undergoing change in racial composition, special initiatives to reduce tensions may be required.[46] Some neighborhoods are cohesive and highly organized, and residents work together to solve problems. In other neighborhoods, it takes more work for community policing to succeed.

COP lost a lot of its popularity after the 2001 terrorist attacks when the focus shifted from hometown security to homeland security. However, in the wake of the Ferguson shooting and other similar incidents, community-oriented approaches are making a resurgence. They were identified as critical in the President's Task Force on 21st Century Policing, a conclusion described in the following Focus on Policing: Task Force on 21st Century Policing.

Police Reform and Community Policing

In 2014, Missouri Governor Jay Nixon appointed the Ferguson Commission, an independent group to conduct a study of the social and economic conditions that impede progress, equality, and safety in the St. Louis region. Among other conclusions, the commission called for enhanced community policing to foster greater trust, satisfaction, and partnership between the community and law enforcement.[47] The Commission is not alone in these calls. In June 2020, President-elect Joe Biden called for a reinvestment in COP—not surprising since he was one of the creators of the Department of Justice Office of Community Oriented Policing Services in the 1990s.[48] Yet, historically marginalized groups argue that community policing did not help them in the past and are skeptical that these efforts will create change now.[49] Community policing does not address systemic racism or the historically challenging relationship between marginalized communities and the police. Accordingly, there is a call for an evidence-based approach,

Focus on Policing

Task Force on 21st Century Policing

On December 18, 2014, President Barack Obama signed an Executive Order establishing the *President's Task Force on 21st Century Policing*. The Task Force members sought expertise from stakeholders and input from the public through listening sessions, teleconferences, and written comments as they worked to identify best practices and make recommendations to the president. The Task Force submitted an initial report to the president on March 2, 2015, and released the final report on May 18, 2015. In the final report, there are six pillars recommended by the task force as crucial to modern policing as follows:

1. Building Trust and Legitimacy
2. Policy and Oversight
3. Technology and Social Media
4. Community Policing and Crime Reduction
5. Training and Education
6. Officer Wellness and Safety

These pillars address the full range of police activity. The fourth pillar calls for the implementation of community policing in communities across the country. Specifically, pillar four focuses on the importance of community policing as a guiding philosophy police and community. Police agencies should work with community residents to identify problems and collaborate on implementing solutions that produce meaningful results for the community. Community policing must be infused throughout the entire police department and should not be just a specialized unit. Every officer must be engaged in the practice. The Task Force took it a step further, arguing that the hiring, training, evaluating, and promoting officers should be based on their ability and track record in community engagement—not just traditional measures of policing.

The Task Force also called for police interventions to be implemented that are rooted in an understanding of procedural justice. The report states that without **procedural justice**—the idea that how individuals regard the justice system is tied more to the perceived fairness of the *process* than to the perceived fairness of the *outcome*.

". . . police interventions can easily devolve into racial profiling, excessive use of force, and other practices that disregard civil rights, causing negative reactions from people living in already challenged communities." The obligation of police is not only to reduce crime but also to do so fairly while protecting the rights of citizens. In short, it matters not just what the police do but how they do it.

The report cites the testimony before the Task Force of Camden County, New Jersey, Police Chief J. Scott Thomson, who noted that "community policing starts on the street corner, with respectful interaction between a police officer and a local resident, a discussion that need not be related to a criminal matter. In fact, it is important that not all interactions be based on emergency calls or crime investigations."

Critical Thinking

1. Do you think that efforts to reach out to the community can pay dividends for policing and if so what are they?

2. What is the downside of police and the public interacting?

Sources: Listening Session on Community Policing and Crime Reduction: Using Community Policing to Reduce Crime (oral testimony of J. Scott Thomson, chief, Camden County [NJ] Police Department, for the President's Task President's Task Force on 21st Century Policing. 2015, Final Report of the President's Task Force on 21st Century Policing. Washington, DC: Office of Community Oriented Policing Services.Force on 21st Century Policing, Phoenix, AZ, February 13, 2015), http://www.cops.usdoj.gov/policingtaskforce.

procedural justice

The idea that how individuals regard the justice system is tied more to the perceived fairness of the *process* than to the perceived fairness of the *outcome*.

keeping the elements of COP that positively affect public safety, discarding those elements that were unsuccessful and opening up to conversations about investing in alternative services in the community. Community policing will likely be part of this effort but it is not the total solution. Increased funding of services for people who are experiencing homelessness, addiction, and poverty can complement police reforms.

Problem-Oriented Policing

Problem-oriented policing (POP) was developed by Herman Goldstein as an alternative to traditional policing. Herman Goldstein spent two years observing on-the-street operations of the police in Wisconsin and Michigan as a researcher with the American Bar Foundation's Survey of the Administration of Criminal Justice, and then participated in the analysis phase of that landmark project. From 1960 to 1964, he was executive assistant to the superintendent of the Chicago Police Department, O. W. Wilson, the widely recognized architect of the professional model of policing. As a result of these experiences, Goldstein could see that a new approach was necessary. He felt police should offer a service that is broad and not limited to law enforcement. Police work was traditionally categorized into vague and general categories: crime, order maintenance, and service. Goldstein argues that this is too broad because real problems are actually more specific. Because crime is so varied and wide in scope, police cannot develop one strategy to fight it. Rather, police need different strategies for each type of crime. Accordingly, Goldstein sought to define policing in terms of more discrete problems with specific solutions to each one.

To do this, police would have to be more innovative and solve recurring problems. Traditional policing did not allow for this because it resulted in police officers tied to the radio responding to calls for service. This approach forces them to be reactive and not proactive. The nature of 9-1-1 systems forces a reactive policing style. In turn, this means that police keep responding to the same crime at the same place over and over. It is important to note that part of the problem is that it is not always the same officer responding to the same address for every call for service. Rather, there are different officers responding who may be unaware that other officers had previously been to the same address to deal with the same problem. So what is the best way to deal with these ongoing and recurrent problems? The answer was focusing on crises before they became problems!

Problem-Oriented Policing Today

Dr. Goldstein's research and writings have inspired many efforts to implement and advance POP in police agencies around the world. As used today, the POP model applies to a style of police management that stresses proactive problem-solving instead of reactive crime fighting. POP is aimed at identifying and then solving problems at the local community level issues. This approach diverges from traditional police models that focus on responding to calls for help in the least possible time, dealing with the situation, and then getting on the street again as soon as possible. Problem-solving may not always be about using a traditional law enforcement response to solve a community problem. Instead, it may be necessary to require officers to engage in social services responses or to partner with other government agencies to solve a problem.

POP strategies require police agencies to identify particular long-term community problems—street-level drug dealers, prostitution rings, gang hangouts—and to develop strategies to eliminate them. Like community policing, being problem-solvers can require that police departments rely on local residents and private resources. This means that police managers must learn how to develop community resources, design efficient and cost-effective solutions to problems, and become advocates as well as agents of reform.[50]

LO4

Compare and contrast COP and POP.

problem-oriented policing (POP)

Developed by Herman Goldstein as an alternative to traditional policing; defines policing in terms of addressing discrete problems with specific solutions to each one.

Exhibit 6.1

Differences between Problem-Oriented Policing and Community-Oriented Policing

	Focus	Objective	Rationale	Method
Problem-Oriented Policing	Specific and recurring problems	To identify and remove the cause of the problems	Prevention is more effective than enforcement	A problem-solving approach
Community-Oriented Policing	Building police community relations in an effort to solve ongoing problems of crime and disorder	Proactive prevention of crime and disorder in partnership with the community	Community support is crucial for police effectiveness	Building relationships with the community, make organizational changes, engage in problem-solving

---

A significant portion of police departments are using special units to confront specific social problems. Some departments employ special units devoted to youth issues ranging from child abuse to gangs. In sum, the term "problem-oriented policing" describes a comprehensive framework for improving the police's capacity to perform their mission. POP impacts virtually everything the police do, operationally as well as managerially. The differences between POP and COP are set out in Exhibit 6.1.

Applying Problem-Oriented Policing

A big part of this approach is having police identify and solve problems at the community level. POP officers are reoriented away from being crime fighters to becoming problem-solvers. A good example of this approach can be found in Newport News, Virginia, where the police have successfully used a POP approach to deal with specific crimes in specific areas. Their experience is set out in the following Focus on Policing: Solving Problems in Newport News, Virginia feature. The Newport News approach spurred development of other POP models aimed at tackling significant crime problems.

In another Focus on Policing, entitled Combating Elder Abuse with POP, a significant social problem is dealt with using a POP approach.

How do police collect information about ongoing problems if different officers respond to calls on varying shifts at the same address for the same problems? That is the job of the crime analyst, discussed in the following Careers in Policing: Crime Analyst feature.

Does Problem-Oriented Policing Work?

Have POP reforms been effective? Reform can be extremely difficult for police agencies to implement—especially one as complex as problem-oriented policing. However, there are some indications that the approach can be successful. Recent research by Ed Maguire, Craig Uchida, and Kimberly Hassell identifies that there are common roadblocks in the implementation of POP. Maguire

Solving Problems in Newport News, Virginia

Newport News is a mid-sized city on the eastern-central peninsula of Virginia. The New Briarfield apartment complex is located in the midtown section of the city, complete with mixed- and low-income housing in close proximity to many local businesses and industry. The New Briarfield apartments faced a problem of high rates of burglaries. Newport News Police implemented a traditional approach and deployed more officers to this area and this reduced the problem significantly. Burglaries in this apartment complex were reduced 35 percent, and robberies in the central business district were reduced by 40 percent. Thefts from vehicles in two downtown areas dropped by over 50 percent. But once the officers were removed, the rate skyrocketed again. Eventually, the apartment complex generated more calls for service than any other area in the city.

The department then engaged in POP and officers used the SARA model. In practice, the police response looked like this:

1. *Scanning*—Crime analysis revealed the continuous problem of burglaries. Police officers then drafted and fielded a survey to see if residents thought this was also a significant problem.

2. *Analysis*—Officers and crime analysts looked at crime patters in the area and analyzed results of the opinion survey of residents. The survey revealed the extent that residents believed that physical deterioration in buildings contributed to burglaries.

3. *Response*—The police department developed a task force to deal with the physical condition of the building and the problem of deterioration.

a. The task force then organized meetings with various government agencies that had responsibilities for the building.

b. The task force developed a strategy and also organized tenants groups to put pressure on city officials to improve the physical condition of the building.

c. For this project, officers in a sense acted as community organizers and liaisons to other government agencies.

4. *Assessment*—This problem-solving project was a huge success. Statistics revealed that there was a drop in crime.

The task force, with the help of the police, was able to clean up the neighborhood and burglaries were reduced by 35 percent. Furthermore, the task force remained active and eventually the citizens and police convinced the local government destroyed the more dilapidated apartments.

Critical Thinking

The situation in Newport News was a good example of the police and citizens working together to solve the problem. Can you name other strategies that could work if the police and community members were to work together to solve community problems?

Sources: Dan Brandon, "The Use and Effectiveness of Problem-Oriented Policing," *Inquiries* 7 (2015), 1–2, http://www.inquiriesjournal.com/articles/1028/the-use-and-effectiveness-of-problem-oriented-policing; William Spelman and John E. Eck, *Problem-Oriented Policing*, U.S. Department of Justice, National Institute of Justice, 1987.

and his associates conducted a systematic content analysis of case summaries and reports completed by police officers in 753 POP cases in Colorado Springs.[51] They find that overall, the police department mostly does a good job of practicing POP in line with Herman Goldstein's original vision. Yet, POP also represents a serious challenge to existing agency routines and that many agencies might not have the capacity to adopt the more technical elements associated with the approach. Specifically, the department had difficulty with partnerships and engaged in inconsistent recordkeeping. The researchers also found that officers did not routinely assess the effectiveness of the responses

Focus on Policing

Combating Elder Abuse with POP

Elder abuse is a particularly important social issue that is becoming ever more significant because of shifts in the U.S. population. Currently there are about 56 million people in the United States over age 65 and the Bureau of the Census predicts that by 2050 the population over age 65 will reach 80 million people; elderly people will then make up more than 20 percent of the population. The National Center on Elder Abuse states that between 8 and 10 percent of elderly people experience abuse each year and an overwhelming number of cases of abuse, neglect, and exploitation go undetected and untreated each year. Another growing problem: financial exploitation, which may be higher than rates of emotional, physical, and sexual abuse or neglect.

Brian Payne has created a POP guide to help relieve the problem of elder abuse. The guide offers instructions on how to utilize the SARA process so that police can begin to address the problem of elder abuse in their communities. The guide offers questions for police to answer as part of their data collection including (but not limited to):

- How many incidents are reported to the agency?
- What are the locations of these incidents?
- What are the demographics of the victims?
- What are the demographics of the offenders?

Analysis: Once the data to answer these questions have been collected and all relevant stakeholders contribute to the conversation, police can begin to look for patterns. Analyzing patterns also allows police agencies to set a baseline for measuring the effectiveness of any new intervention. Payne offers a number of responses for police. First, he suggests that it is important to educate police about the problems of elder abuse and the community services available. Next, developing policies and protocols that communicate the importance of addressing elder abuse can also be a valuable response. This response can also be enhanced by developing a collaborative effort to address elder abuse. Finally, Payne notes that police may need to create new policies and procedures to assist victims. Because the elderly are a vulnerable population often with mental and physical impairments, it is important that police tailor services to ensure that they can in fact seek and get the help that they need. Finally, the police must assess

whether these responses resulted in a decrease of calls for service in cases involving elder abuse and whether the elderly are safer in the community.

An example of how this process can work can be found in the procedures used by the National City, California, police to combat repeated calls for elderly abuse. This town of 50,000, located south of San Diego, has had an ongoing problem policing elder abuse. Police officers responded to numerous calls at one residence over a 10-year period. Within two years alone, they visited the residence on 67 separate occasions. This signaled to the police department that they had a situation that could benefit from the problem-solving approach. Traditional police work failed to eradicate the problems reported at the home and police were still regularly called to respond. After examining the situation through a different lens, the neighborhood policing team recognized that the owner of the home—an elderly woman—was being taken advantage of by her daughter and grandson, who routinely brought people who were members of gangs, people who had substance use disorders, and people who were on parole to the home. Working with Adult Protective Services and other agencies, a public guardian was assigned to the woman and she was moved to an assisted-living facility. The daughter and grandson had to leave the residence and the calls for police to that home stopped. By recognizing that they were dealing with elder abuse, rather than traditional crimes, the neighborhood policing team was able to end the problem.

Critical Thinking

1. The POP method was used to address issues of elder abuse. Based on this model, which other social problems can you address using the SARA model?
2. Is this an effective model of problem-solving?
3. Are there certain crimes that this method would work better with than others? Name some issues that would work well and some that would not.

Sources: Brian K. Payne, "Physical and Emotional Abuse of the Elderly," POP Guide. For more information, visit http://www.popcenter.org/problems/elderly_abuse, accessed June 27, 2022; National City (California) Police Department, "120 East 18th Neighborhood Improvement Project," 2022, Submission for the Herman Goldstein Award for Excellence in Problem-Oriented Policing; and Data from the National Center for Elder Abuse, http://www.ncea.aoa.gov/Library/Data/index.aspx#population.

Careers in Policing

Crime Analyst

Crime analysts are known by many titles: police analysts, management analysts, intelligence analysts, research analysts, and planning analysts among others. Whatever they are called, however, their responsibilities are similar. According to the International Associations of Crime Analysts,[52] crime analysts help police departments in four primary ways:

1. Analysts are responsible for finding series, patterns, trends, and hotspots. Analyses of these trends, patterns, and hotspots provide the who, what, when, where, how, and why of emerging crime in the community that the analyst serves. Information collected by crime analysts is given to sworn personnel who can use this information to develop effective tactics and strategies, interceding as soon as possible, preventing victimization, and reducing crime.

2. Analysts also research and analyze long-term problems. Crime analysis isn't just about immediate patterns and series: analysts also look at the long-term problems that every police department faces. This is a crucial part of both COP and POP.

3. Providing information on demand is another crucial responsibility of crime analysts. Records management systems capture large amounts of varying information. Crime analysts sift through these data and know how to extract the important information that is useful to command staff of the police department.

4. Crime analysts develop and link local intelligence. Crime analysts often know when local information or intelligence fits with state, national, or international intelligence. Analysts are information synthesizers.

developed as part of the problem-solving process. The researchers note that "POP appears to have influenced the edges of the organization although not successfully reaching the middle." This of course is a problem with all new police innovations.

Broken Windows Policing

A third alternative to traditional policing models is referred to as **broken windows** or zero tolerance policing. Inspired by a seminal article by James Q. Wilson and George Kelling entitled "Broken Windows" published in the widely read *Atlantic Monthly* that claimed that signs of neighborhood disorder (e.g., broken windows) have a crime-generating influence at the neighborhood level.[52] Unrepaired broken windows encourage law-abiding people to leave disordered communities and be replaced by offenders who plan to commit crime in those areas. The image of broken windows symbolizes the relationship between disorder, decay, and crime. It is a sign that no one in the community cares or takes ownership over the area so people can do as they please.

 L05

Assess the relationship between the broken windows hypothesis and zero tolerance policing.

broken windows

Idea that signs of neighborhood disorder have a crime-generating influence at the neighborhood level.

On the Web

For more information about Problem-Oriented Policing (POP), visit the Center for Problem-Oriented Policing at http://www.popcenter.org/.

The broken windows model also assumes that there are two types of disorder: physical and social. The former is characterized by not only broken windows, but also vacant buildings, abandoned vehicles, and vacant lots filled with trash. The latter, social disorder, is characterized by persistent panhandlers, lack of civility, noise, and disrespectful youth congregating on street corners. As Wilson and Kelling note, one intoxicated person on a street corner is not enough to change the dynamics of a community but 100 *will* change the dynamic. The increased signs of both social and physical disorder create favorable conditions for crime.

As these conditions take hold, residents experience rapidly expanding levels of fear, causing them to withdraw from community life. Those who do care relocate, if possible, leaving behind abandoned and vacant homes. Stores close and property values decline. As the more stable members of the community flee to safer areas, levels of informal social control decline further and a door is opened for even more serious criminal activity. Once this process begins, it feeds itself: Disorder causes crime, and crime causes further disorder, in a never-ending cycle. Central to understanding this approach is the idea that the care and attention we give demonstrates the value we place on things. When communities are not cared for, this sends the signal that they are not valued. Furthermore, most people (attempt to) respond to the value they perceive others place on matters and things.

Wilson and Kelling argue that the police can play a key role in disrupting this process. If they focus on disorder and petty crime in neighborhoods that have not yet been overtaken by serious crimes such as drug gangs, they can help reduce fear and reduce resident relocation. This means focusing on fear of crime (which hurts neighborhood bonds/informal social control when people are afraid) and neighborhood disorder (which invites other forms of crime). They argue that promoting higher levels of informal social control will help residents themselves take control of their neighborhood and prevent serious crime from infiltrating. Police should focus on disorder problems affecting the quality of life in neighborhoods.

Critical Thinking

What are your thoughts on social disorder contributing to crime? Does this seem like a plausible explanation? Why or why not?

zero tolerance policing
Approach to policing that focuses on controlling minor crime and other signs of social disorder. When minor crimes are ignored, they will escalate into larger crimes.

Nomad_Soul/Shutterstock.com

Zero tolerance policing means that even the most minor offenses should be dealt with formally lest they escalate into more significant crimes. Do you agree with this approach or might it breed resentment if people begin to feel they were unfairly targeted and consequently less likely to cooperate with police in the future.

Zero Tolerance Policing

The broken windows approach was translated into **zero tolerance policing** in New York City under the leadership of New York Police Department (NYPD) Commissioner William Bratton and Mayor Rudolph Guiliani. This approach focuses on controlling minor crime and other signs of social disorder. When ignored, this will escalate. Early intervention through aggressive policing to stop misdemeanors and public order offenses will prevent and reduce felonies. The New York City model greatly relied on the enhanced use of field interrogations to increase intelligence, deter and apprehend offenders, and enhance the citizenry's sense of security. Timely and accurate intelligence is obtained through stop-and-frisk, interrogation, decentralization of command structure, rapid deployment of personnel and resources, and agency cooperation.

Zero Tolerance and Racial Profiling

Stop-and-frisk policies have often unfairly targeted people of color in New York, Boston, and other places. In New York, a federal judge ruled that the NYPD stop-and-frisk policy was unconstitutional after an sophisticated analysis of available data by the New York Civil Liberties Union found that 85 percent of "stops" involved Black or Hispanic people, even though they comprised just half the population. In a single year (2011), the NYPD stopped 685,724 people of whom nearly 9 in 10 people who were stopped were neither ticketed nor arrested.[53] So, while the NYPD focused their attention almost solely on people of color, the result much more often than not was having negative interactions with innocent people.

Another study of Boston Police Department's contact with citizens found that there were over 204,000 reports of police-civilian encounters (field interrogations) from 2007 to 2010. Black citizens were subjected to 63 percent of these encounters, even though they made up just 24 percent of Boston's population. When police-civilian encounters occurred, young Black men were more likely than young White men to be frisked or searched and that young Black men were more likely to be targeted for repeat police-civilian encounters. In over 204,000-plus field interrogations, only 2.5 percent resulted in officer-seized weapons, drugs, or other contraband.[54]

CompStat

In 1994, Police Commissioner William Bratton introduced a data management model in the New York City Police Department called CompStat as part of the zero tolerance policing approach, The **CompStat** process can be summarized in one simple statement: "Collect, analyze, and map crime data and other essential police performance measures on a regular basis, and hold police managers accountable for their performance as measured by these data."[55] The CompStat process is guided by four principles: [56]

> **Accurate and timely intelligence:** In this context, crime intelligence relies on data primarily from official sources, such as calls for service, crime, and arrest data. This data should be accurate and available as close to real time as possible. This crime and disorder data is used to produce crime maps, trends, and other analysis products. Subsequently, command staff use these information products to identify crime problems to be addressed.

> **Effective tactics:** Relying on past successes and appropriate resources, command staff and officers plan tactics that will respond fully to the problem. These tactics may include many different stakeholders, including law enforcement, government, and community partners at the local, state, and federal levels. A CompStat meeting provides the opportunity for developing tactics as well as accountability for developing these tactics.

> **Rapid deployment:** Contrary to the reactive policing model, the CompStat model strives to deploy resources to where there is a crime problem now, as a means of heading off the problem before it continues or escalates. As such, the tactics should be deployed in a timely manner.

> **Relentless follow-up and assessment:** The CompStat meeting provides the forum to "check-in" on the success of current and past strategies in addressing identified problems. Problem-focused strategies are normally judged a success by a reduction in or absence of the initial crime problem. This success or lack thereof, provides knowledge of how to improve current and future planning and deployment of resources.

CompStat

A data-driven approach to police management that uses data to identify problem areas and provides feedback on how well these legal and social problems are being handled by police.

Critical Thinking

Some would argue that the invention of COMPSTAT changed the way policing is done. Explain some of the ways this may be true.

Analyzing the Broken Windows and Zero Tolerance Approaches as Tools for Crime Reduction

Broken windows/zero tolerance policing is controversial because some people perceive it as harassment. Why focus on low-level petty crimes when there are more serious problems? Others feel that zero tolerance policing is remarkably effective.

While some experts claimed that this aggressive approach was responsible for the drastic reductions in crime that took place in New York City during the 1990s, others have found that it comes at a cost to civil liberties. Other less aggressive approaches such as problem-oriented policing can be equally effective.[57]

At the same time, there were questions about protecting the civil rights of citizens when this approach is used. With the implementation of zero tolerance policing, the number of citizen complaints filed before the Civilian Complaint Review Board jumped, as did the number of lawsuits alleging police misconduct and abuse of force.[58] Zero tolerance takes broken windows to its extreme, cracking down on every minor offense possible such as vandalism, panhandling, and graffiti. Police rely on deterrence and do not attempt to address causes of problems, only the resulting behavior. Furthermore, crackdowns on minor offenses bring up questions of what is criminal behavior and what is just socially undesirable.

The broken windows approach has been the focus of a lot of criticism. In an article entitled, "Broken Windows, Neighborhoods, and the Legitimacy of Law Enforcement or Why I Fell in and out of Love with Zimbardo," Tracey Meares discusses why the approach is so attractive to practitioners and public policymakers. Despite the potential of broken windows, however, she argues that the modest outcomes of broken windows policing do not justify the problems these policies create from a procedural justice context. The policy literature ignores this trade-off, and a curriculum framework that emphasizes how the criminal justice system educates citizens may offer a promising alternative. In short, she believes that police should focus more on procedural justice.[59]

Intelligence-Led Policing

Intelligence-led policing (ILP) is a policing business model that incorporates data analysis and criminal intelligence into a strategy that coordinates strategic risk management of threats with a focus on serious, recidivist offenders. It originated in the United Kingdom, but has been increasingly adopted around the world.[60] This approach gained traction in the United States after the terrorist attacks of 9/11, when police looked for ways to combat the evolving threat from abroad.[61] There was a strong desire on behalf of state and local agencies to "do something" in order to prevent a similar attack from occurring again.[62] Intelligence-led policing dramatically shifted from a "tips and leads" policing practice in the United States prior to September 11, 2001, terrorist attacks to a philosophy focused on the prevention and mitigation of threats and crimes through active information sharing and analysis.

How Is Intelligence-Led Policing Different from Traditional Policing?

According to police expert Jerry Ratcliffe, there are three key differences. To begin with, personnel—specifically those personnel who are responsible for the intelligence function within their agency—must be formally trained to comprehend the function of intelligence and information sharing. Next, there must be regular channels to communicate intelligence to personnel making decisions. These strategic and tactical decisions should be driven by intelligence products that result from a formal analytic process. Lastly, there must be changes to organizational structure and accountability to ensure intelligence-related functions are resourced and a priority to the agency.[63]

Intelligence-led policing incorporates data analysis and criminal intelligence into a strategy that tries to pinpoint where crimes will occur and who will be most likely to engage in criminal behavior rather than rely on random patrol, guess work, and luck.

Police departments have had difficulty with the implementation of this approach because of resource issues. Many police departments lack formal policies detailing methods of implementing this approach. Another problem is the lack of sufficient personnel, training, and a lack of intelligence-led decision making. These problems inhibit change toward the ILP paradigm. Interestingly, Jeremy Carter and Scott Phillips found that agency size has little influence on an agency's shift toward ILP. Instead, it is the access to necessary resources and training that appears to pose a significant challenge to law enforcement. Limited resources to develop an intelligence-led approach may result in the capability going underdeveloped or taking the form of other policing practices related to available resources, such as homeland security preparedness.[64] Regardless of these challenges, ILP is an important strategy that has been adopted by agencies across the country.

Predictive Policing

A relatively new concept, predictive policing may be described as harnessing the power of information, geospatial technologies, and evidence-based intervention models to reduce crime and improve public safety. The predictive policing approach does not replace traditional policing. Instead, it enhances existing approaches such as problem-oriented policing, community policing, and intelligence-led policing.

Predictive policing uses computer models for law enforcement purposes, namely anticipating likely crime events and informing actions to prevent crime. Predictions can focus on variables such as places, people, groups, or incidents. Demographic trends, parolee populations, and economic conditions may all affect crime rates in particular areas. Using models supported by prior crime and environmental data to inform different kinds of interventions can help police reduce the number of crime incidents.[65]

What are some of the challenges that police departments face when trying to implement this approach?[66] First, they find that when police departments focus on prediction accuracy rather than tactical utility, they can run into trouble. Larger hotspots might be more accurate for predicting where crime will occur but they are of little use for targeting police operations. For information to be useful for police, there may be some limits on accuracy. Next, misunderstanding the factors behind the prediction can be a problem. Some of the predictive tools are designed in a way that makes it difficult, if not impossible, to highlight the risk factors present in specific areas. Finally, when adopting predictive policing, police departments must be careful not to overlook civil and privacy rights. The very act of labeling areas and people as worthy of further law enforcement attention inherently raises concerns about civil liberties and privacy rights. The U.S. Supreme Court has ruled that standards for what constitutes reasonable suspicion are relaxed in "high-crime areas" (e.g., hotspots). However, what formally constitutes a "high-crime" area, and what measures may be taken in such areas under "relaxed" reasonable-suspicion rules, is an open question.

Despite these challenges, there is some evidence to suggest that predictive policing may be an effective approach. Predictive policing has been implemented in Los Angeles, California, where some evidence suggests that it is working[67] In one instance, the LAPD made use of helicopters for crime prevention[68] Relying on the predictive policing approach, the department has used heat maps, technology, and years of statistics to identify crime "hotspots." Helicopter pilots then fly over hotspots in an effort to deter potential offenders. LAPD officials have found that the strategy is having a positive effect, decreasing incidents of serious crimes when the helicopters conducted more flights. While these findings are encouraging. critics argue that the helicopters can be intrusive for people living in the communities under which they fly because they are loud. Other concerns are that while this tactic might decrease crime in the short term, it might not be as effective in the long term. Potential offenders will find another place to commit crime.

Helping to initiate and encourage predictive policing models, the federal government's Project Safe Neighborhoods (PSN) is a program which is designed to give economic support to community-based predictive violent crime reduction efforts[69] PSN is an evidence-based program that funds local police initiatives that bring a broad spectrum of stakeholders together to identify the most pressing violent crime problems in the community and to develop comprehensive solutions. As part of this strategy for lasting reductions in crime, PSN focuses enforcement efforts on the most violent offenders and partners with locally based prevention and reentry programs. Predictive tools that are encouraged include crime gun intelligence centers (CGICs), which combine intelligence from gunshot detection systems, ballistics, and gun tracing with traditional police work. The goal is to help to develop real-time leads on the "traffickers and trigger pullers," those people who are enabling violence in their communities. Another PSN goal is to bring a broad spectrum of stakeholders to work together to identify the most pressing violent crime problems in the community and develop comprehensive solutions to address them.

Summary

LO1   Discuss the development of community involvement in policing.

The 1960s was a time of turmoil for both the police and the public. Demonstrations on college campuses and in cities across the country were the result of poor relationships with communities of color communities and anger over the Vietnam War. Crime seemed out of control. Lack of trust in and disrespect for the police became the norm. Police administrators began to realize that something must be done to confront the problems of escalating crime rates and poor community relations. In the aftermath of the Kansas City Study, police administrators began to reevaluate how departments could gain community trust, considered a key element of improving police effectiveness. Police departments began experimenting with initiatives to improve the relationship between police and the public. Three of the most prominent efforts were police community relations, foot patrol, and team policing. At this point, community engagement in policing became a priority.

LO2   Explain the concept of community policing.

During the late 1980s, the NIJ funded Executive Sessions at Harvard University, where practitioners and researchers met to discuss the future of policing. They advocated an emphasis on peacekeeping, prevention, and order maintenance in the community. There was agreement that policing should move away from the crime-fighting orientation and the war on crime, and put the focus on community control. Slowly, the era of community policing took hold. The term "community policing" became popular with the passage of the Violent Crime Control and Law Enforcement Act of 1994 and the creation of the Office Community Oriented Policing Services (COPS) under the U.S. Department of Justice.

LO3   Explain the challenge of community policing.

While these community policing programs are being implemented, they still face many challenges. First, community policing involves giving patrol officers a great deal of discretion. Officers are expected to engage in problem solving activities that can be time-consuming and sometimes do not yield measurable results. Furthermore, unchecked discretion can result in the abuse of power. The community can also have an influence on policing and serve as an obstacle to the implementation of COP. Community members might have conflicting priorities regarding local problems on which the police should focus. Another major obstacle is that the approach is difficult to define. There are many different definitions of community policing and ways to implement it. Because community policing looks different in almost every jurisdiction it is implemented in, means that evaluation is difficult.

LO4   Compare and contrast COP and POP.

COP is best known as a philosophy and not a program or special unit. It is based on the concept that police and private citizens can work together in creative ways that can help solve contemporary community problems related to crime, fear of crime, disorder, and neighborhood decay. The main idea is the police cannot fight crime alone—they need the community to be successful! Local police departments must adopt the tactics that are appropriate for the communities that they serve. In contrast, problem-oriented policing (POP) is a style of police management that stresses proactive problem-solving instead of reactive crime fighting. POP is aimed at identifying and then solving problems at the local community-level issues. This approach diverges from traditional police models that focus on responding to calls for help in the least possible time, dealing with the situation, and then getting on the street again as soon as possible.

LO5   Assess the relationship between the broken windows hypothesis and zero tolerance policing.

The broken windows model assumes that there are two types of disorder: physical and social. The former is characterized by not only broken windows, but also vacant buildings, abandoned vehicles, and vacant lots filled with trash. The latter, social disorder, is characterized by persistent panhandlers, lack of civility, noise, and disrespectful youth congregating on street corners. As these conditions take hold, residents experience rapidly expanding levels of fear, causing them to withdraw from community life. Police can play a key role in disrupting this process. If they focus on disorder and petty crime in neighborhoods that have not yet been overtaken by serious crimes such as drug gangs, they can help reduce fear and reduce resident relocation. Police should focus on disorder problems affecting the quality of life in neighborhoods. In contrast, zero tolerance policing focuses on controlling minor crime and other signs of social disorder.

Early intervention through aggressive policing to stop misdemeanors and public order offenses will prevent and reduce felonies. Timely and accurate intelligence is obtained through stop-and-frisk, interrogation, and decentralization.

LO6   Evaluate the effectiveness of police response to crime achieved by broken windows and zero tolerance policies.

Researchers have put broken windows and aggressive policing to the test and found that, indeed, it can be an effective approach to crime reduction. In fact, the downturn in the New York City violent crime rate during the 1990s has been attributed to aggressive police work aimed at lifestyle crimes: vandalism, panhandling, and graffiti. Nonetheless, there has been some serious side effects to using aggressive police tactics: With the implementation of zero tolerance policing, the number of citizen complaints filed has jumped in some jurisdictions, such as New York City, as did the number of lawsuits alleging police misconduct and abuse of force.

LO7   Describe intelligence-led policing and predictive policing approaches.

Intelligence-led policing incorporates data analysis and criminal intelligence into a strategy that coordinates strategic risk management of threats with a focus on serious, recidivist offenders. Intelligence-led policing is a policing business model that incorporates data analysis and criminal intelligence into a strategy that coordinates strategic risk management of threats with a focus on serious, recidivist offenders. Predictive policing harnesses the power of information, geospatial technologies, and evidence-based intervention models to reduce crime and improve public safety. The predictive policing approach does not replace traditional policing. Instead, it enhances existing approaches such as problem-oriented policing, community policing, and intelligence-led policing.

Key Terms

team policing, 159
community policing, 162
community-oriented policing
    (COP), 163
problem solving, 165

procedural justice, 170
problem-oriented policing
    (POP), 171
broken windows, 175
zero tolerance policing, 176

CompStat, 177
intelligence-led policing (ILP),
    178

Notes

1. Elizabeth Simpson, Roundup of the Cops and Robbers Symposium, E-newsletter of the COPS Office, 9, no. 1 (January 2016).
2. President's Task Force on 21st Century Policing, Final Report of the President's Task Force on 21st Century Policing, 2015, Washington, DC: Office of Community-Oriented Policing Services, https://cops.usdoj.gov/pdf/taskforce/taskforce_finalreport.pdf.
3. https://www.fbi.gov/resources/library.
4. George L. Kelling, Tony Pate, Duane Dieckman, and Charles E. Brow. The Kansas City Preventative Patrol Experiment: A Summary Report, 1974.
5. Hubert Williams and Patrick V. Murphy, "The Evolving Strategy of Police: A Minority View" (vol. 13). Washington, DC: U.S. Department of Justice, Office of Justice Programs, National Institute of Justice.
6. Robert A. Brown, "Policing in American History," *Du Bois Review* 16, no. 1 (2019), 189–195, https://www.researchgate.net/profile/Robert_Brown21/publication/339518268_POLICING_IN_AMERICAN_HISTORY/links/5ea0419c45851564fc3479ba/POLICING-IN-AMERICAN-HISTORY.pdf.
7. Jerome H. Skolnick, "The Police and the Urban Ghetto," In Arthur Niederhoffer and Abraham S. Blumberg (eds.), *The Ambivalent Force: Perspectives on Police*, 2nd ed. (Hinsdale, IL: Dryden, 1976), 222.
8. Lawrence W. Sherman, Catherine Milton, Thomas V. Kelly, and Thomas F. MacBride, "Team Policing: Seven Case Studies." Washington, DC: Police Foundation, 1973.
9. Samuel Walker, "Does Anyone Remember Team Policing-Lessons of the Team Policing Experience for Community Policing," *American Journal of Police* 12 (1993), 33.
10. Ibid.
11. David L. Carter, Allen D. Sapp, and Darrel W. Stephens, "The State of Police Education: Policy Direction for the 21st Century," Washington, DC: Police Executive Research Forum, 1989.
12. Dorothy Guyot, "Bending Granite: Attempts to Change the Rank Structure of American Police Departments," *Journal of Police Science and Administration* 7, no. 3 (1979), 253–284.

13. Matthew C. Scheider and Quint Thurman, "A National Evaluation of the Effect of COPS Grants on Police Productivity (Arrests) 1995–1999," *Police Quarterly* 6, no. 4 (2003), 387–409.

14. Matthew J. Hickman and Brian Reaves, *Local police departments 1999.* (Washington, DC: US Department of Justice, Office of Justice Programs, Bureau of Justice Statistics, 2001).

15. Albert Cardarelli, Jack McDevitt, and Katrina Baum, "The Rhetoric and Reality of Community Policing in Small and Medium-Sized Cities and Towns," *Policing* 21 (1998), 397–415.

16. Office of Community Oriented Policing Services, http://www.cops.usdoj.gov/, accessed January 2016.

17. John L. Worrall and Jihong Zhao, "The Role of the COPS Office in Community Policing," *Policing* 26 (2003), 64–87.

18. Office of Community Oriented Policing Services, http://www.cops.usdoj.gov, accessed June 2014.

19. Jihong Zhao, Nicholas Lovrich, and Quint Thurman, "The Status of Community Policing in American Cities," *Policing* 22 (1999): 74–92.

20. David Bayley, "Community Policing: A Report from the Devil's Advocate." In Jack R. Greene and Stephen Mastrofski (eds.), *Community Policing: Rhetoric or Reality*, pp. 225–23. New York, NY: Pracger.

21. Gary Cordner, "Community Policing," *The Oxford Handbook of Police and Policing* (2014), 148.

22. David Kessler, "Integrating Calls for Service with Community- and Problem-Oriented Policing: A Case Study," *Crime and Delinquency* 39 (1993), 485–508.

23. K. Peyton, M. Sierra-Arévalo, D. G. Rand, "A Field Experiment on Community Policing and Police Legitimacy," *Proceedings of the National Academy of Sciences* 116, no. 40 (1990), 19894–19898.

24. J. Rukus, M. E. Warner, and X. Zhang, "Community Policing: Least Effective Where Need Is Greatest," *Crime & Delinquency* 64, no. 14 (2018), 1858–1881.

25. L. Thomas Winfree, Gregory Bartku, and George Seibel, "Support for Community Policing versus Traditional Policing Among Nonmetropolitan Police Officers: A Survey of Four New Mexico Police Departments," *American Journal of Police* 15 (1996), 23–47.

26. A. M. Schuck, "Female Officers and Community Policing: Examining the Connection between Gender Diversity and Organizational Change," *Women & Criminal Justice* 27, no. 5 (2017), 341–362.

27. Anisha Nandi, "Neighborhood Policing Program Builds Relationships to Cut Crime," *CBS News*, March 23, 2018, https://www.cbsnews.com/news/nypd-community-policing-lower-crime/.

28. New York City Police Department, Neighborhood Policing, 2018, .https://www1.nyc.gov/site/nypd/bureaus/patrol/neighborhood-coordination-officers.page

29. Brooks Sutherland, "Boston Police Reach out to Youth," *Boston Herald*, September 25, 2018, http://www.bostonherald.com/news/local_coverage/2018/09/boston_police_reach_out_to_youth#.W6obm1DJ8kg.facebook.

30. Jihong Zhao, Ni He, and Nicholas Lovrich, "Value Change Among Police Officers at a Time of Organizational Reform: A Follow-Up Study of Rokeach Values," *Policing* 22 (1999), 152–170.

31. Charlotte Gill, et al, "Community-Oriented Policing to Reduce Crime, Disorder and Fear and Increase Satisfaction and Legitimacy among Citizens: A Systematic Review," *Journal of Experimental Criminology* 10, no. 4 (2014), 399–428.

32. Jihong Zhao, Matthew Scheider, and Quint Thurman, "A National Evaluation of the Effect of COPs Grants on Police Productivity (Arrests) 1995–1999," *Police Quarterly* 6 (2003), 387–410.

33. Mike Brogden, "'Horses for Courses' and 'Thin Blue Lines': Community Policing in Transitional Society," *Police Quarterly* 8 (2005), 64–99.

34. Ling Ren, Liqun Cao, Nicholas Lovrich, and Michael Gaffney, "Linking Confidence in the Police with the Performance of the Police: Community Policing Can Make a Difference," *Journal of Criminal Justice* 33 (2005), 55–66.

35. Stephen M. Schnebly, "The Influence of Community-Oriented Policing on Crime-Reporting Behavior," *Justice Quarterly* 25 (2008), 223–251.

36. Jack R. Greene, "The Effects of Community Policing on American Law Enforcement: A Look at the Evidence," paper presented at the International Congress on Criminology, Hamburg.

37. Roger Dunham and Geoffrey Alpert, "Neighborhood Differences in Attitudes Toward Policing: Evidence for a Mixed-Strategy Model of Policing in a Multi-Ethnic Setting," *Journal of Criminal Law and Criminology* 79 (1988), 504–522.

38. Scott Lewis, Helen Rosenberg, and Robert Sigler, "Acceptance of Community Policing Among Police Officers and Police Administrators," *Policing* 22 (1999), 567–588.

39. Robin Shepard Engel, *How Police Supervisory Styles Influence Patrol Officer Behavior* (Washington, DC: National Institute of Justice, 2003).

40. Amy Halsted, Max Bromley, and John Cochran, "The Effects of Work Orientations on Job Satisfaction Among Sheriffs' Deputies Practicing Community-Oriented Policing," *Policing* 23 (2000), 82–104.

41. Venessa Garcia, "Constructing the 'Other' Within Police Culture: An Analysis of a Deviant Unit Within the Police Organization," *Police Practice and Research* 6 (2005), 65–80.

42. Allison T. Chappell, "Community Policing: Is Field Training the Missing Link?," *Policing* 30 (2007), 498–517.

43. Michael Palmiotto, Michael Birzer, and N. Prabha Unnithan, "Training in Community Policing: A Suggested Curriculum," *Policing* 23 (2000), 8–21.

44. Lisa Riechers and Roy Roberg, "Community Policing: A Critical Review of Underlying Assumptions," *Journal of Police Science and Administration* 17 (1990), 112–113.

45. John Riley, "Community-Policing: Utilizing the Knowledge of Organizational Personnel," *Policing* 22 (1999), 618–633.

46. Donald Green, Dara Strolovitch, and Janelle Wong, "Defended Neighborhoods: Integration and Racially Motivated Crime," *American Journal of Sociology* 104 (1998), 372–403.

47. The Ferguson Commission. (n.d.) Restoring Relations through Community Policing. https://forwardthroughferguson.org/report/call-to-action/expanding-civilian-oversight/.

48. Joe Biden. We Must Urgently Root Out Systemic Racism from Policing, To Housing Opportunity (Opinion). June 10, 2020. USA Today. https://www.usatoday.com/story/opinion/2020/06/10/biden-root-out-systemic-racism-not-just-divisive-trump-talk-column/5327631002/.

49. Candace Norwood. Calls for reform bring renewed focus on community policing, but does it work? September 18, 2020. https://www.pbs.org/newshour/politics/calls-for-reform-bring-renewed-focus-to-community-policing-but-does-it-work.

50. William Spelman and John E. Eck, *Problem-oriented policing.* US Department of Justice, National Institute of Justice, Research in Brief, 1987, https://www.ojp.gov/pdffiles1/Digitization/102371NCJRS.pdf.

51. Edward R. Maguire, Craig D. Uchida, and Kimberly D. Hassell, "51 Policing in Colorado Springs A Content Analysis of 753 Cases," *Crime & Delinquency* 61, no. 1 (2015), 71–95.

52. James Q. Wilson and George L. Kelling, "The Police and Neighborhood Safety." *The Atlantic Monthly,* March, Broken windows 249, no. 3 (1982), 29–-38, www.theatlantic.com/politics/crime/windows.htm.

53. Donna Lieberman, "What Donald Trump Got Wrong about Stop & Frisk," *Huffington Post,* September 23, 2016, .https://www.nyclu.org/en/publications/op-ed-what-donald-trump-got-wrong-about-stop-and-frisk-huffington-post; New York Civil

Liberties Union, Stop and Frisk Data, 2022, https://www.nyclu .org/en/stop-and-frisk-data, accessed 2023.

54. American Civil Liberties Union, "Black, Brown, and Targeted: A Report on Boston Police Department Street Encounters from 2007–2010," 2015, https://aclum.org/wp-content/uploads /2015/06/reports-black-brown-and-targeted.pdf.

55. Philadelphia Police Department, "The CompStat Process," May 6, 2003, www.ppdonline.org/hq_compstat.php.

56. Bureau of Justice Assistance Police Executive Research Forum, COMPSTAT: Its Origins, Evolution, and Future in Law Enforcement Agencies, 2013, https://bja.ojp.gov/sites/g/files /xyckuh186/files/Publications/PERF-Compstat.pdf.

57. Judith A. Greene, "Zero Tolerance: A Case Study of Police Policies and Practices in New York City," *Crime & Delinquency* 45, no. 2 (1999), 171–187.

58. Judith A. Greene, "Zero Tolerance: A Case Study of Police Policies and Practices in New York City," *Crime & Delinquency* 45, no. 2 (1999), 171–187.

59. Tracey Meares, " Broken Windows, Neighborhoods, and the Legitimacy of Law Enforcement or Why I Fell in and out of Love with Zimbardo", Crime and Delinquency 52 (2015): 609–625.

60. Jerry H. Ratcliffe, "Intelligence-Led Policing," *Encyclopedia of Criminology and Criminal Justice* (Springer: New York, 2014), pp. 2573–2581.

61. D. L. Carter, *Law Enforcement Intelligence: A Guide for State, Local, and Tribal Enforcement Agencies (Report),* 2nd ed. (Office of Community Oriented Policing Services: Washington, DC, 2009).

62. Jeremy G. Carter, Scott W. Phillips, and S. Marlon Gayadeen, "Implementing Intelligence-Led Policing: An Application of Loose-Coupling Theory," *Journal of Criminal Justice* 42, no. 6 (2014), 433–442.

63. J. H. Ratcliffe, *Intelligence-Led Policing.* (Cullompton, UK: Willan Publishing, 2018).

64. Jeremy G. Carter and Scott W. Phillips, "Intelligence-Led Policing and Forces of Organizational Change in the USA,." *Policing and Society* 25, no. 4 (2015), 333–357.

65. National Institute of Justice, Overview of Predictive Policing, 2014, http://www.nij.gov/topics/law-enforcement/strategies /predictive-policing/Pages/welcome.aspx.

66. Walt L. Perry, *Predictive Policing: The Role of Crime Forecasting in Law Enforcement Operations* (Rand RAND Corporation, 2013).

67. George O. Mohler, et al., "Randomized Controlled Field Trials of Predictive Policing," *Journal of the American Statistical Association* 110, no. 512 (2015), 1399–1411.

68. Kate Mather and Richard Winton, "LAPD Uses Its Helicopters to Stop Crimes before They Start," *Los Angeles Times*, March 7, 2015.

69. U.S. Department of Justice, "Department Awards More Than $30 Million to Project Safe Neighborhoods to Combat Violent Crime," October 3, 2018, https://www.justice.gov/opa/pr /justice-department-awards-more-30-million-project-safe -neighborhoods-combat-violent-crime.

Part 3

Challenges of Policing

Chapter 7
Ethical Issues in Policing

Chapter 8
The Changing Rank and File

Chapter 9
Police Discretion

Chapter 10
Police Misconduct: Corruption and Abuse of Power

Chapter 11
Legal Controls

Policing and law enforcement have become challenging occupations, and this section contains five chapters that address some of the significant dilemmas that confound the profession today. We look at ethical issues in policing and how police administrators are attempting to improve the way officers view the job. We also address the different police styles that police employ today. A significant effort is made to address how the police are now more representative of the communities they serve and the increasing role of women and people of color in policing, including the challenges they face and how diversity affects policing. This section also looks at the challenges presented by the discretion given police officers to investigate crimes, make arrests, and use force. The media continually focus on police misconduct, and we look at corruption and abuse of power and what is being done to reduce its occurrence.

7

Ethical Issues in Policing

Learning Objectives

LO1 Discuss the concept of ethical policing in the United States.

LO2 Discuss the elements of democratic policing in the United States.

LO3 Demonstrate disparity and discrimination in policing in the United States.

LO4 Examine contemporary methods of accountability.

LO5 Examine the types of citizen review boards.

LO6 Discuss the application of procedural justice in policing.

Chapter Outline

In 2022, 14 Prince George's County, Maryland, police officers were indicted by a grand jury for an elaborate double-dipping scheme to make money as private security officers while being paid for their regular department shifts. The officers were accused of exploiting a Prince George's County Police Department (PGPD) program known as secondary employment, which allows officers to earn additional income working private security. Often, officers working secondary employment provide security at apartment complexes, concerts, liquor stores, nightclubs, or sporting events. The program allows officers to use their county-issued uniform, badge, gun, and cruiser.

Under department rules in place at the time of the alleged misconduct—from January 2019 to March 2021—officers were allowed to find secondary work themselves or become an employee of a private security firm that brokered the jobs for them. All secondary work was supposed to be approved through the department and performed during off-duty hours.

The indicted officers worked private security shifts at the same time as their on-duty department work, and then concealed the overlap from the police department. They all worked for a fellow Prince George's County officer, Edward "Scott" Finn, who owned a private security company which is at the center of the case.

Finn employed his fellow law enforcement officers to provide security services to apartment complexes and other businesses his company protected and to manage and operate his security business. To drum up business, it is alleged that Finn and his employees provided false information, including arrests, to the apartment complexes to justify their private security services.

To make matters worse, Finn admitted to federal authoties that he underreported a total of more than $1.3 million of income on his 2014 through 2019 individual income tax returns. During that time frame, Finn deposited checks payable to his security business into personal bank accounts and other accounts over which Finn had signature authority. Finn also created false business expenses to lower his tax due by writing checks to relatives and friends for purported services performed and used business funds to purchase a boat, a car, and other items for his personal use. This underreported income resulted in a total tax loss to the government of $367,765. Pleading guilty as charged, Finn faces a maximum sentence of five years in federal prison for tax evasion and will also be required to pay restitution in the full amount of the loss, $367,765.[1]

What do you suppose would be the backlash if an officer, who was not part of this scheme, tipped off the administration? If you were a fellow police officer, would you report this scheme to the higher-ups or would you fear being called a snitch or rat? Does this fear create a blue wall of silence, which demands that officers keep silent about unethical behavior they encounter? And if does, are officers who break the rules allowed to continue without fear of reprisal? What is the ethical thing to do? What are ethics, and how do they affect the police?

LO1

Discuss the concept of ethical policing in the United States.

What Is Ethics, and How Does It Play Out in Policing?

In looking at the profession of policing, it quickly becomes apparent why police officers, probably more than many other professions, should study, understand, and abide by ethical principles. In many ways, the police are the gatekeepers of the criminal justice system. For most citizens, the police represent the most local form of government. But there are several main reasons for police officers to study ethics as follows.

1. Because it is central to decision making and the criminal justice process.
2. To understand how the criminal justice system (and policing) is engaged in coercion.
3. To understand the special duties public servants (police officers) owe to the public they serve.
4. So that police officers can become sensitive to ethical issues they will likely face and develop tools for resolving ethical dilemmas during their careers.
5. For officers to become more professional.
6. To begin developing critical-thinking skills.
7. To quickly recognize the ethical consequences of various actions.

It is critically important for police officers, who are leaders in the community, to avoid a term known as *ethical myopia*, which is the fatal flaw in failing to recognize the importance of ethics in doing police work.[2] Donald C. Menzel, in his book *Ethics Moments in Government,* states that police do not exist to produce a product called "ethics." Instead, the police are expected to provide and produce valuable public services, such as justice, safety, security, and many, many more.[3] Menzel goes on to say that it is important for public servants, like the police to avoid what is known as *ethical illiteracy.* This is when police officers are unable to fully understand or appreciate the intricacies of the complex ethical issues they are likely to face as well as not being able to see all of the consequences of their actions. A large illiteracy blind spot can produce tunnel vision that severely damages a police officer's or whole department's reputation as being a fair and equitable provider of public safety.

Because the police are entrusted with public safety, it is imperative that their decisions follow moral and ethical principles. Do you consider it unethical for a police officer to receive a free meal, given voluntarily by a restaurant owner glad to have officers frequent his establishment, offering their protection during business hours?

Paul Lovichi Photography/Alamy Stock Photo

Defining Ethics

In a broad sense, ethics is a system of moral principles. Ethics as an ideal is concerned with what is not only good for the individual, but also what is good for society as a whole. The word *ethics* is derived from the Greek word *ethos*, which means "character." It speaks to a person's trustworthiness or credibility and is a balance between passion and caution. When an officer engages in unethical behavior, it erodes the public trust and causes great damage to the profession of policing. Many people use the terms *morals* and *ethics* interchangeably; these are different but interrelated terms. Morals generally refer to guiding principles of actions, and ethics tends to refer to specific rules, actions, or behaviors. Ethics tend to have a basis in your values. People tend to make value judgments about people and their actions. Many people equate morals to actions involving one's personal life and ethics as governing one's professional actions. A moral precept is an idea or opinion that's driven by a person's desire to be a good person. An ethical code, on the other hand, is often a set of rules that defines allowable actions or correct behavior, most often in a professional setting.

When discussing ethics, inevitably the next question to ask is what are "values." We often hear the phrase value judgments, but what does that really mean? According to Jay Albanese (2006), values are judgments of worth of people's attitudes, statements, and behaviors.[4] When the police make a value judgment on the behaviors of others, many times a negative consequence will result; that is, ticket, summons, fine, or arrest (or worse). So it is imperative that police officers operate with the highest degree of ethical behavior, to reduce or eliminate undue hardship for community members and their families. Because of the amount of discretion and unsupervised patrol time, it is imperative that people entering the profession of policing adhere to the highest ethical standards.

Ethical Policing

Because the police are entrusted with public safety, it is imperative that their decisions follow moral and ethical principles. It should be noted that virtually every decision that a police officer makes, will have profound, and often long-lasting implications to many people. The slighted police initiated action or decision could have far-reaching implications for all involved. Every police-action will be scrutinized because of the amount of power that the police are given and how they exercise that power is really important to understand. Therefore, it is incredibly important that all police actions take into account the ethical ramifications their decision may hold.

The police have a large amount of discretionary power. They have the power to deprive someone of their liberty through arrest, the power to decide who to investigate, and to initiate an investigation, and the power to issue tickets with fines, or simple warnings.[5] The police also have the discretion whether to use force or not, including deadly force.

Many times when people speak of ethics in policing, they often mention the term *police corruption* (as will be explained in later chapters). From an ethical perspective, there are three types of police corruption: Nonfeasance—failure to perform a legal duty; misfeasance—failure to perform a legal duty in a proper manner; and malfeasance—committing an illegal act.[6] Because of the trust given to the police, it is imperative that they act in ethically legal ways. Due to the nature of the job, the police should be held to a higher standard than ordinary citizens, and their behaviors and actions should be scrutinized more closely. When they act in unethical or illegal ways, they need to be held accountable or else the public trust will be diminished and eroded.

Duty to Intervene

Because of the murder of George Floyd, under the knee of a Minneapolis police officer, many states are trying to pass laws mandating that the police have a "duty to intervene." This legal and ethical standard, which is part of an overall aim at reforming police misconduct, is meant to have officers stop, or at least intervene, when they see wrongdoing (often misuse of force) by fellow officers. It is worth noting that police officers do in fact have a moral obligation to intervene when excessive force is being used by fellow officers. But having a moral obligation to intervene is very different from having a statutory obligation to intervene, particularly when the statutory obligation comes with criminal penalties.

A statutory duty to intervene would require that an officer make a determination whether or not the force they are witnessing is excessive. Often, policing proponents will debate what is reasonable and what is necessary or reasonable force. The bar is not high when an officer sees a fellow officer punching or kicking a suspect that is laying prone on the ground, or is already in handcuffs. Once the imminent threat is over, the use of force should stop. If using the "reasonableness standard," one could ask, would a reasonable person believe that the force they are witnessing is necessary to affect an arrest or stop the resistance to a legal police action?

Before we can discuss the extent of this duty, we first need a working definition of the duty to intervene. One definition of duty to intervene is given by the Second Circuit Court in the case of *Figueroa v. Mazza* (2016):

> A police officer is under a duty to intercede and prevent fellow officers from subjecting a citizen to excessive force, and may be held liable for his failure to do so if he observes the use of force and has sufficient time to act to prevent.[7]

The duty to intervene is often accompanied by departmental policy. In Austin, Texas, their police policy states: "A duty-to-intervene policy creates an affirmative obligation on the part of police officers to stop other officers from engaging in certain conduct prohibited by law or department policy."[8] In Connecticut, they use a more encompassing policy definition:

> Any police officer acting in a law enforcement capacity who witnesses a use of force by another officer (regardless of rank), that the witnessing officer knows to be unreasonable shall intervene and attempt to stop such use of force. "Unreasonable force" is any force applied in a manner inconsistent with this policy or applicable law. The level of intervention should be that level necessary to stop said use of unreasonable force and may involve verbal and/or physical intervention.[9]

These "duty to intervene" policies and laws, many coming out of police accountability legislation, take ethical decisions and make them a statutory obligation. The reminding of officers that they have ethical obligations regarding their actions while on duty is accompanied by defining statutes that further define their actions. Do we still need legislation telling officers that they have a duty to intervene when inherent in their jobs is the fact that they are supposed to intervene when they see wrong doing?

According to Westlaw, *"Officers have an affirmative duty to protect individuals from constitutional violations by fellow officers. To hold an officer liable for failure to intervene it must be shown that the officer knew a person's rights were being violated, had an opportunity to intervene, and chose not to do so.*"[10] Based on case law in *Yang v. Hardin*, the Seventh Circuit goes on to explain that:

> an officer who is present and fails to intervene to prevent other law enforcement officers from infringing the constitutional rights of citizens is liable under § 1983 if that officer had reason to know: **(1)** that excessive force was being used, **(2)** that a citizen has been unjustifiably arrested, or **(3)** that any constitutional violation has been committed by a law enforcement official; and the officer had a realistic opportunity to intervene to prevent the harm from occurring.[11]

According to the Seventh Circuit of the U.S. Court of Appeals, the following outlines what a plaintiff must prove in order to demonstrate that an officer failed to intercede or intervene in a use of force scenario:

1. An officer used excessive force on Plaintiff
2. The Defendant (the officer who Plaintiff alleges should have intervened) knew that the first officer was using/was about to use excessive force on Plaintiff
3. Defendant had a realistic opportunity to do something to prevent harm from occurring
4. Defendant failed to take reasonable steps to prevent harm from occurring
5. Defendant's failure to act caused Plaintiff to suffer harm[12]

The issue of ethics in policing is not a new concept. In 1957, the International Association of Chiefs of Police (IACP) adopted a law enforcement code of ethics. This code is supposed to govern policing in the United States and serves as a general guide to police actions on and off duty. This code of ethics is divided into several parts. First is a general acknowledgment of the duty of a law enforcement officer:

> As a law enforcement officer, my fundamental duty is to serve the community; to safeguard lives and property; to protect the innocent against deception, the weak against oppression or intimidation and the peaceful against violence or disorder; and to respect the constitutional rights of all to liberty, equality, and justice.

The second part of the code of ethics governs the actions of a police officer in the personal or private lives:

> I will keep my private life unsullied as an example to all and will behave in a manner that does not bring discredit to me or to my agency. I will maintain courageous calm in the face of danger, scorn or ridicule; develop self-restraint; and be constantly mindful of the welfare of others. Honest in thought and deed both in my personal and official life, I will be exemplary in obeying the law and the regulations of my department. Whatever I see or hear of a confidential nature or that is confided to me in my official capacity will be kept ever secret unless revelation is necessary in the performance of my duty.

The third section addresses the nature, personal feelings, and attitude of the officer:

> I will never act officiously or permit personal feelings, prejudices, political beliefs, aspirations, animosities or friendships to influence my decisions. With no compromise for crime and with relentless prosecution of criminals, I will enforce the law courteously and appropriately without fear or favor, malice or ill will, never employing unnecessary force or violence and never accepting gratuities.

The final section of this code addresses the public trust that the police must keep sacred as well as their obligation to abide by this code:

> I recognize the badge of my office as a symbol of public faith, and I accept it as a public trust to be held so long as I am true to the ethics of police service. I will never engage in acts of corruption or bribery, nor will I condone such acts by other police officers. I will cooperate with all legally authorized agencies and their representatives in the pursuit of justice.
>
> I know that I alone am responsible for my own standard of professional performance and will take every reasonable opportunity to enhance and improve my level of knowledge and competence. I will constantly strive to achieve these objectives and ideals, dedicating myself before God to my chosen profession... law enforcement.[13]

Whistleblowing

As the nation demanded accountability in policing after the murder of George Floyd, few people think that significant change will happen with officers unwilling to call out bad officer conduct. The culture of police silence is well documented. It makes sense that those who wield significant power should be held accountable for their actions. This is not a different concept for police; this applies to all who have power. But the problem is that in policing, officers tend to not want to hold their colleagues accountable for misconduct.

There is an amazingly strong culture in policing not to expose the wrongdoing of fellow officers. But that culture tends to let bad deeds go unpunished, and uncorrected, leaving the public vulnerable. But officers need to know that federal whistleblower laws protect them from retaliation for reporting violations of fellow officers.

In particular, 42 U.S.C. §1983, part of the Civil Rights Act of 1871, protects whistleblowers from retaliation by public officials for disclosing constitutional violations, including police brutality, to the press, a city council, and other public bodies. Section 1983 is one of the most powerful whistleblower laws, providing the right to a jury trial, injunctive relief, and all economic damages, including compensatory damages and punitive damages.[14]

Critical Thinking

There has been a negative perception of people who tell on others. What is the importance of the whistleblowing process in an ethical organization?

L02

Discuss the elements of democratic policing in the United States.

What Is the Role of the Modern Democratic Police?

The role of the modern democratic police is constantly adapting to the public's expectations for public safety. In its broadest sense, democratic policing involves protecting the constitutional rights of all residents. To achieve democratic policing, there must be accountability for how police departments do their jobs. Community members are less likely to support an agency over which they have little or no say—particularly if the agency has a huge impact on their lives. Therefore, police agencies that don't practice democratic policing are unlikely to have legitimacy. Legitimacy is associated with compliance with the law and acceptance of police authority. It is a necessary condition for police-public cooperation such as reporting crime victimization, acting as a witness or assisting police investigation. Community participation is crucial because police cannot investigate or solve crimes about which they are unaware or lack evidence.

The Policing Project, an independent group aimed at promoting public safety, transparency, equity, and engagement, has identified the following three main elements to democratic policing:

1. There should be robust engagement between police departments and the communities they serve around the policies and priorities of policing.

2. When possible, policing practices should be guided by rules and policies that are adopted in advance of action, are transparent, and are formulated with input from the public.

3. Police departments should develop and use sound metrics of success that encompass all of the goals of policing, including community trust.[15]

Maria Ponomarenko and Barry Friedman argue that this is more than holding officers accountable after something terrible has happened. Rather, there should also be front-end accountability before policing officials take action. Front-end accountability involves questions like: What should the rules be that govern policing? What even counts as misconduct? and What should the proper conduct have been in the first place?[16]

Nicole Glass Photography/Shutterstock.com

There has been a significant effort to bring the police and the community they serve closer together. This all too often happens when tragedy strikes both institutions. Here officers line the streets to watch the funeral procession of Brian Sicknick, who died during the Capitol Riots on January 6, 2021.

There have been ongoing attempts to modernize policing by creating policies and programs that are aimed at creating a truly "democratic" police department. One notable example has been the efforts of Alexander Jones, chief of police in Arlington, Texas. The following Focus on Policing: Modernizing Policing in Arlington, Texas feature sets out his efforts to modernize the Arlington Police Department and bring it closer to the community it serves.

What Is Justice?

Since police officers have an incredible amount of discretion in their daily jobs, the question then becomes, is the ethical object of police action supposed to be "justice" or punishment? If the answer is "justice," then we should define the term. If we use a working definition of justice, it should include the ethical and philosophical idea that people should be treated fairly, properly, and reasonably by the law and the government agents that carry out the law. Justice should include both due processes and fair outcomes. Some may add that justice is when similarly situated individuals receive similar outcomes. Others would say that justice is the outcome when people get what they deserve after a fair and impartial process.

Because the profession of policing is extremely discretion oriented, particularly in instances of low visibility, we have to examine justice in terms of discretionary action. Discretion is the ability to make similar situations have very different outcomes. We know that police officers often operate under the mantra of being "law enforcement" officers, which is often a reactionary term because the very idea of enforcing laws implies action after a law is violated. So we cannot ensure that similarly situated individuals will have similar outcomes, because personal bias (implicit or explicit) often creates disparities in outcomes.

Focus on Policing

Modernizing Policing in Arlington, Texas

Chief Alexander Jones

Arlington, Texas, Police Chief Alexander Jones takes a contemporary view on police-community relations.

In November 2020, Alexander Jones was appointed as the new police chief in Arlington, Texas. Being the 46th largest law enforcement agency in the country, the Arlington Police Department has nearly 900 employees (sworn and professional staff). Chief Jones began his policing career in 1995 in the Baltimore County Police Department. He rose through the ranks to become the bureau chief of community relations and then the colonel of operations, the department's second-highest-ranking officer. In Baltimore County, Jones oversaw 10 police precincts, patrol operations, the Safe School Division, Youth and Community Service Section, and the Support Operations Division. His focus was on community relations and building trust with the communities.

Arlington, Texas, is a thriving city, halfway between the cities of Dallas and Fort Worth, has a population of roughly 393,000 residents, and has several major attractions within its borders. Arlington is home to a major university (University of Texas at Arlington with an enrollment of nearly 40,000 students), the stadiums of the Dallas Cowboys (80,000 capacity) and Texas Rangers (48,000 capacity), as well as Six Flags Theme Park (37,000 capacity) and water park. Two major interstates go through Arlington (I-30 and I-20), so there could easily be upward of 0.5 million people in the city at any one time.

Chief Al Jones is particularly well suited for this city. Rather than subscribing to traditional policing, he believes in the importance of community policing initiatives and bolstering trust with all segments of the population. As a chief, he is a relational leader who takes the time to listen to the concerns of members of his agency as well as community issues to build stronger relationships. Chief Jones is committed to equality under the law for everyone who lives, works, and plays in Arlington. He states that the George Floyd protests are an opportunity to learn about community concerns and taking action to get the community's trust.

Chief Jones immediately started building bridges within the agency as soon as he was hired. His message is that relationship building starts inside the agency; officers must feel respected and engaged within the department so they can then positively connect with communities they serve. He increased communications within the agency so that officers could have a voice and buy-in. He developed a seven-year strategic plan with relational policing as a focus. He believes in empowering officers to make decisions in their patrol beats or districts with a focus on relational policing and building relationships with everyone you encounter. When officers make mistakes, those missteps often turn into teachable moments. Mentoring and coaching the employees in the police department is the rule.

Chief Jones employs what he refers to as a five-tier philosophy known by the acronym T.R.E.A.T.:

1. Transparency—being transparent with your motives and action not only to community members, but also members of the police department so everyone is on the same page.

2. Respect—respect everyone you encounter. All members of the community and the police department must be treated with dignity and respect.

3. Engagement—with the community and the department. Giving people voice and choice.

4. Accountability—being held accountable for your actions and comments inside and outside of the department.

5. Training—all members of the department must understand why they do what they do or why they are being asked to do something. Once they understand the goal, then they can buy into the mission.

Chief Jones regularly puts out a *Chief's brief*; a document explaining the philosophy or actions that the chief is trying to accomplish. He believes that giving information to the officers empowers them. He is a hands-on leader and believes in the concept of managing by walking around and regularly walks around the department and the community. He is a visible leader who regularly goes to officer in-service training to talk to the officers and answer their questions. Jones often shows up at events where officers are working. One of his favorite parts of the job is visiting his officers when they are out in the community feeding people who are experiencing homelessness.

Chief Jones tells his officers and staff that they are a family and sometimes families have disputes, but we still try to make things better together. He is a hands-on leader who often gives fist bumps or hugs to officers, many of whom now expect that level of engagement from him. Jones said he even makes his own photocopies, so he has the chance to get out of the office, walk around the building, and interact with the professional staff.

The Arlington Police Department now engages in *Faith-In-Blue weekends*, which is a time when the police put on programming to connect with the community. Officers also attend church meetings to find out the issues in the community. Officers take community members through police-type scenarios (burglaries, mental health, traffic stops, etc.) so they can see what officers go through. Building better understanding is the key to partnerships. Arlington PD also participates in *Operation Connect*: walking the neighborhoods, knocking on doors, talking to residents, answering questions, and giving pamphlets to community members in areas that have high rates of crimes. These pamphlets are printed in English, Spanish, and Vietnamese, to match the population of the city.

The focus is on building relationships, but also driving down violent crimes and fatal accidents in the area. Chief Jones wants the community to be the eyes and ears of the department by knocking on doors and talking to residents. He said this is not all enforcement, but the focus is on relationships. The chief wants community members on board with policing initiatives, so he loops them in when strategies change. He states that only between 3 to 5 percent of the residents commit serious crimes, so there is no need to punish the other 95 percent of residents as we are doing our jobs. This is a long-term problem that deserves a logical long-term solution, including community partnerships.

The police department puts on an event called "Cooking with Cops." Police officers bring hot dogs, hamburgers, and beverages to communities to build bridges. They also bring police vehicles, dogs, horses, motorcycles, and drones to showcase policing in the community. Roughly 1,500 residents come out to these quarterly events. They also host four Police Activities League (PAL) camps during the summer so officers can hang out with and get to know the youth. In addition, the police hold leadership classes at Boys & Girls Clubs.

To further engage the community, the Arlington Police Department holds a "Coach Five-0" program, where officers get to coach and mentor young people. This program has also grown into another program called "Game-Up Five-0," where officers play video games with local young people. The police just received a grant to provide funds for a dedicated vehicle to house, transport, and play video games. Chief Jones says, "We need these partnerships. Crime is not a policing issue. It's a community issue."

Source: https://www.arlingtontx.gov/city_hall/departments/police/About_Us/Meet_the_Police_Chief.

▶ Disparities in Outcomes

People of color and particularly African American community members are disproportionately under the control of the criminal justice system. One piece of understanding in this outcome is the role of the police as gatekeepers to the criminal justice system. Through negative interactions with the police, citizens enter into the criminal justice system. A 2021 study by Justin T. Picket, Amanda Graham, and Francis T. Cullen found that even though the mission of the police is to protect and serve, many people of color do not feel protected *from* the police. The authors go on to state that most White respondents in their study felt safe, but many Black respondents live in fear of the police. For many Americans, in their study, particularly Black Americans, "being questioned or searched by the police without receiving a good explanation is worse than being robbed or burglarized."[17]

In a 2014 study by the Massachusetts American Civil Liberties Union (ACLU) (discussed later in this chapter), they report that people of color are regularly stopped and searched with no legal justification. In one instance, a teenager says that he has been stopped and searched by the local police upward of 40 times in one year. When he was robbed at gunpoint, he opted not to report it to the local police because of the history of negative contact. He said, "What would [the police] have done for me? I don't trust them after the way they have treated me and my people for so many years."[18]

A Department of Justice report on the Baltimore Police Department (BPD) found that Baltimore city police officers regularly violate constitutional or federal laws in the way they interact with Black people. The report specifically stated that Baltimore police officers regularly engage in patterns or practices of "(1) making unconstitutional stops, searches, and arrests; (2) using enforcement strategies that produce severe and unjustified disparities in the rates of stops, searches and arrests of African Americans; (3) using excessive force; and (4) retaliating against people engaging in constitutionally-protected expression" like peaceful protests. The Department of Justice found that the police department's legacy of zero-tolerance enforcement continues to drive officers to conduct unconstitutional stops, searches, and arrests. Police supervisors instruct officers to make stops with little or no suspicion without sufficient consideration if the actions are constitutional.[19]

Stop and Frisk

Stop and frisk policies are among the most controversial practices in modern policing. These are also known as Field Interrogation Stops or Terry Stops; They are the result of a 1968 court case, *Terry v. Ohio.* In October 1963, Martin McFadden, a Cleveland police detective, conducted a search to prevent a possible armed robbery. Specifically, McFadden conducted a pat-down search on three men whom, he believed, were preparing to rob a store.

Two of the men, John Terry and Richard Chilton, were found to be carrying pistols. They were tried and convicted of carrying

San Francisco police frisk a Black man on a street corner. The racial disparity prevalent in such interactions creates a wedge between police and communities of color.

ChameleonsEye/Shutterstock.com

On the Web

For more information about *Terry v. Ohio,* please visit https://www.oyez.org /cases/1967/67

concealed weapons. They appealed, arguing that evidence used to convict them had been discovered during an illegal search, but their conviction was affirmed by the Ohio Supreme Court. John Terry's case was eventually argued before the U.S. Supreme Court in 1967. The majority opinion was written by Chief Justice Earl Warren, stating that McFadden had the authority to conduct a limited search for weapons in the interest of officer safety. Because both individuals were engaged in suspicious behavior, the police were able to frisk them.

The Supreme Court held that the Fourth Amendment prohibition on unreasonable searches and seizures is not violated when a police officer stops a suspect on the street and frisks them without probable cause to arrest, if the police officer has a reasonable suspicion that the person has committed, is committing, or is about to commit a crime and has a reasonable belief that the person "may be armed and presently dangerous. This is why stop and frisk is also known as a "Terry stop." We will revisit the *Terry* decision in Chapter 11.

What exactly is involved in a stop and frisk? There are two aspects to this tactic. First, police officers can elect to stop a citizen. It should be noted that most field interrogations end this way—with a police officer stopping and talking with a resident. The more controversial piece of this is that given suspicious movements, police officers can also elect to search a citizen. Evidence suggests that police are more likely to stop, frisk, and arrest suspects in predominantly Black or mixed neighborhoods than they are in White areas.

Take, for instance, Operation Impact, a policing strategy that deployed extra police officers to high-crime areas in New York City.[20] Officers were encouraged to conduct investigative "street" stops of citizens suspected of either felony or misdemeanor crimes in these areas. They found that both stops and arrests increased in these high-crime areas. Specifically, arrests for weapons and other felony offenses increased, as did investigative "street" stops.

The increase in "street" stops in these high-crime areas was associated with a small reduction in overall crime and large reductions in burglary offenses. Overall, Operation Impact contributed marginally to overall crime reductions. The other outcome, however, is worth attention. This project generated a high volume of unproductive police stops that had little crime reduction benefit. More than 5 million New Yorkers have been subjected to police stops and street interrogations since the program was initiated and members of the Black and Latino communities were disproportionately targeted for stops. At its height, over 685,000 people were stopped in a single year (2011). Despite its widespread use, 90 percent of those stopped were innocent. Court orders and political fallout resulted in a substantially curtailed use of stop and frisk in New York. Nonetheless, the findings from a study of recent racial and ethnic bias in the stop-and-frisk program suggest discrimination is still present. The findings are set out in Exhibit 7.1.

These stop-and-frisk policies are not limited to New York City. The American Civil Liberties Union (ACLU) published a 2014 report[21] that asserts that Boston police officers often engage in widespread racially biased stop-and-frisk practices, targeting people of color at far greater rates than White people. The report also states that Black citizens in the city studied were subjected to 63 percent of these encounters, even though they made up just 24 percent of

Exhibit 7.1

New York City Stop and Frisk

- Young Black and Latino males between the ages of 14 and 24 account for only 5 percent of the city's population, compared with 38 percent of reported stops. Young Black and Latino males were innocent 80 percent of the time.

- Though frisks are only supposed to be conducted when an officer reasonably suspects the person has a weapon that poses threat to the officer's safety, 66 percent of reported stops led to frisks, of which over 93 percent resulted in no weapon being found.

- Black and Latino people were more likely to be frisked than White people and, among those frisked, were less likely to be found with a weapon.

- Between 2014 and 2017, the New York City Police Department (NYPD) used force on over 21,000 Black and Latino people and over 2,200 White people. Even among those stopped, Black and Latino people were more likely to have force used against them than White people.

- Black and Latino people were disproportionately stopped, regardless of the demographic makeup of the neighborhood. For example, in the 17th precinct, which encompasses Kips Bay and Murray Hill, Black and Latino people make up just 8 percent of the population, but 75 percent of the people were stopped by police.

Source: New York Civil Liberties Union, "Racial Disparities Remain, Despite Significant Decline in Stops," March 14, 2019, https://www.aclu.org/press-releases/nyclu-releases-report-analyzing -nypd-stop-and-frisk-data.

that city's population. The report also showed that controlling for neighborhood-level crime rates do not explain this racial disparity. The report further showed that as the Black population in this city increased as a percentage of the total population, so did the number of police encounters.

The ACLU reports that even after controlling for crime, police officers were more likely to initiate police encounters in Black neighborhoods and to initiate encounters with Black people. When questioned about this disparity, police officials gave no justification for 75 percent of these encounters, simply stating that they were investigatory in nature. More than 200,000 of these stops-and-frisk, investigative encounters over a four-year period yielded no arrests, and only 2.5 percent led to seizure of contraband of any kind.

The Officer Shuffle

Research has confirmed the existence of the officer shuffle, in which disreputable police officers move across police jurisdictions, resigning at the onset of allegations to maintain their police certification and police employment.[22] Officers in the St. Louis area confirmed the existence of the officer shuffle, whereby discredited officers are shuffled to other police agencies amidst allegations of misconduct and violence.[23] This is also true for sexual assault. After conducting a content analysis of newspaper accounts of PSV offenses from 1996 to 2006, Cara Rabe-Hemp and Jeremy

Critical Thinking

What do you think can be done to stop the disproportionate stop-and-frisk occurrences of people of color when it has shown to not increase the amount of contraband found?

Braithwaite found that a group of repeat officers are responsible for the majority of the sexual assaults known to the public. Almost three-quarters of victims in the study were victimized by a repeat or problem-prone offender. Each repeat offender in the sample averaged four reported victims over an average of three years.[24]

So what is to be done to address this small group of problem officers? Rabe-Hemp and Braithwaite suggest several remedies:

1. Strengthen the criminal justice response to sexual assault.
2. Increasing the power and presence of Peace Officer Standards and Training (POST) boards.
3. Greater access to reporting mechanisms for police misconduct.

Critical Thinking

Do you think that police officers who break public trust should be prohibited from ever working in policing again?

Police Accountability

◀ **LO4**

Examine contemporary methods of accountability.

Accountability is a crucial element to a functioning democracy. There are several ways to hold officers and police agencies accountable. First, there are internal methods. Most importantly is the role of the police chief. The chief must speak out against deviance and the rank and file must believe it. This means that it can't just be words, there must also be action to back it up.

Departmental policies and regulations are another way to maintain accountability. This means that in the standard operating procedures, departments must clearly identify what actions, activities and behaviors will not be tolerated. Rules exist to minimize *unarticulated improvisation* and help prevent the inevitable *inconsistencies in police responses* that arise due to police discretion. Rules and regulations are needed to guide officer discretion so that it does not result in patterns of discrimination. Documented policies inform officers of what is acceptable, establishes consistency in operations, provides grounds for discipline, and helps supervisors oversee officers. There is some evidence to suggest that policy changes work. Generally, research concludes that a tightened policy that is rigorously enforced will not only reduce the number of police shootings, but it will also change outcomes for police officers. For example, in a now-classic study, James Fyfe looked at the adoption of a NYPD policy requiring officers to document any discharge of their service weapons. In addition to a decrease in accidental discharges, he found that this restrictive firearms policy also actually resulted in a decline of officer injuries. It is important to remember, however, that these policies must be enforced to be effective.

Internal affairs investigations are another method of accountability. These units act as an internal watchdog. They investigate alleged acts of misconduct by police officers. Investigations can range from citizen complaints, supervisory reports of improper action, and insubordination to equipment violations like firearm discharges. This means that most investigations are reactive, in response to things brought to their attention but they can be proactive too. For internal affairs to be effective, the unit must be linked with the chief and have immediate access as well as enough resources to do a good job.

Gorodenkoff/Shutterstock.com

Accountability can mean that police officers must be willing to tell the truth, even if that means testifying in court if the misbehavior of fellow officers results in criminal charges being filed.

Weingarten Rules

Police agencies must allow officers to have the presence of union officials during disciplinary meetings.

Critical Thinking

One of the biggest complaints about internal affairs is that the police should not be allowed to investigate themselves. What are the pros and cons of having an internal affairs division investigating complaints against officers in their department?

Garrity Rule

An officer cannot be ordered to respond to questions during an investigation of their criminal conduct.

vicarious liability

A situation in which one party is held partly responsible for the unlawful actions of a second or third party.

If police departments do not seriously investigate claims of misconduct, they will lose community support. Internal affairs actions are controlled by agency policy, the Weingarten and Garrity Rules. **Weingarten Rules** comes from *Labor Relations Board v. Weingarten* (1975). The court held that agencies must allow officers to have the presence of union officials (if they request it) in circumstances that relate to information that could be used to discipline an officer.

The **Garrity Rule** comes from *Garrity et al. v. New Jersey* (1967).

Garrity is about differentiating between criminal matters and administrative matters. The essence of the *Garrity* decision is that if an officer is the subject of an internal affairs investigation alleging criminal conduct, then a commanding officer cannot order that officer to respond to questions. But if the inquiry is administrative in nature, the officer should respond.

Without policies in place, agencies can incur **vicarious liability**. If agencies do not have policy regulating behaviors, they will be seen as being *deliberately indifferent*.

Vicarious liability comes from the *Monnell v. New York Department of Social Services* 1978 decision. In *Monnell*, the Supreme Court held that local government units are liable for employee actions.

After internal affairs has completed an investigation, they will dispose to the case in one of the following ways:

1. *Unfounded*—the allegation is found to be false due to incorrect factual information, etc.

2. *Exonerated*—incident took place but the officer did no wrong

3. *Not sustained*—inconclusive (evidence not strong enough to pick sides)

4. *Sustained*—support the accusation and conclude that the officer acted incorrectly

Types of disciplinary actions range from remedial training, oral reprimand, written reprimand, suspension, dismissal, and decertification (i.e., similar to revoking your license). Decertification is typically due to actions related to gross insubordination, drunk on duty, willful neglect of duty, corruption, immorality, etc.

One of the frequently overlooked ways to improve accountability is to the recruitment and selection of good personnel. This may seem fairly obvious—but it is not always considered when discussing accountability. Who you hire may be as important as the policies in place. But it is not enough to hire good officers. Policies must also be in place to retain, promote, and protect good officers and whistle-blowers. Communities and particularly police departments must protect those who come forward and reward the good officers. This is not always the case. In 2008, a Black police officer, Cariol Horne, in Buffalo, New York, was fired for intervening when a White colleague employed a chokehold. In 2021, a court held that she will be given backpay and a pension. Horne served on the Buffalo police force for 19 of the 20 years required to receive a pension.[25] Furthermore, the success of many internal affairs investigations relies on other officers who have come forward.

Early warning systems are another accountability measure that departments can employ. An early warning system is a data-based police management tool designed to identify officers whose behavior is problematic and provide a form of intervention to correct that performance. As an early response, a department intervenes before such an officer is in a situation that warrants formal disciplinary action. The system alerts the department to these individuals and warns the officers while providing counseling or training to help them change their problematic behavior. By 1999, 39 percent of all municipal and county law enforcement agencies that serve populations greater than 50,000 people either had an early warning system in place or were planning to implement one. According to the National Institute of Justice,[26] early warning systems have three basic phases: selection, intervention, and post-intervention monitoring.

- Selecting officers for the program. No standards have been established for identifying officers for early warning programs, but there is general agreement about the criteria that should influence their selection. Performance indicators that can help identify officers with problematic behavior include citizen complaints, firearm discharge and use-of-force reports, civil litigation, resisting-arrest incidents, and high-speed pursuits and vehicular damage.

- Intervening with the officer. The primary goal of early warning systems is to change the behavior of individual officers who have been identified as having problematic performance records. The basic intervention strategy involves a combination of deterrence and education.

- Monitoring the officer's subsequent performance. Agencies must monitor an officer's performance after the initial intervention to see if any changes have been made.

Qualified Immunity

The legal concept of **qualified immunity** shields public officials from lawsuits and monetary liability *when* they perform their duties reasonably. According to this legal doctrine, public officials can only be sued if they violate a clearly established statutory or constitutional right. Typically a legal right is "clearly established," when it is judged that any reasonable government official would have known their actions violated a citizen's rights. As long as a reasonable government worker, such as a teacher or police officer, should know that their behavior was unacceptable and improper, they not only would not have to pay damages but they would not have to go through a trial. So, a teacher who punches a student who did not do their homework or a police officer who shoots a suspect who fails to stop for a red light could be tried and punished since they should be well aware that their behavior is not reasonable or acceptable.

The Supreme Court has considered the concept of qualified immunity in numerous legal cases. One important one, *Safford v. Redding* (2009) is set out in the following Police & the Law: *Safford v. Redding* feature, discusses the concept of qualified immunity in the school setting

So the qualified immunity doctrine would protect police from lawsuits unless it could be proven that they were in violation of a clearly spelled out rule of behavior of which every police officer should be aware. Qualified immunity would protect them from civil action if the police officer could show that they acted in "good faith" and had "probable cause" for their actions. An officer who has violated the Constitution cannot be held liable for damages unless the violation was so "clearly established" in the law that any reasonable officer would have known that their actions were unlawful. Numerous commentators argue that the qualified immunity doctrine is too protective of rogue government agents. Some have called for its abolition. However, as the following Police and the Law: The Defense of Qualified Immunity feature indicates a recent Supreme Court expands the concept of qualified immunity and means it is here to stay.

qualified immunity

A legal principle that grants government officials immunity from civil suits unless the official violated clearly established statutory or constitutional rights of which a reasonable person acting in a similar capacity would be aware.

Police & the Law

Safford v. Redding

Savana Redding was a 13-year-old eighth-grade honors student at Safford Middle School, located about 127 miles from Tucson, Arizona, when on October 3, 2003, she was taken out of class by the school's vice principal. It seems that one of Redding's classmates had been caught possessing prescription-strength ibuprofen (400 mg—the strength of two Advils) and when asked where she got the pills, she blamed Redding, who had no history of disciplinary issues or drug abuse. Though Redding claimed she had no knowledge of the pills, she was subjected to a strip search by the school nurse and another female employee because the school had a zero tolerance policy for all over-the-counter (OTC) medication (which students could not possess without prior written permission). During the search, Redding was forced to strip to her underwear, and her bra and underpants were pulled away from her body. No drugs were found. She later told authorities, "The strip search was the most humiliating experience I have ever had. I held my head down so that they could not see that I was about to cry."

After a trial court ruled that the search was legal, Redding sought help from the American Civil Liberties Union, whose attorneys brought an appeal before the Ninth Circuit Court. Here, the judges ruled that the search was "traumatizing" and illegal, stating that "common sense informs us that directing a 13-year-old girl to remove her clothes, partially revealing her breasts and pelvic area, for allegedly possessing ibuprofen . . . was excessively intrusive." It further went on to say, "The overzealousness of school administrators in efforts to protect students has the tragic impact of traumatizing those they claim to serve. And all this to find prescription-strength ibuprofen."

Rather than let the appellate court decision stand, the school district appealed the case to the U.S. Supreme Court, complaining that restrictions on conducting student searches would cast a "roadblock to the kind of swift and effective response that is too often needed to protect the very safety of students, particularly from the threats posed by drugs and weapons." On June 25, 2009, the Supreme Court held that Redding's Fourth Amendment rights were indeed violated by the search. With Justice David Souter writing

for the majority, the Court agreed that search measures used by school officials to root out contraband must be "reasonably related to the objectives of the search and not excessively intrusive in light of the age and sex of the student and the nature of the infraction."

In Redding's case, school officials did not have sufficient suspicion to extend the search to her underwear. In a separate opinion, Justice John Paul Stevens agreed that the strip search was unconstitutional and that the school administrators should be held personally liable for damages: "It does not require a constitutional scholar to conclude that a nude search of a 13-year-old child is an invasion of constitutional rights of some magnitude." (His opinion was in response to the majority's ruling that school officials could not be held personally liable because the law was unclear before the *Safford* decision. The only justice to disagree with the main finding was Clarence Thomas, who concluded that the judiciary should not meddle with decisions of school administrators that are intended to be in the interest of school safety.

The Court also held that under the qualified immunity doctrine, the person performing the illegal search is still immune from legal action, unless clearly established law shows that the search violated the Fourth Amendment. The Court concluded that the school administrators were not personally liable for damages because "clearly established law [did] not show that the search violated the Fourth Amendment." It reasoned that lower court decisions were disparate enough to have warranted doubt about the scope of a student's Fourth Amendment right. Their behavior is not reasonable or acceptable.

Critical Thinking

1. Considering the threat of school shootings, should students be searched and questioned with less than probable cause?

2. Would it have been reasonable, under the same set of circumstances, for school officials to search Savana's backpack or locker?

Source: *Safford Unified School District v. Redding,* 557 U.S. 364 (2009).

Police & the Law

The Defense of Qualified Immunity

Daniel Rivas-Villegas v. Ramon Cortesluna

In 2021, the Supreme Court ruled on two cases that strengthened the qualified immunity protections for police. The first case, *Daniel Rivas-Villegas v. Ramon Cortesluna* was involved in a 2016 incident in which police in Union City, California, responded to a 9-1-1 call alleging Ramon Cortesluna was going to hurt his girlfriend and her two children. The three victims were trapped in a room when police arrived. They ordered Cortesluna to leave the house and keep his hands up. An officer then shouted, "he has a knife in his left pocket." Cortesluna lowered his hands and was shot with nonlethal bean bag rounds in the stomach and hip. When he got down on the ground, Officer Daniel Rivas-Villegas straddled him and placed his left knee on the left side of Cortesluna's back. Rivas-Villegas was in this position for no more than eight seconds before standing up while continuing to hold Cortesluna's arms, at which point another officer removed the knife and handcuffed Cortesluna, the Court said.

Cortesluna sued, arguing Rivas-Villegas used excessive force in violation of the Fourth Amendment. A federal district court sided with the officer, but the U.S. Court of Appeals for the Ninth Circuit reversed that decision, ruling that "existing precedent put [Rivas-Villegas] on notice that his conduct constituted excessive force." The Supreme Court ruled that "to show a violation of clearly established law, Cortesluna must identify a case that put Rivas-Villegas on notice that his specific conduct was unlawful. The Court decided that Cortesluna "has not done so." They went on to state that neither he nor the appeals court "identified any Supreme Court case that addresses facts like the ones at issue here."

The second case involved a 2016 police incident in which the ex-wife of Dominic Rollice called 9-1-1 and told the dispatcher that her former husband was drunk in her garage and refusing to leave.

Responding to the call, three officers from the Tahlequah, Oklahoma, Police Department, Josh Girdner,

Chase Reed, and Brandon Vick, responded to the call. When they arrived, they approached Rollice and tried to pat him down for weapons, but he refused, and then turned away from the officers and grabbed a hammer from the garage. Bodycam footage showed Rollice grasping the hammer with both hands and raising it to shoulder level and refusing to drop it when officers shouted for him to let it go. Rollice continued to raise the hammer behind his head and took a stance as if he was about to throw the hammer or charge at the officers. Girdner and Vick then shot and killed Rollice.

Rollice's estate sued, alleging the officers violated his Fourth Amendment right to be free from excessive force. The district court found the use of force was reasonable and that qualified immunity applied. But the Tenth Circuit Court of Appeals reversed, ruling that the officers' moves to corner Rollice in the back of the garage led to the use of deadly force.

The Supreme Court reversed the appellate decision, saying none of the precedent cited by the lower court "comes close to establishing that the officers' conduct was unlawful." They went on to say that "We have repeatedly told courts not to define clearly established law at too high a level of generality... Qualified immunity protects all but the plainly incompetent or those who knowingly violate the law.... It must be clear to a reasonable officer that his conduct was unlawful in the situation he confronted."

Taken in sum, the cases indicate that there is little chance that the Court will restrict or even terminate the defense of qualified immunity.

Critical Thinking

1. Critics charge that these cases will encourage police to use violence. Do you agree? Or is the use of violence spontaneous?

2. Are police officers' situational reactions tempered or by a Supreme Court ruling?

Source: *Daniel Rivas-Villegas v. Ramon Cortesluna* 595 U.S. ... (2021) *City of Tahlequah, Oklahoma, Et Al. v. Austin P. Bond, as Special Administrator of the Estate of Dominic F. Rollice, Deceased*, 595 U.S. _____ (2021).

It still remains to be seen what effect these recent Supreme Court decisions will have on states that have banned or curtailed qualified immunity. For example, the defense ended in Colorado when it passed legislation allowing individuals whose rights are violated under the *state* constitution to bring a lawsuit for damages in *state* court.[27]

External of Forms of Accountability

In many public sector organizations, including in policing, proper ethical training and oversight is needed to avoid issues of corruption. Many police officers go through their daily tasks without direct supervision. If the officer is not properly trained in the ethics of police work, then there could be circumstances where they may look the other way when coworkers engage in corrupt activities, or they may engage in these activities themselves. Police officers who are unable to fully grasp the intricacies of simple or complex ethical issues nor to see all of the consequences of one's actions are affected by ethical illiteracy. Sound ethical judgment calls for more than meeting the moral minimum of the law, it calls for professional accountability and oversight.

Special Commissions to Investigate the Police

When unethical police actions go unchecked by supervisors, often they can lead to levels of corruption. When levels of unethical behavior and corruption become pervasive, special commissions are sometimes created to investigate the issues. **Special commissions** are nonpolice personnel often empaneled to investigate police officers or police departments when corruption is pervasive within the department. These commissions are independent and not influenced by internal pressure. But since they are outsiders, they are often resisted by the police force. These commissions tend to be fact-finding in nature and advisory to elected officials. They are often seen as having no real power to enforce, reprimand, or discipline wrongdoing unless they are accompanied by a court-ordered consent decree. Examples of special commissions include the Knapp Commission, Christopher Commission, and Mollen Commission.

Named after its chairman, Judge Whitman Knapp, the **Knapp Commission**, formally known as the **Commission to Investigate Alleged Police Corruption**, was a five-member panel formed in April 1970 to investigate alleged widespread corruption within the NYPD. The creation of this commission was primarily a result of the public exposure of police corruption made by NYPD Officer Frank Serpico and Sergeant David Durk. Its finding that systematic corruption existed resulted in number of recommendations to reduce its occurrence, including:

- Appointment of a special deputy attorney general to investigate corruption
- Reorganization of internal inspection services.
- Elimination of exposure to situations leading to corruption,
- Increasing the risks involved in engaging in corruption,
- Increasing incentives for meritorious police performance,
- Changing the attitudes of both the police and the public toward corruption.

The **Christopher Commission,** formally known as the **Independent Commission on the Los Angeles Police Department** was formed in April 1991, four months after the video-taped beating of Black motorist Rodney King.

special commissions

Groups, made up of independent experts and concerned citizens, that are empaneled to investigate police departments when there is evidence that corruption is pervasive within the department.

Knapp Commission (Commission to Investigate Alleged Police Corruption)

A five-member panel initially formed in April 1970 to investigate alleged widespread corruption within the NYPD.

Christopher Commission (Independent Commission on the Los Angeles Police Department)

Formed in April 1991 to conduct a full and fair examination of the structure and operation of the LAPD, including its recruitment and training practices, internal disciplinary system, and citizen complaint system.

The Christopher Commission was led by Attorney Warren Christopher (who later became U. S. Secretary of State in the Clinton administration). The Christopher Commission was created to conduct "a full and fair examination of the structure and operation of the LAPD," including its recruitment and training practices, internal disciplinary system, and citizen complaint system."[28] The Christopher Commission found that "There is a significant number of officers in the LAPD who repetitively use excessive force against the public and persistently ignore the written guidelines of the department regarding force." The report goes on to say that "The failure to control these officers is a management issue that is at the heart of the problem ... The LAPD's failure to analyze and act upon these revealing data evidences a significant breakdown in the management and leadership of the Department."

The **Mollen Commission**, formally known as **The City of New York Commission to Investigate Allegations of Police Corruption and the Anti-Corruption Procedures of the Police Department**, was led by former Judge Milton Mollen. The Mollen Commission was formed in 1992 to examine and investigate the nature and extent of corruption in the NYPD, evaluate the department's procedures for preventing and detecting corruption, and recommend changes and improvements to police procedures. The Mollen Commission recommended several actions, including increased internal controls and the creation of a permanent independent police commission to perform continuous assessments of the department's systems for preventing, detecting, and investigating corruption and to conduct its own corruption investigations.[29]

Mollen Commission (The City of New York Commission to Investigate Allegations of Police Corruption and the Anti-Corruption Procedures of the Police Department)
Formed in 1992 to examine and investigate the nature and extent of corruption in the NYPD, evaluate the department's procedures for preventing and detecting corruption, and recommend changes and improvements to police procedures.

External Investigations

In the aftermath of the murder of George Floyd, the U.S. Department of Justice conducted an investigation of the Minneapolis Police Department (MPD), which culminated in a 2023 report that concluded it engaged in a pattern of unlawful racial discrimination and excessive force.

The department opened its investigation on April 21, 2021. A team of career attorneys and staff in the Civil Rights Division's Special Litigation Section and the Civil Division of the U.S. attorney's office for the District of Minnesota were for the task. The team conducted numerous onsite tours of MPD facilities; interviewed MPD officers, supervisors, and command staff; spoke with city officials and employees; accompanied behavioral crisis responders and officers on ride-a-longs; reviewed thousands of documents; and watched thousands of hours of body-worn camera footage. Department attorneys and staff also met with community members, advocates, service providers, and other stakeholders in the Minneapolis area.

The department conducted this investigation pursuant to 34 U.S.C. § 12601 (Section 12601), which prohibits law enforcement officers from engaging in a pattern or practice of conduct that deprives people of rights protected by the Constitution or federal law, the Safe Streets Act of 1968, Title VI of the Civil Rights Act of 1964, and Title II of the Americans with Disabilities Act. The investigation employed department data, records, interviews and ride-a-longs and found:

■ Minneapolis officers routinely used excessive force firearms and tasers. They applied neck restraints "without warning" on suspects who committed minor offenses and did not pose a threat to safety.

■ Officers failed to adequately ensure the safety of people in their custody, including ignoring calls for help from people experiencing medical emergencies.

■ There was evidence that officers unlawfully discriminated against Black and Native American people when making arrests and used disproportionate amounts of excessive force against people in these groups.

■ Officers were not held accountable for racist conduct unless there was a significant public outcry.

■ Minneapolis officers routinely violated free speech rights of citizens routinely retaliating against protestors and members of the press who were involved in rallies and protests. They also retaliated against people who questioned or talked back to them during traffic stops and service calls.

■ Unnecessarily dispatched law enforcement to calls for help involving people with mental health of behavioral disabilities, resulting in trauma.

In sum, the DOJ report found Minneapolis officers repeatedly violated citizens First and Fourth Amendments, as well as the federal Civil Rights Act, the Safe Streets Act, and the Americans with Disabilities. While the city had already agreed via state and federal consent decrees to overhaul its policies on vehicle stops and use of force, the report reinforces the need for sweeping changes in the way the police and public interact.[30]

Legal Actions

There is a difference between unethical police behavior and illegal police actions (criminal intent), though it can be argued that most illegal police actions began as unethical behavior that went unchecked or uncorrected by supervising officers. Unethical behavior is typically handled internally by department-level discipline, but police officers can be prosecuted for violations of the law.

In April 2015, former North Charleston, South Carolina, Police Officer Michael T. Slager shot unarmed motorist Walter Scott in the back five times as Scott was running away from Slager during a traffic stop. Slager claimed that Scott had taken the officer's Taser and was charging at the officer at the time of the shooting. A citizen's cell phone video of the incident disproved the officer's claim.[31] The former officer pled guilty to one federal charge of violating Scott's civil rights by using excessive force. He was sentenced to 20 years in prison.[32]

On May 25, 2020, Minneapolis police officers arrested George Floyd on a report that he had used a fake $20 bill. Floyd died after Officer Derek Chauvin pinned him to the ground with a knee until Floyd died. This incident was captured on cell phone video. Chauvin was fired from the Minneapolis police force and tried in state court for the murder of George Floyd. Chauvin was found guilty of murder and manslaughter and was sentenced to 22.5 years in prison.[33] This case led to the George Floyd Justice in Policing Act of 2020 (discussed in Chapter 5), which addresses increases in accountability for police misconduct, restricts the use of certain policing practices deemed reckless, enhances police transparency and data collection, and establishes best practices and police officer training requirements.

On April 11, 2021, former Minnesota Police Officer Kim Potter fatally shot motorist Daunte Wright during a traffic stop for an expired tag. Officer Potter, a 26-year police veteran, drew her gun instead of a Taser and Potter resigned from her police job 2 days later. Potter was indicted and tried for the shooting. A jury found her guilty of first- and second-degree manslaughter in Daunte Wright's death.

Tort Actions

Often unethical actions by the police can cause harm to others. If a person alleges that they have been wronged by the police, they may sue the police for damages, which is known as a *tort action*. A tort is a wrongful act, negligence, or an infringement of a right (other than under contract), leading to civil legal liability. The person who brings the charges in a tort case is known as the plaintiff, and the defendant in the case can be the individual officer, the supervising officers, the police department, the government, or all of the above. The plaintiff will typically name as many people in the lawsuit as possible so that the plaintiff can seek out the person or entity with the most money to compensate the citizen who has been negatively affected by the police action.

In a typical civil suit brought against an officer under state law, a plaintiff alleges that the officer owed them a legal duty; that the office breached that duty; and that the breach caused the citizen some kind of harm, either physical or emotional. The chance of success in a civil suit is much higher than a criminal case because the level of proof needed in a civil case is the *preponderance of the evidence* standard and not the *guilty beyond a reasonable doubt* standard (as in criminal cases).

When examining civil cases, there are two types of torts: *intentional negligence*. Intentional is when an officer commits an act that carries a reasonable certainty of injury or harm (either mental or physical) to another party. These types of cases usually relate to excessive use of force (assault/battery), wrongful death, false arrest or imprisonment, infliction of mental distress, etc.

Negligence, on the other hand, usually involves failure to act reasonably in a situation where it is feasible to foresee that the officer's conduct or actions may have caused harm to another person. Failure to do something typically relates to training, negligent hiring (not checking criminal backgrounds), failure to supervise, negligent retention, etc. By suing the police, you hope to get compensation for the harm that was done (compensatory damages) and/or to punish the officer for their wrongdoing (punitive damages).

The largest tort settlement for police misconduct in American history happened in 2023 when a New Haven man was paralyzed while in police custody. The following Focus on Policing: Randy Cox feature outlines the details of the case and settlement.

When ethical infractions rise to the level of violation of rights, a federal case may be pursued for a civil rights violation lawsuit. **Federal civil rights violation** lawsuits are referred to as violations of Title 42, Section 1983 of the Civil Rights Act of 1871. Section 1983 refers to the deprivation of constitutional rights by any government official. Thus, to be successful in federal court, you must show: (1) you were *deprived of constitutionally guaranteed rights by the officer* and (2) *that the person who perpetrated the wrong doing acted under the color of the law.*

There may be various types of rights violations. Typically, people will claim their Fourth Amendment rights (force as a form of unreasonable seizure), Eighth Amendment rights (force as cruel and unusual punishment), or due process

federal civil rights violation

Contraventions of Title 42, Section 1983 of the Civil Rights Act of 1871, which refers to the deprivation of constitutional rights by any government official.

Focus on Policing

Randy Cox

On June 19, 2022, 36-year-old Richard "Randy" Cox, who was arrested on a weapons charge, was being transported to a police station in New Haven, Connecticut, when he sustained a debilitating injury. Cox was handcuffed behind his back in a police transport van that was not equipped with seatbelts. The van made a sudden stop, and Cox violently slammed head-first into the van's inside wall.

Police body-worn camera video shows that Cox repeatedly asked for help, stating he couldn't move, but the officers did not immediately render medical aid and allegedly assumed he was drunk when they arrived at the police station. Video footage also shows the officers dragging Cox out of the van by his feet and putting him into a wheelchair. Cox was paralyzed due to injuries he sustained while in police custody.

In 2023, the city of New Haven agreed to a historic $45 million settlement with Randy Cox for police misconduct. To date, this is the largest police misconduct settlement in U.S. history. Cox and his legal team previously filed a $100 million civil lawsuit against the City of New Haven and the New Haven Police Department. Of the $45 million settlement, $30 million will be paid by city insurance and the remaining $15 million will be paid out of city coffers. Prior to the Cox settlement, the largest police misconduct settlement in the United States was in 2021 for the police killing of George Floyd in Minneapolis, Minnesota. That settlement was more than $27 million.

New Haven Police Chief Karl Jacobson expressed remorse for what happened to Randy Cox and said, "You can make mistakes as an officer, but you can't treat community members unfairly …You have to give them a voice. Randy had a voice that day and said … 'I broke my neck; I can't move' and we didn't listen to him." New Haven Mayor Justin Elicker added, "When an individual enters police custody, there is an obligation to treat them with dignity and respect and in a manner that ensures their safety and well-being. That did not happen with Randy: He entered policy custody being able to walk, and he left police custody paralyzed with his life and his health forever altered."

Five police officers were charged criminally for their involvement in the arrest and injury to Cox. Four of the five officers were fired by the New Haven Police Department. The fifth officer retired from the police department shortly after the event. At the time of this writing, the case against the five officers is still pending.

Source: https://www.ctpublic.org/2023-06-10/randy-cox-reaches-45-million-settlement-with-city-of-new-haven.

guarantee under the Fourteenth Amendment have been violated to the extent that it shocks judicial conscience. This is a high legal standard so some choose to file in the state system. Regarding civil liability, many plaintiffs file federal lawsuits since attorney fees are covered by the government in federal suits of this nature.

The "violation of civil rights" challenge happened when Michael Slager Shot and killed Walter Scott. Slager pled guilty to violating Scott's civil rights by using excessive force. The Scott family sued the City of North Charleston, South Carolina. The city settled out of court and agreed to pay $6.5 million to the family of Walter Scott.[34] When Minneapolis Officer Derek Chauvin knelt on George Floyd's neck until he died, the Floyd family sued the City of Minneapolis, claiming that the officer violated Floyd's civil rights in the wrongful death. The city settled with the Floyd family for a record $27 million.[35]

In November 2000, the city of Los Angeles paid a record (at the time) $25 million to plaintiffs when multiple convictions were overturned after the LAPD CRASH unit corruption investigation. More than 70 officers were implicated in misconduct, including unprovoked beatings, shootings, planting and covering up evidence, stealing and dealing drugs, and perjury.[36] According to

blue fragility
The level of discomfort or defensiveness felt when police officers are confronted with a level of accountability that they may not be used to or haven't had to deal with in the past.

Focus on Policing

Blue Fragility

A recent teenage brawl at the local mall made its way onto the local news. A video was taken of the event showing a group of boys arguing. Suddenly a White teenager points his finger at a Black teenager's face, and the Black teenager pushes the White teenager's hand away. The White teenager then pushes the Black teenager, who begins to throw punches at the other boy. The White teenager punches back and the Black teenager ends up on the ground. Suddenly, two local police officers arrive and separate the two boys.

When the Black teenager begins to get up, he is pinned to the ground by one officer and rolled on to his stomach, with his hands behind his back. The other officer orders the White teenager to take a seat and then assists in handcuffing the Black teenager. The community is outraged after the video is shown on the news and the department is reluctantly forced to apologize publicly for what took place. The police chief, under public pressure from local officials and clergy, said that there would be an internal affairs investigation.

The Black teen's mother told reporters she was outraged and believed without question that the police actions were based on race: "What made them tackle my son, handcuff him and not the other kid, who watched it all from a distance?" Her son, who was not charged, said he was merely reacting to provocation and was defending himself against bullies. The family hired an attorney and said they intended to sue the police. The family's attorney demanded that the two officers be immediately fired. It is incidents like this that make some officers defensive, guarded, and self-protective.

In 2011, sociologist Robin DiAngelo introduced the term *White fragility*, which in her words is a level of discomfort and/or defensiveness on the part of a White person when they are confronted by information regarding instances of racial inequality and injustice. In the past, they may have been shielded from having to talk about or address racial issues. This concept can be applied to police when they become defensive when their actions are called into question because their behavior, heretofore hidden from the public, has now been observed and recorded. This increased level of defensiveness on the part of a police officer can be referred to as **blue fragility**.

Blue fragility is not an accusatory term, but rather points to the level of discomfort or defensiveness felt when officers are confronted with a level of accountability that they may not be used to or haven't had to address or deal with in the past. There are times when a police officer's actions on the job are called into question and the officer may feel like they are being targeted with unreasonable or undue scrutiny. Often officers are bothered by additional calls for accountability by the public, or additional investigation into their actions. This is particularly true in situations where the police have enjoyed being given the benefit of the doubt from the public for their actions in uniform. This added level of potential responsibility may add angst or anguish to the officer in question. Officers in this situation may become defensive, uncomfortable, and cynical toward anyone questioning their actions and may develop a negative demeanor while the investigation is taking place.

Blue fragility can be overcome by having officers and citizens engage in meaningful dialogue regarding expectations, perceptions, and levels of accountability. When citizens and police officers do not regularly talk about tough situations, when these issues do come up, they tend to take an accusatory tone. Having police officers and community members have regular conversation about what is expected for both sides will help alleviate the levels of discomfort and defensiveness that officers sometimes feel.

Critical Thinking

1. Can you imagine how blue fragility may influence police taking action when they should not and/or failing to take action when they should?

2. Is fragility unique to police officers? Members of what other professions, for example, teachers, may be experiencing "fragility"?

Source: Robin DiAngelo, "White Fragility," *International Journal of Critical Pedagogy* 3, no. 3 (2011), pp 54–70.

the New York City comptroller, the number of civil lawsuits (torts) filed against the NYPD in 2020 was 5,728. The City of New York settled the bulk of them, paying out $205.0 million.[37] It is worth noting that the bulk of the money used to pay police corruption civil suits comes from taxpayer dollars.

Not only does the city government have to pay damages to citizens and families in these suits, but they also have to pay for their cadre of defense attorneys, and the attorney fees for the plaintiff if they win. These expenses represent a rarely discussed but significant cost of police misconduct.[38]

Consent Decrees

Section 14141 of the Violent Crime Control and Law Enforcement Act of 1994, Public Law 103-322 established the legal provision that has allowed the U.S. Department of Justice (DOJ) to intervene in instances where allegations are made that constitutional policing is not followed as a matter of patterns and practices. A **consent decree** is an agreement between the DOJ and a police agency, intended to promote police integrity within an agency to prevent conduct or actions that deprives individuals of their rights, privileges, or immunities protected by the U.S. Constitution. Alternatively, officials can request that the DOJ look into police activities in specific agencies, which may lead to investigations that determine if the statute has been violated. Under several attorneys general, the Civil Rights Division of the DOJ has investigated and negotiated reform efforts with many police agencies. Overall, consent decrees are successful in the short term, but have not been sustainable.[39]

Consent decrees can certainly expedite the changing of policies, but often what is needed is a change of culture within a police department to see real changes in behavior. Change in policing occurs based on the attention given to the three Ps: policy, procedure, or practice. The policy tells you what you are supposed to do as a police officer. The procedure outlines the way you are supposed to accomplish certain tasks. The practice is what happens on the street when officers are doing their daily jobs unsupervised. The "practice" represents the culture of a police department, including what is accepted and what supervisors are willing to address. If a consent decree places more emphasis on practice, then there is a chance that the culture of a department will change in a positive way. While consent decrees were paused during the Trump administration, in 2021, President Joe Biden reinstated the consent decree process.

Mobilizing the Public

A consent decree is a powerful tool because it is believed that corruption flourishes when the public is ignorant of it or tolerates it. With a consent decree, the public can pressure the city officials to make the police department more transparent in its actions and be accountable to the taxpayers. Consent decrees can lessen the effects of the blue wall of silence, exposing negative police action, unethical behavior, and police corruption.

consent decree

An agreement between the U.S. Department of Justice and a police agency intended to promote police integrity within an agency and to prevent conduct or actions that deprives individuals of their rights, privileges, or immunities protected by the U.S. Constitution.

LO5

Examine the types of citizen review boards.

▶ Citizen Review Boards

Because police departments have been perceived as unsuccessful or uncaring about seriously investigating citizen complaints, or the alleged wrongdoing of fellow officers, civilian oversight has become more popular. Civilian review boards began as early as the 1960s. Today, there is a national organization for civilian oversight: National Association for Civilian Oversight of Law

Enforcement (NACOLE). Their mission is to "create a community of support for independent, civilian oversight entities that seek to make their local law enforcement agencies more transparent, accountable, and responsive to the communities they serve." [40]

According to NACOLE, there is no single preferred model of citizen oversight of police. It is unlikely to find two oversight agencies that are the same. However, most oversight systems fall into one of four types:

Type I—A separate agency *investigates citizen complaints and makes a recommendation* about the case and discipline to the chief or sheriff. It is then up to the chief or sheriff to accept or ignore recommendations. Members of the board are appointed and employ full-time professional staff to investigate complaints. This is the most powerful system for citizens.

Type II—Complaints are investigated by internal affairs officers but the civilian review agency examines the internal affairs' investigated complaint file and *makes recommendations regarding discipline*. This is the next level of power for citizens; the main difference is they do not investigate the case like Type I does.

The goal of civilian review boards is to make police accountable for their misbehavior while at the same time making it easier for the public to instigate a formal complaint charging police misconduct. Citizens will be more likely to step forward before a group of people from the community than they would a review board made up of police officers. In some communities such as Topeka, Kansas, citizens groups have been organized to pressure police to create a civilian review board. In this photo, a group called Topekans for Racial Justice calls for the creation of a citizen review board.

Type III—The police department is responsible for investigating and disposing of the complaints. If the complainant is not satisfied with the result, *they can appeal the findings to the citizen review process.*

Type IV—Auditor model. The department has full responsibility of investigating citizen complaints, but an *independent agency has the authority to audit or monitor the performance of the department's internal affairs unit.* Just a few cases are reviewed to keep things "honest." [41]

The Commission on Accreditation for Law Enforcement Agencies, Inc. (CALEA)

CALEA is the agency that provides credentials and approved accreditation for law enforcement agencies. If the standards of the agency are improved, then the agency itself becomes CALEA improved. The accreditation process was established in 1979 and is a process of professional self-governance, much like the American Bar Association for lawyers. But unlike other professions, CALEA accreditation is voluntary and there is no penalty for agencies not getting approved. CALEA establishes minimum standards for all law enforcement agencies.

Some CALEA standards are mandatory while others are optional. The first published standards came out in 1983, and by 1998 over 460 agencies have accreditation, which accounts for 3 percent of total law enforcement population. Of the largest law enforcement agencies, only 22 percent have accreditation. The process is time intensive and expensive (as departments have to redo their entire standard operating procedures and other policies).

Public Interest Groups

The NAACP (National Association for the Advancement of Colored People) and the ACLU (American Civil Liberties Union) were responsible for many of the important Supreme Court cases involving police reforms. Please note that the ACLU is not anti-police but has also defended police officers who are unfairly investigated.

LO6

Discuss the application of procedural justice in policing.

▶ Procedural Justice

Patrol is made more effective when officers treat citizens with dignity and respect.[42] Citizens who are treated respectfully are more likely to be satisfied with their experience with the police.[43] When citizens are treated respectfully, they are more likely to accept police decisions and even to later participate in crime prevention programs.[44] Procedural justice can be explained as "how" authority is exercised. When citizens have contact with the police, the procedural justice that they subjectively experience affects not only their trust and confidence in the police, but also how they identify with the police. In order for modern policing to be effective, the public must trust and believe in the *authority* of the police.

Lister and Rowe make the case in their 2016 book, *Accountability of Policing,* that "police enjoy greater levels of public trust and confidence in circumstances where they are perceived to act on the basis of procedural justice. In this context, procedural justice needs to be done, and to be seen to be done, in order to deliver core aspects of the police mandate."[45] Not only should procedural justice be employed, but it should also be a public process. This level of transparency will help build trust with the community.

According to the final report of The President's Task Force on 21st-Century Policing: "People are more likely to obey the law when they believe that those who are enforcing it have the legitimate authority to tell them what to do . . . . The public confers legitimacy only on those they believe are acting in procedurally just ways."[46]

Research also indicates that precinct-level efforts to ensure that officers are respectful of citizens can help lower the number of complaints and improve community relations.[47] In other words, the police must pay attention to procedural justice, a concern with making decisions that are arrived at through procedures viewed as fair.[48] If people view procedures as unfair, they will be less likely to support police in their crime-fighting efforts.[49]

According to the Community Oriented Policing Services (COPS) office, "often the process is more important than the outcome of the encounter in shaping a community member's assessment of the interaction." For instance, "people who received a traffic citation from an officer who treated them fairly tended to view the police more favorably and

Bob Daemmrich/Alamy Stock Photo

Citizens who are treated respectfully are more likely to be satisfied with their experience with the police and more willing to cooperate when asked. Here in Pflugerville, Texas, a suburb of Austin, residents gather in a neighborhood park for National Night Out. The annual gathering is intended as a crime-fighting effort by fostering communication among neighbors and local police.

were significantly more willing to cooperate with the police than they had been before that encounter."[50]

Another way to conceptualize procedural justice is the concept of banking regarding deposits and withdrawals. Think about police/community interactions as bank transactions—positive interactions are like deposits, and negative interactions are withdrawals. It may take multiple deposits, or positive interactions, to make up for one withdrawal or negative interaction. Deposits strengthen relationships and withdrawals damage them.[51] Employing procedural justice provides an important opportunity for officers to make connections with citizens who are most vulnerable to victimization and experience fear and diminished quality of life.[52]

Summary

LO1 Discuss the concept of ethical policing in the United States.

Ethics is a system of moral principles which speaks to a person's trustworthiness or credibility. An ethical code is often a set of rules that defines allowable actions or correct behavior in a professional setting. When examining the profession of policing, it is apparent that police officers, probably more than many other professions, should understand and abide by ethical principles. In many ways, the police are the gatekeepers of the criminal justice system. For most citizens, the police represent the most local form of government. If an officer engages in unethical behavior, it erodes the public trust and causes great damage to the profession of policing. When the police have the power to detain and arrest, it is important to be ethical because it is central to decision making and the criminal justice process. The police are expected to provide and produce valuable public services, such as justice, safety, and security in an ethical manner.

LO2 Discuss the elements of democratic policing in the United States.

The role of modern policing in a democratic society is constantly adapting to our expectations for public safety. Democratic policing and protecting the constitutional rights of everyone must be paramount. To achieve democratic policing, there must be accountability for how police departments do their jobs. Community members are less likely to support an agency over which they have little or no say. This is particularly true if the agency has a major impact on their lives. Therefore, police agencies that don't practice democratic policing are unlikely to have legitimacy. Legitimacy is associated with compliance with the law and acceptance of police authority. It is a necessary condition for police-public cooperation such as reporting crime victimization, acting as a witness, or assisting police investigation. Community participation is crucial because police cannot investigate or solve crimes about which they are unaware or lack evidence. People want a say in how they are policed.

LO3 Demonstrate disparity and discrimination in policing in the United States.

People of color and particularly the Black community members are disproportionately under the control of the criminal justice system. Through negative interactions with the police, citizens enter the criminal justice system. A 2021 study found that many people of color do not feel protected *from* the police. The authors state that most White respondents in their study felt safe, but many Black respondents live in fear of the police. For many Black people, being questioned or searched by the police without receiving a good explanation is worse than being robbed or burglarized. A 2014 Massachusetts ACLU study reports that people of color are regularly stopped and searched with no legal justification. A Department of Justice report on the Baltimore Police Department found that Baltimore city police officers regularly violate constitutional or federal laws in the way they interact with people of color. The report specifically stated that Baltimore police officers regularly engage in patterns or practices of making unconstitutional stops, searches, and arrests and use enforcement strategies that produce severe and unjustified disparities in the rates of stops, searches, and arrests of Black people.

LO4 Examine contemporary methods of accountability.

Accountability is a crucial element to a functioning democracy; this is especially true in policing. Police accountability starts internally with good policies, proper supervision, and a working internal affairs division. Police leaders must ensure that all officers are abiding by stated policies and engage in corrective actions when they are not. When the police do not do a good job of policing themselves, external forces then step in. Legislatively, elected officials have written bills and laws to increase accountability in policing. One such bill is the George Floyd Justice in Policing Act. This bill increases accountability for police misconduct, restricts the use of certain policing practices, enhances transparency, and establishes best practices and training requirements. There have also been special commissions to investigate police actions and recommend solutions. There are also consent decrees, which are agreements between the U.S. Department of Justice and a police agency intended to promote police integrity within an agency and to prevent conduct or actions that deprive individuals of their rights, privileges, or immunities protected by the U.S. Constitution.

LO5 Examine the types of citizen review boards.

Historically, police departments have been perceived as unsuccessful or uncaring about seriously investigating citizen complaints, or the alleged wrongdoing of fellow officers. Therefore, civilian oversight has become more popular. Civilian review boards began as early as the 1960s. The mission is to create a community of support for independent, civilian oversight entities that seek to make their local law enforcement agencies more transparent, accountable, and responsive to the communities they serve. There is no single preferred model of citizen oversight of police. However, most oversight systems fall into one of four types: Type I, a separate agency investigates citizen complaints and makes a recommendation about the case and discipline to the chief or sheriff; Type II, complaints are investigated by internal affairs officers but the civilian review agency examines the internal affairs investigate complaint file and makes recommendations regarding discipline; Type III, the police department is responsible for investigating and disposing of the complaints; Type IV, the department has full responsibility for investigating citizen complaints but can have an outside auditor.

LO6 Discuss the application of procedural justice in policing.

Procedural justice is when decisions are made through processes that are viewed as fair. Patrol is made more effective when officers treat citizens with dignity and respect. Citizens who are treated respectfully are more likely to be satisfied with the experience with the police. When citizens are treated respectfully, they are more likely to accept police decisions and even to later participate in crime prevention programs. Procedural justice can be explained as "how" authority is exercised. When citizens have contact with the police, the procedural justice that they subjectively experience affects not only their trust and confidence in the police, but also how they identify with the police. In order for modern policing to be effective, the public must trust and believe in the authority of the police. The police enjoy greater levels of public trust and confidence in circumstances where they are perceived to act on the basis of procedural justice. In this context, procedural justice needs to be done, and to be seen to be done, in order to deliver core aspects of the police mandate.

Key Terms

Weingarten Rules, 200
Garrity Rule, 200
vicarious liability, 200
qualified immunity, 201
special commissions, 204
Knapp Commission (Commission to Investigate Alleged Police Corruption), 204

Christopher Commission (Independent Commission on the Los Angeles Police Department), 204
Mollen Commission (The City of New York Commission to Investigate Allegations of Police Corruption and the

Anti-Corruption Procedures of the Police Department), 205
federal civil rights violation, 207
blue fragility, 210
consent decree, 210

Notes

1. Katie Mettler and Steve Thompson, "14 Prince George's Officers Indicted, Accused of Double-Dipping," *The Washington Post*, August 25, 2022, https://www.washingtonpost.com/dc-md-va/2022/08/25/prince-georges-police-officers-indicted/; Internal Revenue Service (IRS), "Prince George's County Police Lieutenant Facing Federal Charges for Attempting to Evade or Defeat Taxes for Years 2014 through 2019," April 2021.
2. Donald C. Menzel, *Ethics Moments in Government: Cases and Controversies* (New York, NY: Routledge, 2010).
3. Ibid.
4. Jay S. Albanese, *Professional Ethics in Criminal Justice: Being Ethical When No One is Looking* (Boston, MA: Pearson Publishing, 2006).
5. Joycelyn M. Pollock, *Ethical Dilemmas and Decisions in Criminal Justice* (Belmont, CA: Cengage, 2007).
6. Jay S. Albanese, *Professional Ethics in Criminal Justice: Being Ethical When No One is Looking* (Boston, MA: Pearson Publishing, 2006).
7. *Figueroa v. Mazza* 2016. 2016/06/03, 14-4116 – U.S. 2nd Circuit.
8. https://www.austintexas.gov/es/document/community-feedback-and-final-recommendations-duty-intervene-cases-improper-or-excessive-use-force-1.
9. https://portal.ct.gov/-/media/POST/GENERAL_NOTICES/2020/20-07-DUTY-TO-INTERVENE-AND-REPORT-with-attachment.pdf.
10. Westlaw, https://content.next.westlaw.com/Browse/Home/CivilRightsLegalMaterialsNews/PoliceConductFailuretoIntervene?transitionType=Default&contextData=(sc.Default)&firstPage=true.
11. Ibid.
12. LEXIPOL, "What You Need To Know About Officer Duty To Intervene. By Laura Scarry," September 11, 2020, https://www.lexipol.com/resources/blog/what-you-need-to-know-about-officer-duty-to-intervene/.
13. IACP Law Enforcement Code of Ethics, https://www.theiacp.org/resources/law-enforcement-code-of-ethics.
14. National Whistleblower Center, https://www.whistleblowers.org/policewhistleblowers/.
15. https://www.policingproject.org/statement-democratic-policing.
16. Maria Ponomarenko and Barry Friedman, "Democratic Accountability and Policing," *Reforming criminal justice: A report of the Academy for Justice on bridging the gap between scholarship and reform,* 2 (2017), 5–26.
17. J. T. Pickett, A. Graham, and F. T. Cullen, "The American Racial Divide in Fear of the Police," *Criminology* (2022), 1–30, https://doi.org/10.1111/1745-9125.12298.
18. American Civil Liberties Union Foundation of Massachusetts, "Black, Brown and Targeted: A Report on Boston Police Department Street Encounters from 2007–2010," October 2014.
19. Agreement in Principle between the Unites States and the City of Baltimore, https://www.justice.gov/opa/file/883376/download.
20. John MacDonald, Jeffrey Fagan, and Amanda Geller, "The Effects of Local Police Surges on Crime and Arrests in New York City," *Columbia Public Law Research Paper*, 14-468 (2015).
21. https://aclum.org/our-work/aclum-issues/racial-justice/ending-racist-stop-and-frisk/.
22. R. L. Goldman, "State Revocation of Law Enforcement Officers' Licenses and Federal Criminal Prosecution: An Opportunity for Cooperative Federalism," *Saint Louis University Public Law Review XXII* (2003), 121–150.
23. M. L. Shockey-Eckles, "Police Culture and the Perceptuation of the Officer Shuffle: The Paradox of Life Behind 'the Blue Wall'" *Humanity & Society* 35 (2011), 290–309.
24. C. E. Rabe-Hemp and J. Braithwaite, "An Exploration of Recidivism and the Officer Shuffle in Police Sexual Violence," *Police Quarterly* 16, no. 2 (2013), 127–147.
25. https://www.cnn.com/2021/04/14/us/buffalo-officer-reinstated-trnd/index.html.
26. https://www.ojp.gov/pdffiles1/nij/188565.pdf.
27. Jay Schweikert, "Colorado Passes Historic, Bipartisan Policing Reforms to Eliminate Qualified Immunity," *Cato Institute*, June 22, 2020.
28. Human Rights Watch: The Christopher Commission Report, https://www.hrw.org/legacy/reports98/police/uspo73.htm.
29. Britannica, https://www.britannica.com/topic/Mollen-Commission.
30. U.S. Department of Justice, "Justice Department Finds Civil Rights Violations by the Minneapolis Police Department and the City of Minneapolis," June 16, 2013, https://www.justice.gov/opa/pr/justice-department-finds-civil-rights-violations-minneapolis-police-department-and-city.
31. *Associated Press*, April 19, 2021, https://apnews.com/article/shootings-police-walter-scott-michael-slager-south-carolina-9bc7b58a116fbc451671da2a96c3c6b9.
32. Sebastian Murdock, "Michael Slager Pleads Guilty in Killing of Unarmed Fleeing Black man Walter Scott, *Huffington Post*, May 2, 2017, https://www.huffpost.com/entry/michael-slager-cop-who-killed-fleeing-black-man-walter-scott-pleads-guilty-to-tk_n_59089734e4b02655f840c8f1?ncid=engmodushpmg00000003&fbclid=IwAR3rbx7B57mObh56eBQMQJgB0bLCqxbnWRbOswnUy-waYfQmd75KcepoKQY.
33. *The New York Times*, https://www.nytimes.com/news-event/trial-of-george-floyd-killing.
34. *The New York Times*, October 8, 2015, https://www.nytimes.com/2015/10/09/us/walter-scott-settlement-reached-in-south-carolina-police-shooting-case.html.
35. *Associated Press*, March 12, 2021, https://apnews.com/article/minneapolis-pay-27-million-settle-floyd-family-lawsuit-52a395f7716f52cf8d1fbeb411c831c7.
36. *Britannica*, Rampart Scandal, https://www.britannica.com/topic/Rampart-scandal.
37. New York City Comptroller's office, April 9, 2021, https://comptroller.nyc.gov/reports/annual-claims-report/.
38. *Chicago Tribune*, September 12, 2019, https://www.chicagotribune.com/investigations/ct-met-chicago-legal-spending-20190912-sky5euto4jbcdenjfi4datpnki-story.html.
39. G. P. Alpert, K. McLean, and S. Wolfe, "Consent Decrees: An Approach to Police Accountability and Reform," *Police Quarterly* 20, no. 3 (2017), 239–249.
40. https://www.nacole.org/mission.
41. U.S. Department of Justice, "Citizen Review of Police: Approaches & Implementation," March 2001, https://www.ojp.gov/pdffiles1/nij/184430.pdf.
42. See generally, Robert E. Worden and Sarah J. McLean, *Mirage of Police Reform: Procedural Justice and Police Legitimacy* (Oakland, CA: University of California Press, 2017).

43. Tom Tyler and Jeffrey Fagan, "Legitimacy and Cooperation: Why Do People Help the Police Fight Crime in Their Communities?" *Public Law and Legal Theory Working Paper Group* (Paper Number 06-99) (New York, NY: Columbia Law School).

44. Arelys Madero-Hernandez, YongJei Lee, Pamela Wilcox, and Bonnie S. Fisher, "Following Their Lead: Police Perceptions and Their Effects on Crime Prevention," *Justice Quarterly* 39, no. 2 (2022), 327–353.

45. Stuart Lister and Michael Rowe, *Accountability of Policing* (Routledge, 2016).

46. Final Report of the President's Task Force on 21st Century Policing (Washington, DC: Office of Community Oriented Policing Services, 2015).

47. Robert Davis, Pedro Mateu-Gelabert, and Joel Miller, "Can Effective Policing Also Be Respectful? Two Examples in the South Bronx," *Police Quarterly* 8 (2005), 229–247.

48. Tom Tyler, "Procedural Justice, Legitimacy, and the Effective Rule of Law." In M. H. Tonry (ed.), *Crime and Justice: A Review of Research* (Chicago, IL: University of Chicago Press, 2003), pp. 283–357.

49. Jacinta M. Gau and Rod K. Brunson, "Procedural Justice and Order Maintenance Policing: A Study of Inner-City Young Men's Perceptions of Police Legitimacy," *Justice Quarterly* 27 (2010), 255–279; Patrick J. Carr, Laura Napolitano, and Jessica Keating, "We Never Call the Cops and Here Is Why: A Qualitative Examination of Legal Cynicism in Three Philadelphia Neighborhoods," *Criminology* 45 (2007), 445–480.

50. Laura Kunard and Charlene Moe, Center for Public Safety and Justice, University of Illinois, COPS Office, 2015, https://cops.usdoj.gov/RIC/Publications/cops-p333-pub.pdf.

51. Ibid.

52. Ibid.

The Changing Rank and File

Learning Objectives

LO1 List the major issues currently facing policing.

LO2 Describe the police subculture.

LO3 Compare and contrast the different police styles.

LO4 Discuss the challenges faced by women in policing.

LO5 Discuss the challenges faced by people of color in policing.

LO6 Define the concept of intersectionality.

LO7 Determine if and how diversity affects policing.

Chapter Outline

UPI/Alamy Stock Photo

On February 23, 2020, 25-year-old Ahmaud Arbery, an unarmed African American man, was jogging in Brunswick, Georgia, when he was pursued and confronted by three neighborhood residents. Travis McMichael and his father, Gregory, who were armed and driving a pickup truck, and their neighbor, William "Roddie" Bryan, who followed Arbery in a second vehicle, trapped him on the road and videotaped the incident. During the confrontation, Arbery was shot and killed.

At trial, evidence revealed that the three defendants pursued Ahmaud Arbery through the neighborhood and tried to box him with their trucks. During the chase, Arbery was running with his hands empty and in plain view. He never spoke a word to the defendants, and never made any threatening sound or gesture; rather, he repeatedly tried to run away from his pursuers. Ultimately, after Arbery had already changed direction multiple times, trying to escape from the defendants, Travis McMichael got out of his truck and pointed a shotgun directly at Arbery. When Arbery tried to defend himself, McMichael shot him in the chest. Arbery, wounded, grabbed for the gun. During a struggle over the gun, Travis McMichael fired two more shots into Ahmaud Arbery, who then stumbled a few steps and fell face-first onto the pavement, where he died in the street.

Evidence at trial also revealed that the defendants, all of whom were White, had strongly held racist beliefs that led them to make assumptions and decisions about Ahmaud Arbery, beliefs that they would not have held if Arbery had been White. Travis McMichael's social media comments and text messages to friends showed that he had for many years associated Black people with criminality and had expressed a desire to see Black people—particularly those he viewed as criminals—harmed or killed, and that he had expressed support for vigilante efforts to catch or harm criminals. Witnesses testified about deeply racist comments Gregory McMichael made to people he barely knew. One witness testified that when he was told that it was "too bad" that Julian Bond, a Black Georgia civil rights leader, had recently passed away; Gregory McMichael angrily responded with a five-minute rant about Black people and said that he wished Bond had "been put in the ground years ago. He was nothing but trouble. Those Blacks are nothing but trouble." William Bryan's text messages revealed that he found out just four days before the shooting, that his daughter was dating a Black man. Bryan referred to the boyfriend as a "ni---" and as a "monkey." There were other messages on social media in which Bryan referred to other Black people using those slurs and another racial slur: "bootlip." When the police spoke to Bryan about Arbery's death, he admitted that he had never seen or heard anything about Arbery before; he just saw a Black guy being chased and figured he must have done something wrong, and that his "instinct" told him that Arbery must be a thief or that maybe had shot someone.

In sum, the evidence at trial proved that race formed a but-for cause of the defendants' actions meaning that, without that factor, the defendants would not have chased down a Black man whom they assumed, without evidence, was a criminal.[1] On August 8, 2022, a U.S. federal judge in the Southern District of Georgia handed down a sentence of life in prison, plus 10 years for Travis McMichael. His father, Gregory McMichael, 66, was sentenced to life in prison plus seven additional years. The third defendant William "Roddie" Bryan, 52, was sentenced for his part in the Arbery death to 35 years in prison.[2]

Do you believe that the national attention this case received influenced the sentencing outcomes? Should all three men be given to what amounts to a life sentence even if only one did the actual shooting? Do you think that a hate crime, such as the murder of Ahmaud Arbery, should be punished more severely than a murder motivated by revenge, jealousy, or greed?

L01

List the major issues currently facing policing.

▶ # The Changing Police Culture

The spring of 2020 was the beginning of a new normal, not just in policing, but across the world. There was a global pandemic as COVID-19 spread and much of the world was in quarantine for months. While people were secluded in their homes, several high-profile killings of Black citizens went viral in a short period of time. All of the killings had direct ties to local police officers. You may recall another case that received national attention after it occurred on March 13, 2020, 26-year-old African American Breonna Taylor, an off-duty emergency medical technician, was fatally shot by Louisville Metro Police Department officers as she slept in her bed in her Louisville apartment. Three plainclothes police officers, executing a no-knock search warrant, entered her apartment. Gunfire was exchanged between Taylor's boyfriend, who woke up believing the officers were intruders. The officers fired over 20 rounds, hitting Taylor eight times. The drug warrant named Taylor's apartment because she was friends with a suspected drug dealer and her car had been seen previously at his house. No drugs were found at the scene.[3]

Incidents like these and many others make it hard to recruit a diverse workforce. It is hard to build trust and legitimacy with communities of color when they see frequent acts of violence toward members of communities of color by police, such as Breonna Taylor and even those acting as self-appointed police such as what occurred in the Arbery case. People tend to empathize with the unarmed victim of police violence and often internalize it. Many in communities of color may experience vicarious trauma from recurring reports of people of color dying at the hands of the police. When citizens see that the police reflect a cross-section of the community, they have greater confidence that police officers will understand their problems and concerns. Police agencies must develop effective strategies for welcoming and supporting officers of color within the police subculture by eliminating discriminatory attitudes and practices.[4] Many cities are reporting hiring and retention issues of police candidates, but it is unclear whether this is due to changes in citizen perceptions of police or something else.[5] Police departments must go above and beyond to find good applicants, particularly applicants of color. Police agencies must be creative in changing their actions and message.

Typically, when the Dallas Police Department hosts its monthly testing for people interested in becoming police officers, about 70 to 80 people show up; but for this event, the department was expecting about 280 people. Why the large turnout? There was a public call by then Dallas Police Chief David Brown for people to join the department after five officers were killed and others injured in a recent targeted ambush. The chief asked young people to stop protesting, to start applying, and to help fix the problems they see in their community. Dallas is not alone, as tensions between police and Black communities across the country have become strained; some police agencies have put out similar calls for help in hopes of recruiting a more diverse force as one way to reestablish community trust.[6]

The recruitment and selection of officers from communities of color is only one element that has resulted in a changing rank and file. The contemporary police officer must be prepared to adapt to this changing police world. In the training academy, young officers learn about the culture of policing. Many enter the academy with the highest aspirations and goals; they want to "serve and protect." Eventually new officers may lose their initial enthusiasm to help the world and become cynical. Research has demonstrated that officer's attitudes change the most after they complete the academy and begin real police work. How does this attitudinal shift happen? Some researchers indicate that the police have a unique subculture that contributes to cynicism and heavily influences working personalities. Police subculture is an often-discussed topic in the media, by researchers and by police themselves. In this chapter, we will review what is known about the inner world of policing and how it is changing in our diverse, multicultural world.

The Police Subculture

A **subculture** is a subdivision within the dominant culture that has its own norms, beliefs, and values. Subcultures have their own unwritten rules, mores, norms, codes, values, and worldview. Subcultures can be both positive and negative. For example, religious people can be part of a subculture. The Amish choose to live in communities that are closed off from the larger culture. They share a common religion and accept prohibitions on electricity, telephone, and automobile use. The Amish choose to only associate with others in their sect. Subcultures can also be negative: prisons often breed a subculture that involves its own language and norms, such as not cooperating with authorities or using violence to resolve conflict.

Subcultures exist for a variety of reasons. They emerge when people in similar circumstances find themselves isolated from mainstream society. People band together for mutual support—they form an alternative culture that reflects their value system. They can also emerge in response to social problems that the dominant culture ignores or refuses to address. To explore the police subculture, we should first understand its values and mores.

All professions have unique characteristics, norms, rules, and levels of authority that distinguish them from other occupations and institutions and create a subculture-like environment. Sometimes the rules, norms, and standard operating procedures are specific to that institution and set them apart from other professions.

 L02

Describe the police subculture.

subculture

A subdivision within the dominant culture that has its own norms, beliefs, and values.

Shiiko Alexander/Alamy Stock Photo

Police experts have long sought to understand the nature of the police experience and how it helps create a unique subculture. Here police officers in Santa Fe, New Mexico, huddle and talk near a police car. What elements of the job do you think creates a blue subculture?

The culture of an organization is also the way members of that organization view and are viewed by the outside world. The culture of an organization becomes the expected behavior of the members of that organization. Organizational culture is often built on past experiences, shared goals and ideals, and the need for self-protection.

Policing is no exception. The culture of policing has developed over time and has adapted to societal norms and expectations. There are specific rules of conduct, use of authority, and legal restrictions that are specific to the profession of policing that are often not to be found in any other organization. There are rules for enforcement and sometimes restriction on activities while doing their job. Most of the time, the police utilize their authority and follow assumed norms well; other times, they deviate from their expected actions or behavior. The mere existence of these specific rules of conduct and professional standards justify the assertion that the police are a complex, rule-bound profession that is engaged in the pursuit of justice and the protection of individual rights. Police experts have long sought to understand the unique nature of the police experience and to determine how the challenges of police work shape the field and its employees. In this section, some of the factors that make policing unique are discussed in detail.

Police Culture

What factors, institutions, and practices define the police culture? Most officers originally join the police department because they want to help people; fight crime; and have an interesting, exciting, prestigious career with a high degree of job security.[7] Recruits often find that the social reality of police work does not mesh with their original career goals. They are unprepared for the emotional turmoil and conflict that accompany police work today.

Membership in the police culture helps recruits adjust to the rigors of police work and provides the emotional support needed for survival.[8] The culture encourages decisiveness in the face of uncertainty and the ability to make split-second judgments that may later be subject to extreme criticism. The police subculture also encourages its members to draw a sharp distinction between good and evil. Police culture is characterized by cynicism, clannishness, secrecy, and insulation from others in society. Together, these elements of police culture have been called the "blue curtain."

Police officers tend to socialize with one another and believe that their occupation cuts them off from relationships with civilians. This decision is based on a number of factors: (1) shift work limits the opportunities to socialize with friends in professions with different work hours, (2) spending time with other police officers means fewer opportunities to be around illegal behavior, and (3) fellow officers understand the stresses associated with the job without explanation. Joining the police subculture means always having to defend fellow officers against outsiders, maintaining a tough exterior, and distrusting the motives and behavior of outsiders.[9]

This unwritten code becomes evident early in a young officer's career. Officers are taught in the police academy that your daily survival is based on your actions and the actions of your fellow officers. Life-and-death scenarios are repeated in training and a bond is formed with other officers, sometimes out of fear of the unknown. The code of silence demands that officers never turn in their peers, even if they engage in corrupt or illegal practices.[10]

Conventional wisdom holds that the police culture can be unpleasant, secretive, and often violent—a view that is often underscored by movies and television. However, police subculture is not some folkway or legend made up by the media. Police experts have found that the experience of becoming a police officer and the nature of the job itself will cause most officers to band together in a unique subculture, which is characterized by cynicism, clannishness, secrecy, and insulation from others in society. In a speech at Georgetown University in February 2015, former FBI Director James Comey shared what he called "hard truths." He said that we need to acknowledge that much of the history of law enforcement is not pretty. A second hard truth is that there is a widespread existence of unconscious bias. The third truth is that many people in law enforcement develop a level of cynicism.[11] **Cynicism** is the belief people are motivated purely by self-interest and will only do what is in their best interest. This level of protection and insulation is referred to as the so-called **blue curtain**.

The *blue curtain*, also referred to as the blue-code, code-of-silence, or the blue-wall-of-silence, is a term for the unwritten rule in policing that officers should not report the misconducts, corruption, or crimes of fellow officers. If an officer is questioned about an incident of misconduct involving another officer, the officer being questioned would claim ignorance of another officer's wrongdoing. Thus, the offending officer is shielded by the blue curtain. The rationale behind this action is that only sworn police officers know what it's like to do the job. So many people and situations are against them, that they have to protect themselves and each other because no one else in society will. This attitude lends itself to the "us-vs.-them" attitude where officers think the world may be against them. This mentality cultivated the ideal of *loyalty over integrity*.[12] When society sees an upswing in crime and violence, the culture of the police tends to be more aggressive and willing to use violence. When the police see situations where they are the targets of attacks or complaints, they tend to band together and insulate fellow officers. The culture of policing is strong and sustaining.

cynicism

The belief that most people's actions are motivated solely by personal needs and selfishness.

blue curtain

The secretive, insulated police culture that isolates officers from the rest of society.

Developing the Blue Curtain

The blue curtain or code of silence can be traced back to union work actions of the latter part of the 1800s and the early part of the 1900s when public and private police were used to infiltrate unions and violently end strikes. Many members of local police departments also were active members of the Ku Klux Klan and they protected each other when conducting racist acts. Little thought or research was given to the police subculture until law enforcement was on the national stage during the 1960s.

Piercing the Curtain

In 1970, the mayor of New York City organized the Knapp Commission to investigate corruption in the New York City Police Department. Officer Frank Serpico and Sergeant David Durk testified about the corruption in the city's police department and that there was a wide-spread culture of hindering the investigation of

Critical Thinking

1. How do you think the blue curtain attitude spreads?

2. As a young officer, what can be done to avoid it?

other officers. He testified that this fraternal understanding among police officers is known as the "code of silence" and the "blue curtain" and that officers view testimony against a fellow officer as betrayal.[13]

In 1991, the Christopher Commission was formed to investigate the unrelenting and brutal beating of motorist Rodney King by Los Angeles police officers. Although there were many officers present who witnessed the beating but did not take part, no officer reported the savage nature of the beating to the department officials. Instead, the officers claimed that the beating was lawful, legitimate, and justified. It was not until a videotape of the incident was made public that it was confirmed that LAPD officers had collectively fabricated their stories.[14]

Although many LAPD officers brushed it off, citizens of Los Angeles were outraged. Two weeks after the videotaped beating, confidence in the police by Black and Hispanic citizens dropped dramatically. Among the Latino population, confidence in LAPD fell from 84 to 31 percent. For Black citizens, who already had less confidence in their local police, the numbers fell from 64 percent to a paltry 14 percent. LAPD approval by White people also fell, but less drastically, from 71 percent to 41 percent.[15]

In 1992, NYC mayor Rudolph Giuliani appointed The City of New York Commission to Investigate Allegations of Police Corruption and the Anti-Corruption Procedures of the Police Department, otherwise known as the Mollen Commission to look at corruption in the ranks of the city's police department. The Mollen Commission stated NYPD officers were deliberately lying to investigators in order to cover up potential police misconduct. The commission found that officers lied in an attempt to conceal inappropriate conduct and that they apparently lied for no other reason than to attempt to protect other officers from reprimand. The Mollen Commission also referred to these actions as "the blue wall of silence." The commission also stated that this is a widespread problem and that the pervasiveness of the code of silence is itself alarming.[16]

Culture within a Culture

Despite these stories, the police subculture is neither unified nor homogenous but rather multifaceted and complex. Often we see specialized units such as SWAT, mobile operations units (motorcycle cops), marine units, mounted officers, and even detectives who feel their brand of policing is a step above the average patrol officer. Even within the detective units, homicide detectives are thought of as being more prestigious than property crimes or juvenile detectives. Some of the more elite units don't conform to the rest of the police department's cultural norms. Many specialized units run like very separate police departments instead of a specialized unit within a department.

Elements of Police Culture

Six core beliefs are historically viewed as being at the heart of the police culture:

■ **Police are the only real crime fighters.** The public wants the police officer to fight crime; other agencies, both public and private, only play at crime fighting.

■ **No one else understands the real nature of police work.** Lawyers, academics, politicians, and the public in general have little concept of what it means to be a police officer.

- **Loyalty to colleagues counts above everything else.** Police officers have to stick together because everyone is out to get the police and make the job more difficult.

- **The war against crime cannot be won without bending the rules.** Courts have awarded criminal defendants too many civil rights.

- **Members of the public are basically unsupportive and unreasonably demanding.** People are quick to criticize police unless they need police help themselves.

- **Patrol work is the pits.** Detective work is glamorous and exciting.[17]

The code of silence also plays a large role in police subculture. This is because policing is fraught with the potential for mistakes. Because officers have to make split-second decisions, there is often not enough time to weigh options. They must rely on training and experience to make the correct decision. Police also have to make complex legal decisions. It is not uncommon to have a group of police officers discussing possible laws broken. This is because they are dealing with complex social realities and challenging people. If a community member is creating disorder, it might not immediately be clear what they should be arrested for—a police officer must decide how to address any situation.

Police Styles

Policing encompasses a multitude of diverse tasks, including peacekeeping, criminal investigation, traffic control, and providing emergency medical service. Part of the socialization of a police officer is developing a working attitude, or style, through which policing is approached. For example, some police officers may view their job as a well-paid civil service position that stresses careful compliance with written departmental rules and procedures. Other officers may see themselves as part of the "thin blue line" that protects the public from wrongdoers. They will use any means to get the culprit, even if it involves cheating, such as planting evidence on an obviously guilty person who so far has escaped arrest. Should the police bend the rules to protect the public? This has been referred to as the "Dirty Harry problem," after the popular Clint Eastwood film character who routinely (and successfully) violated all known standards of police work.[18]

Several studies have attempted to define and classify **police styles** into behavioral clusters. These classifications, called *typologies*, attempt to categorize law enforcement agents by groups, each of which has a unique approach to police work. The purpose of such classifications is to demonstrate that the police are not a cohesive, homogeneous group, as many believe, but individuals with differing approaches to their work.[19] The approach that police take to their task and their attitude toward the police role, as well as toward their peers and superior officers, has been shown to affect their work.[20]

◀ **L03**

Compare and contrast the different police styles.

police styles

The working personalities adopted by police officers that can range from being a social worker in blue to being a hard-charging crime fighter.

Tverdokhlib/Shutterstock.com

Police officers in Miami being prepared for upcoming protests. How would an officer's style influence the way they respond to political dissent and social demonstrations?

An examination of the literature suggests that four styles of police work seem to fit the current behavior patterns of most police agents: the crime fighter, the social agent, the law enforcer, and the watchman.[21]

The Crime Fighter

To crime fighters, the most important aspect of police work is investigating serious crimes and apprehending criminals. Their focus is on the victim, and they view effective police work as the only force that can keep society's "dangerous classes" in check. They are the "thin blue line" protecting society from murderers and rapists. They consider property crimes less significant, and they believe that misdemeanors, traffic control, and social service functions would be better handled by other agencies of government. The ability to investigate criminal behavior that poses a serious threat to life and safety, combined with the power to arrest criminals, separates a police department from other municipal agencies. The crime fighters see diluting these functions with minor social service and nonenforcement duties as harmful to police efforts to create a secure society.

The Social Agent

Social agents believe that police should be involved in a wide range of activities without regard for their connection to law enforcement. Instead of viewing themselves as criminal catchers, the social agents consider themselves community problem-solvers. They are troubleshooters who patch the holes that appear where the social fabric wears thin. They are happy to work with special-needs populations, such as people experiencing homelessness, school kids, and those who require emergency services. Social agents fit well within a community policing unit.

The Law Enforcer

According to this view, duty is clearly set out in law, and law enforcers stress playing it "by the book." Because the police are specifically charged with apprehending all types of lawbreakers, they see themselves as generalized law enforcement agents. Although law enforcers may prefer working on serious crimes—which are more intriguing and rewarding in terms of achievement, prestige, and status—they see the police role as one of enforcing all statutes and ordinances. They perceive themselves as neither community social workers nor vengeance-seeking vigilantes. Simply put, they are professional law enforcement officers who perform the functions of detecting violations, identifying culprits, and taking the lawbreakers before a court. Law enforcers are devoted to the profession of police work and are the officers most likely to aspire to command rank.

The Watchman

The watchman style is characterized by an emphasis on the maintenance of public order as the police goal, not on law enforcement or general service. Watchmen ignore many infractions and requests for service unless they believe that the social or political order is jeopardized. They expect juveniles to misbehave and believe such mischief is best ignored or treated informally. Motorists will often be left alone if their driving does not endanger or annoy others. Vice and gambling are problems only when the currently accepted standards of public order are violated.

Like the watchmen of old, these officers take action only if and when a problem arises. Watchmen are the most passive officers, more concerned with retirement benefits than crime rates.

Police Personality

Along with an independent police culture, some experts believe that police officers develop a unique set of personality traits that distinguish them from the average citizen.[22] To some commentators, the typical police personality can be described as dogmatic, authoritarian, and suspicious.[23] Cynicism has been found at all levels of policing, including chiefs of police, and throughout all stages of a police career.[24] Maintenance of these negative values and attitudes is believed to cause police officers to be secretive and isolated from the rest of society, producing the blue curtain.[25]

The police officer's working personality is shaped by constant exposure to danger and the need to use force and authority to reduce and control threatening situations.[26] Police feel suspicious of the public they serve and defensive about the actions of their fellow officers. There are two opposing viewpoints on the cause of this phenomenon. One position holds that police departments attract recruits who are by nature cynical, authoritarian, and secretive.[27] Other experts maintain that socialization and experience on the police force itself cause these character traits to develop.

Since the first research measuring police personality was published, numerous efforts have been made to determine whether the typical police recruit possesses a unique personality that sets them apart from the average citizen. The results have been mixed.[28] Although some research concludes that police values are different from those of the general adult population, other efforts reach an opposing conclusion. Some have found that police officers are more psychologically healthy than the general population, less depressed and anxious, and more social and assertive.[29] Still other research on police personality has found that police officers highly value such personality traits as warmth, flexibility, and emotion. These traits are far removed from rigidity and cynicism.[30] Thus, no one position dominates on the issue of how the police personality develops—or even whether one exists.

In his classic study of police personality, *Behind the Shield* (1967), Arthur Niederhoffer examined the assumption that most police officers develop into cynics as a function of their daily duties.[31] Among his most important findings were that police cynicism increased with length of service and that military-like police academy training caused new recruits to quickly become cynical about themselves.[32]

Yet, there are some criticisms of the subculture view of the police. First, this view tends to portray officers as isolated, hostile, undemocratic, prejudiced people. This is a subjective interpretation of police that is driven by popular negative stereotypes of the police. It can also be argued that some cynicism can be good. Police officers have a difficult job and are exposed to a great deal of misery. Detachment can help officers deal with an unpleasant part of the job. Since the original research was conducted, there have also been major changes in the law and bureaucratic controls that have modified or curbed the misuse of discretion and authority. For example, *Mapp v. Ohio* (1961) placed the requirement of excluding illegally obtained evidence from court at all levels of the government.

Is the Culture Changing?

One of the main criticisms of the police subculture concept is that because most of the research was conducted in the 1960s and 1970s, it does not account for a changing rank and file. Trina Rose and Prabha Unnithan note that not all police officers feel as though they are part of the in-group. Officers who do not feel as though they are part of the subculture are likely to feel greater occupational stress than those that feel as though they are part of the in group.[33]

One other area that has been of interest to researchers is that contemporary police organizations can also shape the way that police officers shape their personality and style. Thorvald Dahle and Carol Archbold examined how rapid population growth resulting from the oil boom affected police organizations in western North Dakota.[34] They conducted face-to-face interviews with 101 police personnel working in eight police agencies to better understand how rapid population growth affects police organizations (in general), police resources, and the work environment of police organizations that are experiencing population growth. Rapid population growth resulting from the oil boom in western North Dakota has required police agencies to make changes in the way that they were structured and function. In addition, the rapid increase in population has also strained police organizations' resources. They also noted that the number of calls for police service increased dramatically since the oil boom began in 2008. The addition of police officers and needed resources has not kept pace with the rapid population growth.

Ideas of police subculture may be outdated due in large part to rapid changes in the police industry over the past 30 years and cohort effects. Officers hired in different time periods will have different ideals and behaviors than officers hired in previous decades. Furthermore, women and people of color have entered policing in small but noticeable numbers, but have they changed the profession? Is there enough diversification in policing?

The issue dates back to 1965 when Lyndon Johnson established the President's Commission on Law Enforcement and Administration of Justice. The commission's report was issued in 1967 and, among many other findings, the commission considered the lack of officers of color to be one of the central problems in policing at that time. Yet, as Ronald Weitzer points out, almost 50 years later, the 21st Century Task Force on Policing established by President Barack Obama also recommends diversification.[35] In the sections that follow, we will review how women and people of color entered policing and why representation matters.

Who Are the Modern Police?

The composition of the nation's police forces is changing, albeit slowly. Traditionally, police agencies were composed of White men with a high school education who viewed policing as a secure position that brought them the respect of family and friends and a step up the social ladder. It was not uncommon to see police families in which one member of each new generation would enter the force. Policing was therefore a difficult profession to gain a foothold in for new immigrant groups.

The most recent data collected by the Department of Justice on police departments in the United States as part of the Law Enforcement Management and Administrative Statistics Survey (LEMAS) tells us that less than 30 percent of police officers identify as part of an underrepresented group and approximately 12 percent of police officers are women. This level of representation has not always existed. The picture of the police has been changing and will continue to change. Where did this change begin, and how has it evolved?

Women in Policing

Historically, women were discouraged if not barred from becoming police officers because they were believed to lack the skills necessary to effectively fight crime.[36] The history of women in policing began in the territorial west in the 1870s, when a small number of women assisted their spouses who were the elected sheriffs of their counties. Many worked unofficially, but a few were given arrest powers.[37] In northeastern cities, pressure from outside groups such as the Quakers to more humanely address juvenile delinquency first gave women an alternative entrance into policing.[38] These groups believed that women had skills that could prevent crime and benefit youth and women involved in criminal activity.[39]

By the end of the nineteenth century, numerous cities employed jail and prison matrons. These women were hired to handle women and children held in correctional facilities and institutions for the insane. By the 1840s, police matrons were a common feature in most big city police departments. These matrons were not considered police officers. Yet, their role was significant because they constituted the first official recognition of the idea that women were necessary for the appropriate handling of female and juvenile offenders when they were held in custody. Matrons were the forerunners of policewomen. Yet, as a result of this "back door" entrance into policing, female officers failed to be accepted by male officers as "real police officers" and were accorded **token** status.[40]

In 1905, women were appointed as "safety officers" in Portland, Oregon, to protect women and children from the miners and lumberjacks in the area.[41] 1908, Lola Baldwin, 48, was the first woman allowed to have police powers when she was sworn in as a "female detective to perform police service" for the city of Portland, Oregon.[42] She appears to be the first woman hired by a U.S. municipality to carry out regular law enforcement duties. Lola Baldwin, as well as her various municipal supporters, did not view her role as one that was the same as that of uniformed male police officers of the time. Her duties, like those of other early policewomen, emphasized crime prevention and social work rather than law enforcement.

Baldwin never wore a uniform or carried a firearm; rarely flashed her badge; and seldom, if ever, made arrests. Her unit's office was not in the police station but in a local YWCA. In 1909, Alice Stebbins Wells, a minister and social welfare worker, petitioned the Los Angeles City Council and mayor's office, requesting an ordinance that would allow for a woman to be hired in the Los Angeles Police Department. While a student at the Hartford Theological Seminary, she conducted a study that concluded there was a need for women officers. Not only was the measure passed, but on September 12, 1910, Mrs. Wells was appointed as a policewoman with arrest powers in the Los Angeles Police Department (LAPD).[43]

◀ **LO4**

Discuss the challenges faced by women in policing.

token
Done for the sake of appearances or as a symbolic gesture.

Critical Thinking

What can be done to recruit more women into policing?

Roberto Galan/Alamy Stock Photo

Though women did not have police powers until the 20th century, today more than 12 percent of police officers are women. Nonetheless, in some departments, women are still struggling for acceptance and are under appreciated for their job performance.

Wells was an assistant pastor and social worker with two college degrees. The Los Angeles City Council had unanimously passed an ordinance providing for the employment of "one police officer who shall be a woman."[44] Her job was to handle all female and juvenile cases and to investigate social conditions that led some women and children to become involved in crime. The appointment of Wells as a policewoman attracted nationwide newspaper commentary because she was an educated woman and a social worker, and she had deliberately sought and secured the opportunity to work in a police department. To provide some context here, at the same time, male police officers were required to have no more than a high school diploma. Female officers entered policing with college and even masters-level education. This was a huge difference between male and female police officers. Wells went on to become the founder and first president of the International Police Women's Association and traveled throughout America and Canada to promote the hiring of female officers.[45]

Despite their education, women were originally expected to perform their duties in skirts and high heels carrying firearms in their purses and wearing badges labeled "Trooperettes."[46] This greatly limited their ability to be taken seriously and police effectively. Conducting patrol in a skirt and high heels was extremely difficult in good weather, let alone snow or sleet. While women no longer are expected to patrol in high heels or a skirt, issues still exist for women's uniforms. According to Connie Fletcher, "the basic approach is still to take a man's uniform and assume it should fit a woman." Problems with uniforms were and are indicative of the challenges faced by women who tried to break into the career of policing. Entering the profession was difficult.

Legal Challenges

Some relief was gained with the passage of the 1964 Civil Rights Act and its subsequent amendments. Courts have consistently supported the addition of women to police forces by striking down entrance requirements that eliminated almost all female candidates but that could not be proved to predict job performance (such as height and upper-body strength).[47] Women do not perform as well as men on strength tests and are much more likely to fail the entrance physical than male recruits. Critics contend that many of these tests do not reflect the actual tasks that police do on the job.[48]

For many years, women have been excluded based on department height and weight requirements; however, due to legislation and affirmative action policies, these barriers have been removed. The U.S. Equal Employment Opportunity Commission also ruled that a "respondent's height requirement tends to exclude women in significantly greater numbers than it excludes men. Because it is not non-related within the meaning of Title VII, it is unlawful."[49] Educational standards that once required only female applicants to hold college degrees have also been changed to accept all healthy high school graduates.

The Challenges of Women in Police Work

Police departments have had difficulty in hiring, retaining, and promoting female police officers. In 1972, women comprised as little as 2 percent of sworn officers and current estimates indicate that women still only comprise 12 percent of all police officers,[50] with some evidence of a downward trend beginning in 2018.

Of additional concern is the fact that more than half of all police agencies report that no women hold high-level administrative positions.[51] The situation is particularly dire in small and rural agencies that often receive less attention from police researchers. In these small and rural agencies, almost half do not receive applications from women.[52] Even in large agencies, women have made little progress. In a study of the New York Police Department, Salomon Guajardo found that from 2000 to 2013, female officers have made little progress in advancing to supervisory and command positions in the NYPD.[53] Despite this lack of progress, only one in five law enforcement agencies utilize targeted recruitment strategies for women.[54] This means that we are unlikely to see any change in the immediate future.

Studies of policewomen indicate that they are still struggling for acceptance, believe that they do not receive equal credit for their job performance, and report that it is common for them to be sexually harassed by their coworkers.[55] One reason may be that many male police officers tend to view policing as an overtly masculine profession not appropriate for women. Women also report that they get less support from their supervisors. In fact, a recent study found that while male officers tended to report more frequent stressors that took away from their time off duty, such as court appearances and working second jobs, female officers reported experiencing a lack of support from supervisors relative to male officers.[56]

Women have also faced considerable obstacles to promotion within the ranks, although recently this issue has become rather clouded and complex. Some of this pressure is internal and some is external. Carol Archbold and Dorothy Schulz found that female officers were frequently encouraged by their male supervisors to seek promotion, but this dissuaded many of the female officers from seeking promotion for fear that they would be promoted because of their gender status rather than their competencies.[57]

Female officers still also tend to be assigned to tasks that are considered to be more "feminine" such as responding to sexual assaults and juvenile delinquency—as they were in the days of Lola Baldwin. Research suggests that this approach might be somewhat misguided. For example, Jan Jordan (2002) identified professionalism, warmth, and sensitivity as the most important qualities for police officers to possess when they respond to calls involving victims of sexual assault. The female victims that she interviewed felt that male and female officers could have these characteristics.[58] Recent evidence suggests that in fact some female police officers may be *less* sympathetic toward sexual assault victims than male police officers. Ericka Wentz and Carol Archbold found some empirical evidence that women are more likely than men to subscribe to rape myths and victim blaming.[59]

Is the Tide Turning?

Yet, there is some indication that acceptance of female police officers is increasing over time. Cara Rabe-Hemp's research suggests that the workplace experience may be improving for female police officers. Her study revealed that a significant portion of female police officers reported that they have experienced greater acceptance by their male colleagues as their careers have progressed over time.[60] Furthermore, organizations such as the International Association of Women Police (IAWP) have emerged to provide opportunities, support, and training for women in policing.

On the Web

To learn about these organizations go to http://www.iawp.org/ and https://30x30initiative.org/

The IAWP was first organized as the International Police Women's Association in 1915. Their charter was adopted in 1916 in Washington, D.C. The mission of the organization is to strengthen, unite, and raise the capacity of women in policing internationally. IAWP members are in 60 countries and counting. The IAWP provides training, mentoring, peer support, and networking for members and highlights issues affecting women in law enforcement throughout the world. The organization publishes *Women Police Magazine* four times a year with specialized sections designed to improve the lives of female police officers and holds an annual training event.

Most importantly, this organization offers an international network of women police. Other organizations include the National Association of Women in Law Enforcement (NAWLE) and the 30 × 30 Initiative. The latter is a coalition of police leaders, researchers, and professional organizations who have joined together to advance the representation and experiences of women in policing agencies across the United States. Their ultimate goal is to increase the representation of women in police recruit classes to 30 percent by 2030, and to ensure police policies and culture intentionally support the success of qualified women officers throughout their careers.

LO5

Discuss the challenges faced by people of color in policing.

People of Color in Policing

The earliest known date when a Black person was hired as a police officer was 1861 in Washington, DC; Chicago hired its first Black officer in 1872.[61] At first, Black officers experienced a great deal of discrimination. Their work assignments were restricted, as were their chances for promotion. They were often assigned solely to the patrol of Black neighborhoods, and in some cities they were required to call a White officer to make an arrest. White officers held highly prejudicial attitudes, and as late as the 1950s some refused to ride with Black officers in patrol cars.[62] Black people who were able to obtain positions in the few departments willing to open their ranks to officers of color were initially denied desirable job assignments with regard to both position and location. In Miami, they were not permitted to drive departmental vehicles, so they patrolled their beats on foot or by bicycle.[63] As a consequence of unfair assignments, they were further discriminated against in evaluation for promotions,[64] and when Black officers did receive promotions, often their duties differed from those of White officers holding the same positions.[65]

Black Officers During the Civil Rights Era

The 1960s and 1970s marked a great change in U.S. policing. Civil rights demonstrations and riots resulted in clashes between police and primarily Black protestors. For largely the first time, graphic images of police officers turning fire hoses and dogs on Black people made it on television and in the newspapers. Police officers faced widespread criticism. Police were forced to acknowledge that they faced a crisis of legitimacy in the Black community, particularly among Black people residing in low-income, urban areas. One proposal offered as a way to repair this relationship was to hire more Black officers and deploy them in Black communities.[66] The idea was that Black officers could act as a calming force—reducing the anger of Black residents toward the police. Police and citizens would have a shared racial understanding and that this greater rapport would translate into more civil, respectful behavior. This also means that Black officers face **double marginality**.

The Recruitment and Selection of Officers of Color

While some progress has been made in the recruitment and selection of Black police officers, their numbers have not reached the levels suggested above. In the 1930 and 1940s, Black people represented less than 1 percent of all police officers. The percentage of Black officers increased from 9.3 percent in 1987 to 11.7 percent in 2000 and then stalled roughly at that level (i.e., about 12 percent) until 2013. It is possible that this stall may suggest that nationally, Black officers may be closer to full representation. Aggregate statistics, however, do not embody the reality of representation for Black people in American policing. Indeed, representation for Black people is hardly stable across agencies, with some agencies employing no (or few) members of racial minority groups while others are more representative of the communities they serve.[67]

For example, in racially charged Ferguson, Missouri, only 5.6 percent of the police force is Black while 67 percent of the population is Black.[68] It is not unusual for smaller cities like Ferguson to lack diversity, as much of the recent progress in representation from underrepresented populations has been observed in larger agencies. Since racial and ethnic minorities are not distributed across the country equally, the best way to measure progress is to compute an **Equal Employment Opportunity (EEO) Index** at the local level. To do this, you compare the percentage of underrepresented populations to their percentage in the community and see if they are close. For example, if Black people comprise 12 percent of the municipality, they should reflect about 12 percent of the department's personnel to be representative. To calculate an EEO index, you would divide the percentage of the underrepresented group in the police force by the percentage of the population in the community. If the community is 30 percent Latino, and the department is composed of 15 percent Latino officers, the index score is .50.

SuperStock/Alamy Stock Photo

About 12 percent of police officers are Black, increasing more than tenfold from 100 years ago. However, while representation in some agencies reflects the population makeup, other departments have been deficient in recruiting officers from under represented groups.

double marginality
According to Nicholas Alex, the social burden that Black police officers carry by being both racial minority members and law enforcement officers.

Equal Employment Opportunity (EEO) Index
A measure of the representativeness of a police department.

In Table 8.1, you will notice that the percentage of officers of color decreases as department size also decreases. This means that smaller departments have less diversity than large departments.

While the numbers of Black officers have increased over time, those gains are not consistent across agencies of varying sizes. With increased numbers, however, police officers from underrepresented populations now seem more aggressive, more self-assured, and less willing to accept any discriminatory practices by the police department.[70] In a study of Black and White police officers, Lorenzo Boyd has argued that because Black officers tend to see themselves as community stewards in Black neighborhoods, they often outperform their White colleagues at quality-of-life policing.[71] Researchers have found that Black officers are often more willing than White officers to use their authority to take official action;. the higher the percentage of Black officers on the force, the higher the arrest rate for crimes such as assault.[72]

Black in Blue

The experience of Black police officers has not been an easy one. In his classic book *Black in Blue*, written more than 50 years ago, Nicholas Alex pointed out that Black officers of the time experienced what he called *double marginality*.[73] On the one hand, Black officers had to deal with the expectation that they would give members of their own race a break. On the other hand, they often experienced overt racism from their police colleagues. Alex found that Black officers' adaptation to these pressures ranged from denying that Black suspects should be treated differently from White suspects to treating Black offenders more harshly than White offenders (to prove their lack of bias). Alex offered several reasons for why some Black officers were tougher on Black offenders: They desired acceptance from their White colleagues, they were particularly sensitive to any disrespect shown to them by Black teenagers, and they viewed themselves as protectors of the Black community.

Table 8.1   Race and Ethnicity of Full-Time Sworn Personnel in Local Police Departments, by Size of Population Served

Population Served	White (%)	Black/ African American (%)	Hispanic/ Latino (%)	Other (%)	Unknown (%)
All sizes	71.5	11.4	12.5	3.6	1.1
1,000,000 or more	50.4	16.6	27.0	5.6	0.4
500,000–999,999	59.7	21.5	10.9	6.8	1.1
250,000–499,999	68.0	14.8	12.6	4.0	0.6
100,000–249,999	72.9	11.7	10.0	3.4	2.0
50,000–99,999	74.7	7.6	12.9	2.6	2.2
25,000–49,999	86.9	6.0	5.2	1.3	0.6
10,000–24,999	86.9	6.0	5.9	1.8	1.1
2,500–9,999	85.2	4.7	5.5	1.8	0.3

Source: Shelley S. Hyland and Elizabeth Davis, *Local Police Departments, 2016 Personnel* (Washington, DC: Bureau of Justice Statistics, 2019), p. 6.[69]

Because many Black officers found themselves marginalized within their departments, many banded together and formed (or joined) police affiliate organizations based on their shared heritage. Two of the larger associations are the National Association of Black Law Enforcement Officers (NABLEO) and the National Organization of Black Law Enforcement Executives (NOBLE). The mission of NABLEO is to "provide community-based solutions to policing issues which have a direct impact on communities of color and the pivotal roles that African American, Latino, and other criminal justice practitioners of color play."[74] The mission of NOBLE is "to ensure equity in the administration of justice in the provision of public service to all communities, and to serve as the conscience of law enforcement by being committed to justice by action."[75] NOBLE was founded in September 1976 during a three-day symposium to address crime in urban low-income areas. The symposium was cosponsored by the Police Foundation and the Law Enforcement Assistance Administration (LEAA). NOBLE has nearly 60 chapters and represents over 3,000 members worldwide that represent chief executive officers and command-level law enforcement officials from federal, state, county, municipal law enforcement agencies, and criminal justice practitioners. It serves more than 60,000 youths through its major program components which include Mentoring, Education, Leadership Development, and Safety. Since 1976, NOBLE has served as the conscience of law enforcement by being committed to justice by action.

Ron Davis, retired police chief, former director of the U.S. Department of Justice, Office of Community Oriented Policing Services (COPS), the executive director of President Obama's Task Force on 21st Century Policing, and current director of the U.S. Marshals Service, said that, "I have no doubt that the overwhelming majority of police officers in this country are brave and honorable public servants. But despite this, racial disparities still exist and there's a growing divide between officers and civilians along racial lines." Davis goes on to say that "the shooting of unarmed Black men and women, police brutality, and racial disparities in the criminal justice system represent a national crisis that requires a national response." Davis concludes that "blaming the police alone for the inequities of the criminal justice system excuses prosecutors, judges, prison systems, health care disparities, lack of access to mental health services, poor education systems, etc. All of these systems contribute to the crime and violence in our neighborhoods and the overreliance on police to solve problems that extend well beyond our capacity."[76]

Latinos and Officers from Other Underrepresented Populations

Little is known about the experiences of Latinos and other officers from underrepresented populations. In 2003, Latino officers comprised 9.1 percent of all officers. A decade later, Latinos were 11.6 percent of all police officers. Despite this steady growth, there is little research about Latino officers. Ronald Weitzer writes that although there is a growing population of Latinos and Hispanics throughout

Critical Thinking

What are some ways that the police can make their career more attractive to candidates of color?

On the Web

To learn more about NOBLE, visit https://noblenational.org/

the United States, now outnumbering Black people and consisting of the majority in some major cities, not much is known about comparing Latino relations with the police to other racial and ethnic groups.[77] This is particularly challenging given the difficult relationship between some Latino people and the police.

Research suggests that many Latino community members report fear of the police, contributing to their social isolation and exacerbating their mistrust of law enforcement authorities. A substantial portion of Latino respondents report that they would be less likely to voluntarily contact the police if they are the victim of a crime, or to provide information about a crime because they fear that police would use this contact as an opportunity to investigate their immigration status or that of their friends and family members.[78] We also recognize, however, that Latino residents of the United States are not a monolithic group and there are variations in relationships based on country of origin, time in the United States, as well as socioeconomic status.

Most research does not include Latino officers—which is why findings about this ethnic group are largely absent from the chapter.[79] For research purposes, Black and Latino people are often lumped together as simply non-White. This prohibits us from learning whether Latino people are more similar to Black or White people (or not). There has been very little research on patterns of assimilation, ethnic identity, or overall careers of Latino police officers.[80] The same problem exists for officers who are Asian, Native American, and of other racial and ethnic backgrounds. Their exclusion from this chapter is not meant as a lack of interest, but rather reflects the lack of available research. This means that there is still much work to be done in learning about diversity and how it affects policing.

Tensions within Police Departments

There is considerable anecdotal evidence, however, that racial and ethnic changes have been accompanied by tension and conflict. In most large city departments, officers of color belong to separate fraternal organizations (the National Organization of Black Law Enforcement Executives, the National Black Police Officers Association, the Hispanic American Police Association, Asian Peace Officers Association, and various local organizations and chapters). In some departments, officers of color have withdrawn from local police unions, which they criticize for representing White officers at the expense of others. Black police officer associations have spoken out about police use of force, at times criticizing the position of the police union. Litigation over affirmative action often pits an organization that represents officers of color against the local police union.

There are also anecdotal reports that in some departments interracial tensions have escalated into actual violence, including physical fights between different groups of officers in police station houses. Some research describes a shared perception among Black police officers that racist attitudes and institutional obstacles prevent full participation within their departments.[81] A recent study by Norman Conti and Patrick Doreian found that even in a targeted academy program designed to address racial tensions, segregation still existed.[82] The tensions within police agencies, however, are not empirically documented and are deserving of further study. Yet, there is value in diversifying organizations. Exposure to people with different racial and ethnic backgrounds within the workplace helps police understand and connect to the people they encounter on the streets. More research is needed to detail the experiences of officers in racially and ethnically diverse departments.

Intersectionality within Policing

L06

Define the concept of intersectionality.

It would also be helpful to understand the intersection of gender and race in policing.[83] Unfortunately, given the small numbers of women of color in police agencies across the United States, it is difficult to conduct analyses separating women and men of color using the EEO index or any other measure. Women and officers of color still do not comprise a representative proportion of police agencies. **Intersectionality** is a critical perspective that individuals are described by multiple identities: gender, race, religion, and sexual orientation among others.[84] Oppressive institutions such as racism, sexism, and classicism among others are interconnected and can't be examined separately from each other.

For example, the experiences of a Black female police officer will not be identical to those of a White female police officer just because they are both women. Rather, Black women will be treated differently because of the intersection of gender and race. This concept was developed from the tenets of women of color feminist theory and activism and first coined by Black feminist legal scholar Kimberlé Crenshaw in the late 1980s.[85] Intersectionality was originally articulated as a lens to understand the experiences of Black women. The term brought to light, however, that invisibility is a problem for many constituents within groups that claim them as members, but often fail to represent them. It is clear that the intersections of race, gender, sexual orientation, and religion shape experiences.

Most recently, Hillary Potter has taken this approach. Her work highlights the differences between how different identities affect involvement in criminal activity and how traditional theories may not explain their experiences equally. She notes "a Black woman's involvement with crime may be different from a White woman's involvement with crime, both of which may be different than a Latina woman's involvement with crime."[86] Potter has applied this approach as a way to frame offending behaviors. While criminal involvement clearly differs from policing, some of the same concepts can still apply. The experiences of White women in policing likely differ from those of African American and Latina women.

In a study of Black female officers serving in five large municipal departments, Susan Martin found that they perceive significantly more racial discrimination than both other female officers and Black male officers.[87] However, White policewomen were significantly more likely to perceive gender discrimination than Black policewomen. Martin also found that when they were on patrol, Black female officers were treated differently by male officers than White female officers were. Neither group of women was viewed as equals. We need to know more about how intersectionality affects police work. For example, we don't know if the experiences of Black male officers are more similar to other male officers from different racial and ethnic groups or of Black female officers. What we do know is that intersectionality is likely to affect the police subculture in ways that we are not fully aware.

intersectionality

A concept often used in critical theories to describe the ways in which oppressive institutions (racism, sexism, homophobia, transphobia, ableism, xenophobia, classism, etc.) are interconnected and cannot be examined separately from one another.

Jeffrey Isaac Greenberg 8+/Alamy Stock Photo

To improve policing, we need to know more about how intersectionality affects police work. For example, are the experiences of Black male officers similar to those experienced by other men from different racial and ethnic groups? Do Black women in policing share similar attitudes and experiences with women from other ethnic and racial groups?

L07
Determine if and how diversity
affects policing.

▶ Does Diversity Matter?

There is a great deal of conflicting evidence about the importance of diversity. Some of this evidence will be discussed in the section that follows. Black people generally have less confidence in the police than White people and are skeptical of their ability to protect citizens from harm.[88] Black people also seem more likely to have been victimized when well-publicized incidents of police misconduct occur.[89] Black juveniles seem particularly suspicious of police, even when they deny having had negative encounters with them.[90] A **heterogeneous** police force can thus be instrumental in gaining the confidence of communities of color by helping dispel the view that police departments are generally bigoted or biased organizations.

heterogenous
Diverse in character or content.

Representative bureaucracy theory tells us that in fact a heterogenous police department is valuable. Passive representation is indicated by the actual composition of employees working in the organization. Much of the research examining passive representation is descriptive in nature, detailing the racial and socioeconomic status of bureaucratic employees.[91] Active representation refers to how this composition affects policy outputs—whether the inclusion of a diverse group of employees affects the way the organization conducts business. In fact, a central theme of representative bureaucracy is the assumption that passive representation will lead to active representation, whereby bureaucrats act purposely on behalf of their counterparts in the general population.[92] There is a relationship between citizen perceptions of the police as a whole and diversity. Wesley Skogan found a positive association between Black people having representation in the local police force and Black citizens' ratings of police services.[93] Language barriers are another reason for encouraging diversity. Spanish-speaking officers can help with investigations in Spanish-speaking neighborhoods.

Sam Walker, a police historian and civil rights researcher, has repeatedly called for increased diversification in law enforcement and has made it one of the hallmarks of a successful police department.[94] Representative organizations are consistent with the principles of democratic policing.[95] A heterogeneous police force can be instrumental in gaining the confidence of communities of color. The police should strive for diversity particularly in those areas that lack diversity to maintain their legitimacy in a complex democratic society. Recent events have taught us that once trust is eroded, it can be very difficult to rebuild.

Ronald Weitzer notes that the available evidence shows that the vast majority of police officers are "blue," which means that their occupational training and socialization into the profession by fellow officers is more important than their racial background in terms of how they treat citizens.[96] Most studies point to overall similarities in police behavior irrespective of officers' racial background. This point of view was illustrated by protests in Baltimore, Maryland, following the death of Freddie Gray. The Baltimore City Police Department is comprised of a majority of officers of color.[97] Despite the racial diversity of the agency, citizens were outraged by the Baltimore police actions and Gray's subsequent death. Protests erupted throughout the city and the racial makeup of the police department seemed irrelevant.

This is because, as Ivan Sun and Brian Payne found, it's the police socialization process—beginning with training in the academies—that largely determines officers' behaviors. More specifically, their research found that in predominately Black neighborhoods, Black officers were more likely to provide advice or other assistance than other officers. However, Black officers employed coercive actions more frequently as well.[98] Officers of color might be more likely to assimilate into a department's behaviors if there aren't many on staff because they're more isolated.

Similarly, Jacinta Gau and Rod Brunson conducted interviews with 44 citizens in the primarily Black community of East St. Louis. They found that a shared racial background fails to guarantee positive interactions between police and citizens and that Black citizens can in fact be very dissatisfied with Black officers. They note that even in an agency where the vast majority of police officers are Black, corruption, illegality, and generally unprofessional behavior are perceived by the majority-Black public as an apt description of the department.[99]

In short, we are not fully aware of how diversity matters. Policing is a profession that has not yet fully achieved a diverse workforce or passive representation. Until it does, the realization of outcomes associated with active representation may be difficult to fully obtain. This means that there may need to be more diversity before we can expect to see the positive outcomes that are hypothesized to be associated with it. In organizations that are primarily White and male, women and people of color may feel uncomfortable expressing their views. In order to achieve success or get ahead in the organization, female officers and officers of color may instead go with the status quo rather than challenging existing structures.[100]

How Can Police Increase Diversity?

For some time, U.S. police departments have made a concerted effort to attract officers of color, and the gains have been mixed. This effort is being met with mixed results. So why are police departments having trouble recruiting people from underrepresented populations? As discussed in previous chapters, police departments have a long history of discrimination, beginning with Slave Patrols in the pre–Civil War period through shootings in Louisville, Atlanta, Kenosha, Milwaukee, Ferguson, and Charleston.

Because of these incidents, police also have a major image issue. This makes them an unattractive employment alternative, particularly for members of communities of color. Furthermore, in good economic times, young people can get better-paying jobs elsewhere so it is unclear why they would want to work within a subculture that is likely to resist them.

Yet, at the same time, underrepresented populations are growing across the country. For example, racial and ethnic minorities, including citizens of Black, Hispanic, and Asian descent, make up more than 40 percent of New Jersey's population, up from 21 percent in 1990. Diversity within police departments hasn't kept pace. To address this gap in representativeness, there are a number of steps that police departments can take. First, they can increase applicant pools. Increasing the applicant pool is a way to enhance all kinds of diversity, including race, gender, and socioeconomic status.

Jim West/Alamy Stock Photo

Here a diverse group of Ohio State Highway Patrol officers are assigned to protect members of the neo-Nazi National Socialist Movement as they held a rally on the steps of the government office building. How can a diverse police force help protect the public who are involved in politically sensitive demonstrations?

The Boston Police Cadet Program

The Boston Police Cadet Program is an on-the-job training program for Boston's youth seeking a career in law enforcement. The program has a minimum two-year commitment. Cadets rotate throughout the department in various assignments and shifts, including headquarters, district stations, and other specialized units throughout the city. Primary responsibilities include routine clerical and administrative duties, answering phones, data entry, traffic duty, utilizing department vehicles, barrier work, and related duties as required. If selected for appointment, candidates must pass an extensive screening process including drug testing, a preemployment physical, an extensive criminal background check, and a rigorous eight-week cadet training program (both academic and physical in nature) at the Boston Police Academy.[101]

Critical Thinking

1. Are cadet programs a viable way to recruit people into policing?

2. What are the pros and cons?

Source: https://www.boston.gov/departments/police/police -cadet-program

Critical Thinking

What are some of the reasons that diversifying a police department is a positive goal?

Jeremy Wilson and colleagues, as part of the RAND Corporation, report, "Police Recruitment and Retention for the new millennium" developed a number of strategies to assist departments in the recruitment process.[102] Some of these strategies are described below.

1. Integrate the community in the hiring process. In addition to department stakeholders, including community input can better inform decisions on external issues. This means that if a department is having difficulty recruiting, they should meet with the community to get assistance.

2. Wilson and colleagues note that the best recruiters for a department are often its own personnel. Police managers can build professional networks within the department to support recruitment. The goal is to enhance community outreach efforts by making recruitment an overall philosophy rather than a task to be performed. This can include referrals by family, friends, and employees.

3. Police agencies can also create a Department Recruitment Unit. A recruitment unit can be separate from recruitment teams that perform hiring needs assessments or be linked interdepartmentally.

4. Specifically target recruitment efforts in neighborhoods of color that are underrepresented in the department.

5. Police agencies can open department doors and not only allow but also encourage on-site visits. This can be accomplished through the implementation of community policing. Community policing can improve community visibility and, in turn, bolster recruitment efforts.

6. Police departments should attend career and job fairs. Face-to-face interaction and fostering human connections can make recruitment more meaningful and personal for both the department and applicants than flyers, commercials, and electronic media.

7. Youth programs can offer another way to recruit. Explorer programs, internships through local schools, cadet academies, and mentorships with youth

foster special relationships between young adults and departments. For example, the Boston Police Cadet Program offers an opportunity for young people to learn more about a career in policing, make connections, and contribute to their communities. More about the program is included in the box below.

8. Using electronic media is another way to enhance recruiting of different populations. Increasing use of the Internet has lured agencies seeking to attract officers. The interactive potential of Internet media has increased beyond simple advertising. Electronic recruitment techniques are not confined to blogs and websites.

Summary

LO1 List the major issues currently facing policing.

While people were dealing with a pandemic, several high-profile killings of Black citizens went viral in a short period of time. All of the killings had direct ties to local police officers. Citizens were glued to social media and watched the three killings, one of which was in real time, live on the Internet. Incidents like these and many others make it hard to recruit a diverse workforce. It is hard to build trust and legitimacy with communities of color when they see frequent acts of violence toward others in marginalized communities. Many in communities of color may experience vicarious trauma from recurring reports of people of color dying at the hands of the police. When citizens see that the police reflect a cross-section of the community, they have greater confidence that police officers will understand their problems and concerns. Police agencies must develop effective strategies for welcoming and supporting officers of color within the police subculture by eliminating discriminatory attitudes and practices.

LO2 Describe the police subculture.

Police culture helps recruits adjust to the rigors of police work and provides the emotional support needed for survival. The culture encourages decisiveness in the face of uncertainty and the ability to make split-second judgments that may later be subject to extreme criticism. The police subculture also encourages its members to draw a sharp distinction between good and evil. Police culture is characterized by cynicism, clannishness, secrecy, and insulation from others in society.

LO3 Compare and contrast the different police styles.

There are a variety of police styles. Crime fighters consider the most important aspect of police work

as investigating serious crimes and apprehending criminals. Their focus is on the victim, and they view effective police work as the only force that can keep society's "dangerous classes" in check. They are the "thin blue line" protecting society from murderers and rapists. In contrast, social agents believe that police should be involved in a wide range of activities; social agents consider themselves community problem-solvers. They are happy to work with special-needs populations, such as people who are experiencing homelessness, school kids, and those who require emergency services. A third style of policing is known as law enforcers who stress playing it "by the book." They see the police role as one of enforcing all statutes and ordinances. They are professional law enforcement officers who perform the functions of detecting violations, identifying culprits, and taking the lawbreakers before a court. Law enforcers are devoted to the profession of police work and are the officers most likely to aspire to command roles. Finally, the watchman style is characterized by an emphasis on the maintenance of public order as the police goal, not on law enforcement or general service. Like the watchmen of old, these officers take action only if and when a problem arises. Watchmen are the most passive officers and more concerned with retirement benefits than crime rates.

LO4 Discuss the challenges faced by women in policing.

Police departments have had difficulty in hiring, retaining, and promoting female police officers. Of additional concern is the fact that more than half of all police agencies report that no women hold high-level administrative positions. Even in large agencies, women have made little progress. Studies of policewomen indicate that they are still struggling for acceptance, believe that they do not receive equal credit for their job performance, and report that it is common for them to be sexually harassed by their coworkers. Women also report that they get less support from their supervisors. Women have also faced considerable obstacles to promotion within the ranks, although recently this issue has become rather clouded and complex.

LO5   Discuss the challenges faced by people of color in policing.

There is also considerable evidence that the racial and ethnic changes in policing have been accompanied by tension and conflict. In some departments, officers of color have withdrawn from local police unions, which they criticize for representing White officers at the expense of others. Black police officer associations have spoken out about police use of force, at times criticizing the position of the police union. Litigation over affirmative action often pits an organization representing officers of color against the local police union. In in some departments, interracial tensions have escalated into actual violence, including physical fights between different groups of officers in police station houses.

LO6   Define the concept of intersectionality.

It would be helpful to understand the intersection of gender and race in policing. Intersectionality is a critical perspective that individuals are described by multiple identities: gender, race, religion, and sexual orientation among others. Oppressive institutions such as racism, sexism, and classicism, among others, are interconnected and can't be examined separately from each other. The experiences of a Black female police officer will not be identical to those of a White female police officer just because they are both women. Rather, Black female officers will be treated differently because of the intersection of gender and race. It is clear that the intersections of race, gender, sexual orientation, and religion shape experiences.

LO7   Determine if and how diversity affects policing.

There is a great deal of conflicting evidence about the importance of diversity. Black people generally have less confidence in the police than White people and are skeptical of their ability to protect citizens from harm. Black people also seem more likely to have been victimized when well-publicized incidents of police misconduct occur. A diverse police force can be instrumental in gaining the confidence of communities of color by helping dispel the view that police departments are generally bigoted or biased organizations. There is a relationship between citizen perceptions of the police as a whole and diversity. Research found a positive association between Black people having representation in the local police force and Black citizens' ratings of police services. Language barriers are another reason for encouraging diversity. Spanish-speaking officers can help with investigations in Spanish-speaking neighborhoods.

Key Terms

subculture, 221
cynicism, 223
blue curtain, 223
police styles, 225

token, 229
double marginality, 233
Equal Employment Opportunity
    (EEO) Index, 233

intersectionality, 237
heterogeneous, 238

Notes

1. Department of Justice, Office of Public Affairs, Federal Jury Finds Three Men Guilty of Hate Crimes in Connection with the Pursuit and Killing of Ahmaud Arbery, February 22, 2022, https://www.justice.gov/opa/pr/federal-jury-finds-three-men-guilty-hate-crimes-connection-pursuit-and-killing-ahmaud-arbery.
2. Department of Justice, Office of Public Affairs. Federal Judge Sentences Three Men Convicted of Racially Motivated Hate Crimes in Connection with the Killing of Ahmaud Arbery in Georgia, August 8, 2022, https://www.justice.gov/opa/pr

/federal-judge-sentences-three-men-convicted-racially-motivated-hate-crimes-connection-killing.
3. Darcy Costello and Tessa Duvall, "Minute by Minute: What Happened the Night Louisville Police Fatally Shot Breonna Taylor," *USA Today*, May 15, 2020, https://www.usatoday.com/story/news/nation/2020/05/15/minute-minute-account-breonna-taylor-fatal-shooting-louisville-police/5196867002/.
4. Corinne Streit, "Recruiting Minority Officers," *Law Enforcement Technology* 28, no. 2 (2001), 70–72, 74, 75.

5. Trisha N. Rhodes and David H. Tyler, "Is It Cool to Be a Cop? Exploring the Differential Impact of Ferguson on Police Applicants," *Policing: A Journal of Policy and Practice*, paz013, 2019, https://doi.org/10.1093/police/paz013.

6. Jen Fifield, "Does Diversifying Police Forces Reduce Tensions?" The Pew Trust, August 22, 2016, http://www.pewtrusts.org/en/research-and-analysis/blogs/stateline/2016/08/22/does-diversifying-police-forces-reduce-tensions.

7. M. Steven Meagher and Nancy Yentes, "Choosing a Career in Policing: A Comparison of Male and Female Perceptions," *Journal of Police Science and Administration* 16 (1986), 320–327.

8. Michael K. Brown, *Working the Street* (New York, NY: Russell Sage, 1981), p. 82.

9. R. R. Bennett, "Becoming Blue: A Longitudinal Study of Police Recruit Occupational Socialization," *Journal of Police Science and Administration* 12, no. 1 (1984), 47–58.

10. Gary R. Rothwell and J. Norman Baldwin, "Whistle-Blowing and the Code of Silence in Police Agencies: Policy and Structural Predictors," *Crime and Delinquency* 53, no. 4 (2007), 605–632.

11. James B. Comey, Hard Truths: Law Enforcement and Race. Georgetown University. Washington, D.C. February 12, 2015. Speech.

12. Board of Inquiry into the Rampart Area Corruption Incident, www.lapdonline.org/.../pdf/boi_pub.pdf.

13. T. Barker and D. Carter (eds.) *Police Deviance* Cincinnati: Anderson Publishing, 1994). ISBN 978-0-87084-714-1

14. Christopher Commission Report, http://oac.cdlib.org/findaid/ark:/13030/c8765d2h.

15. Ronald Weitzer and Steven A. Tuch, *Race and Policing in America: Conflict and Reform* (Cambridge, MA: Cambridge University Press, 2006).

16. Mollen Commission Final report, https://www.nyc.gov/html/ccpc/assets/downloads/pdf/final_report.pdf

17. Malcolm Sparrow, Mark Moore, and David Kennedy, *Beyond 911: A New Era for Policing* (New York, NY: Basic Books, 1990), p. 51.

18. Carl Klockars, "The Dirty Harry Problem," *Annals* 452 (1980), 33–47.

19. Jack Kuykendall and Roy Roberg, "Police Managers' Perceptions of Employee Types: A Conceptual Model," *Journal of Criminal Justice* 16 (1988), 131–135.

20. Stephen Matrofski, R. Richard Ritti, And Jeffrey Snipes, "Expectancy Theory and Police Productivity in DUI Enforcement," *Law And Society Review* 28 (1994), 113–138.

21. William Muir, *Police: Streetcorner Politicians* (Chicago, IL: University of Chicago Press, 1977); James Q. Wilson, *Varieties of Police Behavior* (Cambridge, MA: Harvard University Press, 1968).

22. Wallace Graves, "Police Cynicism: Causes and Cures," *FBI Law Enforcement Bulletin* 65 (1996), 16–21.

23. Richard Lundman, *Police and Policing* (New York, NY: Holt, Rinehart, and Winston, 1980). See also Jerome Skolnick, *Justice Without Trial* (New York, NY: Wiley, 1966).

24. Micael Bjork, "Fighting Cynicism," *Police Quarterly* 11 (2008), 88–101.

25. William Westly, *Violence and the Police: A Sociological Study of Law, Custom, and Morality* (Cambridge, MA: MIT Press, 1970).

26. Jerome Skolnick, *Justice Without Trial* (New York: Wiley, 1966), pp. 42–68.

27. Milton Rokeach, Martin Miller, and John Snyder, "The Value Gap Between Police and Policed," *Journal of Social Issues* 27 (1971), 155–171.

28. Bruce Carpenter and Susan Raza, "Personality Characteristics of Police Applicants: Comparisons Across Subgroups and with Other Populations," *Journal of Police Science and Administration* 15 (1987), 10–17.

29. Larry Tifft, "The 'Cop Personality' Reconsidered," *Journal of Police Science and Administration* 2 (1974), 268; David Bayley and Harold Mendelsohn, *Minorities and the Police* (New York: Free Press, 1969); Robert Balch, "The Police Personality: Fact or Fiction?" *Journal of Criminal Law, Criminology, and Police Science* 63 (1972), 117.

30. Lowell Storms, Nolan Penn, and James Tenzell, "Policemen's Perception of Real and Ideal Policemen," *Journal of Police Science and Administration* 17 (1990), 40–43.

31. Arthur Niederhoffer, *Behind the Shield: The Police in Urban Society* (Garden City, NY: Doubleday, 1967).

32. Ibid., pp. 216–220.

33. Trina Rose and Prabha Unnithan, "In or out of the Group? Police Subculture and Occupational Stress," *Policing: An International Journal of Police Strategies & Management* 38, no. 2, (2015), 279–294.

34. Thorvald O. Dahle and Carol A. Archbold, ""Just Do What You Can [...] Make It Work!" Exploring the Impact of Rapid Population Growth on Police Organizations in Western North Dakota" *Policing: An International Journal of Police Strategies & Management* 38, no. 4 (2015), 805–819.

35. Ronald Weitzer, "Is American Policing At a Crossroads?," *The Criminologist: The Official Newsletter of the American Society of Criminology* 40, no. 4 (2015), 1–5.

36. S. Miller, *Gender And Community Policing: Walking the Talk* (Boston, MA: Northeastern University, 1999).

37. Dorothy Moses Schulz, *Breaking the Brass Ceiling: Women Police Chiefs and Their Paths to the Top* (Westport, CT: Praeger, 2004).

38. D. M. Schulz, *From Social Worker to Crimefighter* (Westport, CT: Praeger, 1995).

39. Susan Martin, *Breaking and Entering: Policewomen on Patrol*. (Los Angeles, CA: University of California Press, 1980).

40. D. M. Schulz, *From Social Worker to Crimefighter* (Westport, CT: Praeger, 1995).

41. Mary S. Jackson. *Policing in a Diverse Society: Another American Dilemma* (Cambridge, MA: Cambridge University Press, 2018).

42. Gloria Myers, *A Municipal Mother: Portland's Lola Greene Baldwin, America's First Policewoman* (Corvallis, OR: Oregon State University Press, 1995), p. 22.

43. Women in the LAPD, http://www.lapdonline.org/join_the_team/content_basic_view/833.

44. Janis Appier, *Policing Women: The Sexual Politics of Law Enforcement and the LAPD* (Philadelphia, PA: Temple University Press, 1998), p. 10.

45. Mary S. Jackson, *Policing in a Diverse Society: Another American Dilemma* (Cambridge, MA: Cambridge University Press, 2018).

46. Connie Fletcher, *Breaking and Entering: Women Cops Break the Code of Silence to Tell Their Stories From the Inside* (New York, NY: Pocket Books, 1995).

47. *Le Bouef v. Ramsey*, 26 FEP Cases 884 (September 16, 1980).

48. Michael Birzer and Delores Craig, "Gender Differences in Police Physical Ability Test Performance," *American Journal of Police* 15 (1996), 93–106.

49. AELE Law Library of Case Summaries, Employment & Labor Law for Public Safety Agencies: Height Requirement, http://www.aele.org/law/Digests/empl116.html.

50. B. A. Reeves, *Local Police Departments, 2013: Personnel, Policies, and Practices* (Washington, DC: Bureau of Justice Statistics, U.S. Department of Justice, 2015).

51. Ibid.

52. W. T. Jordan, L. Fridell, D. Faggiani, and B. Kubu, "Attracting Females and Racial/Ethnic Minorities to Law Enforcement," *Journal of Criminal Justice* 37 (2009), 333–341.

53. Salomon Alcocer Guajardo, "Women in Policing: A Longitudinal Assessment of Female Officers in Supervisory Positions in the New York City Police Department," *Women & Criminal Justice* 26, no. 1 (2016), 20–36.

54. W. T. Jordan, L. Fridell, D. Faggiani, and B. Kubu, "Attracting Females and Racial/Ethnic Minorities to Law Enforcement," *Journal of Criminal Justice* 37 (2009), 333–341.

55. James Daum and Cindy Johns, "Police Work from a Woman's Perspective," *Police Chief* 61 (1994), 46–49.

56. John M. Violanti, Desta Fekedulegn, Tara A. Hartley, Luenda E. Charles, Michael E. Andrew, Claudia C. Ma, and Cecil M. Burchfiel, "Highly Rated and most Frequent Stressors among Police Officers: Gender Differences." *American Journal of Criminal Justice* (2016), 1–18.

57. Carol A. Archbold and Dorothy M. Schulz, "The Lingering Effects of Tokenism on Female Police Officers' Promotion Aspirations," *Police Quarterly* 11 (2008), 50–73.

58. Jan Jordan, "Will Any Woman Do? Police, Gender and Rape Victims," *Policing: An International Journal of Police Strategies & Management* 25 (2002), 319–344.

59. Ericka Wentz and Carol Archbold, "Police Perceptions of Sexual Assault Victims: Exploring the Intra-Female Gender Hostility Thesis," *Police Quarterly* 15 (2012), 25–44.

60. Cara Rabe-Hemp, "Survival in an 'All Boys Club': Policewomen and Their Fight for Acceptance," *Policing: An International Journal of Police Strategies and Management* 31 (2008), 251–270.

61. Jack Kuykendall and David Burns, "The African American Police Officer: An Historical Perspective," *Journal of Contemporary Criminal Justice* 1 (1980), 4–13.

62. Ibid.

63. Harry W. Mor, "Equality of Opportunity: Discrimination and its Resolution." In *Special Topics in Policing* (Cincinnati, OH: Anderson, 1992).

64. S. Leinen, *Black Police, White Society.* (New York, NY: New York University Press, 1984).

65. J. Kuykendall and D. Burns, "The Black Police Officers: An Historical Perspective." In *The Ambivalent Force: Perspectives on the Police,* 3rd ed. (New York, NY: Holt, Reinhart, and Wilson, 1980).

66. S. H. Decker and R. L. Smith, "Police Minority Recruitment: A Note on Its Effectiveness in Improving Black Evaluations of the Police," *Journal of Criminal Justice* 8 (1980), 387–393; R. M. Kelly and West, G., Jr., The Racial Transition of a Police Force: A Profile of White and Black Policemen in Washington, D.C. In J. R. Snibbe and H. M. Snibbe (eds.), *The Urban Policeman in Transition* (pp. 354–381). Springfield, IL: Charles C. Thomas, 1973.

67. James Daum and Cindy Johns, "Police Work from a Woman's Perspective," *Police Chief* 61 (1994), 46–49.

68. R. Leber, "Ferguson's Police Is 94% White—and That's Basically Normal in the U.S.," *The New Republic* (2014), http://www.newrepublic.com/article/119070/michael -browns-death-leads-scrutiny-ferguson-white-police.

69. Shelley S. Hyland and Elizabeth Davis, *Local Police Departments, 2016 Personnel* (Washington, DC: Bureau of Justice Statistics, 2019), p. 6.

70. Nicholas Alex, *New York Cops Talk Back* (New York, NY: Wiley, 1976).

71. L. M. Boyd, "Light Blue versus Dark Blue: Attitudinal Differences in Quality-of-Life Policing," *Journal of Ethnicity in Criminal Justice* 8 (2010), 37–48.

72. David Eitle, Lisa Stolzenberg, and Stewart J. D'Alessio, "Police Organizational Factors, the Racial Composition of the Police, and the Probability of Arrest," *Justice Quarterly* 22 (2005), 30–57.

73. Nicholas Alex, *Black in Blue: A Study of the Negro Policeman* (New York, NY: Appleton-Century-Crofts, 1969).

74. National Association of Black Law Enforcement Officers, http://nableo.org/.

75. National Organization of Black Law Enforcement Executives, http://noblenational.org/.

76. Ronald Davis, "My Truth About Being a Black Man and a Black Cop," *Huffington Post* (2019), https://www .huffingtonpost.com/entry/opinion-davis-black -police_us_5adf4328e4b061c0bfa22ef8.

77. Ronald Weitzer, "The Puzzling Neglect of Hispanic Americans in Research on Police-Citizen Relations," *Ethnic and Racial Studies* 37, no. 11 (2014), 1995–2013.

78. Nik Theodore and Robert Habans, "Policing Immigrant Communities: Latino Perceptions of Police Involvement in Immigration Enforcement," *Journal of Ethnic and Migration Studies* (2016), 1–19.

79. Ronald Weitzer, "The Puzzling Neglect of Hispanic Americans in Research on Police-Citizen Relations," *Ethnic and Racial Studies* 37, no. 11 (2014), 1995–2013.

80. Norman Conti and Patrick Doreian, "From Here On Out, We're All Blue: Interaction Order, Social Infrastructure, and Race in Police Socialization," *Police Quarterly* 17, no. 4 (2014), 414–447.

81. Kenneth Bolton Jr., "Shared Perceptions: Black Officers Discuss Continuing Barriers in Policing," *Policing: An International Journal of Police Strategies & Management* 26, no. 3 (2003), 386–399.

82. Norman Conti and Patrick Doreian, "From Here On Out, We're All Blue: Interaction Order, Social Infrastructure, and Race in Police Socialization," *Police Quarterly* 17, no. 4 (2014), 414–447.

83. Melissa Morabito and Tara O'Connor Shelley, "Representative Bureaucracy Understanding the Correlates of the Lagging Progress of Diversity in Policing," *Race and Justice* 5, no. 4 (2015), 330–355.

84. Hillary Potter, *Intersectionality and Criminology: Disrupting and Revolutionizing Studies of Crime* (Philadelphia, PA: Routledge, 2015).

85. K. Crenshaw, "Demarginalizing the Intersection of Race and Sex: A Black Feminist Critique of Antidiscrimination Doctrine, Feminist Theory and Antiracist Politics," *University of Chicago Legal Forum* (1989), 139–167.

86. Hillary Potter, "Intersectional Criminology: Interrogating Identity and Power in Criminological Research and Theory," *Critical Criminology* 21, no. 3 (2013), 305–318.

87. Susan Martin, "Outsider Within the Station House: The Impact of Race and Gender on African American Woman Police," *Social Problems* 41 (1994), 383–400, at 387.

88. David Murphy and John Worrall, "Residency Requirements and Public Perceptions of the Police in Large Municipalities," *Policing* 22 (1999), 327–342.

89. Steven Tuch and Ronald Weitzer, "The Polls: Trends, Racial Differences in Attitudes Toward the Police," *Public Opinion Quarterly* 61 (1997), 662; Sutham Cheurprakobkit, "Police–Citizen Contact and Police Performance: Attitudinal Differences Between Hispanics and Non-Hispanics," *Journal of Criminal Justice* 28 (2000), 325–336.

90. G. Hurst Yolander, James Frank, and Sandra Lee Browning, "The Attitudes of Juveniles Toward the Police: A Comparison of African American and White Youth," *Policing* 23 (2000), 37–53.

91. B. Kennedy, "Unraveling Representative Bureaucracy: A Systematic Analysis of the Literature," *Administration & Society* 46 (2012), 395–421.

92. H. F. Pitkin, *The Concept of Representation* (Berkeley, CA: University of California Press, 1967).

93. W. G. Skogan, Citizen Satisfaction with Police Services. In R. Baker and F. A. Meyer Jr. (eds.), *Evaluating Alternative Law Enforcement Policies* (pp. 29-42). Lexington, MA: Lexington Books, 1979.

94. S. Walker, "What a Good Police Department Looks Like: Professional, Accountable, Transparent, Self-Monitoring" (technical report). (Omaha, NE: University of Nebraska Omaha, 2014).

95. P. Manning, *Democratic Policing in a Changing World* (Boulder, CO: Paradigm Publishers, 2010).

96. Ronald Weitzer, "Is American Policing At a Crossroads?," *The Criminologist: The Official Newsletter of the American Society of Criminology* 4 (2015), 1–5.

97. http://dailycaller.com/2015/05/14/most-baltimore-cops -are-minorities/.

98. Ivan Y. Sun and Brian K. Payne, "Racial Differences in Resolving Conflicts: A Comparison between Black and White Police Officers," *Crime & Delinquency* 50, no. 4 (2004), 516–541.

99. Rod K. Brunson and Jacinta M. Gau, "Officer Race Versus Macro-Level Context: A Test of Competing Hypotheses About Black Citizens' Experiences With and Perceptions of Black Police Officers," *Crime & Delinquency* 61, no. 2 (2015), 213–242.

100. Lani Guinier, Gerald Torres, and Lani Guinier, *The Miner's Canary: Enlisting Race, Resisting Power, Transforming Democracy* (Boston, MA: Harvard University Press, 2009).

101. https://www.boston.gov/departments/police/police -cadet-program.

102. Jeremy M. Wilson, Erin Dalton, Charles Scheer, and Clifford A. Grammich, *Police Recruitment and Retention for the New Millennium* (Santa Monica, CA: RAND Corporation, 2010).

Police Discretion

Learning Objectives

LO1   Define the elements associated with police use of discretion.

LO2   Identify the sources of police discretion.

LO3   Compare and contrast the concepts of selective and full enforcement.

LO4   Identify the factors that influence the use of discretion.

LO5   List the ways the legal system influences discretion.

LO6   Compare and contrast the positive and negative aspects of discretion.

LO7   Explain the factors that lead the police to use force.

Chapter Outline

A few years ago, in the early evening, six gunshots rang out in the Wilson-Haverstick housing project in Trenton, New Jersey. One of these shots—from a .45 caliber handgun—struck seven-year-old Tajahnique Lee as she was riding her bicycle to her grandmother's apartment. The bullet passed in one cheek and out the other, knocking out two molars and clipping the tip of her tongue. Tajahnique was rushed to the emergency room at the local Trenton hospital. She survived.

As shocking as this near-tragedy was, the events that have since transpired have become even more troubling for the police. Trenton police believe that the stray bullet that struck Tajahnique was intended for a gang member, affiliated with the Gangsta Killer Bloods, who was driving through the housing complex. The police also believe that the bullet, along with the five others that were shot, came from the gun of a member of the local rival gang known as Sex Money Murder, part of the larger Bloods gang. The police interviewed more than 100 residents and rounded up an equal number of suspected gang members in the days following the shooting. This led to the arrest of two members of Sex Money Murder.

But this would be as far as the police would get. The one eyewitness to the shooting changed his story; others who had cooperated earlier in the investigation refused to talk further with police, and even the shooting victim's grandmother and other family members were not willing to talk with police. One neighbor—who wished to remain anonymous—said of the little girl who was shot: "What are you going to do, testify so they can come back and get the rest of your family?" Faced with little information and no witness willing to testify in court, prosecutors were forced to release the two suspects three weeks later. The case remains unsolved.[1]

Should the police have known that witnesses would not come forward in a case involving a gang called Sex Money Murder? Should they have used their discretion not to act, knowing full well the case would unravel? Or should they follow the full extent of the law?

How can police use their discretionary ability to encourage citizens to come forward and cooperate in solving cases and identifying suspects?

Define and understand the elements associated with police use of discretion.

discretion

The decision to act, or not to act, based on an individual police officer's judgment about the best course of action to take in a given situation.

▶ What Is Discretion?

Police discretion is the decision to act, or not to act, based on an individual police officer's judgment about the best course of action to take in a given situation. It is typically based on experience, training, philosophy, and knowledge as well as situational factors ranging from the time of day to whether a crowd is present. **Discretion** includes the decision to take a specific action, such as writing a crime report, making an arrest, or using force. It can also involve the decision to take informal action, such as when the police decide to let a contrite motorist off with a warning rather than issue a costly ticket as they might issue to a more belligerent driver.

Police use of discretion is most frequently associated with the order maintenance function and includes such activities as mediating disputes instead of making formal arrests and referring people to social service agencies and/or committing a person with a mental illness to health facility rather than arresting them for disorderly conduct. Police must use discretion to make all of these decisions in the course of a typical workday. The patrol officer's discretion often determines whether a noisy neighborhood dispute involves the crime of disturbing the peace or whether it can be controlled with street-corner diplomacy and the combatants sent on their way. Similarly, teenagers milling around in the shopping center parking lot can be brought in and turned over to the juvenile authorities or handled in a less formal and often in a more efficient manner.

Patrol officers are not the only personnel who use discretion as a routine part of the job. Discretion is also involved in the police investigatory process. Detectives must decide, for example, whether to declare a complaint in a case unfounded, to seek a warrant for a search or an arrest, or to conduct a surveillance, or to seek authorization for a wiretap.

Police command staff must also make discretionary decisions about administrative and policing priorities for the entire agency. These discretionary decisions involve the deployment of resources involving where and on what shifts will officers be assigned, whether officers will be directed to be assertive on traffic violations, or to give particular offenses more priority than others.

Even the department's administrative functioning has discretionary elements and decision making: Should educational level be included in the promotion decision; does the department need to reassess its hiring practices to accommodate to the need for diversity; and whether new focused squads should be created, such as an anti-terror unit.

This chapter examines the police use of discretion and looks at the forms it takes.

Police use discretion when deciding to make traffic stops. Do you believe that racial profiling still exists and that Black motorists are more likely to be stopped and ticketed than white drivers? What about the motorist shown in the photo: will he be ticketed or let off with a warning?

Avid_Creative/E+/Getty Images

The Discovery of Discretion

Discretion has always been an element of police work but was only formally identified in the 1950s by researchers at the American Bar Foundation (ABF).[2] Researchers observed the work of municipal police officers in the field and found that officers were not automatons who followed the letter of the law as previously suspected. They discovered that instead, police officers exercised a great deal of discretion in their dealings with the public.[3] Officers were found to have ignored violations of the law at some times but not others. Once police discretion was brought to the attention of the public, the question arose: What should be done to shape and control decision making?

The Use of Discretion

There is little question police officers use discretion in carrying out daily tasks. In some instances, the use of discretion becomes part of the public record. When police deprive people of their liberty, make a formal arrest, use force, or conduct interrogations, their actions typically become part of the public record. However, when they fail to act, there is little oversight on their decision making; their actions fall into what is referred to as **low visibility decision making**.[4] For example, a police officer stops a citizen, believing there is evidence of possible illegal activity. Upon finding no weapons or illegal substances the community member is free to go. Under these circumstances, the police officer's activity is not directly seen or supervised by anyone other than the community member. But because these stops often go unnoticed, we have few ways to determine if the stop was biased and disproportionately affects certain members of the community.

Some may argue that discretion is necessary and that unclear laws and expectations of community members require it. Furthermore, officers encounter a wide magnitude of situations and cannot have uniform responses to apply to their work. Nonetheless, the scope of discretion is not unlimited. Choices are controlled by both the courts and departmental administrative policies. The critical case of *Los Angeles v. Patel* (2015), in which the Supreme Court set out to shape the contours of police discretion is set out below.

low visibility decision making

Police officers often have no oversight on their decision making as much of their work is done alone.

Critical Thinking

Discretion allows officers to treat people differently. What are the pros and cons for discretion?

Sources of Police Discretion

 L02

Identify the sources of police discretion.

Since discretion is integral to how police do their jobs, it is also important to understand the source of that discretion.

Criminal Law

Part of an officer's discretion involves determining if a specific event or action consists of elements that comprise criminal offenses that fall within the boundaries of the law. This is not as easy as it sounds. It is not uncommon to see a group of police officers answering a call for service trying to determine whether a suspect can be arrested and on which charges. According to legal scholar Wayne LaFave in his classic writings, there are five problems with criminal statutes that create difficulties for the police and contribute to the need for discretion.[5]

Unclear law

Legal statutes are often ambiguous and vague. Legislators tend to make laws with little thought to if they can be understood and enforced. Sometimes this is because few politicians have served as police officers, have never actually enforced the law, and are not aware of how statutes can be interpreted. Regardless of the reasoning, a statute without clarity actually invites officers to interpret

Police & the Law

Los Angeles v. Patel (2015)

In 2015, the Supreme Court ruled in 2015 in *Los Angeles v. Patel* to strike down a Los Angeles city ordinance that allowed the police to inspect hotel and motel guest registries without permission from a judge. Police were expected to use their discretion in investigating crimes. They could ask to view the hotel or motel registries as often as they wanted, regardless of whether access to the documents resulted in the apprehension of an offender. A group of motel owners challenged the Los Angeles law. They said they were not troubled by its requirement that they keep records about their guests. But they objected to a second part of the ordinance, which allowed the police to look at the registries at any time without the owners' consent or a search warrant. The Supreme Court was concerned that his ordinance was in violation of citizens' Fourth and First Amendment rights.

In the majority opinion, Justice Sotomayor refers to the Fourth Amendment violation when she wrote that "the ordinance creates an intolerable risk that searches authorized by it will exceed statutory limits, or be used as a pretext to harass hotel operators and their guests." The Court was also concerned that allowing police to review registries affected the First Amendment rights of people staying in or using the facilities of the motels and hotels. In this case, police discretion directly implicated the freedom of those people to participate in political, social, and religious associations that rely on hotels to facilitate their meetings and conferences. By striking down the ordinance, the Supreme Court limited police discretion in their investigations of crime related to hotels and motels in Los Angeles.

Critical Thinking

1. What is truly private these days?

2. If you register in a hotel, do you expect privacy once you give a stranger your driver's license, credit card, and other personal information?

3. Should a line be drawn between what a hotel employee can see and what is available to the police?

Source: *Los Angeles v. Patel,* https://www.oyez.org/cases/2014/13-1175.

things as they see fit. That is why we have the use of discretion and resulting inconsistency.

If a law is unclear, it can be nullified by the courts under the void for vagueness doctrine. In other words, void for vagueness is a rule that applies to laws that are unclear. Vague law is seen as violating due process. This can be challenging for the police. What does "reasonable suspicion" or "probable cause" mean exactly? What is probable cause to one person is a mere hunch to another; hence, some warrantless arrests get overturned by judges. Sometimes criminal statutes can be so vague that they become impossible to enforce. Take the law of *obscenity* that penalizes the production, sale and distribution of offensive materials. Criminal statutes often say something like obscenity is defined as material that is obscene and appeals to prurient interests "per community standards" (Exhibit 9.1). Does this mean by the standards of your grandmother or a teenager? It is worth noting that at one time great works of fiction like Nabokov's *Lolita* and James Joyce's *Ulysses* were considered obscene. In short, there is a lot of room for interpretation in obscenity laws and many other criminal statutes.

Laws Are Often Too Broad

The second problem is that criminal statutes are frequently too broadly written. Broadly written statutes exist to prevent loopholes but this leaves a lot of room for different interpretations and discretionary decisions making by the police.

Exhibit 9.1

What Is Legally Obscene?

The U.S. Supreme Court established the test that judges and juries use to determine whether matter is obscene in three major cases: *Miller v. California*, 413 U.S. 15, 24-25 (1973); *Smith v. United States*, 431 U.S. 291, 300-02, 309 (1977); and *Pope v. Illinois*, 481 U.S. 497, 500-01 (1987). Based on these three cases, the federal law on obscenity contains the following components.

1. Whether the average person, applying contemporary adult community standards, finds that the matter, taken as a whole, appeals to prurient interests (i.e., an erotic, lascivious, abnormal, unhealthy, degrading, shameful, or morbid interest in nudity, sex, or excretion);

2. Whether the average person, applying contemporary adult community standards, finds that the matter depicts or describes sexual conduct in a patently offensive way (i.e., ultimate sexual acts, normal or perverted, actual or simulated, masturbation, excretory functions, lewd exhibition of the genitals, or sado-masochistic sexual abuse); and

3. Whether a reasonable person finds that the matter, taken as a whole, lacks serious literary, artistic, political, or scientific value.

Source: United States Department of Justice, Citizen's Guide to U.S. Federal Law on Obscenity, http://www.justice.gov/criminal-ceos/citizens-guide-us-federal-law-obscenity.

For example, statutes against gambling that leave a lot of room for interpretation. Legislatures really do not expect police to crack down on social gambling. It is not in the interest of public safety to prevent older adults from playing bingo in the town hall; nor is the weekly poker game considered a significant social problem. However, even social gambling can be a slippery slope. Take the risk that high stakes poker games held in players' homes have.[6] With entrance fees ranging from $100 to $1,000 and no security, these games may be attractive to robbers. While in-home poker games are clearly not analogous to casino gambling, they still seem to represent a step up from church bingo.

In defense of policymakers, it can be difficult to write laws that can be applied to every police situation. If every crime incident is somewhat different, lawmakers must write some laws more broadly. Not to mention that many laws have disparate impact on certain segments of the population and not others. Thus, at some level, the law has to be generally broad enough to fit many situations.

Critical Thinking

Why do you think lawmakers tend to make very broad laws that can label people who engage in non-dangerous behavior, for example, social gambling, as law violators?

Conflict with Moral Standards

Public expectations often conflict with moral standards. Many of our laws reflect a moral rather than a criminal standard and simply exist to appease a group of citizens. Thus, the legislator may not have intended strict and full enforcement since there is likely to be substantial differences in public opinion on a specific "moral issue." There have been laws against adultery on record since the founding of the United States. Nonetheless, the public does not really want the police to investigate these types of cases or make arrests for behavior if they involve consenting adults in the privacy of their bedrooms.

Nuisance Behaviors

A fourth problem with criminal law is that it can focus on nuisance behavior rather than truly criminal behavior. There are many criminal laws on the books that regulate behaviors that are essentially noncriminal. Take, for instance, laws regulating public intoxication. Alcoholism is known to be a disease, but we have laws aimed at controlling behaviors precipitated by drinking to excess, public intoxication, minor in possession, and open container laws. When police officers encounter someone publicly inebriated, they have choices: make an arrest, take the person home, help them get public transportation, refer them for treatment, or do nothing. This is a discretionary choice.

Outdated Laws

Another problem with using the criminal law to control police discretion is the existence of outdated laws. Take for instance laws prohibiting possession of small quantities marijuana. These laws may now seem outdated because they make illegal a substance that has been and is still being consumed by a significant number of Americans. It is also legal to possess marijuana in many states, including Colorado and Washington, but illegal in others such as Georgia. Should a college student in possession of 0.50 ounce of marijuana be arrested and sent to court in one state, while being legally within their rights in another? Does this serve a public purpose?

Administrative Rule Making

When an opioid crisis hit Massachusetts and all of New England, Chief Leonard Campanello of the Gloucester, Massachusetts police developed a revolutionary response that was announced on its Facebook page.[7] Under his authority, if a person who is addicted to illegal drugs and requests help from the Gloucester Police Department, an officer will take that person to the hospital, where they will be paired with a volunteer who will help guide them through the process of getting access to treatment. Here, a local police agency partnered with treatment centers to ensure that people who are addicted and need help get that assistance immediately.

What is most unusual is that Chief Campanello also decreed that anyone who comes in seeking help will not be arrested, even if they have drugs or drug paraphernalia in their possession. In response to a growing public health problem, Chief Campanello used his discretion to create an administrative environment where the police treated addiction as a public health problem rather than a criminal justice matter.

Most police departments maintain written rules and policies that are meant to shape and curb police discretion. The Boston Police Department's official rules of conduct contains one on the discharge of firearms that is set out in Exhibit 9.2.

In this situation, an official rule limits the discretion of the individual officer in using deadly force only if no other means are available to control the situation. A police officer must consider other means than using their weapon even if a fleeing felon has committed a crime in which they themselves used deadly force on a victim.

Departmental Work Environment

Work environment also helps shape police officers' use of discretion. Despite what is shown on television and in movies, many municipal and state police officers conduct their work alone, without a partner. It comes as no surprise then

Exhibit 9.2

Discharge of Firearms, Boston Police Department

Sec. 6 Discharge of Firearms: The law permits police officers to use reasonable force in the performance of their duties but only to the degree required to overcome unlawful resistance. This doctrine of "reasonable use of force" applies to the use of firearms as well as to nonlethal force. Also, because of their destructive potential, the use of firearms must be further restricted to the purpose for which they are issued, that of protecting life and limb. The discharge of a firearm by a member of the Department is permissible only when:

(A) There is no less drastic means available to defend oneself or another from unlawful attack which an officer has reasonable cause to believe could result in death or great bodily injury, or

(B) There is no less drastic means available to apprehend a fleeing felon when the officer has probable cause to believe that: (1) the subject has committed a felony during the commission of which they inflicted or threatened to inflict deadly force upon the victim, or (2) that there is substantial risk that the felon in question will cause death or great bodily injury if their apprehension is delayed.

Source: Boston Police Department Rules and Procedures, Rule 303 Section 6, https://static1.squarespace.com/static/5086f19ce4b0ad16ff15598d /t/52af5f30e4b0dbce9d22a80d/1387224880253/Rule+303.pdf.

---

that the level of supervision an officer receives will shape and control their use of discretion.

Within policing, the supervision of frontline officers varies greatly depending upon the agency. Some departments keep close control over officer behavior while others are less vigilant. The term **span of control** refers to the number of subordinates for which a supervisor is responsible, usually expressed as the ratio of supervisors to subordinates. While there is no national standard, The Federal Emergency Management Agency (FEMA) recommends a span of control ratio of one supervisor for every five employees. FEMA recommends that large local law enforcement agencies employ one supervisor for every eight to ten employees (FEMA employs one supervisor for every seven employees).

Departmental span of control is critical because if the decisions of patrol officers remain unchecked and invisible, it may result in a range of problems, from innocent mistakes to widespread corruption. Supervision seems to be a critical element employed to control discretion. Is this tool being used effectively? The Project on Policing Neighborhoods (POPN) that gathered data using systematic observations of patrol officers and lone supervisors (sergeants and lieutenants) in the Indianapolis, Indiana, Police Department (IPD) and the St. Petersburg, Florida, Police Department (SPPD).[8] Trained observers accompanied officers during their shifts and recorded field notes describing police-citizen encounters and other activities in which officers engaged. POPN researchers found that only one officer was present in over half of the citizen contacts and that most incidents did not involve consultation with a supervisor. This means that in fact the work environment of a typical patrol officer is solitary and unsupervised, allowing individual officers a great deal of discretion.

At this point, it should be clear to you that officers exercise a great deal of discretion in the course of their workday. Yet, there still exists the myth that police enforce and confront every criminal violation that they are made aware of. What is the myth of full enforcement and why does it exist?

span of control
The number of subordinates over which a supervisor has authority.

LO3

LO3
Compare and contrast the concepts of selective and full enforcement.

Full v. Selective Enforcement

According to the concept of full enforcement, police confront and deal with each and every single violation that is brought to their attention. Full enforcement is based on the premise that officers take an oath to enforce the law and that they should always enforce it to the fullest.[9] Is full enforcement a myth or reality?

Technically, officers *are* supposed to fully enforce the law. Yet, full enforcement is in fact a myth. In reality, the system would buckle if the police investigated every criminal act to the full extent of the law or arrested every person who, technically, committed a crime. The assembly line of justice would slow down and come to a halt if police made arrests or issued a summons for every legal violation; prosecutors would have too many cases to try and courts would be hopelessly clogged. In reality, there are not enough resources for full enforcement.

More importantly, would anyone want to live in a society with full enforcement? Community members want police to have the power to overlook the speeding violation of someone taking a pregnant person to the hospital to give birth or keep the first-time juvenile offender out of the criminal justice system. Instead, police practice selective enforcement, not enforcing all laws every time an offense occurs. Selective enforcement in reality is due to resource issues, the volume of crime incidents, and choices made by individual officers.

Is Full Enforcement Practical?

Most of us do not want the police to take formal action (e.g., make an arrest and issue a ticket every time we break the law). Would you want to get a ticket for going 66 in a 65 mile per hour zone? Nonetheless, while it may be what the public wants, there are some serious problems that are associated with the widespread use of selective enforcement. When officers selectively enforce the law, they open up themselves and their agencies to lawsuits because they are in some way denying people equal protection under the law. By not openly admitting the difficulty of engaging in full enforcement, agencies are *unlikely* to develop policies that would assist officers to engage in selective enforcement fairly. Without specific policies, agencies and police officers are practicing *unarticulated improvisation*. This means that patrol officers (the least experienced officers in the department) get to make policy decisions without oversight. At best, this could result in inconsistent police practices and other social problems (e.g., public distrust of the police) and at worst blatant racism and discrimination.

Despite the fact that selective enforcement is widespread, police departments are loathe to admit the practice to the public. This is because selective enforcement can be seen as demeaning police authority as well as raising concerns about equal protection and due process. More importantly, admitting to selective enforcement is admitting to violating state law that makes it a crime for officers to not enforce the law or act negligently.

Critical Thinking

As a tax paying citizen, do you expect the police to practice full enforcement at all times? Why or why not?

LO4
Identify the factors that influence the use of discretion.

Factors Influencing Discretion

When approaching a suspected violation of the law, police officers must make a decision whether to use formal or informal sanctions. Informal sanctions include giving a warning, making referral for social services, or doing nothing. Formal sanctions include issuing a citation and arrest. What factors influence police discretion? What causes an officer to issue a warning in one situation and formally arrest in another? Discretionary decisions are usually based on the officer's experience, training, philosophy, and knowledge but there are other factors that affect this decision making as well. Below some of the most important influences on discretion are discussed in some detail:

Situational Factors

Research has shown that situational factors tend to play a large role in police discretion. There are two types of situational factors: legal and extralegal.

Legal variables include offense type (felony vs. misdemeanor), offense severity, and suspect prior record among others. Offense severity is one critical element. There is relatively little, if any, discretion used for the most serious crimes such as murder and aggravated assault.[10] Far more personal discretion is available when police confront a suspect in a minor case involving an alleged simple assault or trespass.

Nonlegal factors include suspect race, gender, age, and attitude. So, a police officer encountering a young Black man accused of shoplifting may take very different action than they would if the suspect was a middle-age White woman, even though both had engaged in the exact same actions.

Victim Factors

Related to offense seriousness is the issue of who brings it to the attention of police. If, for example, a police officer stumbles upon an altercation or break-in, the discretionary response may be different from a situation in which the officer is summoned after a 9-1-1 call from the victim.[11] Police officers are reluctant to take action when a victim decides not to request official action and/or fail to file a complaint. According to Donald Black's observations, police officers held the view "if the victim does not care why should I?" or "if there is no complainant/victim there is no crime."[12] In general, then, the discretion to make an arrest is more likely following a victim complaint and unlikely if the victim does not want to press charges.[13]

Studies also show that the police are responsive if the victim or complainant prefers that they engage in a form of control/intervention (counseling, separate, advice, or referral) that does not include arrest. Police take formal action in about half of the encounters where victims demand an arrest be made while make arrests in less than 20 percent of cases where a victim does not express a preference. When victims request that no arrest be made, the likelihood of formal reaction drops to 7 percent.[14]

The relationship between the parties involved influences decision making and discretion. An altercation between two friends or relatives may be handled differently than an assault on a stranger. A case in point is policing domestic violence cases. Research indicates that police are reluctant to even respond to these kinds of cases because they are a constant source of frustration and futility.[15] Police sometimes intentionally delay responding to domestic disputes, hoping that by the time they get there the problem will be settled.[16] Victims, they believe, often fail to get help or change their abusive situation.[17]

Victims of Sexual Abuse

The use of discretion in sexual abuse and assault cases is unique and somewhat different than may be found in other criminal incidents. Here, victim characteristics are more likely to play a role in shaping police response than for crimes such as robbery or assault. Victims who seem vulnerable are not given top priority. They include those who share such characteristics as intellectual and/or physical disabilities, a history of mental health diagnoses, a history of alcohol and/or drug use, and former reporting sexual assault.[18]

Melissa S. Morabito, April Pattavina, and Linda Williams explored this relationship with data collected from the Los Angeles Police Department and Sheriff's Department.[19] They also found that victim credibility was a significant predictor of arrest: Incidents where police described victims as having mental health concerns or were substance users were significantly less likely to result in arrest than those victims who appeared unimpaired. Not surprisingly, they found that cases involving intimate partners and acquaintances have significantly higher odds of ending in arrest than incidents involving strangers; after all, in these cases, the victim knew the identity of their attacker, reducing the need for "detection."

For cases where the victim and attacker were previously non-acquainted, the results show that the probability of arrest increases where there is strong evidence and a cooperative victim. Another victim factor that influences the decision to pursue a case is victim credibility. Police are more willing to drop investigations when victims provide inconsistent accounts of the incident. Those who seem unsure of what happened, stumble over details, and change their story are the ones whose cases are the ones most likely to be dropped.[20]

Victims are often left out of policing discussions. One way that police departments can better serve victims is through the use of victim advocates. In the section below, we describe the role and responsibilities of victim advocates who are embedded in police agencies:

Environmental Factors

The degree of discretion that an officer will exercise is at least partially defined by the living and working environment.[21] This means that officers may defer to community expectations. For example, in some communities, front stoops are considered to be an extension of the living room. During the summer, when it is hot, it is not unusual to see families congregating in front of their buildings to socialize. This behavior is typical and acceptable and does not require police response. In other communities, this would be considered out of the ordinary and community members might call on the police to intervene. Thus, community values also shape officer decision making.

Overload Hypothesis

overload hypothesis

The theory that police workload influences discretion so that as workload increases, less time and attention can be devoted to new cases, especially petty crimes.

According to the **overload hypothesis**, community crime rates may shape officer discretion. As local crime rates increase, police resources become strained to the breaking point; officers are forced to give less time and attention to each new case. The amount of attention they can devote to less serious crimes decreases, and they begin to treat petty offenders more leniently than officers in less crime-ridden neighborhoods might have done.[22]

Departmental Factors

The number and quality of rules, policies, practices, and customs of the local police department are another influence on discretion.[23] These conditions vary from department to department and strongly depend on the judgment of the chief and others in the organizational hierarchy.[24] Efforts by the administration to limit

Careers in Policing

Victim Advocate

Victim advocates' responsibilities vary depending on the situation and the agency. Generally, they provide advocacy and support services to crime victims, including children and families who have experienced domestic violence and related crimes. Advocates ensure that victims receive the community services made available to them and develop partnerships to promote the long-term effectiveness of such services. In some instances, advocates provide victim-centered education and training to officers as well as community-based organizations. Based on job advertisements for victim advocates, the job includes the following responsibilities:

- Contact victims and direct them to the appropriate services available in the community

- Review crime reports and sort by type

- Review domestic history of the parties involved, write reports, and assign

- Update victim on case status

- Provide information/referrals according to needs

- Offer services to victims, including translation court accompaniment, support, and transportation

- Attend trainings, prepare training materials, and provide victim assistance training to new members and volunteers and interns

- Prepare victim assistance information and reports

- Contact victims for initial assessment and for follow-up to check on well-being; follow up on closed cases

- Assist with victim's compensation filing

- Attend community services/partners meetings and police events and provide appropriate training or informational briefings to the public as required

- Disseminate department or program information, which may be confidential in nature, to appropriate authorities, personnel, or the general public if applicable

or shape the behavior of the officer on patrol may prompt it to issue directives aimed at influencing police conduct. In an effort to crack down on a particular crime—such as adolescent drug use—the department can create a strict arrest and referral policy for those engaging in that crime.

A patrol officer's supervisor can influence discretion especially when the span of control is quite high. Departments with a high ratio of sergeants to patrol officers may experience fewer officer-initiated actions than ones in which fewer eyes are observing the action in the streets.

Supervisory style may also affect how police use discretion. Patrol officers supervised by sergeants who are take-charge types and like to participate in high levels of activity in the field themselves spend significantly more time per shift engaging in self-initiated and community policing or problem-solving activities than in administrative activities. In contrast, officers with supervisors whose style involves spending time mentoring and coaching subordinates are more likely to devote significantly more attention to engaging in administrative tasks.[25]

Department makeup may also affect discretion. Police agencies with higher levels of minority representation in the ranks seem to be less likely to display racial profiling in the use of discretion; for example, in issuing of citations. One reason: Police departments whose officers resemble the citizens that they patrol help foster rapport between officers and citizens that produces more cooperation and less conflict.[26]

Peer Factors

Police discretion is often subject to peer pressure.[27] Police officers experience a degree of social isolation because the job involves strange working conditions and hours, including being on 24-hour call, and an unwillingness to spend time with old friends or family members who may be prone to break the law or that wouldn't understand the stressors that an officer faces. At the same time, officers must handle irregular and emotionally demanding encounters involving the most personal and private aspects of people's lives. As a result, police officers turn to their peers for both on-the-job advice and off-the-job companionship, essentially forming a subculture that provides a source of status, prestige, and reward.

The peer group affects how police officers exercise discretion on two distinct levels. First, in an obvious, direct manner, other police officers dictate acceptable responses to street-level problems by displaying or withholding approval in office discussions. Second, the officer who takes the job seriously and desires the respect and friendship of others will take their advice, abide by their norms, and seek out the most experienced and most influential patrol officers on the force and follow their behavioral models.

Suspect Behavior and Characteristics

Researchers have also found that suspect behavior and characteristics weigh heavily in the use of discretionary powers.[28]

Suspect Demeanor

The attitude and appearance of the offender is one of the most important influences. If an offender is surly, talks back, or otherwise challenges the officer's authority, formal action is more likely to be taken.[29] According to this view, a negative demeanor will result in formal police action.[30] Suspects who behave in a civil manner, accept responsibility for their offense, and admit their guilt are less likely to be sanctioned than those who display a less courteous demeanor.[31]

The role of **suspect demeanor** in the use of discretion is still open to debate. Some studies question whether demeanor actually has an effect on case outcome unless the suspect becomes actively aggressive; using bad language or being defiant may actually have little effect on an experienced officer who is used to that kind of behavior.[32] However, suspects who physically resist a police command are much more likely to receive some form of physical coercion in return and much more likely to be arrested and processed through the system.[33]

Therefore, police officers' response to a suspect's challenge to their authority is dependent on the way the challenge is delivered.[34] Verbal challenges are typically met with verbal responses, and physical with physical, but on occasion, an aggravated or frustrated officer may meet verbal responses with physical force.

Suspect Race

While it should not be the case, it is widely accepted that race also shapes police discretion and decision making. Black citizens are more likely to receive formal treatment (e.g., an arrest, rather than a summons or a warning, than White citizens).[35] In a study of police in two major midwestern cities, Jackson and Boyd (2005) found that the percentage of racial minorities in a patrol area

suspect demeanor
The outward behavior, attitude, and appearance of the offender.

Critical Thinking

Explain how the actions or attitude of a suspect plays into the way discretion is used by police.

has a significant impact on police formal action. As the percentage of minority citizens in the area, the more likely the police would use their law enforcement authority (i.e., arrest).[36] There is also evidence that suspect's race shapes the decision to use force, especially when there is incongruence between officer and suspect race; White officers are more likely to use force if the suspect is Black.[37] Why does race matter?[38] The issue race plays in police decision making and the use of discretion will be revisited and expanded in the following chapter on police misconduct.

Suspect Socioeconomic Status

Whether a suspect appears wealthy and respectable or poor and disreputable should have no effect on police discretion. Yet there are numerous research studies that show that social class plays an important role in police-citizen interactions. Take for instance what happens when a suspect asks why they are being arrested, stopped, searched, and/or detained. In most, but not all, instances, an officer will answer the question, a practice which may diffuse the situation. Nonetheless, not all suspects are treated equally; wealthy citizens are more likely to gain police cooperation than citizens of lower socioeconomic status.[39]

Suspect Gender

A suspect's gender also has an effect on the application of discretion. Research typically shows that female suspects are less likely to be arrested than male suspects; the reason is male police officers are socialized to protect women and act out of "chivalry" to treat women more leniently than men.[40] In contrast, female police officers may act in a more gender-neutral manner and therefore may be less likely to use discretion to benefit women. An example is Amy Farrell's analysis of almost 150,000 traffic stops made in 37 Rhode Island communities. Farrell found that while women are less likely to receive traffic citations than men, the gender makeup of the individual departments has a significant impact on the outcome of traffic stops: the more female police officers in the department the more likely that female drivers will receive citations; the chivalry effect will be neutralized.[41]

Suspect Age

A suspect's age also influences police discretion. Young people tend to be arrested more often and dealt with more harshly than their older counterparts.[42] Older people tend to get more lenient treatment than young adults.

Critical Thinking

Can you list a number of officer-related characteristics that you believe influences their use of discretion?

Ronnie Kaufman/The Image Bank/Getty Images

Do you believe that the personal characteristics of police and citizens influence their interactions? Are police more willing to help an elderly person cross the street while being less accommodating to someone who is young, discourteous, and poor? And would the gender of the officer make a difference in how citizens are treated?

Exhibit 9.3

Factors That Influence Police Discretion

Category	Elements
Crime factors	Offense severity, officer's perceptions of offense severity, reasons for the call, wishes of the complainant
Victim factors	Victim–offender relationship, credibility of the victim
Environmental factors	Community culture and values
Departmental factors	Policies and orders, supervisory style and control
Peer factors	Friendships, norms, subculture
Suspect behavior and characteristics	Suspect demeanor, resistance, race, gender, socioeconomic status, and age
Officer characteristics	Officer's education, experience, and gender

Officer Characteristics

Not only do suspect characteristics influence discretion, so do the characteristics of police officers themselves. Police officer gender may have an impact on discretion. Researchers have found that female officers are less likely to use force than male officers.[43] Because female officers seem to have the ability to avoid violent encounters with citizens and to deescalate potentially violent arrest situations, they are typically the target of fewer citizen complaints.[44] Yet, the research also suggests that there is an interaction between organizational characteristics and individual officer characteristics. Amie Schuck and Cara Rabe-Hemp found that increasing female representation in police organizations causes changes in norms and practices in the organization's institutional structure. They suggest that the relationship between gender diversity and citizen's complaints of inappropriate use of force is a function of the number and quality of rules, policies and mechanisms designed to capture and quantify complaints.[45]

Education influences a police officer's use of discretion. Some research has found that police officers with a bachelor's degree, especially those who were college educated before they became sworn officers, are less likely to abuse their legal authority.[46] Nonetheless, while officer education is a very important issue, researchers have yet to reach any consensus on whether having higher education makes any difference in police us of discretion.[47]

There is some evidence that police officers' career aspirations affect their decision making. One study found that those officers who desired promotion tended to make the most arrests.[48] The factors that influence discretion are summarized in Exhibit 9.3.

LO5

List the ways the legal system influences discretion.

The Criminal Justice System and Police Discretion

Police discretion is also shaped by decision making by other actors in the criminal justice system. It affects how decisions are made and is also influenced by decision making further up the process.

Of all criminal justice decision makers, police discretion is most highly influenced by the county district attorney or local state's attorney. Prosecutors, among the most influential actors in the criminal justice system, have discretion to take a case, to plea bargain, and to decline prosecution (among others). Recent research has uncovered that prosecutors might also influence the police arrest decision. In their study of sexual assault complaints made to the Los Angeles Police Department and Los Angeles Sheriff's Department, Cassia Spohn and Katharine Tellis found that police often consulted with prosecutors prior to making the arrest decision.[49] This means that in some situations, having probable cause was not enough for police to make an arrest. Instead, prosecutors might be influencing police decision making—having enough evidence for probable cause to effect on arrest, is not the same amount of evidence to prove beyond a reasonable doubt that someone is guilty. Police in these cases have a downstream orientation, meaning that they are considering the next phases of the criminal justice system in deciding their own responses to offenders.[50] It is important to think about how prosecutors and police work together and how it affects police business.

The CSI Effect

Prosecutors are always under a lot of pressure to prove cases in court and this can also influence which cases the police decide to present to them. The CSI effect influences prosecutorial decisions and has a trickle-down influence.

The so-called "CSI effect," named for the popular television programs, is concerned with the real-world implications of Hollywood's fictional spin on the forensic sciences and criminal investigations. Prosecutors feel pressured to only bring cases that have forensic evidence because jurors have come to expect this based on their experience watching television. Attempts to satisfy such unrealistic expectations may possibly compromise the pursuit of justice.

nolle prosequi
The decision by a district attorney to drop a case; literally, "will no longer prosecute."

More generally, discretion is needed in the criminal justice system. If discretion is removed from the police, it is then moved to the prosecutor. For example, if police make an arrest for every criminal violation that they see, prosecutors will more carefully select which cases they choose to prosecute. District attorney's or local state's attorney's offices have budgetary constraints and can't hire unlimited staff. Therefore, they may choose to *nolle prosequi* cases that they do not think are in the interest of justice. In this scenario, by limiting police discretion and requiring full enforcement of the law, the discretion moves to the prosecutor.

In some instances, prosecutors are governed by no-drop policies, where they are required to prosecute cases. In these scenarios, the discretion is then shifted to the judge, who must decide what is an appropriate use of the courts time. Because there are too many criminal violations

DNA samples collected from crime scenes are processed in both public and private labs. According to what is known as the "CSI Effect" after watching the popular TV series, jurors expect conclusive forensic evidence from the prosecution if they wish to secure a conviction.

to process through the criminal justice system, we must have discretion somewhere within. The question remains is how that discretion should be spread out throughout the criminal justice actors.

LO6

Compare and contrast the positive and negative aspects of discretion.

Aspects of Police Discretion

It is clear to most of us that discretion is not all bad. We want officers to have the discretion to use their professional judgment based on their experience on the job. We also like it when a police officer gives us a warning rather than a ticket when we don't fully stop at a stop sign or are driving a few miles over the speed limit. What are the positive aspects of discretion?

Positive Aspects

If officers use good judgment, it can help limit the use of the criminal sanction in an already overburdened system. The criminal justice system can't possibly process every criminal violation. Discretion allows police to act as gatekeepers and decide that sometimes an offense should be overlooked or treated informally. Sometimes an arrest can be a bad thing. If you think about a volatile crowd in a protest, officers have to make a decision about how to exercise crowd control. If citizens are acting rowdy or don't have a permit to assemble in a large group, police can choose to make an arrest—but is singling out one person's arrest in a large crowd really in the interest of public safety?

Using Common Sense

Allowing officers to use their common sense to control the situation is another positive aspect of discretion. Although there are a multitude of situations where an officer could arrest someone, this might not always be good public policy. For example, a person experiencing homelessness may be loitering in front of and inside of a place of business, panhandling and trying to stay warm during the winter. Many of these behaviors can be described as criminal: loitering, panhandling, and trespassing among others. In these situations, we may prefer that police refer and offer transport to shelter rather than always make an arrest.

Finally, sometimes individualized justice can be helpful both for community relations and the ultimate goal of public safety. When we think about juveniles for example, as more police officers are assigned to schools, we have seen an increase in criminalization of behaviors that were once considered to be relatively harmless.[51] For instance, students have been arrested for making spitballs or cutting class. In her book *A Return to Justice*, Ashley Nellis argues that the juvenile justice system is not an appropriate response to most acts of delinquency. Rather, Nellis notes that the public benefits far more from a broad based prevention strategy than juvenile incarceration. Similarly, sometimes a warning is enough as is returning a juvenile offender to a parent or guardian for discipline. Accordingly, we really don't always want to throw the book at everyone. It is better public policy to give officers discretion to make these decisions particularly when they involve vulnerable populations such as young people.

Negative Aspects

If properly applied, the exercise of discretion by police may contain and distribute significant social benefits. Nonetheless, unchecked discretion can sometimes deteriorate into discrimination, violence, and other abusive practices. What are some of these specific problems associated with police discretion?

Discrimination and Racism

Discretion implies that not everyone is treated equally under the law. Inequality and discrimination may occur if the police abuse discretion and make decisions based solely on race, ethnicity, or gender. This violates our democratic principle of equal protection under the law as specified in the Fourteenth Amendment to the U.S. Constitution. It can be argued that if officers do not follow the letter of the law, this is a denial of due process. It is important to remember that once a person is arrested, even if they have been exonerated later through the courts, they now have a permanent arrest record that has a long-term effect not only on the treatment they receive from the criminal justice system but also can have an immediate and long-term effect on their private life.

Being arrested can affect a person's ability to obtain a job or even enter certain sectors of employment. Getting arrested signifies an increased risk of unhealthy lifestyle, violence involvement, and violent victimization.[52] Evidence also suggests that young people with arrest records have lower levels of earnings, longer bouts with unemployment, greater work instability, diminished educational levels, and a greater risk of destructive family conflicts. Because this issue is so important, it will be discussed in greater detail in the following chapter.

Procedural Injustice

At best, uncontrolled discretion produces procedural injustice, which eventually results in discriminatory treatment of racial and ethnic minorities. When stories circulate about police abusing their discretion, the result creates public relations and legalistic problems. At worst, procedural injustice can create a lack of trust between police and the communities that they serve. Trust is essential for police to effectively do their jobs. Researchers have found that when officers treat citizens with dignity and respect, the citizens are more likely to be satisfied with the experience, to accept police decisions, and even to participate in crime prevention programs.[53] Research also indicates that precinct-level efforts to ensure that officers are respectful of citizens can help lower the number of complaints and improve community relations.[54] Police must pay attention to procedural justice, a concern with making decisions that are arrived at through procedures viewed as fair.[55] If people view procedures as unfair, they will be less likely to support police in their crime-fighting efforts.[56]

Poor Personnel Management

Poor personnel management and policy development can also be the result of uncontrolled discretion.[57] The myth of full enforcement forces police agencies to create policies that do not acknowledge the use of discretion. This means that new officers must rely on their judgment about the course of action in a multitude of new situations without the benefit of policy to guide them. Officers rarely get guidance from supervisors or policy that aids their decision to use formal versus informal sanctions when responding to a call. If discretion is unregulated and agencies lack guidelines to help officers navigate the complexities of policing, we should expect problems.

Legal Violations

Officers who decide not to arrest someone when they legally can are presumably taking on the responsibilities of judges and juries. It could be argued that they are, in a sense, exonerating that person. The other actors in the criminal justice system do not get the opportunity to weigh the evidence. It can be argued that police who overuse discretion are overstepping their role.

Improper use of discretion can lead to a spate of lawsuits focusing on improper use of power. An example of this is the enforcement of domestic violence laws. In the 1970s, police officers were advised not to make arrests because it was a private family matter. Victims sued their local police departments, arguing that not arresting offenders based on their relationship with the victim is denial of equal protection. Successful lawsuits were filed against police departments across the country for denial of equal protection based on the victim's relationship with the offender. In one such lawsuit, *Thurman v. City of Torrington*, set out below, the court ruled that a police officer may not knowingly refrain from interference in domestic violence cases, and may not "automatically decline to make an arrest simply because the assaulter and his victim are married to each other." The courts ruled that this is a denial of equal protection.

Controlling and Improving the Use of Discretion

Some people believe that discretion should be abolished and that police officers should NEVER be able to nullify the criminal law by choosing not to arrest.[58] This

Police & the Law

Thurman v. City of Torrington (1984)

Between early October 1982 and June 10, 1983, Tracey Thurman, a woman living in the city of Torrington, Connecticut, and others on her behalf, notified the city of Torrington through police officers of the city of repeated threats upon her life and the life of her child made by her estranged spouse, Charles Thurman. Attempts to file complaints by Tracey Thurman against her estranged spouse in response to his threats of death and maiming were ignored or rejected by both individual police officers and the city of Torrington. Only after stabbing and trying to kill Tracey Thurman, was Charles Thurman finally arrested and taken into custody. Tracey Thurman sued the city of Torrington, Connecticut, and the police department, claiming a failure of equal protection under the law. With this lawsuit, filed in 1984, Thurman was the first woman in America to sue a town and its police department for violating her civil rights, claiming the police had ignored the violence because she was married to the perpetrator. The U.S. District Court for Downstate Connecticut agreed with Tracey Thurman's argument and stated:

> City officials and police officers are under an affirmative duty to preserve law and order, and to protect the personal safety of persons in the community. This duty applies equally to women whose personal safety is threatened by individuals with whom they have or have had a domestic relationship as well as to all other persons whose personal safety is threatened, including women not involved in domestic relationships. If officials have notice of the possibility of attacks on women in domestic relationships or other persons, they are under an affirmative duty to take reasonable measures to protect the personal safety of such persons in the community.

Critical Thinking

1. Do you agree that the police should be liable when they do not take action? After all, how can they accurately predict that someone will commit future crimes?

2. Should the police be held legally responsible if, let's say, they arrested Charles Thurman, let him go the next day, and then he stabbed his estranged wife?

Source: *Thurman v. City of Torrington* (1984), http://www.ncdsv.org /publications_thurman_torrington.html.

is unlikely to happen. By taking discretion from the police, we would enhance the discretion that prosecutors, judges, and corrections have in their business dealings. By forcing police to make more arrests, we merely push the discretion to the next phase of the criminal justice system. What can be done to improve the use of discretion?

Improving the quality of discretion is not an easy fix because it involves altering many different police personnel practices. To enhance officer decision making, police departments could provide more comprehensive training around the use of discretion. Another option is to adopt informal bureaucratic controls. This means that the police agency could develop a means of controlling discretion informally to limit mistakes. One way to accomplish this is through more coaching and mentoring of officers (which is never a bad idea).

Informal bureaucratic controls, however, are not always enough and agencies may be required to instead adopt formal bureaucratic controls. Police departments can implement restrictive rules as part of the standard operating procedure (SOP) and evidence suggests that they do control police behavior.[59] SOPs include rules about responding to domestic violence calls, engaging in high-speed pursuits and firearms discharges among others. In a now-classic study, James Fyfe conducted an analysis of the implementation of bureaucratic rules regarding firearm discharges in the NYPD after the department created a regulation requiring officers to justify any firearm discharges with a written report.[60] Fyfe found that the passage of a restrictive firearm discharge policy resulted in an overall decrease in the number of discharges. A side benefit is that officer injuries also decreased.

Another problem associated with the implementation of formal bureaucratic controls is that when there are too many rules (especially if perceived as unfair), it creates an environment conducive to lying—code of silence. Another problem is that SOPs are already quite detailed and adding too many regulations makes it difficult for officers to keep track of their requirements.

Accreditation

Another way of making sure that officers use guided discretion is through accreditation of departmental procedures. The Commission on the Accreditation of Law Enforcement Agencies (CALEA) was created in 1979 to serve as an accrediting body that would improve the delivery of police services.[61] The process is voluntary and there are no penalties for agencies that choose not to be accredited. While the accreditation process can be expensive, it is a way to ensure that all police departments have the minimum policies necessary to guide police discretion. Accreditation gets all departments operating at an enhanced level.

Citizen Oversight

More citizen oversight is another suggested way to reduce the misuse of uncontrolled discretion. By allowing the public to have input on policies and review complaints, agencies can make sure that officer use of discretion is in line with community values and mores.[62] Take for instance what happened when departments began the use of body cameras, a policy designed to increase the transparency of police-citizen interactions. Some departments found that members of the public, rather than applauding this new policy, soon began to question the use of this video footage . Was it a threat to their privacy? Could it fall into the wrong hands and be used against them? Policies are needed to clarify who will have access to the footage and how long the city will be required to keep it. A clear policy in this situation is important to put in place before an incident occurs.[63]

David R. Frazier Photolibrary, Inc./Alamy Stock Photo

The courts can be used as one method of holding police officers accountable for misconduct. Citizens can sue in court if they believe that they were treated unfairly by police. Judgments have been in the millions of dollars.

In some cities, citizen oversight is well documented and regulated. In Hartford Connecticut, there is a Civilian Police Review Board that reviews cases of possible misconduct by Hartford police and produces its own independent findings, separate from the police department's disciplinary process. There is also an inspector general of Hartford that investigates complaints against city officers under a set of reforms passed by the city council. If the findings of the Civilian Police Review Board differ from the findings of the police department (or chief), the case goes to the inspector general for binding arbitration. This oversight adds a level of accountability to the police and serves to help instill much-needed trust in the police department.

Legal Options and the Courts

We know that individuals can sue the local government or specifically the police department if they believe that they have been treated unfairly. The federal government can also sue. These lawsuits are referred to as pattern or practice suits. These suits allege that the defendant has systematically engaged in discriminatory activities. The Department of Justice has sued police agencies that have a history of violating citizen rights. Most departments have settled these suits informally. In one recent case, the Justice Department opened a civil pattern or practice investigation into Baltimore Police Department (BPD), pursuant to the Violent Crime Control and Law Enforcement Act of 1994. The department's investigation of BPD sought to determine whether there are systemic violations of the Constitution or federal law by officers of BPD. The investigation focused on BPD's use of force, including deadly force, and its stops, searches, and arrests, as well as whether there is a pattern or practice of discriminatory policing.

The courts overall play an important role in controlling police discretion. Since we have an adversarial form of justice, it is assumed the system will catch improper use of discretion. To accomplish this, complaints must sometimes go all the way to the Supreme Court to clarify how police are allowed to use their discretion. For example, in *Rodriguez v. United States* (2015), the Court clarified when police are allowed to bring drug sniffing dogs to traffic stops.

LO7

Explain the factors that lead the police to use force.

Police Discretion and the Use of Force

Police have the discretion to use force when necessary and the use of force has been one of the most controversial aspects of policing. When should force be used? How much is proper? Is force being applied equally and without racial and/or ethnic bias? Because police officers are the only government officials who routinely use force within the United States, it is important to know how it is being used and to take steps to make sure it is applied fairly and efficiently.

Police & the Law

Rodriguez v. United States (2015)

In 2012, Dennys Rodriguez was issued a citation after being stopped traveling on the shoulder of the highway—a violation of Nebraska law. The stop was conducted by a Nebraska police officer who happened to have his K-9 dog in his cruiser. When Rodriguez refused to consent to let the drug dog walk around the outside of his vehicle, the officer called for backup, thereby prolonging the stop by an additional eight minutes. The dog alerted the officer to the presence of drugs in the vehicle—specifically, methamphetamine.

Rodriguez was indicted on federal drug charges, but his lawyer moved to suppress the evidence seized from the vehicle on the grounds, among others, that the officer had prolonged the traffic stop without reasonable suspicion in order to conduct the dog sniff. The case eventually made its way to the U.S. Supreme Court. Writing for the majority, Justice Ruth Bader Ginsburg held that "a police stop exceeding the time needed to handle the matter for which the stop was made violates the Constitution's shield against unreasonable seizures" In sum, a traffic stop becomes unlawful if "it is prolonged beyond the time reasonably required to complete the mission of issuing a ticket for the violation."

Critical Thinking

1. Do you agree with the decision in this case? Here, the police took action but the Court ruled that they took too much action under the circumstances.

2. What do you take away from the decisions of *Rodriguez* and *Thurman v. Torrington*: Are the police legally damned if they do, damned if they don't?

Source: *Rodriguez v. United States* (2015), https://www.oyez.org/cases/2014/13-9972.

Situational Factors

Race may be a factor that determines the outcome of police–citizen encounters, but it is certainly not the only one. The suspect's behavior is also a significant determinant of police response than age or race. Recent research by Mark Morgan and his associates finds that suspect resistance exerted a strong influence on the likelihood of police officers using force. Suspects who engage in any form of resistance at the point of arrest may be more likely to be met with force because (1) officers associate noncompliance with degree of guilt, (2) resistance poses an immediate threat to other citizens, and (3) alternative measures (e.g., verbal de-escalation) may not be feasible, given the situational context.[64]

Another study by William Terrill reviewed 3,544 police–suspect encounters and found that situational factors often influence the extent to which force is applied. Use of force seems to escalate when a police officer offers to give a suspect a second chance (such as "Dump the beer out of your car, and I'll let you go"), but when the suspect hesitates or actively defies the order, officers are more likely to react aggressively. People who resist police orders or actually grapple with officers are much more likely to be the target of force than those who are respectful, passive, and noncombative.[65]

Suspect and Police Officer Characteristics

Young men are more likely than older women to be the target of police force. Morgan and his associates find that police officers might view male suspects as being more blameworthy or threatening during the course of an interaction, while having a more sanguine view of female suspects. Likewise, older people may be

A police SWAT team practices a forced entry into a hostage situation. Does police officer style influence the decision to use force? Would a crime control oriented officer, like those shown here, be more likely to use force than one who is more social service oriented? Should officers be trained not to use lethal force and to deescalate, rather than escalate conflict?

treated more leniently than the young because police officers consider them more likely to have committed a crime and more capable of resistance if they chose to fight back.[66]

Officer characteristics may also shape the discretion to use force. Researchers have found that female officers are less likely to use force than male officers.[67] Because female officers seem to have the ability to avoid violent encounters with citizens and to deescalate potentially violent arrest situations, they are typically the target of fewer citizen complaints.[68] More experienced officers have been found to use force less often than rookies and more likely to employ words and gestures designed to deescalate the situation.[69]

The Use of Deadly Force

deadly force

The intentional use of a firearm or other instrument resulting in a high probability of death.

On some occasions the police use of force results in the suspect's death or significant bodily harm. The Federal Bureau of Investigation (FBI) defines **deadly force** as "the intentional use of a firearm or other instrument resulting in a high probability of death."[70] Although the media depict hero cops in a constant stream of deadly shoot-outs in which scores of bad guys are killed, the number of people killed by the police each year is somewhere around 1,000.[71] The trend has been for a decline in the annual number of shootings.

Although these data are encouraging, some researchers believe that the actual number of police shootings is far greater and may be hidden or masked by a number of factors. For example, coroners may be intentionally or accidentally underreporting police homicides by almost half.[72]

The justification for the use of deadly force can be traced to English common law, in which almost every criminal offense was a felony and bore the death penalty. The use of deadly force in the course of arresting a felon was considered expedient, saving the state the burden of trial and execution (the "fleeing felon" rule).[73]

When Deadly Force Can Be Used

The use of deadly force has been restricted by a series of Supreme Court cases. In 1985, in the case of *Tennessee v. Garner*, the U.S. Supreme Court ruled that the fleeing felon rule was unconstitutional and set out guidelines when deadly force can be used.[74] The Court struck down a Tennessee statute that allowed a police officer to "use all the necessary means to effect the arrest" of an individual whom the officer suspected was fleeing or forcibly resisting detention.

The Garner case was a result of a burglary gone wrong. During a chase, a Memphis police officer shot 15-year-old Edward Eugene Garner with a hollow tip bullet to prevent Garner from escaping over a fence. Garner was suspected of breaking into a nearby house (burglary). The officer admitted that before he shot, he saw no evidence that Garner was armed and "figured" he was unarmed. The bullet hit Garner in the back of the head. Garner was taken to the hospital, where he died a short time later.

Garner's father sued the officer and the city, seeking damages for violations of his son's constitutional rights. The district court entered judgment for the defendants because Tennessee law authorized the officer's actions. The court also felt that Garner had assumed the risk of being shot by recklessly attempting to escape. The U.S. Court of Appeals for the Sixth Circuit reversed, holding that killing a fleeing suspect is a "seizure" under the Fourth Amendment and such a seizure would only be reasonable if the suspect posed a threat to the safety of police officers or the community at large.

Justice Byron White wrote for the majority, first agreeing with the Sixth Circuit's determination that apprehension by use of deadly force is a seizure, then framing the legal issue as whether the totality of the circumstances justified the seizure. In order to determine the constitutionality of a seizure, White reasoned, the court must weigh the nature of the intrusion of the suspect's Fourth Amendment rights against the government interests, which justified the intrusion.

The use of deadly force against a subject is the most intrusive type of seizure possible because it deprives the suspect of his life, and White held that the state failed to present evidence that its interest in shooting unarmed fleeing suspects outweighs the suspect's interest in his own survival: "The use of deadly force to prevent the escape of all felony suspects, whatever the circumstances, is constitutionally unreasonable."

In the second case, *Graham v. Connor* (1989), the Court ruled that the issue of whether a police officer used excessive force "requires careful attention to the facts and circumstances of each particular case, including the severity of the crime at issue, whether the suspect poses an immediate threat to the safety of the officers or others, and whether he is actively resisting arrest or attempting to evade arrest by flight."[75] In an unanimous decision, the Court found the "reasonableness of a particular use of force must be judged from the perspective of a reasonable officer on the scene, and its calculus must embody an allowance for the fact that police officers are often forced to make split-second decisions about the amount of force necessary in a particular situation."

The third case, *Kisela v. Hughes* (2018), involved a 2010 shooting incident that took place in Tucson, Arizona.[76] Officers were called to a home following a report that a woman was brandishing a knife. When they arrived, they drew their weapons when they saw Amy Hughes come out of the home's front door holding a kitchen knife. Hughes was told to drop the knife at least twice and, when she refused, Officer Andrew Kisela shot her four times, hitting her in the stomach, hip, arm, and knee. Hughes sued for damages, charging that Kisela had used excessive force.

When the trial court ruled that the force was reasonable, and the Ninth U.S. Circuit Court of Appeals reversed, Kisela then appealed to the Supreme Court. In its decision, the Court ruled that excessive force is an area of the law where the result depends heavily on what happened in each case. Therefore, officers are entitled to immunity unless previous cases clearly tell them a specific use of force is unlawful. In its ruling, the Court was influenced by Kisela's claim that he shot Hughes because he believed she was a threat to her roommate, who was standing only a few feet away. The Court also noted that the officer was separated from the two by a chain-link fence and that Hughes failed to acknowledge two commands to drop the knife. In a dissent, Justice Sotomayor noted that Hughes was holding the knife down at her side, didn't raise it in the direction of her roommate or anyone else, didn't appear agitated, and didn't verbally threaten to harm anyone. She called Kisela's conduct "unreasonable" and pointed out that two other officers didn't fire.

Putting these decisions together, the police use of deadly force is legal only if the officer believes that that suspect presents an imminent danger and that the use of force is the only option available to save the life of the officer or a civilian. Deadly force cannot be used to subdue a nonthreatening, unarmed suspect even if they are attempting to flee the scene of a crime.

Factors Related to the Decision to Use of Deadly Force

Is police use of deadly force a random occurrence, or are there social, legal, and environmental factors associated with its use? The following seven patterns have been related to police shootings:

- **Local and national violence levels.** The higher the levels of violence in a community, the more likely police in the area will use deadly force.[77] A number of studies have found that fatal police shootings were closely related to reported national violent crime rates and criminal homicide rates. Police officers kill civilians at a higher rate in years when the general level of violence in the nation is higher. The perception of danger may contribute to the use of violent means for self-protection.[78]

- **Self-defense.** One reason for the use of deadly force is a claim of self-defense. According to the FBI's most recent annual *Law Enforcement Officers Killed and Assaulted* (LEOKA) report, of the roughly 750,000 police officers in the country, only about 100 law enforcement officers are now being killed in the line of duty each year. Of the more than 100 killed, 55 were feloniously killed and 51 were killed accidentally, for an average of 106 killed in a single year. The likelihood of an officer being killed on duty reflects the crime rate: more officers were killed in the line of duty during the 1990s, when crime rates were higher, than today as crime rates have fallen.

Of the officers who were feloniously killed:

- The average age was 37.
- The average tenure in law enforcement was 10 years.
- Three were female and 52 were male.[79]

Police officers may be exposed to violence when they are forced to confront an emotionally disturbed citizen. On occasion, a distraught person will attack police as a form of suicide.[80] This tragic event has become so common that the term "suicide by cop" has been coined to denote victim-precipitated killings by police. For example, during one 11-year period, more than 10 percent of the shootings by police officers in Los Angeles involved allegedly suicidal people intentionally provoking police.[81]

- **Workload.** A relationship exists among police violence and the number of police on the street, the number of calls for service, the number and nature of police dispatches, the number of arrests made in a given jurisdiction, and police exposure to stressful situations. It can also be noted that officers who work a lot of overtime hours (12- or 16-hour shifts as opposed to a traditional eight-hour shift) may not be as sharp as officers who do not, decreasing their judgment in use of force situations.

- **Firearms availability.** Cities that experience a large number of crimes committed with firearms are also likely to have high police violence rates.

A strong association has been found between police use of force and gun density (the proportion of suicides and murders committed with a gun).[82]

- **Social conflict.** According to the threat hypothesis, more police are killed in cities with a large underclass.[83] The greatest number of police shootings occur in areas that have significant disparities in economic opportunity and high levels of income inequality.[84] Economic disadvantage within marginalized communities coupled with political alienation, leads to a climate in which police–citizen conflict is sharpened. Politically excluded groups may turn to violence to gain ends that those not excluded can acquire with conventional tactics. One conflict-reduction approach is to add marginalized police officers. However, recent research by Brad Smith shows that the mere addition of marginalized officers to a department is not sufficient to reduce levels of police violence.[85] The presence of a Black mayor has also been linked with reductions in the likelihood of police–citizen violence.[86] Such a mayor may help reduce feelings of powerlessness in marginalized communities, which in turn reduces anger against the state, of which the police are the most visible officials. Findings from a recent study of the context of the police use of force are set out in the following Focus of Policing: The Context of Police Use of Force feature.

- **Administrative policies.** The philosophy, policies, and practices of individual police chiefs and departments significantly influence the police use of deadly force.[87] Departments that stress restrictions on the use of force generally have lower shooting rates than those that favor tough law enforcement and encourage officers to shoot when necessary. Poorly written or ambivalent policies encourage shootings because they allow the officer at the scene to decide when deadly force is warranted, often under conditions of high stress and tension.

Race and the Use of Deadly Force

No other issue is as important to the study of the police use of deadly force as racial discrimination. A number of critics have claimed that police are more likely to shoot and kill suspects of color than they are White offenders. In a famous statement, sociologist Paul Takagi charged that police have "one trigger finger for White people and another for Black people."[88] Takagi's complaint was supported by a number of research studies that showed that a disproportionate number of police killings involved minority citizens—almost 80 percent in some of the cities surveyed.[89] At the minimum, Black suspects are shot and killed at a rate that is twice their representation in the population. One reason is that police officers make quicker judgments when interacting with people of color and may decide that force is needed much more quickly than they do with White suspects.[90]

Some pioneering research by James Fyfe helps provide an answer to this question. In his study of New York City shootings over a five-year period, Fyfe found that police officers were most likely to shoot suspects who were armed and with whom they became involved in violent confrontations. Once such factors as being armed with a weapon, being involved in a violent crime, and attacking an officer were considered, the racial differences in the police use of force ceased to be significant. Fyfe found that Black officers were almost twice as likely as White officers to have shot citizens. He attributed this finding to the fact that Black officers work and live in high-crime, high-violence areas where shootings are more common and that Black officers hold proportionately more

The Context of Police Use of Force

Researchers Emma Fridel, Keller Sheppard, and Gregory Zimmerman recently used sophisticated research tools to examine the contexts in which police are more likely to use lethal force and where they are also more likely to be killed in the line of duty.

They note that individual-level factors influence the way force is employed and how it is used. Black officers and younger, more inexperienced officers are more likely to use lethal force than their more experienced counterparts; in contrast, female and unmarried officers are disproportionately victimized.

While these factors are certainly relevant, Fridel and her associates believe the neighborhood context is a critical element of the decision to use force. After reviewing relevant literature and theory, they hypothesize that neighborhoods with concentrated disadvantages are the ones most likely to experience police-citizen violence. One reason is that citizens residing in economically marginalized areas are disproportionately likely to be involved in crime and therefore police presence is higher in these areas. And, being suspicious of authority, people living in lower-class areas are more likely to resist police authority. Increased citizen resistance during police–citizen encounters encourages conflict and as a result in police officers using force against citizens.

In short, the convergence of increased police presence and citizens prone to challenging the police in economically marginalized areas generates higher odds of lethal use of force by the police as well as police lethal victimization. Adding to this combustible mix is the increased rates of civilian gun possession in areas with higher levels of structural disadvantage. Firearm possession may embolden citizens to resist police, elevates police fear, and ensures that suspects armed with a gun will be met with lethal force more frequently than unarmed citizens. They conclude that the greater the level of neighborhood disadvantage the more likely that police–citizen interactions will result in use of force.

To analyze this association more fully, the authors looked at data from 6,416 citizen fatalities and 709 officer fatalities distributed across 1,735 police agencies and 1,506 U.S. places from 2000 to 2016. Using highly sophisticated statistical tools, they found that the odds of a citizen fatality by the police relative to a police fatality varied across social contexts; fatal police–citizen encounters that occurred in places with higher levels of concentrated disadvantage were more likely to result in a police fatality than in a citizen fatality and guns were significantly more likely to be used by citizens involved in police fatalities in economically marginalized places.

Critical Thinking

1. Do police use more violence in economically marginalized neighborhoods because there is more crime in these communities and naturally police are on alert and ready to take aggressive action to thwart attackers?

2. Are police more likely to use force in economically marginalized neighborhoods because residents are powerless and have little recourse if police are in violation of their civil rights?

Source: Emma E. Fridel, Keller G. Sheppard, and Gregory M. Zimmerman "Integrating the Literature on Police Use of Deadly Force and Police Lethal Victimization: How Does Place Impact Fatal Police–Citizen Encounters?," *Journal of Quantitative Criminology* 36 (2020), 957–992.

line positions and fewer administrative posts than White officers, which would place them more often on the street and less often behind a desk.[91]

While Fyfe's research focused attention on the confluence of race, police, and force, it has also created significant debate about its conclusion that Black police officers use as much or more force than White officers. Other researchers dispute this finding. When Eugene Paoline and his colleagues examined police use of force, they found that White officers are actually more coercive toward Black suspects, but Black officers are unaffected by a suspect's race. Conversely, suspects, regardless of their race, are not more likely to display resistance whether the officer they are interacting with is Black or White.[92]

Controlling Deadly Force

Detailed rules of engagement that limit the use of deadly force are common in major cities. As you may recall, the Boston Police Department's official rules of conduct contains one on the discharge of firearms was set out in Exhibit 9.1.

Here an official rule limits an individual officer to use deadly force only if no other means are available to control the situation. A police officer must consider other means than using their weapon even if a fleeing felon has committed a crime in which they themselves used deadly force on a victim. Why should such a rule be created? Because a police officer may have probable cause to believe the offender committed the crime, that is far less than what is needed to prove guilt in a court of law where beyond a reasonable doubt standard is required. It is possible the officer made a mistake or that there were extenuating circumstances in the case (i.e., the perpetrator acted in self-defense).

Some departments have developed administrative policies that stress limiting the use of force and containing armed offenders until specially trained backup teams are sent to take charge of the situation. Administrative policies have been found to be an effective control on deadly force, and their influence can be enhanced if the chief of police gives them the proper support.[93]

There are also training programs designed to instruct officers on how to de-escalate encounters so that deadly force is not needed. While a promising approach reviews the existing programs have yielded inconclusive evidence that they can control or diminish the use of force.[94]

Summary

LO1 Define the elements associated with police use of discretion.

Discretion is the decision by a police officer to take a specific action such as writing a crime report, making an arrest, or using force. It can also involve the decision to take informal action, such as when the police decide to let a contrite motorist off with a warning rather than issue a costly ticket as they might issue to a more belligerent driver. Police use of discretion is most frequently associated with such activities as mediating disputes instead of making formal arrests, referring people to social service agencies, and/or committing a person with a mental illness to a health facility rather than arresting them for disorderly conduct. Police must use discretion to make all of these decisions in the course of a typical workday.

Police officers use a high degree of personal discretion in carrying out daily tasks. When police deprive people of their liberty, make a formal arrest, use force, or conduct interrogations, their actions typically become part of the public record. However, when police ignore an incident for some citizens and not others and use their discretion not to act, their behavior goes unrecorded. Nonetheless, the ability of a police officer to use discretion is not unlimited. Choices can be controlled by both the courts and departmental administrative policies.

LO2 Identify the sources of police discretion.

Discretion is also influenced by departmental written rules and policies. Work environment also helps shape police officers' use of discretion. Some departments keep close control over officer behavior while others are less vigilant. Most police departments maintain written rules and policies that are meant to shape and curb police discretion. Work environment also helps shape police officers' use of discretion. Despite what is shown on television and in movies, many municipal and state police officers conduct their work alone without a partner. It comes as no surprise then that the level of supervision an officer receives will shape and control their use of discretion. Supervision seems to be a critical element employed to control discretion.

Part of an officer's discretion involves determining if a specific event or action consists of elements that comprise criminal offenses that fall within the boundaries of the law. Legal statutes are often ambiguous and vague. Legislators tend to make laws with little thought to if they can be understood and enforced. If a law is unclear, it can be nullified by the courts under the void for vagueness doctrine. Criminal statutes are frequently too broadly written.

LO3   Compare and contrast the concepts of selective and full enforcement.

According to the concept of full enforcement police confront and deal with each and every single violation that is brought to their attention. While technically officers *are* supposed to fully enforce the law, this is not common practice. If the police investigated every potential crime and made arrests the to the full extent of the law or arrested every person who, technically, committed a crime. The assembly line of justice would slow down and come to a halt if police made arrests or issued a summons for every legal violation. Prosecutors would have too many cases to try and courts would be hopelessly clogged. Instead, police practice selective enforcement, not enforcing all laws nor taking action every time an offense occurs. The downside of selective enforcement is the disparate treatment that some members of the community often feel. Many people of color and people of lower economic statuses tend to get the full level of enforcement in their communities.

LO4   Identify the factors that influence the use of discretion.

Many factors influence the use of discretion. Some relate to the crime. Offense severity, who reported the crime, and the wishes of the victim all have influence. If a victim has credibility, police are more likely to take action. There are also community and environmental factors, including local customs and norms. The offender's behavior also plays a role: Suspect demeanor, resistance, race, gender, socioeconomic status, and age have influence. And so too does officer characteristics, such as age, education, and experience.

LO5   List the ways the legal system influences discretion.

The criminal justice system relies on legal statutes that are often ambiguous and vague. Some believe that legislators tend to make laws with little thought of if they can be understood and enforced. Sometimes this is because few politicians have served as police

officers, have never actually enforced the law, and are not aware of how statutes can be interpreted. Most police officers do not have law degrees of advanced legal education, so their interpretation of a well-meaning law may be skewed. Part of an officer's discretion involves determining if a specific event or action consists of elements that comprise criminal offenses that fall within the boundaries of the law, which is a problem because legal statutes are often ambiguous and vague. Criminal statutes are frequently too broadly written, which leaves a lot of room for different interpretations and discretionary decision making by the police.

Regardless of the reasoning, a statute without clarity actually invites officers to interpret things as they see fit. That is why we have the use of discretion and resulting inconsistency. Another problem is that criminal justice policies are often too broad and in some cases contradictory. As a result, there is a lot of room for different interpretations and discretionary decisions made by the police.

LO6   Compare and contrast the positive and negative aspects of discretion.

There are also positive and negative aspects of discretion. If officers use good judgment, it can help limit the use of the criminal sanction in an already overburdened system. Discretion allows police to act as gatekeepers and decide that sometimes an offense should be overlooked or treated informally. Discretion allows officers to use their common sense to control the situation.

Individualized justice can be helpful both for community relations and the ultimate goal of public safety. If properly applied, the exercise of discretion by police may contain and distribute significant social benefits.

On the negative side, unchecked discretion can deteriorate into discrimination, violence, and other abusive practices. Discretion implies that not everyone is treated equally under the law. Inequality and discrimination may occur if the police abuse discretion and make decisions based solely on race, ethnicity, or gender. Being arrested can affect a person's ability to obtain a job or even enter certain sectors of employment. Getting arrested signifies an increased risk of unhealthy lifestyle, violence involvement, and violent victimization. Procedural injustice can create a lack of trust between police and the communities that they serve. Trust is essential for police to effectively do their jobs.

LO7 Explain the factors that lead the police to use force.

There are social, legal, and environmental factors related to police use of force. The higher the levels of violence in a community, the more likely police in the area will use force. Police officers who use force kill at a higher rate in years when the general level of violence in the nation is higher. Workload also affects the use of force: violence is related to the number of police on the street, the number of calls for service, the number and nature of police dispatches, the number of arrests made in a given jurisdiction, and police exposure to stressful situations. A strong association has been found between police use of force and gun density (the proportion of suicides and murders committed with a gun). The greatest number of police shootings occur in areas that have significant disparities in economic opportunity and high levels of income inequality. Departments that stress restrictions on the use of force generally have lower shooting rates than those that favor tough law enforcement and encourage officers to shoot when necessary.

Black, Latino, and Hispanic citizens were more likely than White citizens to experience police threat or use of force as a consequence of police contact. People of color are much more likely to report that police "hassle them." Suspect behavior also influences the use of force. People who resist or merely question the police orders or actually grapple with officers are much more likely to be the target of force than those who are respectful, passive, and noncombative. Female officers are less likely to use force than male officers, most likely because female officers seem to have the ability to avoid violent encounters with citizens.

Key Terms

discretion, 248
low visibility decision
   making, 249

span of control, 253
overload hypothesis, 256
suspect demeanor, 258

nolle prosequi, 261
deadly force, 268

Notes

1. David Kocieniewski, "A Little Girl Shot, and a Crowd That Didn't See," *The New York Times,* July 9, 2007, https://www.nytimes.com/2007/07/09/nyregion/09taj.html.
2. Samuel Walker, "Origins of the Contemporary Criminal Justice Paradigm: The American Bar Foundation Survey, 1953–1969," *Justice Quarterly* 9 (1992), 201–230.
3. Ibid.
4. Jerome Skolnick, *Justice Without Trial: Law Enforcement in Democratic Society (Classics of Law & Society)*, 4th ed. (Quid Pro, LLC Publishing, 2011).
5. Wayne LaFave, *Arrest: The Decision to Take a Suspect Into Custody* (Boston: Little, Brown, 1965).
6. Theresa Vargas, "Risk of Robbery Raising Stakes of Poker Nights," *The Washington Post,* February 21, 2006, http://www.washingtonpost.com/wp-dyn/content/article/2006/02/20/AR2006022001379.html.
7. Sarah DiNatale, "More Than 100 Sent to Drug Treatment in Gloucester Police Program," *Boston Globe,* August 14, 2015.
8. Roger B. Parks, Stephen D. Mastrofski, Christina Dejong, and M. Kevin Gray, "How Officers Spend Their Time with the Community," *Justice Quarterly* 16 (1999), 483–518.
9. Joseph Goldstein, "Police Discretion Not to Invoke the Criminal Process: Low-Visibility Decisions in the Administration of Justice," *Yale Law Journal* (1960), 543–594.
10. Kenneth Litwin, "A Multilevel Multivariate Analysis of Factors Affecting Homicide Clearances," *Journal of Research in Crime and Delinquency* 41 (2004), 327–351.
11. Lawrence W. Sherman, "Causes of Police Behavior: The Current State of Quantitative Research." In A. S. Blumberg and E. Niederhoffer (eds.), *The Ambivalent Force*, 3rd ed., New York: Holt, Rinehart, and Wilson, 1985, pp. 183–195, p. 187.
12. Donald J. Black, "The Social Organization of Arrest," *Stanford Law Review* (1971), 1087–1111.
13. James O. Finckenauer, "Some Factors in Police Discretion and Decision Making," *Journal of Criminal Justice* 4, no. 1 (1976), 29–46.
14. Douglas A. Smith and Christy Ann Visher, "Street Level Justice: Situational Determinants of Police Arrest Decisions," Workshop in Political Theory and Policy Analysis, Indiana University, 1981.
15. Helen Eigenberg, Kathryn Scarborough, and Victor Kappeler, "Contributory Factors Affecting Arrest in Domestic and Nondomestic Assaults," *American Journal of Police* 15 (1996): 27–51.
16. Leonore Simon, "A Therapeutic Jurisprudence Approach to the Legal Processing of Domestic Violence Cases," *Psychology, Public Policy, and Law* 1 (1995), 43–79.
17. Peter Sinden and B. Joyce Stephens, "Police Perceptions of Domestic Violence: The Nexus of Victim, Perpetrator, Event, Self and Law," *Policing* 22 (1999), 313–326.
18. Bjarte Frode Vik, Kirsten Rasmussen, Berit Schei, and Cecilie Therese Hagemann, "Is Police Investigation of Rape Biased by Characteristics of Victims?," *Forensic Science International: Synergy* 2 (2020), 98–106.

19. Melissa Schaefer Morabito, April Pattavina, and Linda M. Williams, "It All Just Piles Up: Challenges to Victim Credibility Accumulate to Influence Sexual Assault Case Processing," *Journal of Interpersonal Violence* 34, no. 15 (2016).

20. Mandeep Dhami, Samantha Lundrigan, and Sian Thomas, "Police Discretion in Rape Cases," *Journal of Police and Criminal Psychology* 35 (2020), 157–169.

21. Gregory Howard Williams, *The Law and Politics of Police Discretion* (Westport, CT: Greenwood, 1984).

22. David Klinger, "Negotiating Order in Patrol Work: An Ecological Theory of Police Response to Deviance," *Criminology* 35 (1997), 277–306.

23. Amie M. Schuck and Cara Rabe-Hemp, "Citizen Complaints and Gender Diversity in Police Organizations," *Policing and Society* (2014), 1–16.

24. Allison Chappell, John Macdonald, and Patrick Manz, "The Organizational Determinants of Police Arrest Decisions," *Crime and Delinquency* 52 (2006), 287–306.

25. Robin Shepard Engel, "Patrol Officer Supervision in the Community Policing Era," *Journal of Criminal Justice* 30 (2002), 51–64.

26. Jeffrey Nowacki and Tyrell Spencer, "Police Discretion, Organizational Characteristics, and Traffic Stops: An Analysis of Racial Disparity in Illinois," *International Journal of Police Science & Management* 21 (2019), 4–16.

27. William A. Westly, *Violence and the Police. A Sociological Study of Law, Custom, and Morality.* (MIT Press, 1971).

28. John McCluskey, William Terrill, and Eugene Paoline III, "Peer Group Aggressiveness and the Use of Coercion in Police–Suspect Encounters," *Police Practice and Research* 6 (2005), 19–37.

29. Nathan Goldman, *The Differential Selection of Juvenile Offenders for Court Appearance* (New York, NY: National Council on Crime and Delinquency, 1963).

30. Joseph Schafer, "Negotiating Order in the Policing of Youth Drinking," *Policing* 28 (2005), 279–300; Richard Lundman, "Demeanor or Crime? The Midwest City Police–Citizen Encounters Study," *Criminology* 32 (1994), 631–653.

31. Joseph Schafer and Stephen Mastrofski, "Police Leniency in Traffic Enforcement Encounters: Exploratory Findings from Observations and Interviews," *Journal of Criminal Justice* 33 (2005), 225–238.

32. Robert E. Worden, Robin L. Shepard, and Stephen D. Mastrofski, "On the Meaning and Measurement of Suspects' Demeanor Toward the Police: A Comment on Demeanor and Arrest," *Journal of Research in Crime and Delinquency* 33 (1996), 324–332.

33. William Terrill and Stephen Mastrofski, "Situational and Officer-Based Determinants of Police Coercion," *Justice Quarterly* 19 (2002), 215–248.

34. William Terrill, *Police Coercion: Application of the Force Continuum* (NY: LFB Scholarly Publishing, 2001).

35. Wendy C. Regoeczi and Stephanie Kent, "Race, Poverty, and the Traffic Ticket Cycle: Exploring the Situational Context of the Application of Police Discretion," *Policing: An International Journal of Police Strategies & Management* 37, no. 1 (2014), 190–205.

36. Arrick Jackson and Lorenzo M. Boyd, "Minority Threat Hypothesis and the Workload Hypothesis: A Community-Level Examination of Lenient Policing in High Crime Communities," *Criminal Justice Studies: A Critical Journal of Crime, Law and Society* 18, no. 1 (2005), 29–50.

37. James Wright and Andrea Headley, "Police Use of Force Interactions: Is Race Relevant or Gender Germane?," *American Review of Public Administration* 50 (2020), 851–864.

38. Geoffrey P. Alpert, John M. Macdonald, and Roger G. Dunham, "Police Suspicion and Discretionary Decision Making During Citizen Stops," *Criminology* 43 (2005), 407–434.

39. Michael T. Rossler and William Terrill, "Police Responsiveness to Service-Related Requests," *Police Quarterly* 15, no. 1 (2012), 3–24.

40. Christy A. Visher, "Gender, Police Arrest Decisions, and Notions of Chivalry," *Criminology* 21 (1983), 5–28.

41. Amy Farrell, "Explaining Leniency Organizational Predictors of the Differential Treatment of Men and Women in Traffic Stops," *Crime & Delinquency* 61, no. 4 (2015), 509–537.

42. Kenneth J. Novak, James Frank, Brad W. Smith, Robin Shepard Engel, "Revisiting the Decision to Arrest: Comparing Beat and Community Officers," *Crime and Delinquency* 48 (2002), 70–98.

43. Peter B. Hoffman and Edward R. Hickey, "Use of Force by Female Police Officers," *Journal of Criminal Justice* 33, no. 2 (2005), 145–151.

44. Steven G. Brandl, Meghan S. Stroshine, and James Frank, "Who Are the Complaint-Prone Officers?: An Examination of the Relationship between Police Officers' Attributes, Arrest Activity, Assignment, and Citizens' Complaints about Excessive Force," *Journal of Criminal Justice* 29, no. 6 (2001), 521–529,

45. Amie M. Schuck and Cara Rabe-Hemp, "Women Police," *Women & Criminal Justice* 16, no. 4 (2005), 91–117.

46. Cody W. Telep, "The Impact of Higher Education on Police Officer Attitudes toward Abuse of Authority," *Journal of Criminal Justice Education* 22, no. 3 (2011), 392–419.

47. Craig Paterson, "Adding Value? A Review of the International Literature on the Role of Higher Education in Police Training and Education," *Police Practice and Research* 12, no. 4 (2011), 286–297.

48. Jason Rydberg and William Terrill, "The Effect of Higher Education on Police Behavior," *Police Quarterly* 13, no. 1 (2010), 92–120.

49. Cassia Spohn and Katherine Tellis, "The Criminal Justice System's Response to Sexual Violence," *Violence Against Women* 18, no. 2 (2012), 169–192. doi:10.1177/1077801212440020.

50. April Pattavina, Melissa Morabito, and Linda M. Williams, "Examining Connections between the Police and Prosecution in Sexual Assault Case Processing: Does the Use of Exceptional Clearance Facilitate a Downstream Orientation?," *Victims & Offenders* (2015), 1–19.

51. Ashley Nellis, *A Return to Justice: Rethinking our Approach to Juveniles in the System* (Washington, DC: Rowman & Littlefield, 2015).

52. Robert Brame, Michael G. Turner, Raymond Paternoster, and Shawn D. Bushway, "Cumulative Prevalence of Arrest from Ages 8 to 23 in a National Sample," *Pediatrics* 129, no. 1 (2012), 21–27.

53. Tom Tyler and Jeffrey Fagan, "Legitimacy and Cooperation: Why Do People Help the Police Fight Crime in Their Communities?," *Public Law and Legal Theory Working Paper Group* (Paper Number 06-99) (New York, NY: Columbia Law School).

54. Robert Davis, Pedro Mateu-Gelabert, and Joel Miller, "Can Effective Policing Also Be Respectful? Two Examples in the South Bronx," *Police Quarterly* 8 (2005), 229–247.

55. Tom Tyler, "Procedural Justice, Legitimacy, and the Effective Rule of Law." In M. H. Tonry (ed.), *Crime and Justice: A Review of Research* Chicago, IL: University of Chicago Press, 2003, pp. 283–357.

56. Jacinta M. Gau and Rod K. Brunson, "Procedural Justice and Order Maintenance Policing: A Study of Inner-City Young Men's Perceptions of Police Legitimacy," *Justice Quarterly* 27 (2010), 255–279; Patrick J. Carr, Laura Napolitano, and Jessica Keating, "We Never Call the Cops and Here Is Why: A Qualitative Examination of Legal Cynicism in Three Philadelphia Neighborhoods," *Criminology* 45 (2007), 445–480.

57. Yvonne Brunetto, Ben Farr-Wharton, Rod Farr-Wharton, Kate Shacklock, Joseph Azzopardi, Chiara Saccon, and Art Shriberg, "Comparing the Impact of Management Support

on Police Officers' Perceptions of Discretionary Power and Engagement: Australia, USA and Malta," *The International Journal of Human Resource Management* 31, no. 6 (2020), 738–759.

58. Kenneth Culp Davis, *Police Discretion* (West Publishing Company, 1975).
59. Jeffrey S. Nowacki, "Organizational-Level Police Discretion An Application for Police Use of Lethal Force," *Crime & Delinquency* 61, no. 5 (2015), 643–668.
60. James J. Fyfe, "Administrative Interventions on Police Shooting Discretion: An Empirical Examination," *Journal of Criminal Justice* 7, no. 4 (1980), 309–323.
61. http://www.calea.org/.
62. Samuel Walker, *Police Accountability* (Belmont, CA: Wadsworth, 2001).
63. http://www.cincinnati.com/story/opinion/editorials/2016/01/18/city-seeing-believing/78986438/.
64. Mark Morgan, Matthew Logan, and Tayte Olma, "Police Use of Force and Suspect Behavior: An Inmate Perspective," *Journal of Criminal Justice* 67 (2020).
65. William Terrill, "Police Use of Force: A Transactional Approach," *Justice Quarterly* 22, no. 1 (2005), 107–138.
66. Mark Alden Morgan, Matthew William Logan, and Tayte Marie Olma, "Police Use of Force and Suspect Behavior: An Inmate Perspective," *Journal of Criminal Justice* 67 (2020), 101673.
67. Joel Garner, Christopher Maxwell, and Cederick Heraux, "Characteristics Associated with the Prevalence and Severity of Force Used by the Police," *Justice Quarterly* 19 (2002), 705–747.
68. Steven Brandl, Meghan Stroshine, and James Frank, "Who Are the Complaint-Prone Officers? An Examination of the Relationship Between Police Officers' Attributes, Arrest Activity, Assignment, and Citizens' Complaints About Excessive Force," *Journal of Criminal Justice* 29 (2001), 521–529.
69. Laura Mangels, Joel Suss, and Brian Lande, "Police Expertise and Use of Force: Using a Mixed-Methods Approach to Model Expert and Novice Use-of-Force Decision-Making," *Journal of Police and Criminal Psychology* 35 (2020), 294–304.
70. Sam W. Lathrop, "Reviewing Use of Force: A Systematic Approach," *FBI Law Enforcement Bulletin* 69 (2000):, 16–20.
71. Washington Post Police Shooting Database, https://www.washingtonpost.com/graphics/investigations/police-shootings-database/.
72. Lawrence W. Sherman and Robert H. Langworthy, "Measuring Homicide by Police Officers," *Journal of Criminal Law and Criminology* 70 (1979), 546–560.
73. Ibid.
74. John H. Blume III, "Deadly Force in Memphis: Tennessee v. Garner," *Cumb. L. Rev.* 15 (1984), 89.
75. Osagie K. Obasogie and Zachary Newman, "The Futile Fourth Amendment: Understanding Police Excessive Force Doctrine Through an Empirical Assessment of Graham v. Connor," *Nw. UL Rev.* 112 (2017), 1465.
76. Kisela v.Hughes 584 U.S. ＿＿ (2018).
77. Brad Smith, "The Impact of Police Officer Diversity on Police-Caused Violence," *Policy Studies Journal* 31 (2003), 147–163.
78. John MacDonald, Geoffrey Alpert, and Abraham Tennenbaum, "Justifiable Homicide by Police and Criminal Homicide: A Research Note," *Journal of Crime and Justice* 22 (1999), 153–164.
79. FBI, "Law Enforcement Officers Killed and Assaulted," 2018, https://ucr.fbi.gov/leoka/2018/resource-pages/about-leoka.
80. Richard Parent and Simon Verdun-Jones, "Victim-Precipitated Homicide: Police Use of Deadly Force in British Columbia," *Policing* 21 (1998), 432–449.
81. "10% of Police Shootings Found to Be 'Suicide by Cop,'" *Criminal Justice Newsletter* 29 (1998), 1.
82. Lawrence Sherman and Robert H. Langworthy, "Measuring Homicide by Police Officers," *Journal of Criminology Law and Criminology* 70 (1979), 546.
83. Brad Smith, "Structural and Organizational Predictors of Homicide by Police," *Policing* 27 (2004), 539–557.
84. Jonathan Sorenson, James Marquart, and Deon Brock, "Factors Related to Killings of Felons by Police Officers: A Test of the Community Violence and Conflict Hypotheses," *Justice Quarterly* 10 (1993), 417–440; David Jacobs and David Britt, "Inequality and Police Use of Deadly Force: An Empirical Assessment of a Conflict Hypothesis," *Social Problems* 26 (1979), 403–412.
85. Brad W. Smith, "The Impact of Police Officer Diversity on Police-Caused Homicides," *Policy Studies Journal* 31, no. 2 (2003), 147–162.
86. David Jacobs and Jason Carmichael, "Subordination and Violence Against State Control Agents: Testing Political Explanations for Lethal Assaults Against the Police," *Social Forces* 80 (2002), 1223–1252.
87. James Fyfe, "Police Use of Deadly Force: Research and Reform," *Justice Quarterly* 5 (1988), 165–205.
88. Paul Takagi, "A Garrison State in a 'Democratic' Society," *Crime and Social Justice* 5 (1974), 34–43.
89. Mark Blumberg, "Race and Police Shootings: An Analysis in Two Cities." In James Fyfe (ed.), *Contemporary Issues in Law Enforcement*, Beverly Hills, CA: SAGE, 1981, pp. 152–166.
90. Kimberly Kahn, Joel Steele, Jean McMahon, and Greg Stewart, "How Suspect Race Affects Police Use of Force in an Interaction over Time," *Law and Human Behavior* 41 (2017), 117–126.
91. James Fyfe, "Shots Fired," Ph.D. dissertation, State University of New York, Albany, 1978.
92. Eugene A. Paoline III, Jacinta M. Gau, and William Terrill, "Race and the Police Use of Force Encounter in the United States," *The British Journal of Criminology* 58, no. 1 (2018), 54–74.
93. Michael D. White, "Controlling Police Decisions to Use Deadly Force: Reexamining the Importance of Administrative Policy," *Crime and Delinquency* 47 (2001), 131.
94. Robin Engel, Hannah McManus, and Tamara Herold, "Does De-escalation Training Work?: A Systematic Review and Call for Evidence in Police Use-of-Force Reform," *Criminology & Public Policy* 19 (2020), 721–760.

10

Police Misconduct: Corruption and Abuse of Power

Learning Objectives

LO1 Describe the varieties of police corruption.

LO2 Explain why police officers engage in corruption for personal gain.

LO3 Describe how corruption can be controlled.

LO4 Recognize what is meant by the term *racial profiling*.

LO5 Describe the effects of police brutality.

Chapter Outline

New York Daily News/Getty Images

Eric Garner was a familiar figure on Staten Island. He was known as a jovial man who sold individual cigarettes, a practice that is against the law (i.e., selling untaxed tobacco). The cops knew him and he had been cited twice already that year near the same spot, in March and May, charged both times with circumventing state tax law. In early July, he was approached by officers who gave him a warning.

Later that month, one of the officers who had given him the earlier warning, Justin Damico, returned, this time with a different partner, Daniel Pantaleo. They decided to do more than issue a warning this time; they decided to make a formal arrest. As the pair sought to subdue Garner, a struggle ensued. The incident, recorded by a friend, showed police applying an illegal chokehold and Garner pleading—"I can't breathe"—11 times during the altercation until he was unconscious on the sidewalk. Little was done to help Garner or give him any form of CPR before an ambulance arrived. He died on the way to the hospital; his cries, seen by millions on the news and the Internet, became a rallying cry for a protest movement that grew even more heated when a grand jury failed to indict the police officers involved. This police action cost the state of New York nearly $6 million. Garner's death is a good example of police discretion gone wrong.

Even if he was found guilty of selling loose cigarettes, the most punishment he would have received was a monetary fine. Should the police have tackled and fought with some-one who was suspected of a petty offense that carries at most a small penalty?

What would have happened if Garner had fought back and injured the police officer? What can be done to avoid such a senseless tragedy?

Is the problem of police misconduct a matter of a "few bad apples" or is it systemic and pervasive? Recent polls find people distrust the police, especially in marginalized com-munities. Black people are much less likely to trust their local police and law enforcement to look out for them and their families than others—36 percent trust the police, compared to 77 percent of White people.[1]

Because police officers are sworn to uphold the law, it is even more shocking when they choose to break it themselves. Police officers carry weapons, are able to take people into custody and deprive them of their liberty; violence is a routine part of the job. Given these responsibilities, it should come as no surprise that community members expect police officers to stick to the letter of the law and refrain from any form of misconduct or illegal behaviors. Given this expectation, we are all liable to take notice when police officers do get involved in controversial behaviors.

This chapter explores two forms of police misconduct that have become the focus of controversy: **police corruption** and police who abuse their power routinely and engage in behavior which violates the law they have sworn to uphold—making false arrests, use of excessive force, falsifying evidence, and violations of civil rights.

Police departments have long wrestled with the problem of defining and controlling illegal and unprofessional behavior by their officers. Is it right for a police officer to take a free cup of coffee or is it a bribe? Should there be a strict **zero tolerance policy** banning police officers from taking any form of gratuity? Is taking a gratuity start of a slippery slope to even greater corruption?

Police corruption has always been a problem since the first U.S. departments were formed in the nineteenth century. In early police departments, it was commonplace for corrupt police officers to systematically ignore violations of laws related to drinking, gambling, and prostitution in return for regular payoffs. Some entered into relationships with professional criminals, especially pickpockets. Illegal behavior was tolerated in return for goods or information. Police officers helped politicians gain office by allowing electoral fraud to flourish. Some senior officers sold promotions to higher ranks within their own police department.[2]

Although most police officers are not corrupt, the officers who are dishonest bring discredit to the entire profession. And corruption is often hard to combat because the police code of silence demands that officers never turn in their peers, even if they engage in corrupt or illegal practices.[3]

police corruption

Acts involving the misuse of authority by a police officer in a manner designed to produce personal gain for themself or for others.

zero tolerance policy

Approach to policing that focuses on controlling minor crime and other signs of social disorder. When minor crimes are ignored, they will escalate into larger crimes.

LO1

Describe the varieties of police corruption.

meat eater

A term used to describe a police officer who actively solicits bribes and vigorously engages in corrupt practices.

grass eater

A term used to describe a police officer who accepts payoffs when everyday duties place them in a position to be solicited by the public.

▶ Varieties of Corruption

Police corruption can include a number of activities. Police corruption involves the abuse of entrusted power, given by law and practice to police officers, to produce personal gain for themself or others.[4]

Scholars have attempted to create typologies categorizing the forms that police corruption can take. In the 1970s, the Knapp Commission, a public body set up to investigate the New York City police, classified abusers into two groups: **meat eaters** and **grass eaters**.[5] Meat eaters aggressively misuse police power for personal gain by demanding bribes, threatening legal action, or cooperating with criminals. Across the country, police officers have been accused, indicted, and convicted of shaking down club owners and other businesspeople.[6] In contrast, grass eaters accept payoffs when their everyday duties place them in a position to be solicited by the public. For example, police officers have been investigated for taking bribes to street-level gambling.[7] The Knapp Commission concluded that the vast majority of corrupt police officers are grass eaters, although the few meat eaters who are caught capture all the headlines. In 1993, another police scandal in New York City prompted the formation of the Mollen Commission, which found that some New York cops were actively involved in violence and drug dealing.

In addition to these concepts, other police experts have attempted to create models to better understand police corruption. Several types of corruption have been identified.[8]

Internal Corruption

This corruption takes place within police agencies, including wage theft, embezzlement, and other crimes. In one case, Chicago police officers conspired to sell relatively new police cars to other officers at cut-rate prices, forcing the department to purchase new cars unnecessarily. There have been instances in which officers seeking promotion have been given or sold promotion exams or paid to have rivals' scores lowered by higher-ups with access to results.[9] In one of the nation's most notorious police scandals, numerous Massachusetts State police troopers received fines and prison sentences for embezzlement when it was found that they submitted false overtime pay claims. Some earned salaried in excess of $200,000 per year, including overtime pay of over $50,000. In order to conceal their scheme, they submitted fraudulent work reports designed to create the appearance that they had worked overtime hours when they had not, and also falsely claimed that they had worked the entirety of overtime shifts while cutting out early.

They fabricated phony traffic tickets using information from earlier citations to "prove" they were on the job. Some of the false claims for overtime involved work on special task forces designed to reduce accidents, crashes, and injuries through the increased presence of troopers targeting vehicles traveling at excessive speeds.[10] The following Focus on Policing: Overtime Scam feature discusses another recent scandal involving overtime pay.

Police officers considered "grass eaters" accept payoffs when their everyday duties place them in a position to be solicited by the public, for example, letting a traffic violator go with a warning rather than a summons.

Critical Thinking

What do you think are some of the causes of police corruption?

External Corruption

External corruption is participation by police in serious criminal behavior in the community. Police may use their positions of trust and power to commit the very crimes they are entrusted with controlling. Specific examples of external corruption are discussed in the sections that follow. But first, let's look at a specific example. In 2020, a federal judge sentenced Eddie Hicks, a former Chicago police sergeant to 13 years in prison for participating in robbery and extortion. Hicks and other officers targeted suspected drug dealers under the guise of police investigations. The four-person crew staged phony drug raids and automobile stops of suspected dealers; threatened them with arrest; then kept the drugs, cash, or weapons they discovered.

A jury convicted Hicks of such crimes as conspiracy to commit racketeering, drug conspiracy, possession of a controlled substance with intent to distribute, carrying a firearm in furtherance of a drug trafficking offense, theft of government funds, and failure to appear for a judicial proceeding. Evidence at trial revealed that Hicks and his robbery crew stole thousands of dollars in cash, multi-kilogram

Focus on Policing

Overtime Scam

In 2020, current and former Boston police officers were arrested and charged in connection with committing over $200,000 in overtime fraud at the Boston Police Department's evidence warehouse. According to the indictment, the officers were assigned to the Department's Evidence Control Unit (ECU) warehouse, where they were responsible for storing, cataloging, and retrieving evidence. ECU officers were eligible to earn overtime pay of 1.5 times their regular hourly pay rate for overtime assignments. According to government prosecutors, beginning in May 2016, the officers under indictment routinely departed two or more hours early from their overtime shifts but then submitted false and fraudulent overtime slips, claiming to have worked the entirety of each shift.

One overtime shift, commonly referred to as "purge" overtime, was focused on reducing the inventory of the evidence warehouse. The shift was supposed to be performed from 4:00 to 8:00 P.M. on weekdays. However, on many days during which the defendant officers claimed overtime payments until 8:00 P.M., the warehouse was actually closed, locked, and alarmed, often well before 8 P.M. and more often by 6:00 P.M. or before. Despite this, it is alleged that the defendants routinely submitted false and fraudulent overtime slips, claiming to have worked from 4:00 to 8:00 P.M. Supervisors, who also left early from this shift, allegedly submitted their own false and fraudulent slips and also knowingly endorsed the fraudulent overtime slips of their subordinates.

Another shift, called "kiosk" overtime, was available to two ECU officers one Saturday, a month from 6:00 A.M. to 2:30 P.M. This shift involved collecting materials, such as unused prescription drugs, and then transporting the materials to an incinerator in a neighboring town. Officers who worked until 10 A.M. routinely submitted overtime slips claiming to have worked 8.5 hours when in fact the defendants frequently completed the work and left after one or two hours of work.

In the three years of the investigation, officers embezzled over $200,000 in overtime pay; more than a few received over $20,000 in pay they did not actually earn. Because some of the overtime pay was taken from funds presented by the U.S. Department of Transportation and U.S. Department of Justice, the Boston officers could be prosecuted under federal law. The charge of embezzlement from an agency receiving federal funds provides for a sentence of up to 10 years in prison, three years of supervised release, and a fine of $250,000 or twice the gross gain or loss. The charge of conspiracy provides for a sentence of up to five years in prison, three years of supervised release, and a fine of $250,000. Sentences are imposed by a federal district court judge based upon the U.S. Sentencing Guidelines and other statutory factors. Some of the officers have already pleaded guilty and some have been sent to prison. For example, Marilyn Golisano, 69, a former clerk for Boston Police Department's (BPD) District A-1 Detectives Unit, was sentenced by a U.S. district court judge to 90 days in prison, followed by three years of supervised release with the first three months to be spent in home confinement. Golisano was also ordered to pay restitution in the amount of $29,000 to the City of Boston. Golisano, who handled the overtime paperwork for the unit, submitted dozens of false and fraudulent overtime slips in 2017 and 2018, claiming she had worked extra hours, with many of those slips bearing forged signatures of her supervisor. Although Golisano's work was done primarily on the computer, Golisano never logged into the BPD computer system at all during many of the overtime shifts she claimed to have worked. Furthermore, on several occasions, when Golisano was supposedly working overtime in downtown Boston, cell phone location information placed Golisano well outside the city.

Critical Thinking

1. Does crime such as this warrant a prison sentence or would civil penalties and dismissal from the force be sufficient?

2. Should police be held to a higher standard than the average citizen since they expect the people they serve to obey the law? If they don't, why should citizens?

Sources: Department of Justice, U.S. Attorney's Office, District of Massachusetts, "Nine Boston Police Officers Arrested for Overtime Fraud Scheme," September 2, 2020, https://www.justice.gov/usao-ma/pr/nine-boston-police-officers-arrested-overtime-fraud-scheme; Department of Justice, U.S. Attorney's Office District of Massachusetts, "Former Boston Police Clerk Sentenced for Overtime Fraud," March 14, 2022, https://www.justice.gov/usao-ma/pr/former-boston-police-clerk-sentenced-overtime-fraud.

quantities of cocaine, hundreds of pounds of marijuana, and several firearms.[11] The following Focus on Policing: Focus on Policing: Planned Theft and New York City Police Officer Jose Tejada feature examines the active criminality of a notorious New York City police officer.

There are different types of external police corruption. The first type is the most common and the most controversial: the acceptance of gratuities, meals, and services. It includes discounts for goods or services like dry cleaning or free meals while on duty. Jim Ruiz and Christine Bono estimate that officers receive close to $ 9,000 a year in gratuities.[12] Not all police departments view accepting gratuities as corruption. Yet others have policies against accepting any free goods or services. These agencies fear a slippery slope—where accepting free coffee may lead to more egregious corruption. For example, gratuities can also be coerced by the police in exchange for extra protection, something that their tax dollars should already be paying for.

Furthermore, while some business owners may offer such gratuities as a way of thanking the police, others may expect something in return. This is the crux of the problem. Police officers can't know which type of business owner that they are dealing with. Other businesses use it to get officers to be seen around their business as a deterrent to potential criminals. Most public opinion surveys show that the public is willing to tolerate free coffee (only 36 percent said it was wrong), but not tolerant of free food.[13]

Kickbacks are another type of external corruption. This is when officers make referrals in exchange for money, Officers could refer an arrestee to certain lawyers or a stranded motorist to particular tow trucks and then receive a portion of the fee paid to the business.

Opportunistic and Planned Theft or Burglary

Officers can engage in opportunistic theft if they take goods from a crime scene for profit (narcotics or money are typical) or from a drunk suspect or drug dealer with large amounts of cash. Some police can commit a planned crime due to unique knowledge of city business hours and security weaknesses or even by stealing from their own evidence rooms. Between 1992 and 1996, 40 police officers in New Orleans were arrested for bank robbery, theft, and other illegal acts. Some additional 200 officers were disciplined.

A **bribe** is a *citizen-initiated* form of corruption. Citizens may bribe the officer to not enforce law. Examples include offering bribes while a speeding ticket is being written to avoid insurance costs increasing. Some bribes might involve community members asking officers to sell ongoing investigation information or when a sting operation will occur. A form of bribing is known as **case fixing**. Community members ask people they know in a police department to make a traffic ticket disappear so they don't have to pay for it. Alternatively, an officer purposely perjured themselves on the witness stand to help someone they know. Bribery is different from **extortion**, which is officer initiated; for example, an officer asks for money or favors to overlook criminal activity.

The Causes of Corruption

No single explanation satisfactorily accounts for the various forms of corruption and abuses of power take.The following factors have all been linked to police misconduct

Critical Thinking

If a friendly business owner wants to show appreciation, do you think the officer should be allowed to accept free gifts like free meals or coffee?

bribe

A gratuity given to a public official in order to have them provide an illegal service.

case fixing

Accepting a gratuity in return for dropping charges or destroying evidence.

extortion

Demanding a gratuity in return for providing a legal service or overlooking an illegal activity.

LO2

Explain why police officers engage in corruption for personal gain.

Focus on Policing

Planned Theft and New York City Police Officer Jose Tejada

Following a two-week trial, a federal jury in Brooklyn, New York, returned a guilty verdict against former New York City Police Officer Jose Tejada on charges of armed robbery conspiracy and narcotics distribution conspiracy; he was sentenced to 18 years in prison. Tejada was a 17-year veteran of the New York City Police Department (NYPD) who, at the time of the robberies, was assigned to the 28th Precinct in Harlem. These charges arose out of the defendant's commission of multiple robberies and attempted robberies in Queens, Manhattan, and the Bronx, some of which he committed while on duty and in uniform; his crimes netted thousands of dollars in cash and multiple kilograms of cocaine. The following are some of the incidents in which Tejada used his position as a police officer to facilitate his crime spree:

- During one attempted robbery on Schley Avenue in the Bronx, Tejada, while on duty and in uniform, used his status as a police officer to demand and gain access to a private residence. The robbery crew mistakenly believed the residents to be drug dealers. In fact, the residents were a family of three, including a teenager, who had no involvement in drug dealing. Tejada and two others unsuccessfully searched the premises for drugs, while Tejada brandished his service weapon to intimidate the innocent family and attempted to handcuff a victim.

- In another robbery on Broadway in Upper Manhattan, Tejada, NYPD Officer Jorge Arbaje-Diaz, and NYPD Auxiliary Officer Yvan Tineo pulled over a car, handcuffed the driver, and stole five kilograms of cocaine hidden inside the car.

- Tejada and Tineo robbed a drug supplier of three kilograms of cocaine at gunpoint on Seaman Avenue in Upper Manhattan.

- In an incident at John F. Kennedy International Airport in Queens, Tejada, Arbaje-Diaz, and Tineo staged the arrest of a corrupt airline employee who was part of a scheme to smuggle narcotics into the United States through incoming commercial flights. The corrupt airline employee wanted Tejada and others to pretend to arrest him at the arrivals terminal while he delivered a drug shipment to his confederates. This staged arrest yielded Tejada, Arbagje-Diaz, and Tineo at least five kilograms of cocaine.

The evidence at trial also showed that Tejada supplied members of the robbery crew with police equipment and paraphernalia to enable them to impersonate police officers. He searched law enforcement databases to determine whether there were outstanding warrants for his own arrest, as well as for the arrest of other members of the robbery crew. Tejada then shared that information with his confederates in an effort to assist them in evading arrest.

Tejada's conviction was one of dozens of convictions in a set of interlocking cases brought in the Eastern District of New York against the members of violent drug robbery crews who impersonated police officers and frequently committed robberies with real officers. Tejada was the third NYPD officer to be convicted in these cases. In total, 52 defendants have been convicted.

Critical Thinking

Is Tejada's sentence of 18 years excessive or too lenient? After all, he did not kill anyone. On the other hand, he helped violent drug crews commit crime.

Source: Drug Enforcement Administration, "Former New York City Police Officer Convicted of Armed Robbery and Drug Trafficking Charges. Officer Assigned to Harlem Precinct Committed Armed Robberies While On Duty and in Uniform in Queens, the Bronx, and Manhattan," June 19, 2014, https://www.dea.gov/press-releases /2014/06/19/former-new-york-city-police-officer-convicted-armed -robbery-and-drug.

Institutions and Practices

The wide discretion that police enjoy, coupled with the low visibility they maintain with the public and their own supervisors, makes them likely candidates for corruption. In addition, the code of secrecy maintained by the police subculture helps insulate corrupt officers from the law. Similarly, police managers, most of whom have risen through the ranks, are reluctant to investigate corruption or punish wrongdoers. Thus, corruption may also be viewed as a function of police institutions and practices.[14]

Moral Ambivalence

Corruption is a function of society's ambivalence toward many forms of vice-related criminal behavior that police officers are sworn to control. Unenforceable laws governing moral standards promote corruption because they create large groups with an interest in undermining law enforcement. These include consumers—people who gamble, wish to drink after the legal closing hour, or patronize a person who engages in sex work—who do not want to be deprived of their chosen form of recreation. Even though the consumers may not actively corrupt police officers, their existence creates a climate that tolerates active corruption by others.[15] Because a vice cannot be controlled and some members of the public apparently want it to continue, the officer may have little resistance to inducements for monetary gain offered by law violators.

Environmental Conditions

Corruption may be linked to specific environmental and social conditions that enhance the likelihood that police officers may become involved in misconduct. For example, in some areas a rapid increase in the marginalized residential population may be viewed as a threat to dominant group interests. Police in these areas may become overly aggressive and routinely use coercive strategies. The conflict produced by these outcomes may lead to antagonism between the police and the marginalized public, and to eventual police misconduct of all types. One study, in which social/ecological conditions in New York City police precincts and divisions were associated with patterns of police misconduct from, found that misconduct cases involving bribery, extortion, excessive force, and other abuses of police authority were linked to trends in neighborhood structural disadvantage, increasing population mobility, and increases in the Latino population.[16]

Corrupt Departments

It has also been suggested that police corruption is generated at the departmental level and that conditions within the department produce and nurture deviance.[17] In some departments, corrupt officers band together and form what is called a "rotten pocket."[18] Rotten pockets help institutionalize corruption because their members expect newcomers to conform to their illegal practices and to a code of secrecy.

Peter Moskos, in his analysis of the indictment of seven Baltimore city police officers, writes "This *is* about bad apples. But it's not *just* about bad apples. There's the barrel that allows these apples to rot."[19] This means that while individual officers are responsible for perpetrating misconduct, there are also systemic reasons why corruption is allowed to flourish.[20] In this case, seven officers were indicted for a bevy of charges, including robbery.

Individual Officer Characteristics

It is also possible that individual-level factors—gender, personality, prior criminal history, and problems in prior jobs—were associated with on-the-job misconduct. There is evidence that these individual level traits are in fact associated with

Focus on Policing

LAPD CRASH

LAPD CRASH units were established by then Chief Daryl Gates to combat the rising problem of gang violence and drug dealing in the city. More than 30 years ago, each of the LAPD's 18 divisions developed an independent Community Resources Against Street Hoodlums (CRASH) unit. The primary goal was to suppress the influx of gang-related crimes and increasing homicides in Los Angeles, which came about primarily from the increase in the drugs trade. Even among the ranks of the specialized CRASH units, some units were thought of as being more elite than others. The CRASH unit in the Rampart Division felt they were the most elite of all of the specialized units in LAPD.

The Rampart Division of the LAPD serves communities to the west of downtown. With roughly 165,000 residents occupying a 5.4-square-mile area, Rampart is one of Los Angeles's most densely populated communities and among the highest violent crime rates in the city. According to the LAPD investigation into corruption in the Rampart Division report, these officers routinely wore jackets and clothing with insignias identifying them as working in the Rampart Division. Officers taking pride in their work assignments is not inherently a bad thing; however, it appeared that their allegiance was taken to an extreme, and officers became more committed to the goals and values of their peer leaders than those of the department.

The investigation into corruption in the Rampart Division uncovered significant evidence that Rampart CRASH had developed its own culture and that it operated as an entity unto itself. This unit routinely made up its own rules and, for all intents and purposes, was left to function with little or no oversight, which perpetuated a feeling of cultural elitism and was a significant contributing factor in corruption. When asked why officers in this division behaved the way they did, officers frequently answered "It's the Rampart Way."

It was found that CRASH officers were awarded plaques for shooting civilians and criminal suspects. These plaques contained red or black playing cards. A red card indicated a suspect was wounded but survived and a black card indicated a suspect had been shot and killed. The black card was considered more prestigious. It was alleged that CRASH officers carried spare (throwaway) guns to plant on civilians and suspects, in order to justify the officers' use of deadly force or to cover up the officers' suspected crime. The

motto of Rampart CRASH was: "We intimidate those who intimidate others."

The investigation found that Rampart CRASH officers were involved in a litany of controversial practices including framing suspects, unprovoked shootings, malicious beatings, perjury, planting of false evidence, stealing and dealing narcotics, witness intimidation, bank robbery, and the covering up of evidence of these activities. This was the most widespread case of documented police misconduct in U.S. history. Many officers took part in or were aware of the misconduct of fellow officers, but like in many other police complaints, the investigations into the corruption of the Rampart CRASH unit were hampered by a lack of cooperation by the officers as well as the code of silence.

More than 70 Los Angeles police officers assigned to, or associated with, the Rampart CRASH unit were implicated in some form of misconduct. Of those 70 officers implicated in wrongdoing, enough evidence was found to bring 58 officers before an internal affairs disciplinary board. The result was that 24 LAPD officers were found to have committed wrongdoing, with 12 suspended, seven forced to resign or retire, and five terminated.

As a result of the investigation into falsified evidence and police perjury, over 100 prior criminal convictions were overturned. The LAPD Rampart-CRASH scandal resulted in over 140 civil lawsuits against the LAPD and the city of Los Angeles, costing over $125 million in total settlements. The full extent of Rampart police corruption is not known, and several rape, murder, and robbery investigations involving Rampart officers remain unsolved.[21]

More than 200 lawsuits and civil claims were filed against LAPD and the City of Los Angeles. More than 100 tainted criminal convictions were thrown out, and thousands more received increased scrutiny and further investigations. Eight officers were convicted of corruption-related crimes. The city attorney's office estimated the potential cost of settling civil suits touched by the Rampart scandal at a $125 million.

Critical Thinking

Do you think the corruption in the LAPD CRASH unit happened simply because of rogue police officers, or because of bad, or lack of, supervision?

Source: Board of Inquiry into the Rampart Area Corruption Incident, www.lapdonline.org/.../pdf/boi_pub.pdf.

Focus on Policing

Gender Differences in Misconduct

It is assumed that female police may engage in less misconduct than their male counterparts; after all, women commit less crime than men, and it stands to reason that they would engage in less professional misbehavior. Another factor may be early socialization: Because young girls are taught not to express negative emotions in response to provocation, they may be less likely to use aggressive or illegal tactics and more likely to use noncriminal coping mechanisms during confrontations.

An important recent study by Janne Gaub sheds some light on the effect gender has on police misconduct. Using a sample of more than 1,500 New York PD officers, her research addressed whether risk and protective factors of police misconduct operate the same way for both male and female police officers. Her data analysis found that there are clear differences in the factors that influence whether male and female police officers are fired for misconduct. One interesting difference was the influence of marriage and divorce. Male police officers were less likely to be dismissed for misconduct if they were married when their career began or got married while employed.

In contrast, marriage was protective for women only if they got married after they joined the NYPD. What is more puzzling is the effect of divorce on police misconduct. Divorced women who joined the NYPD were more likely to engage in misconduct than those who were single or married. Surprisingly, female officers who divorced while already working for the NYPD were far less likely to be fired for misconduct. How can this puzzling outcome be explained? Dr. Gaub concludes that the outcome is related to stress: Female police officers experience stress when they face ostracism and overt hostility from their male counterparts.

Women that are divorced may lack the family support that enables them to cope with this type of job stress, making these women more vulnerable to engaging in misconduct. In contrast, posits Gaub, once women are serving police officers, marriage may have a stabilizing effect on workplace misconduct: If the female officer is removing herself from a negative or dangerous marital situation, her stress level will decline and so will her rate of misconduct. Rather than divorce causing instability, the marital relationship itself causes instability and divorce allows the woman to regain stability in her own life.

Proactive investigation and special units were considerably more protective for women than for men. Status in elite specialized units (e.g., special weapons and tactics units, gang units, and K9 units) means they likely experience significant pressure to conform to the norms of the unit. However, it is possible that this token status works in the opposite way: After working so hard to get into these units, they do not want to ruin the opportunity for themselves and future women by committing crimes.

Conversely, being a supervisor was considerably more protective for men than for women. This is logical, given that (a) supervisors typically have less opportunity to commit misconduct, and (b) men are more likely to be supervisors than are women. Taken together with the findings related to marital status, these findings provide invaluable context that may begin to explain mixed findings in police misconduct research. In fact, additional research should identify the extent to which other characteristics of marginalization within policing supports this theory.

Critical Thinking

Getting married seems to have a positive effect on misbehavior, both among the police and the general public. What is it about marriage that reduces misbehavior? Or is it simply that people who are capable of getting married have more self-control and that personality trait also reduces the likelihood of them getting into trouble?

Source: Janne E. Gaub, "Understanding Police Misconduct Correlates: Does Gender Matter in Predicting Career-Ending Misconduct?," *Women & Criminal Justice* 30 (2020), 264–289.

misconduct and evidence that people who have had issues before joining the police were more likely to engage in misconduct and be terminated than those with clean records. To remedy this problem, police candidates with prior arrests and prior employment problems should be screened out, helping departments to reduce the likelihood of hiring future "bad cops."[22]

LO3

Describe how corruption can be controlled.

Controlling Corruption

How can police misconduct be controlled? One approach is to strengthen the internal administrative review process within police departments. A strong and well-supported internal affairs division has been linked to lowered corruption rates.[23] However, asking police to police themselves is not a simple task. Officers are often reluctant to discipline their peers. One review of disciplinary files of New York City police officers found that many miscreants escaped punishment when their cases were summarily dismissed by the police department without anyone ever interviewing victims or witnesses or making any other efforts to examine the evidence.[24] One reason may be the blue curtain mentality that inhibits police from taking action against their fellow officers. Surveys indicate that police officers are more reluctant than ordinary citizens to report unethical behavior on the part of their colleagues.[25]

Accountability System

accountability system

A system that makes police supervisors responsible for the behavior of the officers in their command.

Another approach, instituted by then–New York Commissioner Patrick Murphy in the wake of the Knapp Commission, is the **accountability system**. This holds that supervisors at each level are directly accountable for the illegal behaviors of the officers under them. Consequently, a commander can be demoted or forced to resign if one of the command officers is found guilty of corruption.[26] However, close scrutiny by a department can lower officer morale and create the suspicion that the officers' own supervisors distrust them. This may be a reason that some officers look the other way when misconduct happens. They do not want to disrupt morale or become pariahs in the department.

Review Boards

Police departments have also organized outside review boards or special prosecutors to investigate reported incidents of corruption. However, outside investigators and special prosecutors are often limited by their lack of intimate knowledge of day-to-day operations. As a result, they depend on the testimony of a few officers who are willing to cooperate, either to save themselves from prosecution or because they have a compelling moral commitment. Outside evaluators also face the problem of the blue curtain, which is quickly closed when police officers feel that their department is under scrutiny. Police officers will often not cooperate when they believe that they or the fellow officers are under scrutiny or may face discipline.

A more realistic solution to corruption, albeit a difficult one, might be to change the social context of policing. Police operations must be made more visible, and the public must be given freer access to police operations. All too often, the public finds out about police problems only when a scandal hits the newspaper. Another option is that some of the vice-related crimes the police now deal with might be decriminalized or referred to other agencies. Although decriminalization of vices cannot in itself end the problem, it could lower the pressure placed on individual police officers and help eliminate their moral dilemmas.

Police Misconduct: Abuse of Power and Biased Policing

Corruption is not the only misconduct engaged in by police officers. Some officers may routinely abuse the power given to them under the law. This occurs when police officers abuse or exploit their discretion to identify a suspect and create or obtain evidence needed to convict them at trial by engaging in planting or manufacturing evidence. For example, about 100 cases involving a group of three Baltimore police officers were put under review by the state's attorney's office when the discovery of body camera footage suggested that one of the officers in the trio had planted evidence at the scene of a drug arrest.[27]

Misconduct extends far beyond corruption to include racial profiling and illegal use of force by police officers.

Racial Profiling and Biased Policing

Early work investigating racial bias in policing was first conducted in the 1960s, spawning the term **racial profiling**, which refers to the practice of stopping, searching, and/or arresting criminal suspects based on their race or ethnicity. The terms driving while Black or DWB and racial profiling became a part of the United States vernacular in 2000 when the New Jersey State Police released thousands of pages of internal documents detailing racial profiling on New Jersey highways. Despite decades of denying the practice, after a series of lawsuits, New Jersey finally admitted that there was a problem after multiple lawsuits.[28] At first, national attention was focused on the disproportionate stopping of Black drivers. *Biased policing,* however, more accurately describes the full range of disparate policing. Stopping Black drivers is just one way race can influence police discretion. Racial profiling is a police-initiated action that relies primarily on race, ethnicity, or national origin rather than individual behavior.[29] More recently, attention and research has focused on the disproportionate use of lethal force, field encounters, searches, and arrests. Biased policing may also include the denial of police services to specific individuals or populations based on their ethnic composition.

racial profiling
Any police-initiated action that relies on the race, ethnicity, or national origin rather than the behavior of an individual or information that leads the police to a particular individual who has been identified as being, or having been, engaged in criminal activity.

Traffic Stops

Traffic stops are perhaps the most well researched and type of biased policing. A number of empirical studies have found that state and local police officers routinely stop and/or search Black motorists at a rate far greater than their representation in the driving pool:

- Brian Withrow looked at police practices in Wichita, Kansas, and found that Black citizens are stopped at disproportionately higher rates than non-Black citizens and that Black, Latino, and Hispanic citizens are more likely to be searched and arrested than non-Black,

AP Images/Colleen Long

Recognizing that profiling is a serious problem, police departments are now training officers to avoid racial stereotypes. Here, New York officers simulate a street stop during a training session. The NYPD is re-training thousands of officers on how to do street stops amid a wave of criticism about the department's controversial stop, question, and frisk policy that has been called racially biased.

non-Latino, and non-Hispanic citizens. Another of his studies, this one from San Jose, California, revealed that Latinos/Hispanics made up 31 percent of the city's population but accounted for 43 percent of the people stopped.[30]

■ Researchers at Northeastern University in Boston used four statistical tests to analyze 1.6 million traffic citations issued in towns across Massachusetts and found the following: ticketing resident people of color disproportionately more than White people, ticketing all people of color disproportionately more than White people, searching people of color more often than White people, and issuing warnings to White people more often than to people of color. According to the study, 15 police departments failed all four tests, 42 failed three tests, 87 failed two tests, and 105 failed one.[31]

■ Richard Lundman's analysis of citizen encounters with police indicates that (a) people of color are more likely to be stopped than White people, but (b) searches of vehicles driven by people of color are no more likely to yield drugs or contraband than searches of vehicles driven by White people.[32]

■ Michael Smith and Geoffrey Alpert found that once Black people, Latinos, and Hispanics are stopped, they are more likely than White people to be searched and arrested. Similar findings were reported by the New Jersey attorney general's office, which found that nearly 80 percent of people searched during traffic stops were Black, Latino, or Hispanic.[33]

■ Jesse J. Kalinowski, Matthew B. Ross, and Stephen L. Ross found that many Black motorists may adjust their driving behavior in response to racial profiling. As a result, they are the only group of motorists less likely to have fatal motor vehicle accidents in daylight, presumably driving more carefully when race is more easily observed; one reason is that Black motorists go slower in daylight than members of other racial groups. This phenomenon is most easily observed within states with high rates of police shootings of Black people.[34]

■ A report sponsored by the American Civil Liberties Union (ACLU) found that Boston police officers often engage in widespread racially biased *stop-and-frisk* practices, targeting people of color at far greater rates than White people. The report also states that Black citizens in the city studied were subjected to 63 percent of these encounters, even though they made up just 24 percent of that city's population. The ACLU report also showed that controlling for neighborhood-level crime rate does not explain this racial disparity.

The report further shows that as the Black population in this city increased as a percentage of the total population, so did the number of police encounters.[35] The ACLU reports that even after controlling for crime, police officers were more likely to initiate police encounters in Black neighborhoods and to initiate encounters with Black people. When questioned about this disparity, police officials gave no justification for 75 percent of these encounters, simply stating that they were investigatory in nature. More than 200,000 of these stop-and-frisk investigative encounters over a four-year period yielded no arrests, and only 2.5 percent led to seizure of contraband of any kind.

The more recent COVID-19 crisis in NYC also provides a window into how bias influences police decision making. In 2020, police officers in New York City were accused of differential enforcement strategies when enforcing distancing rules set up during the COVID-19 epidemic. Media reports showed pictures of swarms of mostly White New Yorkers sitting undisturbed in parks compared with combative encounters between the police and people of color in New York City.[36]

Measuring Bias

To measure bias, there must first be a benchmark—or a baseline to compare police interventions to the larger population. Phillip Atiba Goff and Kimberly Barsamian Kahn note that researchers have long tried to understand the relationship between race and crime.[37] In particular, racial profiling is difficult to measure. The typical way to measure racial profiling is to compare the racial demographics of police stops to the racial demographics of a population. This involves creating a fraction with, for example, the percentage of Black people stopped as the numerator and the percentage of Black people in the population as the denominator.

This means that a community that is 25 percent Black people should have 25 percent of police stops involving Black community members. This, however, is a flawed approach because it assumes that all people driving or walking in a community reside there and this is not always the case. Communities may have visitors who work or shop there without living there. This has been referred to as the *denominator problem*. Researchers have looked for creative ways to get around this problem.

One way is for researchers to look at smaller geographic areas. While it may be difficult to determine who lives or drives through an entire city, smaller geographic units like neighborhoods may be easier to understand.[38] Another way is for researchers to create a denominator is to observe the public.[39] This can be done through a traffic survey or looking at traffic accident data. These methods are not perfect. For example, relying on accident data assumes that all accidents are reported equally—which is not true. Researchers can also observe to see if they can determine the race of drivers or pedestrians to estimate police activity.

The Veil of Darkness Hypothesis

Another way to address the denominator problem is the veil of darkness (VOD) analytical method. As Michele Stacey and Heidi Bonner describe, VOD is an analytical approach that uses changes in natural lighting to assess disparate treatment in traffic stops.[40] The basic benchmark is stops that happen during daylight while the comparison is stops that happen in darkness. If there were no disparate impact, then the proportion of people of color stopped during daylight would be the same as the proportion stopped during darkness because it is more difficult to see a driver's race when it is dark or near dark.[41]

Another way to measure disparity is through the use of police records. Research conducted by Bocar Ba and colleagues suggests that Latino and Black police officers make fewer stops and use force less than their White colleagues—especially in encounters with Black community members.[42] Using data collected through open-records requests from the Chicago Police Department, Ba and his collaborators collected information about officer demographics, language skills, daily shift assignments, and career progression. They were able to then link those files to time-stamped, geo-located records of the same officers' decisions to stop, arrest, and use force in encounters with community members.

This undertaking resulted in a panel of 2.9 million officer shifts and 1.6 million enforcement events by nearly 7,000 officers between 2012 through 2015. What is remarkable about this study is that researchers were able to overcome some of the previous flaws from research—namely, the misconception that officers are evenly distributed throughout a city. In fact, they discovered that White officers work in different environments from officers of color, on average, and that men and women also work during different hours of the day.

For example, in Chicago, Black officers work in districts with 47 percent higher per-capita violent crime than White officers. With the data collected, Ba and colleagues were able to compare the actions of officers of different demographic profiles working in the same specific combination of month and year (e.g., January 2012), day of week, shift time, and assigned beat. This way, they can compare that officers are working in comparable circumstances in comparable places and times and thus having the same opportunity to take enforcement action. Findings suggest that given similar circumstances Black officers make substantially fewer arrests and are much less likely to use force in encounters with Black community members. Findings were similar but not was strong for Latino officers.

In another recent study, Shytierra Gaston used official reports of drug arrests made in St. Louis to understand how neighborhood context affects police discretion.[43] She found that in White neighborhoods drug arrests stem from reactive policing, meaning that community members called the police requesting service. Drug arrests in Black and racially mixed neighborhoods are more often the result of proactive policing—use of officers' discretionary stops based on neighborhood conditions, suspicion of ambiguous demeanor, or minor infractions that first drew their attention to the suspect.

The Effects of Profiling

Racial profiling and biased policing generally is bad public policy. This approach erodes public confidence in police and makes it harder for police officers to do their jobs.[44] If community members distrust police or lack confidence in police, their willingness to engage and cooperate with police is reduced. This reduces police legitimacy and efficacy. If community members are not comfortable reporting crime as victims or witnesses, police departments can't respond to that crime. Community members are less likely to comply with police requests and more likely to file complaints. In short, the effects of biased policing extend well beyond the initial incident. Ben Bowling and Leanne Weber note that stop-and-frisk policies can have a corrosive impact on social solidarity, leading to "feelings of exclusion, resentment, distrust of the police, alienation, social and political disenfranchisement."[45]

Biased policing can also have long-term effects on community members themselves. Disparate arrest and criminal justice involvement can affect employment prospects, housing, and even contact with family members. Beyond that, repeated contact alone can have some severe consequences. Legal scholars Samuel Gross and Katherine Barnes point out that the assumption that a stop-and-search is intrinsically a minor inconvenience is questionable. Its effect can be corrosive for police-community relations, particularly with people of color.

> As the level of the police officer's interest increases, the cost to the innocent citizen escalates rapidly. It's one thing to get a speeding ticket and an annoying lecture . . . it's quite another to be told to step out of the car and to be questioned . . . The questions may seem intrusive and out of line, but you can hardly refuse to answer an armed cop. At some point you realize you are not just another law-abiding citizen who's being checked out . . . like everyone else. You've been targeted. The trooper is not going through a routine so he can let you go . . . he wants to find drugs on you. . . . Those who have not been through this sort of

experience probably underestimate its impact. To be treated as a criminal is a basic insult to a person's self-image and his position in society. It cannot easily be shrugged off.[46]

To be clear, biased policing is not a phenomenon that is limited to the United States. Grace O'Brien points to the over-policing of Aboriginal people in Australia.[47] Advocates have long argued that riots in European countries are the result of disparate stop-and-search policies.[48] In 2020, racial profiling by French policing was challenged in a class-action lawsuit. Three human rights groups: Human Rights Watch, Amnesty International, and Open Society Justice Initiative allege that French police target Black people and people of Arab descent for field contacts. In July 2020, a Black British Olympic gold medalist accused British police of stopping her and her partner for their skin color.[49] While disparate policing remains at issue in the United States, it is not the only country where work remains.[50]

Police Brutality

Police brutality refers to needless and unjustified use of excessive force directed against civilians by police officers. Physical acts range from using excessive force when arresting or detaining a suspect to using violent methods to force confessions and admissions, escalating violence and force unnecessarily. In a broader sense, brutality may also involve verbal threats, harassment, intimidation, and other forms of verbal mistreatment.

Numerous cases of police brutality have made national headlines in addition to the 2020 murder of George Floyd. On March 23, 2020, Daniel Prude, a 41-year-old Black man, was killed after being physically restrained by police officers in Rochester, New York. Around 3 A.M., his brother called the police because he was concerned about Prude's safety because he was having a mental health episode and ran from the house into the street. Prude was experiencing a mental health episode and was walking naked in the street. He was evaluated for odd behavior the day before, but wasn't admitted to the hospital.

Multiple police officers and two emergency medical technicians arrived at Prude's location, where he was naked and bleeding. One officer exited his car and approached Prude, pointing a Taser at him while asking him multiple times to get on the ground. Prude complied, and was then asked by the officer to put his hands behind his back, to which he also complied and was handcuffed. During the arrest, he said, "Yes, sir" several times to the officer.

Prude began to spit so the officers put a mesh bag—known as a spit hood—over his head. They held him face down and pressed his body into the pavement for two minutes and 15 seconds, until he stopped breathing.

LO5
Describe the effects of police brutality.

police brutality

Refers to needless and unjustified use of excessive force directed against civilians. It can include beatings, racial abuse, unlawful killings, or excessive use of riot control agents at protests.

Steve Sanchez Photos/Shutterstock.com

The killing of George Floyd on March 3, 2020, sparked outrage around the country. In Manhattan, hundreds took to the streets protesting against police brutality after Floyd's death at the hands of Minneapolis police. How would you put a stop to race-based and unnecessary violence?

Prude received CPR on the scene and later died of complications from asphyxia after being taken off life support.

Rochester police initially described his death as a drug overdose. It went mostly unnoticed. But nightly protests erupted after body camera video was released nearly six months later, following pressure from Prude's family. The video showed that one officer pushed Prude's face against the ground, while another officer pressed a knee to his back. The police officers who put a hood over his head and pressed his body against the pavement until he stopped breathing did not face criminal charges after a grand jury declined to indict them.

The autopsy report ruled Prude's death a homicide and also included the contributing factors to his death as "excited delirium" and acute intoxication by the drug PCP. The killing first received attention in September 2020 when the police body camera video and written reports were released, along with the autopsy report. Following the report's release, protesters demonstrated outside the Rochester police headquarters and many considered the death to be related to Prude's race. The demonstrations were connected to the Black Lives Matter movement and the string of racial justice events of 2020.

On the night of June 12, 2020, Rayshard Brooks, a 27-year-old Black man, was fatally shot twice in the back by Atlanta Police Department Officer Garrett Rolfe following a drunk driving incident. At approximately 10:42 P.M., Officer Devin Brosnan was responding to a complaint that Brooks was asleep in a car, blocking a Wendy's restaurant drive-through lane. Brosnan encountered Brooks, asleep in his car, and radioed for assistance. Officer Rolfe arrived and conducted a breathalyzer exam, which indicated that Brooks' blood-alcohol level was above the legal limit for driving.

Officers Rolfe and Brosnan began to handcuff Brooks and a struggle ensued. Brooks grabbed a hold of Brosnan's Taser and ran away. With Officer Rolfe in pursuit, Brooks fired the Taser over his shoulder toward Rolfe. Officer Rolfe then fired his weapon three times at Brooks, striking him twice in the back as he fled. A third shot struck an occupied car. Brooks died after surgery.

Footage of the incident was recorded from the officers' body cameras, a cell phone from a witness, and the security system at the restaurant. The videos of the incident and Brooks being shot in the back were widely broadcast. Atlanta Police Chief Erika Shields resigned the next day. Officer Rolfe was fired and Officer Brosnan was placed on administrative duty. Rolfe was charged with felony murder and 10 other offenses. Brosnan with charged with aggravated assault and two counts of violation of oath.

Causes of Brutality

Why does brutality exist and what are its suspected causes?

Class and Status

According to Donald Black's well-received *Theory of Law*, the application of the law—its amount, direction, and content—is not uniform, but controlled by a variety of sociological factors including economic status.[51] Research has supported Black's thesis; police are more likely to use force to control an indigent suspect who victimizes a member of the upper class than when the suspect and victim are members of economically marginalized communities. One reason is that in economically marginalized communities, both in the United States and abroad,

Critical Thinking

Should police officers who are suspected or who have committed corruption be allowed to go through training and retain their jobs, or should they be prohibited from policing anywhere in the country?

aggressive police tactics are welcomed by residents who feel that extrajudicial police violence is preferable to attacks by gangs and violent criminals.[52]

Stress and Strain

Policing can be a stressful occupation and that stress can result in feelings of strain that have directly been related to anger and aggressive responses. A recent study by Stephen Bishopp and his associates measured police strain with such variables as "felonious death of a police colleague," "felonious assault/injury to yourself," "felonious death of a citizen," "severe but nonfatal injury to police colleague," "had to shoot a person in the line of duty," "killed someone in the line of duty," "responded to any call involving an incident which resulted with the death of a child (i.e., a person younger than 12 years of age)," and "used your TASER to subdue a suspect." They found that officers who experience job-related stress and strain were much more likely to verbally physically abuse citizens and that White officers perceived higher levels of strain than Black officers. Nonetheless, the strain-abuse association applied to police officers of both races.[53]

Racial Bias

Racial prejudice is another factor that may unleash an abusive officers who allow race to shape their response. Research shows that White officers are more likely to use force when they engage with a Black suspect than when the suspect is White.[54] One approach to study this phenomenon is to use a laboratory setting to study police responses to stimulus. In one such study, images were shown to participants, who then had less than a second to decide whether they would shoot the target. In some images, the suspects were armed while in others they were holding objects that were not weapons, such as a wallet or cell phone. The analysis showed that the participants were quicker to shoot when an armed person was Black, slower to choose "not to shoot" when an unarmed person was Black, and more willing to shoot Black targets in general.[55]

Race may also play a role when verbal abuse occurs. When interactions recorded on police body cameras are analyzed, they show that race plays a significant role in the way police officers interact with citizens: Police officers talk to Black community members more disrespectfully than to White community members in everyday traffic stops, even after controlling for such relevant factors as officer race, infraction severity, stop location, and stop outcome.[56]

Personality

It has long been suspected that some police officers manifest what is referred to as an authoritarian personality. On the one hand, they exhibit extreme obedience and unquestioning respect for those in authority and are willing to carry out orders even if they contrast with personal beliefs. On the other hand, people who display authoritarian traits expect those they consider subordinate to unquestionably obey their commands and orders. When an authoritarian police officer orders a citizen to get on the ground, exit their car, or show their hands, they expect to be obeyed immediately. Failure to do so may be met with violent and aggressive reaction and submission to the authority of a person external to the self, which is realized through the oppression of subordinate people. The authoritarian personality was first identified after World War II by Theodor Adorno and his colleagues in an effort to understand why Nazi soldiers were willing to obey orders that the average person might find reprehensible.[57]

Policing Style

As you may recall, there have been a number of research studies that show that there are different styles of policing.[58] While some officers see themselves as social workers in blue, others see themselves as crime fighters, who are very aggressive when enforcing the law. Because many of these aggressive officers have an "authoritarian personality," they are willing to use all available means, legal or illegal, to handle a situation because the end justifies the means. Because they are overly aggressive, they become frustrated when forced to perform duties other than enforcing the law. The crime fighter may be the police officer most likely to use brutal or violent methods when identifying suspects, making arrests, and interrogating people in custody.

Effects of Brutality

Police brutality is always illegal. Not only may media reports of police brutality reduce respect for police and fuel demands for social justice, they can also have a measurable effect on crime reporting and crime rates. Citizens may be reluctant to call police, supply information, or make witness statements if they view the police as engaged in illegal activity, a reaction that may present a serious threat to public safety if they lower citizen crime reporting. One study found that in the aftermath of one of Milwaukee, Wisconsin's most publicized cases of police violence against an unarmed Black man, residents of Milwaukee's neighborhoods, especially residents of Black neighborhoods, were far less likely to report crime. The effect lasted for over a year and resulted in a total net loss of approximately 22,200 calls for service; the effect of brutalization on calls for service has not been limited to Milwaukee. As the authors of the study conclude, "Police misconduct can powerfully suppress one of the most basic forms of civic engagement: calling 911 for matters of personal and public safety."[59]

Brutality can also have long-term individual effects on its targets. Take for instance the effects of racial bias in the use of unnecessary force. A national-level survey that asked respondents about how much they "worry" about experiencing police violence found that Black community members worry five times more than their White neighbors; Hispanic and Latino community members worry about police brutality more than four times that of White people. The data from this survey suggest that worrying about police brutality is an emotional injury that people of color disproportionately experience.[60]

The fact that citizens of color experience more brutality and worry about it more than White community members can have long-term effects and produce poor health outcomes. A recent analysis by Alang, McAlpine, McCreedy, and Hardeman found that among Black citizens, police brutality produced five significant long-term outcomes:

1. Fatal injuries that increase population-specific mortality rates;
2. Adverse physiological responses that increase illness and injury;
3. Racist public reactions that cause stress;
4. Arrests, incarcerations, and legal, medical, and funeral bills that cause financial strain;
5. Oppression that causes victims to feel disempowerment.[61]

One answer to these problems is to make it easier for citizens to file complaints and for departments to take them seriously. There are indications that this has indeed happened in some cities. When James Wright studied the complaint process in New Orleans and Indianapolis, he found that in both of these cities Black citizens are more likely to have their complaint sustained when filed against a White officer compared to a White citizen. This indicates that any racial bias in the complaint process seems to be eroding.[62]

Reducing Abuse of Power and Brutality

In order to limit police misconduct and improve police-community relationships, particularly relationships with marginalized communities, the Task Force in 21st Century Policing recommended that police departments increase officer diversity, raise educational requirements for new officers, and implement community policing strategies.[63] Recent research suggests that the task force was correct: increasing educational levels of serving officers can significantly reduce police brutality.[64]

Redirect Training

Another suggestion by the 21st Century Task Force is to redirect police training to include mandatory Crisis Intervention Training (CIT). According to this mandate, police officers would be trained to deal with individuals in crisis or living with mental disabilities as part of both basic recruit and in-service officer training—as well as instruction in disease of addiction, implicit bias and cultural responsiveness, policing in a democratic society, procedural justice, and effective social interaction and tactical skills."[65]

Stress Reduction

Policing is, by its nature, a stressful occupation, filled with danger on the streets and organizational demands for improving performance. There is also evidence that stress, both organizational and situational, is highly correlated with abusive behavior, especially when officers also experience anger rage.

A test of this assumption was recently conducted by Stephen Bishopp and his associates with a large sample of officers in three different agencies throughout the state of Texas. Bishopp found that regardless of race, stress was significantly related to verbally abusing citizens and use of unnecessary force and those who experienced stress-related anger were the ones most likely to engage in abusive behaviors. Contrary to expectations, there were little significant differences between White officers and officers of color.[66]

The stress-anger-abuse paradigm leads directly to the assumption that strain reduction programs can reduce the use of force. Research shows that police officers who enroll in a stress-reduction training program are less likely to use illegitimate force than those not so trained; the greater the number of stress-trained officers on a force, the lower the overall use of force.[67]

The Washington Post/Getty Images

Police officers like those shown here are now being trained to deal with individuals in crisis or living with mental disabilities and drug addiction without resorting to coercive methods. One way of achieving this goal is helping officers deal effectively with job-related stress.

Easing Disciplinary Protections

Some groups like the ACLU have called for legislation making it easier to prosecute police officers whose conduct amounts to criminal violations. One effort has been to pass legislation that eliminates the Law Enforcement Officer Bill or Rights, now a law in 16 states.

The various "Law Enforcement Officers Bill of Rights" gives police officers protections unavailable to other state workers. Most require that police officers be given a formal waiting period before they have to cooperate with internal inquiries into their behavior, expunging misconduct complaint records after a certain period, and ensuring that only fellow officers—not civilians—serve on investigative boards.

A number of experts, legal scholars, and politicians have called for states to rescind or eliminate the Law Enforcement Bill of Rights on the grounds that it both protects police officers charged with misconduct while at the same time dissuades citizens from filing complaints.[68] There are ongoing efforts in Maryland, which has one of the nation's most protective laws, to modify or eliminate the Law Enforcement Bill of Rights. A recent work group made the following recommendations that can be used in place of the Law Enforcement Bill of Rights:

■ Requiring an independent investigation of cases in which officers have shot people or otherwise killed or seriously injured individuals. It did not specify which agency should conduct investigations.

■ Creating a standard for types of force that are not allowed to be used by police, including addressing chokeholds and putting handcuffed individuals facedown.

■ Creating penalties for officers who violate the use-of-force law, including up to 10 years in prison if convicted.

■ Requiring the Maryland Police Training and Standards Commission to maintain a database of officers fired for use-of-force violations.

■ Establishing that officers have a duty to intervene when a colleague is using inappropriate force.

■ Limiting when officers can seek "no-knock" warrants, so they can only ask for them when there is a threat to the safety of officers or individuals.

■ Requiring police departments to create "early warning systems" to identify problematic officers and involving more civilians in police trial boards that review disciplinary cases.[69]

Changing the Police Mindset

Another approach to reducing police abuse of power may involve the mind set of officers who do not understand and/or appreciate the will of the citizens they serve. While some police identify with a "serve and protect" vision of policing, others view themselves as a member of the "thin blue line," who keep the criminal element under control, no matter what the cost to themselves or the public. Changing attitudes and orientations starting with indoctrination in the police academy and through the use of career-long training might help to reorient the job approach into one that both reduces hostility with the public while maintaining efficiency. The following Focus on Policing: Warriors vs. Guardians feature presents evidence of the way police view their job and how those perceptions affect performance.

Focus on Policing

Warriors vs. Guardians

Recent research by Kyle McLean, Scott Wolfe, Jeff Rojek, Geoffrey Alpert, and Michael Smith looked at police professional orientations and how it affects job performance and misconduct. The first orientation held by officers was labeled the "warrior" approach to police work. Those who embraced this view of police work emphasized officer safety and prioritized crime fighting as their primary mission. Warriors saw themselves as neo-soldiers serving on the front lines, that is, the thin blue line, in a battle to preserve order and civilization against the criminal element.

While this may sound harsh and militaristic, there are many citizens who agree that a police officer's role is to combat crime. Nonetheless, the warrior orientation sets police officers apart from the public, few of whom can understand how what the typical police officer routinely encounters: violence, abuse, degradation, and addiction. What develops is a culture and attitude that officers, who risk their lives every day, are beyond reproach and therefore immune from being criticized by the "know-nothing" public.

In contrast, the officer who embraces the guardian mindset prioritizes service over crime fighting. Seeing themselves as a protector of the public, the guardian officer emphasizes building positive relationships between the police and the community. Because police officers are agents of the state, paid by the public, their activities must be subject to the approval of the people they serve. Forming a relationship with the community, increasing the public's trust in police, while at the same time protecting them from harm, is the guardian's highest priority.

Using surveys conducted in two police departments, the researchers set out to assess how these conflicting mentalities were related to police performance. They found that the guardian mindset was associated with greater communication with citizens and less support of attitudes toward use of force misconduct. These officers were more willing to explain their behavior, for example, why they contacted the subject and allowed them to explain their side of the story. In contrast, the warrior mindset was associated with weaker communication with the public, an emphasis on control, and more positive attitudes toward the use and abuse of force.

Critical Thinking

While the researchers found that there was some overlap between the orientations and some officers held attitudes that reflected both orientations, their conclusion was that shifting to a guardian mentality may result in positive policing outcomes. Do you agree?

Source: Kyle McLean, Scott E. Wolfe, Jeff Rojek, Geoffrey P. Alpert, and Michael R. Smith, "Police Officers as Warriors or Guardians: Empirical Reality or Intriguing Rhetoric?," *Justice Quarterly* 37 (2020), 1096–1118.

Consent Decrees

As Yale Law Professor Monica Bell notes, reform may also be accomplished through legal means, such as imposed consent decrees. Take for instance Section 14141 of the Violent Crime Control and Law Enforcement Act of 1994, also known as the Clinton Crime Bill 263. Section 14141 allows the U.S. attorney general to sue a local police department for violating constitutional and legal rights of citizens. Section 14141 of the crime bill permits the Justice Department to investigate any "pattern or practice of conduct by law enforcement officers" that "deprives persons of rights, privileges, or immunities secured or protected by the Constitution or laws of the United States." If violations can be found, the Justice department can sue to "obtain appropriate equitable and declaratory relief to eliminate the pattern or practice." The Department of Justice (DOJ) may use the threat of litigation or actual court practice to force the police agency to consent to demands. While Section 14141 has been used to reform police in a number of departments, including Los Angeles, it was not employed once during the Trump administration.[70]

Increase Wages

Police are not paid sufficiently in many jurisdictions, a condition that encourages them to take on part-time jobs, work overtime, and work paid details. It may encourage police to cut corners, such as getting involved in overtime scandals, as discussed earlier in the chapter. Low wages may also encourage the best, most competent officers to seek other modes of employment. The most skilled and experienced officers may be paid more working for private security agencies than for the local police. It is not uncommon for police officers to earn more in overtime and detail pay than in their base salary. Higher pay may mean less time spent on outside work, greater on-the-job wellness, less stress, improved responses, and more rational decision making.

Summary

LO1   Describe the varieties of police corruption.

Corruption can take on a number of forms. Police officers occasionally engage in serious criminal behavior, the very crimes they are entrusted with controlling, ranging from drug dealing to burglary. Another form of corruption involves bribery and extortion. Bribery is initiated by the citizen; extortion is initiated by the officer. In some cases, an officer solicits (or is offered) regular payoffs to ignore criminal activities, such as gambling or narcotics dealing.

LO2   Explain why police officers engage in corruption for personal gain.

The wide discretion that police enjoy, coupled with the low visibility they maintain with the public and their own supervisors, makes them likely candidates for corruption. In addition, the code of secrecy maintained by the police subculture helps insulate corrupt officers from the law. Corruption is also a function of society's ambivalence toward many forms of vice-related criminal behavior that police officers are sworn to control.

Corruption is also linked to specific environmental and social conditions that enhance the likelihood that police officers may become involved in misconduct. For example, in some areas, a rapid increase in the marginalized group residential population may be viewed as a threat to dominant group interests. Police in these areas may become overly aggressive and routinely use coercive strategies. It has also been suggested that police corruption is generated at the departmental level and that conditions within the department produce and nurture deviance. It is also possible that individual level factors—gender, personality, prior criminal history, and problems in prior jobs—were associated with on-the-job misconduct.

LO3   Describe how corruption can be controlled.

Police departments have also organized outside review boards or special prosecutors to investigate reported incidents of corruption. However, outside evaluators also face the problem of the police code of silence, that is, the blue curtain, which is quickly closed when police officers feel that their department is under scrutiny.

A more realistic solution to corruption would be to change the social context of policing. Police operations must be made more visible, and the public must be given freer access to police operations. Another option is that some of the vice-related crimes the police now deal with might be decriminalized or referred to other agencies. Although decriminalization of a vice cannot in itself end the problem, it could lower the pressure placed on individual police officers and help eliminate their moral dilemmas.

LO4   Recognize what is meant by the term *racial profiling*.

Racial profiling refers to the use of race used inappropriately as a criterion in professional decision making. Racial profiling denotes the practice of targeting or stopping an individual based primarily on their race rather than more appropriate legal factors. Racial profiling occurs when police discretion to stop, search, and arrest citizens is shaped by discrimination and racial prejudice. The assumption is that police officers routinely stop, question, and search Black people, both pedestrians and motorists, to determine levels of criminality. Racial profiling violates civil rights and differentiates on the basis of race or ethnicity. The routine indiscriminately stopping of cars driven by Black people had prompted creation of the term *driving while Black*, denoting the fact that Black motorists are routinely stopped and profiled. A number of empirical studies have found that state and local police officers routinely stop and/or search Black motorists at a rate far greater than their representation in the driving pool. Another practice related to racial profiling is the stopping and frisking of young Black men who have not displayed suspicious behaviors.

In the short term, racial profiling can reduce confidence in police while increasing resentment and suspicion. Racial profiling also increases the chances of arrest, detention, and charges being filed, especially for acts that had little or nothing to do with the original stop. So, racial profiling can illegally force someone to have a criminal record that might not have existed in other circumstances, a record that can have long-term consequences.

LO5 Describe the effects of police brutality.

Policing can be a stressful occupation and that stress can result in feelings of strain that have directly been related to anger and aggressive responses.

Racial prejudice is another factor that may unleash an abusive officer who allows race to shape their response. Research shows that White officers are more likely to use force when they engage with a Black suspect than when the suspect is White. Race may also play a role when verbal abuse occurs. It has long been suspected that some police officers manifest what is referred to as an authoritarian personality. On the one hand, they exhibit extreme obedience and unquestioning respect for those in authority and are willing to carry out orders even if they contrast with personal beliefs. On the other hand, people who display authoritarian traits expect those they consider subordinate to unquestionably obey their commands and orders. There have been a number of research studies that show that there are different styles of policing. Some officers view themselves as "social workers in blue" while helping citizens in need. In contrast, crime fighters are very aggressive when enforcing the law and the officers are most likely to have an "authoritarian personality." Because they are overly aggressive, they become frustrated when forced to perform duties other than enforcing the law.

Key Terms

police corruption, 280
zero tolerance policy, 280
meat eater, 280
grass eater, 280

bribe, 283
case fixing, 283
extortion, 283
accountability system, 288

racial profiling, 289
police brutality, 293

Notes

1. Grace Sparks, "Polling Highlights Stark Gap in Trust of Police between Black and White Americans," *CNN,* June 2, 2020.
2. Samuel Walker, *Popular Justice* (New York: Oxford University Press, 1980), p. 64.
3. Louise Westmarland, "Police Ethics and Integrity: Breaking the Blue Code of Silence," *Policing and Society* 15 (2005), 145–165.
4. Joseph Pozsgai-Alvarez, "The Abuse of Entrusted Power for Private Gain: Meaning, Nature and Theoretical Evolution," *Crime, Law and Social Change* 74 (2020), 433–455.
5. Knapp Commission, *Report on Police Corruption* (New York, NY: Braziller, 1973), pp. 1–34.
6. Elizabeth Neuffer, "Seven Additional Detectives Linked to Extortion Scheme," *Boston Globe*, October 25, 1988, p. 60.
7. Kevin Cullen, "U.S. Probe Eyes Bookie Protection," *Boston Globe*, October 25, 1988, p. 1.
8. Michael Johnston, *Political Corruption and Public Policy in America* (Monterey, CA: Brooks/Cole, 1982), p. 75.
9. William Doherty, "Ex-Sergeant Says He Aided Bid to Sell Exam," *Boston Globe*, February 26, 1987, p. 61.
10. Department of Justice, U.S. Attorney's Office, District of Massachusetts, "Former Massachusetts State Trooper Sentenced in Overtime Abuse Investigation," June 20, 2019.
11. United States Attorney's Office, Northern District of Illinois, "Former Chicago Police Officer Sentenced to 13 Years in Prison for Participating in Robbery and Extortion Crew," October 1, 2020.

12. James Ruiz and Christine Bono, "At What Price a 'Freebie'? The Real Cost of Police Gratuities," *Criminal Justice Ethics* 23, no. 1 (2004), 44–54.

13. M. Jones, "Police Officer Gratuities and Public Opinion," *Police Forum* 7 no. 4 (1997), 8–11.

14. Lawrence Sherman, *Police Corruption: A Sociological Perspective* (Garden City, NY: Doubleday, 1974), pp. 40–41.

15. Samuel Walker, *Police in Society* (New York, NY: McGraw Hill, 1983), p. 181.

16. Robert Kane, "The Social Ecology of Police Misconduct," *Criminology* 40 (2002), 867–897.

17. Lawrence W. Sherman, "Police Corruption—A Sociological Perspective." U.S. Department of Justice, Office of Justice Programs NCJ Number 14985 (1974), p. 194.

18. Robert Daley, *Prince of the City* (New York, NY: Houghton Mifflin, 1978).

19. Italics part of original quote. http://www.copinthehood.com/.

20. Peter Moskos, *Cop in the Hood: My Year Policing Baltimore's Eastern District* (Princeton Press, 2009).

21. Joseph Avrahamy. "Good Cops Get Justice—The Untold Story of the LAPD Rampart Scandal." Insider exclusive. https://insiderexclusive.com/good-cops-get-justice-the-untold-story-of-the-lapd-rampart-scandal/.

22. James J. Fyfe and Robert Kane , "Bad Cops: A Study of Career-Ending Misconduct Among New York City Police Officers." US Department of Justice (2006), p. 763.

23. Lawrence W. Sherman, "Police Corruption—A Sociological Perspective." US Department of Justice, Office of Justice Programs NCJ Number 14985 (1974), p. 194.

24. Kevin Flynn, "Police Dept. Routinely Drops Cases of Officer Misconduct, Report Says," *The New York Times*, September 15, 1999, p. 1.

25. Gary R. Rothwell and J. Norman Baldwin, "Whistle-Blowing and the Code of Silence in Police Agencies," *Crime and Delinquency* 53 (2007), 605–632.

26. Barbara Gelb, *Tarnished Brass: The Decade After Serpico* (New York: Putnam, 1983); Candace McCoy, "Lawsuits Against Police: What Impact Do They Have?" *Criminal Law Bulletin* 20 (1984), 49–56.

27. Kylee Tsuru, "Body Camera Footage Prompts Review of 100 Baltimore Cases," *CNN*, July 20, 2017.

28. https://www.nytimes.com/2000/12/03/nyregion/inside-story-racial-bias-denial-new-jersey-files-reveal-drama-behind-profiling.html.

29. Deborah Ramirez, Jack Mcdevitt, and Amy Farrell, "U.S. Department of Justice, a Resource Guide to Racial Profiling Data Collection Systems," 3 (2000).

30. Brian L. Withrow, "Race-Based Policing: A Descriptive Analysis of the Wichita Stop Study," *Police Practice and Research* 5, no. 3 (2004), 223–240.

31. Amy Farrell, Jack McDevitt, Lisa Bailey, Carsten Andresen, and Erica Pierce, "Massachusetts Racial and Gender Profiling Study: Final Report," (2004).

32. Richard J. Lundman, "Driver Race, Ethnicity, and Gender and Citizen Reports of Vehicle Searches by Police and Vehicle Search Hits: Toward a Triangulated Scholarly Understanding," *Journal of Criminal Law and Criminology* (2004), 309–350.

33. Michael R. Smith and Geoffrey P. Alpert, "Searching for Direction: Courts, Social Science, and the Adjudication of Racial Profiling Claims," *Justice Quarterly* 19, no. 4 (2002), 673–703.

34. Jesse J. Kalinowski , Matthew B. Ross, and Stephen L. Ross, "Endogenous Driving Behavior in Tests of Racial Profiling in Police Traffic Stops," September 3, 2019.

35. https://aclum.org/our-work/aclum-issues/racial-justice/ending-racist-stop-and-frisk/.

36. Live Update, "A Violent Encounter Prompts Concerns about Unequal Policing of Social Distancing," *The New York Times*, May 4, 2020.

37. P. Atiba Goff and K. Barsamian Kahn, "Racial Bias in Policing: Why We Know Less Than We Should," *Social Issues and Policy Review* 6, no. 1 (2012), 177–210.

38. L. A. Fridell, "By the Numbers: A Guide for Analyzing Race Data from Vehicle Stops," (Washington, DC: Police Executive Research Forum, 2014).

39. R. S. Engel J. M. Calnon, "Examining the Influence of Drivers' Characteristics during Traffic Stops with Police: Results from a National Survey," *Justice Quarterly* 21, no. 1 (2004), 49–90.

40. M. Stacey and H. S. Bonner, "Veil of Darkness and Investigating Disproportionate Impact in Policing: When Researchers Disagree," *Police Quarterly* 24, no. 1 (2021), 55–73.

41. Ibid.

42. B. A. Ba, D. Knox, J. Mummolo, and R. Rivera, "The Role of Officer Race and Gender in Police-Civilian Interactions in Chicago," *Science* 371, no. 6530 (2021), 696–702.

43. S. Gaston, "Enforcing Race: A Neighborhood-Level Explanation of Black–White Differences in Drug Arrests," *Crime & Delinquency* 65, no. 4 (2019), 499–526.

44. David Harris, "Racial Profiling: Past, Present, and Future?," *Criminal Justice* 34 (2020), 10–20.

45. Ben Bowling and Leanne Weber, "Stop and Search in Global Context: An Overview," *Policing and Society* 21 (2011), 480–488.

46. Samuel R. Gross and Katherine Y. Barnes, "Road Work: Racial Profiling and Drug Interdiction on the Highway," *Michigan Law Review* 101, no. 3 (2002), 651–754.

47. G. O'Brien, "Racial Profiling, Surveillance and Over-Policing: The Over-Incarceration of Young First Nations Males in Australia," *Social Sciences* 10, no. 2 (2021), 68.

48. D. Oberwittler and S. Roché, "Ethnic Disparities in Police Initiated Contact of Adolescents and Attitudes towards the Police in France and Germany," *Police-Citizen Relations across the World: Comparing Sources and Contexts of Trust and Legitimacy* (2018), 73–107.

49. https://www.nytimes.com/2020/07/07/world/europe/uk-police-bianca-williams-racial-profiling.html.

50. Shytierra Gaston, "Producing Race Disparities: A Study of Drug Arrests across Place and Race," *Criminology* 57 (2019), 424–452.

51. This section relies heavily on the work of Robert Worden. See, Robert Worden, "The 'Causes' of Police Brutality: Theory and Evidence on Police Use of Force." In William A. Geller and Hans Toch (eds.), *Police Violence* (New Haven, CT: Yale University Press, 1996).

52. Jon Gordon, "The Legitimation of Extrajudicial Violence in an Urban Community," Social Forces, 98 (2020), 1174–1195.

53. Stephen Bishopp, Nicole Leeper Piquero, Alex R. Piquero, John L. Worrall, and Jessica Rosenthal, "Police Stress and Race: Using General Strain Theory to Examine Racial Differences in Police Misconduct," *Crime & Delinquency* 66, no. 13–14 (2020), 1811–1838.

54. James Wright and Andrea Headley, "Police Use of Force Interactions: Is Race Relevant or Gender Germane?," *American Review of Public Administration* 50 (2020), 851–864.

55. Yara Mekawi and Konrad Bresin, "Is the Evidence from Racial Bias Shooting Task Studies a Smoking Gun? Results from a Meta-Analysis," *Journal of Experimental Social Psychology* 61 (2015), 120–133.

56. Rob Voigt, Nicholas P. Camp, Vinodkumar Prabhakaran, William L. Hamilton, Rebecca C. Hetey, Camilla M. Griffiths, David Jurgens, Dan Jurafsky, and Jennifer L. Eberhardt, "Language from Police Body Camera Footage Shows Racial Disparities in Officer Respect," *Proceedings of the National Academy of Sciences* 114, no. 25 (2017), 6521–6526, doi: 10.1073/pnas.1702413114. https://www.pnas.org/content/114/25/6521.short.

57. Theodor W. Adorno, Else Frenkel-Brunswik, Daniel Levinson, and Nevitt Sanford. *The Authoritarian Personality, Studies in Prejudice Series, Volume 1* (New York: Harper & Row, 1950).

58. James Q. Wilson, *Varieties of Police Behavior: The Management of Law and Order in Eight Communities* (Cambridge, MA: Havard U Press, 1969); William Muir, *Police: Street Corner Politicians* (Chicago, IL: University of Chicago Press, 1977).

59. Matthew Desmond, Andrew Papachristos, David Kirk, "Police Violence and Citizen Crime Reporting in the Black Community," *American Sociological Review* 81 (2016), 857–876.

60. Amanda Graham, Murat Haner, Melissa M. Sloan, Francis T. Cullen, Teresa C. Kulig, and Cheryl Lero Jonson, "Race and Worrying About Police Brutality: The Hidden Injuries of Minority Status in America," *Victims & Offenders* 15 (2020), 549–573.

61. Sirry Alang, Donna McAlpine, Ellen McCreedy, and Rachel Hardeman, "Police Brutality and Black Health: Setting the Agenda for Public Health Scholars," *American Journal of Public Health* 107 (2017), 662–665.

62. James E. Wright II, "Will They Even Hear Me? How Race Influences Citizen Complaint Outcomes, Public Performance & Management Review," 43, no. 2, 257–277, doi: 10.1080 /15309576.2019.1660188.

63. Kayla Preito-Hodge and Donald Tomaskovic-Devey, "A Tale of Force: Examining Policy Proposals to Address the Issue of Police Violence" June 17, 2020. Available at SSRN: https://ssrn.com /abstract=3629141 or http://dx.doi.org/10.2139/ssrn.3629141.

64. Pamela Wood, "Maryland House work group recommends ditching state's Law Enforcement Officers' Bill of Rights," *Baltimore Sun,* October 15, 2020.

65. President's Task Force on 21st Century Policing. Published 2015. *Final Report of the President's Task Force on 21st Century Policing* (Washington, DC: Office of Community Oriented Policing Services, 2015).

66. Stephen Bishopp, Nicole Leeper Piquero, Alex R. Piquero, John L. Worrall, and Jessica Rosenthal, "Police Stress and Race: Using General Strain Theory to Examine Racial Differences in Police Misconduct," *Crime & Delinquency* 66, no. 13–14 (2020), 1811–1838.

67. Li Danyao, Sean Nicholson-Crotty, and Jill Nicholson-Crotty, "Creating Guardians or Warriors? Examining the Effects of Non-Stress Training on Policing Outcomes," *American Review of Public Administration* 51 (2021), 3–16.

68. Rebecca Tan, "There's a Reason It's Hard to Discipline Police. It Starts with a Bill of Rights 47 Years Ago," *The Washington Post,* August 20, 2020.

69. Pamela Wood, "Maryland House Work Group Recommends Ditching State's Law Enforcement Officer's Bill of Rights," *Baltimore Sun*, October 15, 2020.

70. Monica Bell, "Police Reform and the Dismantling of Legal Estrangement," *Yale Law Journal* 126 (2017), 2054–2150.

Legal Controls

Learning Objectives

LO1 Discuss how the Fourth Amendment controls police.

LO2 Define search and arrest.

LO3 Distinguish between search warrants and arrest warrants.

LO4 Explain when warrants are required.

LO5 Explain a field interrogation (Terry stop).

LO6 Explain the *Miranda v. Arizona* decision.

LO7 Demonstrate the exclusionary rule, including its extensions and exceptions.

Chapter Outline

I n a recent 5–3 decision, *Torres v. Madrid* (2021), the U.S. Supreme Court held that a person may be "seized" by a police officer per the Fourth Amendment to the Constitution even if the person gets away. It seems that police officers intended to execute a warrant in an apartment complex. Though they didn't think she was the target of the warrant, they approached Roxanne Torres in the parking lot. Torres got in a car, but since she was experiencing methamphetamine withdrawal, and didn't notice the officers until one tried to open her car door.

Though the officers wore tactical vests with police identification, Torres claims she only saw the officers had guns. She thought she was being carjacked and drove away. She claims the officers weren't in the path of the vehicle, but they fired 13 shots, hitting her twice. She then drove to a nearby parking lot, asked a bystander to report the attempted carjacking, stole another car, and drove 75 miles to a hospital.

Torres sued the police officers, claiming their use of force was excessive in violation of the Fourth Amendment's prohibition against "unreasonable searches and seizures." The officers argued that Torres couldn't bring an excessive force claim because she was never "seized" per the Fourth Amendment as she got away.

After considering the facts, the Supreme Court ruled that the "application of physical force to the body of a person with intent to restrain is a seizure, even if the force does not succeed in subduing the person." They rested their decision in part on *California v. Hodari D.* (1991), which found that "the mere grasping or application of physical force with lawful authority" as an arrest, "whether or not it succeeded in subduing the arrestee." Citing an English case from 1828, the Court agreed with English lawyers that "[a]ll the authorities, from the earliest time to the present, establish that a corporal touch is sufficient to constitute an arrest, even though the defendants do not submit.'"[1]

The *Torres* case aptly illustrates the role of the courts in controlling and limiting police behavior. Do you agree with the Court in their decision? Should Ms. Torres be allowed to sue the police for illegal seizure even though she was high on drugs, committed car theft, and sundry other crimes?

Charles Brutlag/Shutterstock.com

The Amendments to the Constitution provide the boundaries of what the police can and cannot do when they investigate crime, interrogate suspects, conduct searches, and seize evidence.

Once a crime has been committed and an investigation begun, the police may use various means to collect the evidence needed for criminal prosecution. A number of critical decisions must take place as follows:

- Should surveillance techniques be employed to secure information?

- How can information be gathered to support a request for a search warrant?

- If the suspect is driving a vehicle, can the car be searched without a warrant?

- Can a suspect's phone be tapped or conversations recorded?

- Is there reasonable suspicion to justify stopping and frisking a suspect?

- What are the elements needed in order for an arrest to be considered legal?

- If a suspect has been detained, what constitutes an appropriate interrogation?

- Can witnesses be brought in to identify the suspect?

The U.S. Supreme Court has taken an active role in answering these questions. Its primary concern has been to balance the law enforcement agent's need for a free hand to investigate crimes with the citizen's constitutional right to be free from illegal searches and interrogations. In some instances, the Supreme Court has expanded police power—for example, by increasing the occasions when police can search without a warrant. In other cases, the Supreme Court has restricted police operations—for example, by ruling that every criminal suspect has a right to an attorney when being interrogated by police. Changes in the law often reflect such factors as the justices' legal philosophy and their concern about the ability of police to control crime, their views on the need to maintain public safety versus their commitment to the civil liberties of criminal defendants, and events such as the September 11, 2001, terrorist attacks. In the sections to follow, the influence of the Supreme Court as well as the Constitution will be discussed.

LO1
Discuss how the Fourth Amendment controls police.

Exploring the Fourth Amendment

Some of the key elements of a police investigation are the search for incriminating evidence, the seizure of that evidence, and its use during a criminal trial. The Fourth Amendment protects suspects against unreasonable searches and seizures by placing limitations on what the police can do in their efforts to catch lawbreakers and collect evidence.

The Fourth Amendment states:

The right of the people to be secure in their persons, houses, papers, and effects, against unreasonable searches and seizures, shall not be violated, and no warrants shall issue, but upon probable cause, supported by oath or affirmation, and particularly describing the place to be searched, and the persons or things to be seized.

There are two important parts of the Fourth Amendment, called the "reasonable clause" and the "warrants clause." The reasonable clause stops at "shall not be violated." It simply states that searches and seizures must be reasonable. The warrant clause starts at "and no warrants shall issue . . ." This part of the Fourth Amendment lists warrant requirements. These two Fourth Amendment parts are not necessarily connected. A search can be reasonable without a warrant, but if a warrant is required, it must meet specific requirements.

What Is a Search?

◀ **L02**

Define search and arrest.

The working definition of "search" is straightforward—namely, to look for something. In the search and seizure context, however, "search" has a very distinct meaning. A Fourth Amendment **search** occurs only when a government actor infringes on a person's reasonable expectation of privacy.[2]

A government actor is most often a police officer, in contrast to a private citizen. As a private citizen, a person could enter someone else's property and search for contraband without triggering the Fourth Amendment prohibitions. This person may commit the offense of criminal trespass, but the Fourth Amendment would not be triggered. Police officers' actions almost always trigger the Fourth Amendment.

Assuming a police officer is the one looking for evidence, then what has to happen for the officer to infringe on someone's reasonable expectation of privacy? The officer must be looking in a place where a person could reasonably expect privacy. Usually this includes private property, such as cars, houses, and personal effects (the reality is often quite complicated, however, as the accompanying Police and the Law box about drug dog searches attests). So if an officer looks for contraband in a person's private home, the officer is conducting a search. In contrast, if the officer looks for evidence in a public park, a search has not occurred because the park is public and does not belong to any one individual. Following are three key examples of actions that are *not* considered searches.

search

A government actor's infringement on a person's reasonable expectation of privacy.

Abandoned Property

If a person abandons their property, such as by placing trash at the side of the road for pickup, that person cannot continue to assert privacy in the property. In *California v. Greenwood* (1988), investigators found incriminating information in a person's garbage that was set to be picked up.[3] The Supreme Court ruled that this action did not amount to a search. The officers were authorized to seize the evidence.

Open Fields

In *Oliver v. United States* (1984), the U.S. Supreme Court distinguished between the privacy granted persons in their own home or its adjacent grounds and fields (curtilage) and the lack of expectation of privacy in open fields.[4] The Court ruled that when the police look for evidence in an **open field**, defined as any unoccupied or undeveloped real property outside the curtilage of a home, a search does not occur. What, then, is **curtilage**? It is defined as the grounds or fields attached to and in close proximity to the house. Exhibit 11.1 distinguishes between open fields and curtilage in more detail.

open field

Any unoccupied or undeveloped real property outside the curtilage of a home.

curtilage

Grounds or fields attached to a house.

Exhibit 11.1

Distinguishing Between Open Fields and Curtilage

Open Fields	Curtilage
Park	Yard surrounding house
Public street	Fenced in and secure portion of private property (such as with "No Trespassing" signs)
Remote, unprotected area on private property	Secured outbuildings, such as a detached workshop

---

Fly-overs

In *California v. Ciraola* (1986), the police received a tip that marijuana was growing in the defendant's backyard.[5] The yard was surrounded by fences, one of which was 10 feet high. The officers flew over the yard in a private

---

Police & the Law

Riley v. California, United States v. Wurie, and *Torrey Dale Grady v. North Carolina*

In three cases, the Supreme Court set out the meaning of a search in the age of digital technology.

Riley v. California

The first concerned David Leon Riley, who was stopped for a traffic violation, which eventually led to his arrest on weapons charges. An officer searching Riley incident to the arrest seized a cell phone from Riley's pants pocket. The officer accessed information on the phone and noticed the repeated use of a term associated with a street gang. At the police station two hours later, a detective specializing in gangs further examined the phone's digital contents. Based in part on photographs and videos that the detective found, the State charged Riley in connection with a shooting that had occurred a few weeks earlier and sought an enhanced sentence based on Riley's gang membership. Riley and his attorney argued that the evidence admitted at trial from his cell phone was discovered through a search that violated his Fourth Amendment to be free from unreasonable searches.

United States v. Wurie

On September 5, 2007, Boston police officers spotted an apparent drug deal inside Brima Wurie's car. Police arrested Wurie for distributing crack cocaine and brought him to the police station. Among the items confiscated from Wurie were two cellular phones; officers noticed that one of the phones received numerous calls from a number labeled "my house," visible from the phone's exterior. After consulting a White Pages directory, the police identified the number as belonging to an address in South Boston, associated with the name Manny Cristal. Under interrogation, Wurie claimed that he lived in Dorchester, not in South Boston, and denied that he had sold crack cocaine. Suspecting that Wurie was lying about his address and that he had drugs in his home, the police visited the South Boston address, where a mailbox listed the names Wurie and Cristal. After obtaining a search warrant, the police found and seized 215 grams of crack cocaine, four bags of marijuana, drug paraphernalia, cash, a firearm, and ammunition. Wurie was later charged with possession with intent to distribute, distributing cocaine base, and being a felon in possession of a firearm and ammunition.

Decision

The Court combined these cases and delivered one decision about how police must view smartphones. In both of these cases, the Court agreed that the police engaged in an unreasonable search and seizure. Writing for the Court, Chief Justice John G. Roberts, Jr. affirmed that the

plane at an altitude of 1,000 feet to ascertain whether it contained marijuana plants. On the basis of this information, a search warrant was obtained and executed, and with the evidence against him, the defendant was convicted on drug charges. On appeal, the Supreme Court found that his privacy had not been violated—that a search did not occur. This holding was later expanded in *Florida v. Riley* (1989), when the Court ruled that police do not need a search warrant to conduct even low-altitude helicopter searches of private property.[6] The Court allowed Florida prosecutors to use evidence obtained by a police helicopter that flew 400 feet over a greenhouse in which defendants were growing marijuana plants. The Court said the search was constitutionally permissible because the flight was within airspace legally available to helicopters under federal regulations.

In recent years, the Supreme Court has turned its attention to the use of technology. Some recent cases are included below that explore the search and seizure of cell phones, text messages, and global positioning system (GPS) trackers.

warrantless search exception following an arrest exists for the purposes of protecting officer safety and preserving evidence, neither of which is at issue in the search of digital data. The digital data cannot be used as a weapon to harm an arresting officer, and police officers have the ability to preserve evidence while awaiting a warrant by disconnecting the phone from the network and placing the phone in a "Faraday bag." The Court characterized cell phones as minicomputers filled with massive amounts of private information, which distinguished them from the traditional items that can be seized from an arrestee's person, such as a wallet. The Court also held that information accessible via the phone but stored using "cloud computing" is not even "on the arrestee's person." The Court did hold, however, that some warrantless searches of cell phones might be permitted in an emergency when the government's interests are so compelling that a search would be reasonable.

Grady v. North Carolina

Between 1997 and 2006, Torrey Grady was convicted of two sexual offenses. After being released for the second time, a trial court civilly committed Grady to take part in North Carolina's satellite-based monitoring program for the duration of his life. The program required participants to wear a GPS monitoring bracelet so that authorities can make sure that participants are complying with prescriptive schedules and location requirements. Grady challenged the constitutionality of the program and argued that the constant tracking amounted to an unreasonable search that was

prohibited under the Fourth Amendment. Both the trial court and the North Carolina Court of Appeals held that wearing a GPS monitor did not amount to a search. Grady and his attorney argued that the lower courts were wrong and that a GPS monitor is a search.

Decision

The Court held that the trial court and appellate court both failed to apply the correct law based on the Court's decision in *United States v. Jones*, which held that placing a GPS tracker on the bottom of a vehicle constituted a search under the Fourth Amendment. The Court held that participation in the North Carolina program amounted to a search because requiring someone to wear a bracelet that tracks the person's whereabouts constitutes what the *Jones* decision termed a "physical occupation of] private property for the purpose of obtaining information." The Court remanded the case back to the trial court for a determination of whether or not this "search" was unreasonable under the Fourth Amendment.

Critical Thinking

Why should a device that is carried about openly, used in plain sight, and employed to make phone calls be different from any other openly carried item? As for tracking devices, if they are worn voluntarily to avoid going to prison, why should they be off limits to a police search?

Sources: Riley v. California and US. V. Wurie 134 S.Ct. 2473 (2014); and Grady v. North Carolina 575 U.S. 306 (2015).

Defining an Arrest

The Fourth Amendment does not mention arrests, but it does mention seizures. An arrest is one of the most common types of seizures. Some other actions, such as field interrogations, are also considered seizures.

The arrest power of the police involves taking a person into custody in accordance with lawful authority and holding that person to answer for a violation of the criminal law. Police officers have complete law enforcement responsibility and unrestricted powers of arrest in their jurisdictions. Private citizens also have the right to make an arrest, generally when a crime is committed in their presence.

An arrest occurs when a police officer takes a person into custody or deprives a person of freedom for having allegedly committed a criminal offense. The police stop unlimited numbers of people each day for a variety of reasons, so the time when an arrest occurs may be hard to pinpoint. Some people are stopped for short periods of questioning, others are informally detained and released, and still others are formally placed under arrest. However, a legal arrest occurs when the following conditions exist:

- The police officer believes that sufficient legal evidence—that is, probable cause—exists that a crime is being or has been committed and intends to restrain the suspect.

- The police officer deprives the individual of freedom.

- The suspect believes that they are in the custody of the police officer and cannot voluntarily leave. They have lost their liberty.

LO3

Distinguish between search warrants and arrest warrants.

search warrant

An order, issued by a judge, directing officers to conduct a search of specified premises for specified objects.

arrest warrant

An order, issued by a judge, directing officers to arrest a particular individual.

in-presence requirement

A police officer cannot arrest someone for a misdemeanor unless the officer sees the crime occur. To make an arrest for a crime the officer did not witness, an arrest warrant must be obtained.

Search Warrants and Arrest Warrants

There are two varieties of warrants: **search warrants** and **arrest warrants**. A search warrant is an order, issued by a judge, directing officers to conduct a search of specified premises for specified objects. An arrest warrant is an order, issued by a judge, directing officers to arrest a particular individual.

The Fourth Amendment does not necessitate warrants for all searches and arrests. In some situations, however, warrants are necessary. These situations include:

- **Arrests and searches in private homes or on specific types of private property.** Subject to some limited exceptions, warrants are always required for searches and arrests in private homes.[7]

- **Arrests for minor offenses committed out of view of the arresting officer.** There is no clear definition of "minor offense," but generally this includes misdemeanors. Limiting arrests in this fashion is known as the **in-presence requirement**; a misdemeanor needs to occur in the officer's presence for the arrest to be valid.[8]

An Exception to the In-Presence Requirements

For almost all misdemeanor offenses, the crime must occur in the presence of a police officer. Crimes of domestic violence have historically been difficult for police agencies to address. To enhance police response, some states have created an exception to this requirement for domestic violence misdemeanors. For example, according to California Penal Code §836(c)(1):[9]

> When a peace officer is responding to a call alleging a violation of a domestic violence protective or restraining order…or of a domestic violence protective or restraining order issued by the court of another state, tribe, or territory and the peace officer has probable cause to believe that the person against whom the order is issued has notice of the order and has committed an act in violation of the order, the officer shall, consistent with subdivision (b) of Section 13701, make a lawful arrest of the person without a warrant and take that person into custody whether or not the violation occurred in the presence of the arresting officer.

This means that in cases of domestic violence, the officer does not need to see the misdemeanor offense to make an arrest.

Neil Stanners/Shutterstock.com

In order to protect a citizen's right to privacy, police cannot conduct a search of a person, vehicle, home, or location without a warrant issued by a magistrate or judge. The warrant allows police to search for evidence of a crime and to confiscate any evidence they find. Police can conduct a limited search without a warrant if there are exigent (emergency) circumstances, such as the suspect has a hidden weapon nearby.

Warrant Requirements

◀ **LO4**
Explain when warrants are required.

There are three requirements that must be satisfied before a warrant can be issued. They are probable cause, a neutral and detached magistrate, and particularity.

Probable Cause

A warrant cannot be issued unless it is based on **probable cause**, which is typically defined as a reasonable belief, based on fact, that a crime has been committed and that the person, place, or object to be searched and/or seized is linked to the crime with a reasonable degree of certainty.

Under normal circumstances, a search warrant cannot be obtained unless the request for it is supported by facts, supplied under oath by a law enforcement officer, that are sufficient to convince the court that a crime has been or is being committed.

To establish probable cause, the police must provide the judge or magistrate with information in the form of written affidavits, which report either their own observations or those of private citizens or police undercover informants. If the magistrate believes that the information is sufficient to establish probable cause to conduct a search, they will issue a warrant. Although the suspect is not present when the warrant is issued and therefore cannot contest its issuance, they can later challenge the validity of the warrant before trial.

The Fourth Amendment does not explicitly define probable cause, and its precise meaning still remains unclear. However, police officers have to provide factual evidence to define and identify suspicious activities; they may not simply offer their beliefs or suspicions. In addition, the officers must show how they obtained the information and provide evidence of its reliability. There are several sources of information that officers can use to show probable cause,

probable cause
The evidentiary criterion necessary to sustain an arrest or the issuance of an arrest or search warrant: a set of facts, information, circumstances, or conditions that would lead a reasonable person to believe that an offense was committed and that the accused committed that offense.

including first-hand knowledge, informants' statements, anonymous tips, and telephone tips.

Firsthand Knowledge

Police can obtain a warrant if their investigation turns up sufficient evidence to convince a judge that a crime probably has been committed and that the person or place the police wish to search is probably involved materially in that crime. The ideal source of information is the officer's firsthand knowledge. If the officer witnesses a crime being committed, the warrant requirement can often be disposed of altogether and the officer will make a warrantless arrest (we look at warrantless searches and seizures later). If the officer cannot make a particular arrest or engage in a particular search without a warrant, but they nevertheless have information that could establish probable cause, then the officer's knowledge will be weighted heavily. For example, if during a drug sting operation an officer buys drugs from a suspect on several occasions, this officer's firsthand information will be important in getting a warrant to search the suspect's property.

Sources of Information for Probable Cause

- A police informant whose reliability has been established because they have provided information in the past
- Someone who has firsthand knowledge of illegal activities
- A coconspirator who implicates themself as well as the suspect
- An informant whose information can be partially verified by the police
- A victim of a crime who offers information
- A witness to the crime related to the search
- A fellow law enforcement officer

Informants

Police often rely on informants. Informants can include victims, witnesses, accomplices, and people familiar with the crime or suspects in question. Unfortunately, many informants often act out of self-interest instead of civic duty, and the reliability of the evidence they provide may be questionable. Moreover, their statements reflect only what they have seen and heard and are not substantiated by hard evidence.

The U.S. Supreme Court has been concerned about the reliability of evidence obtained from informants. The Court has determined that hearsay evidence must be corroborated to serve as a basis for probable cause and thereby justify the issuance of a warrant. In the case of *Aguilar v. Texas* (1964), the Court articulated a two-part test for issuing a warrant on the word of an informant. The police had to show (1) why they believed the informant and (2) how the informant acquired personal knowledge of the crime.[10] This ruling restricted informant testimony to people who were in direct contact with police and whose information could be verified.

Anonymous Tips

Because the *Aguilar* case required that an informant be known and that their information be likely to be reliable, it all but ruled out using anonymous tips to secure a search warrant. This was changed in a critical 1983 ruling, *Illinois v. Gates*, in which the Court eased the process of obtaining search warrants by developing a totality-of-the-circumstances test to determine probable cause for issuing a search warrant. In *Gates*, the police received a knowledgeable and detailed anonymous letter describing the drug-dealing activities of Lance and Sue Gates. On the basis of that tip, the police began surveillance and eventually obtained a warrant to search their home. The search was later challenged on the grounds that it would be impossible to determine the accuracy of information provided by an anonymous letter, a condition required by the *Aguilar* case. However, the Court ruled that to obtain a warrant, the police must prove to a judge that, considering the totality of the circumstances, an informant has relevant and factual knowledge that a fair probability exists that evidence of a crime will be found in a certain place.[11] The anonymous letter, rich in details, satisfied that demand.

Telephone Tips

Can the police conduct a search based on an anonymous tip, such as one that is given via telephone? In *Alabama v. White* (1990), the police received an anonymous tip that a woman was carrying cocaine.[12] Only after police observation showed that the tip had accurately predicted the woman's movements did it become reasonable to believe the tipster had inside knowledge about the suspect and was truthful in his assertion about the cocaine. The Supreme Court ruled that the search based on the tip was legal because it was corroborated by independent police work. In its ruling, the Court stated the following:

> Standing alone, the tip here is completely lacking in the necessary indicia of reliability, since it provides virtually nothing from which one might conclude that the caller is honest or his information reliable and gives no indication of the basis for his predictions regarding [Vanessa] White's criminal activities. However, although it is a close question, the totality of the circumstances demonstrates that significant aspects of the informant's story were sufficiently corroborated by the police to furnish reasonable suspicion. . . . Thus, there was reason to believe that the caller was honest and well informed, and to impart some degree of reliability to his allegation that White was engaged in criminal activity.[13]

The *White* case seemed to give police powers to search someone after corroborating an anonymous tip. However, in *Florida v. J. L.*, the Court narrowed that right. In *J. L.*, an anonymous caller reported to the Miami-Dade police that a young Black man standing at a particular bus stop, wearing a plaid shirt, was carrying a gun.[14] The tip was not recorded, and nothing was known about the caller. Two officers went to the bus stop and spotted three Black men. One of them, the 15-year-old J. L., was wearing a plaid shirt. Apart from the anonymous tip, the officers had no reason to suspect that any of the people were involved in any criminal activity. The officers did not see a firearm, and J. L. made no threatening or unusual movements. One officer approached J. L., frisked him, and seized a gun from his pocket. The Court disallowed the search, ruling that a police officer must have reasonable suspicion that criminal activity is being conducted prior to stopping a person. Because anonymous tips are generally considered less reliable than tips from known informants, they can be used to search only if they include specific information that shows they are reliable. Unlike the *White* case, the police in *J. L.* failed to provide independent corroboration of the tipster's information.

Neutral and Detached Magistrate

Warrants can be issued only by neutral and detached magistrates. Any judge is considered a neutral and detached magistrate. Requiring that a judge "sign off"

Critical Thinking

Should anonymous tips be allowed to secure a search warrant when you cannot challenge the credibility of the tipster?

on a warrant brings an element of objectivity to the criminal process. It serves as a check on police officers' decisions concerning who should be arrested and/or searched. The Supreme Court echoed this point over 60 years ago in the important case of *Johnson v. United States* (1948):

> The point of the Fourth Amendment . . . is not that it denies law enforcement the support of the usual inferences reasonable men draw from evidence. Its protection consists in requiring that those inferences be drawn by a neutral and detached magistrate instead of being judged by the officer engaged in the often competitive enterprise of ferreting out crime.[15]

Before a warrant will be issued, a police officer must offer sworn testimony that the facts on which the request for the search warrant is made are trustworthy and true. If the judge issues the warrant, it will authorize police officers to search for particular objects, at a specific location, at a certain time. A warrant may authorize the search of "the premises at 221 Third Avenue, Apt. 6B, between the hours of 8 A.M. and 6 P.M." and direct the police to search for and seize "substances, contraband, paraphernalia, scales, and other items used in connection with the sale of illegal substances." Generally, warrants allow the seizure of a variety of types of evidence, as described below.

Categories of Evidence

Warrants are typically issued to search for and seize a variety of evidence:

- Property that represents evidence of the commission of a criminal offense—for example, a bloody glove or shirt

- Contraband, the fruits of crime, smuggled goods, illegal material, or anything else that is of a criminal nature

- Property intended for use or which has been used as the means of committing a criminal offense—for example, burglary tools, safecracking equipment, and drug paraphernalia

- People may be seized when there is probable cause for their arrest

- Conversation involving criminal conspiracy and other illegalities can be seized via tape recordings and wiretaps

Particularity

Recall that the Fourth Amendment states, in part, that warrants must *particularly* describe "the place to be searched, and the persons or things to be seized." This **particularity** requirement was included in the Fourth Amendment to counteract the use of general warrants by government agents. This was a device used against the colonists by the English crown. British officials had obtained general warrants empowering them to search any suspected places for smuggled goods, placing the liberty of every person in the hands of government officials.[16]

The particularity requirement is also designed to curtail potential abuse that may result from an officer being allowed to conduct a search with unbridled discretion. If a warrant is issued in violation of the particularity clause, the ensuing search is invalid even if the officers actually exercise proper restraint in executing their search. What and who are to be searched must be clearly spelled out. The police cannot search the basement of a house if the warrant specifies the attic;

particularity

The requirement that a search warrant state precisely where the search is to take place and what items are to be seized.

they cannot look in a desk drawer if the warrant specifies a search for a missing piano. However, this does not mean that police officers can seize only those items listed in the warrant. If, during the course of their search, police officers come across contraband or evidence of a crime that is not listed in the warrant, they can lawfully seize the unlisted items. This is referred to as the plain view exception. However, they cannot look in places that are off-limits within the scope of the warrant.

The particularity requirement applies to arrest warrants as well. To satisfy this requirement, the police must clearly specify the name of the individual who is to be arrested. If no name is available, they must provide a sufficiently specific description of the individual.

Critical Thinking

The rule of particularity was first introduced during colonial times. Some argue that it is no longer relevant. What are the pros and cons of using this standard in searches?

Field Interrogation: Stop and Frisk

◀ **LO5**

Explain a field interrogation (Terry stop).

One important exception to the rule requiring a search warrant is the **stop-and-frisk** procedure. This type of search typically occurs when a police officer encounters a suspicious person on the street and frisks or pats down their outer garments to determine whether they are in possession of a concealed weapon. The police officer need not have probable cause to arrest the suspect but simply must be reasonably suspicious based on the circumstances of the case (i.e., time and place) and their experience as a police officer. The stop-and-frisk search consists of the following two distinct components:

stop and frisk

The situation in which police officers who are suspicious of an individual run their hands lightly over the suspect's outer garments to determine whether the person is carrying a concealed weapon; also called a threshold inquiry or pat-down.

1. The stop, in which a police officer wishes to briefly detain a suspicious person in an effort to effect crime prevention and detection.

2. The frisk, in which an officer pats down, or frisks, a person who is stopped, in order to check for weapons. The purpose of the frisk is protection of the officer making the stop.

The stop and the frisk are separate actions, and each requires its own factual basis. Stopping a suspect allows for brief questioning, and frisking affords the officer an opportunity to avoid the possibility of attack. For instance, a police officer patrolling a high-crime area observes two young men loitering outside a liquor store after dark. The two men confer several times and stop to talk to a third person who pulls up alongside the curb in an automobile. From this observation, the officer may conclude that the men are casing the store for a possible burglary. The officer can then stop the suspects and ask them for some identification and an explanation of their conduct.

However, the facts that support a stop do not automatically allow a frisk. The officer must have reason to believe that the suspect is armed or dangerous. In this instance, if the three men identify themselves as security guards and produce identification, a frisk would not be justified. If they seem nervous

San Francisco Chronicle/Hearst Newspapers/Getty Images

Police in San Francisco conduct a post-arrest search of a suspect's outer garments in order to determine whether he was armed or in possession of contraband.

Terry stops

The practice, based on the decision in *Terry v. Ohio*, that gives police officers the right to stop, detain, and pat down a person when there is reasonable suspicion that the suspect was in the act of committing a crime or about to commit a crime. A pat-down is a light touching of the outer garments in order to determine if the person is carrying a gun or contraband; commonly called a stop and frisk.

and secretive and the officer concludes that they are planning a crime, the suspicion would be enough to justify a pat-down.

These stop-and-frisk stops are sometimes called ***Terry* stops** because the 1968 Supreme Court decision in *Terry v. Ohio* gave officers the right to stop and detain a person when there was reasonable suspicion that they were in the act of committing a crime or about to commit a crime. The landmark case of *Terry v. Ohio* (1968) shaped the contours of the stop and frisk.[17] In *Terry*, a police officer found a gun in the coat pocket of one of three men he frisked when their suspicious behavior convinced him that they were planning a robbery. At trial, the defendants futilely moved to suppress the gun on the grounds that it was the product of an illegal search. On appeal, the Supreme Court ruled that if a reasonably prudent police officer believes that their safety or that of others is endangered, they may make a reasonable search for weapons on the person, regardless of whether they have probable cause to arrest that individual for a crime or is absolutely certain that the individual is armed. The *Terry* case illustrates the principle that although the police officer must, whenever possible, secure a warrant to make a search and seizure, still, when swift action is called for based upon on-the-spot observations, the need for the warrant is removed.

What kind of behavior can trigger a *Terry* search? How suspicious does a person have to look before the police can legally stop them and pat them down? In *Illinois v. Wardlow* (2000), the defendant was walking on the street in an area known for narcotics trafficking. When he made eye contact with a police officer riding in a marked police car, he ran away. The officer caught up with the defendant on the street, stopped him, and conducted a protective pat-down search for weapons. A handgun was discovered in the frisk, and the defendant was convicted of unlawful use of a weapon by a felon. The Illinois Supreme Court ruled that the frisk violated *Terry v. Ohio* because flight may simply be an exercise of the right to "go on one's way" and does not constitute reasonable suspicion. However, on appeal, the U.S. Supreme Court reversed the state court, ruling that a person's presence in a "high crime area," in and of itself, is not enough to support a reasonable, particularized suspicion of criminal activity.[18] It held that a location's characteristics are sufficiently suspicious to warrant further investigation and that, in this case, the additional factor of the defendant's unprovoked flight added up to reasonable suspicion. The officers found that the defendant possessed a handgun, and as a result of the pat-down and search, they had probable cause to arrest him for violation of a state law. The frisk and arrest were thus proper under *Terry v. Ohio.*

The Supreme Court's decision in *Arizona v. Johnson* (2009) combined the issue of stop and frisk with a vehicle stop.[19] In that case, police officers serving on a gang task force stopped a vehicle for an infraction, but they did not suspect criminal activity. One officer confronted the driver; another questioned one of the passengers, Johnson. After the officer learned that Johnson had a criminal record, he was asked to exit the vehicle, which he did. The officer then frisked Johnson and found a gun. He was arrested, charged, and convicted of illegally carrying a weapon. The Supreme Court sanctioned the search, reinforcing the *Terry* decision's language that police may need to "act instantly if they have reasonable cause to suspect that the persons temporarily detained are armed and dangerous."[20]

Critical Thinking

Several major cities like Boston, New York, and Chicago rely heavily on Terry stops. How can we ensure that these stops are lawful and are not a recurse to racial profiling?

Are Terry Stops Effective?

Some people might find a Terry stop intrusive, having police touch a person's body just because they seem suspicious. However, the practice may be considered effective if it helps reduce crime. Recent research by Alese Wooditch and David Weisburd analyzed Terry stops in New York City.[21] The specific focus of their research is a sample of cases drawn from a 150-day period in the Bronx, New York City in 2006. Their data set included all non-traffic-related crime incidents and Terry stops that occurred in New York City for the time period of interest as well as the x-y coordinates of the stops and crime incidents, as well as their dates of occurrences. They found that Terry stops produced a modest reduction in crime, which extended over a three-day period. Diffusion of benefits was observed within 300 feet from the location of the stop. These positive effects decreased as the distance from the stop increased.

Search Incident to a Lawful Arrest

Traditionally, a search without a warrant is permissible if it is made incident to a lawful arrest. *Incident* means close in time to an arrest, usually right after the arrest. The police officer who searches a suspect incident to a lawful arrest must generally observe two rules: (1) the search must be conducted at the time of or immediately following the arrest, and (2) the police may search only the suspect and the area within the suspect's immediate control. The search may not legally go beyond the area where the person can reach for a weapon or destroy any evidence. For example, if, shortly after the armed robbery of a grocery store, officers arrest a suspect hiding in the basement with a briefcase, a search of the suspect's person and of the briefcase would be a proper **search incident to a lawful arrest** without a warrant.

> **search incident to a lawful arrest**
>
> An exception to the search warrant rule, limited to the immediate surrounding area.

The legality of this type of search depends almost entirely on the lawfulness of the arrest. The arrest will be upheld if the police officer observed the crime being committed or had probable cause to believe that the suspect committed the offense. If the arrest is found to have been invalid, then any warrantless search, which is incident to the arrest, would be considered illegal, and the evidence obtained from the search would be excluded from the trial.

The U.S. Supreme Court defined the permissible scope of a search incident to a lawful arrest in *Chimel v. California* (1969).[22] According to the *Chimel* doctrine, the police can search a suspect without a warrant after a lawful arrest to protect themselves from danger and to secure evidence. But a search of their home is illegal even if the police find contraband or evidence during the course of that search and if the police would otherwise be forced to obtain a warrant to search the premises. Likewise, police cannot search certain effects obtained during the course of a lawful arrest. In the 2014 landmark decision of *Riley v. California*, the Supreme Court unanimously decided that it is a Fourth Amendment violation to search the cell phone of an arrestee without a warrant.[23] The decision will likely have sweeping implications for other technologies.

Automobile Searches

The U.S. Supreme Court has also established that certain situations justify the warrantless search of an automobile on a public street or highway. Evidence can be seized from an automobile when a suspect is taken into custody in a lawful arrest. In

Carroll v. United States, which was decided in 1925, the Supreme Court ruled that distinctions should be made among searches of automobiles, persons, and homes. The Court also concluded that a warrantless search of an automobile is valid if the police have probable cause to believe that the car contains evidence they are seeking.[24] This same rule is in effect today. The evolution of the Supreme Court's thinking on this issue is described in Exhibit 11.2, *Evolution of Carrol v. US*.

Because police are now confronting such significant social problems as drug trafficking and terrorist activity, the Supreme Court has given them some additional leeway in terms of making stops. For example, in the 2002 case *United States v. Arvizu*, the Court allowed a stop (and eventual search) of a vehicle based on a pattern of suspicious behavior.

■ A vehicle registration check showing that the vehicle was registered to an address in an area notorious for alien and narcotics smuggling

■ The patrol officer's personal experience and knowledge that the suspect had taken a route frequently used by drug smugglers

■ The driver's route having been designed to pass through the area during a border patrol shift change

Although each fact alone was insufficient to justify the stop, together they supported the officer's decision to stop the vehicle.[25]

Scope of the Automobile Search

The legality of searching automobiles without a warrant has always been a trouble spot for police and the courts. Should the search be limited to the interior of the car, or can the police search the trunk? What about a suitcase in the trunk? What about the glove compartment? Does a traffic citation give the police the right to search an automobile? These questions have produced significant litigation over the years. To clear up the matter, the Supreme Court has focused on two types of situations: "pure" vehicle searches and vehicle searches following driver arrests and/or detentions.

A "pure" vehicle search is one in which the police seek to search a vehicle without regard to whether the vehicle is being driven by a person. In other words, these are searches of the vehicle that do not concern the passenger. In *United States v. Ross* in 1982, the Supreme Court held that if probable cause exists to believe that an automobile contains criminal evidence, a warrantless search by the police is permissible, including a search of closed containers in the vehicle.[41] Probable cause is the all-important requirement. In the absence of probable cause, the search will run afoul of the Fourth Amendment, and any resulting evidence will be inadmissible in court. With probable cause, however, the car may be stopped and searched, contraband can be seized, and the occupant can be arrested, all without violating the Fourth Amendment.

What if, however, a driver is stopped for speeding and the officer has no intent—in advance—to search the vehicle? In *Michigan v. Long*, police officers observed a vehicle swerve into a ditch.[42] When officers approached the vehicle, they noticed that the driver was intoxicated and that there was a large hunting knife on the passenger seat. The officers arrested the driver and searched the passenger compartment of the vehicle. Both actions were sanctioned by the Supreme Court. The search was justified on the grounds that it was necessary to protect officer safety.

Exhibit 11.2

Evolution of *Carroll v. United States*

***Carroll v. United States* (1925)**	An automobile can be searched without a warrant if the police have probable cause.[26]
***United States v. Lee* (1927)**	An automobile is any conveyance being used for transportation, including even a motorhome.[27]
***Cardwell v. Lewis* (1974)**	People enjoy a lesser expectation of privacy in their vehicles than in their homes and offices.[28]
***Pennsylvania v. Mimms* (1977)**	During routine traffic stops, officers can order drivers out of their cars and frisk them.[29]
***United States v. Ross* (1982)**	With probable cause, police can search an automobile without a warrant, including any containers within.[30]
***Michigan v. Long* (1983)**	Police can frisk a driver and search the passenger compartment of a vehicle following a valid stop, provided they have reasonable suspicion that the driver poses a danger.[31]
***Michigan Dept. of State Police v. Sitz* (1990)**	Suspicionless seizures of motorists are permissible for purposes of detecting drunk driving.[32]
***Whren v. United States* (1996)**	The constitutional reasonableness of a traffic stop does not depend on an officer's initial motivation. It depends only on whether there was justification to stop the vehicle.[33]
***Maryland v. Wilson* (1997)**	During a routine traffic stop, the officer can order a passenger out of the vehicle and frisk them.[34]
***City of Indianapolis v. Edmund* (2000)**	The police cannot operate roadblocks for the purpose of detecting illegal drugs.[35]
***Illinois v. Lidster* (2004)**	Police are constitutionally authorized to conduct suspicionless vehicle checkpoints for the purpose of gaining information about a crime recently committed in the area.[36]
***Brendlin v. California* (2007)**	Passengers, like drivers, are considered "seized" during traffic stops, meaning they enjoy Fourth Amendment protection from unreasonable searches and seizures.[37]
***Arizona v. Gant* (2009)**	If a motorist is arrested, police may search the vehicle only if it is reasonable to assume the arrestee could access the vehicle *or* the vehicle contains evidence of the offense of arrest.[38]
***Davis v. United States* (2011)**	The postarrest seizure of evidence not connected with the offense of arrest is constitutionally permissible if based on objectively reasonable reliance on appropriate appellate precedent.[39] *Gant* would have invalidated the seizure in this case, but it had not been decided at the time the seizure took place.
***Rodriguez v. United States* (2015)**	Police may not prolong traffic stops to wait for drug-sniffing dogs to inspect vehicles. The Court ruled a police stop exceeding the time needed to handle the matter for which the stop was made violates the Constitution's shield against unreasonable seizures.[40]

reasonable suspicion

A legal standard that is less than probable cause, but more than an unsupported hunch. To achieve the level of reasonableness, the suspicion must be based on specific facts or circumstances and that justifies stopping and even frisking a suspect.

More recently, in *Arizona v. Gant*, the Supreme Court held that a full vehicle search following the driver's arrest is permissible only if it is reasonable to assume the arrestee could access the vehicle *or* the vehicle contains evidence of the offense of arrest.[43] Concerning the latter requirement, if the person was stopped for trafficking in illegal weapons, then with probable cause the police would be authorized to search the vehicle for weapons, even if the driver was arrested, handcuffed, and locked in the back seat of a police car. It is important to note that the *Gant* decision did not overturn *Michigan v. Long*; officers can still search a vehicle's passenger compartment when they have **reasonable suspicion** that the driver, whether or not they are arrested, might gain access to it and obtain a weapon. The following Police & the Law: *Kansas v. Glover* feature covers this issue.

Police & the Law

Kansas v. Glover

While on patrol, Douglas County Kansas Sheriff's Deputy Mark Mehrer ran a registration check on a pickup truck he spotted while on patrol. The officer found that the truck belonged to Charles Glover Jr., whose license has been revoked. The officer stopped the truck based on the assumption that the registered owner was Glover, the truck's legal owner. As it turns out, it was Glover who was the driver; he was then issued a citation for being a habitual violator of Kansas traffic laws.

Before trial, Glover moved to suppress all evidence from the stop, arguing that the stop violated his Fourth Amendment right against unreasonable searches and seizures because the officer lacked reasonable suspicion to pull him over; after all, he only assumed that the owner was also the driver, he had no reasonable knowledge. The state argued that unless he had information to the contrary, a law enforcement officer may infer that the owner of a vehicle is the one driving the vehicle. The knowledge that the owner had his license revoked gave rise to reasonable suspicion to conduct an investigative stop.

After traveling through the state courts, the case found its way to the Supreme Court, which focused on the issue of whether it is reasonable for an officer to suspect that the registered owner of a vehicle is the one driving the vehicle without any information to the contrary.

In an 8–1 decision, the Court concluded that the stop was reasonable because, under the Fourth Amendment,

it is logical for an officer to assume that the driver of a vehicle is its owner, and if the owner's license is revoked, to conduct an investigative stop of the vehicle. In its decision, the Court ruled that under the Fourth Amendment, a police officer may make a "brief investigative traffic stop" when they have "a particularized and objective basis," based on commonsense and knowledge of human behavior, to suspect legal wrongdoing. The police officer's commonsense inference was that the vehicle's owner was most likely the driver, which provided sufficient suspicion to stop the vehicle. It does not matter that a vehicle's driver is not always its registered owner; the officer's judgment was based on commonsense judgment and experience. Thus, he had reasonable suspicion, and the traffic stop did not violate the Fourth Amendment.

Critical Thinking

1. *Glover* shows that reasonable suspicion is based both on objective observation and observable facts and also on common sense and experience. Would it have been reasonable to pull the car over if, in this case, the driver was a woman?

2. In making decisions to stop, search, and arrest, should police be limited to what they observe rather than to what they infer or suspect? When would it be unreasonable to assume the owner was actually the driver?

Source: *Kansas v. Glover* 589 U.S. ___ (2020); 140 S. Ct. 1183; 206 L. Ed. 2d 412.

Searching Drivers and Passengers

Can police officers search drivers and passengers during routine traffic stops? In 1977, the Supreme Court ruled in *Pennsylvania v. Mimms* that officers could order drivers out of their cars and frisk them during routine traffic stops. Officers' safety outweighed the intrusion on individual rights.[44] In 1997, the Court held in *Maryland v. Wilson* that the police had the same authority with respect to passengers.[45] In the *Wilson* case, a state patrol officer lawfully stopped a vehicle for speeding. While the driver was producing his license, the front-seat passenger, Jerry Lee Wilson, was ordered out of the vehicle. As he exited, crack cocaine dropped to the ground. Wilson was arrested and convicted of drug possession. His attorney moved to suppress the evidence, but the U.S. Supreme Court disagreed and extended the *Mimms* rule to passengers. The Court noted that lawful traffic stops had become progressively more dangerous to police officers and that thousands of officers were assaulted and even killed during such stops. The decision means that passengers must comply when ordered out of a lawfully stopped vehicle.

In 2007, the Supreme Court decided another vehicle search case, this one dealing with searches of passengers. In *Brendlin v. California*, a car was stopped to check its registration.[46] After stopping the vehicle, the officers learned that a passenger, Brendlin, was a parole violator. The officers arrested him, searched him, and found an orange syringe cap on his person. A pat-down search of the driver also revealed contraband. She was also arrested. Then the car was searched incident to the driver's arrest, and methamphetamine paraphernalia was discovered. Brendlin challenged the search, seeking to have the evidence excluded, but the California Supreme Court held that Brendlin was not "seized" in the traffic stop. This meant he could not even challenge his arrest and subsequent search. Not surprisingly, the U.S. Supreme Court disagreed, holding that Brendlin *was* seized. This case was important because the Court held that anyone detained in a traffic stop, not just the driver, is "seized." This means such people can challenge the police action on constitutional grounds.

In 2015, the Supreme Court ruled on the use of police dogs during traffic stops. In *Rodriguez v. United States*, K-9 Officer Morgan Struble was driving alone with his drug-sniffing companion when he saw Rodriguez's car drift over the shoulder line and then jerk back onto the road. Struble stopped the car; asked for an explanation; and took Rodriguez's license, registration, and proof of insurance to run a records check back in his patrol car. Struble returned to Rodriguez's car, began to question a passenger, and then went back to his patrol car to run a records check on the passenger. Officer Struble decided to conduct a dog sniff of Rodriguez's car and he wanted another officer there for safety. With the records check still negative, Struble went back to Rodriguez's car again, finished writing a warning ticket, and asked permission to walk his dog around the car. Rodriguez declined and Struble ordered him from the car and did it anyway, finding methamphetamine.

Rodriguez moved to suppress the evidence found in the search, claiming the dog search violated his Fourth Amendment right to be free from unreasonable seizures. The district court denied the motion. On appeal, the U.S. Court of Appeals for the Eighth Circuit affirmed, holding the search was constitutional because the brief delay before employing the dog did not unreasonably prolong the otherwise lawful stop. The Supreme Court disagreed and ruled that the police may not prolong traffic stops to wait for drug-sniffing dogs to inspect vehicles. The Court held that the use of a K-9 unit after the completion of an otherwise lawful traffic stop exceeded the time reasonably required to handle the matter and therefore violated the Fourth Amendment's prohibition against unreasonable searches and seizures.

Consent Searches

Police officers may also undertake warrantless searches when the person in control of the area or object consents to the search. Those who consent to a search essentially waive their constitutional rights under the Fourth Amendment. Ordinarily, courts are reluctant to accept such waivers and require the state to prove that the consent was voluntarily given. In addition, the consent must be given intelligently, and in some jurisdictions, consent searches are valid only after the suspect is informed of the option to refuse consent.

Voluntariness

The major legal issue in most consent searches is whether the police can prove that consent was given voluntarily. In general, consent cannot be the result of "duress or coercion, express or implied."[47] For example, in the case of *Bumper v. North Carolina* (1968), police officers searched the home of an older woman after informing her that they possessed a search warrant.[48] At the trial, the prosecutor informed the court that the search was valid because the woman had given her consent. When the government was unable to produce the warrant, the court decided that the search was invalid because the woman's consent was not given voluntarily. On appeal, the U.S. Supreme Court upheld the lower court's finding that the consent had been illegally obtained by the false claim that the police had a search warrant.

In most consent searches, however, voluntariness is a question of fact to be determined from all the circumstances of the case. In *Schneckloth v. Bustamonte* (1973), the defendant helped the police by opening the trunk and glove compartment of the car. The Court said this action demonstrated that the consent was voluntarily given.[49] Furthermore, the police are usually under no obligation to inform a suspect of the right to refuse consent.[50] Failure to tell a suspect of this right does not make the search illegal, but it may be a factor used by the courts to decide whether the suspect gave consent voluntarily.

Implied Consent

All states have some form of implied consent laws that give law enforcement officers the right to search and seize evidence without a warrant if a citizen wishes to engage in a particular activity, such as getting on an airplane or driving a car. Take, for example, requiring drivers to submit to a breathalyzer or other tests for intoxication. A person refusing such a request can have their license suspended or revoked. But what about a driver who is unconscious and therefore cannot authorize a search? This was the situation the Supreme Court faced in the case of *Mitchell v. Wisconsin* (2019). Gerald P. Mitchell was arrested for operating a vehicle while intoxicated. He became lethargic on the way to the police station, so the arresting officers took him to a hospital. An officer attempted to read him a statutorily mandated form that set out Wisconsin's implied consent law, but the semiconscious Mitchell was too inebriated to indicate his understanding

Critical Thinking

Many people who are stopped by the police do not know that they may not have to consent to a search. Others consent out of fear of repercussions if they don't. How can we balance the officer's ability to do a consent search with the citizen's Fourth Amendment rights?

or consent; he soon then fell unconscious. Without a warrant, the police asked hospital workers to draw Mitchell's blood, which revealed his blood alcohol concentration to be .222. Later charged with operating while intoxicated and with a prohibited alcohol concentration, Mitchell's attorneys moved to suppress the results of the blood test on the grounds that his blood was taken without a warrant or his consent. In return, the state argued that under the implied-consent statute, police did not need a warrant to draw his blood. The trial court sided with the state and allowed the results of the blood test into evidence and Mitchell was convicted.

In its decision, the Court noted that blood alcohol concentration (BAC) tests are searches subject to the Fourth Amendment. As such, a warrant is generally required before police may conduct a BAC test. In this case, an "exigent circumstances" exception allows the government to conduct a search without a warrant "to prevent the imminent destruction of evidence." The Court had previously held that the short-lived nature of blood-alcohol evidence alone does not automatically qualify BAC tests and that other factors must be considered. However, the situation involving an unconscious driver gives rise to exigency because officials cannot conduct a breath test and must instead perform a blood test to determine BAC.[51]

Third-Party Consent

Can a person give consent for someone else? In *United States v. Matlock* (1974), the Court ruled that it is permissible for one co-occupant of an apartment to give consent to the police to search the premises in the absence of the other occupant, as long as the person giving consent shares common authority over the property and no present cotenant objects.[52] What happens if one party gives consent to a search while another interested party refuses? This is what happened in the 2006 case of *Georgia v. Randolph*. Police were called to Scott Randolph's home because of a domestic dispute. His spouse told police that Randolph had been using a lot of cocaine and that drugs were on the premises. One officer asked Randolph whether he could conduct a search of the home, and Randolph said no. Another officer asked his spouse for permission, and she not only said yes but also led the officer upstairs to a bedroom where he allegedly found cocaine residue. The Supreme Court held that because Randolph was present when the police came to his home, they were required by the Fourth Amendment to heed his objection to the search; the seizure of the drugs was ruled illegal.[53]

Bus Sweeps

Today, consent searches have additional significance because of their use in drug control programs. On June 20, 1991, the U.S. Supreme Court, in *Florida v. Bostick*, upheld the drug interdiction technique known as the **bus sweep**, in which police board buses and, without suspicion of illegal activity, question passengers, ask for identification, and request permission to search luggage.[54] Police in the *Bostick* case boarded a bus bound from Miami to Atlanta during a stopover in Fort Lauderdale. Without suspicion, the officers picked out the defendant and asked to inspect his ticket and identification. After identifying themselves as narcotics officers looking for illegal drugs, they asked to inspect the defendant's luggage. Although there was some uncertainty about whether the defendant consented to the search in which contraband was found, and about whether he was informed of his right to refuse consent, the defendant was convicted.

bus sweep

Police investigation technique in which officers board a bus or train without suspicion of illegal activity and question passengers, asking for identification and seeking permission to search their baggage.

The Supreme Court was faced with deciding whether consent was freely given or the nature of the bus sweep negated the defendant's consent. The Court concluded that drug enforcement officers, after obtaining consent, may search luggage on a crowded bus without meeting the Fourth Amendment requirements for a search warrant or probable cause.

This case raises fundamental questions about the legality of techniques used to discourage drug trafficking. Are they inherently coercive? In *Bostick*, when the officers entered the bus, the driver exited and closed the door, leaving the defendant and other passengers alone with two officers. Furthermore, Terrance Bostick was seated in the rear of the bus, and officers blocked him from exiting. Finally, one of the officers was clearly holding his handgun in full view. In light of these circumstances, was this a consensual or a coercive search? The Supreme Court ruled, despite the coercive circumstances, that the search was appropriate because consent had been given voluntarily.

Free to Go

What if a police officer stops a motorist and asks for consent to search the vehicle? Must the officer inform the driver that they are "free to go" before asking consent to search the vehicle? In *Ohio v. Robinette* (1996), the Court concluded that no such warning is needed to make consent to a search reasonable. Robert D. Robinette was stopped for speeding. After checking his license, the officer asked whether Robinette was carrying any illegal contraband in the car. When the defendant answered in the negative, the officer asked for and received permission to search the car. The search turned up illegal drugs. The Supreme Court ruled that police officers do not have to inform a driver that they are "free to go" before asking whether they can search the car. According to the Court, the touchstone of the Fourth Amendment is reasonableness, which is assessed by examining the totality of the circumstances.[55] In this case, the search was ruled a reasonable exercise of discretion.

Plain View

plain view doctrine

The principle that evidence in plain view of police officers may be seized without a search warrant.

The Supreme Court has also ruled that police can search for and seize evidence without the benefit of a warrant if it is in plain view.[56] For example, if a police officer is conducting an investigation and notices, while questioning some individuals, that one has drugs in their pocket, the officer can seize the evidence and arrest the suspect. Or if the police are conducting a search under a warrant, authorizing them to look for narcotics in a person's home, and they come upon a gun, the police can seize the gun, even though it is not mentioned in the warrant. The 1986 case of *New York v. Class* illustrates the **plain view doctrine**.[57] A police officer stopped a car for a traffic violation. Wishing to check the vehicle identification number (VIN) on the dashboard, he reached into the car to clear away material that was obstructing his view. While clearing the dash, he noticed a gun under the seat—in plain view. The U.S. Supreme Court upheld the seizure of the gun as evidence because the police officer had the right to check the VIN; therefore, the sighting of the gun was legal.

The doctrine of plain view was applied and further developed in *Arizona v. Hicks* (1987).[58] In that case, the Court held that moving a stereo component in plain view a few inches to record the serial number constituted a search under the Fourth Amendment. When a check with police headquarters revealed that the item had been stolen, the equipment was seized and offered as evidence at James Hicks' trial. The Court held that a plain view search and seizure could be justified only by probable cause, not reasonable suspicion, and suppressed the evidence against the defendant. In this case, the Court decided to take a firm stance on protecting Fourth Amendment rights. The *Hicks* decision is uncharacteristic in an era when most decisions have tended to expand the exceptions to the search warrant requirement.

Plain Touch

If the police touch contraband, can they seize it legally? Is "plain touch" like plain view? In the 1993 case of *Minnesota v. Dickerson*, two Minneapolis police officers noticed the defendant acting suspiciously after leaving an apartment building they believed to be a crack house. The officers briefly stopped Timothy Dickerson to question him and conducted a pat-down search for weapons. The search revealed no weapons, but one officer felt a small lump in the pocket of Dickerson's nylon jacket. The lump turned out to be one-fifth of a gram of crack cocaine, and Dickerson was arrested and charged with drug possession. In its decision, the Court added to its plain view doctrine a plain touch or plain feel corollary. However, the pat-down must be limited to a search for weapons, and the officer may not extend the "feel" beyond that necessary to determine whether what is felt is a weapon.[59]

Although *Dickerson* created the plain feel doctrine, the Supreme Court limited its scope in *Bond v. United States*.[60] In that case, a federal border patrol agent boarded a bus near the Texas–Mexico border to check the immigration status of the passengers. As he was leaving the bus, he squeezed the soft luggage that passengers had placed in the overhead storage space. When he squeezed a canvas bag belonging to the defendant, he noticed that it contained a "brick-like" object. The defendant consented to a search of the bag, the agent discovered a "brick" of methamphetamine, and the defendant was charged with and convicted of possession. The court of appeals ruled that the agent's manipulation of the bag was not a search under the Fourth Amendment.

On appeal, however, the Supreme Court held that the agent's manipulation of the bag violated the Fourth Amendment's rule against unreasonable searches. Personal luggage, according to the Court, is protected under the Fourth Amendment. The defendant had a privacy interest in his bag, and his right to privacy was violated by the police search.

Electronic Surveillance

The use of wiretapping to intercept conversations between parties has significantly affected police investigative procedures. Electronic devices enable people to listen to and record the private conversations of other people over telephones, through walls and windows, and even over long-distance phone lines. Using these devices, police are able to intercept communications secretly and obtain information related to criminal activity.

The oldest and most widely used form of electronic surveillance is wiretapping. With approval from the court and a search warrant, law enforcement officers place listening devices on telephones to overhear oral communications of suspects. Such devices are also often placed in homes and automobiles. The evidence collected is admissible and can be used in the defendant's trial.

Critical Thinking

Many police departments use helicopters for patrol. If you live in a house that has a 6-foot privacy fence around your yard, and if a police helicopter is flying low and observes illegal substances in your yard, do you think that should fall under "plain view"? Why or why not?

Many citizens believe that electronic eavesdropping through hidden microphones, radio transmitters, telephone taps, and bugs represents a grave threat to personal privacy.[61] Although the use of such devices is controversial, the police are generally convinced of their value in investigating criminal activity. However, opponents believe that these techniques are often used beyond their lawful intent to monitor political figures, harass suspects, or investigate cases involving questionable issues of "national security."

In response to concerns about invasions of privacy, the U.S. Supreme Court has increasingly limited the use of electronic eavesdropping in the criminal justice system. In *Katz v. United States* (1967), the Court ruled that when federal agents eavesdropped on a phone conversation using a listening device that could penetrate the walls of a phone booth, they had conducted an illegal search and seizure.[62] The *Katz* doctrine is usually interpreted to mean that the government must obtain a court order if it wishes to listen in on conversations in which the parties have a reasonable expectation of privacy, such as in their own homes or on the telephone. Meanwhile, public utterances or actions are fair game. *Katz* concluded that electronic eavesdropping is a search, even though there is no actual trespass. Therefore, it is unreasonable, and a warrant is needed.

Surveillance Law

It can be relatively painless to secure a warrant for an ordinary search, but the police have to jump through many more hoops when it comes to electronic surveillance. There are two key laws that restrict government wiretap authority. The first, the Federal Wiretap Act (more formally called Title III of the Omnibus Crime Control and Safe Streets Act), was adopted in 1968 and revised in 1986.[63] It requires court approval of all real-time eavesdropping on electronic communications, including voice, e-mail, fax, Internet, and those connected with criminal investigations. More recently, this authority has been used to support eavesdropping on communications between suspected terrorists. The Patriot Act, the controversial antiterrorism legislation enacted after 9/11, has expanded the number of criminal statutes for which such wiretaps can be authorized.

The second key statute controlling wiretaps and eavesdropping is the Foreign Intelligence Surveillance Act (FISA) of 1978.[64] It authorizes wiretapping of any alien the government believes is a member of a foreign terrorist group or is an agent of a foreign power. In the case of U.S. citizens, there must be probable cause that the person targeted for a wiretap is involved in criminal activity; otherwise, there is no such requirement for aliens. FISA warrants are authorized by the secret Foreign Intelligence Surveillance Court, which meets in a heavily secured room within the U.S. Justice Department. The court is staffed by 11 judges, appointed by the chief justice of the U.S. Supreme Court, who serve seven-year terms.

Just as the Patriot Act altered the Federal Wiretap Act, it also altered FISA. It did so by allowing prosecutors to gather evidence in cases involving national security crimes. In 2007, President Bush signed into law the controversial Protect America Act. It removed the warrant requirement for surveillance of foreign intelligence targets that the government "reasonably believes" are operating outside the United States. The law was especially controversial because it permitted electronic surveillance of all communications, including some domestic ones that involved foreign targets. Because of a sunset clause, the law expired in early 2008, but portions of it were replaced by the FISA Amendments Act of 2008. At present, the FISA Amendments Reauthorization Act of 2017 was been signed into law, continuing to keep these alterations to FISA in place. This area of law continues to change.

Technologies for Local Police

The Federal Wiretap Act and FISA have limited applicability to local law enforcement. Most terrorism investigations and related surveillance activity tend to be federal affairs. For example, most FISA warrants are sought by the Federal Bureau of Investigation (FBI). Yet there are plenty of technological advances that have benefited local law enforcement officials. Gone are the days of crude wiretaps outside phone booths and other antiquated devices. Now the police can avail themselves of several technological advances to help them keep tabs on the criminal element. Some devices even permit listening to, and looking in on, the activities of *everyone*, not just criminals. These devices are controversial because there is no warrant requirement; examples include surveillance cameras and GPS tracking devices.

Surveillance Cameras

Many large cities (including Baltimore, Chicago, Los Angeles, Dallas, Washington, and New York) have installed, in public locations, security cameras that can be monitored by officers from a distance. Since 2006, Washington, DC, has installed dozens of cameras across the city. Initially they were used as investigative tools, so that officers could go back through recorded video and find evidence of crimes committed in the cameras' view. They were eventually monitored on a regular basis.[65] The cameras have proved helpful on more than one occasion, but critics claim that these "prying eyes" violate people's privacy.

ShotSpotter

Some cities have employed a gunfire locator or gunshot detection system called ShotSpotter. This is a system that detects, locates, and alerts the police of gunfire in less than 60 seconds. It conveys the location of gunfire or other weapon fire using acoustic, optical, potentially other types of sensors, as well as a combination of such sensors and digital cameras. There are some concerns with this approach. Suffolk County, New York's ShotSpotter system experienced so many false alarms that the company had to adjust its algorithms to be more discriminating. Even after the adjustment, a report by Suffolk County police to the county legislature stated that, over an eight-month period, only 6.5 percent of ShotSpotter's 212 activations could be confirmed as an actual gunshot. Over 30 percent were confirmed as false alarms.[66]

GPS Tracking Devices

In *United States v. Jones* (2012), The Supreme Court decided on the constitutionality of GPS tracking of criminal suspects.[67] Without a warrant, police installed a GPS tracking device on Antoine Jones' vehicle and tracked his movements for a month. They were able to use the evidence obtained from the tracking device to successfully build a drug trafficking case against Jones, who was ultimately sentenced to life in prison. Interestingly, the Supreme Court sided with Jones and reversed his conviction, concluding that the use of the GPS tracking device constituted a search and needed to be supported by probable cause and a warrant.

On its face, the *Jones* case seems somewhat at odds with former Supreme Court cases involving tracking devices. In one case, *United States v. Knotts*, the Court held that it was constitutional for police to use a "beeper," a less sophisticated tracking device, to monitor a suspect's movements.[68] The difference in *Knotts*, however, was that the beeper was placed in a container with the consent of its owner who then passed it off to Knotts. In other words, Knotts was not the victim of any sort of government trespass. Moreover, the government tracked Knotts' movements only in public areas. A similar decision was reached in *United States v. Karo*, another case in which the tracking device was inserted into a container *before* it came into the possession of the individual whose movements were tracked.[69] *Jones* is distinguished from these cases because, according to the Court, the police trespassory attached the tracking device to Jones' vehicle.

Interrogation

After a suspect is taken into custody, it is routine to question them about their involvement in the crime. The police may hope to find out about coconspirators or even whether the suspect was involved in similar crimes. This is a particularly unsettling time, and the arrestee may feel disoriented, alone, and afraid. Consequently, they may give police harmful information that can be used against them in a court of law. Exacerbating the situation is the fact that the interrogating officers sometimes use extreme pressure to get suspects to talk or to name their accomplices. Because of these concerns, the Supreme Court has issued rulings that protect criminal suspects from police intimidation, the most important of which was set down in the 1966 case of *Miranda v. Arizona*.[70]

L06

Explain the *Miranda v. Arizona* decision.

The *Miranda* Warning

In the landmark case of *Miranda v. Arizona* (1966), the Supreme Court held that suspects in custody must be told that they have the following rights if they are subjected to interrogation:

- They have the right to remain silent.
- If they decide to make a statement, the statement can and will be used against them in a court of law.
- They have the right to have an attorney present at the time of the interrogation, or they will have an opportunity to consult with an attorney.
- If they cannot afford an attorney, one will be appointed for them by the state.

Miranda warning

The requirement that when a person is custodially interrogated, police inform the individual of the right to remain silent, the consequences of failing to remain silent, and the constitutional right to counsel.

The police must give this information—collectively known as the **Miranda warning** to a person in custody before questioning begins.

Some suspects choose to remain silent. However, simply remaining silent is not the same as invoking *Miranda* protection. As the Supreme Court recently decided, if a suspect does not assert their *Miranda* rights and makes a self-incriminating voluntary statement in response to police questioning, that statement can be used in court.[71] To enjoy the benefits of *Miranda*, then, the suspect must state that they intend to remain silent. Also, the suspect can insist on having counsel present.

A suspect's constitutional rights under *Miranda* can be given up (waived). A suspect can choose to talk to the police or sign a confession. However, for the waiver to be effective, the state must first show that it was voluntary and that the defendant was aware of all of their *Miranda* rights. People who cannot understand the *Miranda* warning because of their age, intellectual or cognitive disabilities, or language problems may not be legally questioned without an attorney present. If they can understand their rights, they may be questioned.[72]

Once the suspect asks for an attorney, all questioning must stop until the attorney is present. And if the criminal suspect has invoked their *Miranda* rights, police officials cannot reinitiate interrogation in the absence of counsel even if the accused has consulted with an attorney in the meantime.[73] This rule was recently modified to some extent; it doesn't apply if the suspect has been released from custody for at least two weeks.[74]

Even if the suspect has invoked their *Miranda* rights and demanded an attorney, the police can question the offender about another, separate crime (as long as they give the *Miranda* warning for the second crime as well); for example, say a person is arrested on burglary charges and requests an attorney. The next day, police question them about a murder after reading the suspect their *Miranda* rights. They decide to waive their rights and confesses to the murder without a lawyer being present. The murder confession would be legal even though the suspect had requested an attorney in the burglary case, because they are two separate legal matters.[75]

The *Miranda* Rule Today

The Supreme Court has used case law to define the boundaries of the *Miranda* warning since its inception. Although statements made by a suspect who was not given the *Miranda* warning or received it improperly cannot be used against them in a court of law, it is possible to use illegally gained statements and the evidence they produce in some well-defined instances:

■ If a defendant perjured themselves, evidence obtained in violation of the *Miranda* warning can be used by the government to impeach their testimony during trial.[76]

■ At trial, the testimony of a witness is permissible even though their identity was revealed by the defendant in violation of the *Miranda* rule.[77]

Initial errors by police in getting statements do not make subsequent statements inadmissible. A subsequent *Miranda* warning that is properly given can cure the condition that made the initial statements inadmissible.[78] However, if police intentionally mislead suspects by questioning them before giving them a *Miranda* warning, their statements made after the warning is given are inadmissible in court. The *Miranda* rule would be frustrated were the police permitted to undermine its meaning and effect.[79]

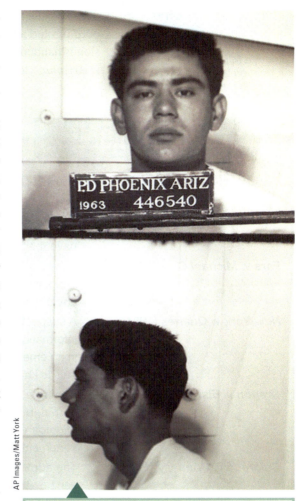

AP Images/Matt York

The booking photos of Ernesto Miranda. The arrest of Miranda on March 13, 1963, led to the landmark self-incrimination case that resulted in the so-called *Miranda* rights, which include the right to remain silent and have a lawyer present if they so choose, paid for by the state, before what they tell police can be used against them in a court of law.

On the Web

For more information about *Miranda v. Arizona*, visit http://www.law.cornell.edu /supremecourt/text/384/436

public safety doctrine

The principle that a suspect can be questioned in the field without a *Miranda* warning if the information the police seek is needed to protect public safety.

Over the years, the Supreme Court has decided a number of cases that have both limited and expanded the reach of *Miranda*. Indeed, a new *Miranda* decision is handed down nearly every term. See Exhibit 11.3, "Evolution of *Miranda v. Arizona*," for a summary of several of these important decisions.

Exhibit 11.3

Evolution of *Miranda v. Arizona*

***Miranda v. Arizona* (1966)**	Any person subjected to custodial interrogation must be advised of their Fifth Amendment right to be free from compelled self-incrimination and to have the assistance of counsel.[84]
***Fare v. Michael C.* (1978)**	The *Miranda* warning applies only to the right to have an attorney present. The suspect cannot demand to speak to a priest, a probation officer, or any other official.[85]
***New York v. Quarles* (1984)**	A suspect can be questioned in the field without a *Miranda* warning if the information the police seek is needed to protect public safety. For example, in an emergency, suspects can be asked where they hid their weapons.[86] This is known as the **public safety doctrine**.
***Oregon v. Elstad* (1985)**	Admissions made in the absence of *Miranda* warnings are not admissible at trial, but post-*Miranda* voluntary statements are admissible. A post-*Miranda* voluntary statement is admissible even if an initial incriminating statement was made in the absence of *Miranda* warnings.[87]
***Colorado v. Connelly* (1986)**	The admissions of defendants with intellectual and cognitive disabilities can be admitted in evidence as long as the police acted properly and there is a preponderance of the evidence that the defendants understood the meaning of *Miranda*.[88]
***Moran v. Burbine* (1986)**	An attorney's request to see the defendant does not affect the validity of the defendant's waiver of the right to counsel. Police misinformation to an attorney does not affect waiver of *Miranda* rights.[89] For example, a suspect's statements may be used if they are given voluntarily, even though their family has hired an attorney and the statements were made before the attorney arrived. Only the suspect can request an attorney, not their friends or family.
***Colorado v. Spring* (1987)**	Suspects need not be aware of all the possible outcomes of waiving their rights for the *Miranda* warning to be considered properly given.[90]
***Minnick v. Mississippi* (1990)**	When counsel is requested, interrogation must cease and cannot be resumed until an attorney is present.[91]
***Arizona v. Fulminante* (1991)**	The erroneous admission of a coerced confession at trial can be ruled a harmless error that would not automatically result in overturning a conviction.[92]
***Davis v. United States* (1994)**	A suspect who makes an ambiguous reference to an attorney during questioning, such as "Maybe I should talk to an attorney," is not protected under *Miranda*. The police may continue their questioning.[93]
***Chavez v. Martinez* (2003)**	Failure to give a suspect a *Miranda* warning is not illegal unless the case becomes a criminal issue.[94]
***United States v. Patane* (2004)**	A voluntary statement given in the absence of a *Miranda* warning can be used to obtain evidence that can be used at trial. Failure to give the warning does not make seizure of evidence illegal per se.[95]

***Missouri v. Seibert* (2004)**	*Miranda* warnings must be given before interrogation begins. The accused in this case was interrogated and confessed in the absence of *Miranda* warnings. *Miranda* rights were then read, at which point the accused "re-confessed." The pre-*Miranda* questioning was improper.[96]
***Maryland v. Shatzer* (2010)**	*Miranda* protections do not apply if a suspect is released from police custody for at least 14 days and then questioned. However, if the suspect is rearrested, then *Miranda* warnings must be read.[97]
***Florida v. Powell* (2010)**	The *Miranda* warnings do not require that the suspect be advised that they have the right to have an attorney present during questioning. It is sufficient to advise the suspect that they have the right to talk with a lawyer before questioning and to consult a lawyer at any time during questioning.[98]
***Berghuis v. Thompkins* (2010)**	Unless a suspect asserts their *Miranda* rights, any subsequent voluntary statements given after the warnings are admissible in court. Simply remaining silent does not imply that a suspect has invoked *Miranda* protection.[99]
***J.D.B. v. North Carolina* (2011)**	Children may be more prone to confessing to crimes they did not commit, and this needs to be taken into consideration in deciding whether a police interrogation is also custodial. In other words, the suspect's age factors into the *Miranda* custody analysis.[100]
***Bobby v. Dixon* (2011)**	Murder confession is admissible because it was voluntary and *Miranda* rights were both read by police and waived by the suspect—this, despite the fact that *Miranda* rights were *not* read in a previous interrogation of the suspect arising out of the same criminal act.[101]
***Salinas v. Texas* (2013)**	The Fifth Amendment's privilege against self-incrimination does not extend to defendants who simply decide to remain mute during questioning. Long-standing judicial precedent has held that any witness who desires protection against self-incrimination must explicitly claim that protection.[102]
***Vega v. Tekoh* (2022)**	The Court held that Miranda rights are not constitutionally guaranteed and a violation of Miranda is not a violation of the Fifth Amendment.[103]

The Impact of *Miranda*

After *Miranda* was decided, law enforcement officials became concerned that the Supreme Court had gone too far in providing defendants with procedural protections. Subsequent research indicates that the decision has had little effect on the number of confessions obtained by the police and that it has not affected the rate of convictions.[80] It now seems apparent that the police formerly relied too heavily on confessions to prove a defendant's guilt. Other forms of evidence, such as witness statements, physical evidence, and expert testimony, have generally proved adequate to win the prosecution's case. Blaming *Miranda* for increased crime rates in the 1970s and 1980s now seems problematic, given that rates are down and *Miranda* is still the law.[81]

Critics have called the *Miranda* decision incomprehensible and difficult to administer. How can one tell whether a confession is truly voluntary or has been elicited by pressure and coercion? Aren't all police interrogations essentially coercive?[82] These criticisms aside, the Supreme Court is unlikely ever to reverse course. In the 2003 case *of Dickerson v. United States*, for example, the Court made it clear that the *Miranda* ruling is here to stay and has become enmeshed in the prevailing legal system.[83] In that case, the Court invalidated a federal statute enacted shortly after the *Miranda* decision that said any confession could be used against a suspect if it was voluntarily obtained.

Not surprisingly, police administrators who in the past might have been wary of the restrictions imposed by *Miranda* now favor its use.[104] One survey found that nearly 60 percent of police chiefs believe that the *Miranda* warning should be retained, and the same number report that abolishing *Miranda* would change the way that the police function.[105] To ensure that *Miranda* rules are being followed, many departments now routinely videotape interrogations, although research shows that this procedure is not a sure cure for police intimidation.[106]

With the ongoing war on terrorism, law enforcement officers may find themselves in unique situations involving national security and forced to make an immediate decision about whether the *Miranda* rule applies. It is also important to note that *Miranda* is an American creation. *Miranda*-like warnings are not always required in other countries. The following Focus on Policing: Interrogation Law in Other Countries feature discusses how interrogation is conducted abroad.

Focus on Policing

Interrogation Law in Other Countries

The Fifth Amendment ensures that those suspected of criminal activity cannot be forced to incriminate themselves and that they have the right to counsel. The Supreme Court's *Miranda* decision requires the police to advise certain criminal suspects of these important protections. In no other area of criminal procedure is the police required to advise suspects of their rights.

Miranda and the Fifth Amendment's self-incrimination clause are controversial. On the one hand, they help protect the innocent from being forced to confess. On the other hand, is justice served when the one person who may know most about a particular crime is under no obligation to talk?

To gain an appreciation for the significance of the right to counsel in the United States—and for the *Miranda* decision—it is helpful to take a look at interrogation laws in some other countries. Neither *Miranda*-like warnings nor the right to counsel are uniquely American creations. Several other countries have similar procedures, but to varying degrees. Here we look at three of them: the United Kingdom, France, and China.

The United Kingdom

The United Kingdom has no single constitutional document as the United States does. Police interrogation is instead governed by the Police and Criminal Evidence Act and the Code of Practice for the Detention, Treatment, and Questioning of Persons by Police Officers.

In the United Kingdom, if a suspect is taken into custody and the police intend to question the suspect, they are required to advise them that there is no obligation to talk. The British approach is somewhat stricter than that employed in the United States because police are required to advise the suspect of the right to silence as soon as there are reasonable grounds to believe they have committed an offense. The *Miranda* rule applies only when there is custody and interrogation.

There is also a right to counsel in the United Kingdom, but the suspect generally receives assistance only when they ask for it. If a suspect exercises their rights and refuses to answer police questions, the court is later permitted to draw adverse inferences from this action. For example, the prosecutor can comment at trial that the suspect failed to answer questions. This can work against them at trial. In the United States, the prosecutor *cannot* comment on a defendant's pretrial silence.

France

In contrast to the United States and the United Kingdom, France is known for long having put

The Exclusionary Rule

L07

Demonstrate the exclusionary rule, including its extensions and exceptions.

No review of the legal aspects of policing would be complete without a discussion of the **exclusionary rule**, the principal means used to restrain police conduct. The Fourth Amendment guarantees individuals the right to be secure in their persons, homes, papers, and effects against unreasonable searches and seizures. The exclusionary rule provides that all evidence obtained by illegal searches and seizures is inadmissible in criminal trials. Similarly, it excludes the use of illegal confessions under Fifth Amendment prohibitions.

exclusionary rule

The principle that prohibits using illegally obtained evidence in a trial.

For many years, evidence obtained by unreasonable searches and seizures that consequently should have been considered illegal was admitted by state and federal governments in criminal trials. The only criteria for admissibility were whether the evidence was incriminating and whether it would assist the judge or jury in ascertaining the innocence or guilt of the defendant. How the evidence was obtained was unimportant; its admissibility was determined by its relevance to the criminal case.

society's interest in crime control ahead of individual rights and liberties. France's interrogation law provides evidence of this. First, there is no clear requirement that a suspect be advised that they are not required to answer police questions. Second, the right to counsel is limited. Suspects do not have the right to counsel immediately following their detention; the right does not apply until 20 hours after the person has been detained for ordinary offenses. For more serious cases, such as those involving drug rings or terrorism, the right to counsel does not attach for up to 72 hours from the detention. Finally, the accused has the right to consult with counsel only for a limited time; there is no right to have counsel present during police interrogations.

China

In its earlier days, the People's Republic operated without much regard for individual rights. To this day, there are criticisms that its government curtails citizens' freedoms, but legal reforms have brought China's criminal justice system somewhat in line with that of other modernized nations. The 1979 Criminal Procedure Law (CPL), which was significantly amended in 1996, has led to considerable progress in terms of protections afforded to those accused of criminal activity.

The CPL requires that before an interrogation, the police must give the suspect an opportunity to make a statement about their involvement (or lack of involvement) in the crime. This presumably protects the suspect from having the police proceed under the assumption that they are guilty. Critics have argued that the police routinely ignore this requirement and use psychological pressures to extract confessions. In any case, there is no recognized right to freedom from self-incrimination in China. The CPL prohibits the use of torture, but this does not protect a suspect from incriminating themself. There *is* a right to counsel, but it attaches only after the police have completed their first interrogation.

Critical Thinking

1. What is your take on *Miranda*? Should the state provide people with free legal advice after their arrest?

2. What would be the effect of giving police a free hand to interrogate suspects? Would it lead to greater levels of abuse or merely help in solving crimes?

Sources: National Association of Criminal Defense Lawyers, Foreign Countries on Recording Custodial Interrogations, Information on the policy and history of recording custodial interrogations in foreign countries. February 25, 2019, https://www.nacdl.org/Content /ForeignCountriesonRecordingCustodialInterrogations; Yue Ma, "A Comparative View of the Law of Interrogation, *International Criminal Justice Review,* 17(2007), 5–26; Christopher Slobogin, "An Empirically Based Comparison of American and European Regulatory Approaches to Police Investigation," *Michigan Journal of International Law* 22 (2001), 423–456.

In 1914, however, the rules on the admissibility of evidence underwent a change of direction when the Supreme Court decided the case of *Weeks v. United States*.[107] The defendant, Fremont Weeks, was accused by federal law enforcement authorities of using the mail for illegal purposes. After his arrest, the home in which Weeks was staying was searched without a valid search warrant. Evidence in the form of letters and other materials was found in his room and admitted at the trial. Weeks was then convicted of the federal offense based on the incriminating evidence. On appeal, the Supreme Court held that evidence obtained by unreasonable search and seizure must be excluded in a federal criminal trial.

Thus, for the first time, the Court held that the Fourth Amendment barred the use of evidence obtained through illegal search and seizure in a federal prosecution. With this ruling, the Court established the exclusionary rule. The rule was based not on legislation but on judicial decision making. Can the criminal go free because the constable blunders? That became the question.

In 1961, the Supreme Court made the exclusionary rule applicable to the state courts in the landmark decision of *Mapp v. Ohio*. In *Mapp*, police officers forcibly searched a home while using a fake warrant. The Court held that although the search had turned up contraband, it violated the Fourth Amendment's prohibition against unreasonable searches and seizures, so the illegally seized evidence could not be used in court. Justice Tom Clark, delivering the majority opinion of the Court, made clear the importance of this constitutional right in the administration of criminal justice:

> There are those who say, as did Justice [then Judge Benjamin] Cardozo, that under our constitutional exclusionary doctrine "[t]he criminal is to go free because the constable has blundered." In some cases this will undoubtedly be the result. But . . . there is another consideration—the imperative of judicial integrity. . . . The criminal goes free, if he must, but it is the law that sets him free. Nothing can destroy a government more quickly than its failure to observe its own laws, or worse, its disregard of the charter of its own existence.[108]

fruit of the poisonous tree
Secondary evidence obtained from a search that violates the exclusionary rule.

The exclusionary rule has also been extended to include derivative, or secondary, evidence, which is also called **fruit of the poisonous tree**.[109] This doctrine applies not only to evidence obtained directly from a violation of the Fourth Amendment but also to evidence indirectly obtained from such a violation. For example, if the police, without probable cause and a warrant, searched a private home and found a key to a locker at a nearby bus station, a subsequent search of the locker would be considered fruit of the poisonous tree.

Current Status of the Exclusionary Rule

In the 1980s, a more conservative U.S. Supreme Court gradually began to limit the scope of the exclusionary rule. It created three major exceptions:

- **Independent source exception.** This rule allows admission of evidence that has been discovered by means wholly independent of any constitutional violation. So if police enter a drug dealer's home with an arrest warrant and, while arresting them, illegally search for and seize evidence such as drug

On the Web

For more information about *Mapp v. Ohio*, visit http://www.law.cornell.edu/supremecourt/text/367/643

paraphernalia, the illegally seized material may be allowed in court if, independently, a warrant had been issued to search the apartment for the same evidence but had not yet arrived at the scene.[110]

■ **Good faith exception.** In *United States v. Leon* (1984), the Court ruled that evidence seized by police relying on a warrant issued by a detached and neutral magistrate can be used in a court proceeding, even if the judge who issued the warrant erred in drawing up the document.[111] In this case, the Court articulated a **good-faith exception** to the exclusionary rule: evidence obtained with a less than adequate search warrant may be admissible in court if the police officers acted in good faith when obtaining court approval for their search. However, deliberately misleading a judge or using a warrant that the police know is unreasonably deficient would be grounds to invoke the exclusionary rule. In a subsequent case, *Arizona v. Evans*, the Court ruled that the exclusionary rule was designed as a means of deterring police misconduct, not to punish police for honest mistakes; it does not apply when they have acted in objectively reasonable reliance on an apparently valid warrant but later find out it was technically faulty.[112] In 2009, the Supreme Court decided *Herring v. United States*, another good-faith case.[113] Officers searched Herring based on a warrant listed in a neighboring county's database. Unbeknownst to them, the warrant had been recalled months earlier. The Supreme Court sanctioned the search and further noted that the exclusionary rule will be violated only when there is "systemic error or reckless disregard of constitutional requirements."[114]

good-faith exception
The principle that evidence may be used in a criminal trial even though the search warrant used to obtain it was technically faulty, as long as the police acted in good faith when they sought the warrant from a judge.

■ **Inevitable discovery rule.** This rule holds that evidence obtained through an unlawful search or seizure is admissible in court if it can be established, to a very high degree of probability, that police investigation would be expected to lead to the discovery of the evidence. In the case that established the rule, *Nix v. Williams* (1984), police illegally interrogated a suspect and found the location of the victim's body. The evidence obtained was allowed at trial when the Court ruled that because the body was lying in plain sight and many police officers were searching for the body, it would have been obtained anyway, even without the information provided by the illegal interrogation; this is now referred to as the **inevitable discovery rule**.[115]

inevitable discovery rule
The principle that evidence can be used in court even though the information that led to its discovery was obtained in violation of the *Miranda* rule if a judge finds it would have been discovered anyway by other means or sources.

In these and other cases, the Supreme Court has made it easier for the police to conduct searches of criminal suspects and their possessions and then use the seized evidence in court proceedings. The Court has indicated that, as a general rule, the protection afforded the individual by the Fourth Amendment may take a back seat to concerns about public safety if criminal actions pose a clear threat to society.

Summary

LO1 Discuss how the Fourth Amendment controls police.

The Fourth Amendment controls searches and seizures. The Fourth Amendment contains two parts: the reasonableness clause and the warrants clause. Each clause is independent because a search can

be reasonable without a warrant, but if a warrant is required, certain steps must be taken.

LO2 Define search and arrest.

A search occurs when a government actor infringes on a person's reasonable expectation of privacy. When police look through abandoned property, look in open fields, or use aerial surveillance, they do not "search." An arrest occurs when a police officer takes a person into custody or deprives a person of freedom for having allegedly committed a criminal offense.

LO3   Distinguish between search warrants and arrest warrants.

A search warrant is an order, issued by a judge, directing officers to conduct a search of specified premises for specified objects. An arrest warrant is an order, issued by a judge, directing officers to arrest a particular individual.

LO4   Explain when warrants are required.

Warrants are required in two key situations: arrests and searches in private homes or on specific types of private property. Arrests for minor offenses committed out of view of the arresting officer also require a warrant.

LO5   Explain a field interrogation (Terry stop).

An exception to the rule requiring a search warrant is the stop-and-frisk procedure, also known as a Terry stop. This type of search typically occurs when a police officer encounters a suspicious person on the street and frisks or pats down their outer garments to determine whether they are in possession of a concealed weapon. The police officer need not have probable cause to arrest the suspect but simply must be reasonably suspicious based on the circumstances of the case (that is, time and place) and their experience as a police officer.

LO6   Explain the *Miranda v. Arizona* decision.

Miranda v. Arizona requires police officers to advise people who are both in custody and interrogated of their constitutional right (from the Fifth Amendment) not to incriminate themselves. Suspects who are advised of their *Miranda* rights are told: (1) they have the right to remain silent; (2) if they decide to make a statement, the statement can and will be used against them in a court of law; (3) they have the right to have an attorney present at the time of the interrogation, or they will have an opportunity to consult with an attorney; and (4) if they cannot afford an attorney, one will be appointed for them by the state. The Supreme Court has modified the *Miranda* rule to some extent over the years. Mostly, its decisions have relaxed the *Miranda* rule. The impact of *Miranda* on law enforcement, such as through lost convictions, has been fairly minimal.

LO7   Demonstrate the exclusionary rule, including its extensions and exceptions.

The exclusionary rule provides that all evidence obtained by illegal searches and seizures is inadmissible in criminal trials. The exclusionary rule has been extended to include "fruit of the poisonous tree," or indirect evidence. Exceptions to the exclusionary rule include independent source, good faith, and inevitable discovery.

Key Terms

search, 307
open field, 307
curtilage, 307
search warrant, 310
arrest warrant, 310
in-presence requirement, 310
probable cause, 311

particularity, 314
stop and frisk, 315
search incident to a lawful arrest, 317
reasonable suspicion, 320
bus sweep, 323
plain view doctrine, 324

Miranda warning, 328
public safety doctrine, 330
exclusionary rule, 333
fruit of the poisonous tree, 334
good-faith exception, 335
inevitable discovery rule, 335

Notes

1. *Torres v. Madrid*, 592 U.S. —(2021).
2. *Katz v. United States*, 389 U.S. 347 (1967).
3. *California v. Greenwood*, 486 U.S. 35 (1988).
4. *Oliver v. United States*, 466 U.S. 170 (1984).
5. *California v. Ciraola*, 476 U.S. 207 (1986).
6. *Florida v. Riley*, 488 U.S. 445 (1989).
7. *Payton v. New York*, 445 U.S. 573 (1980).
8. *Welsh v. Wisconsin*, 466 U.S. 740 (1984).
9. California Penal Code - PEN § 836 http://codes.findlaw.com/ca/penal-code/pen-sect-836.html.
10. *Aguilar v. Texas*, 378 U.S. 108 (1964).
11. *Illinois v. Gates*, 462 U.S. 213 (1983).
12. *Alabama v. White*, 496 U.S. 325 (1990).
13. Ibid., at 325, 326.
14. *Florida v. J. L.*, No. 98-1993 (2000).
15. *Johnson v. United States*, 333 U.S. 10 (1948), pp. 13–14.

16. Mark I. Koffsky, "Choppy Waters in the Surveillance Data Stream: The Clipper Scheme and the Particularity Clause," *Berkeley Technology Law Journal* 9 (1994), 131.

17. *Terry v. Ohio*, 392 U.S. 1 (1968).

18. *Illinois v. Wardlow*, 120 S.Ct. 673 (2000).

19. *Arizona v. Johnson*, 555 U.S. 323 (2009).

20. *Terry v. Ohio*, p. 24.

21. Alese Wooditch and David Weisburd, "Using Space–Time Analysis to Evaluate Criminal Justice Programs: An Application to Stop-Question-Frisk Practices," *Journal of Quantitative Criminology* (2015), 1–23.

22. *Chimel v. California*, 395 U.S. 752 (1969).

23. *Riley v. California*, 573 U.S. ___ (2014).

24. *Carroll v. United States*, 267 U.S. 132 (1925). See also James Rodgers, "Poisoned Fruit: Quest for Consistent Rule on Traffic Stop Searches," *American Bar Association Journal* 81 (1995), 50–51.

25. *Carroll v. United States*, 267 U.S. 132 (1925).

26. *United States v. Lee*, 274 U.S. 559 (1927).

27. *Cardwell v. Lewis*, 417 U.S. 583 (1974).

28. *Pennsylvania v. Mimms*, 434 U.S. 106 (1997).

29. *United States v. Ross*, 456 U.S. 798 (1982).

30. *Michigan v. Long*, 463 U.S. 1032 (1983).

31. *Michigan Dept. of State Police v. Sitz*, 496 U.S. 444 (1990).

32. *Whren v. United States*, 517 U.S. 806 (1996).

33. *Maryland v. Wilson*, 519 U.S. 408 (1997).

34. *City of Indianapolis v. Edmond*, 531 U.S. 32 (2000).

35. *Illinois v. Lidster*, 540 U.S. 419 (2004).

36. *Brendlin v. California*, 551 U.S. 249 (2007).

37. *Arizona v. Gant*, 556 U.S. 332 (2009).

38. *Davis v. United States*, 564 U.S. ___ (2011). 556 U.S. 332.

39. *United States v. Arvizu*, 534 U.S. 266 (2002).

40. *Rodriguez v. United States,* 575 U. S. ___ (2015).

41. *United States v. Ross*, 456 U.S. 798 (1982). See also Barry Latzer, "Searching Cars and Their Contents: U.S. v. Ross," *Criminal Law Bulletin* 6 (1982), 220; Joseph Grano, "Rethinking the Fourth Amendment Warrant Requirements," *Criminal Law Review* 19 (1982), 603.

42. *Michigan v. Long*, 463 U.S. 1032 (1983).

43. *Arizona v. Gant*, 556 U.S. 332 (2009); also see New York v. Belton, 453 U.S. 454 (1981) and Thornton v. United States, 541 U.S. 615 (2004).

44. *Pennsylvania v. Mimms*, 434 U.S. 106 (1977).

45. *Maryland v. Wilson*, 65 U.S.L.W. 4124 (1997).

46. *Brendlin v. California*, 551 U.S. 249 (2007).

47. *Schneckloth v. Bustamonte*, 412 U.S. 218 (1973).

48. *Bumper v. North Carolina*, 391 U.S. 543 (1968).

49. *Schneckloth v. Bustamonte*, 412 U.S. 218 (1973).

50. *Ohio v. Robinette*, 519 U.S. 33 (1966).

51. 18-6210 *Mitchell v. Wisconsin* (06/27/2019).

52. *United States v. Matlock*, 415 U.S. 164 (1974).

53. *Georgia v. Randolph*, 547 U.S. 103 (2006).

54. *Florida v. Bostick*, 501 U.S. 429 (1991).

55. *Ohio v. Robinette*, 519 U.S. 33 (1996).

56. *Coolidge v. New Hampshire*, 403 U.S. 443 (1971).

57. *New York v. Class*, 475 U.S. 106 (1986).

58. *Arizona v. Hicks*, 480 U.S. 321 (1987).

59. *Minnesota v. Dickerson*, 508 U.S. 366 (1993).

60. *Bond v. United States*, 120 S.Ct. 1462 (2000).

61. Gary T. Marx, *Undercover: Police Surveillance in America* (Berkeley: University of California Press, 1988).

62. *Katz v. United States*, 389 U.S. 347 (1967).

63. 18 U.S.C. §§ 2510–20.

64. 50 U.S.C. §§1801–11, 1821–29, 1841–46, and 1861–62.

65. Allison Keith, "Police Go Live Monitoring D.C. Crime Cameras," *Washington Post*, February 11, 2008, A1.

66. Suffolk County, NY Legislature. http://legis.suffolkcountyny.gov /pdf/2013/shotspotter_june2013.pdf.

67. *United States v. Jones*, 565 U.S. ___ (2012).

68. *United States v. Knotts*, 460 U.S. 276 (1983).

69. *United States v. Karo*, 468 U.S. 705 (1984).

70. *Miranda v. Arizona*, 384 U.S. 436 (1966).

71. *Berghuis v. Thompkins*, 560 U.S. (2010).

72. *Colorado v. Connelly*, 479 U.S. 157 (1986).

73. *Minnick v. Mississippi*, 498 U.S. 46 (1990).

74. *Maryland v. Shatzer*, 559 U.S. (2010).

75. *Texas v. Cobb*, 532 U.S. 162 (2001).

76. *Harris v. New York*, 401 U.S. 222 (1971).

77. *Michigan v. Tucker*, 417 U.S. 433 (1974).

78. *Oregon v. Elstad*, 470 U.S. 298 (1985).

79. *Missouri v. Seibert*, 542 U.S. 600 (2004).

80. Michael Wald and others, "Interrogations in New Haven: The Impact of Miranda," *Yale Law Journal* 76 (1967), 1519. See also Walter Lippman, "Miranda v. Arizona—Twenty Years Later," *Criminal Justice Journal* 9 (1987), 241; Stephen J. Schulhofer, "Reconsidering Miranda," *University of Chicago Law Review* 54 (1987), 435–461; Paul Cassell, "How Many Criminals Has Miranda Set Free?," *Wall Street Journal*, March 1, 1995, p. A12.

81. "Don't Blame Miranda," *The Washington Post*, December 2, 1988, p. A26. See also Scott Lewis, "Miranda Today: Death of a Talisman," *Prosecutor* 28 (1994), 18–25; Richard Leo, "The Impact of Miranda Revisited," *Journal of Criminal Law and Criminology* 86 (1996), 621–648.

82. Ronald Allen, "Miranda's Hollow Core," *Northwestern University Law Review* 100 (2006), 71–85.

83. *Dickerson v. United States*, 530 U.S. 428 (2000).

84. *Miranda v. Arizona*, 384 U.S. 436 (1966).

85. *Fare v. Michael C*, 439 U.S. 1310 (1978).

86. *New York v. Quarles*, 467 U.S. 649 (1984).

87. *Oregon v. Elstad*, 470 U.S. 298 (1985).

88. *Colorado v. Connelly*, 479 U.S. 157 (1986).

89. *Moran v. Burbine*, 475 U.S. 412 (1986).

90. *Colorado v. Spring*, 479 U.S. 564 (1987).

91. *Minnick v. Mississippi*, 498 U.S. 146 (1990).

92. *Arizona v. Fulminante*, 499 U.S. 279 (1991).

93. *Davis v. United States*, 512 U.S. 452 (1994).

94. *Chavez v. Martinez*, 538 U.S. 760 (2003).

95. *United States v. Patane*, 542 U.S. 630 (2004).

96. *Missouri v. Seibert*, 542 U.S. 600 (2004).

97. *Maryland v. Shatzer*, 559 U.S. 98 (2010).

98. *Florida v. Powell*, 559 U.S. ___ (2010).

99. *Berghuis v. Thompkins,* 560 U.S. 370 (2010).

100. *J.D.B. v. North Carolina*, 564 U.S. ___ (2011).

101. *Bobby v. Dixon*, 565 U.S. ___ (2011).

102. *Salinas v. Texas* (2013) 570 US _ (2013)

103. https://www.supremecourt.gov/opinions/21pdf/21-499_gfbh .pdf.

104. Marvin Zalman and Brad Smith, "The Attitudes of Police Executives Toward Miranda and Interrogation Policies," *Journal of Criminal Law and Criminology* 97 (2007), 873–942.

105. Victoria Time and Brian Payne, "Police Chiefs' Perceptions About Miranda: An Analysis of Survey Data," *Journal of Criminal Justice* 30 (2002), 77–86.

106. G. Daniel Lassiter, Jennifer Ratcliff, Lezlee Ware, and Clinton Irvin, "Videotaped Confessions: Panacea or Pandora's Box?," *Law and Policy* 28 (2006), 192–210.

107. *Weeks v. United States*, 232 U.S. 383 (1914).

108. *Mapp v. Ohio*, 367 U.S. 643 (1961).

109. *Silverthorne Lumber Co. v. United States*, 251 U.S. 385 (1920).

110. *Segura v. United States*, 468 U.S. 796 (1984).

111. *United States v. Leon*, 468 U.S. 897 (1984).

112. *Arizona v. Evans*, 514 U.S. 260 (1995).

113. *Herring v. United States*, 555 U.S. 135 (2009).

114. Ibid., p. 11.

115. *Nix v. Williams*, 467 U.S. 431 (1984).

Part 4

Contemporary Issues in Policing

This final section contains two chapters that touch upon some of the challenges police officers and administrators face in our changing society. Some are social issues, such as how police work affects the health and well-being of police officers. There is also the issue of budget constraints facing contemporary city administrations and their effect on modern policing. Is greater work stress being placed on officers because they are expected to do more with less? Another issue is how social media is affecting police work, especially when their encounters with the public are being recorded and shown on the national and local news. We also look at technology and how it impacts policing today, ranging from the effect of body-worn cameras to thermal imaging devices.

Chapter 12
Modern Challenges of the Job

Chapter 13
Technology and the Future of Policing

12

Modern Challenges of the Job

Learning Objectives

LO1 Identify how police work affects the health and well-being of police officers.

LO2 Explore how budget constraints affect modern policing and the work of the individual officer.

LO3 Describe the relationship between the media and the police.

LO4 Compare and contrast the positive and negative aspects of how police use social media to engage the community.

LO5 Discuss the strategies for policing protests and how they have changed over time.

Chapter Outline

The Stresses of Modern Policing
Officer Health and Well-being
Traffic Safety
Shift Length and Sleep Problems
Officer Injuries
COVID-19 and the Police

Mental Health and Suicide Risks
The Budget Crisis
Furloughs and Salary Reductions
Police and the Media
Crime Dramas and the Police
Social Media and the Police

Policing Protests
Black Lives Matter and Ferguson, MO
Protests in Baltimore, MD, and the Freddie Gray Incident
Riots and Washington, DC: Storming the Capitol

Jose Perez/B...

One of the most popular TV series of all time has been the *Law and Order* franchise which actually includes nine separate shows, including not only the original *Law and Order* and another focusing on the *Special Victims Unit*, but at one time or another, *Criminal Intent, Organized Crime, True Crime, Law and Order LA, Trial by Jury, Conviction*, and even *a Law and Order UK* set in London. A new Law and Order series set in Toronto was announced for 2024.

For more than 20 years, the original *Law and Order* and *Law and Order SVU* have followed a familiar pattern. They are filmed on location in New York and the plots are typically inspired by the latest headlines: Hollywood producer accused of rape, famous singer molests young girls, or a reporter is killed just before they expose a major scandal. The opening usually shows some civilians, for example, a couple out for dinner, discovering a victim either dead or in extremis. As the detectives arrive, crime scene people are already there telling them that the victim had been strangled or still alive, on the way to the emergency room. The first half of the show concentrates on the investigation of the crime by the police; the second half follows the prosecution of the same crime in court. The detectives, especially in *SVU*, are sensitive to the victims and their families. They think nothing of meeting with them on their own time and relating their personal experiences as a means of comfort. There are always two detectives who work together: the veteran and the junior detective, who is learning the ropes but still quite competent. Then there is the boss, a lieutenant or a captain, who oversees the investigation and handles personal problems. When they first arrive at the crime scene, they are met by the first responding officer or a crime scene unit (CSU) forensic technician, who will inform the two lead detectives on everything known at that point. It's during their preliminary crime scene examination that the featured detectives will make their first observations and will come up with some theories followed by a throw-away gag line. The police and the prosecutors work well together and you get the feeling they are all part of the same team. The real enemy: snarky defense attorneys who try to get their guilty clients off on technicalities.

While the *Law and Order* franchise is reassuring and paints the police in the most positive light possible, critics lament the fact that the show does not give a totally accurate description of policing today: The police are always dedicated to their job and the rule of law. They rarely drink or take substances to stay awake or go to sleep. Since the TV detectives only work on one case at a time, they are thorough and careful as they collect evidence, interview witnesses, and then make an arrest. Never do they manhandle suspects or fudge how they found the evidence. They work closely with the medical examiner's office and crime lab, who very quickly produce results and are rarely if ever wrong in their conclusions. While some of the crimes bring out protesters who are concerned about racial profiling or political preferences, the police always arrest the correct guilty party and the district attorney rarely if ever loses a jury trial. Even the criminals have a lot of class. Most sound like they majored in English literature at Columbia or NYU (referred to as "Hudson University" on the show). But, despite their impressive intelligence and vocabulary, they make a telling error that allows the detectives to wrap up the case in an hour of TV time.

Is it a disservice to the public to paint such a flattering picture of the police? Does the media create an expectation of police performance that cannot be met—an expectation that leads to disappointment and dissatisfaction with local police agencies? Would the public prefer a TV series that actually shows the reality of modern policing?

LO1

Identify how police work affects the health and well-being of police officers.

Shorex.koss/Shutterstock.com

While police officers on TV shows like *Law and Order* identify criminals, bring them to trial, and watch while they are sentenced to prison, all in about 40 minutes, this scenario has little connection to the real world of policing. The job can be extremely stressful, most crimes go unsolved, and few cases result in an actual trial. As a result, the stresses of policing can take a toll on an officer's mental and physical health.

The Stresses of Modern Policing

While the *Law and Order* franchise is entertaining, the show does not give a totally accurate description of policing today: Modern policing is marked by stresses that were previously unknown to earlier generations. The challenges faced by police officers are ever evolving and range from the health and well-being of police officers and their self-care to dealing with budgetary crises, relationships with the media, and policing protests. These dangers and stresses are sometimes not ones that quickly come to mind. For example, the 24-hour news cycle gives reporters great incentive to pay attention to everything that the police do. Each of these issues is dealt with in the sections that follow.

Officer Health and Well-being

A great deal of attention has been paid to the safety of police officers. This attention is, in fact, well deserved. Police work can be tough, stressful, and dangerous. Officers are put in dangerous situations regularly. This can range from a traffic stop to arresting an armed suspect or responding to a domestic violence call, or even self-harm, like the rising rates of officer suicide. There is near-universal agreement about the dangers these activities pose. However, when we think of officer wellness and safety, we must go beyond the immediate dangers in the field and recognize the stress and psychological strain these activities can cause.

Pillar 6 of the Final Report on 21st Century Policing, published by the Office of Community Oriented Policing Services. deals specifically with officer wellness and safety. "The wellness and safety of law enforcement officers is critical not only to themselves, their colleagues, and their agencies but also to public safety."[1] The "bulletproof cop" does not exist. The officers who protect us must also be protected—against incapacitating physical, mental, and emotional health problems as well as against the hazards of their job. A significant amount of injuries and deaths of officers are not due to the interaction with criminal offenders but rather the outcome of officers' poor physical health due to poor nutrition, lack of exercise, sleep deprivation, and substance abuse.[2] Pillar 6 addresses such issues as; physical, mental, and emotional health; vehicular accidents; officer suicide; shootings and assaults; and the partnerships with social services, unions, and other organizations that can support solutions.[3]

Officer suicide is a major problem. A national study using data from the National Occupational Mortality Surveillance found that police died from suicide 2.4 times as often as from homicides.[4] When we hear the old adage that there is a "war on cops," if we delve deeper, one may find that this war is an internal war. According to the organization Blue H.E.L.P. (a nonprofit organization that has been collecting law enforcement suicide information since 2016), police suicides have been outpacing police homicides. There were 196 officer suicides in 2019, 148 in 2020, 143 in 2021, and 160 in 2022. Suicide claims more law enforcement lives than felonious killings or accidental deaths in the line of duty.[5] According to the Marshall Project, more officers die of suicide than die of shootings and traffic accidents combined. While many deaths may be self-inflicted, a result of posttraumatic stress disorder (PTSD) or depression, they are classified as unknown cause in an effort to shield the department from bad publicity and lawsuits brought by family members.[7] While suicides have become a serious concern, the number of police officers killed in the line of duty has pretty much been decreasing steadily since 1974, with the exception of the September 11, 2001, terrorist attacks on the United States.[8]

More officers are killed or removed from service because of vehicle accidents; chronic diseases such as high blood pressure; and other problems that often stem from high stress environments, poor nutrition, and lack of exercise[9] rather than being shot in the line of duty. Officers are exposed to exhaust fumes from spending time in their cars and methamphetamine laboratories. The health concerns are numerous. Police officers assigned to shift work and overtime have an even harder time maintaining healthy nutrition and regular exercise. Working evening shifts also results in the exposure of more stressful events than those officers working during the day.[10] In short, the threats to officer safety and well-being largely come from the routine aspects of police work. These are concerns that will be discussed in greater detail below.

Traffic Safety

The Prince George's County Police Department experienced three officer deaths as a result of traffic crashes in less than two years. In one of these crashes, the driver was ejected while the passenger survived with minimal injuries because he was wearing his seatbelt. As a result, the department implemented a driver safety program that focuses on the three primary contributing factors to injuries

Careers in Policing

Dispatcher

A police dispatcher is the gatekeeper for most police departments. They are the people whom answer calls for service, gathers information from the caller, and then directs the response of police officers and emergency service providers to the correct location. While on the line during an emergency call, they may be requited to keep the caller calm and focused until emergency personnel arrive. This might include guiding callers through first aid procedures ranging from stopping bleeding to delivering a baby. They may also be asked to use automated dispatch and law enforcement systems and databases to enter, research, and retrieve information and provides support to emergency teams. In some jurisdictions, they will monitor security and fire alarm systems and coordinate responses in an emergency. In others, they are asked to monitor CCTV systems for unusual or suspicious activity and then respond to CCTV alerts, actively monitor observed activity, and dispatch resources as needed.

To qualify as a dispatcher, candidates must have at least a high school diploma or GED. However, higher education in a relevant field like criminal justice or law enforcement can certainly be helpful in securing a position. Prior work experience, in a relevant area that stresses communication skills, is also of great benefit, especially if it involves solving problems over the phone or interacting with people in stressful, time-sensitive situations. It is also helpful if you can provide evidence that you are calm under pressure and do not let your emotions take control of decision making. In some departments, dispatcher candidates may be tested by being monitored while taking a simulated emergency call. Once hired, dispatchers will go through extensive training including material on policies, practices, equipment, regulations, and so on; the ability to handle emergencies with calm confidence is a must. Among the skills they are required to possess include knowledge of:

- Principles and practices of data collection and report preparation.

- Basic principles of recordkeeping.
- Police department policies and standard operating procedures.
- Terminology and procedures used in public safety dispatching.
- Operation of computer-aided communications equipment, including multiple telephone lines and radio systems.
- City and county geography, maps, streets, landmarks, and driving directions.
- Applicable federal, state, and local laws; regulatory codes, ordinances, and procedures relevant to assigned area of responsibility.
- Modern office practices, methods, and computer equipment and applications related to work.
- English usage, grammar, spelling, vocabulary, and punctuation.
- Type 35 wpm.
- Memorize codes, names, street locations, and other information.
- Read and interpret maps and other pertinent documentation.
- Terminology and procedures used in public safety dispatching.
- Operate modern office equipment including computer equipment and specialized software applications.

Currently, starting pay for dispatchers in larger jurisdictions can be as high at $72,000 per year.

associated with vehicle crashes: excessive speed, lack of seatbelt use, and driver inattention. The program encourages officers to slow down (which allows the driver more reaction time), to wear a seatbelt to minimize injury during a crash, and to pay attention by eliminating distractions from electronic devices.[11]

Prince George County is not alone in its concern for officer traffic safety. Police officers spend a great deal of time in their cars—it is the nature of the job. Officers sustaining injuries in vehicular crashes missed five fewer days and spent less time in rehabilitation when wearing seatbelts. Research also suggests a connection between higher vehicle speed and a greater severity of injuries following a crash.[12] While fatal traffic accidents are a relatively rare event, they are still of great concern to officers. Each year about 35 to 40 officers are killed in on-duty traffic-related accidents.[13] The **National Highway and Traffic Safety Administration (NHTSA)** conducted an analysis of almost 30 years' worth of crash data and found that 42 percent of all law enforcement officers killed in traffic crashes were not wearing seat belts. The number may actually be higher because NHTSA could not determine whether or not the officer was wearing a seat belt in 13 percent of the cases.[14] Another issue that affects both officer and citizen safety is that of distracted driving. Not all police departments have policies on distracted driving, which means that officers can talk on the phone or text while driving.[15] Media reports suggest that distracted driving results in more accidents than we might expect.[16]

Shift Length and Sleep Problems

Shift length is an issue of concern to officers and chiefs. Driving these concerns have been issues of safety, health, performance, quality of life, fatigue, and efficiency. Concern about shift length and fatigue is not limited to the police. The well-known impact of fatigue on safety has led the federal government to regulate the work hours of private, for-profit workers—train engineers, truck drivers, commercial pilots, and nuclear power plant operators. Surprisingly there are no corresponding regulations for the police despite the importance of their job. Traditionally, police departments relied on a five-day, eight-hour scheduling framework with three standard shifts (day, evening, midnight) in each 24-hour period. However, since at least as early as the 1970s, law enforcement agencies have adopted alternate schedule configurations or **compressed work weeks (CWW).**[17] Poor nutrition and fitness are also serious threats, as is sleep deprivation. Many errors in judgment can be traced to fatigue, which also makes it harder to connect with people and control emotions.[18] Research on CWWs in policing is quite limited. What do we know?

In 2010, the Police Foundation conducted a multisite randomized experiment where officers were randomly assigned to one of three conditions: (a) five consecutive 8-hour days, (b) four consecutive 10-hour days, and (c) three consecutive 12-hour days. Results suggest that 10-hour shifts have advantages over eight-hour shifts but that these advantages do not extend to 12-hour shifts. Officers working 10-hour shifts became significantly more sleep per night (over half an hour) than those on eight-hour shifts and had a significantly higher quality of work life. Also, those on 10-hour shifts worked the least amount of overtime of the three groups, potentially resulting in cost savings.[19] Officers assigned to 12-hour shifts had significantly lower average levels of alertness at work and were sleepier than those on eight-hour shifts, something that was not true for those on 10-hour shifts.

Longer work days in a CWW are very popular among police officers. Among the many benefits believed to result from longer shifts are the ability to increase coverage during peak hours of activity, improve officer job satisfaction and morale, increase performance, reduce response time, reduce crime, reduce costs for officers and agencies (e.g., commuting, overtime, and sick leave), limit

National Highway and Traffic Safety Administration (NHTSA)

NHTSA was established by the Highway Safety Act of 1970 and is dedicated to achieving the highest standards of excellence in motor vehicle and highway safety. It works daily to help prevent crashes and their attendant costs, both human and financial.

compressed work weeks (CWW)

A non-traditional work with longer than eight-hour shifts.

fatigue, improve teamwork, allow for increased in-service training during periods of overlap, increase days off for personal pursuits/family activities, and reduce accidents and complaints against officers.[20]

But does this benefit extend beyond 10- or 12-hour shifts? What happens if a police department offers 13-hours-and-20-minute shifts? This would mean officers work for three days and have four days to rest. Leonard Bell and colleagues studied the impact of a longer-than-average compressed workweek on police officers' sleep, cognitive abilities, health, quality of life, and work performance. In one precinct of the Phoenix Police Department, officers worked three consecutive 13-hour-and-20-minute shifts per week for six months. Officers were assessed using tests of sleep quality, vigilance, and quality of life as well as measures of salivary cortisol. Data were also analyzed for Professional Standards Bureau complaints, shooting qualifications, vehicular accidents, self-initiated calls, adult bookings, field interrogations, overtime, and time off for the six months of the study period and the same six months of the previous year.

Officers working 13:20-hour shifts experienced significant decreases in hours of sleep, overall quality of sleep, concentration, cognitive processing, and quality of life. Increases were also observed in fatigue, daytime dysfunction due to sleepiness, reaction time, anticipatory errors, and Professional Standards Bureau complaints. There were no significant differences in most indices of work performance or differences due to working day or night shifts. Officers overwhelmingly preferred 10-hour shifts. Their research indicates that there are no apparent advantages but considerable liabilities associated with 13:20-hour shifts for police officers.[21]

Officer Injuries

Firearms are one of the leading causes of deaths for law enforcement officers feloniously killed in the line of duty. Line-of-duty deaths and assaults on officer information are collected by the Federal Bureau of Investigation (FBI) Law Enforcement Officers Killed and Assaulted program (LEOKA). The data collected by this program come from a survey provided to law enforcement agencies that have faced a line-of-duty death. The survey instrument is a comprehensive assessment and provides a great deal of detail regarding the incident and includes a brief narrative in most cases. While there is a delay in findings each year, this data source represents the most comprehensive source currently available and provides quality information regarding the line-of-duty death picture each year. The number of assaults on officers is believed to be much higher than the number officially reported through this program. However, this is the most comprehensive resource available for assaults and provides some insight into the risks officers face.

The full range of injuries experienced by police officers as a result of their jobs is largely unknown. After a citizen encounter, police officers may be unaware that they are injured or may not report it to the agency because they believe that it is too minor. Injuries that are reported are more likely to be those related to higher profile calls for service, such as homicides or robberies, as compared to lower status calls for service that actually represent the majority and may represent a larger number of injuries.[22] This means that we lack data about the extent of officer injuries.

In order to begin to better understand the injuries sustained by law police officers, the International Association of Chiefs of Police (IACP) conducted a multi-department assessment of line-of-duty injuries. Eighteen different agencies participated in this study and tracked all reported injuries over the course of one year. All available information pertinent to each injury was documented and entered into a database using a standardized reporting instrument built for this study. The IACP collected all data and partnered with George Mason University to perform an analysis of the data and develop strategies and resources for injury prevention. Reportable injuries were defined as any injury resulting in pain or discomfort that occurred during the performance of the individual's duties as a police officer, including both on- and off-duty employment.

Among other findings, the report notes that police encounters with suspects under the influence of alcohol and/or drugs resulted in more severe officer injuries. These findings suggest that the closer offenders are monitored after an arrest through police-probation/police strategic partnerships, the better the chance of neutralizing threats and reducing officer injuries. Overall findings showed that the majority of injuries were those that would not be collected by traditional collection mechanisms, such as the Federal Bureau of Investigation's Law Enforcement Officers Killed and Assaulted program or the Uniform Crime Report data. This means that we know very little about the extent of officer injuries and local police departments must begin collecting more detailed information about these injuries.

One of the other factors affecting officer injuries is the use of body armor. Bullet- and stab-resistant vests are instrumental to officer survival as body armor has saved the lives of more than 3,000 officers. Armor vests can only save lives when they are actually worn and an increasing percentage of police departments have instituted "mandatory wear" policies.[23] The Bulletproof Vest Partnership (BVP) Program[24] assists law enforcement agencies in acquiring soft body armor for their personnel. BJA provides funds to state, local, and tribal jurisdictions to help purchase vests. There are limitations to the effectiveness of body armor. There is no such thing as bulletproof armor. Ballistic-resistant body armor provides protection against penetrating bullets and the blunt trauma associated with bullet impacts, but it will not stop all bullets. Some armor vests only protect against handgun bullets, while some others protect against rifle bullets.[25]

COVID-19 and the Police

The COVID-19 pandemic changed many aspects of policing but most concerning, it made the job much more dangerous. Of the 264 police officers who died in the line of duty in 2020 across the United States, 145 officers died of COVID-19, according to the National Law Enforcement Officers Memorial Fund (NLEOMF).[26] In 2020, 2021, and 2022, COVID-19 was the leading cause of death for police officers. COVID-19 was responsible for more police officer deaths than gun violence, car accidents, and all other causes combined. It should be noted that there are likely many more officers whose deaths will be related to the pandemic that still need to be confirmed according to the Officer Down Memorial website. To put this in perspective, 70 officers were killed on 9/11 in what had previously been the largest incident cause of death for police officers. The COVID-19 outbreak has outpaced 9/11 and not enough is known about the lingering effects of the virus on those who have recovered. The State of Texas has reported the most COVID-19-related deaths, followed by Louisiana, Florida, and New Jersey. COVID-19 was the single highest cause of law enforcement deaths occurring in 2020 and 2021. Despite those numbers, police departments and

Critical Thinking

It was reported that COVID-19 was the leading cause of death of police officers in 2021 and 2022. What can be done to convince officers to get vaccinated and take precautions for this disease?

unions in cities across the country have pushed back against mandates requiring vaccines for public employees, filing lawsuits, and threatening resignation. It should also be mentioned that correctional officers have been affected by COVID at much higher rates than police officers.[27]

Mental Health and Suicide Risks

Police officers are more likely to die by suicide than to die in the line of duty, according to research. Experts suggest that chronic workplace stress may place officers at increased risk for suicide and mental health issues, such as posttraumatic stress disorder and substance abuse.[28] "Police officers are at a higher risk of suicide than any other profession. In fact, suicide is so prevalent in the profession that the number of police officers who died by suicide *is more than triple* that of officers who were fatally injured in the line of duty."[29]

Due to stressors in the police profession, officers may be at risk for a variety of personal and mental health–related concerns. Organizational stressors involved in police work include unconventional shifts, excessive paperwork, and poor administrative support.[30] Researchers have also found relatively high prevalence rates of depression among police officers,[31] and officers are also especially prone to developing PTSD because they are exposed to so many instances of violence, many of which threaten their immediate safety.[32]

Today, police officers face a significant amount of trauma on a daily basis. The constant exposure to devastation, life-threatening situations, and the physical strain of working long hours can lead to feelings of hopelessness and anxiety. In addition to the threat of physical harm, officers are constantly witnessing devastating and disturbing events such as murder, suicide, and domestic violence. During their careers, a typical police officer witnesses on average roughly 188 critical incidents. The exposure to horrendous accidents and actions can lead to multiple mental health issues that often go untreated. For example, the rates of posttraumatic stress disorder and depression among police officers is reportedly *five times higher* than that of the general public.[33]

Take for instance research on internet child exploitation investigations that suggest that viewers experience salient emotional, cognitive, social, and behavioral consequences due to viewing these materials and their reactions can be short and long term.[34] They frequently interact with people experiencing their worst moments and are exposed to acute psychological stress that accompanies that trauma.[35] The stress associated with engaging in these activities negatively impacts officers' health and performance in a variety of ways, including sleep difficulties and emotional responses at work.[36] Adina Bozga and colleagues find that the exposure to this type of trauma over time has profound psychological consequences and should be treated as an important organizational issue.[37] This trauma can also affect satisfaction, long into retirement,[38] and can also impact family members of the officer.[39]

Furthermore, because policing involves shift work, there are also consequences to working hours that may differ from friends and family. Officers may not get to spend much time with their families and work–family conflict has also been shown to negatively correlate with measures of psychological health.[40] John Violanti and colleagues have been studying officers in Buffalo, New York, for decades and have found that some of these effects are more profound for female officers than their male peers.[41]

A related issue is the dual role of police officers as military reserves. Law enforcement professionals represent 10 percent of those activated, thus posing unique challenges and opportunities for public safety agencies in remaining staffing levels but also addressing the issues associated with deployment.[42] For some officers, the lingering effects of their deployments may provide challenges they did not anticipate. For example, veterans may be overly sensitive and hyper-aware of danger. They may have difficulty relating to the seemingly small problems complained about by their colleagues.[43] It is important for police managers to recognize the need to address the emotional and behavioral effects of combat deployment on the returning citizen soldier–police officer.

However, police officers have historically refrained from seeking professional mental health services.[44] In police culture, a major obstacle that impedes the maintenance of psychological health is the stigma attached to asking for help. Police culture values strength, self-reliance, controlled emotions, and competency in handling personal problems. These values do not align with help-seeking leaving the sense of having lost control by asking someone else to help fix the problem. Supervisors can unintentionally reinforce the value of being too self-reliant by not encouraging peers and subordinates to seek help when significantly distressed.[45]

Yet, recent research suggests that police officers are more at risk than the general public. John Violanti and Andrea Steege find that there are a significantly higher proportion of deaths from suicide for law enforcement officers compared to all deaths in the United States among people who were employed during their lifetime. Law enforcement personnel are 54 percent more likely to die of suicide than those with a more typical occupation.[46] According to recent findings, the states of Texas, California, New York, and Florida experience the highest rates of officer suicides, with each state reporting at least 10 police suicides. In fact, the New York City Police Department (NYPD) even received national attention in for its high rate of officer suicides. The New York City Police Commissioner declared a mental health crisis as the city wrestled with the suicide deaths of nine police officers. At least six of the nine deaths in the NYPD involved a gun, many using their own service weapon.

According to Blue H.E.L.P., a nonprofit that works to reduce stigmas tied to mental health issues for those in law enforcement, in 2022 there were 160 current or former officers who died by suicide, compared with 196 in 2019.[47] New York State had the highest number of suicides, 27, followed by California, 23; Texas, 19; and Florida, 15. Among those 27 in New York, 10 were New York Police Department officers. "The tempo for the New York City Police Department is unforgiving—job demands, financial restraints and living in New York is a challenge," according to Jon Adler, the former Bureau of Justice Programs director at the Department of Justice and a former police officer in New York.[48]

The Fear of Stigma

In spite of the pervasiveness of mental health issues amongst the police, there is still a significant **stigma** around officers asking for help. Many officers view asking for help as a sign of weakness, or that if an officer were to acknowledge that they have a possible problem with mental health concerns, then many may perceive that something is wrong with them. Moreover, many police officers fear that openly talking about their personal struggles may result in stigma from other officers, career setbacks, and ultimately the shame and indignity of having their weapons removed. Officers who suppress their feelings on the job and continue to

stigma
A set of negative and often unfair beliefs that a society or group of people have about something.

hide those feelings can become cut off or distant from human emotions and daily kindness. Even the best adjusted officer can become skilled at feeling nothing at all in key moments of crisis.

The fear of being ostracized and no longer accepted is real and daunting to most officers. It is the issue that causes many officers to turn to substance use in an attempt to self-medicate their feelings and forget the terrible things they see on duty. This self-medication, however, is having a deadly result on officers. Using alcohol and/or drugs can lead to a downward spiral in which both work performance and relationships suffer. Alcohol is a depressant and can often dull the senses. Alcohol, like many other drugs, has the ability to slow down an overactive mind that was pushed to the limit by stress, worry, and trauma. This can then increase feelings of depression, which in turn leads to further substance abuse. Substance use is also one of the main contributing factors to suicide. Of the 89 completed suicides in the NYPD over the years, 72 percent had alcohol in their system at the time of suicide.[49]

Confronting the Problem

In order to reduce suicide rates among police officers, mental health advocates are stressing the importance of overcoming the idea that seeking help is a sign of weakness and that support in the form of professional counseling, support groups, and chaplains is readily available. Turning to other officers for help doesn't always work. Policing is infamous for creating an authoritarian culture of repression and omission. This culture shift begins in basic training. When police cadets learn to be police officers, they often lose their individual identities. They cease being individual people with independent thoughts, feelings, and opinions. They are all officers, and they are all the same; they are all blue.[50]

Even if a police officer doesn't want to admit that they have a problem, emotional distress will eventually surface. Often that distress comes in the form of physical illness. In a study of this issue, funded by the National Institute of Occupational Safety and Health, researchers examined more than 400 police officers with questionnaires, blood tests, stress monitoring, and more. The researchers found that officers older than 40 had a higher risk of a heart attack when compared to national standards. They also found that officers had higher levels of cholesterol and cortisol (a chemical associated with stress).[51]

So what can be done to address mental health concerns among police officers? Supervision can be key for encouraging police officers to seek necessary help. Specifically, a supervisor who shares a personal example of going through a rough time and recovering after receiving confidential, professional help from a police psychologist can normalize the problem, make help-seeking behavior seem less threatening, and increase the willingness of other officers to ask for help.[52] Psychological services should also be targeted toward police. Psychological services to law enforcement personnel are unique when compared to traditional clinical practice. For example, police psychologists must be informed about multiple laws, statutes, and cases that guide their activities in providing intervention services. Police psychologists must also have a working knowledge of law enforcement organizational dynamics and be aware of and sensitive to police culture.[53] One program, In Harm's Way, focuses on law enforcement suicide prevention training and support. It aims to decrease suicide a by increasing the probability that officers contemplating taking their own life will seek help from mental health professionals. It provides training and resources for officers and agencies.

Critical Thinking

What ways can police departments start the conversation about self-help and suicide prevention in a profession that is based on ideals of courage and bravado?

Examples of resources include a law enforcement suicide prevention toolkit with downloadable templates of materials to assist in presenting a suicide prevention training in an agency, reducing the stigma of requesting help, and encouraging officers to support one another.[54]

The Budget Crisis

There have been calls for reducing police budgets and using the money for social services. While the defund movement was short lived, critics may achieve their goals simply because of the strain being put on local budgets. Take what happened a few years ago in New Haven, Connecticut. Police cruisers in New Haven had holes in the floorboards, cracks in fenders and bumpers, metal that stuck out of torn seats and ripped uniforms, gas gauges that did not work, and radio equipment that malfunctioned. The police union, frustrated by years of these problems, and the funding cuts that slowed the purchase of new vehicles, filed a complaint with the state Board of Labor Relations, saying the poor condition of the fleet was creating unsafe work conditions. New Haven appears to be an extreme example of police departments nationwide that are dealing with deteriorating vehicles and budget cuts.[55] In recent years, cities all across the country have been forced to do more with fewer resources. Services have been curtailed, employees have been **furloughed**, and capital improvements have been delayed—if not canceled altogether. Throughout history, police department spending has rarely landed on the chopping block, but these days all public agencies have had their budgets slashed. The economy has improved since 2008, and a number of criminal justice agencies have resumed hiring and are once again expanding, but shrinking—or at least stagnant—budgets remain a real issue.

furloughed
A period of time when an employee is told not to come to work and is not paid.

With the COVID-19 pandemic and the shutdown of society in much of 2020, fewer people went out shopping, dining, and being entertained, so the tax base of cities, towns, and states was greatly reduced. This reduction in tax revenue meant that fewer tax dollars were available for municipal services, like the police. This created a huge budget crisis nationally. Take for instance what happened in Portland, Oregon. Facing a $20 million shortfall in the city's general fund, mostly due to fewer taxes collected during the 2020 pandemic, the mayor proposed a $5.7 billion budget in which the city's police department would sustain the biggest cut of any city department. The Portland Police would have to sustain a $9 million reduction in funding.[56]

In another instance, when the Seattle Police Department leadership informed the city council that the police overspent their budget by $5.4 million in 2020, the council expressed its intent to cut the same amount from the police budget in 2021. The city council hoped that the $5.4 million would support the participatory budgeting process in the spring.[57]

Often, reductions in police budgets give much-needed money to crime prevention programs. In a move that signals a major reckoning of the role of Oakland Police, the City Council voted to slash $18 million from the police department's $674 million budget over two years and instead spend the money for violence

Light And Dark Studio/Shutterstock.com

Due to tight state and local budgets, not to mention the effects of the "defund the police" movement, some departments have faced extreme funding issues. Some have actually had to furlough personnel and cut programs.

prevention and social services.[58] Police departments across the country have adopted a range of creative—and controversial—strategies to respond to mandates that they limit spending. Some have placed limits on overtime, putting caps on the amount of extra work officers can put in.[59] Other cities have left hundreds of positions unfilled.[60] Still others have offered senior officers early retirement. The list goes on.

Consolidation Efforts

One of the most interesting policing trends in this new era of austerity is "consolidation." Consolidation refers to merging historically separate functions and sharing responsibilities.[61] For example, merging two police departments together reduces staffing needs as does merging police and fire services into a single agency. As another example, sharing SWAT responsibilities among several agencies in a given jurisdiction helps reduce the costs of training and maintaining several separate teams. Even charging for certain services, such as responding to excessive false security system alarms, can fall under the consolidation umbrella, as doing so spreads out the costs of crime control.

In 2012, researchers at Michigan State University surveyed state residents about their perceptions of such consolidation. A sizable majority of respondents expressed concern that consolidation will hurt service quality. Nearly two-thirds of respondents agreed or strongly agreed that service would suffer with consolidation.

Despite what people think about consolidation, the practice has been around for some time. It is not a thought exercise. For example, Sunnyvale, California, was one of the first cities to merge police, fire, and emergency medical services. All the way back in 1950, the city created a single "Department of Public Safety," and to this day, all new hires get police, fire, *and* medical training. In fairness, though, some formerly consolidated agencies have since abandoned the approach. For example, Eugene, Oregon, abandoned consolidation because doing so created another layer of administration between city management and the police and fire chiefs.

Furloughs and Salary Reductions

In the last decade in response to shrinking budgets, cities have also furloughed and laid off more law enforcement officers, or left more vacancies unfilled than at any time in recent memory. Simultaneously, police officer salary and benefit reductions are becoming more common. For example, the Community Oriented Policing Services (COPS) Office found that an estimated 10,000–12,000 police officers and sheriff's deputies were laid off in 2011, approximately 30,000 law enforcement jobs were unfilled, and 53 percent of counties had fewer staff than they had in October 2010.[62] In short, police departments are not filling empty positions, which leaves them with fewer personnel to do the same work.

What does this mean for patrol officers and police departments? In practice, budget constraints mean that police officers and their departments can't address all crimes that occur in the communities that they serve or do so with aging equipment. While selective enforcement is standard for police departments in the United States, budget shortfalls can exacerbate the problem. For example, the COPS Office reports that:[63]

■ Some agencies have stopped responding to all motor vehicle thefts, burglar alarms, and non-injury motor vehicle accidents.

- Agencies have also reported decreases in investigations of property crimes, fugitive tracking, a variety of white collar crimes, and even low-level narcotics cases.

- Many agencies have greatly reduced training opportunities for their officers.

- Investments in technology and communications systems are being slashed in many agencies facing budget reductions.

With many of the service cutbacks comes a reduction in direct face-to-face contacts between citizens and police personnel. This is particularly challenging as police departments work to enhance community engagement.[64]

Police and the Media

In April 2015, a North Charleston police officer stopped Walter Scott, a Black man, reportedly for a broken brake light. The video from the officer's dash camera shows the officer returning to his car and moments later, Walter Scott exits his car and flees the scene, ostensibly because he owes child support and is fearful of being incarcerated and losing a new job. The officer, Michael Slager, followed Scott to a lot behind a pawn store. After an altercation and while Scott was again fleeing the scene, Officer Slager fired eight shots at Scott, striking him five times, including three in the back, and then handcuffed Scott's arms behind his back. Slager claimed in his police report that Scott took control of his Taser and that the officer feared for his life in a scuffle after the traffic stop. The video didn't show Scott taking the stun gun. A witness recorded the shooting on his cell phone and shared the footage with the victim's family. Walter Scott's family turned the footage over to the media only after they felt as though the incident was being incorrectly characterized by the press and the police department. Slager was quickly fired and subsequently arrested. He was indicted and was sentenced to 20 years in prison after pleading guilty in Scott's death. U.S. District Judge David Norton, in issuing the sentence, said Slager shot Scott with "malice and recklessness" and then gave false testimony to investigators.[65]

The *Scott* case is one of many that relied on video footage showing the police acting inappropriately. Beginning in the 1960s, with news cameras capturing footage of the police response to civil rights protests, and amateurs armed with cell phone cameras capturing such events as the Scott shooting, video accounts of the police have served to both shape community perceptions and to hold police accountable for their actions. While historically, the media have been responsible for recording footage of and reporting stories that are important to us, in modern times, this has changed. This first became apparent with the Rodney King beating, where a man with a video camera captured footage of police officers engaged in the beating of an unarmed motorist. The witness accidentally caught the incident on film, but now with a video camera on every cell phone, citizens have also been recording events that are important to us. This footage is often very quickly shared with the media and the internet, with news reporting 24 hours a day. The public has a seemingly insatiable appetite for information about crime and the police that is fed by these news outlets.

The image and public perceptions of the police are also shaped by entertainment media and shows such as *Law and Order,* discussed in the opening vignette,

◀ LO3

Describe the relationship between the media and the police.

as well as *COPS, NCIS, The Wire*, and *Criminal Minds*, to name just a few. This is an important influence on the public's perception of the police. Another large change has been the use of social media by the police and the public. Social media has served as another way to share information either by the public or the police—that the media may not elect to cover. Police departments have also made use of social media as a way to enhance community engagement and share information with the communities that they serve. In the sections that follow, the role of the media as well as the use of social media by the police will be discussed.

Despite the important role of the PIO and the formal system of communications used by police departments, the relationship with the media can be difficult to manage. On many days, it feels impossible to watch the news or read a newspaper without coming across a negative story about the police. In fact, the media has accurately portrayed that the police within the United States are facing a crisis. Beginning in the summer of 2014, there were many highly publicized events involving the deaths of Black men by police. This resulted in a great deal of media attention. Researchers have long examined the relationship between mass media and perceptions of the police.

Careers in Policing

Public Information Officer

What about the media coverage of the police? Many large police departments rely on public information officers (PIOs). PIOs are responsible for maintaining official communications between the police department and the press. A PIO is responsible for disseminating an agency's message and enhancing interaction among the agency, the media, and the public. It may not be reasonable or necessary for smaller agencies to hire or maintain a full-time PIO. A PIO should have a strong background in police operations, but that does not mean that they must come from the ranks of sworn personnel. Larger departments may also have media relations or Public Information Offices. For example, the Cambridge Police Department has a Public Information Office. The Public Information Office is the central location for all press contacts and media requests, as well as an important point of contact for members of the community seeking information from the police.

According to their website, the Cambridge (MA) Police Department Public Information Office has the following responsibilities:[66]

- It shall be the responsibility of the police commissioner or a designee thereof, to act as the official spokesperson of the Cambridge Police Department in conducting and maintaining an active liaison with the news media.

- Assisting news personnel in covering routine news stories and at the scene of incidents.

- Availability to the media of a police spokesperson at night and on weekends when needed.

- Preparing and distributing news releases.

- Arranging for, and assisting at, news conferences.

- Coordinating and authorizing the release of information about victims, witnesses, and suspects.

- Assisting in crisis situations.

- Coordinating and authorizing the release of information concerning confidential agency investigations and operations.

It is well understood that the media can help shape public perceptions of police legitimacy. This research has evolved as coverage of shootings in Ferguson, Missouri; Cleveland, Ohio; and Charleston, South Carolina, have raised questions for the public about how and when the police use force in encounters with the public.

Mainstream media coverage of police use of force and these shootings has increased. Since there are no reliable statistics about use of deadly force by the police across departments, it is difficult to tell if shootings have also increased. So why is there increased coverage? Increased coverage may be because with the use of cell phone cameras, there is more concrete evidence of police use of force. Whereas before there were only witness accounts of shooting, now there are recorded images. Citizens are also becoming more sensitive to the actions of the police and are demanding more attention to the issue in the press. The increased interest in criminal activity has other implications for the police as well. Police investigators have expressed fear that they have lost control over representations of their work in media stories. Their major worry is that they are no longer able to maintain secrecy over their investigative activities and techniques. This could have a significant negative impact on their work as offenders can become too familiar with their practices.[67] There is an important and careful distinction between providing transparency for the public but also maintaining professionalism in investigations. It has become an increasingly difficult boundary.

This media coverage not only affects citizens' perceptions of the police but also the self-image of police officers. Research reveals that citizens' perceptions of the police can also impact officers' sense of **self-legitimacy**.[68] Police care about their portrayal in the media.[69] Oscar Rantatalo found that for special police units, newspaper articles that positively portrayed police activities—for example depicting the unit as heroic and elite—enhanced police officers' identifications.[70] These articles positively reinforced officers' perceptions of themselves and their work. Negative depictions, however, caused officers to question and reframe their work in their departments. Furthermore, officers who were less motivated to do their job as a result of negative publicity were significantly less likely to view themselves as legitimate authority figures.[71] In short, police officers are also highly affected by the media portrayal of their work. This sense of self-legitimacy matters a great deal as officers who express high levels are more committed to their organizations and less quick to threaten citizens with force.[72] This suggests a somewhat circular relationship between legitimacy and police use of force where officers who have greater feelings of self-legitimacy may be less likely to use force that then threatens legitimacy in the community.

self-legitimacy
The confidence that police officers have in their authority as a law enforcement officer.

Crime Dramas and the Police

Crime dramas—specifically those that focus on police work—are a huge source of entertainment. These shows, such as the *Law and Order* franchise discussed in the opening vignette, also influence the way that people think about the police. Evidence suggests that viewing television news and crime-based reality programs significantly increases confidence in the police, particularly when the police are portrayed positively. Yet, there are some challenges associated with entertainment media depictions of the police. First, there are limitations to the positive effects of media on citizen perceptions. Valerie Callanan and Jared Rosenberger find that consumption of crime-related media increased confidence in the police among White respondents but had no effect on Latinos or Black people.[73]

Next, police work on television and in the movies is not indicative of real life. Kathleen Donovan and Charles Klahm note these depictions are often simplistic and do not portray the true nature of police work.[74] They also posit that media portrayals can hurt police by creating unrealistic expectations for the public of police capabilities. Police in crime dramas are highly effective, often solving complicated cases one at a time and within an hour (with commercial breaks). This effectiveness is also undoubtedly related to the unlimited resources that police in crime dramas have at their disposal. In reality, clearance rates are much lower and cases are rarely solved so neatly and quickly. Detectives have large caseloads and can rarely focus on one case at a time.

These crime shows may cause the public to expect the police to be much more adept at solving crime than real life allows. Finally, police dramas may also encourage becoming a police officer for many of the wrong reasons. Laura Huey and Ryan Broll discuss how the media glamorizes police work, particularly criminal investigations. This could be disappointing for new investigators who find that the dirty work associated with the job is far from glamorous.[75] Investigating homicides or interviewing victims of violent crimes are far from the Hollywood depiction. Instead, the work of an investigator is more mundane and certainly less filled with surprises than on television!

Critical Thinking

How can the romanticized version of policing in crime dramas help and hurt the efforts of police in solving crimes and recruiting new officers?

LO4

Compare and contrast the positive and negative aspects of how police use social media to engage the community.

Social Media and the Police

How do police departments use social media? Social media represents an additional way for police departments to communicate with the public. In some ways, social media provides an opportunity to bolster the community policing mission. The use of Facebook and Twitter offer new ways for police to listen to the public and work together to achieve shared goals. First, social media can be a way to reach underserved parts of the community. Young people, who may not attend community meetings or feel comfortable engaging with the police in public, may be more apt to engage in dialogue through a social media platform. The informal nature of social media may be another reason why some community members feel comfortable communicating with the police through these platforms.

The most comprehensive information available comes from the International Association of Chiefs of Police (IACP). According to one IACP Social Media survey, 96.4 percent of agencies they surveyed use some kind of social media with 83.4 percent reporting that the intent was for citizen engagement and community outreach.[76] Lori Brainard and Mariglynn Edlins find that the 10 largest police departments are all using social media tools as part of their work.[77] The most common social media tools utilized by the police are Facebook, X, and YouTube. They conclude, however, that even among the largest police departments, not enough resources have been dedicated to make these social media tools a real way to engage the community in dialogue.

The use of social media can also be a double-edged sword for police departments. The downsides of this approach should not be dismissed. Social media accounts must be monitored and messages coordinated. Police departments must decide what kind of content should be shared through these platforms and ensure that the message is consistent. The police, however, are not the only ones creating content. Police departments must also monitor these accounts to keep track of the content created by the public that is put on their sites. This can include not only hate or inappropriate speech but also reflects the possibility of cyberattacks or even just spam slowing down department sites. Monitoring social media accounts can be a huge responsibility for a larger police department that will require the dedication of resources. For smaller departments, it may not be possible to dedicate personnel to maintaining social media—resources may be few and far between.

Police departments are also using social media as a way to share pertinent information with the communities that they serve. For example, following the Boston Marathon bombing on April 15, 2013, Commissioner Ed Davis instructed his media relations office to utilize all social media tools. The goal of command staff at the Boston Police Department (BPD) was to share accurate information with the public about what the police were doing but also about potential danger. BPD was able to inform the public about the casualties, road closures, and the status of the investigation. Most notably, BPD was able to correct misinformation that was spreading throughout Boston. In particular, Reddit users were conducting their own parallel investigation as citizen journalists. This group was, however, quick to spread incorrect information—at times whipping an already frightened public up into a frenzy. They identified a "suspect" whom BPD determined not to be related to the case. BPD was able to refute this by releasing the names of the actual suspects and correcting misinformation as it spread.[78]

Social media has also changed the nature of citizen response to critical incidents. For example, the shooting of Michael Brown in Ferguson, Missouri, became a national-level police issue rather than one constrained to Ferguson or even Missouri. The use of social media has become a way for citizen journalists to funnel information directly to more mainstream news outlets. In summary, social media can be a useful tool both for police departments to share public safety information with the community but also for the community to keep tabs on police initiatives and conduct.

Source: Penn Hills Police Department

https://twitter.com/PennHillsPolice
@PennHillsPolice

Police are now using social media to enlist the public in crime prevention projects, to distribute information, to learn about citizen concerns, and to reach underrepresented elements of the community.

Critical Thinking

Name some ways in which social media can be good tools for the police.

Policing Protests

◀ **LO5**

Discuss the strategies for policing protests and how they have changed over time.

On November 28, 1999, trade officials from 125 member countries began to land in Seattle.[79] Two anti-World Trade Center Organization (WTO) protests consisting of several hundred people occurred downtown. The next day, three large demonstrations decried WTO policies. Thousands of protesters marched through downtown Seattle, with several hundred dressed in bright green sea turtle costumes, deriding WTO "free trade" as harmful to the environment and animal welfare. Several brief standoffs occurred between police in riot gear and protester groups, but they ended without incident. A state of emergency was declared on the first official day of the WTO conference. Protesters clogged city streets and shut down the opening WTO session, triggering police use

Pascal J. Le Segretain/Sygma/Getty Images

Public protests have become a familiar element of American life. Today, police departments focus on protecting free speech while limiting the use of force. The January 6 riot at the Capitol building in Washington, D.C., is a poignant example of what happens when law enforcement officers are caught unawares and unprepared to control demonstrators.

escalated force

A situation in which the militancy of protestors was met by increased militancy by the police.

of tear gas and rubber bullets to disperse the crowds. More than 35,000 people marched from an AFL-CIO labor rally at the Seattle Center to the downtown area. Meanwhile, images of masked "anarchists" smashing windows, spraying graffiti, and damaging patrol cars shocked the public.

The Seattle protests are certainly not unique and such incidents have become a feature of American life since the 1960s with the advent of civil rights and Vietnam War protests. While there have been protests and riots throughout American history, what makes these different is that they are now captured on film, tape, or cell phone. For the first time, Americans can now watch on the nightly news how police interact with citizens protesting government policies. As a result of this dramatic change, police response to protests has changed dramatically. Accordingly, it is important to understand the evolution of the police response to protests to have context for current police practices.

During the 1960s and early 1970s, the police operated under a philosophy of **escalated force** in which the militancy of protestors was met by increased militancy by the police. Any show of force or violence by the protestors was met with overwhelming force in return.[80] Not surprisingly, there was quite a bit of violence associated with this approach and it also brought negative attention from the media—hurting the image of the police. There were also major constitutional issues associated with this strategy. Citizens of the United States are guaranteed the right to free speech and assembly. The tactics associated with "escalated force" denied those rights.

In response to this violence at demonstrations and the poor public relations, a new approach termed *negotiated management* emerged. This approach was based on greater cooperation between police and demonstrators and an effort to avoid violence. The new approach called for the protection of free speech rights, toleration of community disruption, ongoing communication between police and demonstrators, avoidance of arrests, and limiting the use of force to situations where violence is occurring.[81] This became the predominant strategy used by the police during the 1980s and 1990s. This **negotiated management** approach was considered to be an abject failure after viewing the incredibly violent exchanges between the police and protesters during the 1999 WTO protests in Seattle, Washington, on television.

Alex Vitale argues that a third strategy is used by some police departments—**command and control**[82] or has also been described as **strategic incapacitation**. The underlying premise of "command and control" or "strategic incapacitation"[83] is to emphasize the extent to which the police attempt to micromanage all important aspects of demonstrations in an attempt to eliminate any disorderly or illegal activity during the demonstration. This approach is distinguished from negotiated management because it sets clear and strict guidelines on acceptable behavior with very little negotiation with demonstration organizers. It is also inflexible to changing circumstances and will frequently rely on high levels of confrontation and force in relation to even minor violations of the rules established for the demonstration. Force is used, however, only for

negotiated management

An approach based on greater cooperation between police and demonstrators and an effort to avoid violence.

command and control

The use of authority to take decisions and to issue directives, orders, instructions to police officers as they conduct operations.

strategic incapacitation

Policing designed to deliberately contain and hamper and neutralize protest movements, limiting their growth, size, and political effectiveness.

the police to regain control over the demonstration. This can also be described as strategic incapacitation, where protesters who are breaking the rules are targeted by the police.

Black Lives Matter and Ferguson, MO

After the death of Trayvon Martin and the acquittal of his killer, George Zimmerman, in 2013, Alicia Garza, Patrisse Cullors, and Opal Tometi created the beginnings of the Black Lives Matter movement on social media. The movement was developed to draw attention to the ways in which Black people are deprived of basic human rights and dignity.[84] While it began as a grassroots effort in the Black community, it has quickly become an international activist movement and is now quickly recognized. Guided by 13 principles, which include diversity, restorative justice, and globalism, to name a few, the Black Lives Matter movement is a decentralized network comprised and led by a cadre of everyday freedom fighters, as diverse as the tapestry of America itself with membership that spans the intersections of race, gender, nationality, and identity.[85]

In 2014, following the shooting of Michael Brown by Ferguson Police Officer Darren Wilson, residents began to gather near the site of Brown's shooting to demonstrate and memorialize. Mr. Brown's death prompted weeks of demonstrations and a response from the police that included tear gas and rubber bullets. In response, Black Lives Matter supporters flooded into Ferguson from cities across the country to protest the shooting. Nightly protests ensued. Responsibility for policing the protests was taken away from the Ferguson Police Department and fell to the St. Louis County Police Department instead. The National Guard was deployed to help maintain order. Confrontations between protesters and police continued. *Time Magazine* named Ferguson protesters as their Person of the Year.[86]

A grand jury made the decision not to indict Officer Wilson and this set off a wave of anger among those who had gathered outside the Ferguson Police Department awaiting the announcement. As the night wore on, the situation grew more intense. Buildings were set on fire and looting was reported in several businesses. Seven months after the shooting death of Brown, the Department of Justice Civil Rights Division issued a report into policing and court practices in the Missouri city. Investigators determined that in "nearly every aspect of Ferguson's law enforcement system," Black people are impacted a severely disproportionate amount. On February 9, 2015, the Ferguson City Council voted to reject the consent decree that the city's negotiating team had negotiated. Unable to reach a mutually agreed upon court-enforceable settlement to remedy the department's findings, lawsuit was filed, seeking declaratory and injunctive relief to remedy the unlawful conduct identified by the department's investigation.

A year later on the anniversary of Michael Brown's death, St. Louis County issued a state of emergency following an escalation in violence. Demonstrators were calling for more action to be taken following the release of a federal report that alleged overwhelming racial bias in the town›s policing. The Department of Justice responded to the refusal of Ferguson to comply and filed a lawsuit against the city of Ferguson, Missouri, alleging a pattern or practice of law enforcement conduct that violates the Constitution and federal civil rights laws.

The lawsuit, filed pursuant to Section 14141 of the Violent Crime Control and Law Enforcement Act of 1994 and Title VI of the Civil Rights Act of 1964 (Title VI), alleges that the City of Ferguson, through its police department and municipal court:

- conducts stops, searches, and arrests without legal justification, and uses excessive force, in violation of the Fourth Amendment;

- interferes with the right to free expression in violation of the First Amendment;

- prosecutes and resolves municipal charges in a manner that violates due process and equal protection guaranteed by the Fourteenth Amendment; and

- engages in discriminatory law enforcement conduct against Black people in violation of the Fourteenth Amendment and federal statutory law.[87]

There was another outcome of this tragic event. Protests in Ferguson, Missouri, brought images of police using military equipment to control crowds. These images brought attention to a government program entitled 1033, which was part of the National Defense Authorization Act of Fiscal Year 1997. The goal of the program was to transfer excess military equipment to civilian agencies. The public was uneasy with images of police-driven tanks on the streets of Ferguson. On January 16, 2015, President Barack Obama issued Executive Order 13688, "Federal Support for Local Law Enforcement Equipment Acquisition," to identify actions that can improve federal support for the appropriate use, acquisition, and transfer of controlled equipment by state, local, and tribal law enforcement agencies (LEAs). Among other issues, this executive order, which establishes federal government-wide prohibited equipment lists, which identify categories of equipment that LEAs will not be able to acquire via transfer from federal agencies or purchase using federally provided funds (e.g., tracked armored vehicles, bayonets, grenade launchers, large-caliber weapons and ammunition).[88] This meant that some agencies had to return items that they had previously received under the program.

Ferguson effect

An allegation that police have shown restraint in doing their jobs in the wake of criticism following these widely publicized tragedies.

Since the shooting of Michael Brown, in Ferguson, on August 9, 2014, the subsequent civil unrest, there has been speculation that a **Ferguson effect** has ended the great crime decline. This claim was also repeated by former FBI Director James Comey that there is a "Ferguson effect," meaning that police have shown restraint in doing their jobs in the wake of criticism following these widely publicized tragedies. The thinking behind this is that police officers are holding back on making stops for fear of ending up the next YouTube "bad cop" sensation.[89]

If police are engaged in de-policing, we would in fact expect crime to be on the rise. If offenders know that the police will not respond to criminal activity, they might step up their offending behaviors. David Pyrooz and colleagues tested this claim—to see in fact if crime rose after the shooting and civil unrest in Ferguson. They examined felony offenses in 81 of the 150 largest cities across the United States for 12 months before and after the shooting of Michael Brown. The researchers found no evidence to support the claim of a systematic post-Ferguson change in overall, violent, and property crime trends. These findings are not surprising as Pyrooz and colleagues note that changes in crime trends are rarely the result of random shocks but rather are slow changes.[90]

Critical Thinking

Assuming that the Ferguson effect is real, what are the ways that police administrators can combat that issue?

Protests in Baltimore, MD, and the Freddie Gray Incident

On April 12, 2015, Baltimore Police Department officers arrested Freddie Gray, a 25-year-old Black man who had sustained injuries to his neck and spine while in transport in a police vehicle. On April 18, 2015, after Gray's subsequent coma, the residents of Baltimore protested in front of the Western district police station; Gray died a week after his arrest. Further protests were organized after Gray's death became public knowledge, amid the police department's continuing inability to adequately or consistently explain the events following the arrest and the injuries.

Spontaneous protests started after the funeral service, although several included violent elements. Civil unrest continued with at least 20 police officers injured, at least 250 people arrested, 285 to 350 businesses damaged, 150 vehicle fires, 60 structure fires, and 27 drug stores looted.[91] On the fifth day of protests, the governor deployed state troopers to assist with crowd control. Thirty-two troopers with expertise in crowd control arrived in Baltimore to be in place for help whenever the Baltimore City Police department asked. After Gray's funeral, violence erupted and a state of emergency was declared in Baltimore. The governor called in the National Guard and state police, requesting as many as 5,000 reinforcements from neighboring states. Mayor Stephanie Rawlings-Blake of Baltimore instituted a weeklong citywide curfew from 10 P.M. to 5 A.M. in an effort to reduce nightly violence.

In May 2015, six officers were charged in Gray's death and protests quieted; a year later the officers were either acquitted or the charges were dropped. Baltimore officials reached a $6.4 million settlement with the family of Freddie Gray, an agreement they say is the right step for a city still recovering from riots and demonstrations sparked by the 25-year-old's death from an injury sustained in police custody. In response to the protesters and death of Freddie Gray, the governor promised to sign a recently passed bill that would enable all Maryland police departments to outfit officers with body cameras that record audio and video. The law would create an exception to the state's wiretapping law that requires two-party consent for any audio to be recorded.

Riots and Washington DC: Storming the Capitol

In January 2021, White supremacist pro-Trump rioters mobbed the U.S. Capitol, forcing congressional representatives into hiding before being evacuated and ultimately ending; five people were killed in the attack.[92]

The attack began with peaceful protests in Washington, DC, that quickly escalated to an attack as rioters mobbed the U.S. Capitol with pipes and chemical irritants harming more than 50 police officers. Police had responded to violent events across the Capitol complex, including two reports of pipe bombs that were determined to be hazardous and harmful.[93] They battered doors, broke windows, and scaled the walls, rampaging through the building while inhabitants called for help. In the end, it took more than 2 hours to restore order and the Capitol Police arrested only 14 rioters. The lack of preparation for a planned attack was shocking, with regular crowd-control methods, such as an armed perimeter, the use of mounted units, and police dogs, noticeably missing.[94] The chief of the Capitol Police turned in his resignation the following day.

More than 1,000 defendants have been arrested and charged with crimes, including over 200 who assaulted police officers. More than 500 defendants pleaded guilty in the attack and some have received long prison sentences.[95] Several other defendants have agreed to cooperate with the government.[96] According to sources on Capitol Hill and the Capitol Police union, as well as testimony from Metropolitan Police Chief Robert Contee, more than 150 officers were injured in the attack.[97]

Many of those arrested had ties to the military as well as state, local, and federal law enforcement agencies. Records indicate that more than 50 of those arrested in the attack are active-duty or former military members. At least 25 have served in the U.S. Marines, 21 have served in the Army, 2 served in the Navy, and 2 served in the Air Force. One defendant was a sergeant with the Army Special Forces, the Green Berets.

At least 15 of those arrested were either former police officers or were employed as law enforcement officers at the time of the riot. One off-duty Drug Enforcement Agency agent was accused of carrying his government-issued weapon to the Capitol riot. Prosecutors say he posed for pictures while flashing his DEA badge and climbed onto the Peace Monument to film himself as he delivered a "monologue." He is no longer employed at the agency. Of the seven active police officers involved in the riot, at least six have been fired. A police officer with Windermere Police Department in Florida resigned after the FBI arrested him at his police department. A Chicago police officer who was arrested and accused of entering the Capitol building on January 6, has been relieved of his position.

A North Cornwall Township, Pennsylvania, police officer was fired after being charged with, among other crimes, obstruction of law enforcement during a civil disorder. A Houston police officer and Monmouth County correctional police officer both resigned after they were arrested, and two Virginia police officers were fired after prosecutors charged them for their conduct at the Capitol. Prosecutors have charged at least one former police chief with conspiring to obstruct an official proceeding. Prosecutors have also charged former officers with the New York Police Department with lunging at a Capitol police officer with a flagpole after NYPD's close work with the FBI Joint Terrorism Taskforce.[98]

As the police are thrust into situations like domestic terrorism, it broadens the scope of what local police officers do. One of the challenges of the job is that there is no longer an ideal view of a symbolic assailant. The actions of the January 6th rioters showed that people from all walks of life are susceptible to political rhetoric and calls to action. The police may find that they are enforcing laws that are broken, not by deranged, drug-induced criminals, but by typical citizens from middle America. One of the challenges of the job is learning how to treat suspected criminals with dignity and respect while ensuring that their rights are not violated as they are being taken into custody. All of these factors combined, on a daily basis, contribute to the stress of the job, which is why officer wellness is so important.

Summary

LO1   Identify how police work affects the health and well-being of police officers.

Modern policing is marked by stresses that were previously unknown to earlier generations. A significant number of injuries and deaths of officers are not due to the interaction with criminal offenders but rather the outcome of officers' poor physical health due to poor nutrition, lack of exercise, sleep deprivation, and substance abuse. Officer suicide is a major problem and COVID-19 was the leading cause of death for officers. More officers are killed or removed from service because of chronic diseases such as high blood pressure, and other problems that often stem from high-stress environments, poor nutrition, and lack of exercise rather than being shot in the line of duty.

LO2 Explore how budget constraints affect modern policing and the work of the individual officer.

In recent years, cities across the country have been forced to do more with fewer resources. Policing services have been curtailed, employees have been furloughed, and capital improvements have been delayed or canceled. Often, reductions in police budgets give much-needed money to crime prevention programs. Many police departments have adopted a range of creative and controversial strategies to respond to limited spending. Some have placed limits on overtime. Other cities have left hundreds of positions unfilled. Still others have offered senior officers early retirement. Some areas have merged their police departments to cut down on duplication of services and staff.

LO3 Describe the relationship between the media and the police.

Many large police departments rely on media relations or public information officers for maintaining official communications between the police department and the press. It is often hard to watch the news or read a newspaper without coming across a negative story about the police. There were many highly publicized events involving the deaths of Black men by police. Mainstream media coverage of police use of force and these shootings has increased partially because of the availability of cell phone cameras and video footage. This media coverage not only affects citizens' perceptions of the police but also the self-image of police officers.

LO4 Compare and contrast the positive and negative aspects of how police use social media to engage the community.

Social media represents an additional way for police departments to communicate with the public and increase their community policing mission. Social media offers new ways for police to listen to the public and work together to achieve shared goals. Police departments must also monitor these accounts to keep track of the content created by the public that is put on their sites. On the other hand, following the Boston Marathon bombing, the Boston police media relations office utilized social media to share accurate information with the public about what the police were doing but also about potential danger.

LO5 Discuss the strategies for policing protests and how they have changed over time.

The police response to protests has changed over time. During the 1960s and early 1970s, the police operated under a philosophy of ''escalated force'' in which the militancy of protestors was met by increased militancy by the police. Not surprisingly, there was quite a bit of violence associated with this approach and it also brought negative attention from the media—hurting the image of the police. In response to this violence at demonstrations and the poor public relations, a new approach termed *negotiated management* emerged. This approach was based on greater cooperation between police and demonstrators and an effort to avoid violence. The new approach called for the protection of free speech rights, toleration of community disruption, ongoing communication between police and demonstrators, avoidance of arrests, and limiting the use of force to situations where violence is occurring.

Key Terms

National Highway and Traffic Safety Administration (NHTSA), 345
compressed work weeks (CWW), 345

stigma, 349
furloughed, 351
self-legitimacy, 355
escalated force, 358
negotiated management, 358

command and control, 358
strategic incapacitation, 358
Ferguson effect, 360

Notes

1. The Final Report of The President's Task Force on 21st Century Policing, https://cops.usdoj.gov/pdf/taskforce/taskforce_finalreport.pdf.
2. Ibid.
3. Ibid.
4. Ibid.
5. FBI, "Officers Feloniously Killed," *2019 Law Enforcement Officers Killed and Assaulted*; FBI, "Officers Accidentally Killed," *2019 Law Enforcement Officers Killed and Assaulted*; Blue H.E.L.P., "Suicides to Date by Year,"
6. Andy O'Hara, "It's Time We Talk About Police Suicide," The Marshall Project. October 3, 2017. https://www.themarshallproject.org/2017/10/03/it-s-time-we-talk-about-police-suicide.
7. Ibid.
8. *USA Today*, December 30, 2013, https://www.usatoday.com/story/news/nation/2013/12/30/law-enforcement-deaths/4247393/.
9. Joseph B. Kuhns, Edward R. Maguire, and Nancy R. Leach, *Health, Safety, and Wellness Program Case Studies in Law Enforcement* (Washington, DC: Office of Community Oriented Policing Services, 2015).
10. Claudia C. Ma, Michael E. Andrew, Desta Fekedulegn, Ja K. Gu, Tara A. Hartley, Luenda E. Charles, John M. Violanti, and Cecil M. Burchfiel, "Shift Work and Occupational Stress in Police Officers," *Safety and Health at Work* 6, no. 1 (2015), 25–29.
11. Joseph B. Kuhns, Edward R. Maguire, and Nancy R. Leach, *Health, Safety, and Wellness Program Case Studies in Law Enforcement* (Washington, DC: Office of Community Oriented Policing Services, 2015).
12. Ibid.
13. Federal Bureau of Investigation, Crime Data Explorers, 2023, https://cde.ucr.cjis.gov/LATEST/webapp/#/pages/home.
14. John R. Batiste, Michael L. Wagers, and Richard J. Ashton, "Preventing Traffic-Related Line-of-Duty Deaths," *The Police Chief* 78 (July 2011), 52–55.
15. Ibid.
16. http://kdvr.com/2014/02/03/distracted-police-officers-cause-hundreds-of-crashes-in-metro-denver/.
17. Karen L. Amendola, David Weisburd, E. Hamilton, Greg Jones, Meghan Slipka, and Anneke Heitmann, "The Shift Length Experiment: What We Know About 8-, 10-, and 12-Hour Shifts in Policing," The Police Foundation. National Institute of Justice, 2011.
18. https://cops.usdoj.gov/pdf/taskforce/taskforce_finalreport.pdf.
19. Ibid.
20. Ibid.
21. Leonard B. Bell, Thomas B. Virden, Deborah J. Lewis, and Barry A. Cassidy, "Effects of 13-Hour 20-Minute Work Shifts on Law Enforcement Officers' Sleep, Cognitive Abilities, Health, Quality of Life, and Work Performance The Phoenix Study," *Police Quarterly* (2015), 1098611115584910.
22. International Association of Chiefs of Police, Reducing Officer Injuries: Final Report, https://www.theiacp.org/resources/document/reducing-officer-injuries-final-report, accessed July 11, 2013.
23. Brian A. Reaves, *Local Police Departments, 2013: Equipment and Technology* Department of Justice, Office of Justice Programs, Bureau of Justice Statistics, NCJ 248767, Washington, http://www.bjs.gov/content/pub/pdf/lpd13et.pdf.
24. www.ojp.gov/bvpbasi.
25. http://www.nij.gov/topics/technology/body-armor/pages/welcome.aspx#note2.
26. https://dailymedia.case.edu/wp-content/uploads/2021/01/02214818/2020-LE-Officers-Fatalities-Report-opt.pdf.
27. https://www.washingtonpost.com/business/2020/09/02/coronavirus-deaths-police-officers-2020/.
28. Suicide Prevention Resource Center, "Why Suicide Is a Top Cause of Death for Police Officers and Firefighters," August 2, 2019, https://www.sprc.org/news/why-suicide-top-cause-death-police-officers-firefighters.
29. Jean Hilliard, "New Study Shows Police At Highest Risk For Suicide of Any Profession," September 14, 2019, https://www.addictioncenter.com/news/2019/09/police-at-highest-risk-for-suicide-than-any-profession/.
30. Hans Toch, *Stress in Policing* (American Psychological Association, 2002).
31. Katrina J. Lawson, John J. Rodwell, and Andrew J. Noblet, "Mental Health of a Police Force: Estimating Prevalence of Work-Related Depression In Australia Without A Direct National Measure 1, 2," *Psychological Reports* 110, no. 3 (2012), 743–752.
32. Tahera Darensburg, Michael E. Andrew, Tara A. Hartley, Cecil M. Burchfiel, Desta Fekedulegn, and John M. Violanti, "Gender and Age Differences in Posttraumatic Stress Disorder and Depression Among Buffalo Police Officers," *Traumatology* 12, no. 3 (2006).
33. Jean Hilliard, "New Study Shows Police At Highest Risk For Suicide Of Any Profession," September 14, 2019, https://www.addictioncenter.com/news/2019/09/police-at-highest-risk-for-suicide-than-any-profession/.
34. Martine Powell, Peter Cassematis, Mairi Benson, Stephen Smallbone, and Richard Wortley, "Police Officers' Perceptions of their Reactions to Viewing Internet Child Exploitation Material," *Journal of Police and Criminal Psychology* 30, no. 2 (2015), 103–111.
35. John M. Violanti and Anne Gehrke, "Police Trauma Encounters: Precursors of Compassion Fatigue," *International Journal of Emergency Mental Health* 6, no. 2 (2004), 75–80.
36. A. D. MacEachern, A. A. Dennis, S. Jackson, and D. Jindal-Snape, "Secondary Traumatic Stress: Prevalence and Symptomology Amongst Detective Officers Investigating Child Protection Cases," *Journal of Police and Criminal Psychology* 34, no. 2 (2019), 165–174.
37. A Adina Bozga, Almuth McDowall, and Jennifer Brown, "'Little Red Sandals': Female Police Officers' Lived Experience of Investigating Sexual Violence," *Policing: An International Journal* 44, no. 1 (2020), 32–48.
38. Patrick Parnaby and Ryan Broll., "After 10–7: Trauma, Resilience and Satisfaction with Life among Retired Police Officers," *Policing: An International Journal* 44, no. 2 (2021), 230–245, https://doi.org/10.1108/PIJPSM-07-2020-0125.
39. Karen L. Amendola, Maria Valdovinos Olson, Julie Grieco, and Teresina G. Robbins, "Development of a Work–Family Conflict Scale for Spouses or Partners of Police Officers," *Policing: An International Journal* 44, no. 2 (2021), 275–290, https://doi.org/10.1108/PIJPSM-07-2020-0127.
40. Aslaug Mikkelsen and Ronald J. Burke, "Work-Family Concerns of Norwegian Police Officers: Antecedents and Consequences," *International Journal of Stress Management* 11, no. 4 (2004), 429.
41. J. M. Violanti, S. L. Owens, D. Fekedulegn, C. C. Ma, L. E. Charles, and M. E. Andrew, "An Exploration of Shift Work, Fatigue, and Gender Among Police Officers: The BCOPS Study," *Workplace Health & Safety* 66, no. 11 (2018), 530–537.

42. ACP and the Bureau of Justice Assistance, Office of Justice Programs, U.S. Department of Justice, *Law Enforcement Leader's Guide on Combat Veterans: A Transition Guide for Veterans Beginning or Continuing Careers in Law Enforcement* (July 2010), http://www.theiacp.org/PublicationsGuides/ContentbyTopic/tabid/216/Default.aspx?id=1298&v=1.

43. Scott Allen et al., "Keeping Our Heroes Safe: A Comprehensive Approach to Destigmatizing Mental Health Issues in Law Enforcement," *The Police Chief* 81 (March 2014), 34–38.

44. Kerry M. Karaffa and Julie M. Koch, "Stigma, Pluralistic Ignorance, and Attitudes Toward Seeking Mental Health Services Among Police Officers," *Criminal Justice and Behavior* (2015), 0093854815613103.

45. Scott Allen et al., "Keeping Our Heroes Safe: A Comprehensive Approach to Destigmatizing Mental Health Issues in Law Enforcement," *The Police Chief* 81 (March 2014), 34–38.

46. John M. Violanti and Andrea Steege, "Law Enforcement Worker Suicide: An Updated National Assessment," *Policing: An International Journal* 44, no. 1 (2020), 18–31, https://doi.org/10.1108/PIJPSM-09-2019-0157.

47. *ABC News*, January 2, 2020, https://abcnews.go.com/Politics/record-number-us-police-officers-died-suicide-2019/story?id=68031484.

48. Ibid.

49. American Addiction Centers, "Substance Abuse Among Police," June 11, 2019, https://americanaddictioncenters.org/police.

50. Ibid.

51. Ibid.

52. John M. Violanti and Andrea Steege, "Law Enforcement Worker Suicide: An Updated National Assessment," *Policing: An International Journal* 44, no. 1 (2020), 18–31, https://doi.org/10.1108/PIJPSM-09-2019-0157.

53. Herbert M. Gupton et al., "Support and Sustain: Psychological Intervention for Law Enforcement Personnel," *The Police Chief* 78 (August 2011), 92–97.

54. In Harm's Way: Law Enforcement Suicide Prevention, http://policesuicide.spcollege.edu.

55. http://triblive.com/usworld/nation/9972211-74/police-vehicles-cruisers.

56. Rebecca Ellis, "Under Portland Mayor's Proposed $5.7 Billion Budget, Police Bureau Would See Biggest Cut," *OBP Portland,* April 29, 2021, https://www.opb.org/article/2021/04/29/oregon-ted-wheeler-portland-police-budget-cuts/.

57. Paul Faruq Kiefer, "Council Vote Leaves Cuts to Seattle Police Department Budget Unresolved," *South Seattle Emerald,* May 12, 2021, https://southseattleemerald.com/2021/05/12/council-vote-leaves-cuts-to-seattle-police-department-budget-unresolved/.

58. Rick Hurd, "Oakland Police Chief: New $18 Million Budget Cut Leaves City Less Safe," *East Bay Times,* June 28, 2021, https://www.eastbaytimes.com/2021/06/28/oakland-police-chief-new-18-million-budget-cut-leaves-city-less-safe/.

59. Jeff Horseman, "Temecula to Plug Budget Gap with Overtime Limits," *Press-Enterprise*, February 23, 2010, p. A4.

60. Carrie Johnson, "Double Blow for Police: Less Cash, More Crime," *Washington Post*, February 28, 2009.

61. For more on consolidation trends, see http://policeconsolidation.msu.edu/, accessed June 2014.

62. Jim Bueermann, "Being Smart on Crime with Evidence-based Policing," *NIJ Journal* 269 (March 2012), https://www.ncjrs.gov/pdffiles1/nij/237723.pdf.

63. U.S. Department of Justice, Office of Community Oriented Policing Services, *The Impact of the Economic Downturn on American Police Agencies,* October 2011.

64. Bernard K. Melekian, "Policing in the New Economy: A New Report on the Emerging Trends from the Office of Community Oriented Policing Services," *The Police Chief* 79 (January 2012), 16–19.

65. Matthew Vann and Erik Ortiz, "Walter Scott Shooting," December 2016, https://www.nbcnews.com/storyline/walter-scott-shooting/walter-scott-shooting-michael-slager-ex-officer-sentenced-20-years-n825006.

66. City of Cambridge, https://www.cambridgema.gov/GIS/mapsbydepartment/publicinformationoffice.

67. Laura Huey and Ryan Broll, "'All It Takes Is One TV Show to Ruin It': A Police Perspective on Police-Media Relations in the Era of Expanding Prime Time Crime Markets," *Policing and Society* 22, no. 4 (2012), 384–396.

68. Ben Bradford and Paul Quinton, "Self-Legitimacy, Police Culture and Support for Democratic Policing in an English Constabulary," *British Journal of Criminology* (2014), azu053.

69. Scott E. Wolfe and Justin Nix, "The Alleged 'Ferguson Effect' and Police Willingness to Engage in Community Partnership," *Law and Human Behavior* 40, no. 1 (2015), 1–10.

70. Oscar Rantatalo, "Media Representations and Police Officers' Identity Work in a Specialized Police Tactical Unit," *Policing and Society* 26, no. 1 (2016), 97–113.

71. Justin Nix and Scott E. Wolfe, "The Impact of Negative Publicity on Police Self-Legitimacy," *Justice Quarterly* (2015), 1–25.

72. Justice Tankebe and Gorazd Meško, "Police Self-Legitimacy, Use of Force, and Pro-Organizational Behavior in Slovenia," *Trust and Legitimacy in Criminal Justice* (New York, NY: Springer International Publishing, 2015), pp. 261–277.

73. Valerie J. Callanan and Jared S. Rosenberger, "Media and Public Perceptions of the Police: Examining the Impact of Race and Personal Experience," *Policing & Society* 21, no. 2 (2011), 167–189.

74. Kathleen M. Donovan and Charles F. Klah, "The Role of Entertainment Media in Perceptions of Police Use of Force," *Criminal Justice and Behavior* (2015), 0093854815604180.

75. Laura Huey and Ryan Broll, "'I Don't Find It Sexy at All': Criminal Investigators' Views of Media Glamorization of Police 'Dirty Work,'" *Policing and Society* 25, no. 2 (2015), 236–247.

76. International Association of Chiefs of Police, *Technology & Social Media* (n.d.), http://www.iacpsocialmedia.org/.

77. Lori Brainard and Mariglynn Edlins, "Top 10 US Municipal Police Departments and Their Social Media Usage," *The American Review of Public Administration* 45, no. 6 (2015), 728–745.

78. Edward F. Davis, Alejandro A. Alves, and David Alan Sklansky, "Social Media and Police Leadership: Lessons from Boston," (2014), 10.

79. Lynsi Burton, "WTO Riots in Seattle: 15 Years Later," November 29, 2014. http://www.seattlepi.com/local/article/WTO-riots-in-Seattle-15-years-ago-5915088.php.

80. C. McPhail, D. Schweingruber, and J. D. McCarthy, "Protest Policing in the United States, 1960/1995." In D. Della Porta and H. Reiter (eds), *Policing Protest: The Control of Mass Demonstrations in Western Democracies* (Minneapolis, MN: University of Minnesota Press).

81. D. Schweingruber, "Mob Sociology and Escalated Force: Sociology's Contribution to Repressive Police Tactics," *Sociological Quarterly* 41 no. 3 (2000), 371/390.

82. Alex S. Vitale, "From Negotiated Management to Command and Control: How the New York Police Department Polices Protests," *Policing & Society* 15, no. 3 (2005), 283–304.

83. Patrick F. Gillham, Bob Edwards, and John A. Noakes, "Strategic Incapacitation and the Policing of Occupy Wall Street Protests in New York City, 2011," *Policing and Society* 23, no. 1 (2013), 81–102.

84. L. M. Boyd and K. C. Dumpson, "Black Lives Matter: The Watchdog For The Criminal Justice System." In B. Berry (ed.), *Appearance Bias and Crime* (Cambridge, MA: Cambridge University Press, 2019).

85. Ibid.

86. Alex Altman, "Ferguson Protestors, the Activists," *Time Magazine*, December 10, 1014. http://time.com/time-person -of-the-year-runner-up-ferguson-protesters/.

87. Department of Justice, "Justice Department Files Lawsuit to Bring Constitutional Policing to Ferguson, Missouri," February 10, 2016, https://www.justice.gov/opa/pr/justice-department -files-lawsuit-bring-constitutional-policing-ferguson-missouri.

88. Evan Perez, Kevin Liptak, and Allison Malloy, "Obama Will Restrict Grenade Launchers, Military Equipment from Local Police," *CNN Politics*, May 18, 2025, https://www.cnn.com /2015/05/18/politics/bayonets-police-white-house/index.html.

89. Evan Perez, Shimon Prokupecz, and Wesley Bruer, "FBI Chief Tries to Deal with the 'Ferguson Effect,'" *CNN Politics*, October 25, 2015, http://www.cnn.com/2015/10/26/politics/fbi-comey-crime -police/.

90. David C. Pyrooz, Scott H. Decker, Scott E. Wolfe, and John A. Shjarback, "Was There a Ferguson Effect on Crime Rates in Large US Cities?," *Journal of Criminal Justice* 46 (2016), 1–8.

91. Jessica Anderson, "Baltimore Riots," *Baltimore Sun*, April 28, 2015.

92. Evan Perez and Paul LeBlanc, "Federal Murder Investigation to Be Opened in Capitol Police Officer's Death," *CNN Politics,* https://www.cnn.com/2021/01/08/politics/capitol-police-officer -killed/index.html.

93. Jennifer Elias, Kevin Breuninger, and Marty Steinberg, "More Than 50 Police Officers Were Hurt at pro-Trump Riot at the Capitol That Also killed 4," January 7, 2021, https://www.cnbc .com/2021/01/07/four-dead-after-pro-trump-rioters-storm -capitol.html.

94. Shaila Dewan, Neil MacFarquhar, Zolan Kanno-Youngs, and Ali Watkins, "Police Failures Spur Resignations and Complaints of Double Standard," *The New York Times,* January 7, 2021, https://www.nytimes.com/2021/01/07/us/Capitol-cops-police .html.

95. Madison Hall, "At Least 476 Rioters Have Pleaded Guilty for Their Role in the Capitol Insurrection So Far. This Table Shows Them All," *INSIDER*, February 16, 2023, https://www.insider .com/capitol-rioters-who-pleaded-guilty-updated-list-2021-5.

96. Clare Hymes, Cassidy McDonald, and Eleanor Watson, "What We Know about the 'Unprecedented' Capitol Riot Arrests," *CBS News*, August 11, 2021, https://www.cbsnews.com/news /capitol-riot-arrests-latest-2021-07-22/.

97. Ibid.

98. Ibid.

Chapter 13

Technology and the Future of Policing

Learning Objectives

LO1 Trace the development of police technology.

LO2 Identify the problems associated with modern technology.

LO3 Compare and contrast the various types of soft technology.

LO4 List and discuss the uses of hard technology.

Chapter Outline

Ashley Thomas Photography/Shutterstock.com

At the crack of dawn, Dallas police detonated a "bomb robot" at the community center hideout of Micah X. Johnson, who was a suspect in the shooting deaths of five police officers. Johnson was a lone gunman whose motivation seemed to be anger at the police shooting young Black men. The robot was deployed after seven more officers were shot during a standoff with the suspect that involved several hours of unsuccessful negotiation. This was the first time that a bomb disposal robot had been used in this way on U.S. soil. The robot, manufactured by Northrop Grumman, is the "Remotec Andros" model, a remotely controlled bomb disposal unit commonly used by police, military, and other first responders around the world. It is wheeled, weighs around 485 pounds, and has a robotic arm with grippers.[1]

The U.S. military had used this technology before with remote-controlled robots for tasks such as surveillance and investigating suspect bombs. Some are equipped with two-way intercoms and even cameras to allow for police to negotiate with suspects without risk. When deployed for bomb disposal, they often use small explosives in order to trigger the larger bomb. In this case, the perpetrator was killed by the explosion but the robot was unharmed. Incidents such as the Dallas standoff raise many questions about how and when this type of military technology should be used by police.

Do you agree that using robotic technology in a lethal manner is a huge concern and one that will require discussion and regulation in the future?

Will the law on search and seizure have to be totally revised to account for technology that allows monitoring and recording of citizen behavior?

Which is more important to you, respect for privacy or enforcement of the law?

LO1

Trace the development of
police technology.

▶ # How Did Police Technology Develop?

Why has the use of advanced technology by local police departments become a
national issue? Budget realities demand that police leaders maximize efficiency.
Technology is one method of increasing productivity at a relatively low cost.
The introduction of technology has already been explosive. In 1964, only one
city, St. Louis, had a police computer system; by 1968, 10 states and 50 cities
had state-level criminal justice information systems. Today, nearly every law
enforcement organization relies on computer technology.[2]

Police departments are now employing advanced technology in all facets of
their operations, from assigning patrol routes to gathering evidence. Similarly,
investigators are starting to use advanced technology to streamline and enhance
the investigation process. Gathering evidence at a crime scene and linking clues
to a list of suspects can be a tedious job for many investigators. Yet linkage is
critical if suspects are to be quickly apprehended before they are able to leave
the jurisdiction, intimidate witnesses, or cover up any clues they may have left
behind. It is now difficult to imagine the modern police without technology such
as cars, radio communication, and access to criminal record data among other
advancements. We now turn to the advent of technological policing, which surprisingly occurred much earlier that you might think.

Developing New Technologies

August Vollmer, considered to be the father of modern policing and the professionalization movement, developed an administrative reform agenda that among
other elements included advancements in science and technology. Vollmer's
reform agenda included:

- Raising personnel standards in selection and training

- Adopting civil service protections for municipal police

- Creating rules and regulations to make officers more accounTable

- Encouraging the use of scientific technology for police

- Helping create the Uniform Crime Reports (UCR)

- Experimenting with the use of crime labs (1916) and lie detectors (1921) and
  other technology[3]

Vollmer's interest in science and technology helped propel professionalization and bureaucratization of the police. These technological advances helped
improved policing but still carried with them some baggage. Take for instance
the telephone, which was created in 1876, but did not heavily impact policing
until the mid-twentieth century. The telephone allowed citizens to call the police
whenever they wanted, allowing them more contact with police officers. The contact, however, occurred in an impersonal way: people became socialized to say "I
am calling the cops," instead of dealing with problems informally and within the
community. As a result, they expected police to respond instantly and have the
ability to solve every type of problem imaginable. Not surprisingly, local police
officers have had and continue to have a problem meeting those expectations.

Another technological advance, the patrol car, was also a mixed blessing for
the police. The patrol car removed officers from the street and away from the
citizen. The car allowed for quicker access to citizens and calls for service but

removed the police from everyday contact and positive reinforcement from the law-abiding public. By the 1920s, the use of the car was widespread. The car allowed officers to cover a larger geographical area and to quickly respond to calls for service.

Conventional wisdom also held that police cars would also deter crime if people saw a car patrolling. The two-way radio was another technological advancement that dramatically changed police operations. The two-way radio was widespread in the 1930s and it eliminated communication problems. The radio was valuable because it increased supervision and internal communications. Supervisors could readily find patrol officers and information could be shared across departments. The two-way radio also allowed the department to dispatch officers quickly to calls for service.[4]

Influence of the Law Enforcement Assistance Administration

These technological advancements during the reform era were just the beginning. Technology is constantly changing due to scientific discoveries as well as the needs of police. The 1970s witnessed many structural changes in police agencies themselves. The end of the Vietnam War significantly reduced tensions between students and police. However, the relationship between police and people of color was still tense at best. Local fears and distrust, combined with conservative federal policies, encouraged police departments to control what was perceived as an emerging minority group "threat."[5]

Increased federal government support for criminal justice greatly influenced police operations.[6] During the decade, the Law Enforcement Assistance Administration (LEAA) devoted a significant portion of its funds to police agencies. Although a number of police departments used this money to purchase little-used hardware, such as anti-riot gear, most of it went to supporting innovative research on police work and advanced training of police officers. Perhaps most significant, LEAA's Law Enforcement Education Program helped thousands of officers further their college education. Hundreds of criminal justice programs were developed on college campuses around the country, providing a pool of highly educated police recruits. LEAA funds were also used to import or transfer technology originally developed in other fields into law enforcement. Technological innovations involving computers transformed the way police kept records, investigated crimes, and communicated with one another. State training academies improved the way the police learned to deal with such issues as job stress, community conflict, and interpersonal relations.

Technological Revolution

◀ **L02**
Identify the problems associated with modern technology.

Police departments have evolved into organizations that rely on technology that today, extends way beyond radios and patrol cars. Neighboring agencies are now linked so they can digitally share information on cases, suspects, and warrants. On a broader jurisdictional level, the Federal Bureau of Investigation (FBI) implemented the National Crime Information Center (NCIC) in 1967. This system provides rapid collection and retrieval of data about people wanted for crimes anywhere in the 50 states. Some police departments are using computerized imaging systems to replace mug books. Photos or sketches are stored digitally and are easily retrieved for viewing. Several software companies have developed identification programs that help witnesses create a composite picture of the perpetrator. A vast library of photographed or drawn facial features can be digitized and accessed on a terminal screen. Witnesses can scan thousands of noses, eyes, and lips until they find those that match the suspect's. Eyeglasses, mustaches, and beards can be added; skin tones can be altered. When the composite is created, an attached camera prints a hard copy for distribution.

Advances such as these generally fall into two broad categories: hard technology and soft technology.[7] Hard technology includes new materials and equipment that police use to catch criminals and prevent crime. Soft technology primarily consists of software and information systems. Innovations in this area include new programs, crime classification techniques, system integration, and data sharing. Additional examples of hard and soft technology appear in Exhibit 13.1. In the following subsections, we explore in more detail several of the key technological innovations that have improved police capabilities in recent years.

Technological Problems and Issues

While many experts many applaud the advances in law enforcement technology, others are more cautious with their praise. In her research, Ruha Benjamin discusses "the New Jim Code," which means that the criminal justice system uses technologies that are promoted as more objective or progressive than previous systems, but actually reflect and reproduce existing inequalities.[8] Examples of the code are not limited to the criminal justice system but are particularly pertinent to the increased use of technology by police agencies. One example is the use of gang databases by police agencies to track gang activity in their community. These gang databases include primarily Black and Latinx community members—some even as young as toddlers who are noted to be self-professed gang members.

Exhibit 13.1

Overview of Soft and Hard Technologies Experimented with in Policing

Soft Technologies

Hotspot Crime Mapping

CompStat

Social Media

Predictive Analytics

Hard Technologies

Body-Worn Cameras (BWCs)

Thermal Imaging

Gunshot Detection Technology

Lethal and Nonlethal Weaponry

Drones

Biometrics

License Plate Readers

Source: J. Byrne and D. Hummer, "Technology, Innovation and 21st Century Policing." In Michael McGuire and Tom Holt (eds.)., *Handbook of Technology, Crime, and Justice* (London: Routledge, 2016).

The "New Jim Code" is further exemplified by automated risk assessments, which are used to determine the likelihood of a person committing a crime. Often these risk assessments flag Black defendants as future offenders twice as often as their White peers because they include their home neighborhood characteristics, financial, education, and employment history. It is impossible to separate the effects of racism and the differential opportunities afforded to communities of color from these assessments. As a result, Benjamin argues that they reproduce existing discrimination but in a more technologically savvy way.[9]

Soft Technology

◀ **L03**

Compare and contrast the various types of soft technology.

soft technology

Processes that are used to optimize the effectiveness and efficiency of an organization.

Soft technology refers to organized yet intangible processes that are used to optimize the processes of an organization. Every organization can benefit when experienced members who have developed "know how" over the years can translate that knowledge into processes that enhance administrative effectiveness and efficiency. Soft technologies are associated with the operation of the organization and the fulfillment of its functions. They may improve both achievement of the mission and shape the vision.

The organization and management of the company are carried out within the framework of a process that, although not technological in terms of hard technologies, does involve a series of optimized processes in the same sense as in technology. They are designed to improve the general functioning of any type of organization or institution, be it in the private of public sector. Through the use of soft technologies, human resources can become more efficient. Consequently, through its use, a public agency such as the police can achieve short- and long-term objectives in a manner that benefits the public. What are some of the most noTable soft technologies that have been applied to police work?

CompStat

The use of soft technology received a boost with the **Computer Statistics (CompStat) program** in New York City, which was designed as a means of directing police efforts in a more productive fashion.[10] CompStat originated with Charts of the Future, the creation of Jack Maple, a former transit police officer. On 55 feet of wall space, he mapped every train station in New York City and every train. He marked every violent crime, robbery, and grand larceny that occurred and noted the solved and the unsolved crimes. Charts of the Future became the basis for CompStat.

William Bratton, commissioner of the NYPD, wanted to revitalize the department and break through its antiquated bureaucratic structures. He installed a computerized system that gave local precinct commanders up-to-date information about where and when crime was occurring in their jurisdictions. Part of this CompStat program, twice-weekly "crime-control strategy meetings," brought precinct commanders together with the department's top administrators, who asked them to report on crime problems in their precincts and relay what they were doing to turn things around.

Those involved in the strategy sessions had both detailed data and electronic pin maps that showed how crime clustered geographically in the precinct and how

Computer Statistics (CompStat) program

A computerized system that gave local precinct commanders up-to-date information about where and when crime was occurring in their jurisdictions. Precinct commanders were given reports on crime problems and strategies to turn things around.

Computerized crime mapping technology enables police and other law enforcement agencies to analyze data sources such as arrests, complaints, contacts, and related factors within a community or other geographical areas and then incorporate this data into computerized mapping software.

crime mapping
Computer mapping programs that can translate addresses into map coordinates allowing police to identify problem areas for particular crimes, such as drug dealing.

patrol officers were being deployed. The CompStat program required local commanders to demonstrate their intimate knowledge of crime trends and to develop strategies to address them effectively. When the assembled police administrators presented their ideas, the local commander was required to demonstrate, in follow-up sessions, how he had incorporated the new strategies in the local patrol plan. CompStat proved extremely successful and made a major contribution to the dramatic decline in New York City's crime rate during the past decade. CompStat-like programs have since been implemented in other jurisdictions around the country.[11]

Crime Mapping

It is now recognized that there are geographic "hotspots" where a majority of crimes are concentrated.[12] Computer mapping programs that can translate addresses into map coordinates allow departments to identify problem areas for particular crimes, such as drug dealing. Computer maps allow police to identify the location, time of day, and linkage among criminal events and to concentrate their forces accordingly. Crime maps offer police administrators graphic representations of where crimes are occurring in their jurisdiction. Computerized **crime mapping** gives the police the power to analyze and correlate a wide array of data to create immediate, detailed visuals of crime patterns.

The simplest maps display crime locations or concentrations and can be used to help direct patrols to the places they are most needed. More complex maps can be used to chart trends in criminal activity, and some have even proven valuable in solving individual criminal cases. For example, a serial rapist may be caught by observing and understanding the patterns of their crime so that detectives may predict where they will strike next and stake out the area with police decoys.

Crime mapping makes use of new computer technology. Instead of antiquated pin maps, computerized crime mappings let the police detect crime patterns and pathologies of related problems. It enables them to work with multiple layers of information and scenarios, and thus identify emerging hotspots of criminal activity far more successfully and target resources accordingly. Most police agencies throughout the United States now use mapping techniques. The New York City Police Department's CompStat process relies on computerized crime mapping to identify crime hotspots.[13]

The Chicago Police Department has developed the popular CLEARMAP Crime Incident web application. By visiting the department's webpage, anyone can search a database of reported crime within the city and map incident locations.[14] The system was awarded a prestigious Harvard Innovations in American Government award.

Some mapping efforts cross jurisdictional boundaries.[15] Examples of this approach have included the Regional Crime Analysis System in the greater Baltimore–Washington area and the multijurisdictional efforts of the Greater Atlanta PACT Data Center. The Charlotte–Mecklenburg Police Department (North Carolina) has used data collected by other city and county agencies in its crime mapping efforts. By coordinating the departments of tax assessor, public works, planning, and sanitation, police department analysts have made links between disorder and crime that have been instrumental in supporting the department's community policing philosophy. Crime maps alone may not be a panacea for significantly improving police effectiveness. Many officers are uncertain about how to read maps and assess their data. To maximize the potential of this new technique, police agencies need to invest in training and infrastructure before crime mapping can have an impact on their service efficiency.

Mapping serves other purposes besides just resource allocation. Law enforcement officials in the state of Washington have developed a new Internet-based mapping system that provides critical information about public infrastructures to help them handle terrorist or emergency situations. The initiative, known as the Critical Incident Planning and Mapping System,[16] provides access to tactical response plans, satellite imagery, photos, floor plans, and hazardous chemical locations.

Mapping technology has recently been combined with GPS (global positioning system), a network of orbiting satellites that transmits signals to a por-Table device that tracks the precise whereabouts of a person or thing. Officers in one gruesome case found various parts of a man's badly decomposed body in Lake Powell, in Utah's Bryce Canyon National Park. They used a digital camera equipped with GPS technology to snap pictures of the exact locations where body parts and related evidence were found. The officers were then able to view all the photo locations on a map, which helped them determine that the body broke apart over time due to wave action, not because of foul play.[17] GPS technology is also used for a wide range of other applications, such as keeping track of the exact locations of officers' patrol cars.[18]

Using Artificial Intelligence (AI): Data Mining and Predictive Policing

In the classic science fiction movie *Minority Report*, pre-crime chief John Anderton, played by Tom Cruise, heads a futuristic police unit that uses people with psychic power ("precogs") to identify and catch criminals *before* they commit crimes. Does the ability to predict future crimes exist only in the realm of science fiction or is it possible that it may soon be a reality? Today, artificial intelligence is just beginning to be used by law enforcement agencies to help prevent crimes and its use may expand rapidly in the near future. Two initiatives now being used are data mining and predictive policing.

In an effort to identify crime patterns and link them to suspects, many departments use computer software to conduct analysis of behavior patterns, a process called **data mining**.[19] By discovering patterns in crimes such as burglary, especially those involving multiple offenders, computer programs can be programmed to recognize a particular way of working a crime and thereby identify suspects most likely to fit the profile. The analysis of large data sets has led to what is now called predictive policing.

As you may recall (refer to Chapter 6), predictive policing tries to harness the power of information, geospatial technologies, and evidence-based intervention models to reduce crime and improve public safety. This two-pronged approach—applying advanced analytics to various data sets in conjunction with intervention models—can move law enforcement from reacting to crimes into the realm of predicting what and where something is likely to happen and deploying resources accordingly.[20]

data mining

Using sophisticated computer software to conduct analysis of behavior patterns in an effort to identify crime patterns and link them to suspects.

The predictive policing approach does not replace traditional policing. Instead, it enhances existing approaches such as problem-oriented policing, community policing, intelligence-led policing, and hotspot policing. Predictive policing uses computer models for law enforcement purposes, namely anticipating likely crime events and informing actions to prevent crime. Predictions can focus on variables such as places, people, groups, or incidents. Demographic trends, parolee populations, and economic conditions may all affect crime rates in particular areas. Using models supported by prior crime and environmental data to inform different kinds of interventions can help police reduce the number of crime incidents.

While technology plays an important role in the analysis process, police themselves must:

- find relevant data

- preprocess the data so they are suiTable for analysis, notably by adding identifying details and addressing any systematic data exclusions or biases

- design and conduct analyses in response to ever-changing crime conditions

- review and interpret the results of these analyses to exclude erroneous findings (e.g., hotspots over water), and integrate the findings with contextual knowledge

- analyze the integrated findings in light of other demands and constraints facing the agency and make recommendations about how to act on them

- take action to exploit the findings and assess the impacts of those actions.[21]

Critical Thinking

What are the ramifications of computers predicting which behaviors a person "might" Exhibit?

LO4

List and discuss the uses of hard technology.

hard technology

Equipment that is designed to help police prevent crime, identify suspects, and bring them to justice. These include such devices as less-than-lethal weapons, drones, thermal imagers, and body armor.

Hard Technology

In contrast to soft technology, **hard technology** typically involves tangible equipment that is designed to help police prevent crime, identify suspects, and bring them to justice. These include, but are not limited to, devices such as less-than-lethal weapons, drones, thermal imagers, and body armor equipment. Law enforcement agencies today employ a wide variety of hard technology to deal with crime and enforce the law. Some of the more important technological innovations are set out below.

Thermal Imaging Cameras

You may recall when Dzhokhar Tsarnaev, the Boston Marathon bomber, was on the run from the police. Eventually, the local police received a tip from a homeowner who suspected someone was hiding in a covered boat sitting in his driveway. Because the boat was covered, law enforcement agents responding to the call could not confirm if someone was actually on the boat, their exact position, and whether they were armed. To obtain this information, they employed a thermal imaging device mounted to a helicopter. As it passed over the boat, the images clearly showed someone lying prone on the floor of the boat, slowly moving about. Aided by the visual information from the helicopter, a special weapons and tactics (SWAT) team was able to approach the boat and apprehend the suspect.

The device used to apprehend the Boston Marathon bomber, which can be mounted on aircraft or handheld, uses a specially created lens that focuses the infrared light emitted by all of the objects in view. All objects emit infrared energy, known as a heat signature. An infrared camera detects and measures the infrared energy of objects. The camera converts that infrared data into an electronic image that shows the apparent surface temperature of the object being measured. The light is then scanned by an array of infrared-detector elements that create a temperature pattern called a *thermogram* that is translated into electric impulses that are translated by the **thermal imaging camera** into an image.

This process is also known as "night vision." Thermal imaging helps law enforcement officials detect everything from marijuana-growing operations to suspects hiding from officers in foot pursuits. While effective, some believe that this device, used without a warrant, is an intrusion on personal privacy. The following Police & the Law: *Kyllo v. United States* feature shows how the Supreme Court dealt with this issue.

thermal imaging camera
A device that detects radiation in the infrared range of the electromagnetic spectrum, used in law enforcement to detect variations in temperature (warm images stand out against cool backgrounds).

Police & the Law

Kyllo v. United States

The Constitution does not cover these new technologies. The founding fathers might not have considered that technologies such as gun detector technology or thermal imaging would even exist. As such, as new technologies emerge, it is up to legislators to make laws and the Supreme Court to interpret them as they pertain to the police. One example is thermal imaging. In the case *Kyllo v. United States* (2001), federal agents believed that marijuana was being grown in Danny Kyllo's home. Agents used a thermal imaging device to scan the home. The scan of Kyllo's home took only a few minutes and was performed from the passenger seat of a vehicle across the street from the front of the house and also from the street in the back of the house. The device they used was able to detect heat and able to determine if the home had the high-intensity lamps needed for indoor marijuana growth. The scan showed in fact that the garage roof and a wall were relatively hot compared to the rest of the home and nearby homes. The agents concluded that Kyllo was using halide lights to grow marijuana in his house. This observation was supported by tips from informants, utility bills, as well as the thermal imaging. Consequently, a federal magistrate judge issued a warrant authorizing a search of Kyllo's home, where agents found an indoor growing operation involving more than 100 plants. Kyllo was indicted on one count of manufacturing marijuana, in violation of 21 U.S.C. § 841(a)(1). He unsuccessfully moved to suppress the evidence seized from his home and then entered a conditional guilty plea. The lower court ruled that there was no objectively reasonable expectation of privacy because the thermal imager did not expose any intimate details of Kyllo's life, only hotspots on his home's exterior. On appeal, the Supreme Court reversed this decision, ruling that when the government uses a device that is not in general public use to explore details of a residence that would have been unknowable without physical intrusion, the surveillance is a Fourth Amendment "search," and is presumptively unreasonable without a warrant. Justice Scalia specifically noted that the device can tell you things that the average person would not be able to tell standing outside the house: obtaining information regarding the interior of a home, which could not otherwise have been obtained without physical intrusion into a constitutionally protected area, such as Kyllo's private residence, constituted a search, at least where the technology was not in general public use. Since thermal imaging technology was not in general public use, such a surveillance was a search and was presumptively unreasonable without a warrant. Whether the search warrant was supported by probable cause without the surveillance evidence was for the trial court to determine in the first instance.

Critical Thinking

Thermal imaging technology has become more prevalent and is being used by police departments around the nation. If a case identical to Kyllo were to work its way up to the Supreme Court today, would the justices have come to the same conclusion?

Source: *Kyllo v. US* 533 U.S. 27 (2001).

Less-Than-Lethal Weapons

In order to curb or reduce the use of deadly force, law enforcement agencies have adopted a number of different types of less-than-lethal weapons. This is not a new idea, since police have been arming themselves with a form of nonlethal weaponry since the mid-nineteenth century when wooden clubs or batons were given and used by most officers. Today, according to the National Institute of Justice, there are seven types of less-lethal device technologies:

- **Conducted energy devices.** Some conducted energy devices (CEDs), such as the Taser, can induce involuntary muscle contractions that temporarily incapacitate people. Others deter an individual from a course of action. These include stun guns and stun belts.

- **Directed energy devices.** This technology uses radiated energy to achieve the same effect as blunt force, but has a lower probability of injury.

- **Chemicals.** These chemicals include pepper spray (also known as OC— oleoresin capsicum), tear gas, and stink bombs.

- **Distraction.** This equipment temporarily incapacitates people while causing little harm. Examples include the laser dazzler, bright lights, and noise.

- **Vehicle-stopping technology.** This equipment can stop cars during high-speed chases.

- **Barriers.** These include nets, foams, and physical barriers.

- **Blunt force.** Projectiles used in crowd-control deter people from a course of action.[22]

Of these, CEDs such as the Taser have become increasingly popular. Tasers produce 50,000 volts of electricity that can stun and temporarily disable people with involuntary muscle contractions. While Tasers make people easier to arrest and/or subdue without serious injury, in most cases their use is not without controversy. There are safety concerns. There are well-documented cases of permanent damage and even death linked to Taser use by untrained or poorly trained officers. When CEDs are properly used as an alternative to deadly force, they can help reduce injuries to officers and suspects alike.

In a study that compared seven law enforcement agencies that use CEDs with six agencies that do not, researchers found:

- A 70 percent decrease in officer injuries associated with the use of CEDs. During the two years before CEDs were used, 13 percent of the officers involved in use-of-force incidents required medical attention. When CEDs were deployed, the percentage requiring medical attention declined to 8 percent.

- A 40 percent decrease in suspect injuries associated with the use of conducted energy devices. During the two years before the agencies began using CEDs, 55 percent of the suspects required medical attention, while 40 percent required medical attention after the agencies started using the devices.[23]

Detection Technology

Cities can purchase devices that literally "listen" for gunfire so that officers can quickly be directed to the place where guns were recently fired. Companies have also developed gun detectors that officers can use to determine who is carrying an illegally concealed weapon. Millivision, one of the leaders in this area, has developed a porTable gun detection device that officers can use from a distance. It does not reveal any anatomical information, only the outline of a gun.[24] Police departments even use closed-circuit television cameras to monitor certain urban areas from a distance.[25] Another device can "listen" for a person hidden in the trunk of a vehicle. This is useful in the traffic stop context, when police officers are vulnerable to attack. The so-called enclosed space detection system (ESDS) has been developed for police to ascertain whether one or more people are hidden in a vehicle. It works by detecting the motion of the vehicle caused by the shock wave produced by a beating heart.[26] The following Focus on Policing: Gunshot Locators feature reviews gunshot locators in greater detail.

Focus on Policing

Gunshot Locators

Faced with a surge in the number of shootings, the city of Gary, Indiana, installed the ShotSpotter gunshot location system (GLS). The device uses a network of weatherproof acoustic sensors that locate and record gunshots. Most gunshots emit sound waves for a distance of up to two miles. The GLS sensors determine the direction from which the sound came. When several sensors are used in conjunction with one another, they can triangulate and determine the exact location where the gunshots were fired. Using this technology, the Gary Police Department seized 27 semiautomatic handguns in a single night. It happened over New Year's Eve because the department knew from previous experience that many guns were fired into the air near midnight.

Technology

ShotSpotter, the leading manufacturer of gunshot location systems, bases its product on the same technology that geologists use to pinpoint an earthquake's epicenter. In fact, the original concept was conceived by a U.S. Geological Survey seismologist. With at least three sensors, the system ties into a geographic information system (GIS) and maps the gunshot's location with a dot on a city map. Gunshots show up as red dots; different colors are used for other loud noises. The map then shows a dispatcher the gunshot's location, information that is then used to send the nearest officer to the scene.

An added feature of GLS technology is that it can be integrated with surveillance cameras so that both gunshots *and* shooters can be detected. ShotSpotter also markets the Rapid Deployment System (RDS), a porTable version of its gunshot detector that can be used by SWAT teams and other first responders. A few other companies have developed similar gunshot detection technologies. These include the SECURES Gunshot Detection and Localization System and the Safety Dynamics SENTRI. The Safety Dynamics product is especially adept at distinguishing gunshots from other noises in loud areas. Chicago used SENTRI in its "Operation Disruption," a crackdown on gun violence.

Advantages

The obvious advantage of gunshot location technology is rapid response by police. With real-time information

(Continued)

on gunshot locations, police officers can be rapidly dispatched to the scene and given a realistic opportunity to apprehend the shooter. A related advantage is an improved ability to provide medical treatment for gunshot victims.

In one unfortunate example, 35-year-old landscaper Jose Villatoro was fatally shot as he was mowing a yard outside a Washington, DC, apartment complex. Neighbors reported hearing the shot, but they did not call police because gunshots were so common in the area. Perhaps ShotSpotter or a similar device could have saved his life.

Gunshot location systems have also given police a better chance of locating forensic evidence at crime scenes. This occurred in a Washington, DC–area sniper case, where a man was shooting people from a freeway overpass. He was turned in by someone, but a gunshot locator the FBI installed assisted agents in locating spent shell casings.

ShotSpotter and similar technologies also provide a more complete picture of gun usage across the United States. Gun violence is typically measured using injury and death statistics. Yet, many argue that this presents an incomplete picture of the totality of gun violence. These numbers do not account for all the times when a gun is fired and the bullet simply misses its mark. In 2015, there were 165,531 separate gunshots recorded in 62 different urban municipalities nationwide, including places such as San Francisco, Washington, DC, and St. Louis. Jillian Carr and Jennifer Doleac found that ShotSpotter showed evidence of severe underreporting of gun violence.

Limitations

While gunshot locators clearly help authorities identify the whereabouts of shooters. They have been credited for significant reductions in gunfire in several cities, but whether the devices themselves are responsible cannot be known for sure. Another concern is that despite built-in mechanisms to prevent false positives, the devices sometimes alert authorities to a gunshot when in fact none occurred. ShotSpotter and similar technologies are also incapable of detecting shots fired in private residences—thus presenting an incomplete picture of gun usage. Finally, gunshot locators are prohibitively expensive for many cities. The cost to cover one square mile is approximately $150,000, followed by an additional $100,000 to $120,000 for every other square mile covered. If cameras are added to the technology, the cost can add up to millions of dollars to cover a relatively small area within a single city.

Critical Thinking

While gun shot locators work, do you think they can actually deter crime? Is someone high or drunk, enraged and angry, likely to think about gun locators before they commit a violent act?

Source: Jillian Carr and Jennifer L. Doleac, "The Geography, Incidence, and Underreporting of Gun Violence: New Evidence Using ShotSpotter Data," *Incidence, and Underreporting of Gun Violence: New Evidence Using ShotSpotter Data,* April 26, 2016, http://jenniferdoleac.com/wp-content/uploads/2015/03/Carr_Doleac_gunfire_underreporting.pdf.

License Plate Readers

License plate readers (LPRs) are high-speed cameras and information systems that read vehicle license plates in real time using optical recognition technology. It is both a scanning and an information technology. The LPR looks like a camera and is mounted on a vehicle or at a fixed location. The LPR can scan the license plates of moving or parked vehicles. Once a plate is scanned, the license plate number, date, time, and location of the observation, as well as a photo, are stored on a server. The technology then compares the data against an existing database of plates that are of interest to law enforcement, such as lists of stolen vehicles or vehicle owners with open warrants. If a match is made, a signal alerts the officer to proceed with further confirmation and investigation. Hundreds of cars can be scanned in this manner in very short periods of time.

LPRs may be used for many purposes, ranging from stolen vehicle enforcement to more complex surveillance and predictive functions. LPRs can be assigned to mobile patrol units or deployed at fixed locations. While LPRs serve an important surveillance function, they can also be viewed as information technologies, as the data they collect can be stored, analyzed, and searched for investigative purposes.[27] LPRs may help police reduce crime through deterrence and the apprehension (and thus incapacitation) of offenders.[28]

LPR technology is becoming increasingly common among police agencies. According to the Police Executive Research Forum, a large majority of agencies (85 percent) in their membership plan to acquire or increase their use of LPRs during the next five years. On average, these same agencies expect that 25 percent of their vehicles will have LPRs on board in five years.[29]

One of the major issues with LPRs is inaccurate data. License plate readers are entirely dependent on the quality of data in which the images are compared to. Data collected from LPR devices are compared to "hot lists" that consist of information about vehicles that have been stolen or are under surveillance. Privacy can be a concern for the use of LPRs. Access to an LPR database should be restricted to police users who have a specific and approved reason to access the database for a lawful purpose that includes both a need to know and a right to know the information. There are many other decisions that must be made about the use of LPRs, including when an officer can turn it on and in what circumstances it will be used.

Christopher Koper and colleagues recently evaluated LPRs to establish their utility in crime reduction.[30] They conducted an experiment using 18 crime hotspots in a suburban jurisdiction. Nine of these locations were randomly selected to receive additional patrols over 11 weeks. Officers used mobile computing technology primarily for surveillance and enforcement (e.g., checking automobile license plates and running checks on people during traffic stops and field interviews). They noted both advantages and disadvantages to using mobile technologies. Officers did not often use technology for strategic problem-solving and crime prevention. Basic applications of mobile computing may have little if any measurable impact on crime reduction in the field. Koper and his colleagues note that greater training and emphasis on strategic uses of technology for problem-solving and crime prevention, and greater attention to its behavioral effects on officers, might enhance its application for crime reduction.

Closed-Circuit Television (CCTV)

Another advancement that police departments have experimented with is closed-circuit television (CCTV). CCTV programs use surveillance cameras in public and private areas in an attempt to prevent property and personal crime. Some systems use a bulletproof casing, night-vision capability, motion detection, and advanced zoom and automatic tracking capacities, but many more existing systems are much simpler. More common CCTV installations include a number of cameras connected to a control room where human operators watch a bank of television screens. Not all CCTV systems are police-monitored—but many are. There are many challenges associated with maintaining a CCTV system including:[31]

1. Assessing your needs and budget before investing
2. Planning ahead for maintenance, infrastructure, and other ongoing costs
3. Planning camera locations to maximize the view-shed

4. Considering integration with other technology (e.g., gunshot detection systems, crime mapping software)

5. Balancing privacy protection with system utility

6. Weighing the costs and benefits to using active monitoring

7. Integrating camera systems with existing practices and procedures

8. Setting and managing realistic expectations for video footage quality

9. Using surveillance systems to complement, not replace, routine policing, investigations, and legal proceedings

10. Incorporating video evidence with witness testimony in court

But how does this relate to patrol? CCTV is not a physical barrier. It is still highly situational, and does have some crime prevention capacity in the right situations. The primary preventative goal is to change the offender's perception so that the offender believes if they commit a crime, they will be caught. For this crime prevention process to succeed, two elements must exist:

1. The offender must be aware of the cameras' presence.

2. The offender must believe the cameras present enough risk of capture to negate the rewards of the intended crime.

The integration of CCTV with proactive police activity has been found to generate a crime control benefit greater than what has generally been believed. Standalone camera deployment seems particularly effective in the case of street-level crime. Overall reductions in violence and social disorder have been achieved when departments use a special operator to monitor cameras and directly communicate with patrol cars dedicated to responding to incidents observed by the operator.[32]

In sum, CCTV systems appear to be a promising method to increase police effectiveness. This conclusion is supported by a recent analysis of over 40 years of CCTV data collected in a variety of studies. The evidence suggested that CCTV can provide crime reduction benefits and that, if anything, its use should be expanded, especially when focusing on protection of vehicles and other property.[33] The largest and most consistent effects of CCTV were observed in parking lots where potential thieves were deterred by visible and omnipresent video cameras. Evidence of other significant crime reductions within other settings, particularly residential areas, was also uncovered. CCTV had the greatest benefits when police deployed multiple interventions, such as community outreach or rapid response patrol. CCTV is not without its critics.

Advocates have expressed privacy concerns and the potential effect that CCTV could have on public life. In particular, there is concern that video footage could be used to violate the civil liberties of community members.[34] For example, there is the potential for inappropriate surveillance or the misuse of video footage by government employees. Nancy LaVigne and colleagues note that CCTV may also give potential victims a false sense of security, which causes them to let their guard down.[35] In terms of logistics, there is some concern that

CCTV is a powerful tool for preventing and solving crimes. It enables police officers to monitor public spaces and private properties, gather evidence, and track the movements of suspects. It deters would-be criminals who know they are being watched.

Michael Vi/Shutterstock.com

CCTV can displace crime to areas where there are fewer cameras.[36] In addition, the cost of setting up a functional CCTV system may not be warranted given the amount of crime in a community.[37]

Automatic Vehicle Location (AVL) Systems

Another effort utilized by police involves automatic vehicle location (AVL) systems. AVL provides a way of automatically determining and transmitting the geographic location of a vehicle. This data, from one or more vehicles, may then be collected by a vehicle tracking system for a picture of vehicle travel.

Criminologist David Weisburd and his colleagues examined whether information on where the police patrol drawn from **automatic vehicle location (AVL)** systems could be used to increase the amount of directed patrol time at high-crime police beats and crime hotspots, and whether such increases would lead to reductions in crime. They examined 232 police beats that were randomly allocated to an experimental or control condition. In the experimental condition, the police commanders knew the amount of time that police spent in beats and crime hotspots. This information was not provided to commanders in the control condition. Over a 13-week period, assigned patrol time, unallocated patrol time, total patrol time, and crime were tracked at both police beats and crime hotspots.

Weisburd and his colleagues found that information generated from AVL can in fact be used to increase directed patrol time at crime hot spots, and that these increased levels of patrol will lead to reductions in crime.[38] Before implementation, departments should discuss under what circumstances AVL will be used and whether data generated will be used to discipline officers or evaluate their performances. There are many considerations for both officers and the community associated with its adoption.

automatic vehicle location (AVL)

AVL provides a way of automatically determining and transmitting the geographic location of a vehicle.

High-Definition Surveying (HDS)

Traditionally, to investigate and evaluate a crime scene, detectives relied on photographic evidence and two-dimensional drawings. However, it can be difficult to visualize the positional relationships of evidence with two-dimensional tools. Now, through a combination of laser and computer technology, high-definition surveying (HDS) creates a virtual crime scene that allows investigators to maneuver every piece of evidence.

High-definition surveying gives law enforcement a complete picture of a crime scene. HDS reflects a laser light off objects in the crime scene and back to a digital sensor, creating three-dimensional spatial coordinates that are calculated and stored using algebraic equations. An HDS device projects light in the form of a laser in a 360-degree horizontal circumference, measuring millions of points and creating a "point cloud." The data points are bounced back to the receiver, collected, converted, and used to create a virtual image of any location. A personal computer can now take the data file and project that site onto any screen.

Not only does HDS technology allow the crime scene to be preserved exactly, but the perspective can also be manipulated to provide additional clues. For instance, if the crime scene is the front room of an apartment, the three-dimensional image allows the investigator to move around and examine different points of view. Or if a victim was found seated, an investigator can later show a jury what the victim might have seen just before the crime occurred. If witnesses outside said that they looked in a living room window, an investigator can zoom around and view what the witnesses could or could not have seen through that window. HDS technology can also limit crime scene contamination.

Investigators may inadvertently touch an object at a crime scene, leaving their fingerprints, or they may move or take evidence from the scene, perhaps by picking up fibers on their shoes. Evidence is compromised if moved or disturbed from its resting place, which may contaminate the scene and undermine the case. HDS technology is a "standoff" device, allowing investigators to approach the scene in stages by scanning from the outer perimeter and moving inward, reducing the chances of contamination. The investigative and prosecutorial value of virtual crime scenes is evident. If an HDS device is used at the scene, detectives, prosecutors, and juries can return to a crime scene in its preserved state. Showing a jury exactly what a witness could or could not have seen can be very valuable.

Biometrics

biometrics

Automated methods of recognizing a person based on a physiological or behavioral characteristic.

Biometrics is the measurement and statistical analysis of people's unique physical and behavioral characteristics. The technology is mainly used for identification and access control or for identifying individuals who are under surveillance. It is an automated method of recognizing a person based on a physiological or behavioral characteristic.[39] Some biometric measures, such as fingerprint identification, have been used for years by law enforcement to identify criminals. However, recent improvements in computer technology have expanded the different types of measures that can be used for identification. Biometrics is now used to identify individuals based on voice, retina, facial features, and handwriting identification, just to name a few. The central issue is that biometric authentication technologies pose privacy and security concerns: once biometric data has been compromised, there is no way to undo the damage.

The field of biometrics can be used by all levels of government, including the military and law enforcement, and is also helpful in private businesses. Financial institutions, retail shopping, and health and social fields can all use biometrics as a way to limit access to financial information or to secure Internet sites. As opposed to current personal identification methods, such as personal identification numbers (PINs) used for bank machines and Internet transactions, biometric authenticators are unique to the user and as a result cannot be stolen and used without that individual's knowledge.

The process of recording biometric data occurs in four steps. First, the raw biometric data are captured or recorded by a video camera or a fingerprint reading device. Second, the distinguishing characteristics of the raw data are used to create a biometric template. Third, the template is changed into a mathematical representation of the biometric sample and is stored in a database. Finally, a verification process will occur when an individual attempts to gain access to a restricted site. The individual will have to present their fingerprint or retina to be read and then matched to the biometric sample on record. Once verification is made, the individual will have access to restricted areas.

Currently, a number of programs are in effect. Immigration and Customs Enforcement has been using hand geometry systems at major U.S. airports to check frequent international travelers. Casinos around the country have started to implement facial recognition software into their buildings so that security is notified when a known cheater enters their premises. Although biometrics are touted as a huge technological advancement, this pioneering field has been stalled due to concerns regarding privacy, human rights, and systematic prejudice, with some biometrics technologies, such as facial and voice recognition, shown to produce racial and ethnic bias that could see innocent people jailed or refused essential benefits. MIT researchers pointed to the imagery data sets used to develop these facial recognition technologies, found to be 77 percent male and 83 percent White, as the reason behind the disparity in performance.[40]

Integrated Automated Fingerprint Identification Systems

The use of computerized automated fingerprint identification systems such as the FBI's Integrated Automated Fingerprint Identification System (IAFIS) is growing in the United States. Using mathematical models, IAFIS can classify fingerprints and identify up to 250 characteristics (minutiae) of the print. These automated systems use high-speed silicon chips to plot each point of minutiae and count the number of ridge lines between that point and its four nearest neighbors, which substantially improves their speed and accuracy over earlier systems.

Some police departments report that computerized fingerprint systems are allowing them to make over 100 identifications per month from fingerprints taken at crime scenes. IAFIS files have been regionalized. The Western Identification Network (WIN), for example, consists of eight central site members (Alaska, Idaho, Montana, Nevada, Oregon, Utah, Wyoming, and Portland Police Bureau), two interface members (California and Washington), multiple local members, and six federal members (Drug Enforcement Administration, Federal Bureau of Investigation, Immigration and Naturalization Service, Internal Revenue Service, Postal Inspection Service, and Secret Service).[41] When it began, the system had a centralized automated database of 900,000 fingerprint records; today, with the addition of new jurisdictions (Alaska, California, and Washington), the system's number of searchable fingerprint records has increased to more than 14 million. IAFIS can now search through 8 million fingerprints in 75 minutes, a task that would take more than 40 years by hand.

IAFIS has the ability to perform a number of functions that include the following:

- Searching a set of known fingerprints against an existing database and returning with results that are better than 99 percent accurate.

- Searching a latent print from a crime scene or evidence against a database.

- Searching a latent from a crime scene against a latent on file from other crime scenes.

- Interfacing of IAFIS with other criminal justice information systems for added efficiency.

- Interfacing of IAFIS with digital mug shot systems and live scan fingerprint capture devices.[42]

Technology is constantly improving the effectiveness and reliability of the IAFIS system, making it easier to use and more efficient in identifying suspects.[43]

DNA Testing

DNA, or deoxyribonucleic acid, is genetic material found in human cells and those of almost all other organisms. Nearly every cell in a person's body has the same DNA. Human DNA consists of about 3 billion bases, and more than 99 percent of those bases are the same in all people. The order, or sequence, of these bases determines the information available for building and maintaining an organism, similar to the way in which letters of the alphabet appear in a certain order to form words and sentences.[44]

DNA Profiling

DNA profiling

The identification of a criminal suspect by matching DNA samples taken from their person with specimens found at the crime scene.

DNA profiling is a procedure that gained national attention during the O. J. Simpson trial allows suspects to be identified on the basis of the genetic material found in hair, blood, and other body tissues and fluids. When DNA is used as evidence in a rape trial, DNA segments are taken from the victim, the suspect, and blood and semen found on the victim. A DNA match indicates a 4-billion-to-1 likelihood that the suspect is the offender.

Every U.S. state and nearly every industrialized country now maintains DNA databases of convicted offenders.[45] These databases allow comparison of crime scene DNA to samples taken at other crime scenes and to offenders known to the police. The United States has more than 3 million samples of offenders/arrestees in its state and federal DNA databases. The United States is not alone in gathering this material: Great Britain requires that almost any violation of law results in the collection of DNA of the violator.[46]

Leading the way in the development of the most advanced forensic techniques is the Forensic Science Research and Training Center, operated by the FBI in Washington, DC, and Quantico, Virginia. The lab provides information and services to hundreds of crime labs throughout the United States. The National Institute of Justice is also sponsoring research to identify a wider variety of DNA segments for testing and is involved in developing a polymerase chain reaction (PCR)-based DNA-profiling examination using fluorescent detection that will reduce the time required for DNA profiling.

The FBI is now operating the Combined DNA Index System (CODIS), which has assisted in nearly 50,000 investigations. CODIS is a computerized database that allows DNA taken at a crime scene to be searched electronically to find matches against samples taken from convicted offenders and from other crime scenes. To this end, the FBI has the National DNA Indexing System (NDIS), which contains:

- DNA profiles from genetic evidence collected at crime scenes. This is generally relegated for serious crimes as resources are limited and police agencies must make choices about which crimes to pursue.

- The NDIS also contains data from convicted offenders, and most states require that they provide genetic samples.

Early on, the CODIS linked evidence taken from crime scenes in Jacksonville, Florida, to ones in Washington, DC, thereby tying nine crimes to a single offender.[47] When Timothy Spence was executed in Virginia on April 27, 1994, he was the first person convicted and executed almost entirely on the basis of DNA evidence.[48] More recently, CODIS has been expanded to include a wealth of information, including profiles of individuals convicted of crimes—and even of arrestees, if state law permits.[49] Critics of this information gathering cite concerns that some arrestees are innocent and that retaining data from innocent persons could be improperly used and constitute a violation of privacy and civil liberties.[50]

Using DNA evidence has become crucial to many investigations and juries now expect that cases will include this type of evidence. DNA evidence—and the forensic sciences in general—are not without some problems, however. A recent study reported that although there is widespread knowledge about the utility of forensic evidence, it is not being adequately used by law enforcement agencies.[51] The authors found that a significant number of unsolved homicides and rapes with forensic evidence had not been submitted to laboratories for analysis. And when cases with DNA evidence make it to trial, jurors are sometimes confused by the complexities involved.[52]

Drones

A drone refers to an unpiloted aircraft. Another term for it is an "unmanned aerial vehicle," and is many times equipped with cameras for still pictures or video recordings. Police departments across the country have purchased small unmanned surveillance vehicles, not unlike the drones used to track terrorists in Iraq and Afghanistan, for the purpose of tracking drug dealers and other people of interest. Historically, the Federal Aviation Administration (FAA) made it very difficult for law enforcement agencies to secure approval for conducting drone patrols. In February 2012, however, President Barack Obama signed a law requiring the FAA to write rules on how it would license police and other public safety agencies to fly drones at low altitudes, making it likely that small aircraft containing high-definition cameras, sensors, and recording equipment would soon be flying over many more American cities. Later that year, the FAA released its first list of agencies that were authorized to fly drones. That list has since expanded.[53]

■ Hundreds of law enforcement agencies are now authorized to fly drones, but it is not clear that many of them are doing so. In addition, the FAA generally places limitations on drone use, such as by limiting them to a defined block of airspace and/or daytime hours.[54]

■ Supporters of drone use in domestic law enforcement see the technology as a valuable tool necessary for apprehending law breakers. The police cannot be everywhere, they claim, so an extra set of "eyes" in the sky could prove helpful in fighting crime. Supporters also argue that gun detectors, security cameras, tracking devices, and other technologies are already in use, so drones are just one more tool that can be added to the law enforcement arsenal. Drones are also affordable compared to new helicopters and airplanes. Critics, however, claim that drone use, though perhaps useful for catching criminals, will also let "Big Brother" peer into the private lives of law-abiding citizens.

Critical Thinking

Can the use of drones be considered an invasion of privacy or a violation of the Fourth Amendment? Why or why not?

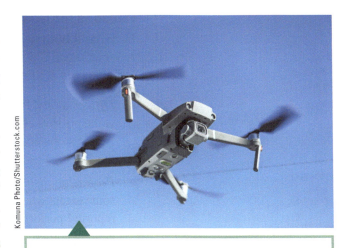

Komuna Photo/Shutterstock.com

Police drones are mainly used for surveillance. The advantage is that they can replace helicopters that require specially trained pilots. A drone can be kept in the trunk of a patrol car and deployed at a moment's notice. Drones allow officers to maintain focus on what's happening around them and safely navigate obstacles without the threat of engaging in chases that threaten harm to officers and civilians.

Body-worn cameras are widely used by police and law enforcement agencies in the United States. They are worn by officers in the performance of duties that require them to have contact with the public. They can then determine whether police acted appropriately during the interaction. Despite their widespread use there is little definitive evidence that they are an effective technology that can improve police relations with the public.

Artas/iStock/Getty Images

In-Car and Body-Worn Cameras (BWCs)

During the 1990s, lawsuits alleging racial bias in police traffic stops began to be filed. This, coupled with some questionable shootings and other police–suspect encounters, prompted many agencies to install cameras in their patrol cars. Between 2000 and 2004, the Office of Community-Oriented Policing Services in the U.S. Justice Department awarded over $20 million in grants to local police departments so they could purchase and install in-car camera systems. Before the funding program, 11 percent of state police and highway patrol vehicles were equipped with cameras. A few years later, nearly 75 percent of these agencies were able to equip their police cars with cameras.

More recently, a number of police departments around the country have begun equipping their officers with body-worn cameras. While dashboard cameras and cameras mounted on weaponry have either a limited view shield or are only activated in certain instances, body-worn cameras have the capability to provide a continuous loop of an officer's activity from a first-person perspective. It has been argued that the technology could be extremely beneficial in a number of areas (as is any video evidence) and enhancing the public's perception of procedural fairness.[55] That is, officers will be inclined to respect the due process of law if police and citizens are recorded. Proponents, especially within policing, contend BWCs are a preferred technology because of the ability for third parties to see an incident in its entirety from the perspective of the officer.[56]

Reasons for Cameras

In-car and body-worn cameras offer several advantages. The International Association of Chiefs of Police (IACP) came up with several reasons why this technology is desirable:

Critical Thinking

Although many officers are/were opposed to them, please list some positive reasons to have a body-worn camera.

- *Officer safety.* Perhaps the single most beneficial feature of an in-car camera is the positive effect it can have on officer safety. Having a recording of, say, traffic stops enables the officers to view it and critique their actions after the fact.

- *Professionalism and performance.* Officers report altering their behavior to some extent when in front of the camera. The IACP found that many officers reported performing to the best of their ability, knowing their actions were being recorded. Other officers argue that a camera's recordings are useful for preparing courtroom testimony; there is less need to rely on memory, which bolsters an officer's credibility when they are testifying.

- *Defense against complaints.* A recording of a police–citizen contact helps protect the officer and the department for which they work from meritless complaints or lawsuits. The IACP study revealed that roughly half of citizen complaints are withdrawn once complainants are made aware that a camera recorded the alleged incident. BWCs have repeatedly exonerated officers.[57]

- *Leadership benefits.* Police administrators regard in-car cameras as desirable because they aid in investigations of misconduct and promote accountability of officers working in the field. Years of research on public perceptions of police have revealed that professionalism and courtesy promote citizen satisfaction and support. Cameras help further this.

- *Training.* Just as individual officers may review the recordings from their in-car cameras, so can training personnel use the recordings to arm trainees with the knowledge they need and stories of "what not to do."

- *Improve police legitimacy.* Body-worn cameras have been shown to improve police legitimacy, convincing the public that police can act appropriately among community members that police departments play an appropriate role in implementing rules governing public conduct. Placing BWCs on police officers has been suggested as a potentially important response to police legitimacy crises.

Criticisms of Cameras

Cameras are not supported by all concerned. To this day, some agencies have yet to install cameras because of resistance on the part of line officers and their collective bargaining units. In Montgomery, Alabama, officials agreed to install in-car cameras in the city's police cruisers years ago, mainly in response to one officer's shooting of an unarmed suspect, but union officials say the cameras threaten officer privacy. Critics make these points about in-car cameras:

- *Distraction from the job.* If cameras encourage officers to be on their best behavior, then some of them may obsess over the camera so much that their actions amount to performing for the camera rather than focusing on the task at hand. A small number of officers in the IACP study reported that the cameras distracted them from violators. Sometimes the officers would even worry more about positioning the camera for optimal viewing than about guarding their own safety.

- *Too much reliance on the camera.* Some officers also reported relying more on recordings of their stops than on their own memory. This could be detrimental from a court testimony standpoint, and some officers reported that their note-taking skills suffered as a consequence of heavy reliance on technology.

- *Too much information.* There is a concern that the cameras reveal too much information. Union challenges, such as those in Montgomery, Alabama, underscore the controversy associated with requiring that officers always be on their toes because a camera is recording their every move. Is this desirable? Many agencies compromise by setting the cameras to turn on only when the vehicle's flashing lights and/or siren are turned on.

- *Stress and job performance.* The IACP study found that some officers reported increased stress levels associated with the cameras. A small percentage reported reduced job satisfaction. Some officers even reported making fewer traffic stops because of the presence of a camera.

- *Technology challenges.* There are challenges associated with implementing body-worn cameras. For example, Round Lake Park, Illinois, Police Department BWC. For more than eight months, BWCs were recording the entire shift, even as officers were taking bathroom breaks and involved in other non-essential police work. This was a misuse of technology.[58]

Assessments of BWC

The first assessment of BWCs in the United States was conducted in Rialto, California. The evaluation showed that with BWCs there was a reduction in overall citizen complaints.[59] Specifically, during the 12-month Rialto experiment, use of force by officers wearing cameras fell by 59 percent and reports against officers dropped by 87 percent against the previous year's Figures. Interestingly, complaints and use of force decreased even when the cameras were not in use—presenting a spillover effect. The evaluation also noted that there is great training potential in BWC footage. The footage "could be used to mentor officers about how they conduct themselves specifically." Junior officers train with their own footage and potentially improve their own performance.

Since the Rialto study was undertaken in 2012, other evaluations have also shown evidence of positive impacts of BWC use for policing agencies generally and officers specifically. Most notably, there was a decrease in overall complaints, an increase in complaints ruled unfounded, an increase in arrests, better success in prosecution of domestic violence cases, and no decrease in citizen contacts; the use of BWC technology has been shown to reduce arrests in neighborhoods whose residents are predominantly people of color.[60] Officers, however, reported no change in paperwork burden or ease of use of the technology.

Wesley Jennings and colleagues found in a study of BWC use by the Orlando Police Department that BWCs reduced force and external complaints and also improved evidence collection and report writing.[61] There is also evidence of variation in departmental acceptance of BWCs both before and after they were deployed: some had negative perceptions of BWCs while others were more positive. Once activated, officers seemed to approve of BWCs, finding them easy to use and comfortable, though most remained uncertain whether their use could actually impact citizen behaviors.[62]

As promising as these new technologies are, in times of economic downturn, it is often difficult to maintain them after budget cutbacks. According to the Police Executive Research Forum, technology is one of the first components of a policing agency to be impacted (after hiring freezes and layoffs) when budgets are decreased.[63]

Summary

LO1 Trace the development of police technology.

August Vollmer, considered to be the father of modern policing and the professionalization movement, developed an administrative reform agenda that, among other elements, included advancements in science and technology. Another advance was the patrol car, which allowed for quicker access to citizens and calls for service. By the 1920s, the use of cars was widespread. The two-way radio was used in the 1930s and it eliminated communication problems. The radio was valuable because it increased supervision and internal communications. In the 1970s, federal government support for criminal justice greatly influenced police operations. During the decade, the Law Enforcement Assistance Administration (LEAA) funded innovative research on police work and advanced training of police officers. Technological innovations involving computers transformed the way police kept records, investigated crimes, and communicated with one another. State training academies improved the way police learned to deal with such issues as job stress, community conflict, and interpersonal relations.

LO2 Identify the problems associated with modern technology.

While many experts may applaud the advances in law enforcement technology, others are more cautious with their praise. In her research, Ruha Benjamin discusses "the New Jim Code," which is described as using technology that reflects and reproduces existing inequalities, but is promoted as more objective or progressive than previous systems. The new technology includes materials and equipment that police use to catch criminals and prevent crime, such as body-worn cameras (BWCs), thermal imaging, and gunshot detection technology. It also involves software and information systems that improve the effectiveness of police operations.

LO3 Compare and contrast the various types of soft technology.

Soft technology relies on the gathering and processing of information to improve police operations. Take for instance the identification of geographic "hotspots" where a majority of crimes are concentrated. Computer mapping programs can translate addresses into map coordinates that allow departments to identify problem areas for particular crimes, such as drug dealing or burglary. Computer maps are used to identify the location, time of day, and linkage among criminal events and to concentrate police forces accordingly. The simplest maps display crime locations or concentrations and can be used to help direct patrols to the places they are most needed. Mapping technology has recently been combined with GPS.

Another well-known element of soft technology is to identify crime patterns through a process called data mining. By discovering patterns in crimes, computers can be programmed to recognize a particular way of working a crime and thereby identify suspects most likely to fit the profile. The analysis of large data sets has led to what is now called *predictive policing*.

LO4 List and discuss the uses of hard technology.

Hard technology typically involves tangible equipment that is designed to help police prevent crime, identify suspects, and bring them to justice. These include but are not limited to such devices as as less-than-lethal weapons, drones, thermal imagers, and body armor equipment. Law enforcement agencies today employ a wide variety of hard technology to deal with crime and enforce the law. Take for instance the use of small, unmanned surveillance drones, for the purpose of tracking drug dealers and monitoring neighborhoods. Hundreds of law enforcement agencies are now authorized to fly drones. Supporters of drone use in domestic law enforcement see the technology as a valuable tool necessary for apprehending law breakers. They have an extra set of "eyes" in the sky, helpful in fighting crime. Supporters also argue that gun detectors, security cameras, tracking devices, and other technologies are already in use, so drones are just one more tool that can be added to the law enforcement arsenal. Drones are also affordable compared to new helicopters and airplanes. Critics, however, claim that drone use, though perhaps useful for catching criminals, will also let "Big Brother" peer into the private lives of law-abiding citizens. Another approach relies on the measurement and statistical analysis of people's unique physical and behavioral characteristics referred to as biometrics. The technology is mainly used for identification and access control or for identifying individuals who are under surveillance. Biometrics is now used to identify individuals based on voice, retina, facial features, and handwriting identification, just to name a few.

Key Terms

soft technology, 373
Computer Statistics (CompStat) program, 373
crime mapping, 374
data mining, 375
hard technology, 376
thermal imaging camera, 377
automatic vehicle location (AVL), 383
biometrics, 384
DNA profiling, 386

Notes

1. Peter W. Singer, "Police Used a Robot to Kill—The Key Questions," *CNN*, July 16, 2016, http://www.cnn.com /2016/07/09/opinions/dallas-robot-questions-singer/.
2. Lois Pliant, "Information Management," *Police Chief* 61 (1994), 31–35.
3. William M. Oliver, *August Vollmer: The Father of American Policing* (Durham, NC: Carolina Academic Press, 2017).
4. Ibid.
5. Pamela Irving Jackson, *Minority Group Threat, Crime, and Policing* (New York, NY: Praeger, 1989).
6. For an overview of early federal support for local law enforcement, see John L. Worrall, "The Effects of Local Law Enforcement Block Grants on Serious Crime," *Criminology and Public Policy* 7 (2008), 325–350.
7. James Byrne and Gary Marx, "Technological Innovations in Crime Prevention and Policing: A Review of the Research on Implementation and Impact," *Cahiers Politiestudies Jaargang* 20 (2011), 17–40, at 20.
8. Ruha Benjamin, *Race after Technology: Abolitionist Tools for the New Jim Code* (New York, NY: Wiley, 2019).
9. Ibid.
10. William Bratton, *Turnaround: How America's Top Cop Reversed the Crime Epidemic* (New York, NY: Random House, 1998).
11. James J. Willis, Stephen D. Mastrofski, and David Weisburd, "CompStat and Bureaucracy: A Case Study of Challenges and Opportunities for Change," *Justice Quarterly* 21 (2004), 463–496.
12. This section is based on Derek Paulsen, "To Map or Not to Map: Assessing the Impact of Crime Maps on Police Officer Perceptions of Crime*," International Journal of Police Science and Management* 6 (2004), 234–246; William W. Bratton and Peter Knobler, *Turnaround: How America's Top Cop Reversed the Crime Epidemic* (New York, NY: Random House, 1998), p. 289; Jeremy Travis, "Computerized Crime Mapping," *NIJ News*, January 1999.
13. James J. Willis, Stephen D. Mastrofski, and David Weisburd, "Making Sense of COMPSTAT: A Theory-Based Analysis of Organizational Change in Three Police Departments," *Law and Society Review* 41 (2007), 147–188.
14. Chicago Police Department, http://gis.chicagopolice.org/, accessed May 2014.
15. Nancy G. La Vigne and Julie Wartell, *Mapping Across Boundaries: Regional Crime Analysis* (Washington, DC: Police Executive Research Forum, 2001).
16. http://www.youtube.com/watch?v=9JNqPsh7kmU, accessed May 2014.
17. Kevin Corbley, "GPS Photo Mapping in Law Enforcement," *Law Enforcement Technology* 35 (2008), 96, 98–101.
18. Geoffrey Gluckman, "Eye in the Sky: GPS Has Changed the Way Law Enforcement Does Fleet Management," *Law Enforcement Technology* 33 (2006), 68, 70–75.
19. Rebecca Kanable, "Dig into Data Mining," *Law Enforcement Technology* 34 (2007), 62, 64–68, 70.
20. National Institute of Justice, "Overview of Predictive Policing," June 9, 2014, Department of Justice.
21. Walter L. Perry, Brian McInnis, Carter C. Price, Susan C. Smith, and John S. Hollywood, "Predictive Policing: The Role of Crime Forecasting in Law Enforcement Operations," (Rand Corporation, 2013) p. 117.
22. National Institute of Justice, "Types of Less-Lethal Devices," *NIJ*, http://www.nij.gov/topics/technology/less-lethal/pages /types.aspx.
23. NIJ, "Less-Lethal Technology: Conducted Energy Devices," http://www.nij.gov/topics/technology/less-lethal/Pages /conducted-energy-devices.aspx.
24. Millivision, http://www.millivision.com/technology.html, accessed May 2014.
25. Rebecca Kanable, "Setting Up Surveillance Downtown," *Law Enforcement Technology* (February 2008), http://www.officer .com/article/10249122/setting-up-surveillance-downtown, accessed May 2014.
26. Oak Ridge National Laboratory, http://infohouse.p2ric.org /ref/16/15985.htm, accessed May 2014.
27. Christopher S. Koper, Cynthia Lum, James J. Willis, Dan J. Woods, and Julie Hibdon, "Realizing the Potential of Technology in Policing: A Multisite Study of the Social, Organizational, and Behavioral Aspects of Implementing Police Technologies," National Institute of Justice, December 2015.
28. Christopher S. Koper, Bruce G. Taylor, and Daniel J. Woods, "A Randomized Test of Initial and Residual Deterrence from Directed Patrols and Use of License Plate Readers at Crime Hot Spots," *Journal of Experimental Criminology* 9, no. 2 (2013), 213–244.
29. Police Executive Research Forum, Critical Issues in Policing Series "How Are Innovations in Technology Transforming Policing?," January 2012, http://www.policeforum.org/assets /docs/Critical_Issues_Series/how%20are%20innovations%20 in%20technology%20transforming%20policing%202012.pdf.
30. Christopher S. Koper, Cynthia Lum, and Julie Hibdon, "The Uses and Impacts of Mobile Computing Technology in Hotspot Policing," *Evaluation Review* 39, no. 6 (2015), 587–624.
31. Nancy G. La Vigne, Samantha S. Lowry, Joshua A. Markman, and Allison M. Dwyer, "Evaluating the Use of Public Surveillance Cameras for Crime Control and Prevention," Washington, DC: US Department of Justice, Office of Community Oriented Policing Services. Urban Institute, Justice Policy Center (2011).
32. Eric L. Piza, Andrew M. Gilchrist, Joel M. Caplan, Leslie W. Kennedy, and Brian A. O'Hara, "The Financial Implications of Merging Proactive CCTV Monitoring and Directed Police Patrol: A Cost–Benefit Analysis," *Journal of Experimental Criminology* 12, no. 3 (2016), 403–429.
33. Eric L. Piza, Brandon C. Welsh, David P. Farrington, and Amanda L. Thomas, "CCTV Surveillance for Crime Prevention. A 40-Year Systematic Review with Meta-analysis," *Journal of Criminology and Public Policy* 18 (2019), 135–159.
34. Nancy G. La Vigne, Samantha S. Lowry, Joshua A. Markman, and Allison M. Dwyer, "Evaluating the Use of Public Surveillance Cameras for Crime Control and Prevention," Washington, DC: US Department of Justice, Office of Community Oriented Policing Services. Urban Institute, Justice Policy Center, 2011, https://www.urban.org/sites/default/files /publication/27556/412403-evaluating-the-use-of-public -surveillance-cameras-for-crime-control-and-prevention_1.pdf.
35. Ibid.
36. E. L. Piza, J. M. Caplan, L. W. Kennedy, A. M. Gilchrist, "The Effects of Merging Proactive CCTV Monitoring with Directed Police Patrol: A Randomized Controlled Trial," *Journal of Experimental Criminology* 11, no. 1 (2015), 43–69.
37. Matthew P. J. Ashby, "The Value of CCTV Surveillance Cameras as an Investigative Tool: An Empirical Analysis," *European Journal on Criminal Policy and Research* 23, no. 3 (2017), 441–459.
38. David Weisburd, Elizabeth R. Groff, Greg Jones, Breanne Cave, Karen L. Amendola, Sue-Ming Yang, and Rupert F.

Emison, "The Dallas Patrol Management Experiment: Can AVL Technologies Be Used to Harness Unallocated Patrol Time for Crime Prevention?," *Journal of Experimental Criminology* 11, no. 3 (2015), 367–391.

39. "Introduction to Biometrics," http://www.biometrics.org /introduction.php Fernando L. Podio, "Biometrics— Technologies for Highly Secure Personal Authentication," *ITL Bulletin* (National Institute of Standards and Technology), May 2001.

40. https://www.raconteur.net/technology/biometrics-ethics-bias/.

41. Western Identification Network, http://www.winid.org/winid/, accessed May 2018.

42. Kenneth R. Moses, et al., "Automated Fingerprint Identification System (AFIS)," Scientific Working Group on Friction Ridge Analysis Study and Technology and National Institute of Justice (eds.), *SWGFAST-The Fingerprint Sourcebook* (2011), 1–33.

43. Weipeng Zhang, Yan Yuan Tang, and Xinge You, "Fingerprint Enhancement Using Wavelet Transform Combined with Gabor Filter," *International Journal of Pattern Recognition and Artificial Intelligence* 18 (2004), 1391–1406.

44. Medisine Plus, "What is DNA?," U.S. National Library of Medicine (n.d.) https://medlineplus.gov/genetics/understanding /basics/dna/.

45. Frederick Bieber, Charles Brenner, and David Lazer, "Finding Criminals Through DNA of Their Relatives," *Science* 312 (2006), 1315–1316.

46. Ibid.

47. "FBI's DNA Profile Clearinghouse Announces First 'Cold Hit,'" *Criminal Justice Newsletter* 16 (1999), 5.

48. "South Side Strangler's Execution Cited as DNA Evidence Landmark," *Criminal Justice Newsletter* 2 (1994), 3.

49. Federal Bureau of Investigation, "CODIS: Combined DNA Index System," http://www.fbi.gov/about-us/lab/biometric-analysis /codis, accessed May 2014.

50. Karen Norrgard, "Forensics, DNA Fingerprinting, and CODIS," *Nature Education* 1 (2008), 1.

51. Kevin. J. Strom and Matthew J. Hickman, "Unanalyzed Evidence in Law-Enforcement Agencies: A National Examination of Forensic Processing in Police Departments," *Criminology and Public Policy* 9 (2010), 381–404.

52. Valerie Hans, David Kay, Michael Dann, Erin Farley, and Stephanie Albertson, "Science in the Jury Box: Jurors' Comprehension of Mitochondrial DNA Evidence," *Law and Human Behavior* 35 (2011), 60–71.

53. "Drone List Released by FAA Shows Which Police Departments Want to Fly Unmanned Aerial Vehicles," *Huffington Post*, http:// www.huffingtonpost.com/2013/02/08/drone-list-domestic-police -law-enforcement-surveillance_n_2647530.html, accessed May 2014. Refer to http://tinyurl.com/b8nvtsr for a list of agencies currently authorized to fly drones (accessed May 2018).

54. Federal Aviation Administration, "Fact Sheet—Unmanned Aircraft Systems (UAS)," http://www.faa.gov/news/fact_sheets /news_story.cfm?newsId=14153, accessed May 2018.

55. Alana Saulnier, Ryan Lahay, William P. McCarty, and Carrie Sanders, "The RIDE Study: Effects of Body-Worn Cameras on Public Perceptions of Police Interactions," *Criminology and Public Policy, Special Issue: Cutting-Edge Research in Police Policy and Practice* 19 (2020), 833–854.

56. James Byrne and Don Hummer, "Policing and Technology." In M. McGuire and T. Holt (eds.), *The Routledge Handbook of Technology, Crime, and Justice* (New York, NY: Routledge), pp. 375–389.

57. Michael E. Miller, "A Body Cam Caught a Cleveland Cop Acting Heroically. So Why Are Cops Afraid of Them?," October 9, 2015, https://www.washingtonpost.com/news/morning-mix /wp/2015/10/09/a-body-cam-caught-a-cleveland-cop-acting -heroically-so-why-are-cops-afraid-of-them/.

58. Chuck Goudie, "What Happens When Police Body Cams Don't Shut Off?," *ABC Eyewitness News 7*, Chicago, May 16, 2016, http://abc7chicago.com/news/what-happens-when-police -body-cams-dont-shut-off/1341468/.

59. Barak Ariel, William A. Farrar, and Alex Sutherland, "The Effect of Police Body-Worn Cameras on Use of Force and Citizens' Complaints Against the Police: A Randomized Controlled Trial," *Journal of Quantitative Criminology* 31, (2015), 509–535, https://doi.org/10.1007/s10940-014-9236-3.

60. Jessica Huff, "Do Body-Worn Cameras Reduce Disparities in Police Behavior in Minority Communities? Evidence of Nuanced Influences across Black and Hispanic Neighborhoods," *Criminology & Public Policy*, 21 (2022), 1–41; Charles M. Katz, David E. Choate, Justin R. Ready, and L. Nuño, "Evaluating the Impact of Officer Worn Body Cameras in the Phoenix Police Department," *Phoenix, AZ: Center for Violence Prevention and Community Safety, Arizona State University* (2014).

61. Wesley G. Jennings, Mathew D. Lynch, and Lorie A. Fridell, "Evaluating the Impact of Police Officer Body-Worn Cameras (BWCs) on Response-to-Resistance and Serious External Complaints: Evidence from the Orlando Police Department (OPD) Experience Utilizing a Randomized Controlled Experiment," *Journal of Criminal Justice* 43, no. 6 (2015), 480-486.

62. Janne E. Gaub, David E. Choate, Natalie Todak, Charles M. Katz, and Michael D. White, "Officer Perceptions of Body-Worn Cameras Before and After Deployment: A Study of Three Departments," *Police Quarterly* 19 no. 3, (2016), 275–302, https://doi.org/10.1177/1098611116653398

63. PERF (Police Executive Research Forum), *Policing and the Economic Downturn: Striving for Efficiency Is the New Normal* (Washington, DC: Police Executive Research Forum, 2013).

Glossary

accountability system A system that makes police supervisors responsible for the behavior of the officers in their command.

active shooter An individual actively engaged in killing or attempting to kill as many people as possible using a firearm.

Arizona Counter Terrorism Information Center A statewide intelligence system designed to combat terrorism. It consists of two divisions; one is unclassified and draws together personnel from various public safety agencies and the other operates in a secretive manner and is made up of personnel from the FBI's Joint Terrorism Task Force.

arrest To deprive a person of their freedom of movement. A police officer can legally arrest someone if a warrant has been issued or without a warrant if probable cause exists that the person has committed a crime at the time of the arrest.

arrest warrant An order, issued by a judge, directing officers to arrest a particular individual.

August Vollmer First police chief of Berkeley, California, and a leading figure in the development of the field of criminal justice in the United States.

automatic vehicle location (AVL) AVL provides a way of automatically determining and transmitting the geographic location of a vehicle.

bear arms The ability or requirement to keep weapons in defense of the city or town.

beats Specific zones designated as areas of police patrol.

bending granite Refers to the fact that police departments are reluctant to innovate and are set in their ways.

biometrics Automated methods of recognizing a person based on a physiological or behavioral characteristic.

blue curtain The secretive, insulated police culture that isolates officers from the rest of society.

blue fragility The level of discomfort or defensiveness felt when police officers are confronted with a level of accountability that they may not be used to or haven't had to deal with in the past.

bona fide occupational qualifications Employment standards linked to specific job tasks.

Bow Street Runners A group of private police out of Bow Street in London.

bribe A gratuity given to a public official in order to have them provide an illegal service.

broken windows Idea that signs of neighborhood disorder have a crime-generating influence at the neighborhood level.

Bureau of Alcohol, Tobacco, Firearms, and Explosives (ATF) Federal agency with jurisdiction over the illegal sale, importation, and criminal misuse of firearms and explosives and the distribution of untaxed liquor and cigarettes.

bus sweep Police investigation technique in which officers board a bus or train without suspicion of illegal activity and question passengers, asking for identification and seeking permission to search their baggage.

case fixing Accepting a gratuity in return for dropping charges or destroying evidence.

Christopher Commission (Independent Commission on the Los Angeles Police Department) Formed in April 1991 to conduct a full and fair examination of the structure and operation of the LAPD, including its recruitment and training practices, internal disciplinary system, and citizen complaint system.

clearance The identification of the offender and the development of sufficient evidence to charge them and take them into custody.

command and control The use of authority to take decisions and to issue directives, orders, instructions to police officers as they conduct operations.

community-oriented policing (COP) I concept that police and private citizens working together in creative ways can help solve contemporary community problems related to crime, fear of crime, disorder, and neighborhood decay.

community policing An attempt to involve the community as active partners with the police in solving community problems such as crime or quality-of-life issues.

compressed work weeks (CWW) A non-traditional work with longer than eight-hour shifts.

CompStat A data-driven approach to police management that uses data to identify problem areas and provides feedback on how well these legal and social problems are being handled by police.

Computer Statistics (CompStat) program A computerized system that gave local precinct commanders up-to-date information about where and when crime was occurring in their jurisdictions. Precinct commanders were given reports on crime problems and strategies to turn things around.

consent decree An agreement between the U.S. Department of Justice and a police agency intended to promote police integrity within an agency and to prevent conduct or actions that deprives individuals of their rights, privileges, or immunities protected by the U.S. Constitution.

constable The primary municipal law enforcement agent in urban areas.

crime control model A view of justice that places primary emphasis on the protection of citizens and the control of criminal behavior.

crime mapping Computer mapping programs that can translate addresses into map coordinates allowing police to identify problem areas for particular crimes, such as drug dealing.

CSI effect Refers to the influence television shows like *CSI: Crime Scene Investigation*, have on jurors and, as a result, juries now place heavy emphasis on forensic science in making their decisions and reaching a verdict.

curtilage Grounds or fields attached to a house.

cynicism The belief that most people's actions are motivated solely by personal needs and selfishness.

data mining Using sophisticated computer software to conduct analysis of behavior patterns in an effort to identify crime patterns and link them to suspects.

deadly force The intentional use of a firearm or other instrument resulting in a high probability of death.

defunding the police A call for budgeting less money for police and reinvesting those monies in other (preventative) public safety strategies. It has become a prominent idea in the national conversation around police reform.

Department of Homeland Security Agency assigned the mission of preventing terrorist attacks within the United States, reducing America's vulnerability to terrorism, and minimizing the damage and aiding the recovery from attacks that do occur.

discretion The decision to act, or not to act, based on an individual police officer's judgment about the best course of action to take in a given situation.

DNA profiling The identification of a criminal suspect by matching DNA samples taken from their person with specimens found at the crime scene.

double marginality According to Nicholas Alex, the social burden that Black police officers carry by being both racial minority group members and law enforcement officers.

downstream orientation When detectives consider the prosecutor's response when making decisions about a case.

Drug Enforcement Administration (DEA) The federal agency that enforces federal drug control laws.

due process model A view of justice that emphasizes the protection of the rights of the accused person as they move through the system.

Equal Employment Opportunity (EEO) Index A measure of the representativeness of a police department.

escalated force A situation in which the militancy of protestors was met by increased militancy by the police.

exclusionary rule The principle that prohibits using illegally obtained evidence in a trial.

extortion Demanding a gratuity in return for providing a legal service or overlooking an illegal activity.

federal civil rights violation Contraventions of Title 42, Section 1983 of the Civil Rights Act of 1871, which refers to the deprivation of constitutional rights by any government official.

Ferguson effect An allegation that police have shown restraint in doing their jobs in the wake of criticism following these widely publicized tragedies.

foot patrol A policing initiative that took officers out of cars and has them walking in neighborhood beats.

Frank Serpico A former NYPD detective, best known for whistleblowing on police corruption.

fruit of the poisonous tree Secondary evidence obtained from a search that violates the exclusionary rule.

furloughed A period of time when an employee is told not to come to work and is not paid.

fusion center Often located in police departments, a mechanism for sharing information and intelligence within specific jurisdictions and across levels of government.

Garrity Rule An officer cannot be ordered to respond to questions during an investigation of their criminal conduct.

George Floyd Justice in Policing Act of 2020 Bill that increases accountability for law enforcement misconduct, restricts the use of certain policing practices deemed reckless, enhances police transparency and data collection, and establishes best practices and training requirements for cadets and in-service training for veteran officers.

good-faith exception The principle that evidence may be used in a criminal trial even though the search warrant used to obtain it was technically faulty, as long as the police acted in good faith when they sought the warrant from a judge.

grass eater A term used to describe a police officer who accepts payoffs when everyday duties place them in a position to be solicited by the public.

hard technology Equipment that is designed to help police prevent crime, identify suspects, and bring them to justice. These include such devices as less-than-lethal weapons, drones, thermal imagers, and body armor.

heterogenous Diverse in character or content.

hostage and barricaded suspect incidents Incidents in which a suspect, usually armed with high-powered weapons or multiple weapons, has confined themselves in a building, structure, or area with limited access and egress and have taken a victim or victims hostage.

hotspot policing Focusing police patrol on small units of geography like street blocks or even single addresses that have extremely high levels of criminal activity.

hue and cry Bystanders summoned to assist law enforcers.

in-presence requirement A police officer cannot arrest someone for a misdemeanor unless the officer sees the crime occur. To make an arrest for a crime the officer did not witness, an arrest warrant must be obtained.

inevitable discovery rule The principle that evidence can be used in court even though the information that led to its discovery was obtained in violation of the *Miranda* rule if a judge finds it would have been discovered anyway by other means or sources.

intelligence-led policing A policing business model that incorporates data analysis and criminal intelligence into a strategy that coordinates strategic risk management of threats with a focus on serious, recidivist offenders.

internal affairs An element of a law enforcement agency investigating incidents and plausible suspicions of lawbreaking and professional misconduct attributed to officers on the force.

Internet crime Any illegal activity involving one or more components of the Internet, such as websites, chat rooms, and/or email. Internet crime involves the use of the Internet to communicate false or fraudulent representations to consumers. These crimes may include, but are not limited to, advance-fee schemes, nondelivery of goods or services, computer hacking, or employment/business opportunity schemes.

INTERPOL The world's largest international police organization, with members from 195 countries.

intersectionality A concept often used in critical theories to describe the ways in which oppressive institutions (racism, sexism, homophobia, transphobia, ableism, xenophobia, classism, etc.) are interconnected and cannot be examined separately from one another.

justice of the peace Assists the shire reeve or constable in maintaining order.

Knapp Commission (Commission to Investigate Alleged Police Corruption) A five-member panel initially formed in April 1970 to investigate alleged widespread corruption within the NYPD.

law enforcement The activities of an agency of the Federal, State or local government, authorized by law to engage the prevention, detection, investigation, or prosecution of violations of the criminal law.

low visibility decision making Police officers often have no oversight on their decision making as much of their work is done alone.

mass shootings Shootings that involve four or more victims, taking place in a public location, with victims chosen randomly or for symbolic purposes.

meat eater A term used to describe a police officer who actively solicits bribes and vigorously engages in corrupt practices.

***Miranda* warning** The requirement that when a person is custodially interrogated, police inform the individual of the right to remain silent, the consequences of failing to remain silent, and the constitutional right to counsel.

Mollen Commission (The City of New York Commission to Investigate Allegations of Police Corruption and the Anti-Corruption Procedures of the Police Department) Formed in 1992 to examine and investigate the nature and extent of corruption in the NYPD, evaluate the department's procedures for preventing and detecting corruption, and recommend changes and improvements to police procedures.

National Criminal Intelligence Sharing Plan A formal intelligence-sharing initiative that identifies the security and intelligence-sharing needs recognized in the wake of the 9/11 terrorist attacks.

National Highway and Traffic Safety Administration (NHTSA) NHTSA was established by the Highway Safety Act of 1970 and is dedicated to achieving the highest standards of excellence in motor vehicle and highway safety. It works daily to help prevent crashes and their attendant costs, both human and financial.

negotiated management An approach based on greater cooperation between police and demonstrators and an effort to avoid violence.

nolle prosequi The decision by a district attorney to drop a case; literally, "will no longer prosecute."

open field Any unoccupied or undeveloped real property outside the curtilage of a home.

order maintenance Police practice that involves handling minor offenses and conflicts and disorderly conduct

before they escalate into serious crimes.

overload hypothesis The theory that police workload influences discretion so that as workload increases, less time and attention can be devoted to new cases, especially petty crimes.

particularity The requirement that a search warrant state precisely where the search is to take place and what items are to be seized.

peacekeeping The goal of policing to create a secure and stable neighborhood environment.

plain view doctrine The principle that evidence in plain view of police officers may be seized without a search warrant.

police brutality Refers to needless and unjustified use of excessive force directed against civilians. It can include beatings, racial abuse, unlawful killings, or excessive use of riot control agents at protests.

police corruption Acts involving the misuse of authority by a police officer in a manner designed to produce personal gain for themself or for others.

police legitimacy Refers to the public belief that there is a responsibility and obligation to voluntarily accept and defer to the decisions made by authorities.

police reform A way to reimagine policing in the twenty-first century, in order to produce a more effective, more efficient, more user-friendly version of public safety.

police styles The working personalities adopted by police officers that can range from being a social worker in blue to being a hard-charging crime fighter.

Policing The maintenance of public order, law enforcement, and crime prevention by police officers, the duly sworn agents of the civil authority of government.

Posse Comitatus Act Bars federal troops from participating in civilian law enforcement except when expressly authorized by law.

probable cause The evidentiary criterion necessary to sustain an arrest or the issuance of an arrest or search warrant: a set of facts, information, circumstances, or conditions that would lead a reasonable person to believe that an offense was committed and that the accused committed that offense.

problem-oriented policing Developed by Herman Goldstein as an alternative to traditional policing; defines policing in terms of addressing discrete problems with specific solutions to each one.

problem solving The process of engaging in the proactive and systematic examination of identified problems to develop and rigorously evaluate effective responses.

procedural justice The idea that how individuals regard the justice system is tied more to the perceived fairness of the *process* than to the perceived fairness of the *outcome*.

public safety doctrine The principle that a suspect can be questioned in the field without a *Miranda* warning if the information the police seek is needed to protect public safety.

qualified immunity A legal principle that grants government officials immunity from civil suits unless the official violated clearly established statutory or constitutional rights of which a reasonable person acting in a similar capacity would be aware.

racial profiling Any police-initiated action that relies on the race, ethnicity, or national origin rather than the behavior of an individual or information that leads the police to a particular individual who has been identified as being, or having been, engaged in criminal activity.

reasonable suspicion A legal standard that is less than probable cause, but more than an unsupported hunch. To achieve the level of reasonableness, the suspicion must be based on specific facts or circumstances and that justifies stopping and even frisking a suspect.

right-wing A description referring generally to an individual, a political party, or faction that advocates very conservative policies and typically favors socially traditional ideas. Hierarchy, separatism, and inequality may be seen as natural results of traditional right-wing ideology.

school shooting An armed attack involving the use of a firearm at any educational institution, such as an elementary, middle, or high school or university.

search A government actor's infringement on a person's reasonable expectation of privacy.

search incident to a lawful arrest An exception to the search warrant rule, limited to the immediate surrounding area.

search warrant An order, issued by a judge, directing officers to conduct a search of specified premises for specified objects.

self-legitimacy The confidence that police officers have in their authority as a law enforcement officer.

sheriff (formerly shire reeve) The lead law enforcement person in county and rural areas.

shire reeve (later became sheriff) The lead law enforcement person in county and rural areas.

situational crime prevention (SCP) Crime prevention strategies that are aimed at reducing criminal opportunities that arise from the routines of everyday life.

slave patrols A government-sponsored force paid to patrol specific areas to prevent insurrection by those enslaved against the White community.

social contract A condition in which citizens give up some individual liberties or rights in exchange for some common security provided by the government.

soft technology Processes that are used to optimize the effectiveness and efficiency of an organization.

span of control The number of subordinates over which a supervisor has authority.

special commissions Groups, made up of independent experts and concerned citizens, that are empaneled to investigate police departments when there is evidence that corruption is pervasive within the department.

stigma A set of negative and often unfair beliefs that a society or group of people have about something.

stop and frisk The situation in which police officers who are suspicious of an individual run their hands lightly over the suspect's outer garments to determine whether the person is carrying a concealed weapon; also called a threshold inquiry or pat-down.

strategic incapacitation Policing designed to deliberately contain and hamper and neutralize protest movements, limiting their growth, size, and political effectiveness.

subculture A subdivision within the dominant culture that has its own norms, beliefs, and values.

suspect demeanor The outward behavior, attitude, and appearance of the offender.

swatting A practice of calling 9-1-1 and faking an emergency that draws a response from law enforcement. The purpose is to harass or injure a victim.

team policing Continuous decentralized patrol services in a specific geographic area by a team of officers, usually under the direction of a sergeant or lieutenant.

Terry v. Ohio A Supreme Court case that established that the police could stop, detain, question, and search a person based only on an officer's reasonable suspicion.

The National Commission on Terrorist Attacks Upon the United States Also known as the 9-11 Commission, an independent, bipartisan commission created by congressional legislation and President George W. Bush in 2002 to prepare a full and complete account of the circumstances surrounding the September 11, 2001, terrorist attacks, including preparedness for and the immediate response to the attacks.

thermal imaging camera A device that detects radiation in the infrared range of the electromagnetic spectrum, used in law enforcement to detect variations in temperature (warm images stand out against cool backgrounds).

thief takers Private citizens who were paid to catch criminals.

token Done for the sake of appearances or as a symbolic gesture.

U.S. Marshals Service Federal agency whose jurisdiction includes protecting federal officials, transporting criminal defendants, asset forfeiture, and tracking down fugitives.

vicarious liability A situation in which one party is held partly responsible for the unlawful actions of a second or third party.

vice squads Police units assigned to enforce morality-based laws, such as those addressing prostitution, gambling, and pornography.

vigilante A self-appointed private citizen who undertakes law enforcement in their community without legal authority.

watch and ward The establishment of groups of men to deter crime, stand watch at the city gates, and provide law enforcement.

Weingarten Rules Police agencies must allow officers to have the presence of union officials during disciplinary meetings.

zero tolerance policing Approach to policing that focuses on controlling minor crime and other signs of social disorder. When minor crimes are ignored, they will escalate into larger crimes.

Name Index

Subject Index

Page numbers followed by "e" denote exhibits.

Page numbers followed by "e" denote exhibits.